Complete Babylonian

Teach Yourself®

Complete Babylonian

A comprehensive guide to reading and understanding Babylonian, with original texts

Martin Worthington

First published in Great Britain in 2010 by Hodder Education. An Hachette UK company.
This edition published in 2018 by John Murray Learning.

British Library Cataloguing in Publication Data: a catalogue record for this title is available from the British Library.

Library of Congress Catalog Card Number: on file.

ISBN: 978 1 473 62780 2

eISBN: 978 1 473 62781 9

3

Typeset by MPS Ltd

Printed and bound in Great Britain by CPI Group (UK) Ltd., Croydon, CR0 4YY.

John Murray Learning policy is to use papers that are natural, renewable and recyclable products and made from wood grown in sustainable forests. The logging and manufacturing processes are expected to conform to the environmental regulations of the country of origin.

Carmelite House
50 Victoria Embankment
London EC4Y 0DZ
www.hodder.co.uk

Also available in ebook

Contents

Meet the author

They're all dead, but *we*'re not (yet)!
And what a picture we can get!
Of how they lived and worked and wrote:
of farmer, merchant, and king that smote.

Archives here, letters there,
spells and word-lists, contracts binding.
So much to read, so much to learn,
The mass of words is simply blinding.

And all inscribed in an ancient tongue
the world let go, but should have not!
For it's neat and tidy, and *so* much fun,
and great to learn – if you know what's what:

Accuse the accusative, veto the vetitive,
string up the suffixes, and preach at the precative!
Find the infinitive, and get at the root,
then the language is yours – and a culture to boot!

I met it first in 'ninety-seven,
in Amélie's courses at UCL.
Like standing by the doors of heaven,
and glimpsing through an old world, swell.

Great teachers, grammars, and works auxiliar
went on to make it quite familiar.
For points remaining a trifle vexed,
research continues ... *you* might be next!

That, dear reader, is why this book
was penned to guide and to inform.
So do peruse it, and have a good look
at those dainty wedges called Cuneiform.

Credits

Cover spot UV © British Institute at Ankara

Gurney, O.R. and Finkelstein, J.J. 1957: *The Sultantepe Tablets* 1 (British Institute of Archaeology at Ankara Occasional Publication 3). London 1957: fig. 38.

By kind permission of the author and publishers, Table 51 in Unit 48.2 is based on the corresponding columns of Table 6.2 in Leonid Kogan, "Proto-Semitic Phonetics and Phonology", in: Stefan Weninger (ed.), *The Semitic Languages: An International Handbook*, Berlin: De Gruyter Mouton, 2011, p. 55.

Acknowledgements to the first edition

It is a very pleasant duty to thank the many people without whom this book would never have been written. David Cook and Amélie Kuhrt, for guiding my interests to the Ancient World in general and Mesopotamia in particular; Annette Zgoll and Nicholas Postgate, who first taught me Babylonian; my parents, for boundless and bountiful moral support; Oliver Stadon, for his constant interest and encouragement; Riccardo Bernini, for his *esprit*; the Master and Fellows of St John's College, Cambridge, for both the opportunity to write the book and the ideal setting to do it in; and, last but not least, Ginny Catmur of Hodder, for taking on an unconventional project and being wonderfully supportive at every turn.

I am also much indebted to the friends and colleagues, too numerous to mention, with whom I have had the pleasure of discussing Babylonian grammar and philology over the years, both in and out of the classroom; and to those who commented constructively on draft sections of this course: Pat Boyde, David Conlon, Stephanie Dalley, Matthew Dolan, Charlie Draper, Aasha Joshi and Elizabeth Whitton.

The entire manuscript was read by Nicholas Postgate, Eric Smith and Aage Westenholz, whose acumen and keen attention to detail eliminated several inaccuracies, inconsistencies, and instances of unclear expression. For any faults which remain I bear sole responsibility.

This book is dedicated to the memory of Eleanor Marie Pierisa Parodi Worthington, *ahātiya ša itti ilāni*, and, in gratitude, to her friends Nunzia, Francesco, Monia and Flavia.

Urbino, 12th January 2010

Note to the second edition

The largest changes vis-à-vis the first edition (2010, re-issued in a corrected printing in 2012) consist in the introduction of cuneiform, the inclusion of the reading sections, and the addition of several units. Many further changes of various shapes and sizes were made throughout – some in the wake of new discoveries, some because there were things I should have known in 2010, but didn't! For any such cases which apply to the present edition, I tender advance apologies.

Not a few modifications were made at the instigation of readers, who contacted me with questions and alerted me to corrigenda of various kinds. Receiving this feedback from users of the volume known to friends and family as 'TYB' (now 'TYB2') has been hugely rewarding. The most detailed observations came from Simon Fitton-Brown and David Tibet, but many others stepped forward too. In addition to Simon and David, I would like to thank Emilio Alvarez, Jenaro Álvarez, Irving Finkel, Wendy Fraser, Lucia Itria, Dana Kounovská, Bill McGrath, Darran McManus, Cindy Mouchon, Peerapat Ouysook, Mojdeh Pourhamzeh, Daniel Semler, Chris Stapleton, and Larry Stillman.

I also owe much to students with whom I had the pleasure of dissecting Babylonian and Assyrian grammar at the University of Cambridge, the School of Oriental and African Studies, the Russian State University for the Humanities, Sichuan University, and the Institute for the Study of the Ancient World. It was in such contexts that I realized my presentation of construct forms (Unit 10.2) could be made simpler and clearer, and that the 'airport rule' (Unit 7.1) was so named.

Special thanks go to Alex Barker, Mark Chetwood, George Heath-Whyte, Scarlett Long and Katie Shields, with whom I read *The Poor Man of Nippur* in the academic year 2016–17. The flair and enthusiasm which they brought to reading the story have much to answer for in its now being available as an open-access film in the original language, for the use of Babylonian learners everywhere (see Reading H).

Among my colleagues, I am indebted to Brit Kaerger for suggesting I sharpen my presentation of the imperative and precative; and to Henry Stadhouders for alerting me to the need to talk about 'predicative complements'.

My thanks are also due to Kate Pool of the Society of Authors for giving generously of her time and advice, and to Victoria Roddam, Christina Wood, Michelle Armstrong and Emma Green of John Murray Learning for their near-saintly editorial patience.

Tom Gillam created the Cuneifyplus tool (http://cuneifyplus.arch.cam.ac.uk), and especially the function that automates the creation of sign lists. If you study cuneiform, I am sure you will quickly come to be as grateful to Tom as I am.

Preparing the second edition was one of my activities during a Visiting Research Scholarship at the Institute for the Study of the Ancient World (ISAW) of New York University, during the academic year 2017-2018. I am much indebted to the Institute and its community for making this possible.

Much more Babylonian (and Assyrian) is now available online than was the case in 2010. More will no doubt appear with every year that passes – until books are forgotten, computers burned out, and it is only the clay tablets of old which remain ...

Prague, 15th August 2018

What *is* Babylonian?

Babylonian is an ancient Semitic language which was spoken in the south of what is now Iraq. It was written in cuneiform (i.e. 'wedge-shaped') script. The earliest known writings in Babylonian date from shortly after 2000 BC, but Babylonian personal names which appear in documents written in another language (Sumerian) show it was spoken (though not written down) even earlier. It probably died out as a vernacular (i.e. everyday) language around 500 BC, but continued to be used for scholarship and religious cult well into the first century AD, perhaps even later. Over its long history it underwent some changes, but on the whole it was remarkably stable.

Babylonian's closest relative was Assyrian, which was spoken in the north of what is now Iraq. Together, Babylonian and Assyrian form the 'Eastern' branch of the Semitic family. They have no direct descendants. The two are so similar that they are often regarded as 'dialects' of a single language, 'Akkadian'. Since anyone who has learned Babylonian is a good 90% of the way to a working knowledge of Assyrian, the main differences between Babylonian and Assyrian are described in Unit 41.

LANGUAGE TIP

The term 'dialects' is misleading for Akkadian/Babylonian/Assyrian, inasmuch as it usually denotes secondary varieties, distinct from the 'main' language. For example, there is (standard) German, and then there are German dialects. But in the case of Akkadian, if you take out the 'dialects' Babylonian and Assyrian, there is nothing left!

There is a widespread supposition that, the further back one goes into the past, the less information survives about it. If this were true, it would leave the Babylonians and Assyrians, whose civilizations far pre-date the Greeks and Romans, pretty badly off. Fortunately for them, however, the above supposition is simply not true: written sources in Babylonian and Assyrian are measured in the hundreds of thousands. This is because they did most of their writing on clay tablets, which have proven to be often one of the most durable media ever used.

The possibility of learning about the Babylonians and Assyrians from their own writings is, however, a comparatively recent development. For after their languages died out the world forgot how to read the cuneiform script, and with the passage of centuries the Babylonians and Assyrians were virtually lost to history. For a long time, the only known sources of knowledge about them were scattered mentions in the Bible and Greek historians.

It was only in the nineteenth century that rediscovery began through excavation, and the process got going in earnest with the decipherment of the cuneiform script. This was principally achieved by Edward Hincks, an Irish clergyman. The story of decipherment is ably charted by Peter Daniels in his chapter 'Edward Hincks' Decipherment of Mesopotamian Cuneiform' in *The Edward Hincks Bicentenary Lectures* (edited by Kevin Cathcart; University College Dublin, 1994, pp. 30-57). Daniels finds that Hincks' discoveries were much used by Henry Rawlinson, an officer in the British army, who ended up taking most of the credit.

For several years, the question of whether the cuneiform script and the languages written in it really had been deciphered was controversial, so in 1857 the Royal Asiatic Society conducted an experiment: a cuneiform composition was sent to four different scholars (including Hincks and Rawlinson) who were requested to produce a translation without consulting with each other. The translations were to be compared, and if they were found sufficiently similar, the decipherment could be said to be sure – and thus it turned out. The full report, accessible at https://www.jstor.org/stable/25228700, makes for fascinating reading even today.

So picturesque an event was bound to catch the public imagination. Sure enough, when the 'Modern Major-General' in Gilbert and Sullivan's *The Pirates of Penzance* boasts that his skills include the ability to write 'Babylonic cuneiform', this is an allusion to the extracurricular activities of major-general Henry Rawlinson.

As scholars began to translate Babylonian and Assyrian writings, it became clear that there were astonishing discoveries to be made.

Perhaps the most striking of these was George Smith's discovery of the Babylonian account of the Flood, with many parallels to the story told in *Genesis*. But it was also found that the Babylonians had used 'Pythagoras's Theorem' over a thousand years before the birth of Pythagoras, and that many of the constellations which we inherited from the Greeks go back to Babylonian originals.

Exciting discoveries continue to be made as new tablets are found, translated and studied. In July 2007, Michael Jursa discovered a tablet in the British Museum which confirmed the name of the Chief Eunuch of Nebuchadnezzar as given in the Biblical Book of Jeremiah. In 2016, Mathieu Ossendrijver discovered that Babylonian scholars of the seventh century BC used geometric methods to track the movements of Jupiter, something previously thought to have been an innovation of European scholars in the fourteenth century AD. These discoveries were reported in the news all over the world.

But how well do we actually understand Babylonian, which stopped being spoken two and a half millennia ago? The answer is: astonishingly well. If (an admittedly rather remote contingency) the survival of the human race depended on modern scholars writing a letter in Babylonian and getting the ghost of Nebuchadnezzar to believe it was written during his lifetime, we can be pretty confident that the human race would survive.

For sure, there are gaps in our knowledge. For example, there are still rare words whose meaning is not clear, and rare grammatical forms or constructions which are poorly understood. Some verbal forms are not yet attested, so we do not know what they looked like. What is more, extant writings give us little sense of real-life conversation, so that we are not always sure how simple things such as **yes** or **hello** were said in daily life. However, even where our knowledge is hazy, it is growing by the year: as new sources are found and studied, and new linguistic patterns identified, our understanding advances, and doubts are laid to rest. We are learning more about Babylonian and Assyrian (and the people who wrote them) all the time. Theirs may be dead civilizations, but they nonetheless make for a very lively subject of study!

One of the consequences of these ongoing gains in knowledge is that scholarship about Babylonian and Assyrian becomes outdated much more quickly than in other fields: whereas a grammar of Latin or Greek written 50 years ago could still be recommended unreservedly today, a 50-year-old grammar of Babylonian or Assyrian would no longer be up-to-date. Though most of it would still be very useful, on some points it would be wrong, and on many points it would say nothing where we can now say something. If one were to go even further back to the nineteenth-century grammars of, say, Archibald Henry Sayce or Friedrich Delitzsch, an even bigger chasm would loom: brilliant – *seriously* brilliant – though they were in their day, to put them in the hands of a beginner today would be downright misleading.

A similar caveat applies to translations. A 50-year-old translation of Cicero or Demosthenes could (though it might sound old-fashioned) be trusted today. By contrast, a 50-year-old translation of a Babylonian composition would almost certainly be outdated in several respects: it would be quite likely for new manuscripts of the composition to have come to light, filling in gaps or providing textual variants; the meanings of certain words or phrases would almost certainly have become clearer, so at least some of the translator's question marks could be done away with; better understanding of the grammar might mean that some of the sentences would have to be translated in a different way. Sometimes, such problems arise even with comparatively recent translations.

The fact that translations of Babylonian become less reliable with age is a very good reason for learning the language: this enables you to form independent judgments about what a passage means, without being dependent on potentially outdated sources.

And how about the language itself? For a start, we are lucky that the cuneiform writing system included vowels. This means that we can study the languages written in it at a much greater level of precision than languages whose writing system did not record vowels. Thus our knowledge of Babylonian and Assyrian is vastly superior to that of, for instance, Ancient Egyptian: cuneiform allows us to distinguish different words and verbal tenses which in a writing system such as hieroglyphs would look identical. What is more, it gives us a good idea of how Babylonian and Assyrian were pronounced, making them very satisfying to learn.

Babylonian is very different from English in both vocabulary and grammar, but 'different' does not mean 'difficult'. Its structures are so regular (and, one is tempted to add, so logical) that you can quickly come to understand it on its own terms.

One of the central concepts in how Babylonian works is that, being a Semitic language (like Arabic and Hebrew), it builds its words out of groups of three letters known as 'roots'. Roots convey a general meaning, from which more specific meanings are derived by putting the relevant root through regular patterns (this means adding particular combinations of vowels and consonants). Thus take the three letters *dmq*, which convey the general idea of **goodness**: put them through one pattern and you get the adjective *damqu*, meaning **good**; put them through another pattern and you get the adjective *dummuqu*, meaning **very good**; put them through yet another pattern and you get the word *mudammiqu*, meaning **someone who makes (things) good**. By learning the patterns, which are usually quite simple, you massively extend your range of vocabulary, as each pattern can be applied to many different roots.

In English, whether a noun is the subject or object of a sentence is indicated by word order: the subject usually precedes the verb, the object usually follows it. Thus **man** is subject in **man sees dog**, but object in **dog sees man**. In Babylonian, by contrast, the subject and object are marked by endings: the subject takes *-u* and the object takes *-a*. So – to employ an unholy amalgam of Babylonian and English – a Babylonian could say **manu sees doga** and **doga sees manu**, both meaning **man sees dog**, whereas **mana sees dogu** and **dogu sees mana** would both mean **dog sees man**. (Actually, a Babylonian would usually put the verb at the end of the sentence, and say **dogu mana sees** or **manu doga sees**; but that is a different story …)

There are many other things about Babylonian which might surprise an English speaker. For example, it does not use articles (words like **a** and **the**); it does not always use singulars and plurals in the same way English does; the word for **you** changes, depending on who is being addressed (a man, a woman, a group of women, or a group which includes at least one man). But one gets used to all these things, and in the end they will seem quite natural to you – just as they did to the millions of people who spoke Babylonian as a mother tongue.

Learning a foreign language always takes some effort, but as languages go Babylonian is not difficult. The catch, if any, lies in the cuneiform script: this is extremely taxing, and takes years of study to master. Thankfully, mastery of the script is not necessary for understanding the language. This course is designed so that, if you wish, you can learn Babylonian in 'transliteration', i.e. converted from the ancient script into the alphabet we use today. If you do this, you will have learned to read, in the original language, the large body of Babylonian compositions which modern scholars have edited. Alternatively, you can elect to learn the cuneiform script, of which this course teaches two varieties.

Complete Babylonian is not truly 'complete' – not least because we have a lot left to discover! But it will give you a good working knowledge of the language, equipping you to understand and enjoy the textual treasures which the Babylonians (and Assyrians) have left us, including letters, omens, incantations, proverbs, and great works of literature.

Part one

Getting started

1 Introduction

In this unit you will learn:

- **about the history of Babylonian and Assyrian**
- **about the cuneiform script and how it works**
- **what a 'composite text' is.**

Babylonian is a very beautiful and highly regular language, and one which vaunts a vertiginously vast, varied, and vibrant body of writings. It is a member of the Semitic family, and so is related to Arabic, Hebrew, Aramaic, and Ethiopic. It was spoken – and, happily for us today, written – in the south of ancient Iraq. It was alive from before 2000 BC to at least 500 BC, and continued to be used as a language of scholarship and cult even after dying out as a vernacular tongue. It was usually written on clay tablets (ranging in size from a postage stamp to a large book), but other surfaces (clay prisms, stone monuments) were also used. The latest Babylonian writings which can be precisely dated are astronomical almanacs from 74 to 75 AD.

Decipherment was achieved in the 1850s, and though the language is now well understood, the number of scholars proficient in it is extremely small, so that great numbers of ancient documents have yet to be studied, and startling discoveries continue to be made. As an academic subject at university level, this makes Assyriology (i.e. the language-based study of ancient Iraq) one of the most exciting fields in the humanities. One does not, however, have to study Assyriology full-time, let alone devote oneself to it professionally, in order to enjoy the cultural and linguistic delights which a knowledge of Babylonian has to offer. The language is not overly complicated, and though at first glance the unfamiliarity of the vocabulary seems a large hurdle, most grammatical principles are simple, and progress is correspondingly fast.

Babylonian's closest relative was Assyrian (which was spoken in the north of ancient Iraq). The two are so similar that they are often viewed as dialects of a single language, 'Akkadian'. This course will explain the main ways in which Assyrian differs from Babylonian, thereby providing a basic knowledge of Assyrian.

For a preview of the sorts of things you will be reading, have a look at the Key to the exercises. The exercises are all taken *verbatim* from original Babylonian sources. (For sentences longer than one word, the source is specified in the Key.)

1.1 Periods of the language

For a language with such a long recorded history, Babylonian was astonishingly stable. Though different stages or 'periods' are recognized, each with its own characteristics, they are so similar that someone who has mastered the language of one period will not have to work hard to learn that of another.

The language of the second millennium is conventionally divided into two periods: Old Babylonian (c. 2000–1500 BC), and Middle Babylonian (c. 1500–1000 BC). During the second millennium BC, the vernacular language was also (give or take the odd archaism, poetic licence of various kinds, and such stylistic traits as generally characterize literary language) the language of literature. In the first millennium BC, a deeper cleavage developed between the language of literature ('Standard Babylonian') and the vernacular ('Neo-Babylonian'): the former remained close to the language of the second millennium (Old and Middle Babylonian), while the latter underwent a number of changes. This course introduces you to the language of the second millennium and to the literary language of the first (Standard Babylonian). Proficiency in these will enable you to read the great works of Babylonian literature and scholarship, and it will also provide you, should you require it, with a solid foundation for studying the vernacular language of the first millennium (Neo-Babylonian). Exercises are given separately for Old and Middle Babylonian on the one hand (they are very similar) and Standard Babylonian on the other. You may wish to do both sets of exercises in parallel, or first complete one set and then work through the other.

1.2 Reading fragments

Most cuneiform manuscripts (i.e. inscribed clay tablets) are fragmentary. Often scholars have managed to piece multiple fragments of the same manuscript back together, but even so the proportion of manuscripts on which all the original cuneiform signs are perfectly preserved is small. It is fortunate, therefore, that a given work is often extant on multiple manuscripts: even though each of these may be fragmentary, together they often give a complete or near-complete text. This is especially common for first millennium literary and scholarly works. (By contrast, letters of all periods tend to be extant on only one manuscript.)

LANGUAGE TIP

It is one of the exciting things about Assyriology that new (fragments of) manuscripts are being found all the time. Thus, for example, in 1930 The Epic of Gilgameš ('Standard' version) was known from 108 inscribed clay fragments. By 2003 this number had grown to 184; thanks to the new sources, breaks could be filled, and the text of the Epic is becoming more complete.

When modern editors have multiple manuscripts at their disposal, they usually produce a 'composite text', taking one bit from one manuscript, another bit from another manuscript, and so on, and putting variants at the bottom of the page in the so-called 'apparatus criticus'. Especially in editions of first millennium manuscripts, the result is an eclectic entity, heterogeneous in both spelling and grammar: it does not reflect the intentions of a single scribe, but amalgamates the habits and intentions of many scribes. The Standard Babylonian exercises in this course are mostly taken from modern editors' composite texts. Do not be surprised, then, if Standard Babylonian sentences seem to be internally inconsistent in spelling, etc.

1.3 Other books

It would be a very good idea, while learning Babylonian, to familiarize yourself with other facets of Mesopotamian (i.e. ancient Iraqi) culture and history. This would provide useful background knowledge to bear in mind when translating the sentences in this course. You might start by reading translations of epics and myths, to get a feel for the sort of things that Babylonian stories talked about. To this end, one can recommend A.R. George's *The Epic of Gilgamesh* (Penguin Classics, 2003), Stephanie Dalley's *Myths from Mesopotamia* (Oxford World's Classics, 2008), and (with a bigger selection) B. R. Foster's *Before the Muses: An Anthology of Akkadian Literature* (CDL Press, 2005).

An excellent and beautifully illustrated one-volume introduction to the history and culture of Mesopotamia is Michael Roaf's *Cultural Atlas of Mesopotamia* (Andromeda, 1999). More detailed are Marc van de Mieroop, *A History of the Ancient Near East* (Blackwell, 2006) and Amélie Kuhrt, *The Ancient Near East*, 2 vols. (Routledge, 1997).

If you like drinking from multiple wells (often a good idea in language learning), other introductions to Babylonian are: Richard I. Caplice, *Introduction to Akkadian*, 3rd ed. (Pontifical Biblical Institute, 1988) and J. Huehnergard, *A Grammar of Akkadian*, 3rd ed. (Eisenbrauns, 2011). Caplice's book is very condensed, Huehnergard's more fulsome. You might also find it rewarding to equip yourself with a copy of *A Concise Dictionary of Akkadian* (see Unit 42.2) and start consulting it alongside the Glossary at the end of this course.

Beware of recent reprints of venerable books – owing to the rapid pace of discovery, scholarship about Babylonian grammar and philology ages quite quickly.

1.4 Babylonian words recognizable today

There is more Babylonian around us than one might think. As we now know, there is a trace of it even in the English language. Our word **alcohol** comes to us through Arabic, **al** being the Arabic word for **the** (we also have it in **algebra**, which we likewise borrowed from Arabic). The element **cohol** goes back to the Babylonian and Assyrian word *guhlu*, which meant a type of eye-paint – what we now refer to with the related word **kohl**. And some scholars think that the English verb to **babble** derives from **Babel** (as in **the tower of Babel**), itself stemming from *bābili*, the Babylonian word for the city of Babylon.

Moreover, many Arabic and Hebrew words which have found their way into English are recognizably similar to their Babylonian relatives (sometimes slightly masked by sound changes, see Units 47, 46.7, and 48). Here is a selection of cases:

Alkali: from Ar. *al-qaliy* **the-ashes** – related to Bab. *qalû* **to roast**
Alpha: from Phoenician *alp* (a close relative of Hebrew *aleph*) **ox** – related to Bab. *alpu* **ox**
Amen: from Heb. *'amen* **certainly** – related to Bab. *imittu* (from *imintu*) **right** (opposite of left)
Bethlehem: from Heb. *bayith leḥem* **house of bread** – related to Bab. *bītu* **house** and *lêmu* **to consume** (food)

Checkmate: from Persian *shah* **king** and Ar. *māta* **he has died** – related to Bab. *mâtu* **to die**
Cherub: from Heb. *kerūv* **(a type of angel)** – related to Bab. *karābu* **to bless**
Cider: from Heb. *šikar* **(a drink)** – related to Bab. *šikaru* **beer**
Cotton: from Ar. *qutn* **cotton** – related to Bab. *qutnu* **thinness**
Dragoman: from Ar. *tarjumān* **interpreter** – related to Bab. *targumannu*
Halal: from Ar. *ḥalāl* **lawful** – related to Bab. *elēlu* **to be pure**
Kebab: from Ar. *kabāb* **roasted meat** (via Turkish) – related to Bab. *kabābu* **to burn**
Kosher: from Heb. *košer* **proper** – related to Bab. *kašāru* **to be successful**
Mattress: from Ar. *maṭraḥah* **place** (*ma-*) **where something is thrown** from Ar. *ṭaraḥa* **to throw** – related to Bab. *ṭerû* **to beat**
Rabbi: from Hebrew *rav* **master** – related to Bab. *rabû* **great**
Safari: from Ar. *safar* **journey** (via Kiswahili) – related to Bab. *šapāru* **to send**
Shibboleth: from Heb. *šiboleth* **ear of corn** – related to Bab. *šubultu*
Souk: from Ar. *sūq* **marketplace** – related to Bab. *sūqu* **street**
Tell (mound): from Ar. *tall* **mound** – related to Bab. *tillu*

For more on the relations between Babylonian, Hebrew and Arabic, see Unit 48.

1.5 The cuneiform script and its varieties

The cuneiform script was used for over 3,000 years, and changed a great deal across time and space, giving rise to many different varieties. Some sign shapes are fairly stable across different varieties, others change so much as to be hardly recognizable. This course introduces you to two varieties of the script: Monumental Old Babylonian and Cursive Neo-Assyrian.

It is a constant of the cuneiform world that monuments tend to use older sign forms than those current for everyday use in the same period. 'Monumental Old Babylonian' actually originated during the Ur III dynasty (c. 2100–2000 BC), when it was used to write the many thousands of Sumerian administrative records which survive from this period. If you see a clay tablet in a museum, the chances are in favour of its being an Ur III administrative document, in Sumerian language. In Old Babylonian times (c. 1800–1500 BC), everyday documents such as letters were written in a cursive script ('Cursive Old Babylonian', not taught here). However, the Ur III script was used in some Old Babylonian monumental inscriptions (usually in stone), such as the stele which bears the lawcode of Hammurapi and is now housed in the Louvre museum. Monumental Old Babylonian was also used for royal inscriptions in later periods, particularly by Nebuchadnezzar II of Babylon (605–562 BC). His 'East India House' inscription (in Monumental Old Babylonian) is on display in the British Museum.

In Neo-Assyrian times, the cursive and monumental scripts were quite similar (more so than in the Old Babylonian period). This course introduces you to cursive Neo-Assyrian sign forms, as found on clay tablets from Assurbanipal's libraries at Nineveh. Knowing these, you should be able to recognize Neo-Assyrian monumental sign forms fairly easily.

In the interests of facilitating learning, and enabling you to reinforce your knowledge within the confines of available space, it has been necessary to compress documents written in several varieties of the script into these two. While this may not seem very 'purist', conversion from one variety of a script to another was no rarity in ancient times: Assyrians often converted Babylonian literature into their own version of the script, while leaving the language (more or less) unchanged. This reflects the wider point that the variety of script need not match the variety of language.

Cuneiform is an inherently three-dimensional script, so any representation of it on a printed page is bound to contain a distortion. Even when one has learned to read a passage of paper cuneiform quite fluently, looking at the original inscription is always a very different experience. The transition from 2D to original 3D takes time and patience. Therefore, even after all your hard work with this course, you will still not have learned how to sight-read an ancient tablet in a museum. But you will have acquired a strong foundation which will assist you in travelling down that thorny path.

Indeed, the experience of reading in Ancient Mesopotamia was probably very different from ours: people wrote less, read less (there is no evidence of 'reading for pleasure'), and had less experience of sight-reading. Tablets were often hard to read, whether because of individual handwriting, or because of the tricks with light and shadow that three-dimensional cuneiform is subject to. Rather than reading a tablet with the ease which you or I bring to a newspaper, ancient readers very likely often had to puzzle their way through it, much as modern Assyriologists do today. The goal of sight-reading real (three-dimensional) cuneiform 'fluently' may, then, be something of a chimera – which gives you leave to go about it at any pace you like. That said, with practice it is not too taxing to acquire fluency in reading passages one has already studied, and doing so will refine in many ways your understanding of how written Babylonian works.

SELF CHECK

	I can ...
	... explain what Babylonian is, how it relates to Assyrian, Hebrew and Arabic, and report something of its history
	... explain what the cuneiform script is, and the difference between its cursive and monumental varieties.

2 How to use this course

In this unit you will learn:

- **how to get the most out of this course**
- **that there are different ways of working through it**
- **that jumping around between different parts of it can be useful.**

The function of this course is to provide you with the resources with which you can learn Babylonian. As it is you who is doing the learning, you have to remain in control of what you are learning, and exercise some initiative in learning it.

A book of language instruction is not (alas!) like a good novel, to be read at even speed from cover to cover. Some sections are straightforward and can be read quite quickly, while others need to be absorbed carefully and slowly. You will judge which pace is right for you from one section to another.

It should also be stressed that there is an in-built tension in language instruction books between presenting information in the order most suited to the needs of learners who come to it for the first time, vs. presenting it in the order that makes most sense in terms of the language's structures. The problem with the former procedure is that it can be difficult to find information when one wants to look back over it, and also that by dismembering things which naturally belong together it misses opportunities to get the linguistic structures to cohere in the learner's head. The problem with the latter route is that it can make things unnecessarily daunting.

This course adopts a compromise position: the information is arranged more or less as in a reference grammar, following the language's structures. But lots of help is given in the exercises (explaining things anticipated from later units), and there are numerous cross-references, which you are encouraged to explore. Ultimately, a language is an enormous and complex system in which countless things interweave and interlock, so that any attempt to present it in linear steps must entail an element of distortion. Hopping backwards and forwards between units to make your own paths through the material is, therefore, perfectly sensible.

Since the standard reference grammar of Babylonian is in German (see Unit 42.6), more information has been provided in the present course than would normally be given in a work for beginners. Accordingly, it is not necessary to have mastered everything on a page (or even in a unit) before moving on to the next. Sometimes it suffices to get the gist, and to remember where to look up the information when the need for more detailed understanding arises. In deciding what to learn and what not to learn you might be guided by the 'most important things to remember' sections at the end of units.

2.1 The examples

Like the exercises, the examples are all taken *verbatim* from original sources. For longer or more interesting items, a reference to the source is provided. (To decipher the reference, consult the list of abbreviations at the end of the course, just before the Index.)

The abbreviations OB, MB and SB (Old Babylonian, Middle Babylonian, Standard Babylonian) are used to show which stage of the language an example belongs to.

It is a very good idea not just to read the examples casually, but to work through them, copying them out by hand, looking up the words, and ensuring one understands how they work. (Occasionally, examples incorporate grammatical features which will be explained in later units; it is, therefore, a good idea to re-read earlier examples in the light of knowledge acquired.)

2.2 The exercises

The exercises are not tests of whether you have mastered a unit, but a way of helping you to master it. It is, therefore, perfectly natural to refer back to the unit while doing them – this is not 'cheating'! Similarly, there is no shame in making a mistake (even the same one several times). The crucial thing is to understand the nature of any mistakes one has made, and how to avoid repeating them. With practice, one shuffles bad habits off.

For your convenience, the word or words in an exercise which display the rules explained in the foregoing unit are marked in bold.

In the early stages of learning a foreign language, translating a sentence is no easy matter. It is, therefore, a good idea to be methodical. The ideal would be to copy out the 'transliterated' sentence into a notebook, then to write down the vocabulary as one looks it up, then to write down the 'normalization' (as will be explained later, transliteration and normalization are two different ways of writing Babylonian in the Roman alphabet; see Unit 4) and translation. Leave plenty of space everywhere (e.g. writing every vocabulary item on a new line), both for clarity of presentation and to insert any additional annotations. Treated thus, a five-word sentence can easily take up half a side of A5 and (in the first few weeks of learning) occupy one for several minutes. (Experienced language learners will have their own methods of learning, and work out short cuts.)

Do not be afraid of being creative in how you approach the exercises! Sometimes, you may wish to translate directly from the normalization (provided in the Key), rather than from the transliteration. One can also learn a lot simply by reading the Key, carefully comparing the normalization and translation and looking things up to make sure one understands how they correspond. Indeed, some readers may wish to do this first, and then do the exercises a few days later. You can even create your own English–Babylonian exercises, taking the translations provided in the Key and translating these back into the original language. For this purpose you may wish to compile an English–Babylonian word list.

For all these purposes (and others), you will probably find it useful to make a photocopy of the Key (perhaps also of the Glossary), to save you having to leap back and forth across the course.

Sometimes, the source from which the exercise was taken is damaged. This is indicated with square brackets, e.g. [*l*]*a* means 'the left-hand side of the cuneiform sign representing *la* is broken'; ⸢*l*⸣*a* means 'part of the left-hand side of the cuneiform sign representing *la* is broken'. While learning the language you can ignore such brackets, but it is good to get used to seeing them, as you will regularly meet them in editions.

Often a sentence can be interpreted in several ways, and the Key to the exercises gives multiple interpretations. If one looks at the full passage from which the sentence is taken, it is usually obvious which of these interpretations applies.

Not all units contain the same number of exercises. The number in a given unit is partly determined by the importance and difficulty of the grammatical phenomenon to be practised, and partly by the frequency with which the phenomenon will be encountered in exercises in other units.

2.3 Units 44–47

Units 44–47 gather together related points which recur through the course. They have been placed at the end because it would be daunting to encounter them at the beginning, but you will be referred to them periodically. It will be useful to read them through at some point, and revisit them from time to time.

2.4 Learning vocabulary

This course is structured so that *you* decide which words to learn, and when. You are not expected to learn a list of words in one unit before moving on to the next. A list of common words is provided at the end of the course, and a list of Babylonian/Assyrian words with cognates in Hebrew and Arabic is provided in Unit 1.4.

You could get away with learning virtually no words, and looking them up in the Glossary as you need them; but after a while this would get tedious, so it is a good idea to learn words which you find yourself looking up frequently. Learning words will solidify your command of the language, and help you get under its skin.

Most people will find it useful to develop associations for words they want to learn. For example, to help yourself remember the word *nūnu* (which means **fish**), you might imagine yourself saying 'Nu-nu-nu-nu-nu, this fish is not fresh!' to an uncooperative fishmonger. Speaking words aloud is a great help in learning them.

You should also bear in mind an important difference vis-à-vis English: English has many more words than Babylonian (or Assyrian), so each Babylonian word has to do more 'work' than its English counterparts (i.e. carry more meanings). For example, there is no separate word in Babylonian for 'to declare'. Thus Babylonian witnesses have to 'say' (*qabûm*) where in English they would more specifically 'declare' or 'state'.

As a learner of Babylonian vocabulary, the key thing is to learn the basic meaning of the word (e.g. 'say' for *qabû*), and not to be too discombobulated if along the way you encounter the same word with slightly modified meanings (e.g. 'state', 'declare', 'assert', etc.).

The advantage to you is that there are fewer foreign words to learn: with many a modern language you would have to learn separate words for 'say', 'declare' and 'state', but Babylonian covers all of these (and more) with just *qabû*.

2.5 Learning grammar

According to a widespread perception, grammar is the shoal of piranha in the merry stream of language learning. This perception, which is entirely erroneous, has two likely sources.

One is that grammatical information (e.g. verbal endings) is often presented in tables. Some learners tend to regard tables as distracting interruptions to the main text (like many people's view of the songs in *The Lord of the Rings*) and pass over them with just a cursory glance. Unsurprisingly, they have difficulty learning grammar! But even among learners who do look at tables, many expect to 'read' them with the same speed they would normal text, and then find they are not learning as quickly as they want. The trick is to realize that a table presents information in much more dense a fashion than normal text (think how long it would take to explain every table cell in words!), and that it needs to be studied more slowly.

Another reason why many people get frustrated by grammar is grammatical terminology. The trick here is to realize that, often, the actual terms are completely arbitrary; it is the concepts and categories which they stand for that really matter. Accordingly, when a grammatical term is introduced, the term itself is much less interesting than *why* it is being introduced.

For example, instead of speaking of verbs as having 'person', 'number', 'gender', 'tense', etc., we could instead borrow the animals of Shaolin Kung Fu, and speak of verbs as having a 'tiger-quality', a 'monkey-quality', a 'snake-quality', a 'crane-quality' and a 'dragon-quality'. What really matters is that we understand that there is a difference between pairs such as **you eat** and **he eats** (i.e. 'person'), **I eat** and **we eat** (i.e. 'number'), **he eats** and **she eats** (i.e. 'gender'), **he eats** and **he ate** (i.e. 'tense'). The nomenclature with which we describe these differences is simply a matter of convention.

Finally, when learning sequences of sounds by heart, whether they be just endings (e.g. 'possessive suffixes', Unit 11) or full words (e.g. the present tense of the verb), rhythm is very important. In the same way that some people find it more convenient to learn telephone numbers as two-digit sets of numbers, and others three, experiment with saying the endings with different rhythms, at different speeds (fortified by the maxim that, in language learning, if you don't sound ridiculous, you're not doing it properly).

2.6 Two types of linguistic knowledge

Languages are not structured in an even way, so that the amount of things you know always matches the amount of things you can do. Sometimes you can learn just one little thing, and this suddenly expands hugely the range of things you can say. Sometimes you have to learn all sorts of peculiar rules to manage to say something which is really quite simple.

An example of the first kind (quick expansion) is English plurals: give or take a few exceptions, all you have to do is add **s** (sometimes pronounced **z**, sometimes with a preceding **e**) to the end of a word, and that makes it plural. Thus with a single simple rule you go from having **an idea**, **a chocolate**, and **a castle** to the even more attractive scenario of having **ideas**, **chocolates** and **castles**.

By contrast, learners of English (quite understandably) writhe and fume over the past tense. Why can't all verbs be like **to treat** (past tenses **I treated**, **I have treated**)? Why do I have to learn **'sing, sang, sung'**, **'dig, dug, dug'**, let alone **'smite, smote, smitten'**, when all I want to do is form a past tense? One shares the sentiment, but there is no good answer, beyond the fact that human languages were not devised by computers.

Considering plurals and past tenses, Babylonian is the other way round: plurals are a bit finnicky, while past tenses are extremely straightforward.

When negotiating one's way through what sometimes seems like the labyrinth of a new language, it is often useful to make oneself aware of the two types of knowledge described above, for self-congratulation and self-encouragement: 'Ha! Look how much new stuff I can do with this'; 'These rules all seem very complicated, but at least the objective behind them – e.g. to form plurals – is a simple one'.

2.7 The readings

Interspersed between the units are readings from original Babylonian sources (some, while being in Babylonian, were composed by Assyrians). Two of them pertain to the grisly life of the Assyrian king Sennacherib, who was murdered by one of his sons, but you will also encounter incantations and a Babylonian folk tale.

Reading connected passages is the best way to consolidate one's grip over a dead language. You may find it helpful to listen to the recordings at https://www.soas.ac.uk/baplar/recordings/. The best way to use the passages is to work with them aloud: read them to family and friends, speak them out, and don't be shy to try different intonations and voices for them. Once you spend time with them, you will find that bits of them start to stick in your mind. That is a huge step forward.

The translations are provided so that, though you will want or need to look up words in the Glossary first time round, on subsequent occasions you can study the Babylonian text with minimal hassle, flicking your eyes to the opposite page for quick reminders, as necessary.

The readings will give you insights into Ancient Mesopotamian culture, but they will also give you a sense of the philological uncertainties which Assyriologists have to deal with.

2.8 Learning cuneiform

Usually, when learning a foreign language, it is essential to learn the script that goes with it. Thus someone learning English would be ill-advised not to learn the Roman alphabet, just as learners of Russian or Arabic cannot dispense with the relevant script.

The case of Babylonian is different: there exists, both online and in print, a large (and rapidly growing) body of Babylonian converted ('transliterated') into Roman script. It is, then, perfectly possible to enjoy Babylonian as a language without engaging directly with the script (though one has to know something about how it works).

The drawbacks of such an approach are: 1) one has to rely on the editors' interpretations: cuneiform signs can often be read in different ways, and there is sometimes room for disagreement about what the correct reading is; being able to read the script enables one to formulate independent judgments; 2) one can only read what has been transliterated (much has only been published as a scale drawing); 3) one misses out on the feeling of authenticity of reading an original source.

Conversely, the advantage of dealing with Babylonian in transliteration only is that cuneiform is jolly difficult! Indeed, in the first edition of this course I left it out, for fear that it might scare readers off. In this second edition I have added electronically generated signs, but it is still possible to work through the course in transliteration only. Indeed, that is probably what I would advise independent learners to do in the first instance.

Different people have different ways of learning signs. Copying them out by hand, wedge for wedge, is a useful exercise at the beginning, as it causes one to notice all sorts of details which one might not otherwise take heed of. Beyond that, some people like to study signs as isolated entities, on flashcards. Others prefer to look at passages of connected text which they already understand, comparing the cuneiform with the transliteration (one finger on each). See what works best for you.

I would advise you to make great use of the Cuneifyplus tool, created by Tom Gillam on the basis of previous materials created by Steve Tinney. This is freely available at http://cuneifyplus.arch.cam.ac.uk. Its main function is that it converts transliterations to cuneiform, allowing you to construct your own exercises and to resolve all sorts of small doubts (e.g. 'I know what *šá* looks like, but I wonder what *šà* looks like …').

But the Cuneifyplus tool also generates bespoke sign-lists. For example, if you type (or copy) in the following made-up sentence, *er-šam ina er-ši-im ša-ap-lim ú-še-šib* (**I got the wise man to sit down on the lower bed**), and request the Assurbanipal font, you will get this output:

𒅕 : *er*
𒌑 : *šam, ú*
𒀸 : *ina*
𒅆 : *ši, lim*
𒅎 : *im*
𒊭 : *ša*
𒀊 : *ap*
𒊺 : *še*
𒉺 : *šib*

This means that it would take these nine cuneiform signs to write the passage, and that two of them are used with two different readings each. This can be done for any passage you are studying.

In learning cuneiform, it is also useful to be aware of differences between ancient and modern reading (see Unit 1.5). Having to work out where words started and stopped was another issue, though on narrow tablets with only one or two words to a line this was a lesser problem.

Thus, except perhaps within highly formulaic settings, such as short administrative records, it is doubtful whether many people (or even anyone at all) in Ancient Mesopotamia sight-read cuneiform as easily as we read a newspaper. Let that be an encouragement to you, as you grapple with the script!

SELF CHECK

	I can ...
	... understand what the present course is trying to do, and the different ways I might work through it.

3 *Pronunciation*

In this unit you will learn:

- **how Babylonian is conventionally pronounced**
- **where you can hear examples of modern scholars reading it.**

Since we cannot hear native speakers of Babylonian, we do not know exactly how the language was pronounced, and in any case there must have been considerable variation across time and space. However, the pronunciations reconstructed by modern scholars are probably good approximations of how the language was pronounced by literate individuals in certain periods.

The decipherers of Babylonian assumed that it had more or less the same sounds as other Semitic languages, especially Arabic. This assumption was confirmed in outline when scholars found Babylonian words written in the Aramaic and Greek alphabets. These confirmed that, for example, the sound which the decipherers had identified as *l* was indeed some sort of **l**.

There are, however, many **l** sounds. British English has two: the **l** in **low**, which sits high in the mouth, is different from the **l** in **ball**, which is pronounced deep in the throat. We can be confident that the Babylonian sound which we transcribe as *l* was, so to speak, a member of the **L**-family. Many subtleties in the pronunciation of Babylonian are still being discovered from patterns in cuneiform spellings.

3.1 The sounds of Babylonian

It is suggested that individual sounds be pronounced as follows. Most letters should cause English speakers no difficulty (where no extra indication is given, pronounce as in English).

' – a glottal stop, like **tt** in the Cockney pronunciation of **bottle**: to the ear of an English speaker, this is a hiatus between sounds more than a sound in its own right. (See also the additional notes.)

a – as in **pat**.
b
d
e – as in **bed**.
g – as in **go**.
h – as in Scottish **loch**, German **Reich**. (As a reminder that it was not pronounced as in English **hotel**, some books print it as *ḫ*.)
i – like **ee** in **bee**.
(*j* – some books use this instead of *y*; pronounce as in **yes**.)
k

l
m – as in **mum**. (After the Old Babylonian period, single *m* between vowels was probably pronounced **w**, but do not let this worry you.)
n
p
q – this was probably a **k** followed by a glottal stop. This sound being very alien to modern Western languages, for convenience most Assyriologists pronounce it as a heavy **k**, articulated with the back of the tongue. (Some books print it as *ḳ*.)
r – probably rolled, as in Scots. Unlike in British English (e.g. **barn**, where the **r** simply lengthens the **a**), it is always pronounced. Thus make sure to distinguish, for example, *mārtu* **daughter** from *mātu* **land**.
s – as in **sit**.
ṣ – this was probably a **s** followed by a glottal stop. This sound being very alien to modern Western languages, it is conventionally pronounced **ts** as in **bits**.
š – **sh** as in **shop**.
t
ṭ – this was probably a **t** followed by a glottal stop. This sound being very alien to modern Western languages, it is conventionally pronounced as a heavy **t**.
u – like **oo** in **pool**, but shorter.
w
y – as in **yes**. (Some books use **j** instead of **y**.)
z – as in **Zorro**.

Notes: Double consonants (as in *libbu* **heart**, *idukkū* **they kill**) are actually pronounced double (i.e. long), as in many modern languages (but not British English).

q, *ṣ* and *ṭ* (the so-called 'emphatics'): though to an English speaker these look like combinations of two different sounds (**k** + glottal stop, **s** + glottal stop, **t** + glottal stop), speakers of Babylonian would have perceived them as single sounds (i.e. as one phoneme). Something similar happens with the English sound **x** (as in **box**): this is also made up of two different sounds (**k** and **s**), but English speakers nonetheless perceive the combination as a single sound.

Little is yet known about the placement of the accent in Babylonian words, and even less about overall sentence intonation. For the purposes of learning the language, simply stress words in whatever way you find most natural.

The sibilants (*s*, *ṣ*, *š*, *z*) are perhaps the most hotly debated Babylonian sounds in modern scholarship. To complicate matters, it is generally thought that they changed over time. The suggested pronunciations are conventional.

In Old Babylonian, written *h* was used to represent the sound **h**, the glottal stop and perhaps also other guttural sounds.

3.2 Short and long vowels

A given Babylonian vowel could be pronounced short or long. (Long ones probably lasted about twice as long as short ones.) The length of a vowel can affect the meaning (e.g. *mutu* **man** vs. *mūtu* **death**). For an example of long and short vowels in English, compare the **a** in **bat** with the **a** in **father**: the former is short, the latter is long. But here there is the complication that the sound ('quality') of the vowels is different, as well as their length ('quantity'). In normalization (see Unit 4.4) long vowels are identified as such with a horizontal line (a 'macron'): *ā, ē, ī, ū*.

Vowels resulting from contraction of two other vowels (see Unit 47.1) were, at least at the end of a word, probably pronounced in a third way (i.e. different from both long and short), but we do not know exactly how. Possibly they were (at least sometimes) pronounced bisyllabically (i.e. as two syllables), so that e.g. *rabû* **great** was pronounced *ra-bu-u*. Many scholars simply pronounce them long. In normalization, contracted vowels usually bear circumflex accents: *â, ê, î, û*.

LANGUAGE TIP

You will sometimes (especially in words from middle weak roots – see Unit 25) encounter vowels resulting from contraction which are normalized with a macron instead of a circumflex accent. This is because the two 'parent' vowels did not belong to two separate syllables, but formed a diphthong (i.e. they were not really two fully separate vowels). For example, *bītu(m)* **house** from original *baitum*: this was pronounced as in English **(fish) bait**, not **ba-it**.

3.3 Modern recordings

Many French scholars use circumflex accents for both long and contracted vowels when normalizing (i.e. they do not use macrons). Hence if you read an edition by a French scholar you may well encounter *â, ê, î, û* where you would expect to find *ā, ē, ī, ū*.

Particularly in the early stages of learning Babylonian, it may be helpful to listen to modern scholars reading the language aloud, just as you would in a classroom. For this, you can consult the online archive of recordings called 'Babylonian and Assyrian Poetry and Literature: An Archive of Recordings' (BAPLAR): https://www.soas.ac.uk/baplar/recordings/.

SELF CHECK

	I can ...
	... read Babylonian aloud in accordance with modern scholarly conventions.

4 *Writing Babylonian in Roman characters*

In this unit you will learn:

- **how Babylonian and Assyrian spelling is different from English spelling**
- **what 'transliteration' is, and what conventions it uses**
- **what 'normalization' is, and what conventions it uses.**

Regardless of whether you plan to learn the cuneiform script, in studying Babylonian it is important to understand something of how the script worked (esp. 'syllabic' vs. 'sumerographic' spellings), and of the two ways in which cuneiform is converted into Roman characters ('transliteration' and 'normalization'). Like the Roman alphabet, the cuneiform script reads from left to right.

4.1 Syllabic vs. sumerographic spellings

Cuneiform signs represent syllables, and writers of Babylonian usually spelled each word out syllable by syllable. (The rules for how to divide a Babylonian word into syllables -'syllabification'- are given in Unit 47.5.) Sometimes, however, they instead wrote down the equivalent word in Sumerian (a different language), for the Babylonians held Sumerian culture, from which they had inherited the cuneiform script, in great esteem. These two ways of writing are known as 'syllabic' vs. 'sumerographic', and they used the same repertoire of cuneiform signs. Thus the word *eqlum* **field** might be written *eq-lum* (syllabic) or a.šà (sumerographic).

Sumerographic and syllabic spelling could be combined, e.g. a.šà-*lum* to spell *eqlum* **field** (on italic vs. non-italic see section 4.3). In such cases, the syllabic component of the spelling is known as a 'phonetic complement' to the sumerographic component.

This is similar to the spelling of English **2nd**: the element **2** carries meaning but in itself does not spell out pronunciation (in the same way that a sumerogram does not spell out the Babylonian pronunciation), while the element **nd**, which does spell out pronunciation, is added to show that the word **second** (not **two**) is meant. One could say that **nd** is a phonetic complement. In Babylonian, phonetic complements often show which ending a word has, rather than disambiguate between two different words.

Regardless of how a Babylonian word was spelled (syllabically or sumerographically), it was usually read aloud in Babylonian. Accordingly, one of the things you will learn in this course is to convert sumerographic spellings (also known as 'sumerograms'; some books call them 'logograms') into their Babylonian equivalents.

4.2 The element of choice in syllabic spellings

In writing modern English, we have very narrow margins of choice over how to spell words. Occasionally, we can capitalize words which are normally not capitalized (**a Really Good Idea**), or substitute archaic spellings (**ye olde curiosity shoppe**) for their modern equivalents. Generally, however, the spelling of each word is fixed.

This was not so in Babylonian: the cuneiform script allowed a large element of individual choice in spelling. We have already seen that one could choose to spell a word syllabically or sumerographically. But even syllabic spellings raised choices of their own.

First, most syllables could be represented by several different signs, so one could choose which sign to use. Second, a syllable of the type consonant+vowel+consonant (e.g. *gub*) could be split into two signs, consonant+vowel and vowel+consonant (e.g. *gu-ub*). Thus when writing the syllable *gub* one could choose whether or not to split it. If it was not split, a sign had to be chosen among the several which could represent *gub*; if it was split, one sign had to be chosen among several which could represent *gu*, and another among the several which could represent *ub*. Third, one could decide whether to spell double consonants double or not. Fourth, one could decide whether to mark long vowels as such. (This was done with an 'extra' vowel, e.g. *ba-a-bu* for *bābu* **gate**; the 'extra' vowels are known as plene spellings.) Fifth, one had the choice of whether to represent a word as it was actually spoken, or to undo assimilations, etc. which had occurred in the spoken language (see Unit 44.5).

Thus a given word can turn up in many different spellings. For instance, the word *imaqqut* **he falls** could be written as *i-ma-qut* (three signs), *i-maq-qut* (three signs), *i-maq-qu-ut* (four signs), *i-ma-qu-ut* (four signs), *i-ma-aq-qut* (four signs), *i-ma-aq-qu-ut* (five signs).

4.3 Transliteration

Transliteration is a system of conventions for converting cuneiform into Roman characters. The aim of transliteration is to write Babylonian in the Roman alphabet in such a way as to keep a one-to-one correspondence with the original cuneiform, so that the reader can see how the word was spelled in cuneiform (i.e. exactly which cuneiform signs were used).

To indicate which cuneiform sign is being used to write a given syllable, numbers are used to distinguish between different cuneiform spellings of that syllable. For example, considering the syllable *tum*, one sign representing *tum* is transliterated as tum_1, another as tum_2, another as tum_3, another as tum_4, etc. This system is applied to all syllables.

Additional conventions in this system of numbering are that: the subscript $_1$ is normally omitted; the subscripts $_2$ and $_3$ are often replaced with acute and grave accents respectively, so that tum_2 can also be written *túm*, and tum_3 as *tùm*. (These accents have nothing to do with pronunciation, as they would, for example, in French.) When Assyriologists read a transliteration aloud sign by sign, they say the numbers: *túm* or tum_2 = '*tum* two'; 'one' is normally omitted.

The following conventions are also used in transliteration:

- syllabic spellings are in italic, sumerographic spellings in non-italic
- in syllabic spellings, signs are joined into words by hyphens (e.g. *iz-za-kar*); in sumerographic spellings they are joined into words by dots (e.g. anše.kur.ra)
- when a word includes both types of spelling (sumerographic and syllabic), the two types are joined by a hyphen (e.g. dù-*ma*; a.šà-*lum*)
- in this course, 'determinatives' (see the list of sumerograms at the end of the course) are placed in superscript.

As a result of all these conventions, a typical line of transliterated Babylonian looks like this:

gu_4 *pa-a-šu* dù-*ma i-qab-bi iz-za-kár a-na* anše.kur.ra *na-'i-id qab-li*

Each unit in this line (gu_4, *pa*, *a*, *šu*, *dù*, *ma*, *i*, *qab*, etc.) represents one cuneiform sign.

4.4 Normalization

Normalization is another way of converting cuneiform into Roman characters. It consists in writing Babylonian more or less as if it were a modern language: hyphens and dots between signs are abandoned (except for the particle *-ma*, discussed in later units), sumerographic spellings are turned into the Babylonian words they represent, etc. Unlike transliteration, normalization does not indicate how a word was spelled in cuneiform.

When normalizing, you have to use your knowledge of the language to decide where to double consonants and where to add marks of vowel length (e.g. *ā*) or contraction (e.g. *â*). The line of transliteration cited in 4.3 …

gu_4 *pa-a-šu* dù-*ma i-qab-bi iz-za-kár a-na* anše.kur.ra *na-'i-id qab-li*

… would be normalized as follows:

alpu pâšu īpuš-ma iqabbi izzakkar ana sīsî na'id qabli

This means **The ox opened its mouth and spoke, saying to the horse, expert in battle, …**.

Transliterations do not normally use the letter *y*. You have to decide, on the basis of your knowledge of the language, when to normalize *i* as *y* (e.g. *i-na bi-ti-ia* as *ina bītiya* **in my house**).

The most important things to remember

1. In cuneiform, words can be spelled syllabically or sumerographically. When used syllabically, cuneiform signs represent syllables.
2. In syllabic spellings, most cuneiform signs can represent several different syllables, and most syllables can be represented by several signs.
3. In cuneiform spelling, long vowels and double consonants are not necessarily marked as such.

4 In cuneiform spelling, a syllable of the type consonant + vowel + consonant can be split into two signs: consonant+vowel and vowel+consonant (e.g. *gu-ub* for the syllable *gub*).

5 The two systems of conventions for transcribing cuneiform into Roman characters are 'transliteration' and 'normalization'.

6 In transliteration, syllabic spellings are italic and sumerograms are non-italic.

7 In normalization, Babylonian is written (more or less) as it was pronounced.

8 In normalization, sumerograms are converted into Babylonian.

9 In normalization, double consonants and markers of vowel length or contraction are inserted where necessary.

10 In normalization, a line over a vowel means it is long; a circumflex accent over it means it results from contraction of two vowels (see Unit 47.1).

SELF CHECK

	I can ...
	... explain how Babylonian spelling is different from English spelling
	... explain what 'transliteration' and 'normalization' are, and how they relate to each other, and to the original cuneiform
	... explain what sumerograms are.

5 Roots and patterns

In this unit you will learn:

- **what a 'root' is**
- **how Babylonian words are derived from roots according to regular patterns.**

Most Babylonian words (including nouns, adjectives and verbs) are formed according to regular patterns, by adding sounds to groups of three letters. These groups of letters, which typically consist of three consonants, are known as 'roots'. Roots are marked with the square root symbol √, so that, for example, √*nṣr* means 'the root *nṣr*'. (It does not imply that any mathematics is involved!)

A root has a basic meaning associated with it, and the meanings of the words derived from it are related to this basic meaning. For example, √*nṣr* is associated with the basic meaning of **guarding**. From it are derived the words *nāṣiru* **a guard**, *niṣru* **protection**, *niṣirtu* **a guarded thing**, i.e. **treasure**, **secret**, *naṣāru* **to guard**, *maṣṣarūtu* (from *manṣarūtu*) **safekeeping**, *naṣru* **guarded**, etc.

Given knowledge of a word's root, the meaning of the root, and the meaning conveyed by the pattern through which the word is formed, one can usually get a good idea of what the word is likely to mean. For example, for the word *nērebu*: if one knows it comes from √*'rb*, that the meaning of this root is **to enter**, and that the pattern from which *nērebu* is formed can denote the place associated with the root (see Unit 46.1), one will not be surprised to learn that *nērebu* means **place of entering**, i.e. **entrance**!

To describe the patterns through which words are derived from roots, we will use *PRS* to represent the three root letters. This provides convenient shorthand: we can simply say 'the pattern *taPaRRaSī*' instead of saying 'the letters *ta*, followed by the first root letter, followed by the letter *a*, followed by the second root letter, same again, followed by the letter *a*, followed by the third root letter, followed by *ī*'.

The pattern can be turned into an actual word by substituting *P*, *R* and *S* with the relevant root letters. For example, the pattern *PāRiSu* means 'the (male) person who performs the action of the root'. Thus for √*nṣr* (**guarding**) the *PāRiSu* form is *nāṣiru*, and means **a guard**; for √*mhṣ* (**beating**), the *PāRiSu* form is *māhiṣu*, and means **a beater**, **someone who beats**.

In specifying patterns we will use the symbol *v* to mean 'a short vowel' and the symbol *v̄* to mean 'a long vowel'. For example, the pattern *iPRvS* means 'the letter *i*, followed by the first root letter, followed by the second root letter, followed by a short vowel, followed by the third root letter'. Which vowel to insert in place of *v* or *v̄* will be explained from unit to unit as you learn new patterns.

Exercise 5.1

Put the roots √*rkb* **to ride**, √*šrq* **to steal**, and √*hbš* **to be swollen** through the following patterns: *PaRSāku*, *PaRSāta*, *PaRSāti*, *PaRiS*, *PaRSat*, *PaRSānu*, *PaRSātunu*, *PaRSātina*, *PaRSū*, *PaRSā*.

Exercise 5.2

Put the roots √*nks* **to cut**, √*pšš* **to anoint**, √*pṭr* **to loosen**, and √*bqm* **to pluck out** through the following patterns: *uPaRRiS*, *tuPaRRiS*, *tuPaRRiSī*, *uPaRRiS*, *nuPaRRiS*, *tuPaRRiSā*, *uPaRRiSū*, *uPaRRiSā*. (The repetition of *uPaRRiS* is deliberate. You will see why in Unit 16.2.)

SELF CHECK

	I can ...
	... explain what roots and patterns are, and why they are important in learning Babylonian.

Part two

Nouns and adjectives

6 Overview of nouns and adjectives

In this unit you will learn:

- **some general features of Babylonian nouns and adjectives, and how the language treats them.**

Like English, Babylonian has nouns (words denoting things, e.g. **king**, **road**, **happiness**) and adjectives (words which qualify nouns, e.g. **good**, **fast**, **ugly**). This unit introduces you to several facts about them; you do not need to absorb them all before moving on. (See also Unit 46.)

> **LANGUAGE TIP**
> Babylonian (at least in its written forms) uses adjectives much less often than English, and one seldom finds two adjectives qualifying the same noun. In part this is because Babylonian likes to use nouns connected by **of** instead of adjectival expressions: **a chariot of kingliness** instead of **a kingly chariot**; **a dwelling of peace** instead of **a peaceful dwelling**.

6.1 A, the, some, any

Babylonian has no articles, neither definite (**the**) nor indefinite (**a**, **an**).
šarru(m) = **king**, **a king**, or **the king**; *ilū* = **gods** or **the gods**

The translation is determined by context. Babylonian also usually leaves **some** and **any** unexpressed. Insert one of these in translation when you judge that the sense requires it.

> **LANGUAGE TIP**
> Indispensable though they may seem to us, articles (words such as **a**, **the**) are comparatively rare in the world's languages as a whole. That they cluster so densely in the languages of Western Europe is probably no coincidence but the result of mutual influence over the centuries (a so-called 'areal phenomenon').

6.2 Grammatical 'case'

In Babylonian, the dictionary form (and indeed every other form) of nouns and adjectives can be analysed as a 'stem' + a grammatical ending, e.g. *šarru(m)* **king** = *šarr* + *u(m)*. This ending varies with the grammatical function (subject, object, etc.) which the word serves in the sentence.

The principle that a word changes in accordance with the function it serves in the sentence occasionally manifests itself in English, e.g. **I** (subject) vs. **me** (other functions). (With English **I/me**, however, the entire word changes, rather than just the ending.)

When Babylonian nouns and adjectives vary their endings according to the role which they play in the grammar of the sentence, they are said to change 'case'. A small minority do not change their ending according to case; they are said to be 'indeclinable'.

6.3 The three cases

Old and Middle Babylonian had three cases, known as 'nominative', 'accusative' and 'genitive'. (On vocatives see 6.4.) The nominative case is used for the subject of the sentence, and also where no other case is obviously necessary (e.g. in lists of words). The accusative case is used for the direct object. It can also be used with adverbial meaning (see Unit 36.5).

> **LEARNING TIP**
> To remember that the accusative is used for the direct object, think of the sentence **I accuse <u>you</u>!**

The genitive case is used after all prepositions (words like **in**, **to**, **of**), and in constructions meaning **of** (see Unit 10).

In all plurals (nouns, adjectives, masculine, feminine), the accusative and genitive endings are the same. (Some books therefore amalgamate accusative plural and genitive plural into a single case, the 'oblique', which exists only in the plural.)

6.4 Vocatives

In Old Babylonian, vocatives (words calling out to people, e.g. **O my friend**) sometimes display no case vowel.

OB *sābīt* **O ale wife** (from *sābītum*)

Strictly speaking, one could say that Old Babylonian has a vocative case, on a par with the nominative, accusative and genitive cases. However, vocatives are so rare that one can get away with thinking about them as isolated oddities, without going to the trouble of learning an extra case as such. (The same is true of the locative, treated in Unit 36.9–10.)

Later in the language, the nominative is often used.

SB *bēlu* **O lord**

When nouns with possessive suffixes (see Unit 11) are used as vocatives, they appear in the form which serves for nominative and accusative.

bēlī **O my lord**

6.5 Grammatical 'gender'

English has two genders for people (masculine, feminine) and one for objects (neuter): **he**, **she**, **it**. Babylonian has only two genders: masculine and feminine.

> **CULTURE TIP**
> In most assemblages of cuneiform sources, male names are attested much more frequently than female ones. This is probably connected to the fact that women were generally more distant from the world of writing. There are, however, notable exceptions to this: some women were fully literate.

Since there is no neuter (**it**) gender, the masculine and feminine genders are used for all nouns. Thus, if one translated super-literally, animals and inanimate objects would be referred to as **he** and **she** rather than **it**.

The grammatical gender of nouns denoting living beings is intuitively predictable: living beings of male sex (**man**, **boy**, **bull**, **king**, **billy goat**) have masculine gender, and living beings of female sex (**woman**, **girl**, **cow**, **queen**, **nanny goat**) have feminine gender. For other words, grammatical gender can usually be deduced from the 'dictionary form' (i.e. the form used in the Glossary at the end of this course): if *t* appears after the root letters, the gender is feminine; if not, the gender is usually masculine. (You will become proficient in identifying the root letters as your study of Babylonian proceeds.)

Feminine equivalents of masculine nouns and adjectives are formed by adding *t* or *at* (which in some words changes to *et*, see Unit 47.7) to the masculine stem. This *t* is known as the 'feminine *t*'.

bēlu **lord** → *bēl***t***u* **lady**
šarru **king** → *šarr***at***u* **queen**
rīmu **wild bull** → *rīm***t***u* **wild cow**
damqu **good** (m.) → *damq***at***u* **good** (f.)

If a noun which does not have *t* after the three root letters is feminine, this is stated in the Glossary (see e.g. *īnu(m)* **eye**).

Knowing a noun's gender is important, because it determines the form of words which qualify it or refer to it. For instance, if one wanted to say **its** in Babylonian, this would super-literally be **his** (*-šu*) or **her** (*-ša*), depending on whether the referent was masculine or feminine.

Babylonian adjectives have separate forms for masculine and feminine. They are listed in the Glossary by their masculine forms.

rīmu <u>*kadru*</u> <u>**rampaging**</u> **wild bull**
rīmtu <u>*kadirtu*</u> <u>**rampaging**</u> **wild cow**

6.6 Grammatical 'number'

In English, nouns can be either singular (**man**, **ship**) or plural (**men**, **ships**). In Babylonian there is another possibility, known as 'dual' (used for pairs of things, such as hands, eyes, etc.). Being in the singular, dual or plural is known as a word's 'number'. Nouns have different forms for singular, dual and plural. Adjectives also have different forms for singular and dual/plural (dual and plural adjectives are identical). The fact that adjectives change from singular to plural is unfamiliar to English speakers.

6.7 Position of adjectives

Adjectives normally follow the nouns they qualify, e.g. *šarru* <u>*rabû*</u> **the** <u>**great**</u> **king**, but in poetic language the opposite can happen. In poetry, a noun and its adjective can even be separated by a verb.

OB *patrī* *išpukū* *rabûtim* **They cast great swords** (Gilg. II 167)

6.8 Agreement between nouns and adjectives

Adjectives agree with the nouns they qualify in case, gender and number. Thus if a noun is nominative feminine plural, an adjective qualifying it will also be nominative feminine plural.

6.9 Agreement between nouns in apposition

A word is in 'apposition' to another word when it is juxtaposed to it and functions like an epithet of it, e.g. **That's my daughter Marigold** – **Marigold** is in apposition to **my daughter**. In Babylonian, nouns in apposition agree in case with the nouns they qualify.
SB *ina qibīt aššur bēliya* **By the command of Assur, my lord** (Asar. 57: v.4)

Assur (an indeclinable name) stands in the genitive case, so **my lord**, which is in apposition to Assur, also stands in the genitive case (see Unit 11.5).

6.10 Words functioning as nouns

Adjectives, both masculine and feminine, can be used as nouns, e.g. *ṭābu* **good** (m. sg.) can mean **a/the good man**, *ṭābtu* **good** (f. sg.) can mean **a/the good woman**.

Feminine adjectives are often used as abstract nouns:
ṭābtu **good** (f. sg.) can also mean **goodness**
kīttu **firm, true** (f. sg.) can also mean **truth**
lemuttu **evil** (f. sg.) can also mean **evil(ness)**

When they are so used, this is indicated in the Glossary (see e.g. *ṭābu(m)* **good**; the *m* in brackets is explained in 6.11).

As will be explained in Unit 22, infinitives of verbs can be used as singular nouns.

6.11 Mimation

Many grammatical tables in this course, especially those for nouns and adjectives, display an *m* in brackets at the end of a form. This means that the *m* can be present, but need not be. This *m* is known as 'mimation' (from *mīm*, the Arabic name of the letter M). When it occurs at the end of a word (without the particle *-ma*), this *m* is usually present in Old Babylonian, and usually absent in later periods. It began to be lost in the spoken language already in the Old Babylonian period, but, owing to their liking for traditional spellings, scribes wrote it sporadically (and at times haphazardly) even after it had completely vanished from the spoken language. When the word was followed by the particle *-ma*, mimation was 'protected', and continued to exist even in the first millennium BC.
OB *šarrum* and *šarrum-ma*; SB *šarru* but *šarrum-ma* (maybe also *šarru-ma*)

Mimation is supplied in brackets in the Glossary. When a word is cited in isolation in the main text of the course, mimation is usually omitted.

6.12 Names and epithets

Names and epithets sometimes stand in the nominative even though the grammar would lead one to expect genitive or accusative. This is known as the 'honorific' use of the nominative. Some names do not have a 'case vowel'.

LANGUAGE TIP

Unlike modern Western names, whose original meanings are no longer recognizable, Babylonian names usually had a clear meaning. They varied in length from just one word (e.g. *šallūru*, lit. **plum**) to an entire sentence. In this course, when several words form a name, they are joined by an en dash (–).

6.13 Babylonian singulars corresponding to English plurals

In English, if one were to behold a pile of slain warriors, one would speak of **the bodies of the warriors** – **bodies** because there are many of them. Instead, Babylonian would usually say **the body of the warriors**, because each warrior only has one body. Similarly, where English would say **the cats lifted their tails**, Babylonian would usually say **the cats lifted their tail** – the idea being again that each cat is only lifting one tail. Occasionally, however, Babylonian behaves like English.

6.14 -er and -est

In English, we have special forms of the adjective: one ending in **-er** (the comparative: **bigger**, **lighter**), one in **-est** (the superlative: **biggest**, **lightest**). Babylonian adjectives do not have special comparative or superlative forms. The idea of something being more or less than something else is conveyed by *eli* (literally **upon**, **over**), which in this usage translates as **than**.

SB <u>*eli*</u> *balṭūti ima''idū mītūti* **The dead will be numerous <u>upon</u> the living**, i.e. **The dead will be more numerous <u>than</u> the living** (ID Nin. 20)

CULTURE TIP

Babylonian poets sometimes borrowed phrases or lines from each other. The most striking case (from which the previous example is taken) is that of four lines in which the goddess Ištar threatens to bring up the dead to devour the living. They occur almost verbatim in *The Epic of Gilgameš*, *Ištar's Descent* and *Nergal* and *Ereškigal*.

The idea of something being **...est** seems simply to be conveyed by context, particularly in conjunction with *ina* **among**:

SB <u>*šūturāku*</u> *ina ilāti* (Gula Hymn 4)

While this sentence could be translated as **<u>I am very great</u> among the goddesses**, the sense is very probably **<u>I am the greatest</u> among the goddesses**.

6.15 And, or

Babylonian often omits to say **and** and **or** between nouns. When you feel that one of these is necessary, supply it in translation.

6.16 Compound words

Babylonian has very few compound words. They are formed like genitive constructions (see Unit 10), except that the second word does not necessarily have the genitive ending but ends in *-u(m)*, *-a(m)*, *-i(m)* depending on its case, like any normal noun or adjective. *eṣemṣēru* **backbone** (from *eṣemtu* **bone** and *ṣēru* **back**) *ašarēdu* **foremost** (from *ašru* **place** and *(w)ēdu* **sole, single**)

The most important things to remember

1 The endings of Babylonian nouns and adjectives change according to the word's grammatical 'case' (which is determined by its role in the sentence), its number (sg., dual or pl.) and its gender (m. or f.).

2 The nominative case is used for the subject.

3 The accusative case is used for the direct object.

4 The genitive case is used after all prepositions.

5 The grammatical gender of Babylonian nouns and adjectives can be masculine or feminine.

6 All feminine adjectives and most feminine nouns have *t* (the 'feminine *t*') before the vowel *u* in the dictionary form.

7 In prose, adjectives directly follow the nouns they qualify; in poetry, adjectives can precede them and/or be separated from them.

8 Adjectives agree in number, gender and case with the nouns they qualify.

9 Adjectives can be used as nouns.

10 In Old Babylonian, many nouns and adjectives ended in *m* ('mimation'), which was lost in later periods of the language.

SELF CHECK

	I can ...
	... generally navigate my way around how Babylonian nouns and adjectives behave
	... explain what a grammatical 'case' is
	... (in time:) explain how Babylonian's three cases are used
	... explain what 'grammatical gender' is
	... explain what 'mimation' is.

7 Nouns and adjectives, singular

In this unit you will learn:

- **that the endings for nouns and adjectives change over time**
- **how to inflect singular nouns and adjectives.**

This unit will introduce you to the forms of singular nouns and adjectives.

As was said in Unit 6.2, nouns and adjectives change their ending depending on their grammatical 'case', which is determined by the role they play in the grammar of the sentence. The subject of the sentence stands in the 'nominative' case, the object stands in the 'accusative' case, and words introduced by prepositions (**in**, **on**, **of**, etc.) stand in the 'genitive' case. The endings for the three cases are the same for singular nouns and singular adjectives.

7.1 Old and Middle Babylonian

In Old and Middle Babylonian (i.e. c. 1900–1000 BC), the case endings for singular nouns and adjectives are as follows:

Nominative	(subject)	*-u(m)*
Accusative	(object)	*-a(m)*
Genitive	(after prepositions)	*-i(m)*

For the *m* in brackets, see Unit 6.11.

LEARNING TIP

The sequence nominative accusative genitive forms the acronym 'nag'; the sequence *-u -a -i* can be remembered easily by thinking of the sounds in the sentence **you are free**.

The case endings are added directly to the word's stem. When the stem ends in a consonant, it can be found by removing the case ending and mimation from the dictionary form (i.e. the form under which it is listed in the Glossary).

šarru(m) **king** → stem *šarr-*

šarratu(m) **queen** → stem *šarrat-*

The singular forms of these two words in the three cases are as follows:

	king	**queen**
nom.	*šarru(m)*	*šarratu(m)*
acc.	*šarra(m)*	*šarrata(m)*
gen.	*šarri(m)*	*šarrati(m)*

When the word stem ends in a vowel, this vowel and the case vowel contract (see Unit 47.1), so that the stem vowel disappears and the dictionary form bears a circumflex accent on the case vowel, e.g. *rubû* **nobleman** (from *rubāu*; stem *rubā-*). In such cases the word stem is provided in the Glossary, so that you can see which vowel has contracted with the case ending.

An exception to vowel contraction is that Old Babylonian *ia* (with either vowel long or short) usually stays uncontracted (except in the city of Mari, where it regularly contracts to *ê*; see Unit 47.1).

annī- **this**
nom. (*anniu(m)* →) *annû(m)*
acc. (*annīa(m)* →) *annâ(m)* (Old Bab. *annīam*)
gen. (*annīi(m)* →) *annî(m)*

Some books insert ʼ between any two adjacent vowels which have not contracted, e.g. *annīʼam* instead of *annīam*; the meaning does not change.

In all periods, the sequence *ai* (with either vowel long or short) contracts to *ê*.

LEARNING TIP
With a cheerful anachronism, the fact that *a*+*i* = *ê* can be remembered as 'the airport rule'.

rubā- **nobleman**
nom. (*rubāu(m)* →) *rubû(m)*
acc. (*rubāa(m)* →) *rubâ(m)*
gen. (*rubāi(m)* →) *rubê(m)*

Note: the feminine equivalents of masculine nouns and adjectives whose stem ends in a vowel do not have stems ending in a vowel, because *t* is added to the masculine stem (see Unit 6.5). The vowel before *t*, if short, is lengthened:

stem *annī-*
m. *annû(m)* **this** → f. *annītu(m)* **this**
stem *rubā-*
m. *rubû(m)* **nobleman** → f. *rubātu(m)* **noblewoman**
stem *kanu-*
m. *kanû(m)* **cherished** → f. *kanūtu(m)* **cherished**

7.2 Standard Babylonian

Around 1000 BC, short vowels at the end of words ceased to be pronounced distinctly. The effects of this change in writing vary from one manuscript (i.e. cuneiform tablet) to another, according to the habits, training and skill of the writer. On some first millennium manuscripts, short vowels at the end of a word seem to be written virtually at random. On others, they are written in accordance with the rules of second millennium grammar.

When translating first millennium literature, the rule of thumb is that you will often, but not always, see second millennium endings; and that endings are not an infallible guide to the role which words play in a sentence's grammar. When the endings are awry from the standpoint of second millennium grammar, be guided by the context.

Many Standard Babylonian manuscripts were written by Assyrian scribes. (Indeed, our single most important source for Babylonian literature and scholarship is the libraries of the Assyrian king Assurbanipal.) Many of the sentences in the exercises and examples are taken from such manuscripts.

CULTURE TIP

The Assyrian king Assurbanipal (who reigned from 668 until c. 627 BC), raised as a scholar rather than a future ruler, assembled enormous libraries of cuneiform manuscripts in his capital Nineveh. They are the largest known before that of Alexandria. Excavated in the 19th century, the tablets are now in the British Museum.

First millennium Assyrian scribes often use their own case system (see Unit 41.4), so that word endings are more regular than on Babylonian manuscripts, but it is possible to translate correctly without being aware of this. Since Assyrian often has *e* where Babylonian has *i*, do not be surprised to encounter *e* instead of *i* while doing Standard Babylonian exercises.

The sign *me* is a particular case. This can be read *mì*, and since it is much quicker to write than mi_1, it is likely that many of its appearances should in fact be read *mì*. Thus, on the basis of spellings like *a-me-lu*, the first-millennium form of *awīlum* **man** is often normalized *amēlu*. But it was probably *amīlu* (*a-mì-lu*) – pronounced *awīlu*.

7.3 Adjectives, masculine and feminine

As noted in Unit 6.6, Babylonian adjectives have different forms for masculine and feminine. The masculine form is used when qualifying a masculine noun, the feminine form when qualifying a feminine noun. In the Glossary, the feminine form is given after the masculine form.

	gracious god	**gracious goddess**
nom.	*ilu(m) damqu(m)*	*iltu(m) damiqtu(m)*
acc.	*ila(m) damqa(m)*	*ilta(m) damiqta(m)*
gen.	*ili(m) damqi(m)*	*ilti(m) damiqti(m)*

LANGUAGE TIP

The stem of feminine singular adjectives always ends in *t*.

Exercise 7.1, Old Babylonian

Normalize the following sentences and translate them into English. (On square brackets, used to indicate a damaged or lost sign on the original, see Unit 2.2.)

Examples: *ma-tum* *ki-ma* ***li-i*** *i-ša-ab-bu* (*išabbu* **it is bellowing**); (AH II i 3)

⇒ *mātum kīma lî išabbu* **The country is bellowing like a bull**

a-wa-tum an-ni-tum šar-ra-am *i-ka-ša-a[d]* (*ikaššad* **it will reach**) (AbB 5, 125: 6′–8′)

⇒ *awātum annītum šarram ikašša[d]* **This word will reac[h] the king**

a-na ***šar-ri-im*** *a-qá-ab-bi* (*aqabbi* **I will speak**)

aš-šu ***mi-ni-im*** *ta-ak-la-šu* (*taklašu* **you detained him**) *i-na* ***ka-ap-ri-im ba-ru-um*** *ú-ul i-ba-aš-ši* (*ul ibašši* **there is not**)

na-ak-ru-um *i-na* ***ma-tim*** *na-di-i* (*nadi* **he has settled**)

ú-ku-ul-tam *šu-bi-lim* (*šūbilīm* **send to me!**)

i-na ***bi-ti-im ri-qí-im*** *wa-aš-ba-ku* (*wašbāku* **I am living**)

iš-tu ***ú-ri-im*** *a-ma-qú-ut* (*amaqqut* **I will jump down**)

šu-ku-un (*šukun* **set!**) ***a-da-na-am***

an-za-am *ku-šu-ud* (*kušud* **defeat!**)

i-lu-um*-ma* (don't translate *-ma*) *ù* ***a-wi-lum*** *li-ib-ta-al-li-lu* (*libtallilū* **may they be thoroughly mixed**) *pu-hu-ur i-na* ***ṭi-iṭ-ṭi***

ru-u'-tam *id-du-ú* (*iddû* **they threw**) *e-lu* ***ṭi-iṭ-ṭi***

Exercise 7.2, Old and Middle Babylonian

The last two sentences are MB.

ri-ig-ma *ú-še-eb-bu-ú* (*ušebbû* **they made resound**) *i-na* ***ma-tim***

ú-bu-ut (*ubut* **destroy!**) ***bi-ta*** *bi-ni* (*bini* **build!**) ***e-le-ep-pa ma-ak-ku-ra*** *zé-e-er-ma* (*zēr-ma* **spurn ...! and**) ***na-pí-iš-ta*** *bu-ul-li-iṭ* (*bulliṭ* **preserve!**)

a-na (*ana* **onto**) ^{giš}***di-im-tim*** (^{giš} is a 'determinative') *a-na mi-ni-im i-ti-ni-il-li* (*ītenelli* **he constantly goes up**)

am-mi-nim (*ammīnim* = *ana mīnim*) *it-ti* ***na-ma-aš-te-e*** *ta-at-ta-na-la-ak* (*tattanallak* **you roam through**) ***ṣe-ram***

ha-ri-im-tum *iš-ta-si* (*ištasi* **she called out to**) ***a-wi-lam***

li-ip-te-kum (*liptekum* **may he open for you**) ***pa-da-nam pe-hi-tam***

i-di-in (*idin* **give!**) *a-na* ***šar-ri-im ka-ak-ka-am da-an-na-am***

a-na ***u$_4$-mi-im an-ni-i-im*** *uz-na-ia i-ba-aš-ši-a* (*uznāya ibaššiā* **my attention is focused** *ana* **on**)

ši-ru-um *a-na* ***ši-ri-i[m]*** *i-na-zi-iq* (*inazziq* **it worries** *ana* **about**)

a-ga-a ṣi-i-ra *tu-up-pi-ra-šu* (*tuppirāšu* **you** (pl.) **crowned him with**)

a-ša-re-du-ta ṣi-ru-ta *qar-du-ta ta-qi-ša-šu* (*taqīšāšu* **you** (pl.) **bestowed upon him**)

Exercise 7.3, Old and Middle Babylonian

For the sumerograms, look up the Babylonian word in the list at the end of the course, and put it into the case (nominative, accusative or genitive) which is appropriate to the grammatical context. The last sentence is MB.

geštin ***ṭà-ba-am šu****-bi-lam* (*šūbilam* **send to me!**)

kù.babbar *ù* **ì.giš** *ú-ul i-di-nu-nim* (*ul iddinūnim* **they did not give to me**)

i-na **é.gal-*lim*** *an-ni-im ir-bi* (*irbi* **he grew up**) *mi-il-kum ša* **munus** *im-ta-qú-ut* (*imtaqut* **fell**) *ana šà-šu* (*ana libbišu* **into his heart**)

kaš *iš-ti-a-am* (*išti'am* **he drank**)

is-sà-qar-am (*issaqqaram* **he spoke**) *a-na* **kar.kid**

šuku *ú-ul ni-šu* (*nīšu* **we have**)

gun ***ù ma-da-ta*** *ugu-šu-nu ú-kin* (*elišunu ukīn* **I imposed upon them**)

Exercise 7.4, Standard Babylonian

Remember that *e* may occur where you expect *i*; see section 7.2.

ga-me-lu (or: *ga-mì-lu*) *ul a-mur* (*āmur* **I could find**)

a-dan-na *i-te-eq* (*īteq* **he/she/it passed**)

ki-ma ***šu-uš-kal-li*** *ú-kàt-ti-man-ni* (*ukattimanni* **it enveloped me**) ***šit-tú***

ina ***hu-ha-ri*** *šá* ***e-re-e*** *sa-hi-ip* (*sahip* **he is caught**)

da-a-a-na (*dayyāna*; see Unit 44.10) ***ṣal-pa mi-se-ra*** *tu-kal-lam* (*tukallam* **you make (s/o) experience (s/th)**)

ú-rap-pa-áš (*urappaš* **he will enlarge**) ***kim-ta meš-ra-a*** *i-ra-áš-ši* (*irašši* **he will acquire**)

sa-ar-tu *le-pu-uš* (*lēpuš* **I will commit**)

[*ni*]-*ṣir-ta* *i-mur-ma* (*īmur-ma* **he saw ..., and**) ***ka-tim-ti*** *ip-tu* (*iptu* **he opened**)

iṣ-ṣa-lim (*iṣṣalim* **it turned black**) ***ur-pa-tum pe-ṣi-tum***

mu-tum *ki-ma* ***im-ba-ri*** *i-za-an-nun* (*izannun* **it was raining down**) *ugu-šú-un* (*elišun* **upon them**)

i-na ***pu-uz-ri*** *ú-lid-an-ni* (*ūlidanni* **she gave birth to me**) *iš-kun-an-ni* (*iškunanni* **she placed me**) *i-na* ***qup-pi šá šu-ri***

na-ruq-qu ra-kis-tú *i-din-šú* (*idinšu* **give him!**)

The most important things to remember

1. In Old and Middle Babylonian (second millennium BC), singular nouns and adjectives have the same endings.
2. The three cases are clearly distinguished:
3. *-u(m) for* nominative.
4. *-a(m)* for accusative.
5. *-i(m)* for genitive.
6. The bracketed *m* ('mimation') is usually present in Old Babylonian, and usually absent later. Otherwise, singular nouns and adjectives have the same endings in Old and Middle Babylonian.
7. In Standard Babylonian (first millennium BC), the case system no longer works properly: the vowels at the end of singular nouns and adjectives are sometimes written at random.

8 A given adjective has both masculine and feminine forms.

9 The 'stem' of a noun or adjective can be found by removing *-u(m)* from the dictionary form.

10 If the dictionary form ends in *-û(m)*, with a circumflex accent on the *u*, this means that the stem ends in a vowel.

SELF CHECK

	I can ...
	... inflect (i.e. give the forms for) singular nouns and adjectives, for the variety or varieties of Babylonian I'm interested in (Old, Middle, Standard, or a combination of these)
	... (if studying more than one variety): explain how forms changed over time
	... explain why the endings of 'Standard Babylonian' will often be, or appear to be, quite irregular.

8 *Nouns, plural*

In this unit you will learn:

- **how to inflect plural nouns**
- **why feminine plurals can be tricky**
- **that some nouns change gender from singular to plural.**

Masculine nouns and feminine nouns have different endings in the plural. Any given noun has the same endings for genitive plural and accusative plural. (For plural adjectives see Unit 9.)

8.1 Old and Middle Babylonian, masculine

In Old and Middle Babylonian (second millennium BC), the case endings for masculine plural nouns are as follows:

nom. *-ū*	acc. *-ī*	gen. *-ī*

The endings are added directly to the word stem (to identify the stem see Unit 7.1).

	singular	plural
nom.	*šarru(m)* **king**	*šarrū* **kings**
acc.	*šarra(m)*	*šarrī*
gen.	*šarri(m)*	*šarrī*

Masculine nouns which originated as adjectives or which look like adjectives sometimes take adjectival endings in the plural (e.g. *eṭlu(m)* **young man**, nom. pl. *eṭlūtu(m)*; these endings are described in Unit 9.1).

8.2 Old and Middle Babylonian, feminine

In Old and Middle Babylonian (second millennium BC), the case endings for feminine plural nouns are as follows:

nom. *-ātu(m)*	acc. *-āti(m)*	gen. *-āti(m)*

To add the feminine plural endings to a noun, one takes the noun in its dictionary form, removes the ending *-u(m)*, the feminine *-t-* (if present), and (if present) a preceding short vowel, which can only be *a* or *e*. The appropriate plural ending is added to what remains.

nom. sg.	nom. pl.
šarratu(m) **queen**	*šarrātu(m)*
kaššāptu(m) **witch**	*kaššāpātu(m)*
īnu(m) **eye**	*īnātu(m)*

If the noun is related to an *e*-verb (see Unit 14.13), the plural endings *-ātu(m)* and *-āti(m)* usually change to *-ētu(m)* and *-ēti(m)*.

bēltu(m) **lady** (*bêlu* **to rule**) → nom. pl. *bēlētu(m)*
erretu(m) **curse** (*erēru* **to curse**) → nom. pl. *errētu(m)*
unīqu(m) **female goat kid** (*enēqu* **to suckle**) → nom. pl. *unīqētu(m)*

Spotting relations between nouns and verbs will become easier as you become familiar with the patterns according to which Babylonian nouns are formed (see Unit 46).

8.3 Standard Babylonian

In vernacular Babylonian of the first millennium, cases were no longer distinguished in the plural: masculine nouns simply ended in *-ī* or *-ānī*, feminine nouns in *-āt-* followed by an indistinct vowel (usually spelled *i*).

sg.	pl.
m. *ilu* **god**	*ilī* or *ilānī* **gods**
m. *šarru* **king**	*šarrī* or *šarrānī* **kings**
f. *šarratu* **queen**	*šarrāti* (also *-āte* and *-ātu*, more rarely *-āta*) **queens**
f. *kaššāptu* **witch**	*kaššāpāti* (also *-āte* and *-ātu*, more rarely *-āta*) **witches**

Occasionally, *-ānī* appears as *-ēnī*. As in the second millennium, when the noun is related to an *e*-verb, *-āt-* changes to *-ēt-*.

erretu **curse** (*erēru* **to curse**) → pl. *errēti*

Most Standard Babylonian manuscripts follow the system of the contemporary vernacular language, but a minority use second millennium endings. Assyrian manuscripts usually spell *-ī* as *-ē* and *-āti* as *-āte*.

LANGUAGE TIP

The long *ī* in the masculine plural suffix *-ānī* probably often shortened to *i* (and was perhaps pronounced indistinctly). Consequently, many Assyriologists normalize the suffix as *-āni* (as did the first edition of this course): *šarrāni* **kings**. However, historically *-āni* is *-ān+ī*, where the latter is the old masculine plural ending *-ū/ī/ī*. To reflect this, it is better to normalize *-ānī*.

8.4 Changes caused by feminine plural endings

Sometimes, the addition of the feminine plural ending results in changes. These changes are the same in Old, Middle, and Standard Babylonian. In describing the changes, we will cite words in their Middle Babylonian forms (which differ from Old Babylonian ones in the absence of mimation, and from Standard Babylonian ones in the final vowel).

1 Sometimes, in the singular, a consonant in contact with the feminine *t* has become assimilated to it (on assimilation see Unit 47.9). Since in the plural it is no longer in contact with *t*, the consonant usually regains its original form.

nom. sg.	nom. pl.
kīttu (from *kīntu*) **firmness**	*kīnātu*
ittu (from *idtu*) **ominous sign**	*idātu*
šuttu (from *šuntu*) **dream**	*šunātu*

2 Babylonian allows two consecutive syllables ending in a short vowel to occur only at the end of a word; if they occur elsewhere, the vowel of the second syllable is elided (i.e. removed, see Unit 47.4).

Accordingly, the feminine plural ending sometimes induces vowel elision:

nom. sg.	nom. pl.
puluhtu **fear**	(*puluhātu* →) *pulhātu*
damiqtu **good thing**	(*damiqātu* →) *damqātu*

These two phenomena ('undone' assimilation and vowel elision) can occur in one and the same form:

nom. sg.	nom. pl.
pirittu (from *piridtu*) **terror**	(*piridātu(m)* →) *pirdātu(m)*
maruštu (from *maruṣtu*) **distress**	(*maruṣātu(m)* →) *marṣātu(m)*

8.5 Vowel contraction in plurals

When the vowel of the plural ending is itself preceded by a vowel, the two vowels usually contract (see Unit 47.1). This happens in both masculine and feminine nouns.

rubû **nobleman** (from *rubāu*) → nom. pl. *rubû* (from *rubāū*)
awātu **word** → nom. pl. *awâtu* (from *awaātu*)

However, in Old Babylonian the sequence *ia* often stays uncontracted.

rabītu **big thing** → Old Bab. nom. pl. *rabiātum*
(but *rabâtum* also possible)

In the Old Babylonian city of Mari, the sequence *ai* (either vowel long or short) contracts to *ê*.
rabītu(m) **big thing** → OB Mari nom. pl. *rabêtum*

The sequence *ai* (either vowel long or short) contracts to *ê* in all periods.

rubû **nobleman** (from *rubāu*) → acc./gen. pl. *rubê*
mû **water** (from *māū*) → acc./gen. pl. *mê*
šamû **heaven** (from *šamāū*) → acc./gen. pl. *šamê*

8.6 Nouns which occur in the plural only

Some nouns occur only in the plural.

nišū **people** (f.!)
mû **water, the waters**
šamû **heaven, the heavens**
dadmū **villages, the inhabited world**

libbātu(m) **anger**

In the Glossary they are marked 'pl. only'. (Some books mark them with '*plurale tantum*' or 'pl. tant.')

8.7 Change of gender from singular to plural

Some nouns are masculine in the singular but feminine in the plural. (The opposite does not happen.)

bītu **house** → *bītātu* **houses**

eqlu **field** → *eqlētu* **fields**

In the Glossary such cases are marked with 'pl. *-ātu*' (or 'pl. *-ētu*').

> **LANGUAGE TIP**
> In the noun *bītu* **house**, the *t* at the end of the stem is not the 'feminine *t*' but a root letter: the root is √*bīt* (middle weak, see Unit 25). In the singular, *bītu* is masculine.

8.8 Unusual plurals

A few nouns have masculine plural endings, but are nonetheless grammatically feminine (i.e. they take feminine plural adjectives and feminine plural verbal endings; feminine plural suffixes refer to them).

nišū **people**; *ṣēnū* **sheep and goats**

Three short masculine nouns double the stem consonant when the plural is formed:

abu **father** → nom. pl. *abbū* **fathers** (or perhaps *abbû*, from *abbāū*)
ahu **brother** → nom. pl. *ahhū* **brothers** (or perhaps *ahhû*, from *ahhāū*)
iṣu **tree** → nom. pl. *iṣṣū* **trees**

In Old Babylonian, two frequently used masculine nouns insert *-ā-* between the stem and the plural ending. (The *ā* is never visible, as it always contracts with the plural ending.)

awīlu **man** → nom. pl. *awīlû* (from *awīlāū*)

ṣuhāru **young man** → nom. pl. *ṣuhārû* (from *ṣuhārāū*)

This is rare in other periods.

In Old Babylonian, the masculine plural ending *-ānū/-ānī* occurs mostly with *ālu(m)* **town**.

ālu(m) **town** → OB nom. pl. *ālānū*

Exercise 8.1, Old Babylonian

a-wi-lu-ú *bi-tam ip-lu-šu* (*iplušū* **they broke into**)

šar-ru-tam ša (translate *ša* as **over**) ***ni-ši*** *i-ši-im-kum* (*išīmkum* **he destined you for**) *ᵈen-líl*

na-ab-lu *im-ta-aq-qù-tu* (*imtaqqutū* **they gradually died down**)

me-le-em-mu *i-ha-li-qú* (*ihalliqū* **they are escaping**) *i-na qí-ši-im*

li-ib-ba-tim *im-ta-la* (*imtala* **he has become full of**)

ši-bi *ú-kál-lam* (*ukallam* **he will display**)

ša-am-mu *i-na* a.šà-*lim ú-ul i-ba-aš-šu-ú* (*ibaššû* **there are**)

tup-pa-am a-na ***me-e*** *ad-di* (*addi* **I threw**)

mu-ú *ú-ul i-ba-aš-šu-ú* (*ibaššû* **there are**)

al-pu *ša-al-mu* (*šalmū* **they are healthy**)

a-wi-lu-ú *i-na nu-pa-ri-im ka-lu-ú* (*kalû* **they are detained**)

a-lam ut-te-er (*uttēr* **he turned** *ana* **into**) *a-na* ***ti-li*** *ù* ***kàr-mi***

a-wi-le-e *wu-[u]š-ši-ir* (*wuššir* **release!**)

Exercise 8.2, Standard Babylonian

When normalizing sumerograms, use Middle Babylonian forms.

i-na ***di-ma-a-ti*** *si-hir-ti* uru (*sihirti āli* **round the town**) *a-lul pag-ri-šú-un* (*ālul pagrīšun* **I hung their bodies**)

a-na ***pul-ha-a-ti ša*** **ùg**^{meš} *i-šim-šu* (*išīmšu* **he solemnly appointed him** *ana* **as**) ^{d}*en-líl*

da-mi *ki-ma im-ba-ri ú-šá-az-na-[an]* (*ušaznan* **he makes rain down**) (said of a demon)

ina ***ka-ma-a-ti*** *rab-ṣu* (*rabṣū* **they were sitting**)

^{d}***a-nun-na-ki*** *iš-šu-ú* (*iššû* **they carried**) ***di-pa-ra-a-ti***

lu kám-⸢su⸣ ina šap-li-ka (*lū kamsū ina šaplika* **may they bow down beneath you**) lugal^{meš} idim^{meš} (*kabtūtu* **magnates**) *u* nun^{meš}

The most important things to remember

1. In the plural, masculine and feminine nouns have different endings.
2. In Old and Middle Babylonian, masculine plural nouns end in *-ū* (nominative), *-ī* (accusative), *-ī* (genitive).
3. In Old and Middle Babylonian, feminine plural nouns end in *-ātu(m)* (nominative), *-āti(m)* (accusative), *-āti(m)* (genitive).
4. In all periods, any given noun always takes the same ending for accusative plural and genitive plural.
5. In Standard Babylonian, masculine plural nouns usually end in *-ī* (also spelled *-ē*) or *-ānī*, regardless of case.
6. In Standard Babylonian, feminine plural nouns usually end in *-āti* (also spelled *-āte*), regardless of case.
7. Adding the feminine plural ending to a noun sometimes causes a vowel within the stem to be elided, according to the rule given in Unit 47.4. ('Within a word, two consecutive syllables ending in a short vowel can only appear at the end of the word; in other positions, the vowel in the second syllable is lost.')

8 Adding the feminine plural ending to a noun sometimes 'undoes' an assimilation which had taken place in the singular.

9 The gender of some nouns changes from singular to plural.

10 Some nouns occur only in the plural. These include *mû* **water**, *šamû* **heaven** and *nišū* **people**. (The last-named is feminine.)

SELF CHECK

	I can ...
	... inflect (i.e. give the forms for) plural nouns, for the variety or varieties of Babylonian I'm interested in (Old, Middle, Standard, or a combination of these)
	... (if studying more than one variety): explain how forms changed over time
	... explain why feminine plurals are tricky
	... explain what vowel elision is and how it works
	... explain what vowel contraction is and how it works.

9 *Adjectives, plural*

In this unit you will learn:

▸ **how to inflect plural adjectives.**

Like nouns, adjectives have the same endings for accusative plural and genitive plural. Feminine plural adjectives behave exactly like feminine plural nouns.

9.1 Old and Middle Babylonian, masculine

In Old and Middle Babylonian (c. 1900–1000 BC), the case endings for masculine plural adjectives are as follows:

nom. *-ūtu(m)* acc. *-ūtī(m)* gen. *-ūtī(m)*

The endings are added directly to the word stem (on word stems see Unit 7.1), e.g. *damqu* **good**:

	sg.	pl.
nom.	*damqu(m)*	*damqūtu(m)*
acc.	*damqa(m)*	*damqūti(m)*
gen.	*damqi(m)*	*damqūti(m)*

The bracketed *m* ('mimation') is usually present in Old Babylonian, and usually absent in Middle Babylonian (see Unit 6.11).

9.2 Old and Middle Babylonian, feminine

In Old and Middle Babylonian (c. 1900–1000 BC), the case endings for feminine plural adjectives are the same as the endings for feminine plural nouns (see Unit 8.2):

nom. *-ātu(m)* acc. *-āti(m)* gen. *-āti(m)*

The bracketed *m* ('mimation') is usually present in Old Babylonian, and usually absent in Middle Babylonian (see Unit 6.11). As with nouns (see Unit 8.2), if the adjective is related to an *e*-verb, *-ātu(m)* and *-āti(m)* change to *-ētu(m)* and *-ēti(m)*.

The feminine plural ending is added in the same way as for nouns.

9.3 Standard Babylonian

In the vernacular language of the first millennium, masculine plural adjectives ended in *-ūt-* followed by an indistinct vowel, usually spelled as *i* (*e* on Assyrian manuscripts). Thus the usual ending in writing was *-ūti*, regardless of grammatical case. Most manuscripts behave thus, but a minority use second millennium endings.

Feminine plural adjectives behave exactly like feminine plural nouns, and the same applies to them as was said in Unit 8.3: they usually end in *-āti* (*-āte* on Ass. manuscripts), regardless of grammatical case. As with nouns (see Unit 8.4), the feminine plural endings can induce changes: 'undoing' of assimilation, and vowel elision.

nom. sg.	nom. pl.
damiqtu(m) **good**	(*damiqātu(m)* →) *damqātu(m)*
lemuttu(m) (from *lemuntu(m)*) **evil**	(*lemunētu(m)* →) *lemnētu(m)*

9.4 Plurals of adjectives of dimension

In addition to taking plural endings, adjectives of dimension (**big**, **small**, **long**, **short**, etc.) sometimes (perhaps always) double their second root letter when forming the plural.

nom. sg.	nom. pl.
rabû(m) **big**	*rabbûtu(m)*
ṣehru(m) **small**	*ṣehherūtu(m)*

LANGUAGE TIP

Spellings such as *ra-bu-tum* are ambiguous: it is not clear whether the middle consonant was pronounced double but spelled single, or actually pronounced single. In such cases of doubt, one can normalize *ra(b)bûtum*.

9.5 Plurals of adjectives as nouns

When masculine plural adjectives are used as nouns (e.g. *damqu* meaning **the good one**, *alīlu* meaning **the powerful one** – see Unit 6.10), they usually take adjective endings.

<u>šībūti</u> upahhir **He gathered <u>the elders</u>** (AH I 386)

Sometimes they take noun endings. There is no difference in translation.

CULTURE TIP

It is likely that most people in Ancient Mesopotamia did not know which year they were born in, and so could not determine exactly how old they were.

9.6 Adjectival endings on plural nouns

Nouns which originated as adjectives or which look as if they might have can take adjectival endings in the plural.

eṭlu **young man** → nom. pl. *eṭlūtu* **young men**

Exercise 9.1, Old Babylonian

pa-ši iš-pu-ku (*išpukū* **they cast**) ***ra-bu-tim***

mi-ri ***da-an-nu-tim*** *a-li-li uš-*[*ta-li-ik*] (*uštālik* **he sent forth**)

in e-pé-ri ***ra-bi-ù-tim*** (the non-contraction is an archaism) suhuš.suhuš*-šu* (*išdīšu* **its roots**, said metaphorically of a city) *ki-ma* sa.tu*-im* (sp. *šadîm*) *ú-ki-in* (*ukīn* **he made firm**)

še-ri-ik-ta-ša (*šeriktaša* **her dowry**, accusative; **her** refers to a dead woman) dumu^{meš} ***mah-ru-tum*** (i.e. from an earlier marriage) *u* ***wa-ar-ku-tum*** (i.e. from a later marriage) *i-zu-uz-zu* (*izuzzū* **they shall divide**)

pu-uš-qí ***wa-aš-ṭú-tim*** *ú-*[*p*]*e-et-ti* (*upetti* **I found ways out of**) ***eṭ-lu-tum*** *ú-na-šá-qu* (*unaššaqū* **they kiss**) *ši-pi-šu* (*šēpīšu* **his feet**)

at-ta-na-al-la-ak (*attanallak* **I was walking about**) *i-na bi-ri-it* (*ina birīt* **among** + genitive) ***eṭ-lu-tim***

Exercise 9.2, Old Babylonian

Pay particular attention to the sumerograms: look up the Babylonian word in the list at the back of the book, and put it into the case (nominative, accusative or genitive) which is appropriate to the grammatical context:

zú.lum (plural!) ***wa-at-ru-tim*** *ša i-na* ^{giš}kiri$_6$ *ib-ba-aš-šu-ú* (*ša … ibbaššû* **which grew...**) *be-el* ^{giš}kiri$_6$*-ma i-*⌜*le*⌝*-*[*qé*] (*bēl kirîm-ma ileqqe* **it is the owner of the orchard who will receive**)

dingir (plural!) **gal.gal** (nom. pl. of *rabû* **great**) *ib-bu-ú-nin-ni* (*ibbûninni* **they called me**)

gu$_4^{\text{hi.a}}$ *ù* ùz (plural!) máš$^{\text{hi.a}}$ *ša-am-mi* ***na-ap-šu-tim*** *li-ku-lu* (*līkulū* **they should eat**)

Exercise 9.3, Standard Babylonian

it-bu-ú-ma (*itbû-ma* **they arose**) *ma-li-ke-e* ***rab-bu-tu***

^{d}utu *a-na* (*ana* **against**) ^{d}*hum-ba-ba id-kaš-šum-ma* (*idkâššum-ma* **he roused**) *me-he-e* ***ra-bu-tu***

21 uru^{meš}*-šú-nu* (*ālānīšunu* **their towns**, m. pl.) ***dan-nu-ti*** *ù* uru^{meš}*-ni* **tur^{meš}** *šá li-me-ti-šú-nu al-me* kur*-ud* (*almi akšud* **I besieged (and) conquered**)

ugu *tam-le-e šu-a-tu*$_4$ (*šuātu* **that**) é.gal^{meš} ***rab-ba-a-ti*** *a-na mu-šab be-lu-ti-ia* (*ana mūšab bēlūtiya* **as my lordly residence**) *ab-ta-ni* (*abtani* **I built**)

ú-še-el-la-a (*ušellâ* I **will bring up**) ***mi-tu-ti*** gu$_7$ (*ikkalū* **they will eat**) ***bal-ṭu-ti***

ki-ma kaš^{meš} (singular) *a-šat-ta-a* (*ašattâ* **I will drink**) a^{meš} ***dal-hu-te***

up-pi-is-si-ma (*uppissi-ma* **treat her!**) *ki-ma* garza^{meš} ***la-bi-ru-t*[*i*]**

mal-ki ***šep-ṣu-ti*** *e-du-ru ta-ha-zi* (*ēdurū tāhāzī* **they feared doing battle with me**)

gim *ar-me a-na* (*ana* **onto**) *zuq-ti* ***šá-qu-ti*** *ṣe-ru-uš-šú-un e-li* (*ṣēruššun ēli* **I went up against them**) *a-na* ùg^{meš}*-šú* (*nišīšu* **his people**, f. pl.) ***dal-pa-a-te*** *ú-še-ṣi* (*ušēṣi* **I sent out**) *nu-u-ru*

ugu (translate *eli* as **at**) *ep-še-e-ti* ***an-na-a-ti*** *lìb-bi i-gug* (*libbī īgug* **my heart became furious**)

har-ri na-hal-li na-at-bak kur*-i* (translate *natbāk šadî* as plural) *me-le-e* ***mar-ṣu-ti*** *i-na* ^{giš}gu.za *áš-ta-am-di-ih* (*aštamdih* **I sped across**)

The most important things to remember

1. In the plural, masculine and feminine adjectives have different endings.
2. In Old and Middle Babylonian, feminine plural adjectives have the same endings as feminine plural nouns: *-ātu(m)* (nominative), *-āti(m)* (accusative), *-āti(m)* (genitive).
3. In Old and Middle Babylonian, masculine plural adjectives have different endings from masculine plural nouns: *-ūtu(m)* (nominative), *-ūti(m)* (accusative), *-ūti(m)* (genitive).
4. As with nouns, any adjective has the same forms for accusative plural and genitive plural.
5. Like feminine nouns, Standard Babylonian feminine plural adjectives usually end in *-āti* (also spelled *-āte*), regardless of grammatical case; the final short vowel can vary.
6. Standard Babylonian masculine plural adjectives usually end in *-ūti* (also spelled *-ūte*), regardless of grammatical case; the final short vowel can vary.
7. As with nouns, the feminine plural ending can cause vowel elision according to the rule given in Unit 47.4. ('Within a word, two consecutive syllables ending in a short vowel can only appear at the end of the word; in other positions, the vowel in the second syllable is lost').
8. Adding the feminine plural ending to an adjective sometimes 'undoes' an assimilation which had taken place in the singular.
9. Masculine adjectives used as nouns can take noun or adjective endings in the plural.
10. Adjectives of dimension sometimes (perhaps always) double the middle root letter in the plural.

SELF CHECK

	I can ...
	... inflect (i.e. give the forms for) plural adjectives, for the variety or varieties of Babylonian I'm interested in (Old, Middle, Standard, or a combination of these)
	... (if studying more than one variety): explain how forms changed over time
	... explain how plural adjective endings differ from noun endings.

10 *The construct state*

In this unit you will learn:

- **what it means for a Babylonian noun to have a 'state'**
- **how the 'construct state' arose**
- **how to form it**
- **why forming it can be quite tricky**
- **how to use it.**

One way to say **of** in Babylonian, which you have already met in the exercises, is to use the preposition *ša* **of** followed by the genitive case.

kunukku ša šarri **The seal of the king**
ana kunukki ša šarri **For the seal of the king**

Another way of saying **of** dispenses with *ša*. It is done like this: the second word stands in the genitive, while the first word stands in a form known as the 'construct' form. This way of expressing **of** is best understood by considering its origin, which is explained in 10.1.

On how one might choose between different ways of expressing **of**, see Unit 30.3.

10.1 The origin of construct forms

In the ancestor language of Babylonian, the notion of **of** could be expressed by the genitive case alone (as happens e.g. in Latin or German). Thus, in the phrase **the land of the enemy**, **the enemy** would stand in the genitive case (*nakrim*), meaning **of the enemy**; **the land** would stand in whatever case was appropriate for its grammatical role in the sentence. (The examples are in non-italic, to indicate that they are not Babylonian as we know it.)

mātu nakrim (with **land** in the nominative)
māta nakrim (with **land** in the accusative)
māti nakrim (with **land** in the genitive)

Forms such as these sometimes appear in documents written in the parent (or aunt and uncle) languages of Babylonian, collectively known as 'Old Akkadian', in about 2400–2100 BC. (The question of mimation, or lack thereof, on the first word is complicated.) As time passed, the habit of running the two words together in speech eroded the short final vowel at the end of the first word (i.e. its case vowel). This resulted in a single form for all three cases:

māt nakrim **the land of the enemy**

This is the form which occurs in Babylonian as we know it, and this principle applies to all singular words. However, if the case vowel is preceded by two consonants (e.g. *libbu* **heart**, *kunukku* **seal**, *mahru* **front**, *širiktu* **gift**), refinements set in. For if no change had occurred other than the loss of the case vowel, one would have ended up with a word ending in two consonants (*libb*, *kunukk*, *mahr*, *širikt*), which Babylonian does not tolerate (see Unit 47.13). In such cases, a 'helping' vowel is inserted: *libbi*, *mahar*. Which vowel to insert and where (after or between the two consonants) is determined by factors which will be explained later in this unit.

Plurals underwent the same development as singulars. However, in masculine plurals the ending was 'protected' by being long (and/or to make the pl. different from the sg.), and so was not eroded.

OB <u>*kakkabū*</u> *šamāī* **<u>The stars</u> of heaven**, nominative (Gilg. II 6) (the non-contraction is poetic)

In feminine plurals, the short final vowel was eroded, so the ending of the construct form is *-āt* (or *-ēt*) in all three cases.

OB <u>*ummānāt*</u> *nakrim* **<u>The troops</u> of the enemy**

10.2 Singular construct forms

If stated in words, the rules for producing the construct form of singular words sound diabolically complicated. Thankfully, there is a short cut: compare the word whose construct state you want to form with the examples below, and find the one that matches it in terms of

- the number of syllables
- whether it has the 'feminine *t*'
- whether the stem ends in a single consonant, a double consonant, two different consonants, or a vowel (in the latter case the dictionary form would have a circumflex accent, like *rubû* **lord**, stem *rubā-*).

Pattern 1 (stem ends in a single consonant) – the construct state is the same as the stem

bītu **house** → *bīt*
(Exception: Old Babylonian nouns related to III-weak verbs – see Unit 23 – often have construct forms ending in a vowel, e.g. *tībi nakrim* **attack of the enemy** from *tībum* **attack**, related to *tebû* **to arise**.)

Pattern 2 (stem ends in two different consonants; no feminine *t*) – add the vowel which appears after the first root letter

mahru **front** → *mahar*
šipru **work** → *šipir*
murṣu **illness** → *muruṣ*

(Adjectives used as nouns follow a slightly different rule: the 'helping vowel' need not be the same as the vowel earlier in the word. However, it is rare to encounter such cases.)

Pattern 3 (two-syllable word; stem ends in two different consonants; one is the feminine *t*) – add *a* before the 'feminine *t*'

šubtu **dwelling** → *šubat*
ṣibtu **interest** → *ṣibat*

In words from the same root as *e*-verbs (see Unit 14.13) the *a* is subject to *e*-colouring:
bēltu **lady** → *bēlet*

Pattern 4 (stem ends in two identical consonants; two-syllable word) – add *i* to the stem

libbu **heart** → *libbi*
šikittu **shape** → *šikitti*
kīttu **truth** → *kītti*

Pattern 5 (stem ends in two identical consonants; three-syllable word): remove one stem-final consonant

kunukku **seal** → *kunuk*

Pattern 6 (stem ends in feminine 6; three-syllable word) – add *i*

širiktu **gift** → *širikti*

> **LANGUAGE TIP**
> The *-i* added at the end of some words in the construct state was probably not pronounced as a full *i* sound, but more like the first **a** in **banana** (the so-called 'schwa' sound).

Pattern 6 (stem ends in a vowel) – the form is variable

The construct form can be just the stem, or the stem with the appropriate case vowel. (In the latter case, the two vowels usually contract.)

kussû **throne** (from *kussiu*) → *ina kussi šarrūtiya* or *ina kussî šarrūtiya* **on the throne of my kingship**

Sometimes in Standard Babylonian the vowel at the end of the stem is lost. This happens especially with G participles of III-weak verbs (see Units 23 and 35).

nāšû **bearer** (from *nāšiu*) → *nāš bilti* **tribute bearer** (lit. **bearer of tribute**)

Sometimes in Standard Babylonian one finds *-Ce-e*:

SB <u>*a-ṣe-e*</u> *abul ālišu* **the <u>exiting</u> of the gate of his city**, i.e. **(the action of) going out of his city gate** (construct state of *(w)aṣû*) (Chic. iii.30)

10.3 Plural construct forms

The formation of plural construct forms follows the same principles as singular ones: mimation is lost, as are final short vowels (but not long ones). The question of double consonants or two consonants does not arise, so plural construct forms are much easier than singular ones.

For masculine plural nouns, construct forms are the same as non-construct ones, ending in *-ū* (nom.), *-ī* (acc.), *-ī* (gen.):

nom. *šarrū* acc. *šarrī* gen. *šarrī*
OB <u>*ilū*</u> *mātim itrurū* **<u>The gods</u> of the land trembled** (SEAL 1.1.2.1: 42, Anzû)

CULTURE TIP

In the *Anzû* poem, Anzû (a mythical bird-like creature) steals the Tablet of Destinies from the god Enlil. He thus usurps mastery of the Universe, and becomes all-powerful. He can only be defeated through a ruse suggested by Ea, the god of wisdom (who elsewhere comes up with the plan to cheat the Deluge by tipping off the Babylonian Noah).

When masculine plural adjectives are used as nouns, they can be put in the construct form. If this happens, they may take the same endings as nouns; alternatively, the construct form of the masculine plural adjectival ending is *-ūt* for all three cases.

For feminine plural nouns (and adjectives used as nouns), there is only one construct form for all three cases. It ends in *-āt* (or *-ēt*):

<u>*ummānāt*</u> *nakri* **<u>The troops</u> of the enemy**

The first millennium masculine plural ending *-ānī* remains such (or *-āni* – see Unit 8.3, Tip box) in the construct state (i.e. *i* is not lost, even if it is shortened).

10.4 Terminology and the idea of a noun's 'state'

In discussing Babylonian grammar, it is useful to have a word for a noun's being or not being in the construct form. By convention, this is known as a noun's 'state'. When a noun is, so to speak, free-floating (as in Units 7 and 8), it is in the 'basic state'; when it is in the construct form, it is in the 'construct state'. There are other states, which you will meet in future units: when it has possessive suffixes, a noun is in the 'possessive state' (see Unit 11); when it has stative suffixes, it is in the 'predicative state' (see Unit 18.8). These 'states' are mutually exclusive: a noun can never be in two of them at the same time.

The case endings which you learned in Units 7 and 8 are those of the basic state. In the construct state, one form serves all cases (except for masculine plurals). The structure 'noun in the construct state + genitive' is known as a 'genitive construction'. Except for *lā* **not** and the rare particle *-mi* (of variable meaning), nothing can separate a construct from the genitive which depends on it.

Another state of the noun, the 'endingless state', will be discussed in Unit 40.

It is important to realise that case and state are two different things. Thus a noun can be in the genitive case and the construct state; in the genitive case and the basic state; in the nominative case and the construct state; etc.

The principle that a noun in the construct state (let's call it 'noun A') will normally be followed by a noun in the genitive case (let's call it 'noun B') tells us nothing about the case of noun A, or the state of noun B. These will be determined by the grammatical context.

10.5 Chains of construct forms

To say something like **X of Y of Z**, one can use a 'chain' of construct forms.

OB *līt ummān nakrim* **A defeat of the army of the enemy** (OBE 156: 6)

MB *muštēšir kiššat ilī* **Keeper-in-good-order of all of the gods** (RIMA 2, 12 i.1)
MB *hāyiṭ ṣalpāt ayyābē* **Espier of the treachery of the enemies** (RIMA 2, 12 i.7–8)
SB *muštēšir nūr kiššati* **Keeper-in-good-order of the light of the Universe** (epithet of the sun god) (BWL 128: 34)

In such chains, the first noun (e.g. *līt*) is in the construct state; its case (which one cannot tell from looking at it) is determined by the grammar of the sentence: nominative if the whole phrase is the subject of the sentence, accusative if the whole phrase is the direct object, genitive if the whole phrase follows a preposition. The second noun (e.g. *ummān*) is in the construct state and (though one cannot tell this from looking at it) in the genitive case. The third noun is in the basic state and (as the ending shows) in the genitive case.

In principle, chains of nouns in the construct state could go on for ever, but: (a) it is rare for very long chains to be necessary; (b) when chains of construct states get long, they tend to be interrupted with *ša* **of**.

SB *mušaklilat pilludê ša ilī* **Perfectly-carry-out-er** (f.) **of the rites of the gods** (BWL 267: 1–2)

Genitive constructions cannot be used to express **X-and-Y of Z**. For this, one has to use *ša* **of**.

10.6 Construct forms followed by multiple genitives

To say something like **X of Y and (of) Z**, the construct state is followed by more than one noun with the genitive ending.

MB *šāgiš <u>lemni</u> u <u>ayyābi</u>* **Slaughterer of <u>evildoer</u> and <u>foe</u>** (RIMA 2, 12 i.11)
SB *ilat <u>kuzbi</u> u <u>dādī</u>* **Goddess of <u>allure</u> and <u>sex appeal</u>**

u **and** often appears between two such genitives, but it is not obligatory.

CULTURE TIP
Babylonians were not prudish: their literature abounds with explicit sexual references.

10.7 Adjectives qualifying nouns involved in genitive constructions

When an adjective qualifies a noun which is involved in a genitive construction, the adjective stands (as usual) in the same case as the noun it qualifies. For the purpose of determining the adjective's position, the entire genitive construction counts as a single noun: usually the adjective follows it, but in poetry it can precede it.

OB *mupahhir nišī <u>saphātim</u> ša isin* **The (re)assembler of the <u>scattered</u> people of Isin** (CH Prologue ii.49–51)
SB *kīma <u>ezzi</u> tīb mehê* **Like the <u>furious</u> onslaught of a storm** or **Like the onslaught of a <u>furious</u> storm** (Asar. 58: 16)
SB *bīt uzni <u>ṣīrte</u> <u>šuklulu</u>* **Perfect house of the exalted ear** (temple name; BTT p. 78, 151); *ṣīrte* (f., gen.) goes with *uzni* (f., gen.) and *šuklulu* (m., nom.) goes with *bīt* (m., nom.)

An adjective qualifying a noun cannot appear *within* a genitive construction.

10.8 Translating genitive constructions

Owing to differences in how Babylonian and English sometimes use singulars and plurals (see Unit 6.13), one occasionally encounters singular construct forms which, so as to become English-sounding English, need to be translated as plurals.

pagar muqtablīšunu **The body of their warriors**, i.e. **The bodies of their warriors**

Sometimes it is clear from the context that the translation requires more than just **of**.

OB *āl sunqim* **A town of famine**, i.e. **A town beset by famine**
SB *šārat lētīšu* **The hair of his cheeks**, i.e. **The hair on his cheeks**

Possessive suffixes at the end of a genitive construction can qualify the entire construction. Thus *šārat lētīšu* could mean **his cheek-hair** as well as **the hair on his cheeks**.

10.9 The archaic construct ending *-u*

Sometimes, singular nouns in the construct state display the ending *-u*. By the Old Babylonian period and later, this is an archaism.

OB *ina libbu erṣetim* **In the midst of the netherworld** (Gilg. VA+BM i.11′)

Exercise 10.1, Old Babylonian

ri-mi (*rimi* **sit on!**) ***pa-ra-ak*** *šar-ru-tim*

i-ša-lu (*išālū* **they asked**) ***tab-sú-ut*** dingir^{meš} *e-ri-iš-tam* ^{d}*ma-mi*

ab-ša-nam li-bi-il (*lībil* **let him bear**) ***ši-pí-ir*** ^{d}*en-líl*

i-na (*ina* **from**) ***ši-i-ir*** *i-li e-ṭe-em-mu li-ib-ši* (*libši* **let there come into being**)

ik-ta-ab-ta (*iktabta* **it has become burdensome for me**) ***ri-gi-im*** *a-wi-lu-ti*

ù a-na-ku (*u anāku* **as for me**) *ki-i a-ša-bi* (from *aššābu* **someone who dwells**) *i-na* ***bi-it*** *di-im-ma-ti ša-hu-ur-ru ri-ig-mi* (*šahurru rigmī* **my cry is silent**)

qí-iš-tum ig-re-e-šu (*igrešu* **it attacked him**)

iš-ku-un (*iškun* **it brought**) *ek-le-tam a-na* (*ana* **on**) ***nu-úr*** *ša-ma-i*

i-ša-at *li-ib-bi mu-ti na-pi-ih-tum ib-li* (*ibli* **it became extinguished**)

^{d}iškur ***be-el*** hé.gál ***gú-gal*** *ša-me-e ù er-ṣe-tim re-ṣú-ú-a* (*rēṣūya* **my helper**, nominative) *zu-ni i-na ša-me-e mi-lam i-na na-ag-bi-im li-ṭe*$_{4}$*-er-šu* (*līṭeršu* **may he deprive him of**)

i-na ***a-al*** *sú-un-qì-im wa-aš-ba-a-ku* (*wašbāku* **I am living**)

šu-up-ši-ik *i-li ra-bi-[m]a* (*rabi-ma* **it was great**)

CULTURE TIP

According to the Babylonian Story of the Flood (*Atra-hasīs*), from which the last sentence is taken, mankind was created to work: the lesser gods rebelled against the higher gods because of all the agricultural work they had to do, so the higher gods created mankind to do it for them.

Exercise 10.2, Middle Babylonian

šal-ma-at *qu-ra-di-šu-nu* (*qurādīšunu* **their warriors**, m. pl. gen.) *i-na* ***mit-hu-uṣ*** *tu-ša-ri ki-ma ra-hi-ṣi lu-ke-mir* (*lukemmir*, for *lū ukemmir* **I truly piled up**)

kur *kat-mu-hi* dagal-*ta a-na si-hir-ti-ša ak-šud* (*ana sihirtiša akšud* **I conquered in its entirety**)

kur-*a mar-ṣa ù ger-re-te-šu-nu* (*gerrētešunu* **their, i.e. the mountains' paths**, f. pl. acc.) *pa-áš-qa-a-te i-na* ***aq-qúl-lat*** urudu^meš^ *lu ah-si* (*lū ahsi* **I truly hewed my way through**)

um-ma-na-at ^kur^ *pap-he-e ... it-ti* ***um-ma-na-at*** **kur** *kat-mu-hi-ma* (do not translate-*ma*) *ki-ma šu-ú-be uš-na-il* (*ušna"il* **I laid low**; ŠD preterite, see Unit 14.10)

pa-gar *muq-tab-li-šu-nu* (*muqtablīšunu* **their warriors**, m. gen. pl.) *a-na gu-ru-na-a-te i-na* ***gi-sal-lat*** kur-*i lu-qé-ri-in* (*luqerrin* **I truly stacked**)

Exercise 10.3, Standard Babylonian

a-na ***šá-hat*** kur-*e pa-áš-qa-te ip-par-šid-du* (*ipparšiddū* **they fled**) *mu-ši-tíš*

ki-ma ***ša-pá-at ku-ni-i-ni*** *iṣ-li-ma ša-pá-tu-š[a]* (*iṣlimā šapātuša* **her lips turned dark**)

mu-ut *bu-bu-ti ù ṣu-mi* ⸢*li-mu-ta*⸣ (*limūta* **may he die**)

um-ma-na-at ^d^*aš-šur gap-šá-a-te ad-ke-e-ma* (*adke-ma* **I called up**)

The most important things to remember

1 Babylonian can express **X of Y** by putting the two words next to each other: X is put into a special form known as the 'construct state', and its case is usually invisible; Y is put in the genitive case, and other things being equal stays in the 'basic state'.

2 Constructions like this are known as 'genitive constructions'.

3 One can form a chain of nouns in the construct state, and a noun in the construct state can be followed by multiple genitives.

4 Adjectives qualifying nouns involved in genitive constructions usually follow the entire construction, and always agree in case, gender and number with the nouns they qualify.

5 Masculine plural nouns have the same form in the construct state as they do in the basic state (nominative *-ū*, accusative *-ī*, genitive *-ī* in Old and Middle Babylonian; *-ī*, *-ē* or *-ānī* in Standard Babylonian).

6 Masculine plural adjectives used as nouns usually form the construct state with the ending *-ūt* in all three cases.

7 Feminine plural nouns (and adjectives used as nouns) form the construct state with the ending *-āt* (or *-ēt*) in all three cases.

8 The rules for forming the construct state of singular nouns are intricate.

9 For nouns with stems ending in a single consonant, the singular construct state is formed by removing the case vowel (e.g. *bītu* → *bīt*).

10 For other nouns, how to make the construct form depends on the number of syllables in the dictionary form of the noun, and what the noun stem ends in.

SELF CHECK

	I can ...
	... explain what the 'construct state' is
	... translate genitive constructions
	... explain which three factors determine how a given noun looks in the construct state
	... use the patterns in Unit 10.2 to put a noun in the construct state, by analogy with the one that resembles it in the three relevant ways
	... (in time:) recite the construct forms of the example nouns.

11 *Possessive suffixes*

In this unit you will learn:

- **that Babylonian usually expresses 'my', 'your', 'her', etc. through suffixes**
- **what these suffixes are**
- **how to add them to nouns**
- **that they can also be used with some prepositions.**

This unit is basically about how to say **my**, **your**, **his**, **her**, **its**, **our**, **your**, **their** in Babylonian. Whereas English has self-standing words for this, Babylonian instead uses suffixes which one adds to the relevant word. Thus, from the standpoint of an English speaker, it is as if Babylonian said **housemy** instead of **my house**, **palacetheir** instead of **their palace**, etc. These suffixes are known as 'possessive suffixes'.

Possessive suffixes can attach themselves to nouns (including verbal infinitives, participles, and adjectives used like nouns). The same suffixes are also used with some (but not all) prepositions. A noun with a possessive suffix is in the 'possessive state' (as distinct from the basic state, construct state, etc. – see Unit 10.4).

We will first present the suffixes, then explain what form a given word assumes before them (we will treat plurals before singulars, as they are easier). There is not much difference between second and first millennium forms, so we will treat them together.

11.1 The suffixes

Babylonian possessive suffixes are as in Table 1. For the first person singular suffix, one uses *-ī* after a consonant, and *-ya* after a vowel. (But sometimes, after *u*, *-ya* appears as *-'a*.)

Table 1

1st sg.	*-ī, -ya*	'my'
2nd sg. m.	*-ka*	'your'
2nd sg. f.	*-ki*	'your'
3rd sg. m.	*-šu*	'his'
3rd sg. f.	*-ša*	'her'
1st pl.	*-ni*	'our'
2nd pl. m.	*-kunu*	'your'
2nd pl. f.	*-kina*	'your'
3rd pl. m.	*-šunu*	'their'
3rd pl. f.	*-šina*	'their'

The gender distinction which English makes in the third person singular (**his**, **her**) is made in both the second and third persons, singular and plural. Thus, for example, the suffix for **your** changes depending on whether one speaks to a man, a woman, a group of men, or a group of women. (A mixed group counts as masculine.)

Some of these suffixes also have 'short forms', which mostly occur in poetry. They have the same meaning as normal forms. For *-kunu*, *-kina*, *-šunu*, *-šina*, the short forms are *-kun*, *-kin*, *-šun*, *-šin*. For *-ka*, *-ki*, *-šu*, *-ša*, the vowel of the suffix is dropped; in Old Babylonian the vowel preceding a 'shortened' suffix is usually the case vowel (nom. *u*, acc. *a*; gen. is rare), while Standard Babylonian generally has *u* for both nom. and acc.

libbaka **your heart** → SB 'short form' *libbuk*

11.2 Learning the suffixes

Here are some associations which may help you in learning the suffixes:

-ī	think of English **I** (though remember that *-ī* is pronounced like **ee** in **see**).
-ka	think of saying **your** to a man called Karl.
-ki	think of saying **your** to a woman called Kim.
-šu	think of saying **his** about Franz Schubert.
-ša	think of saying **her** about Charlotte Brontë.
-ni	think of the American President Richard Nixon talking about '**our** country'.
-kunu -kina -šunu -šina	you can probably learn these as a string of sounds, like a poem.

11.3 Possessive suffixes and vowel elision

The rules of vowel elision (see Unit 47.4) do not apply to possessive suffixes. Thus *šarrašunu* **their king** does not become *šarrašnu*, and *ummānātušunu* **their troops** does not become *ummānātušnu* – at least in writing. It is, however, possible that the spellings are traditional, and that (in some varieties of the language) vowels were elided.

11.4 Possessive suffixes after plural nouns

To add a suffix to a plural noun, remove mimation (if present) and add the suffix after the case vowel.

ummānātu(m) **troops** → *ummānātušu* **his troops**, *ummānātušunu* **their troops**

têrēti(m) **instructions** → *têrētišunu* **their instructions**

qurādī **warriors** → *qurādīšu* **his warriors**

Since, after mimation (if present) is removed, plurals end in a vowel, the possessive suffix for the first person singular after plural nouns is *-ya* not *-ī*.

šībū **witnesses** → *šībūya* **my witnesses**

In Old and Middle Babylonian, plurals with possessive suffixes decline, just as they would without suffixes.

šībūya **my witnesses** (nom.), *šībīya* **my witnesses** (acc./gen.)
tuppātuya **my tablets** (nom.), *tuppātiya* **my tablets** (acc./gen.)

CULTURE TIP

Though cuneiform tablets were made of clay, and inscribed by hand while the clay was still damp, it is rare for a tablet to have fingerprints.

11.5 Possessive suffixes after singular nouns in the genitive

For singular nouns, how to add a possessive suffix depends on the noun's grammatical case (nominative, accusative, genitive). We will first give the rules for nouns in the genitive, which are simplest. For the genitive, the rules are the same as for plurals: remove mimation (if present), and add the suffix.

ina bīti(m) **in the house** → *ina bītišunu* **in their** (m.) **house**
ša rubê(m) **of the lord** → *ša rubêki* **of your** (f. sg.) **lord**
bīt ili(m) **the temple of the god** → *bīt ilišunu* **the temple of their** (m.) **god**

LANGUAGE TIP

Some Assyriologists normalize the genitive *i* as long before possessive suffixes: *ina bīti(m)* **in the house** → *ina bītīšu* **in his house**. There are good reasons for thinking that this is truer to Babylonian pronunciation, but nonetheless this course normalizes the *i* as short: this has the advantage for learners of distinguishing sg. and pl. (*ina kakkišu* **with his weapon** vs. *ina kakkīšu* **with his weapons**).

11.6 Possessive suffixes after singular nouns in the nominative/accusative

a) Nouns with stems ending in a vowel

Remove mimation (if present), and add the suffix:

rubû(m) **nobleman** → *rubûšu* (nom.), *rubâšu* (acc.)

(Nouns with stems ending in *-i* or *-ī* sometimes add the suffix directly onto the stem, e.g. *murabbīšu* **the one who brought him up** (nom./acc.); the genitive conforms to the normal pattern: *murabbîšu*.)

LANGUAGE TIP

The noun *pû* **mouth** has two stems: *pā-* and *pī-*. The stem *pā-* gives rise to the possessive forms *pûšu* (nom.) and *pâšu* (acc.) **his mouth**; the stem *pī-* gives rise to the possessive form *pīšu* **his mouth** (nom./acc.). (In the genitive, possessive forms from both stems have *î*: *pîšu* **his mouth**.)

b) Nouns with a stem ending in consonants

Nominative and accusative have identical forms. The general principle is that one adds the suffix to the word stem.

With the first person singular suffix *-ī*, this works without complications:

bītu(m) **house** → *bītī* **my house**
libbu(m) **heart** → *libbī* **my heart**
biltu(m) **tribute** → *biltī* **my tribute**
napištu(m) **life** → *napištī* **my life**

With other suffixes, it works without complications when the stem ends in a single consonant:

bītu(m) **house** → *bītka* **your** (m. sg.) **house**
mayyālu(m) **bed** → *mayyālšu* **his bed**

However, when the stem ends in two consonants, adding suffixes other than *-ī* directly to the stem would create a sequence of three consonants, which Babylonian does not allow (see Unit 47.13). Accordingly, a 'helping' vowel must be inserted. If it is a double consonant (whether or not the feminine *t* is involved), insert *a*.

lemuttu(m) **evil(ness)** → *lemuttašu* **his evil(ness)**

In other cases, start from the construct state of the same noun (see Unit 10), and do the following:

- if the construct state ends in a single consonant, add the suffix directly to this form
- if the construct state ends in *i*, change *i* to *a* and then add the suffix to the resulting form

If a noun has two alternative forms of the construct state, it may have two alternative forms with possessive suffixes.

Some examples with *-ka* **your** (m. sg.) are given in Table 2.

Table 2

basic state, nom.	construct state, nom./acc./gen.	possessive state, nom./acc.
kalbu(m) 'dog'	*kalab*	*kalabka* 'your dog'
šipru(m) 'work'	*šipir*	*šipirka* 'your work'
libbu(m) 'heart'	*libbi*	*libbaka* 'your heart'
ummu(m) 'mother'	*ummi*	*ummaka* 'your mother'
šarru(m) 'king'	*šar, šarri*	*šarraka* 'your king'
šubtu(m) 'dwelling'	*šubat*	*šubatka* 'your dwelling'
napištu(m) 'life'	*napišti*	*napištaka* 'your life'

Occasionally, literary language inserts *a* before the suffix where in prose it would be absent. (This can result in the elision of a vowel in the previous syllable.)

rigmaka instead of *rigimka* (both **your shout**)

11.7 Sound changes involving possessive suffixes

When a suffix beginning with *š* immediately follows a sibilant or dental sound (*s*, *š*, *ṣ*, *z*, *t*, *d*, *ṭ*), these two sounds coalesce into *ss*.

rupšu(m) **breadth** → *rupussa* **her breadth** (from *rupuš+ša*)
bītu(m) **house** → *bīssu* **his house** (from *bīt+šu*)

murṣu(m) **disease** → *murussu* **his disease** (from *muruṣ+šu*)
biltu(m) **tribute** → *bilassunu* **their** (m.) **tribute** (from *bilat+šunu*)
šubtu(m) **dwelling** → *šubassa* **her dwelling** (from *šubat+ša*)
bēltu(m) **lady** → *bēlessina* **their** (f.) **lady** (from *bēlet+šina*)
mihṣu(m) **strike, blow** → *mihissu* **his strike** (from *mihiṣ+šu*)

Like any double consonant, this *ss* need not be spelled double in cuneiform. In Old Babylonian it often appears as *zz*.

11.8 Unassimilated spellings

After the Old Babylonian period, scribes often use spellings in which the assimilation is not complete, i.e. the *š* of the suffix has turned to *s*, but the preceding sound has not.

qí-bit-su **his command** (sp. *qibīssu*, from *qibītšu*).

In Standard Babylonian, one even finds spellings where the assimilation has not taken place at all.

It is highly probable that all these spellings were pronounced in the same way, perhaps as *ts*.

11.9 A special case: nouns from III-weak roots

Masculine nouns from III-weak roots (i.e. masculine nouns related to III-weak verbs, on which see Unit 23) exhibit two types of dictionary form: that in which the case vowel has contracted with another vowel (e.g. *rubû* **lord**), and that in which it has not (e.g. *kīlu* **imprisonment** from *kalû* **to detain**, *tību* **attack** from *tebû* **to arise**). Some nouns have both types of form (e.g. *būšu/bušû* **goods, property**). To add suffixes to nouns whose dictionary forms include a circumflexed vowel (like *rubû*), see section 11.6 a). Nouns like *kīlu* and *tību* behave differently:

nom. *tībūšu*, acc. *tībāšu*, gen. *tībīšu* (or *tībišu*)

ahu **brother**, *abu* **father** and *māru* **son** usually also behave like this:

nom. *abūšu*, acc. *abāšu*, gen. *abīšu* (or *abišu*) **his father**
nom. *ahūšu*, acc. *ahāšu*, gen. *ahīšu* (or *ahišu*) **his brother**
nom. *mārūšu*, acc. *mārāšu*, gen. *mārīšu* (or *mārišu*) **his son**

11.10 Translating possessive suffixes

The literal meaning of the possessive suffixes when they are attached to nouns is **my**, **your**, **his**, etc. However, the overall sense can change with the context. This happens also in English. Consider the two sentences **I applaud the judges: their judgment was just** and **He rendered their judgment before midday**. In the first sentence, **their judgment** means **the judgment which they gave**; in the second, it means **the judgment which they received**. Some Babylonian examples:

dīnī **my legal verdict** = both **the legal verdict which I rendered** and **the legal verdict about me**

ṭēmšu **his report** = both **the report which he issued** and **the report about him**
libbātuya **my anger** = both **the anger I feel** and **the anger (which someone else feels) towards me**

Usually it will be clear from the context which of the possible meanings is intended. (The translation of possessive suffixes attached to infinitives is treated in Unit 22.2.)

11.11 Suffixed nouns with adjectives

When a noun bearing a possessive suffix is qualified by an adjective, the adjective usually follows the noun+suffix complex (but in poetry it can precede it). The adjective agrees with the noun in case, number and gender, just as it would if the suffix were absent.

LANGUAGE TIP

Adjectives agree with nouns in case even when, owing to the presence of a suffix, this is not visible on the noun. For example, *bīssu* **his house** could be nominative or accusative; **his empty house** is *bīssu rīqu(m)* in the nominative, and *bīssu rīqa(m)* in the accusative. In the genitive it is *bītišu rīqi(m)*.

OB *ṭēmšunu gamram adīni ul almad* **I have not yet heard their full report** (ARM 26/2, 411: 26)
OB *awâtiya šūqurātim lišme* **May he hear my precious words** (CH Epilogue xlviii.12–14)
SB *kī qibītišunu ṣīrti* **In accordance with their exalted command** (Asar. 40–41: 20)

11.12 Possessive suffixes referring to 'dangling' words

Sometimes, a word or phrase at the start of a Babylonian sentence appears to be 'dangling', i.e. it only fits into the overall grammar of the sentence inasmuch as it is referred to by a suffix.

OB *bēletum māratka atta kaqqassa* (from *kaqqadša*) *t[u]kabbi[t]* **Your daughter Beletum, you have made her head heavy**, i.e. **You have honoured your daughter Beletum** (AbB 9, 129: 6–7)
SB *šumma amīlu muhhašu umma ukāl* **If a man, the top of his head has fever**, i.e. **If the top of a man's head is feverish**

Such constructions are especially common in law codes, omens and medical prescriptions. In Old and Middle Babylonian, 'dangling' words usually stand in the nominative, more rarely the accusative. In Standard Babylonian it is often difficult to tell their case.

CULTURE TIP

Babylonian and Assyrian medical prescriptions often contain revolting or peculiar-sounding ingredients (sailor's excrement, dog's tongue, lion fat, etc.). These were not meant to be understood literally, but served as cover names for plants. Similar substitutions were operated by medieval alchemists.

11.13 Possessive suffixes anticipated by *ša*

Poetic language sometimes employs a variant of the 'dangling construction', in which *ša X* (**of X**) is followed by a suffix referring back to X.

SB *<u>ša antum</u> ina šamê illakā dimāša* **<u>Of Antum</u>, in heaven her tears were flowing,** i.e. **Antum's tears were flowing in heaven** (*dimāša* is a dual form – see Unit 12) (Schlaf, 98: 4)

For a summary of the various ways in which Babylonian expresses possession and genitival relations (the notion of **of**) see Unit 30.2.

11.14 Possessive suffixes attached to prepositions

Possessive suffixes can attach themselves to some (but not all) prepositions (Unit 11.3 still applies). This works, for example, for *itti* **with**, *eli* **over**, *balu* **without**, *mahar* **before, in front of** (but not with *ana* or *ina*):

itti **with** → *ittiya* **with me**, *ittiša* **with her**, etc.
eli **over** → *elikunu* **over you** (m. pl.), *elika* **over you** (m. sg.), etc.
mahar **in front of** → *maharki* **in front of you** (f. sg.), *maharšu* **in front of him**, etc.
OB *urrī u mūšī <u>elišu</u> abki* **I cried <u>over him</u> day and night** (Gilg. VA+BM ii.5')

Before suffixes, *aššu(m)* **because of, for the sake of** assumes the form *aššumi*:
aššu(m) **for the sake of** → *aššumiya* **for my sake**, *aššumika* **for your** (m. sg.) **sake**, etc.

> **LEARNING TIP**
> Though it is still useful to call them 'possessive suffixes' (to make it clear which set of suffixes one is talking about), when possessive suffixes attach to prepositions they do not have a possessive meaning.

Exercise 11.1, Old Babylonian

a-ba-šu *wu-ši-ir* (*wuššir* **let ... go!**)

ma-ṣa-ra-tu-ia *da-an-na* (*dannā* **they** (f.) **are strong**)

[*t*]*e-re-tu-ia* *ša-al-ma* (*šalmā* **they** (f.) **are in good order**)

a-ta-mar (*ātamar* **I have seen**) ***pa-ni-ki***

i-la-a-tim a-na ***šu-ub-ti-ši-na*** *li-ša-al-li-mu* (*lišallimū* **they** (m.) **should deliver safely**)

pa-ni-ši-na *ú-na-wi-ir* (*unawwir* **I brightened**)

bé-li ni-ik-ka-sí-ia *li-pu-uš* (*līpuš* **he should do**)

mar-hi-tum li-ih-ta-⌜ad-da-a-am⌝ (*lihtaddâm* **let her enjoy herself**, Gtn precative)
i-na su-ni-⌜ka⌝

ni-pa-ti-šu *li-wa-aš-še-ru* (*liwaššerū* **they should release**)

i-na (*ina* **owing to**) ***ri-ig-mi-ka*** *i-li* (*ili*, irregular construct state of *ilum*) *bi-tim ú-ul i-ṣa-al-lal* (*iṣallal* **he can sleep**)

ṣu-har-re-ni (sp. *ṣuhārêni*) [*ṭ*]*ú-ur-da*[*m*] (*ṭurdam* **send to me!**)

ša-pí-ir-ni *mi-nam ni-ip-pa-al* (*nippal* **we will answer**)

ša-at-ta-am du-um-mu-qú-um i-na ***li-ib-bi-ka*** *li-ib-ši* (*libši* **let there be**)

é ***mu-ub-bi-ri-šu*** *i-tab-ba-al* (*itabbal* **he shall take**)

Exercise 11.2, Old Babylonian

da-a-a-nu ***a-wa-a-ti-šu-nu*** *i-im-ma-ru* (*immarū* **they will inspect**)

i-na ***ut-li-ia*** *ni-ši* kalam *šu-me-rí-im ù ak-ka-di-im ú-ki-il* (*ukīl* **I held**)

le-ú-ti *ša-ni-nam ú-ul i-šu* (*īšu* **has**)

a-wa-ti-ia *šu-qú-ra-tim i-na* na.ru-*ia aš-ṭur* (*aštur* **I inscribed**)

e-lu-tim i-ta-qí (*ittaqqi* **he poured**) ***ni-qí-šu***

ni-pa-ti-ka *iš-tu nu-pa-ri-im šu-ṣí-a-am* (*šūṣi'am* **release!**)

wa-ar-du-ú-a *ù* ***al-pu-ú-a*** *ú-ku-la-am li-im-hu-ru* (*limhurū* **they should receive**)

li-ba-ti-ia *ma-lu-ú* (*malû* **they** (m.) **are full of**)

qá-qá-ad-ka *lu me-si* (*lū mesi* **let it be washed**)

be-el hu-ul-qí-im ***hu-lu-uq-šu*** *i-le-qé* (*ileqqe* **he will take (back)**)

a-ha-ka *ṭù-ur-da-am-ma* (*ṭurdam-ma* **send to me!**) ***a-ha-at-ki*** *ma-ar-ṣa-at* (*marṣat* **she is ill**)

CULTURE TIP

As shown by Old Babylonian letters from the city of Mari, awareness of the possibility of contagion existed already in the 18th century BC: someone writes that, since so-and-so is ill, nobody is to use the same cup as her.

Exercise 11.3, Standard Babylonian

ina šùl-me u ha-de-e (*hadû* = **joy**, stem *hadā-*) *a-na* **kur.kur**^{meš}***-šú-nu*** gur^{meš}*-šú-nu-ti* (*utīršunūti* **I sent them back**)

an-nu-ú ma-a-ru (literary equivalent of *mār*) ***ri-du-ti-ia***

it-ti ***lìb-bi-ia*** *a-tam-mu* (*atammu* **I communed**)

ṣu-lul-šú-nu du_{10} **ugu-*ia*** *it-ru-ṣu* (*itruṣū* **they spread**)

ep-še-ti-šú-nu *lem-né-e-ti ur-ru-hi-iš áš-me* (*ašme* **I heard of**)

ṣu-bat ***ru-bu-ti-ia*** *ú-šar-riṭ* (*ušarriṭ* **I tore**)

lìb-bi *i-gug-ma* (*īgug-ma* **it became furious, and**) *iṣ-ṣa-ri-ih* (*iṣṣarih* **it became hot (with rage)**) ***ka-bat-ti***

^{d}giš.gím.maš *ina šà* unug^{ki} *i-na-aṭ-ṭa-la* (*inaṭṭala* **he was seeing**) ***šu-na-te-ka***

id-di (*iddi* **he flung off**) *mar-šu-ti-šu it-tal-bi-šá* (*ittalbiša* **he clad himself in**) ***za-ku-ti-šu***

meh-ret ***um-ma-ni-ia*** *aṣ-bat* (*aṣbat* **I seized**)

Exercise 11.4, Standard Babylonian

ina ***giš-par-ri-ia*** *ul ip-par-šid* (*ipparšid* **he could escape**)

im-si (*imsi* **he washed**) ***ma-le-šu*** *ub-bi-ib* (*ubbib* **he cleansed**) ***til-le-šu***

ur-ki pi-te-ma (*pitê-ma* **open!**) ***ku-zu-ub-ki*** *lil-qé* (*lilqe* **so he can take**) *ki-ma ez-zi ti-ib me-he-e as-su-ha* (*assuha* **I tore out**) ***šu-ru-su-un***

zi-kir-šu-nu *kab-tu it-ta-'i-id* (*itta'id* **he strictly observed**)

šal-lat-sún *ka-bit-tu áš-lu-la* (*ašlula* **I plundered**)

pi-ta-a (*pitâ* **open for me!**) ***ba-ab-ka***

a-na ***ki-šuk-ki-ia*** *i-tu-ra* (*itūra* **it turned** *ana* **into**) *bi-i-tu*

ki.sikil^{meš} tur^{meš} *ina* ***ur-ši-ši-na*** *tuš-ta-mit* (*tuštamīt* **you have killed**)

ma-lak ***ger-ri-ia*** *a-na ru-qe-e-te iṭ-ṭul* (*iṭṭul* **he/she observed**)

The most important things to remember

1 Babylonian usually says **my**, **your**, etc. by adding suffixes to nouns. Nouns with these suffixes are said to be in the 'possessive state'.

2 The same suffixes can be added to some prepositions; when this happens, the suffixes no longer have possessive meaning.

3 You need to learn the suffixes.

4 How to add the suffixes to nouns is a complex business: it depends on how the noun's stem ends, and on the noun's grammatical case.

5 For all nouns in the genitive case (singular and plural), suffixes are added to the forms in the basic state, after removing mimation (if present), e.g. *ina bīti(m)* **in the house** → *ina bītišu* **in his house**, *ana rubê(m)* **to the lord** → *ana rubêšu* **to his lord**, *ana nišī* **to the people** → *ana nišīšu* **to his people**.

6 For nouns with stems ending in vowels, the suffix is usually added to the forms in the basic state, after removing mimation (if present), e.g. *rubâ(m)* **lord** (accusative sg.) → *rubâšu* **his lord** (accusative sg.).

7 For nominative or accusative singular nouns with stems ending in consonants, the first person suffix *-ī* is added to the noun stem, e.g. *šarru(m)*, *šarra(m)* **king** → *šarrī* **my king**.

8 For nominative or accusative singular nouns with stems ending in double consonants, *a* is inserted before all suffixes except that of the first person (e.g. *kunukku(m)* **seal** → *kunukkašu* **his seal**). (The first person has *-ī*: *kunukkī* **my seal**.)

9 When a suffix beginning with *š* comes into contact with a preceding sibilant or dental, the two sounds coalesce into *ss*, e.g. *bītšu* → *bīssu* **his house**, *qaqqadša* → *qaqqassa* **her head**.

10 The rule of vowel elision (Unit 47.4) does not apply to possessive suffixes.

SELF CHECK

	I can ...
	... explain what possessive suffixes are
	... translate possessive suffixes
	... (in time:) recite the possessive suffixes
	... explain how possessive suffixes are attached to nouns
	... explain when suffixes starting with *š* result in *ss*
	... explain how 'dangling' constructions work.

Reading A: The epithets of Assurnaṣirpal II

Mesopotamian inscriptions often have long sequences of epithets, especially for gods and kings. These can seem boring to modern audiences, but when examined by trained historians they reveal all sorts of interesting patterns.

> **CULTURE TIP**
> The Assyrian king Sennacherib only assumed the title *šar kibrāt arbā'i* **king of the four edges** once he had actually campaigned in the North, South, East and West – probably showing that he wanted to 'earn' the title. He also used different epithets in inscriptions at Nineveh (the political capital) and Assur (the religious capital), reflecting the different orientation of the two centres.

Here you will read the epithets of Assurnaṣirpal II, king of Assyria, as they appear in the first ten lines of the Standard Inscription, which he had carved all over his palace at Nimrud. Examples of the Standard Inscription can be seen in museums worldwide.

The lines have been rearranged into meaningful units. The original line numbers are given in the transliteration, in bold. Commas have been inserted in the normalization to separate different 'chunks' of the epithets.

Cuneiform

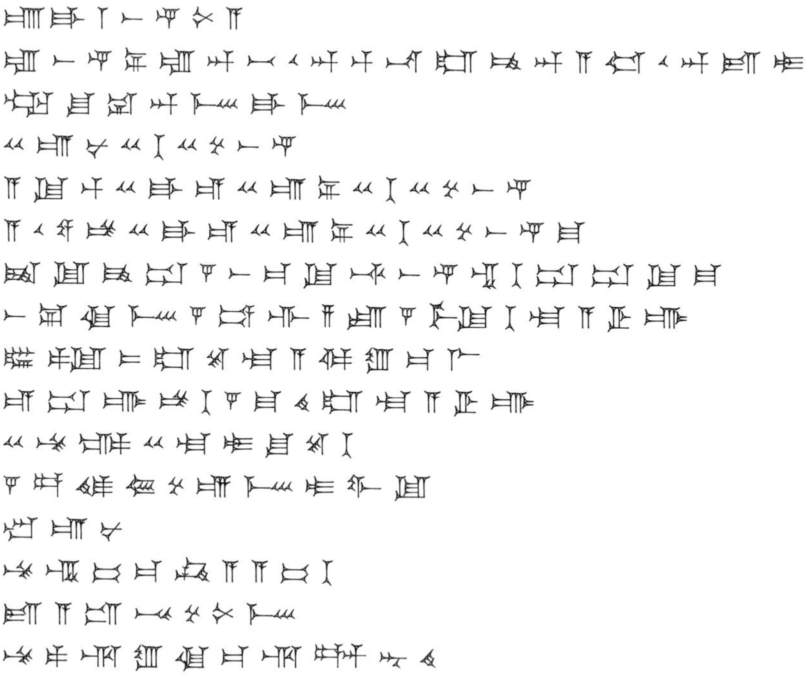

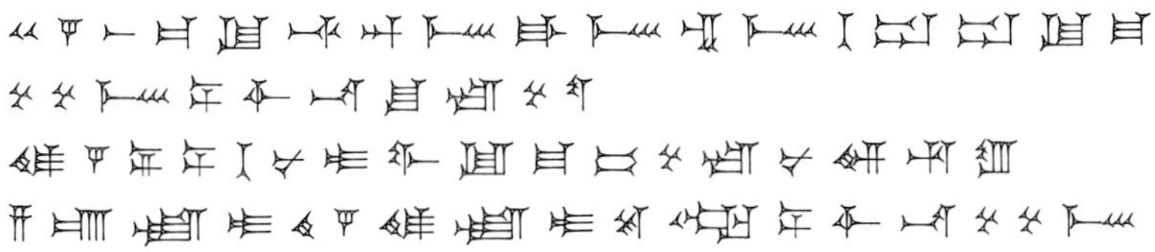

Transliteration

1 é.gal ^{m}*aš-šur*–pap–a

šid *aš-šur ni-šit* ^{d}bad *u* ^{d}maš *na-ra-am* ^{d}*a-nim u* ^{d}*da-gan*

ka-šu-uš **2** dingir^{meš} gal^{meš}

man *dan-nu* man šú man kur *aš-šur*

a tukul–maš man gal-*e* man *dan-né* man šú **3** man kur *aš-šur*

a 10–erim.táh man gal-*e* man *dan-né* man šú man kur *aš-šur-ma*

eṭ-lu qar-du šá ina ^{giš}*tukul-ti aš-šur* en-*šú* **4** du.du-*ku-ma*

ina mal-ki^{meš} *šá kib-rat* 4-*ta šá-nin-šú la-a* tuku-*ú*

^{lú}sipa **5** *tab-ra-te la a-di-ru* ^{giš}lal

e-du-ú gap-šú šá ma-hi-ra la-a tuku-*ú*

man *mu-šak-niš* **6** *la kan-šu-te-šú*

šá nap-har kiš-šat un^{meš} *i-pe-lu*

níta *dan-nu*

mu-kab-bi-is **7** gú *a-a-bé-šú*

da-a-iš kul-lat kúr^{meš}

mu-pa-ri-ru ki-iṣ-ri mul-tar-he

man *šá ina* ^{giš}*tukul-ti* **8** dingir^{meš} gal^{meš} en^{meš}-*šú* du.du-*ku-ma*

kur.kur^{meš} dù-*ši-na* šu-*su* kur-*ud*

hur-šá-ni **9** dù-*šú-nu i-pe-lu-ma bi-lat-su-nu* **10** *im-hu-ru*

ṣa-bit li-i-ṭé šá-kín li-i-te ugu dù-*ši-na* kur.kur^{meš}

Normalization

The normalization uses Middle Assyrian case endings (see Unit 41), and uncontracted (i.e. Assyrianizing) *rabie*. There may well have been variability in such matters if/when the inscription was read aloud.

ēkal aššur–nāṣir–aple

iššiak aššur, nišīt enlil u ninurta, narām anim u dagan

kašūš ilē rabûte

šarru dannu, šar kiššate, šar māt aššur

apil tukultī-ninurta, šarre rabie, šarre danne, šar kiššate, šar māt aššur apil addu–nērārī, šarre rabie, šarre danne, šar kiššate, šar māt aššur-ma

eṭlu qardu ša ina tukulti aššur bēlišu ittanallaku-ma

ina malkē ša kibrāt erbetta šāninšu la iraššû

rē'i (or: *rē'û*) *tabrâte lā ādiru tuqunte*

edû gapšu ša māhira lā iraššû

šarru mušakniš lā kanšūtešu

ša naphar kiššat nišē ipēlu (or: *ipellu*)

zikaru dannu mukabbis kišād ayyābēšu

dā'iš kullat nakrē (or: *nakrūti*)

muparriru kiṣri multarhē

šarru ša ina tukulti ilē rabûte bēlēšu ittanallaku-ma

mātāte kališina qāssu ikšud(u)

huršānē kališunu ipēlu-ma bilassunu imhuru

ṣābit līṭē šākin līte eli kališina mātāte

Translation

Palace of Assurnaṣirpal ('Assur is the protector of the heir', see Unit 29),

***iššiakku*-ruler of Assur, chosen by Enlil and Ninurta, beloved of Anum and Dagan,**

***kašūšu*-weapon of the great gods,**

mighty king, king of the Universe, king of the land of Assur,

son of Tukultī-Ninurta ('My trust is Ninurta', see Unit 29), **great king, strong king, king of the Universe, king of the land of Assur,**

(who was) son of Adad-nērārī ('Adad is my helper')**, likewise** (*-ma*, see Unit 30.7) **great king, strong king, king of the Universe, king of the land of Assur,**

valiant man who marches in the trust of Assur, his lord, and

acquires no rival (lit. **does not acquire his rival**) **among the kings of the four rims,**

shepherd of wonderment who does not fear battle (lit. **non-fearer of battle**),

huge flood who acquires no opponent,

king who makes submit (lit. **make-submit-ter of**) **those who are insubmissive to him,**

who ruled (or **rules**) **over the totality of all the people,**

mighty man who tramples (lit. **trampler of**) **the neck of his enemies,**

who thrashes (lit. **threshes**) **the entirety of enemies,**

who scatters the host of the arrogant,

king who marches in the trust of the great gods, his lords, and

(who)se hand conquered the lands in their entirety,

(who) ruled over the mountains in their entirety and received their tribute,

who seizes (lit. **seizer of**) **hostages, who achieves victory over the lands in their entirety ...**

Notes

1 It's curious how Assurnaṣirpal gives his father and grandfather – but not himself – the title 'great king'; **2** note the variable word order in *mātāte kališina* vs. *kališina mātāte*; **3** it can be difficult to tell whether strings of epithets are all on the same level, or whether some are epithets of other epithets. For example, *rē'û tabrâte lā ādiru tuqunte* could be taken as meaning **Assurnaṣirpal is an amazing shepherd and he doesn't fear battle** (*rē'û tabrâte* and *lā ādiru tuqunte* are on the same level), or **Assurnaṣirpal is an amazing shepherd who doesn't fear battle** (*rē'û tabrâte* **amazing shepherd** is qualified by *lā ādiru tuqunte* **non-fearer of battle**). The translation reflects one way of understanding the structure of the epithets, but other ways are possible.

You can read the rest of Assurnaṣirpal's Standard Inscription at http://oracc.museum.upenn.edu/riao/Q004477. You can listen to a recording of the extract above at http://www.bbc.co.uk/programmes/p03krt5v. The recording has minor variants from the version given here and – *mea culpa*! – omits the line about Tukultī-Ninurta.

12 *The dual*

In this unit you will learn:

- **that Babylonian has special forms to mean 'two' of a noun**
- **what these forms are.**

In addition to the singular and plural, Babylonian has 'dual' forms, to indicate two of something.

īnān **two eyes**

Early in the language's history, the dual was probably used every time two of something was mentioned. However, already in the Old Babylonian period it was being ousted by the plural. From the Old Babylonian period onwards, the dual is chiefly used for body parts which occur in pairs. After the Old Babylonian period, most appearances of the dual are archaizing.

Some nouns are used in the dual even though there is only one item: *rēšān*, lit. **two heads**, can simply mean **head**. When translating duals into English, it is often appropriate just to use a plural, without specifying **two**: *īnāšu* **his eyes**.

12.1 Dual forms of nouns

Like the plural, the dual has identical forms for accusative and genitive. The dual endings in the basic state (see Unit 10.4) are as follows. (The *n* is usually present in Old Babylonian, and often absent in Standard Babylonian.)

nom. *-ā(n)* acc. *-ī(n)* gen. *-ī(n)*

The dual endings in the construct and possessive states (see Unit 10.4) are:

nom. *-ā* acc. *-ī* gen. *-ī*

OB *<u>īnī</u> awīlim šarrum inassa[h]* **The king will tear out the man's <u>eyes</u>** (YOS 10, 26: iii.51)

OB *<u>uznāya</u> ibaššiānikku* **<u>My ears</u> are** (i.e. **my attention is trained**) **on you** (AbB 7, 115: 27')

OB *<u>īnāka</u> eliša lib[b]ašiā* **May <u>your</u>** (m. sg.) **<u>eyes</u> be upon her** (AbB 9, 223: 9–10)

OB *pīka libbaka liwa"ir u libbaka liwa"ir <u>birkīka</u>* **May your** (m. sg.) **mouth instruct your heart, and may your heart instruct <u>your legs</u>** (Akkade 62: 15–16)

OB *<u>išdī</u> dūri* **The foundation** (lit. **the two roots**) **of the wall** (acc./gen.)

MB *ša eṭli qardi <u>purīdāšu</u> ittūrā* **The valiant man's legs** (lit. **of the valiant man, <u>his legs</u>**) **turned back** (BBSt. 6: i.21)

In the first millennium, when the dual endings were no longer current in the spoken language and the rules of usage had been forgotten, there arose a tendency to use the ending *-ā(n)* 'hypercorrectly', i.e. to use it not just in the nominative but also in the accusative and genitive.

SB *kīma šadîm ullâ rēšāša* **I raised its** (the temple's) **top** (lit. **head**) **like a mountain** (VAB 4, 138: ix.27–28)

12.2 Adjectives qualifying duals

Plural and dual forms of adjectives are identical (or one could say that plural adjectives are used for dual nouns).

OB *ina panīn namrūtim* **with bright faces** (AbB 13, 164: 10)

12.3 Duals as subjects of verbs

When duals are the subject of verbs, the verbal prefixes and suffixes are the same as for the 3rd person feminine plural (to be studied in later units).

SB eli *dūr appiya illakā dimāya* **My tears coursed down my cheeks** (lit. **over the wall of my nose**) (Gilg. XI 139)

Here, the dual renders the idea of two streams of tears, one flowing from each eye.

CULTURE TIP

It is not known for certain how one said **to sneeze** in Babylonian. A possible candidate is the verb *šehēqu* (attested only once), but probably there were other ways too. It is likely that these occur in medical writings, but have yet to be properly understood.

The most important things to remember

1 Except for nouns denoting body parts which occur in pairs, duals are archaic already in the Old Babylonian period. They are ousted by plurals.

2 There is no special dual form for adjectives: plural forms are used to qualify dual nouns.

3 The dual endings in the basic state are *-ān* (nominative), *-īn* (accusative), *-īn* (genitive). After the Old Babylonian period the *n* is sometimes lost.

4 In the construct and possessive states, the *n* is lost: *-ā* (nominative), *-ī* (accusative), *-ī* (genitive).

SELF CHECK

	I can ...
	... explain what the dual is
	... (in time:) recite the dual endings for the basic state
	... (in time:) recite the dual endings for the construct and possessive states.

13 *Prepositions*

In this unit you will learn:
- **what prepositions are**
- **how Babylonian uses them.**

Prepositions are grammar-words like **of, for, to, from, by, like, at, beside, notwithstanding**. In English (and usually in Babylonian) they govern nouns. Multi-word items such as **because of, apart from, as per, for the sake of,** are known as 'compound prepositions' – Babylonian has them too.

Babylonian prepositions are followed by nouns in the genitive case (see Unit 6.3; if the noun is in the construct state, the case may have no visible markers). Occasionally, prepositions are followed by adverbs (see Unit 36.11). The complex 'preposition + noun' is known as a 'prepositional phrase'. Prepositions have many different meanings. Watch out for how they are used, and learn from seeing them 'in action'.

LANGUAGE TIP

It is rare in Babylonian for prepositions and the nouns they govern to be separated by line breaks (i.e. for the preposition to stand at the end of a line). This is probably because the complex 'preposition + noun' was thought of as a single 'word'.

13.1 Prepositions with and without suffixed pronouns

Some prepositions, e.g. *eli* and *itti*, can be followed by suffixed pronouns (see Unit 11.14), e.g. *elišu* **over him**. Prepositions which cannot be followed by suffixed pronouns include *ina* **in**, *ana* **to**, *kī* **like**, *kīma* **like**.

In order to say things like **to him** (with *ana*), Babylonian can either use an independent (i.e. non-suffixed) pronoun (see Unit 37), or a prepositional phrase with a possessive suffix: *ana ṣērišu* **to him** (lit. **to his back**). In such cases, one sometimes has the impression that the noun in the prepositional phrase (here *ṣēru* **back**) simply acts as a link between the preposition and the possessive suffix (*ana ... šu*), and does not really contribute to the meaning.

13.2 Prepositional phrases qualifying nouns

In English, there is a clear difference between **the man in the office wrote a novel** and **the man wrote a novel in the office**: in the first case, the phrase in the office qualifies **the man** (i.e. he is **the-man-in-the-office**), whereas in the second it does not. In Babylonian, word order is much less helpful in making such distinctions, so ambiguities can arise. In the spoken language such ambiguities may have been eliminated through intonation. In the written language, when it is necessary to make it clear that a prepositional phrase qualifies a noun, *ša* **of** is often used instead of other prepositions. Thus, literally, **the-man-in-the-house** would be **the-man-of-the-house**.

OB *alpī ša kaprim assuham* **I have transferred the-oxen-of the-settlement** (i.e. **the oxen which were in the settlement**) (AbB 14, 59: 12) – whereas *alpī ina kaprim assuham* could have meant **In the settlement I transferred the oxen**.
OB *kīma kīsi ša qātišunu liṣṣurūki* **May they protect you like the-money-bag-of-their-hand** (i.e. **the money bag in their hand**) (AbB 6, 1: 11–12) – whereas *kīma kīsi ina qātišunu liṣṣurūki* could have meant **May they protect you with their hand like a money-bag**.

When it is necessary to keep the original preposition, *ša* **who / which** is used in addition to it, producing a verbless subordinate clause (see Unit 30.14).

OB *ayyûm-ma ina šarrānī ša itti bēliya išariš idabbub* **Which of** (lit. **among**) **the kings who are with my lord will talk straight?** (ARM 10, 11: 18–20) – without *ša*, the sentence could have been interpreted as **Which of the kings will talk straight with my lord?**

13.3 Short forms of *ina* and *ana*

The prepositions *ina* and *ana* sometimes appear in the 'short forms' **in** and **an**. When this happens, *n* usually assimilates to a following consonant. The meaning is the same.

ippuhri **in the assembly** (from *inpuhri = ina puhri*)
aṣṣēriya **to me** (lit. **to my back**) (from *anṣēriya = ana ṣēriya*)

A good way to think of why the short forms come into being is to imagine *ina* or *ana* and the following word being pronounced as if they constituted a single word. In this composite word, the rules of vowel elision induce elision of the *a* (see Unit 47.4), after which *n* assimilates to the following consonant (see Unit 47.9).

ina puhri → pronounced as *inapuhri* → *a* elided → *inpuhri* → *n* assimilated → *ippuhri*

13.4 Prepositions exclude each other

Babylonian does not usually allow two consecutive prepositions. In situations where English would have **as** or **like** followed by another preposition (**he spoke as through gritted teeth**), Babylonian uses only *kīma* **as, like**, which ousts the other preposition. In such cases, one adds the ousted preposition to the translation, but in brackets.

OB *kīma bēliya u bēltiya uznāya ibaššiānikkum* **My attention is** (lit. **my two ears are**) **focused on you as (on) my lord and lady** (AbB 11, 106: 13'–14')
OB *kīma addim u šamšim ana kâšim taklāku* **I trust in you as (in) Adad and Šamaš** (AbB 4, 161: 38–39)

In both these examples, *kīma* has ousted *ana*.

LANGUAGE TIP

Since two consecutive prepositions are not allowed, when it follows a preposition the sumerogram ugu must be read *muhhi* (not *eli*): *ina/ana* ugu = *ina/ana muhhi*.

13.5 Prepositions introducing clauses

All (or nearly all) Babylonian prepositions can double as 'subordinators' (sometimes called 'subordinating conjunctions'), introducing a clause rather than a noun or noun phrase. This function will be discussed in Unit 30.10.

13.6 The suffix -*a*

A small number of nouns (esp. *panu* and *mahru*) occasionally display a suffix -*a* instead of the expected case vowel after prepositions. This is an archaism, and may be an old adverbial ending.

eli ša pana **Than before** (lit. **Upon that of before**)

> **CULTURE TIP**
>
> The Babylonian story known today as *The Poor Man of Nippur*, in which a pauper exacts threefold revenge on the mayor who treated him unjustly, is very similar to stories circulating in many other times and places, from Sicily (Beppe) to Medieval Germany (Till Eulenspiegel). It is Reading H in this course.

13.7 Particularity of *ša*

As well as just **of**, *ša* can mean **the person of ...**, **the thing of ....** In this usage, it can have special plural forms *šūt* **the men of ...** and *šāt* **the women of ....**

OB *šūt abnim* **The stone ones** (lit. **The ones of stone**) (Gilg. VA+BM iv.22)
SB *anāku* <u>*ša enzi*</u> **I'm** <u>**the guy with**</u> (lit. **of**) <u>**the nanny goat**</u> (Poor Man of Nippur 146)

In this function, *ša* is not a preposition but a pronoun.

The most important things to remember

1 When a preposition governs a noun, the noun is in the genitive case.

2 Some prepositions can be followed by 'possessive' suffixes.

3 *ina* and *ana* occasionally display the 'short forms' **in** and **an**; the *n* assimilates to a following consonant.

4 As well as meaning **of**, *ša* can mean **the person of ...**, **the thing of ....**

5 Babylonian does not allow two consecutive prepositions.

6 Where English uses a prepositional phrase to qualify a noun (e.g. **the-man-in-the-office**), Babylonian often replaces the preposition with *ša* **of**.

SELF CHECK

	I can ...
	... explain what a preposition is.

Part three

Strong verbs

14 *Overview of verbs*

In this unit you will learn:

- **what the 'dictionary form' of a verb is**
- **that Babylonian has four verbal 'systems'**
- **what these are, and what they mean**
- **that Babylonian has 'strong' and 'weak' verbs, and what this means**
- **that Babylonian has '*a*-verbs' and *e*-verbs', and how this affects verb forms**
- **how to tell from the dictionary form whether a verb is strong or weak, and an *a*-verb or an *e*-verb**
- **that each Babylonian verb has one (or two) 'theme vowels', and what this means.**

This unit introduces you to some of the key concepts underpinning the behaviour of Babylonian verbs. (Unless otherwise stated, the following observations apply to both 'weak' and 'strong' verbs.)

14.1 Position of the verb in the sentence

In prose the verb normally stands at the end of its clause, hence also at the end of the sentence. This word order is unusual in Semitic languages as a whole, and is probably the result of influence from Sumerian. In poetry the position of the verb is much freer. The exercises in this course contain both prose and poetry, so you will see the verb assume a variety of positions.

In English, the position of the verb is different in statements and questions (**You can ...**; **Can you ...?**). This is not so in Babylonian. Thus, unless they begin with a clear question word (who?, what?, why?, when?, where?, etc.), many written Babylonian sentences could be interpreted as either statements or questions, and it is context which guides the reader. (In the spoken language, statements and questions were almost certainly distinguished by intonation, but often this is not reflected in writing; see Unit 44.9.)

14.2 General principles of inflection

A Babylonian verbal form consists of a 'core', to which prefixes and suffixes are added. The 'core' is determined by the tense and system (on these see later in this unit). The prefixes and suffixes are determined by the grammatical characteristics (person, number and gender) of the subject.

When the subject of an English sentence is a pronoun (I, you, he, she, it, we, you, they), in the corresponding Babylonian sentence it is not necessary to use the pronoun: the verbal form alone suffices, as the subject is marked by the prefix and suffix.

amqut **I fell**, *nimqut* **we fell**, *tamqutī* **you** (f. sg.) **fell**

In these examples, *mqut* is the verbal core (meaning **fell**); *a-*, *ni-*, and *ta…ī* are the prefixes and suffixes which mark the subject.

It is possible also to use the independent (i.e. non-prefixed, non-suffixed) pronouns, but this is not necessary. Often (but not always) the independent pronouns are used to emphasize who the action is being done by:

anāku amqut ***I* fell, I *myself* fell**
nīnu nimqut ***we* fell, we *ourselves* fell**
atti tamqutī ***you*** (f. sg.) **fell, you** (f. sg.) ***yourself* fell**

The independent pronouns (*anāku* **I**, etc.) are presented in Unit 37.

14.3 Agreement between subject and verb

a) A Babylonian verb and its subject usually agree in number (as in English) and in gender. A group comprising masculine and feminine subjects is treated as masculine plural. Instances of non-agreement arise when a singular noun implicitly refers to a group of people. The verb can then agree with the group which the noun represents rather than the noun itself (like saying **the committee think …** in English).

MB ^{kur}*adauš tīb tāhāziya danna lū <u>ēdurū</u>* **Mount Adauš** (i.e. its inhabitants) **truly <u>feared</u>** (pl.) **my mighty onslaught** (RIMA 2, 18: iii.66–7)

b) A string of singular subjects can, as in English, be treated as plural, and take a plural verb (**the rat and the toad live by the river**). Sometimes, however, such a string is treated as singular, and takes a singular verb.

OB *ālum u halṣum <u>šalim</u>* **The city and the district <u>is well</u>**, i.e. **The city and the district are well** (AbB 9, 90: 4–5)
OB *šizbum u himētum ana kispim ša abim <u>ihhaššeh</u>* **Milk and butter/ghee <u>is needed</u> for the funerary rite of** (the month of) **Abum** (AbB 14, 7: 5–7)

> **CULTURE TIP**
> In Tablet VI of The Epic of Gilgameš, the funerary rites for Enkidu involve bowls of butter/ghee (*himētu*) and honey. This has been compared to Book XXIII of the *Iliad*, where jars of grease and honey are placed beside the dead Patroclus.

c) Occasionally, when the subject consists in several nouns, the noun which is uppermost in the speaker's mind prevails over others, so that the verb agrees with it rather than with the group as a whole.

OB *šamšī-adad u ummānātušu <u>qerub</u>* **Šamši-Adad and his troops <u>is nearby</u>** (AbB 8, 15: 40–2)
OB *šarrum u ummānātum <u>šalmā</u>* **The king and the troops <u>are well</u>** (verb is f. pl. rather than m. pl.; the non-agreement cannot be rendered in English) (ARM 10, 157: 24–5)

14.4 Variables impinging on inflection

The inflection of a Babylonian verb depends on the following variables:

- person (1st, 2nd, 3rd)
- number (singular, dual, plural)
- gender (masculine, feminine)
- tense (present, preterite, perfect, stative, precative, imperative, infinitive)
- system (G, N, D, Š, Gt, Dt, Št, Gtn, Ntn, Dtn, Štn) – the notion of 'system' is explained in 14.6.

(As noted in future units, some of what we are calling 'tenses' should, strictly speaking, be described in terms of 'mood' and 'aspect' in addition to, or even rather than, 'tense'. We use 'tense' to keep things simple.)

14.5 Verbs of being and verbs of doing

In English, verbs usually denote an action: **to speak**, **to go**, **to make**, etc. This is also true of many Babylonian verbs: *qabû* **to speak**, *alāku* **to go**, *epēšu* **to make**, *šakānu* **to put**, *nâku* **to have sex with**, *baṭālu* **to cease**, etc.

However, there are also many Babylonian verbs which translate into English as **to be** + adjective: *damāqu* **to be good**, *lemēnu* **to be evil**, *kânu* **to be firm**, *danānu* **to be strong**, *enēšu* **to be weak**, *šaqû* **to be high**, etc.

These two types of verb can be called 'verbs of doing' and 'verbs of being'. This distinction is grammatically significant, as the two types sometimes behave slightly differently. You will be alerted to these differences as they come up.

14.6 The four systems

A Babylonian verb can follow four different systems of inflection: G, N, D, Š. In one system (G) the verb has a basic meaning close to that of the root, whereas the other three systems modify this basic meaning (see examples below).

Not all verbs are used in all four systems. For any given verb, the dictionaries indicate which systems it appears in, and which meaning it has in each of them. A minority of verbs do not appear in the G system. (Their dictionary form is the infinitive of the system where they appear most frequently.)

There are some rules of thumb for how a verb's meaning changes from one system to another, and we give these below. However, there are exceptions. The safest way to ascertain what a verb means in a particular system is to look it up. (Note: Other books call systems 'stems'.)

14.7 The G system

'G' can be usefully thought of as standing for 'general'. (It is in fact borrowed from German grammarians of Babylonian, who use it as an abbreviation of *Grund-*, i.e. 'basic'.) This system is so called because it usually conveys what we perceive as the most general, or basic, meaning of the verb. This system has the meaning which is closest to that inherent in the root, e.g. the meaning of the root √*nṣr* is **guarding**, and in the G system the verb *naṣāru* means **to guard**.

14.8 The N system

This system is so called because all its forms can be analysed as containing an *n* somewhere before the first root letter (though it may have assimilated to the following consonant): *naPRiS*, *iPPaRRaS* (from *inPaRRaS*), etc. (It is not certain that this is historically accurate, but it is a good way to think of it.)

For verbs that take a direct object in the G system, the N system usually forms the passive of the meaning in the G system. For example, the verb *šarāṭu* means **to tear apart** in the G system, but when put into the N system it means **to be torn apart**. For verbs that do not take a direct object in the G system, the meaning of the N system should be sought in the Glossary (later, in the dictionaries). Often it means **to become ...** (i.e. it has an 'ingressive' function).

A good way to think about how these uses combine is that the N system means **to become PaRS-**. For a verb like *mahāṣu* **to beat**, the *PaRS-* form (= *mahṣ-*) means **beaten**, so the N system would mean **to become beaten**, i.e. **to be beaten**. For a verb like *damāqu* **to be good**, the *PaRS-* form (= *damq-*) means **good**, so the N system means **to become good**.

That the N system can be used to express both the passive and the ingressive (i.e. the notion of becoming) is not so strange when considered against English **get**, which has the same functions: **He got thrown out** (passive) vs. **He got lucky** (ingressive).

LANGUAGE TIP

In fact, English **get** is considerably more complicated than the N system: it can also form the causative (**They got me to do this**), as well as meaning **to possess** (**I've got tickets for the opera**), **to acquire** (**I'll get them tomorrow**), **to arrive** (**I get home tomorrow**) and **to take revenge on** (**I'll get you for that**). Set against this, the Babylonian N system is a piece of cake!

14.9 The D system

'D' stands for 'doubling'. This system is so called because in all its forms the middle root letter is doubled (except when it is 'weak'), e.g. *PuRRiS*, *uPaRRiS*, *uPtanaRRaS*, etc. The D system has several different functions.

a) It turns a verb of **being** into a verb of **making be**. For example, the verb *damāqu* means **to be good** in the G system, but when put into the D system it means **to make good, to improve**.

b) It intensifies the meaning in the G system. For example, the verb *šebēru* means **to break** in the G system, but when put into the D system it means **to smash**.

c) Sometimes the D system has the same meaning as the G system, but it indicates that the action is performed on a plurality of objects. (In this case there is often no difference in translation between the G and D systems.)

14.10 The Š system

This system is named after the letter *š* (whose name is pronounced 'sheen'), because in all its forms there is a *š* which appears somewhere before the three root letters, e.g. *šuPRiS*, *ušaPRiS*, *uštanaPRaS*, etc. The Š system usually forms the 'causative' of the meaning in the G system. 'Causative' embraces the ideas of **causing**, **allowing**, **enabling**, and even **helping**.

kašādu G **to arrive** → Š **to cause (s/o) to arrive**, **to get (s/o) to arrive**, **to make (s/o) arrive**, **to allow (s/o) to arrive**, **to enable (s/o) to arrive**, **to help (s/o) to arrive**

The idea of making a verb causative without recourse to a verb such as *to make*, *to get*, or *to cause* is not wholly alien to the English language. Several English verbs have a causative equivalent:

to fall → **to fell** (**to cause to fall**)
to lie → **to lay** (**to cause to lie**)
to sit → **to set** (**to cause to sit**)
to rise → **to raise** (**to cause to rise**)
(and, originally, **to drink** → **to drench**)

An important difference, however, is that in English the pairs are perceived today as two separate verbs, whereas in Babylonian the G and Š systems were (in the vast majority of cases) almost certainly perceived as two incarnations of the same verb.

If a verb takes one direct object in the G system, it will usually take two direct objects in the Š system. For example, the Babylonian verb **to eat** (*akālu*) takes one direct object in the G system (i.e. the thing eaten); when put into the Š system, it takes two direct objects (the thing eaten, and the person who is made or allowed to eat it).

(There is also a so-called ŠD system, formed by inserting *š* before the first root letter of D system forms. It usually has the same meaning as either the D system or the Š system. This is rare, and not taught here. An instance appears in Exercise 10.2.)

14.11 The derived systems

The four systems (G, N, D, Š) give rise to further systems, which are derived by the addition of the infixes *-tan-* or *-t-*. The infix *-tan-* gives rise to the Gtn, Ntn, Dtn and Štn systems (pronounced 'gee tee en', etc.). In each of these cases, the meaning is that of the parent system (G, N, D, Š), with an extra nuance of repetition or graduality. In translation this can often be rendered by such phrases as **constantly**, **again and again**, **bit by bit**, **progressively**. For example, see the verb *šebēru* **to break**:

G **to break (s/th)** → Gtn **to break (s/th) again and again**
N **to be broken** → Ntn **to be broken again and again**
D **to smash (s/th)** → Dtn **to smash (s/th) again and again**
Š **to cause (s/o) to break (s/th)** → Štn **to cause (s/o) to break (s/th) again and again**

LANGUAGE TIP

'Infix' is a word like 'prefix' and 'suffix'; but instead of indicating that the relevant bit is added at the beginning of a word (prefix) or the end (suffix), it indicates that the relevant bit is inserted *in*to the word.

The infix *-t-* gives rise to the Gt, Dt, and Št systems (pronounced 'gee tee', etc.). (The existence of an Nt system is debated; if it does exist, it is extremely rare. Be that as it may, it is not taught here.) The meanings of the *-t-* infix will be explained in Unit 34.

14.12 Strong and weak verbs

Babylonian verbs from roots with three consonants are known as 'strong' verbs. Verbs which have fewer than three root consonants are known as 'weak': 'first weak' (I-weak), 'second weak' (II-weak), and 'third weak' (III-weak) according to which letter is missing. Some verbs ('doubly weak') are missing the first and third consonant.

Weak verbs do their best to inflect like strong verbs, but are not always successful. Owing to particularities in their inflection, verbs whose first root letter is *w* (I-*w* verbs) will be treated together with weak verbs.

14.13 *a*-verbs and *e*-verbs

Some verbs display *e* or *ē* where one would expect *a* or *ā* (but this never affects the ventive suffix *-a(m)*, treated in Unit 19.5; for prefixes and suffixes see Unit 45.2). These are known as *e*-verbs (as opposed to *a*-verbs), and the fact of having *e* instead of *a* is known as *e*-colouring. Examples: *emēdu* **to impose**, *leqû* **to take**.

If a verb has an *e* in its dictionary form, it is an *e*-verb. If it has an *a* in its dictionary form, it is an *a*-verb. If it is neither, one has to look beyond the dictionary form (but this is rare). If the dictionary allows by-forms with *e* and *a*, it can behave as either.

For almost all *e*-verbs in Old Babylonian, the shift from *a* to *e* was caused by the disappearance of a guttural consonant (see Unit 47.7). The few Old Babylonian *e*-verbs whose *e*-colouring did not arise through loss of a guttural consonant include *lemēnum* **to be evil**, *qebērum* **to bury**, *qerēbum* **to draw near**, *ṣehērum* **to be small** and *šebērum* **to break**. After the Old Babylonian period, *e*-colouring begins to spread through the language. In Middle Babylonian, certain D and Š system forms of *a*-verbs look as if they come from *e*-verbs, esp. *uPeRRiS* for expected *uPaRRiS* and *ušePRiS* for expected *ušaPRiS*.

In vernacular Babylonian of the first millennium, *e*-colouring appeared in many forms of what were originally *a*-verbs. Occasionally, such forms find their way into literary manuscripts.

Nouns and adjectives related to *e*-verbs also display *e*-colouring, e.g. *lemnu* **evil** (related to *lemēnu* **to be evil**), formed according to the pattern *PaRS-* (see Unit 18.1–2) but with *e* instead of *a*.

14.14 The dictionary form

The 'dictionary form' of most Babylonian strong verbs follows the pattern *PaRāSu(m)*, e.g. *maqātu* **to fall**, *kašādu* **to conquer**, *lamādu* **to learn**, *šapāru* **to send**, etc. (This form is known as the 'G infinitive'.) The dictionary forms of *e*-verbs follow the same patterns as *a*-verbs, except that *a* and *ā* change to *e* and *ē*. Owing to their missing one or more root consonants, weak verbs cannot conform exactly to the pattern *PaRāSu*.

By looking at the dictionary form of a verb, one can tell whether it is strong or weak (and, if weak, which type of weak verb). The various combinations (strong, weak, *a*, *e*) are summarized in Table 3. The verbs *izuzzu* **to stand**, *išû* **to have** and *edû* **to know** have irregular dictionary forms (i.e. they do not follow, or attempt to follow, the pattern *PaRāSu*).

Table 3

	a-verbs	*e*-verbs
strong	*maqātu(m)* 'to fall'	*lemēnu(m)* 'to be evil'
I-weak	*abātu(m)* 'to destroy'	*erēbu(m)* 'to enter'
II-weak	*kânu(m)* 'to be firm'	*ṭênu(m)* 'to grind'
III-weak	*banû(m)* 'to build'	*leqû(m)* 'to take'

Verbs which do not occur in the G system are listed in dictionaries by the infinitive of the system in which they appear most frequently.

N *naprušu* **to fly** D *(w)uššuru* **to release**

14.15 Theme vowels

Every Babylonian verb has either one or two vowels which appear regularly at certain points in its inflection in the G and N systems. These vowels are known as 'theme vowels', and are indicated in the Glossary at the end of this course (in brackets after the dictionary form). For strong verbs, the possible theme vowels are: *a/u* (e.g. *šakānu* **to put**), *a* (e.g. *ṣabātu* **to seize**), *i* (e.g. *paqādu* **to entrust**), or *u* (e.g. *maqātu* **to fall**). Occasionally, a verb's theme vowel changed as the language evolved. Such cases are noted in dictionaries.

14.16 Impersonal masculine plurals

In English, one can avoid specifying who it is that does something by using the passive: **It is said that Florence is beautiful**, **The piano will be tuned tomorrow**: we are not told who says that Florence is beautiful, nor who will tune the piano. This is known as the 'impersonal' use of the passive. Babylonian also produces impersonal sentences, but instead of the passive it uses a notional 3rd person masculine subject (**they**).

šumma mārum abāšu imtahaṣ rittašu inakkisū **If a son has struck his father, 'they' will cut off his hand**, i.e. **... his hand will be cut off** (CH § 195)

English occasionally does this too (**They say that Urbino is beautiful** = **It is said that Urbino is beautiful**). Babylonian is, however, more thoroughgoing than English in this usage: any 3rd person masculine plural verb which does not have an obvious subject could be impersonal (but it is also possible that there is a real subject in the background).

OB *nipâtišu liwaššerū* **They should release his debt slaves** or **'They' should release his debt slaves**, i.e. **His debt slaves should be released** (AbB 5, 130: r.2'–3')

Context will usually show which applies. If you are confident that a sentence is impersonal, you are free to translate it with an English passive.

14.17 To be able

Babylonian does have a verb meaning **to be able** (*le'û*), but usually the concept is left unexpressed. For verbs in the present and preterite, add **can**, **could**, etc., in translation if you feel the sense requires it.

14.18 Negation

In Old and Middle Babylonian, assertions are negated by *ul*; questions are negated by *lā* if there is a question word (who?, why?, when?, etc.) and by *ul* if there is no question word. Subordinate clauses (see Unit 30) are negated by *lā*. In vernacular Babylonian of the first millennium, *lā* ousted *ul*. Standard Babylonian generally follows second millennium rules for negation, but occasionally, under the influence of contemporary vernacular language, *lā* appears instead of *ul*. For *lā* + present as a negative command, see Unit 15.1.

14.19 Commands and wishes

This section explains the landscape of wishes and commands in Babylonian. It will not teach you any new Babylonian forms, but rather will help you orient yourself through the units where new forms appear.

In Babylonian, wishes and commands are not very clearly distinguished. This may sound odd, but it can occasionally be a grey area in English: when the Lord's Prayer says **give us this day our daily bread**, the grammar is that of a command; but most people who have uttered the line through the ages probably didn't perceive themselves as giving the recipient of the prayer an order, rather as voicing the wish or hope that bread would be given on a daily basis.

For Babylonian, there is a family of verbal forms which basically express commands, but whose function can blur into voicing wishes or hopes, and it is not always easy to decide which function is in play. The grammar of these expressions varies depending on whether a verb of doing or a verb of being is at issue.

LANGUAGE TIP

Just as in English, commands cannot occur in subordinate clauses. (Subordinate clauses will be treated in Unit 30.)

Babylonian can address commands not just to **you** (as in English), but also to a third party, or to oneself. English has a somewhat roundabout way of issuing commands to a third party, using expressions like **Mary should do it**, **Alex must do it**, **Let John do it**. The latter case is especially blurry, because there is some ambiguity over whether this is a command issued directly to John, or whether I am telling *you* that *you* should **let John do it**. Babylonian is much neater: there is a bespoke form of the verb, which does without helping verbs (**should**, **must**, **let**, etc.).

In discussing the verbal forms used for commands/wishes, one faces a terminological quandary, the reason being that different types of verbal form can be used for **you** vs. the other addressees. This creates an asymmetry: a command to **you** and a command to, for example, **him** are both, in terms of their function, command forms. But if we call them command forms, we obscure the fact that they use different verb forms. Conversely, if our terminology follows the form, and we assign two different labels to them, we obscure the fact that they have the same function.

There is no easy way out of this catch-22, so it is all the more important to be aware of it. This book will often use terms based on form ('imperative', 'precative', 'cohortative', etc.), but it should be stressed that this does not imply a substantive difference in function.

With all these provisos, the 'map' of forms for positive wishes/commands in Babylonian looks as follows (it will be useful to refer back to this while tackling the following units):

Positive

		ACTION	STATE
SG	I	precative	*lū*+stative (= precative of state)
	you m.	imperative	*lū*+stative (= precative of state)
	you f.	imperative	*lū*+stative (= precative of state)
	he	precative	*lū*+stative (= precative of state)
	she	precative	*lū*+stative (= precative of state)
PL	we	cohortative	*lū*+stative (= precative of state)
	you m.	imperative	*lū*+stative (= precative of state)
	you f.	imperative	*lū*+stative (= precative of state)
	they m.	precative	*lū*+stative (= precative of state)
	they f.	precative	*lū*+stative (= precative of state)

As this indicates, we have four different forms for expressing positive commands (or wishes): imperative, precative, *lū*+stative, cohortative.

The imperative is used only in the second person. The precative is not used in the second person. *lū*+stative can be used for any person.

Negative

Negative commands (and wishes) have their own forms, which have to be learned in addition to positive ones:

		ACTION	STATE
SG	I	*lā*+present ; or vetitive	*lā*+stative ; or vetitive
	you m.	*lā*+present ; or vetitive	*lā*+stative ; or vetitive; or *lā*+present
	you f.	*lā*+present ; or vetitive	*lā*+stative ; or vetitive; or *lā*+present
	he	*lā*+present ; or vetitive	*lā*+stative ; or vetitive
	she	*lā*+present ; or vetitive	*lā*+stative ; or vetitive

PL	we	*lā*+present ; or vetitive (?)	*lā*+stative ; or vetitive
	you m.	*lā*+present ; or vetitive	*lā*+stative ; or vetitive; or *lā*+present
	you f.	*lā*+present ; or vetitive	*lā*+stative ; or vetitive; or *lā*+present
	they m.	*lā*+present ; or vetitive	*lā*+stative ; or vetitive
	they f.	*lā*+present ; or vetitive	*lā*+stative ; or vetitive

lā+present is the negative equivalent of the imperative.

This is enough to make one's head spin, but in reality the negative forms are quite rare. Also, Babylonians themselves seem to have been a bit confused about them. As with all things, it is practice through reading which will consolidate your grasp of the phenomena.

The most important things to remember

1 Babylonian verbs usually agree in gender and number with the subject.

2 They inflect in four different systems (and in their sub-systems):

- the G system has the most general meaning, and that which is closest to the meaning of the root;
- the N system usually has a meaning corresponding to the passive of the G system;
- the D system is used in various ways, one being to change verbs of being into verbs of doing;
- the Š system usually has a meaning corresponding to the causative of the G system.

3 Babylonian verbs can be strong or weak (the latter are missing one or more root letters).

4 Babylonian verbs (both strong and weak) fall into *a*-verbs and *e*-verbs. They inflect in the same way, except that *e*-verbs usually have *e/ē* where *a*-verbs have *a/ā*.

5 The dictionary form of most verbs is the G system infinitive (*PaRāSu(m)*). For verbs which do not occur in the G system, the infinitive of the system in which they occur most frequently is used.

6 In statements, verbs are negated by *ul*. In questions, they are negated by *lā* if there is a question word, by *ul* if there is not. Subordinate clauses (introduced in Unit 30) are negated by *lā*.

SELF CHECK

	I can ...
	... generally navigate my way around how Babylonian verbs behave
	... explain what a verbal 'system' is
	... (in time:) explain which meanings are associated with the four systems
	... explain the difference between a strong and weak verb
	... explain the difference between an *a*-verb and an *e*-verb
	... explain what impersonal constructions are, and how Babylonian expresses them.

15 *The present*

In this unit you will learn:

▸ **how to make present forms of the verb.**

The Babylonian tense which this course calls the 'present' tense can actually correspond to various tenses in English, not just the English present tenses.

15.1 Uses of the present

The Babylonian present is used to refer to the future (cf. English **I am going to the cinema tomorrow**), more rarely to the present. It can also refer to the past, but usually only with 'durative' verbs, i.e. verbs whose action is perceived as lasting for a period of time (unlike **to chop**, which happens in a single instant).

A particularity of the present is that *lā* + present = **must not ..., should not**.

CULTURE TIP

Babylonian and Assyrian do not have a word for **time**. Their speakers could of course refer to the passage of time in terms of days, months, years, reigns, etc., but one cannot literally translate into Babylonian or Assyrian a sentence such as **How much time has passed?**

15.2 Forms in the G, N, D and Š systems

Using the system explained in Unit 5, whereby PRS represent a verb's three root letters, the present forms of strong verbs conform to the patterns in Table 4. This may seem intimidating, but the pattern is actually quite simple: the 'core' of each column stays the same:

G *PaRRvS* N *PPaRRvS* D *PaRRaS* Š *šaPRaS*

Table 4

	G	N	D	Š
1st. sg.	*aPaRRvS*	*aPPaRRvS*	*uPaRRaS*	*ušaPRaS*
2nd sg. m.	*taPaRRvS*	*taPPaRRvS*	*tuPaRRaS*	*tušaPRaS*
2nd sg. f.	*taPaRRvSī*	*taPPaRRvSī*	*tuPaRRaSī*	*tušaPRaSī*
3rd sg.	*iPaRRvS*	*iPPaRRvS*	*uPaRRaS*	*ušaPRaS*
1st pl.	*niPaRRvS*	*niPPaRRvS*	*nuPaRRaS*	*nušaPRaS*
2nd pl.	*taPaRRvSā*	*taPPaRRvSā*	*tuPaRRaSā*	*tušaPRaSā*
3rd pl. m	*iPaRRvSū*	*iPPaRRvSū*	*uPaRRaSū*	*ušaPRaSū*
3rd pl. f	*iPaRRvSā*	*iPPaRRvSā*	*uPaRRaSā*	*ušaPRaSā*

v means: a short vowel which changes from verb to verb.

What changes are the prefixes and suffixes, which vary with the person, gender and number of the subject. In isolation, these prefixes and suffixes are as in Table 5.

Table 5

	G and N	D and Š
1st sg.	*a-*	*u-*
2nd sg. m.	*ta-*	*tu-*
2nd sg. f.	*ta-...-ī*	*tu-...-ī*
3rd sg.	*i-*	*u-*
1st pl.	*ni-...*	*nu-*
2nd pl.	*ta-...-ā*	*tu-...-ā*
3rd pl. m.	*i-...-ū*	*u-...-ū*
3rd pl. f.	*i-...-ā*	*u-...-ā*

15.3 Observations on the prefixes and suffixes

The suffixes (*-ī*, *-ā*, *-ū*) are the same in all four systems. The prefixes of the D and Š systems can be thought of as simplification of those of the G and N systems, whereby the consonants (*t*, *n*) stay the same but vowels (*a*, *i*) have been changed to *u*. Whereas first and third person singular are different in the G and N systems, they are identical in the D and Š systems.

Within a given system, all second person forms (masculine, feminine, singular, plural) have the same prefix, though they may have different suffixes. The same applies for third person forms. The 3rd person plural suffixes *-ū* (m.) and *-ā* (f.) are related to the plural morphemes *-ūt-* (m.) and *-āt-* (f.) (see Units 8.2 and 9.1).

LANGUAGE TIP

'Morphemes' are bits of words which carry meaning in their own right, and cannot be divided further. For example, the English word **shopper** is made up of the morphemes **shop** and **-er**; **disorganized** of **dis-**, **organize** and **-(e)d**; **antidisestablishmentarianism** of **anti-**, **dis-**, **establish**, **-ment**, **-arian**, and **-ism**.

15.4 The vowel in the G and N systems

In the G and N systems it is necessary to insert a vowel which varies from verb to verb. This vowel is indicated by the symbol *v* in Table 4, and the vowel to insert is known as the 'theme vowel' (see Unit 14.15). Each verb's theme vowel is indicated in the Glossary (in brackets after the infinitive). For verbs which have the two theme vowels *a/u*, insert the first of these (*a*).

iPPaRRvS (3rd sg. present, N system)

paqādu (i) **to entrust** → *ippaqqid* **he/she/it is being entrusted**
ṣabātu (a) **to seize** → *iṣṣabbat* **he/she/it is being seized**
našāku (a/u) **to bite** → *innaššak* **he/she/it is being bitten**

taPaRRvSī (2nd f. sg. present, G system)

paqādu (i) **to entrust** → *tapaqqidī* **you** (f. sg.) **are entrusting**
ṣabātu (a) **to seize** → *taṣabbatī* **you** (f. sg.) **are seizing**
našāku (a/u) **to bite** → *tanaššakī* **you** (f. sg.) **are biting**

15.5 The present forms of *parāsu* in the G, N, D and Š systems

As well as understanding how Babylonian verbs work in principle, you need to learn the forms. Different people have different ways of doing this: some prefer to do it visually, writing them out several times, others by reciting them like a poem, others still by these two methods combined. You will know, or discover, what works best for you. Whatever your method, you will find it easier in the long run to learn the forms of an actual verb rather than the pattern in the abstract. Accordingly, Table 6 shows the forms of the verb *parāsu* **to separate** for you to commit to memory. (This is best done column by column rather than row by row.)

Table 6

	G system	N system	D system	Š system
	'I separate'	**'I am separated'**	**'I separate'**	**'I cause to separate'**
1st sg.	*aparras*	*apparras*	*uparras*	*ušapras*
2nd sg. m.	*taparras*	*tapparras*	*tuparras*	*tušapras*
2nd sg. f.	*taparrasī*	*tapparrasī*	*tuparrasī*	*tušaprasī*
3rd sg.	*iparras*	*ipparras*	*uparras*	*ušapras*
1st pl.	*niparras*	*nipparras*	*nuparras*	*nušapras*
2nd pl.	*taparrasā*	*tapparrasā*	*tuparrasā*	*tušaprasā*
3rd pl. m.	*iparrasū*	*ipparrasū*	*uparrasū*	*ušaprasū*
3rd pl. f.	*iparrasā*	*ipparrasā*	*uparrasā*	*ušaprasā*

LANGUAGE TIP

The meanings of *parāsu* include **to cut off**, **to wean**, and **to render a verdict** (in a lawsuit). These all derive from the basic idea of separating: to separate into two parts; to separate a child from the breast; to draw a line of right and wrong to separate litigants.

15.6 Sound changes

When *n* comes into contact with a following consonant, it fully assimilates (i.e. becomes identical) to it (see Unit 47.9). In the present tense, this happens in the Š system to verbs whose first root letter is *n*.

ušaPRaS for *našāku* **to bite** → *ušaššak* **he causes to bite** (from *ušanšak*)

After the Old Babylonian period, double voiced 'stop' consonants (*bb*, *dd*, *gg*) occasionally nasalize (see Unit 47.11).

imaggur **he agrees** → *imangur*

Exercise 15.1, Old Babylonian

Render the Babylonian present tense as an English present or future according to what you think works best in the context of the sentence. (An exclamation mark means that the preceding sign is badly written on the tablet.)

a-al-šu ***ú-ha-al-la-aq***

šu-ut-tam ***i-pa-aš-šar***

i-na-aṭ-ṭal *ù* ***ip-pa-al-la-as***

sí-sí-ik-tum da-ri-tum bi-ri-ni ***ik-ka-aṣ-ṣa-ar***

i-na u_4*-mi ša da-an-na-tim* ***i-ṣa-ab-ba-at*** *qá-at-ka*

er-ṣe-tum ***i-ra-am-mu-um***

nam-ri-ri ša i-lim ***ta-na-ṭa-a-al*** (ignore the 'extra' *-a-*)

a-na-ku (*anāku* **Me, . . .**) *e-li-ka* ***a-ha-ab-bu-ub***

mu-ru-uṣ li-ib-bi-im ma-di-iš ***a-na-aṭ-ṭa-al***

ki-ir-ba-an mun *i-na lu-ba-ri-im* ***ta-ra-ak-ka-as!*** *i-na ki-ša-di-šu* ***ta-ra-ak-ka-a*****[s]** *ba-li-iṭ* (*baliṭ* **he will be well**)

Exercise 15.2, Old Babylonian

a-na-ku (*anāku* **I**) *mu-ša-am ù ka-ṣa-tam* (see Unit 36.5) *šu-na-ti-ka-ma* (ignore *-ma*) ***a-na-ṭa-al***

túg*ṣú-ba-a-at* (*ṣubāt*: singular, but treated as if plural) *a-wi-le-e ša-at-tam a-na ša-at-tim* (*šattam ana šattim* **year by year**) ***i-da-am-mi-qú*** *at-ti* (*atti* **you** (f. sg.)) túg*ṣú-ba-a-ti ša-at-tam a-na ša-at-ti-im* ***tu-qá-al-la-li***

ku-ru-ma-ti-ši-n[*a*] ***ta-ma-ha-r*****[*i*]**

šum ha-ba-li-im (*habālu(m)* = **wrongdoing**) *pa-ga-ar-ki* (*pagarki* **for yourself**) ***ta-ša-ak-ka-ni***

é ***ú-da-ab-ba-ab***

ṭe$_4$*-ma-am an-ni-a-am ma-ah-ri-šu* (*mahrīšu* **before him**) ***a-ša-ak-ka-an***

a-na m[*i*]*-ni-im bi-ti* ***tu-pá-la-ah***

ši-ip (sp. *šēp*) d*nin-šubur ù* d*nin-si*$_4$*-an-na be-li-ia* ***a-na-aš-ši-iq*** *mi-im-ma la* ***ta-na-ku-di***

pa-nu-šu la ***i-ṣa-li-mu***

Exercise 15.3, Old Babylonian

Look up the Babylonian readings of the sumerograms in the list at the end of the course, and remember to put the word in the correct form.

é.gal-*lam la* ***ú-da-ba-ab***

nun kur *la ša-tam* (*lā šâtam* **other than his own**) *qá-sú* (**by his hand**, Unit 36.5) *i-ka-šad*

nun kur kúr-*šú* ***ú-na-ka-ap***

muš lú ***i-na-ša-ak***

érin-*ka* sag a.šà-*ša ú-ul* ***i-ka-šad***

érin-*ni li-it* érin kúr ***i-ša-ak-ka-an***

dim *i+na* (*ina* **in**) kur ***i-ra-ah-hi-iṣ***

é lú ***is-sà-ap-pa-ah***

kur *a-na* (*ana* **in**) *dan-na-tim* ***i-pa-hu-ur***

dumu lugal gu.za *a-bi-šu* ***i-ṣa-bat***

uru^{ki} *šu-ú* (šū **this**) ***iṣ-ṣa-ab-ba-at*** *ú-lu-ma* (*ūlū-ma* **or**) *ú-ul* ***iṣ-ṣa-ab-ba-at*** (question)

é.gal-*am la* ***ú-da-ab-ba-bu***

Exercise 15.4, Old and Middle Babylonian

The last five sentences are MB.

a-ra-an-šu-nu i-na mu-úh-hi-k[a] ***iš-ša-ak-ka-an***

am-tam a-na ma-am-ma-an ú-ul ***a-na-ad-di-in***

aš-ša-as-sú la ***i-h[a]-al-la-lu***

a-wa-tu-ia ma-ti i-in-ki ***i-ma-ha-ra***

hi-ṭì-it gú.un-*šu i-na mu-úh-hi-ka* ***iš-ša-ak-ka-an***

i-na ni-iš dingir *li-ib-ba-ku-nu* ***ú-na-pa-šu***

ap-kal-lum qí-bit-su ma-am-man ul ***ú-šam-sak***

[in]a qá-ti-šu el-le-ti pa-áš-šu-ra ***i-rak-kas***

^{giš}má-*šú* ***ú-ma-har***

me-lam-mu-šú ***ú-sa-ah-ha-pu*** *na-gab za-ia-a-ri*

⸢*ul*⸣ ***[i]š-ša-ka-an*** *sa-li-mu ba-lu mi-it-hu-ṣi*

Exercise 15.5, Standard Babylonian

qip-ta-šú ***a-tam-ma-ah***

ùg^{meš} kur.kur *kul-lat-si-na* ***ta-paq-qid***

da-a-a-na ṣal-pa mi-se-ra tu-kal-lam

ma-hir ṭa-a'-ti la muš-te-še-ru ***tu-šá-az-bal*** *ar-na*

i-šad-da-ad *i-na miṭ-ra-ta za-ru-ú* ^{giš}má

i-šar-ra-ak *ter-din-nu a-na ka-ti-i ti-ú-ta*

[ana za]-ma-a-ru qu-ub-bi-ia ***ú-šá-aṣ-rap***

mi-lik (for older *milka*) *šá an-za-nun-ze-e* ***i-ha-ak-kim*** *man-nu*

at-ta a-na ši-bu-ti-šú-nu ***taš-šak-kin*** (sp. *taššakkan*)

mu-ka-aš-ši-di ***ik-ka-aš-šad***

The most important things to remember

1 The present is formed by adding prefixes and suffixes to a 'core'. The core changes with the verb's system, the prefixes and suffixes with the grammatical characteristics of the subject.

2 The third person singular forms in the four systems for the verb *parāsu* **to separate** are: G *iparras*, N *ipparras*, D *uparras*, Š *ušapras*.

3 In the G and N systems the vowel between the second and third root letters changes from verb to verb: it is the verb's theme vowel (for verbs with the two theme vowels *a/u*, use *a*).

4 One set of prefixes and suffixes is used for the G and N systems, another for the D and Š systems. You need to know them. (You will probably find it easier to learn them as part of actual forms than in the abstract.)

5 The Babylonian present can be translated as an English present or future tense, and in past narrative as an English past tense (**I did, I was doing**) – usually this happens only with durative verbs.

SELF CHECK

	I can ...
	... explain what the 'present' tense is used for
	... recall the forms of the present for *parāsu(m)* in the G system
	... (in time:) recall the forms of the present in the other systems
	... recall which theme vowel (when there are two) is used in the present
	... convert a present form to the dictionary form, in order to look up the verb in the Glossary.

16 *The preterite*

In this unit you will learn:

▶ **how to make preterite forms of the verb.**

The preterite is fundamentally a past tense.

16.1 Uses of the preterite

In Old Babylonian, the preterite usually corresponds to an English preterite (**I ate**), but occasionally a natural-sounding English translation requires an English perfect (**I have eaten**).

After the Old Babylonian period, in vernacular language the preterite was gradually ousted by the perfect, and in first millennium vernacular the usual way of referring to the past in non-negated main clauses was the perfect. However, the preterite continued to be used in Standard Babylonian, more or less as in Old Babylonian.

A special use of the preterite is to make so-called 'performative' utterances, which are those where the very fact of speaking the utterance does what the utterance says. In translation one inserts **hereby** (as in **I hereby pronounce you man and wife**, **I hereby declare the meeting open**).

SB <u>*alsikunūši*</u> *ilānī mušīti* **<u>I hereby call upon you</u>, O gods of the night** (*alsi* = 1st sg. pret. *šasû*) (*Maqlû* I 1)

16.2 Forms in the G, N, D and Š systems

Using the system explained in Unit 5, the preterite forms of strong verbs conform to the patterns shown in Table 7.

Table 7

	G system	N system	D system	Š system
1st sg.	*aPRvS*	*aPPaRvS*	*uPaRRiS*	*ušaPRiS*
2nd sg. m.	*taPRvS*	*taPPaRvS*	*tuPaRRiS*	*tušaPRiS*
2nd sg. f.	*taPRvSī*	*taPPaRSī*	*tuPaRRiSī*	*tušaPRiSī*
3rd sg.	*iPRvS*	*iPPaRvS*	*uPaRRiS*	*ušaPRiS*
1st pl.	*niPRvS*	*niPPaRvS*	*nuPaRRiS*	*nušaPRiS*
2nd pl.	*taPRvSā*	*taPPaRSā*	*tuPaRRiSā*	*tušaPRiSā*
3rd pl. m.	*iPRvSū*	*iPPaRSū*	*uPaRRiSū*	*ušaPRiSū*
3rd pl. f.	*iPRvSā*	*iPPaRSā*	*uPaRRiSā*	*ušaPRiSā*

v means: a short vowel which changes from verb to verb.

The principle is the same as for the present, i.e. the 'core' of each column stays the same:

G *PRvS*	D *PaRRiS*
N *PPaRvS* (but *v* is sometimes elided)	Š *šaPRiS*

What changes are the prefixes and suffixes, which vary with the person, gender and number of the subject. These prefixes and suffixes are the same as those for the present, and the same comments apply (see Unit 15.3).

LANGUAGE TIP

The only difference between present and preterite in the D and Š systems is the vowel between the second and third root letter, which is *a* for the present, *i* for the preterite: *uPaRRaS*, *ušaPRaS* (present) vs. *uPaRRiS*, *ušaPRiS* (preterite).

16.3 The vowel in the G and N systems

In the G and N systems it is necessary to insert a vowel which varies from verb to verb. This vowel is indicated by the symbol *v* in Table 7. For the G system, this is the theme vowel. For verbs with the two theme vowels *a/u*, insert the second of these (*u*).

In the N system, for all verbs whose theme vowel is not *u* insert *i*. Verbs with theme vowel *u* are (except for the I-weak verb *epēšu*, see Unit 24) rarely attested in the N preterite. Some have *u*, others have *i*.

iPPaRvS (3rd sg. preterite, N system)
  for *paqādu* (*i*) **to entrust** = *ippaqid* **he/she/it was entrusted**
  for *ṣabātu* (*a*) **to seize** = *iṣṣabit* **he/she/it was seized**
  for *našāku* (*a/u*) **to bite** = *innašik* **he/she/it was bitten**

taPRvSī (2nd sg. f. preterite, G system)
  for *paqādu* (*i*) **to entrust** = *tapqidī* **you** (f. sg.) **entrusted**
  for *ṣabātu* (*a*) **to seize** = *taṣbatī* **you** (f. sg.) **seized**
  for *našāku* (*a/u*) **to bite** = *taššukī* **you** (f. sg.) **bit** (from *tanšukī*)

16.4 A sound change: vowel elision

Vowel elision (see Unit 47.4) occurs in N system preterites which have a suffix as well as a prefix:

taPPaRSī (from *taPPaRvSī*, syllabified *taP–Pa–Rv–Sī*)
taPPaRSā (from *taPPaRvSā*, syllabified *taP–Pa–Rv–Sā*)
iPPaRSū (from *iPPaRvSū*, syllabified *iP–Pa–Rv–Sū*)
iPPaRSā (from *iPPaRvSā*, syllabified *iP–Pa–Rv–Sā*)

16.5 A sound change: assimilation of *n*

When *n* comes into contact with a following consonant, it assimilates (i.e. becomes identical) to it (see Unit 47.9). In the preterite, this happens in the G and Š systems to verbs whose first root letter is *n*.

iPRvS for *našāku* **to bite** → *iššuk* **he/she/it bit** (from *inšuk*)
ušaPRiS for *našāku* **to bite** → *ušaššik* **he/she/it caused (s/o) to bite** (from *ušanšik*)

LANGUAGE TIP

In principle, assimilation of *n* could also happen to N preterites of verbs whose second root letter is *n*, when as a result of vocalic elision this is in contact with the third root letter. However, such forms are not yet attested.

Exercise 16.1, Old Babylonian

li-ib-bi ***im-ra-aṣ***

šu-mi ú-ul ***iz-ku-ur***

il-ba-aš *li-ib-ša-am*

ip-hur *um-ma-nu-um i-na ṣe-ri-šu* (*ina ṣērišu* **round him**)

iš-hu-uṭ *li-ib-ša-am*

ib-ri-iq *bi-ir-qum* ***in-na-pí-ih*** *i-ša-tum*

ši-bu-ti ***ú-pa-ah-hi-ir*** *a-na ba-bi-šu*

[i-n]a še-re-ti ib-ba-ra ***ú-ša-az-ni-in***

ip-ru-u' *ma-ar-ka-sa e-le-ep-pa* ***ip-ṭú-ur***

a-bu-ba a-na ku-ul-la-at ni-ši ***ú-za-am-me-er***

Exercise 16.2, Old Babylonian

qí-iš-tum ig-re-e-šu (*igrešu* **it attacked him**) ***iš-ku-un*** *ek-le-tam a-na* (translate *ana* as **in place of**) *nu-úr ša-ma-i*

li-ib-bi ma-di-iš ***iz-zi-iq***

ši-ir a-wi-lim ***is-hu-ul***

ni-iš šar-ri i-na pí-i-šu ***aš-ku-un***

hu-ub-tam ***ih-bu-ut***

ki-ma ni-iṭ-li-ia it-ti-ša ***ad-bu-ub***

di-nam a-n[a] (translate *ana* as **about**) *a-hi-šu ú-ul* ***ag-mu-ur***

⸢re⸣-eš$_{15}$*-ka* ***ú-ka-ab-bi-it***

a-na mi-nim qá-at-ka i-na zu-um-ri-ia ***ta-as-sú-úh***

⸢i⸣-lu ma-tim ***it-ru-ru-ma iš-ši-⸢qú⸣*** *še*$_{20}$*-pí-šu*

Exercise 16.3, Old Babylonian

a-na ša-pí-ri-ia mi-nam ***ú-ga-al-li-il***

i-na e-bu-ri ^{še}*am ú-ul* ***id-d[i]-nu*** (translate *nadānu* as **to give out**) *i-na pu-úh-ri ši-la-ti* ***id-bu-ba***

a-na e-pé-ši-im (translate *epēšum* as **undertaking**) *an-ni-i-im ki-i la* ***ta-ap-la-ah***

ap-pa-šu ***ip-lu-úš****-ma* (*-ma* **and**) [*ṣe*]*-re-tam* ***iš-ku-un***

qa-qa-ad-ka ***ú-ka-bi-it***

ṣa-bu-um ša be-lí-ia ***ip-hu-ur***

a-wa-tim wa-at-ra-tim-ma (do not translate *-ma*) *ha-ià-su-mu* (*hayasumu*, personal name) *a-na ṣe-er be-lí-ia* ***iš-pu-ur***

a-di-ni ṭe$_4$*-ma-am ú-ul* ***al-ma-ad***

i-ša-tam i-na li-ib-bi qí-ir-ti ***ip-pu-uh-ma*** (*-ma* **and**) ^{giš}*di-im-tum* ***im-qú-ut***

kù.babbar *ú-ul* ***ni-im-hu-ur***

lú^{meš} *šu-nu-ti* (*šunūti* **those**) *a-hi a-na mi-nim* ***ih-su-ús***

^{anše}*ha-a-ru-um* ***iq-qà-ṭì-il***

anše$^{\text{hi.a}}$ *a-na ge-er-ri-im* ***ih-ha-aš-hu***

Exercise 16.4, Middle Babylonian

In literary Middle Babylonian, D and Š preterites often display *e*-colouring, see Unit 14.13.

a-na šú-a-tú (*ana šuātu* **to that one**) *né-me-qa* **šúm***-šú* (*iddinšu* or *iddinaššu* **he gave**) zi*-tam da-rí-tam ul* **šúm***-šú* (*iddinšu* or *iddinaššu* **he gave**)

^{m}*a-da-pa* (personal name, indeclinable) *ša šu-ú-ti* [*k*]*a-ap-pa-ša* ***iš-bi-ir*** (see Unit 11.13)

am-mi-ni ša šu-ú-ti ka-ap-pa-ša ***te-e-eš-bi-ir*** (see Unit 11.13)

a-na gi-sal-lat kur*-i ša-qu-ti ki-ma* mušen (pl.) ***ip-pár-šu*** (see Unit 14.14, bottom; and exercise 32.1, Language tip box)

šal-ma-at qu-ra-di-šu-nu i-na ba-ma-at kur*-i a-na qù-ru-na-a-te* ***lu-qé-rin*** (sp. *lū uqerrin*; *lū* = **truly**)

ša-gal-ti um-ma-na-te-šu-nu (*-te-* sp. *-ti-*) dagal^{meš} *ki-ma ri-hi-il-ti* ^{d}iškur *lu* ***áš-kun***

ul ***iš-nu-un*** *ma-ti-ma ina* (*ina* **among**) man^{meš}*-ni kúl-la-ti qa-bal-šu ma-am-ma*

a-na re-ši-šu-nu ***ú-še-pi-ik*** *ša-am-na*

iš-ku-un ^{d}*a-nu me-eṭ-ṭa la pa-da-a e-lu tar-gi-gi*

^{d}*nin-urta qar-du* sag-ed dingir^{meš} ^{giš}tukul^{meš}*-šu-nu* ***ú-še-be-er***

Exercise 16.5, Standard Babylonian

^{lú}maš.maš *ina ki-kiṭ-ṭe-e ki-mil-ti ul* ***ip-ṭur***

qer-bi-ia ***id-lu-hu***

$^{\text{na4}}$*a-gúr-ri ina* $^{\text{na4}}$za.gìn ***ú-šab-šil***

da-nu-um ^{d}*en-líl u* ^{d}*é-a* ***ú-rap-pi-šú*** *ú-zu-un-šú* *ta-na-da-a-ti* (sp. *tanādāt*; normalize *tanādāt(i)*) lugal *i-liš* (*iliš* **to (those of) a god**) ***ú-maš-šil*** *ù pu-luh-ti* é.gal *um-man* ***ú-šal-mid***

am-mì-ni ^{lú}ì.du$_{8}$ (*ata* **O doorman**) ***ta-at-bal*** aga gal-*a ša* sag.du-*ia*

ik-pu-ud-ma (do not translate *-ma*) *lìb-ba-šu le-mut-tu*

ú-nak-ki-is *kap-pi-šú ab-ri-šu nu-bal-˹li-šú˺*

ana 20 d[ann]a (*ana ešrā bīrī* **at 20 leagues**) ***ik-su-pu*** *ku-sa-pa ana* 30 danna (*ana šalāšā bīrī* **at 30 leagues**) ***iš-ku-nu*** *nu-bat-ta*

Exercise 16.6, From The Epic of Erra

Render *-ma* after verbs as **and**.

kur^{meš} (use *šadû*) ***ub-bit****-ma* (*ubbit* **he annihilated**) *bu-ul-šú-nu* ***ú-šam-qit***

ta-ma-a-ti ***id-luh****-ma mi-šir-ta-ši-na* ***ú-hal-liq***

a-pi ù qí-i-ši ***ú-šah-rib****-ma ki-i* ^{d}gìra *iq-mi* (*iqmi* **he burned**)

CULTURE TIP

The Epic of Erra was used as a talisman: manuscripts of it were perforated and hung up, to guard against outbreaks of plague.

The most important things to remember

1. Like the present, the preterite is formed by adding prefixes and suffixes to a 'core'. The core changes with the verb's system, the prefixes and suffixes with the grammatical characteristics of the subject.
2. The third person singular forms in the four systems for the verb *parāsu* **to separate** are: G *iprus*, N *ipparis*, D *uparris*, Š *ušapris*.
3. In the G and N systems the vowel between the second and third root letters changes from verb to verb. In the G system it is the verb's theme vowel (*u* for verbs with theme vowel *a/u*). In the N system it is usually *i*.
4. The same prefixes and suffixes are used as for the present.
5. The Babylonian preterite can usually be translated with an English preterite (**I did**).
6. For verbs with *n* as first root letter, this assimilates to the second root letter when they come into contact (e.g. *iddin* **he/she gave**, from *nadānu(m)* **to give**).
7. In the N system, the rule of vowel elision (Unit 47.4) comes into force when there is a vowel after the third root letter.

SELF CHECK

	I can ...
	... explain what the 'preterite' tense is used for
	... recall the forms of the preterite for *parāsu*(*m*) in the G system
	... (in time:) recall the forms of the preterite in the other systems
	... recall which theme vowel (when there are two) is used in the preterite
	... convert a preterite form to the dictionary form, in order to look up the verb in the Glossary
	... explain what is special about verbs whose first root letter is *n*, and how this affects their forms.

17 *The perfect*

In this unit you will learn:

- **how to make perfect forms of the verb.**

The perfect is fundamentally a past tense. In all four systems, the 'core' includes an infix *-ta-* (*-te-* in *e*-verbs).

> **LANGUAGE TIP**
> The perfect tense was discovered by Assyriologist Benno Landsberger and only described in print in 1952, in the Akkadian grammar by Landsberger's pupil Wolfram von Soden (*Grundriss der akkadischen Grammatik*).

17.1 Uses of the perfect

In Old Babylonian the perfect had a meaning very similar to the English perfect (**I have eaten**). As Babylonian developed, the perfect gradually supplanted the preterite in the vernacular language, and by the first millennium it became the normal vernacular tense for referring to the past, corresponding to both the English perfect (**I have eaten**) and the English preterite (**I ate**).

One often meets the sequence 'preterite-*ma* perfect'. In this usage, both verbs usually translate as English preterites (**I did X, and (then) I did Y**).

In Old Babylonian letters, the perfect often translates into English as a present + **herewith**.

OB *aštaprakkum* **Herewith I am sending to you** (m. sg.) ...

In subordinate clauses, the Babylonian perfect can (like the English perfect) refer to the future. (Subordinate clauses will be treated in Unit 30.)

OB *tuppī kīma <u>teštemû</u> šulumka šupram-ma libbī linūh* **When <u>you have heard</u> my letter, write to me how you are, so that my mind can be at ease** (AbB 13, 175: 15–18)

17.2 Forms in the G, N, D and Š systems

Using the system explained in Unit 5, the perfect forms of strong verbs conform to the patterns shown in Table 8. (In *e*-verbs *a* changes to *e*.) The principle is the same as for the present and preterite, i.e. the 'core' of each column stays the same:

G *PtaRvS* (though *v* is sometimes elided) D *PtaRRiS* N *ttaPRvS* Š *štaPRiS*

Table 8

	G	N	D	Š
1st sg.	*aPtaRvS*	*attaPRvS*	*uPtaRRiS*	*uštaPRiS*
2nd sg. m.	*taPtaRvS*	*tattaPRvS*	*tuPtaRRiS*	*tuštaPRiS*
2nd sg. f.	*taPtaRSī*	*tattaPRvSī*	*tuPtaRRiSī*	*tuštaPRiSī*
3rd sg.	*iPtaRvS*	*ittaPRvS*	*uPtaRRiS*	*uštaPRiS*
1st pl.	*niPtaRvS*	*nittaPRvS*	*nuPtaRRiS*	*nuštaPRiS*
2nd pl.	*taPtaRSā*	*tattaPRvSā*	*tuPtaRRiSā*	*tuštaPRiSā*
3rd pl. m.	*iPtaRSū*	*ittaPRvSū*	*uPtaRRiSū*	*uštaPRiSū*
3rd pl. f.	*iPtaRSā*	*ittaPRvSā*	*uPtaRRiSā*	*uštaPRiSā*

v means: a short vowel which changes from verb to verb.

What changes are the prefixes and suffixes, which vary with the person, gender and number of the subject. These prefixes and suffixes are the same as those for the present and preterite, and the same comments apply (see Unit 15.3).

17.3 The vowel in the G and N systems

In the G and N systems it is necessary to insert a vowel which varies from verb to verb. This vowel is indicated by the symbol *v* in Table 8 and is the same as the vowel in the present of the G and N systems (i.e. = the theme vowel; when a verb has the two theme vowels *a/u*, then insert *a*).

17.4 Sound changes

In the G system, when suffixes are added to the core, the vowel between the second and third root letter is elided (see Unit 47.4).

šakānu **to put** → *taštaknī* **You** (f. sg.) **have put** (from *taštakanī*)

As in other tenses, *n* assimilates to a following consonant.

nadānu **to give** → *attadin* **I have given** (from *antadin*)

The *t* of the perfect infix changes to *d*, *ṭ*, *s*, *z* and *ṣ* when it directly follows these consonants.

dabābu **to speak** → *addabub* **I have spoken** (from *adtabub*)
ṣabātu **to seize** → *iṣṣabat* **He/she/it has seized** (from *iṣtabat*)
zabālu **to bring** → *izzabil* **He/she/it has brought** (from *iztabil*)
sahāru **to search for** → *issahur* **He/she/it has searched for** (from *istahur*)

After the Old Babylonian period, *št* changes to *lt*.

šakānu → *iltakan* **He has put** (from *ištakan*)
šapāru **to send** → *taltapar* **You** (m. sg.) **have sent** (from *taštapar*)

However, owing to their liking for traditional spellings, writers often use *št* rather than *lt* even after the Old Babylonian period. For further changes (*gt* → *gd*; *mt* → *md*, *nd*) see Unit 47.10.

Exercise 17.1, Old Babylonian

li-ib-bi **tu-ul-te-mi-in**

[li]-ib-ba-šu **im-ta-ra-aṣ**

tu-uš-ta-am-ri-iṣ *li-ib-bi ù mu-ru-uṣ li-ib-bi ra-bi-a-am a-na pa-ni-ia* (*ana panīya* for **me**) **ta-aš-ta-ka-an**

ri-ig-ma-am e-li-ia **ta-aš-ta-ka-a[n]**

hi-iṣ-pa-tum ka-bi-it-tum a-na pa-ni-ia **ip-ta-rik**

ú-sa-a-tim ra-bi-a-tim i-na mu-úh-hi-ia **ta-aš-ta-ka-an**

ki-ša-ad-ka ka-aq-qá-r[a]-am **uš-ta-ak-ši-id**

síg *ša* é.gal **iš-ta-aq-lu**

a.šà-*am* **am-ta-kar**

[l]ú*ša-ar-ra-qí šu-nu-ti* (*šunūti* **those**) **aṣ-ṣa-ba-at**

ri-ig-ma ra-bi-a-am **iš-ta-ak-na**

mi-ša-ra-am i-na ma-ti **aš-ta-ka-an**

Exercise 17.2, Middle Babylonian

m*a-da-pa* (personal name, indeclinable) *ma-ar* d*é-a ša šu-ú-ti ka-ap-pa-ša* **iš-te-bi-ir**

ma-ar ši-ip-ri ša d*a-ni* **ik-ta-al-da** (see Unit 47.9)

ša-am-na [il-q]ù-ni-šu-um-ma (*ilqûniššumma* **they brought to him, and**; preterite) **it-ta-ap-ši-iš**

[k]úl-la-at kur-*ia* **ta-al-ta-la-al**

Exercise 17.3, Standard Babylonian

mi-li **it-tah-su**

mi-šit-tu **im-ta-qut** *eli* uzu[meš]*-ia*

lu-u'-tu **im-ta-qut** *eli bir-ki-ia*

im-ha-aṣ pe-en-ša (*pēnša*, variant of *pēmša*)

it-ta-ša-ak *ú-ba-an-šá*

ig-dam-ra *maš-šak-ki-ia* [munus]ensi[meš]

as-li-ia ina ṭu-ub-bu-hi (*ina ṭubbuhi* **through slaughter (for sacrifices)**) dingir[meš] **ig-dam-ru**

qu-ra-du d*èr-ra ana šu-an-na* uru lugal dingir[meš] **iš-ta-kan** *pa-ni-šú*

tam-ha-ṣi-šu-ma (*-šu* means **him**, as object of *tamhaṣī*; *-ma* is **and**) *kap-pa-šu* **tal-te-eb-[ri]**

qaq-qad ú-ri-ṣi ana (translate *ana* as **in place of**) *qaq-qad* lú **it-ta-din**

CULTURE TIP

Babylonian rituals against demons often used scapegoats. These might be statuettes or live animals (not just goats). In either case, the demon was invited (or commanded) to transfer his or her unwelcome attentions to the scapegoat, and leave the patient alone.

The most important things to remember

1. Like the present and preterite, the perfect is formed by adding prefixes and suffixes to a 'core'. The core changes with the verb's system, the prefixes and suffixes with the grammatical characteristics of the subject.
2. The third person singular forms in the four systems for the verb *parāsu* **to separate** are: G *iptaras*, N *ittapras*, D *uptarris*, Š *uštapris*.
3. In the G and N systems the vowel between the second and third root letters changes from verb to verb. It is the same as the corresponding vowel in the present.
4. The same prefixes and suffixes are used as for the present and preterite.
5. The Babylonian perfect can often be translated with an English perfect (**I have done**), but sometimes context requires an English preterite (**I did**).
6. The *t* of the *-ta-* infix assimilates to immediately preceding *d*, *ṭ*, *s*, *z* and *ṣ*.
7. In verbs with *n* as first root letter, *nt* changes to *tt*.
8. After the Old Babylonian period, *št* changes to *lt*, e.g. *iltapar* **he has sent** matching Old Babylonian *ištapar*.
9. In the G system, the rule of vowel elision (Unit 47.4) comes into force when there is a vowel after the third root letter: 2nd sg. m. *taptaras* but 2nd sg. f. *taptarsī*, etc.

SELF CHECK

	I can ...
	... explain what the 'perfect' tense is used for
	... recall the forms of the perfect for *parāsu(m)* in the G system
	... (in time:) recall the forms of the perfect in the other systems
	... recall which theme vowel (when there are two) is used in the perfect
	... convert a perfect form to the dictionary form, in order to look up the verb in the Glossary
	... explain which sound changes perfect forms are subject to.

18 *The stative and the verbal adjective*

In this unit you will learn:

- **how to make stative forms of the verb**
- **how statives relate to the verbal adjective**
- **that nouns can be put in the stative**
- **that accusatives with the stative do not necessarily express the direct object**
- **that *lū* before the stative expresses a command or wish.**

There is a 'core' form of the Babylonian verb to which two different sets of endings can be added, producing two different grammatical forms: the 'verbal adjective', and the stative. Their meanings will be explained in this unit.

The verbal adjective is an adjective, and takes adjectival endings (described in Units 7 and 9). The stative is a tense of the verb, and takes its own set of suffixes (*-āku*, *-āta*, etc.), which are different from those of the present, preterite and perfect. The stative takes no prefixes.

18.1 The core forms for statives and verbal adjectives

Using the system explained in Unit 5, the 'core' forms of statives and verbal adjectives conform to the patterns shown in Table 9. (In *e*-verbs, *a* changes to *e*.)

Table 9

G	N	D	Š
PaRvS	*naPRuS*	*PuRRuS*	*šuPRuS*

v means: a short vowel which changes from verb to verb.

In the G system, owing to the rules of vowel elision (see Unit 47.4), the vowel between the second and third root letters is elided when suffixes beginning with a vowel are added.

For most adjectives related to strong verbs, in the G system the vowel represented by the symbol *v* is *i*. A few (almost all of which are verbs of being), however, have *a* or *u*. In this course, when the vowel is not *i*, this is stated in the Glossary (see e.g. *lemēnu* **to be evil**: the Glossary gives the stative as *lemun*). The core vowel in the G system is also visible in certain feminine singular G verbal adjectives.

18.2 The verbal adjective

Most adjectives in Babylonian, including many which you have already met, are 'verbal adjectives'. They are called 'verbal' because they are intimately related to the verb, e.g. inasmuch as they follow the four systems – otherwise, there is nothing special about them. (The idea of adjectives somehow being related to verbs occurs also with English past participles, e.g. **broken**.)

For verbs of being, the verbal adjective corresponds in English to the adjective used in translating the infinitive of the verb.

lemēnu **to be evil** → *lemnu* **evil**
marāṣu **to be ill** → *marṣu* **ill**
šupšuqu **to be very difficult** → *šupšuqu* **very difficult**

For verbs of doing which take a direct object, the verbal adjective usually means 'having undergone the action of the verb' (i.e. it has a passive sense). It can be translated with the English past participle (**broken**, **enhanced**).

parāsu **to separate** → *parsu* **separated**

For verbs of doing which do not take a direct object, the verbal adjective usually means 'performing the action of the verb' or 'having performed the action of the verb'. It can be translated with the English present participle (**sleeping**) or past participle (**fallen**).

ṣalālu **to be asleep** → *ṣallu* **sleeping, asleep**
maqātu **to fall** → *maqtu* **fallen**

Feminine singular verbal adjectives are produced by adding *-t-* or *-at-* (*-et-* for adjectives related to *e*-verbs) to the core. The meaning is the same. When *-t-* is added, the G system core vowel is visible; when *-at-* (or *-et-*) is added, the core vowel is elided (see Unit 47.4).

damāqu **to be good** → f. sg. *damiqtu*, *damqatu* **good**
lemēnu **to be evil** → f. sg. *lemuttu* (from *lemuntu*), *lemnetu* **evil**
rapāšu **to be broad** → f. sg. *rapaštu*, *rapšatu* **broad**

LANGUAGE TIP
Verbal adjectives in the N system are rare.

18.3 The stative

The stative is so called because, rather than describing an action, it describes a state (though this distinction is often obscured in translation). It can refer both to the present and the past – more rarely to the future. The stative only has suffixes (not prefixes), and these are different from the suffixes used by the present, preterite and perfect. Unlike the present, preterite and perfect, the stative has different markers for 3rd singular masculine and feminine subjects, and for 2nd plural masculine and feminine subjects. It is rare to use the stative in the N system.

18.4 Translating statives

How to translate a stative depends on whether the relevant verb can take a direct object in other tenses (e.g. present, preterite, perfect) of the same system.

For verbs which do not take a direct object in other tenses of the same system (this includes all verbs of being), the stative signifies that the subject of the verb is in a state resulting from performing the action. (Since the future use of the stative is comparatively rare, we do not include future translations in the following examples, though they are theoretically possible.)

maqit **He is/was in the state resulting from falling**, i.e. **He has/had fallen**
ṣalil **He is/was in the state resulting from lying down**, i.e. **He is/was lying down**
maruṣ **He is/was in the state resulting from being ill**, i.e. **He is/was ill**
damiq **He is/was in the state resulting from being good**, i.e. **He is/was good**

For verbs which do take an object in other tenses of the same system, the stative can be translated in four ways:

- so that the subject is/was/will be in a state of performing the action
- so that the subject is/was/will be in a state of having performed the action
- so that the subject is/was/will be in a state of undergoing the action
- so that the subject is/was/will be in a state of having undergone the action.

Context indicates which translation is appropriate. Here are some examples. (Future translations are again omitted on grounds of rarity.)

našik (from *našāku* **to bite**)
He is/was in the state of biting, i.e. **He is/was biting; He is/was in the state of having bitten**, i.e. **He has/had bitten; He is/was in the state of being bitten**, i.e. **He is/was being bitten; He is/was in the state of having been bitten**, i.e. **He has/had been bitten**
kašid (from *kašādu* **to reach**)
He is/was in the state of reaching, i.e. **He is/was reaching; He is/was in the state of having reached**, i.e. **He has/had reached**; **He is/was in the state of being reached**, i.e. **He is/was being reached; He is/was in the state of having been reached**, i.e. **He has/had been reached**
mahiṣ (from *mahāṣu* **to beat**)
He is/was in the state of beating, i.e. **He is/was beating; He is/was in the state of having beaten**, i.e. **He has/had beaten; He is/was in the state of being beaten**, i.e. **He is/was being beaten; He is/was in the state of having been beaten**, i.e. **He has/had been beaten**

This array of possible meanings is bewildering when first encountered, but in context it is usually obvious which meaning applies.

LANGUAGE TIP

In a formal linguistic description of Babylonian grammar, the difference between the stative and other forms of the verb would be said to be one of 'aspect' rather than one of tense. For the purposes of learning to translate, however, one can simply think of the stative as a tense.

18.5 Statives with an accusative

Statives can take an accusative. When the other tenses (e.g. present and preterite) of the same verb in the same system take a direct object, then the accusative can be translated as a direct object, like it would be for the other tenses (e.g. present and preterite).

OB *<u>âm</u> hašhū* **They need <u>grain</u>** (AbB 12, 47: 8)
OB *ûm <u>girram</u> parik* **The grain is lying across <u>the road</u>** (AbB 7, 84: r.10')
OB *šunu <u>manna</u> palhū* **<u>Whom</u> do they fear?** (AbB 3, 10: 12)
OB *<u>mê</u> lū ramkāta* **May you be bathed in <u>water</u>** (Gilg. BM+VA: iii.11)

It is, however, possible for the stative to take an accusative even if other tenses of the same verb in the same system do not. This is known as the 'accusative of respect': one translates literally as **in respect of ...**, **with respect to ...** and then paraphrases as the context and English idiom suggest. (This is a sub-type of the 'adverbial accusative', see Unit 36.5.)

OB *ištu rēš šattim <u>murṣam dannam</u> marṣāku* **Since the beginning of the year I have been ill <u>with respect to a strong disease</u>**, i.e. **... with a strong disease** (ARM 26/2, 403: 3–4)
OB *šuttuh <u>lānam</u> damiq zumram* **It (the snake) is very long in respect of form, it is beautiful in respect of body**, i.e. **It is very long in form, beautiful in body** (SEAL 5.1.20.1: 1–2)

CULTURE TIP
In Tablet XI of The Epic of Gilgameš, Gilgameš has procured the 'plant of life', but it is stolen by a snake while he bathes. There is an obvious affinity with the role of the snake in the Genesis story.

18.6 Forms of the stative in the G, N, D and Š systems

Using the system explained in Unit 5, the stative forms of strong verbs conform to the patterns shown in Table 10.

Table 10

	G system	N system	D system	Š system
1st sg.	*PaRSāku*	*naPRuSāku*	*PuRRuSāku*	*šuPRuSāku*
2nd sg. m.	*PaRSāta*	*naPRuSāta*	*PuRRuSāta*	*šuPRuSāta*
2nd sg. f.	*PaRSāti*	*naPRuSāti*	*PuRRuSāti*	*šuPRuSāti*
3rd sg. m.	*PaRvS*	*naPRuS*	*PuRRuS*	*šuPRuS*
3rd sg. f.	*PaRSat*	*naPRuSat*	*PuRRuSat*	*šuPRuSat*
1st pl.	*PaRSānu*	*naPRuSānu*	*PuRRuSānu*	*šuPRuSānu*
2nd pl. m.	*PaRSātunu*	*naPRuSātunu*	*PuRRuSātunu*	*šuPRuSātunu*
2nd pl. f.	*PaRSātina*	*naPRuSātina*	*PuRRuSātina*	*šuPRuSātina*
3rd pl. m.	*PaRSū*	*naPRuSū*	*PuRRuSū*	*šuPRuSū*
3rd pl. f.	*PaRSā*	*naPRuSā*	*PuRRuSā*	*šuPRuSā*

v means: a short vowel which changes from verb to verb.

This may seem intimidating, but the pattern is actually quite simple: the 'core' of each column stays the same:

G *PaRvS* (though *v* is usually elided)
N *naPRuS*
D *PuRRuS*
Š *šuPRuS*

What changes is the suffixes, which vary with the person, gender and number of the subject. In isolation, these are as in Table 11.

Table 11

	G, N, D, Š
1st sg.	*-āku*
2nd sg. m.	*-āta*
2nd sg. f.	*-āti*
3rd sg. m.	-Ø
3rd sg. f.	*-at*
1st pl.	*-ānu*
2nd pl. m.	*-ātunu*
2nd pl. f.	*-ātina*
3rd pl. m.	*-ū*
3rd pl. f.	*-ā*

Ø means: nothing.

18.7 Observations on the stative suffixes

The same set of suffixes is used in all four systems. Most stative suffixes are different from the suffixes used by the present, preterite and perfect. The third feminine singular ending *-at* is related to the 'feminine *t*' which appears in nouns and adjectives. The third person plural suffixes *-ū* (m.) and *-ā* (f.) are related to the plural morphemes *-ūt-* (m.) and *-āt-* (f.) introduced in Units 8.2 and 9.1. There are strong similarities between several stative suffixes and the corresponding independent pronouns (see Unit 37), e.g. *-āta* and *atta* **you** (m. sg.).

18.8 The stative of nouns

Stative suffixes can be added to nouns, producing clauses which in English translation use a form of the verb **to be**. The tense to be used in translation is, as for the stative of verbs, determined by context. The stative ending is added to the dictionary form of the noun after the case vowel and (if present) the feminine *t* (and, if present, preceding short *a* or *e*) have been removed.

šarrāku I **am/was/will be a king**, **I am/was/will be a queen**
OB *sinnišāku* **I am/was/will be a woman** (ARM 10, 31: r.7')

A stative ending cannot co-exist with a possessive suffix. Nor can it be added to a noun which is modified by an adjective. To say things like **I am your king**, **I am a good king** or **I am your good king**, a different construction is used (see Unit 29). When a noun takes stative endings, it is said to be in the 'predicative state' (cf. Unit 10.4).

18.9 *lū* + stative

When the stative is directly preceded by the particle *lū*, the overall sense is that of a command or wish: **let it ..., may it ..., it should ....**

OB *lū šalmāta lū balṭāta* **May you** (m. sg.) **be well, may you** (m. sg.) **be healthy**
OB *ina* u_4 4 kam (Babylonian reading uncertain; *erbet ūmī* ?) *daltī lū kamsat* **My door should be finished (with)in four days** (AbB 3, 34: 19)

LANGUAGE TIP

Since in English **should be** can express uncertainty as well as obligation, to avoid ambiguity one can translate *lū* + stative with **must**, though this may be somewhat stronger than the Babylonian.

18.10 G statives of verbs of being from *PRR* roots

Verbs of being which have PRR roots (i.e. roots with identical second and third root letters, e.g. √*dnn*) can form the 3rd m. sg. G stative according to the pattern *PV̄R*. (This applies to I-weak verbs as well as to strong verbs, see Unit 24.7.)

danānu **to be strong** → *dān* **he/it is strong** (but *dannāku* **I am strong**, etc.)

The reason for this oddity is that PRR roots originally had only two root letters: 3rd m. sg. G statives (like *dān*) preserve the older form. The second root letter was reduplicated (√*dn* → √*dnn*) to bring the biliteral roots into line with the prevailing triliteral pattern. During the first millennium, the pattern *PV̄R* was gradually ousted by the pattern *PaRvS*.

18.11 The intensifying Š system stative

The Š system stative is not always causative. For verbs which are verbs of being in the G system, the Š stative can convey the same meaning as the G stative, but more intensely. (In English this is conveyed with words such as **very**.)

SB *niṭâtuya šumruṣā* **My beatings are/were very painful** (BWL 44: 99)

CULTURE TIP

The Babylonian poem *ludlul bēl nēmeqi* **I will praise the lord of wisdom** (from which the above example is taken) recounts, in the first person, the suffering (and finally the deliverance) of a righteous man. In this, it bears affinities with the Biblical Book of Job.

This is known as the 'elative' use of the Š system.

18.12 Rarer forms of the stative endings

Occasionally, the endings *-āku*, *-āta* and *-āti* appear respectively as *-āk*, *-āt*, *-āt*.

OB *aššum ṣuhārti annītim ṭēmī ul ṣabtāk* **I have not made up my mind about this girl** (AbB 4, 152: 9–10)

In literary Old Babylonian, *-āta* occasionally appears as *-āti*.

Exercise 18.1, Old Babylonian

te-re-tum ma-di-iš ***la-ap-ta***

i-na-an-na ša-at-tum ***ga-am-ra-at***

a-na-ku (*anāku* **I myself**) *ni-iš* dingir-*lim* ***za-ak-ra-ku***

ma-al-lu-ú ra-ab-bu-tum na-ra-am ***pa-ar-ku***

ha-al-ṣum ša be-lí-ia ***ša-lim***

ki-ri-ih a-lim ***da-an***

^{lú}kúr *a-na ma-a-ti-ia* ***qé-ru-ub***

bi-sa a-na bi-ti-ia ***qú-ru-ub***

šu-ut (*šūt* **they**) *ki-ma ka-ak-ka-bi ú-ga-ri* ***sà-ah-pu***

ma-ra-at-ki ***ša-al-[m]a-at***

Exercise 18.2, Old Babylonian

bu-bu-tum i-na mu-uh-hi-ia ***ka-am-ra-at***

a-wi-lum ***wa-ša-aṭ***

ša-pí-ir-ni lu-ú ***ba-li-iṭ***

a-wa-tum i-ni ú-ul ***ma-ah-ra-at***

li-ib-bi ***lu-um-mu-un***

lú *šu-ú* ***mu-úš-ke-en***$_6$

ib-ri lu-ú ***it-ba-ra-nu*** *a-na ù at-ta* (*anā u atta* **I and you**)

ge-ru-um ***da-an***

^{m}*bé-e-ia-a* (*bēyā*, personal name; indeclinable) *a-na mi-nim* ***na-zi-iq***

Exercise 18.3, Old Babylonian

From a prayer to the gods of the night, describing night time. (Use the present tense in translation.)

⸢***pu***⸣***-ul-lu-lu*** *ru-bu-ú*

wa-aš-ru-ú *sí-ik-ku-ru ši-re-tum* ***ša-ak-na-a***

ha-ab-ra-tum ni-šu-ú ***ša-qú-um-ma-a***

pe-tu-tum ***ud-du-lu-ú*** *ba-a-bu*

Exercise 18.4, Old and Middle Babylonian

The last two sentences are MB.

i-na qá-ti ha-ab-ba-[ti] i-ša-tum ***na-ap-ha-at*** *ma-a-tam i-ik-ka-[al]* (*ikkal* **it is consuming**)

ṣú-ha-rum i-na ma-a-at šu-bar-tim (*šubartum* = name of a country) ***wa-ši-ib***

i-na ká.dingir.ra$^{\text{k[i]}}$ ***wa-ši-ib***

e-ru-ú ***ma-hi-ir*** *ú-ku-ul-tam ki-ma né-ši-im na-e-ri* *ṭe$_4$-em-ka lu-ú* ***sa-di-ir***

a-bu-ni lu ***ša-lim*** *lu* ***ba-li-iṭ***

a-ša-al šar-ri ***ku-ub-bu-ra-at***

uz-na-a-tum ù ki-ša-da-t[um] ***nu-uk-ku-sà***

a-wi-lu-ú ma-di-iš ***ṣú-ur-ru-mu***

te-re-tum ***lu-up-pu-ta***

re-de-nu *a-na ma-an-ni ka-ar-ra* ***la-ab-ša-ta***

i-na ma-ti-ni i-lu ši-na (*šina* **two**) ***ha-al-[q]ú***

Exercise 18.5, Standard Babylonian

aš-ša-as-su ***a-mat***

ši-ir-a-nu-ú-a ***nu-up-pu-hu***

meš-re-tu-u-a ***su-up-pu-ha***

kip-pat kur.kur *ina qé-reb* an-e ***šaq-la-a-ta***

lu-ú ***sa-ni-iq*** *pi-i-ka lu-ú* ***na-ṣir*** *at-mu-ka*

i-lu a-na šar-ra-bi ul ***pa-ri-is*** *a-lak-ta*

kal ^{giš}gigir ***šu-ug-mu-ra-ku***

lem-né-ta-ma *kab-ta-ti tu-šam-ri-iṣ*

pa-áš-qat *né-ber-tum* ***šup-šu-qat*** *ú-ru-uh-šá*

Exercise 18.6, Standard Babylonian

From The Epic of Erra. Erra (the plague god) describes himself and his destructive powers:

ina a[n]-e *ri-ma-ku ina* ki-tim *la-ab-ba-ku*

ina kur *šar-ra-ku ina* dingir^{meš} *ez-za-ku*

ina ^{d}*í-gì-gì qar-da-ku ina* ^{d}*a-nun-na-ki gaš-ra-ku*

ina [b]*u-lim ma-hi-ṣa-ku ina* kur-*i šu-ba-ku*

ina a-pi ^{d}gìra-[ku] *ina qí-ši ma-*⸢*ag*⸣*-šá-rak*

ina a-lak har-ra-nu (sp. *harrāni* **campaign**) *ú-ri-in-na-ku*

Exercise 18.7

Erra is eulogized by his servant Išum (do not translate *-ma*; *-ka* = **you**, direct object):

gi-mir par-ṣi-ma ha-am-ma-ta dingir^{meš}*-ma pal-hu-ka*

^{d}*í-gì-gì šah-tú-ka* ^{d}*a-nun-na-ki-ma gal-tu-ka*

The most important things to remember

1 The stative is formed by adding suffixes (not prefixes) to a 'core'; these are different from the suffixes used in the present, preterite and perfect. You need to know them.

2 The 3rd m. sg. stative has no ending: it is the same as the 'core'.

3 The cores in the four systems for the verb *parāsu* **to separate** are G *paris* N *naprus* D *purrus* Š *šuprus*.

4 In the G system, adding suffixes to the core results in vowel elision (as per the rule stated in Unit 47.4).

5 For any verb in any system, the core of the stative is the same as the stem of the masculine verbal adjective.

6 The verbal adjective adds adjectival endings (nominative sg. -*u*, accusative sg. -*a*, genitive sg. -*i*, etc.) to the core, while the stative adds its own endings (-*āku*, etc.).

7 The stative describes a state rather than an action (but the difference is often lost in translation). The tense in translation is determined by context.

8 The stative can take an accusative; sometimes this translates as a direct object, and sometimes it is necessary to translate it as an 'accusative of respect'.

9 Stative endings (-*āku*, -*āta*, etc.) can be added to nouns, giving the meaning **I am/was ...**, **You are/were ...**, etc.

10 *lū* before a stative (including nouns with stative endings) expresses a command or wish.

SELF CHECK

	I can ...
	... explain what the 'stative' is, and how to translate it
	... explain why 'verbal' adjectives are so called
	... explain how the stative and verbal adjectives are related in form
	... recite the stative endings
	... recite the G stative of *parāsu(m)*
	... explain how the forms of the stative are different from those of the other tenses
	... explain what happens to the meaning when a stative is preceded by *lū*
	... explain what an accusative might mean when used with a stative, other than the direct object.

19 *Verbs with accusative, dative and ventive suffixes*

In this unit you will learn:

- **that Babylonian uses suffixes to express 'me', 'you', etc. and 'to me', 'to you', etc.**
- **what these suffixes are**
- **what the 'ventive' suffix is, and what it means**
- **the forms of the ventive suffix.**

Babylonian verbs have two sets of suffixes which correspond to English pronouns. One set is used for the direct object (e.g. **I saw <u>him</u>**). These are known as 'accusative suffixes'. The other set is used for the indirect object (e.g. **I gave the book <u>to him</u>**). These are known as 'dative suffixes'. (On 'ventive' suffixes see 19.5.)

The dative and accusative suffixes are somewhat similar to the possessive suffixes (see Unit 11.1). However, dative and accusative suffixes are always attached to verbs, never to nouns, whereas possessive suffixes are always attached to nouns, never to verbs.

For the purposes of suffixes, infinitives (see Unit 22) count as nouns: they can take possessive suffixes, not dative or accusative suffixes. (Though possessive suffixes after infinitives can express the direct object – see Unit 22.2.)

19.1 The accusative and dative suffixes

Table 12 displays the accusative and dative suffixes. Since they are easily confused with possessive suffixes (which, however, only attach to nouns, never to verbs), these are also listed for comparison. The bracketed *m* is usually present in Old Babylonian, and usually absent in later stages of the language (see Unit 6.11).

Table 12

	Accusative	Dative	Possessive
1st sg.	*-ni* (but see 19.6)	*-a(m), -(m), -ni(m)*	*-ī, -ya*
2nd sg. m.	*-ka*	*-ku(m)*	*-ka*
2nd sg. f.	*-ki*	*-ki(m)*	*-ki*
3rd sg. m.	*-šu*	*-šu(m)*	*-šu*
3rd sg. f.	*-ši*	*-ši(m)*	*-ša*
1st pl.	*-niāti, -nâti*	*-niāši(m), -nâši*	*-ni*
2nd pl. m.	*-kunūti*	*-kunūši(m)*	*-kunu*
2nd pl. f.	*-kināti*	*-kināši(m)*	*-kina*
3rd pl. m.	*-šunūti*	*-šunūši(m)*	*-šunu*
3rd pl. f.	*-šināti*	*-šināši(m)*	*-šina*

19.2 The first person singular dative suffix

Which of the three forms (*-am*, *-m*, *-nim*) the 1st pers. sg. dative suffix assumes depends on what subject suffix (if any) it is following.

- After *-ū* and *-ā* (3rd m. pl., 3rd f. pl., 2nd pl.): *-nim* (later *-ni*, later still *-nu*).
- After *-ī* (2nd f. sg.): *-m* (later *-Ø*, so that dative and non-dative forms are identical).
- After *-Ø* and *-at* (3rd sg. m. and f. stat.): *-am* (later *-a*). (Though it is rare after *-at*.)
- If the verb form (in any tense or system) includes no subject suffix (e.g. *išpur* **he sent**): *-am* (later *-a*).

Some examples are given in Table 13.

Table 13

	without dat.	with dat., OB	with dat., SB
1st sg.	*addin*	*addinam*	*addina*
2nd sg. m.	*taddin*	*taddinam*	*taddina*
2nd sg. f.	*taddinī*	*taddinīm*	*taddinī*
3rd sg.	*iddin*	*iddinam*	*iddina*
1st pl.	*niddin*	*niddinam*	*niddina*
2nd pl.	*taddinā*	*taddinānim*	*taddināni*
3rd pl. m.	*iddinū*	*iddinūnim*	*iddinūni*
3rd pl. f.	*iddinā*	*iddinānim*	*iddināni*

19.3 Sound changes involving dative and accusative suffixes

The suffixes sometimes give rise to sound changes (which you have already met in different contexts in previous units).

a When a dative or accusative suffix beginning with *š* immediately follows a sibilant or dental sound (*s*, *ṣ*, *š*, *z*, *t*, *d*, *ṭ*), the two sounds coalesce into *ss*. (Like all double consonants, this need not be spelled double in cuneiform. In OB it often appears as *zz*.)

niṭṭarad + *šu* = *niṭṭarassu* **We have dispatched him**

As with possessive suffixes (see Unit 11.8), after the Old Babylonian period partially assimilated or non-assimilated spellings are sometimes used.

iṣ-ṣa-bat-su for *iṣṣabassu* **He/she seized him/it**

b When a dative or accusative suffix beginning with a consonant immediately follows *n*, *n* often assimilates to the suffix's initial consonant. (Like all double consonants, the resulting double consonant need not be spelled double in cuneiform.)

iddin + *šim* = *iddiššim* **He/she gave (it) to her**

c The addition of the suffixes *-am* (later *-a*) and *-anni* can result in vowel elision in the G and N systems (see Unit 47.4).

ištakan **He/she has put**	→	*ištaknam* **He/she has put for me**
		ištaknanni **He/she has put me**
ṭurud **Dispatch!**	→	*ṭurdam* **Dispatch to me!**
		ṭurdanni **Dispatch me!**
iššakin **It was placed**	→	*iššaknam* **It was placed for me**

19.4 Accusative replaces dative

In the first millennium, there is a tendency for the accusative suffix to oust the dative suffix.

SB *ana ištar ālika lū kanšāta-ma liddin<u>ka</u> pir'a* **You should bow down (in prayer) to the goddess of your town, so that she will grant offspring <u>to you</u>!** (*liddin* **so that she will grant**) (BWL 108: 13)

> **CULTURE TIP**
> Ištar, goddess of war and sex, was widely thought of as *the* goddess *par excellence*. For this reason, her name gave rise to the noun *ištaru*, simply meaning **goddess**.

19.5 The ventive suffix

By the Old Babylonian period, the dative suffix of the first person singular (*-am/-m/-nim*) had acquired a second function ('ventive'). It continued to perform these two different functions (1st sg. dative; 'ventive') throughout the language's history. Though in origin it is one and the same suffix doing two different things, it is useful to think in terms of two different suffixes which happen to look identical and behave identically.

The major function of the ventive suffix is to act like an arrow, indicating (or highlighting) that the action described in the sentence is happening towards or for someone. This function is best seen with verbs of motion, e.g the verb *alāku*: when it lacks the ventive suffix, it means **to go**; when it has the ventive suffix, it means **to come**. (Hence the name 'ventive', from the Latin word *venio* **I come**.)

illik **He/she went**; OB *illikam* SB *illika* **He/she came**

This also works for *ṭehû* **to go/come near**, *(w)arādu* **to go/come down**, *elû* **to go/come up**, etc.

It is not hard to see how this function grew out of the first person dative suffix: if one thinks of *alāku* as originally meaning **to walk**, forms such as **he walked to me** acquired a meaning of their own (**he came**), so that the suffix started being used even for other persons (**he came to you**). In a conversation, the ventive applied to verbs of motion usually acts as an arrow pointing at the speaker or addressee (but not a third party).

In English, the ventive suffix is – apart from verbs of motion – often not visible in translation. If, however, you want somehow to acknowledge its existence and function to yourself, then when saying words such as **to** in the corresponding English sentence, stab your finger through the air in the direction of an imaginary goal.

There are also, particularly in the first millennium BC, uses of the ventive which so far we simply don't understand. In such cases one leaves it untranslated, and trusts in posterity.

19.6 The ventive suffix followed by dative and/or accusative suffixes

The ventive suffix can be followed by all but one dative, and all accusative suffixes. The first person singular dative suffix never appears together with the ventive suffix, because in origin they are one and the same.

The first person singular accusative suffix is almost always preceded by the ventive suffix. Here the ventive suffix has ceased to convey meaning in its own right, and basically become part of the accusative suffix. Thus the ending *-anni/-nni/-ninni* can simply be translated as **me**, without worrying about the erstwhile ventive component.

išpuranni **He/she sent me**
SB *biblāt libbiya tušakšidanni* **You** (m. sg.) **allowed me to attain my heart's desire** (Asar. 98: r.29)

Other dative and accusative suffixes are frequently preceded by the ventive suffix. In most such cases, the ventive suffix is left untranslated in English.

When the ventive suffix is followed by a dative or accusative suffix, the *m* of the ventive suffix assimilates to the initial consonant of the dative or accusative suffix.

aṭarrad + *am* + *ku(m)* = OB *aṭarradakkum* SB *aṭarradakku* **I will send (it) to you**

LANGUAGE TIP
You may wonder why the *m* of the ventive suffix assimilates to a following consonant, whereas other *m*s do not usually assimilate. The reason is thought to be that the *m* of the ventive suffix goes back to an original *n*.

19.7 Loss of *n* in the ventive suffix *-ni(m)-*

In Standard Babylonian, the *n* of the ventive suffix *-ni(m)* is sometimes lost when *-ni(m)* is followed by a dative or accusative suffix. The vowels which are thus made adjacent stay uncontracted.

SB *iṣṣurūinni* (from *iṣṣurūninni* = *iṣṣurū* + *nim* + *ni*) **They guarded me**
SB *utukku lemnu tušaṣbitāinni* (from *tušaṣbitāninni* = *tušaṣbitā* + *nim* + *ni*) **You** (pl.) **got** (or: **helped, allowed, enabled**) **an evil** *utukku*-**demon to seize me** (Maqlû V 60)

19.8 Dative and accusative suffixes together

It is possible for a verbal form to have both a dative and an accusative suffix (although forms such as this are rare). If this happens, the dative suffix precedes the accusative suffix and the *m* of the dative suffix assimilates to the following consonant. For example:

OB *awīlum panānum ul hasis inanna mannum ihsusakkuššu* (= *ihsus-am-kum-šu*; ventive, dative, accusative) **The man was not mentioned previously – who has mentioned him to you** (m. sg.) **now?** (AbB 14: 144, 29–30)

CULTURE TIP
The Babylonian adjective *panû* **past, previous** derives from *panu* **front**, and *(w)arkû* **later**, subsequent from √*wrk* **back** (see Unit 46.2 for how). Thus in Babylonian one looks at the past, with the future behind one. In English we have the opposite conception, but the Babylonian idea makes sense inasmuch as one can only see what has already happened.

19.9 'Redundant' suffixes

Sometimes, accusative or dative suffixes pick up a word or phrase in the sentence in a way which, to English speakers, seems redundant. The suffix probably added emphasis to the sentence. It need not be translated.

SB *šamaš ana humbaba idkâššum-ma* (*idke* **he roused** + *am* + *šum* + *ma*) *mehê rabbûtu* **Šamaš roused the great storm winds against Humbaba** (Gilg. V 137)
SB *ana pizallūri šutummu epussi* (from *epuš-ši*, stative of *epēšu* **to make** + 3rd sg. f. dat. *-ši*) **The storehouse is made for the gecko** (BWL 236: ii.11–13)

19.10 'Missing' suffixes

Sometimes Babylonian verbs lack a dative or accusative suffix where an English speaker would expect one to be used.

OB *šumma paspasū imaqqutūnikk*[*um*] *šūbilam* **If some ducks fall on you** (i.e. **if you happen to come by some ducks**), **send (them) to me!** (AbB 7, 154: 27–29)

> **LANGUAGE TIP**
> In linguistic jargon, cases of 'missing' suffixes are said to display 'zero anaphora' (where 'anaphora' means referring back to something previously mentioned).

Exercise 19.1, Old Babylonian

ma-di-iš ***i-da-al-hu-ni-in-ni***

ni-iš dingir^{meš} ***ú-ša-áz-ki-ir-šu***

li-ib-ba-šu ma-di-iš ***ma-ru-uṣ-kum***

am-mi-nim ^{m}*še-ep*–^{d}en.zu *tu-da-ab-ba-ab* [*l*]*a* ***tu-da-ab-ba-ab-šu***

aš-šum hi-bi-il-ti-šu ***ú-lam-mi-da-an-ni***

ši-it-tum ra-hi-a-at ni-ši ***im-qù-***⌜***us***⌝***-sú***

i-na te-er-ti-šu la ***ta-na-sà-ah-šu***

pu-ha-am ul ***id-di-nu-ni-a-ši-***[***im***]

ni-iš i-li-im [*l*]*a* ***tu-ša-az-ka-ri-šu***

mu-ú ***ik-šu-du-ni-a-ti***

Exercise 19.2, Old Babylonian

i-na-tum ***ša-ak-na-šu-nu-ši-im***

ge-er-ru-um pa-ri-is-ma a-di i-na-an-na ú-ul ***aš-pu-ra-ak-ki-***[***im***]

a-ka-la-am iš-te-en ú-ul ***i-di-nam***

a-na mi-ni-im i-pí-ir-ša ta-ap-ru-sà i-pí-ir-ša ***id-na-a-ši-im*** *a-na a-ha-ti-ia ú-ul ad-di-in a-na ka-a-šum* (*ana kâšum* **to you** (m. sg.)) ***a-na-ad-di-na-ak-kum***

an-ni-a-tum ***dam-qá-k*[*u*]*m***

ša-at-ta-am 4 (*erbet* **four**) gu$_4^{hi.a}$ ***a-ṭa-ar-ra-da-ak-kum***

be-lí ù be-el-ti aš-šu-mi-ia da-ri-iš u$_4$-mi ***li-ba-al-li-ṭú-ku-nu-ti***

a-na-ku (*anāku* **Me, ...**) *mu-ur-ṣú* ***iṣ-ba-ta-ni***

a-na ^{d}giš *ki-ma i-li-im* ***ša-ki-iš-šum*** *me-eh-rum*

Exercise 19.3, Middle Babylonian

lugal *ṭè-e-ma* ***iš-kun-šu***

ul ***ú-*[*š*]*e-el-lim-šu*** *ina mah-ra* (see Unit 13.6) *hi-mil-ta-šu* sig$_5$*-ta ul am-gur*

pa-ni ba-nu-ti ša ^{d}*a-ni šu-nu* (*šunu* **those ones**) ***ú-ka-la-mu-ka***

Exercise 19.4, Standard Babylonian

na-piš-ta-šu ***ú-šat-bak-šu***

šal-lat-su-nu ka-bit-tu ***ta-šal-la-la*** *ana qé-reb šu-an-na*^{ki}

ki-ma šu-uš-ka-al-li ***ú-kàt-ti-man-ni*** *šit-tú*

a-sak-ku mar-ṣu ***it-taš-kan-šú*** (translate *šakānu* as **to assign**)

iš-šak-na-nim-ma (ignore *-ma*; translate *šakānu* as **to assign**) *i-da-at pi-rit-ti*

šá-lim-tu ***ša-ak-na-as-su*** (translate *šakānu* as **to decree**)

muš ***iṣ-ṣa-bat-su*** *ina* (*ina* **by**) *kap-pi-šú*

The most important things to remember

1. Babylonian verbs have suffixes for pronoun direct objects ('accusative suffixes') and pronoun indirect objects ('dative suffixes').
2. The accusative and dative suffixes (which attach to verbs, not nouns) are similar to, but different from, the possessive suffixes (which attach to nouns, not verbs). You need to know them.
3. Dative suffixes originally had mimation (though it is generally lost after the Old Babylonian period); accusative suffixes did not.
4. The first person singular dative and accusative suffixes change their form depending on what immediately precedes them.
5. The first person singular dative suffix developed an additional meaning, representing direction. In this function it is known as the 'ventive' suffix.
6. The ventive suffix turns verbs of going into verbs of coming.
7. The ventive suffix often precedes dative and accusative suffixes, in which case it can be left untranslated.

8 When the ventive suffix precedes another suffix, its mimation assimilates to the following consonant (even in periods where mimation would otherwise be lost), e.g. *išpur* + *am* + *ši(m)* = SB *išpurašši* **He sent to her**.

9 Sometimes, the presence or absence of a dative or accusative suffix seems odd to an English speaker.

SELF CHECK

	I can ...
	... explain what accusative endings are, and what they are used for
	... explain what dative endings are, and what they are used for
	... explain how the ventive ending originated, what it is and how it is used
	... recall the three forms of the ventive ending, and explain when which is used
	... (in time:) recite the accusative and dative endings.

20 *The imperative: commands to an interlocutor*

In this unit you will learn:

- **the forms of the imperative, i.e.**
- **how to tell someone to do something**
- **how to tell someone** *not* **to do something.**

In giving a command to an interlocutor (i.e., in grammatical terms, a second person addressee), the construction changes depending on whether the command is positive (**do X!**) or negative (**don't do X!**).

20.1 Negative commands

Negative commands to the second person (i.e. instructions to someone *not* to do something) are expressed with *lā* + the 2nd person present:

lā tapallah **Do not fear!** (said to 2nd m. sg.)

OB *šalmāku* <u>*lā tanakkudī*</u> **I am well, <u>do not worry</u>!** (said to 2nd f. sg.) (AbB 7, 112: 4)

The construction '*lā* + 2nd present' does not (so far) have a particular grammatical name. One can call it 'negative command' or 'negative imperative'. With the latter, it is important to remember that the 'negative imperative' is not formed by putting a negation in front of the imperative.

20.2 Positive commands

Positive commands to the second person, i.e. instructions to someone to do something, have their own special form (called 'the imperative' from Latin *impero,* **I command**).

There are different imperative forms for m. sg., f. sg. and pl. (the pl. form works for all genders). The Key to the exercises indicates after the translation to whom commands are addressed.

Like other verbal tenses, the imperative can take ventive, accusative, and/or dative suffixes.

20.3 Forms in the G, N, D and Š systems

Using the system explained in Unit 5, the imperative forms of strong verbs conform to the patterns shown in Table 14.

Table 14

	G system	N system	D system	Š system
m. sing.	*PvRvS*	*naPRiS*	*PuRRiS*	*šuPRiS*
f. sing.	*PvRSī*	*naPRiSī*	*PuRRiSī*	*šuPRiSī*
pl.	*PvRSā*	*naPRiSā*	*PuRRiSā*	*šuPRiSā*

v means: a short vowel which changes from verb to verb.

The 'core' of each column stays the same:

G *PvRvS* (but the second *v* is elided when suffixes are added)
N *naPRiS*
D *PuRRiS*
Š *šuPRiS*

To this 'core', suffixes (but not prefixes) are added to mark the person, number and gender of the subject. In its non-use of prefixes, the imperative differs from the present, preterite and perfect. The suffixes used in the imperative are the same suffixes which appear in the corresponding forms of the present, preterite, and perfect. The same suffixes are used for all four systems.

LANGUAGE TIP

Across all four systems, the form of imperative has a very close relationship to the form of the preterite.

20.4 The vowel in the G system

The vowel in the G imperative depends on the vowel in the G preterite. Verbs with *i* or *u* in the G preterite use this same vowel in the imperative:

muqut **fall!** (from *maqātu* **to fall**, pret. *imqut*)
šukun **put!** (from *šakānu* **to put**, pret. *iškun*)
piqid **entrust!** (from *paqādu* **to entrust**, pret. *ipqid*)

For verbs with preterite vowel *a*, the vowelling in the imperative is usually *PiRaS*, but a few verbs have *PaRaS*:

limad **learn!** (from *lamādu* **to learn**, pret. *ilmad*)
pilah **fear!** (from *palāhu* **to fear**, pret. *iplah*)
rikab **ride!** (from *rakābu* **to ride**, pret. *irkab*)
ṣilal **lie down!** (from *ṣalālu* **to lie down**, pret. *iṣlal*)
tikal **trust!** (from *takālu* **to trust**, pret. *itkal*)
ṣabat **seize!** (from *ṣabātu* **to seize**, pret. *iṣbat*)
tabal **take away!** (from *tabālu* **to take away**, pret. *itbal*)

LANGUAGE TIP

Imperatives in the N system are rarely used.

20.5 *n* as first root letter

When *n* is the verb's first root letter, this undergoes different modifications in different systems. In the G system, *n* as first root letter disappears altogether:

usuh **pull out!** m. sg. (from *nasāhu* **to pull out**, pret. *issuh*)
uqur **destroy!** m. sg. (from *naqāru* **to destroy**, pret. *iqqur*)
idin **give!** m. sg.; *idnī* f. sg.; *idnā* pl. (from *nadānu* **to give**, pret. *iddin*)

The reason may be that the formation of the imperative is closely related to that of the preterite. Since *n* as first root letter disappears through assimilation in the G preterite (e.g. *iddin* **he/she gave**), so it disappears in the G imperative (e.g. *idin* **give!**).

In the N and Š systems, *n* as first root letter is in contact with a following consonant, to which it assimilates.

Exercise 20.1, Old Babylonian

In addition to normalizing and translating the following positive commands, produce their negative equivalents in normalization and translation.

dingir–***pi-la-ah*** *qa-qa-ad-ki* ***ku-ut-mi-ma*** (do not translate *-ma*)

qá-ti ***ṣa-ba-at***

šar-ra-am ***lu-um-mi-id***

ša-am-mi ***ú-ku-um***

mu-ug-ri-in-ni

it-ti-šu i-ša-ri-iš ***du-bu-ub***

a-na ba-la-ṭi-ka-ma ***ku-ru-ub***

am-tam ***id-nam***

Exercise 20.2, Old Babylonian

Same instructions as in Exercise 20.1. (Ignore square brackets when producing the negated equivalents.)

pa-ga-ar-ka ***ú-ṣú-ur***

bi-ta ***ṣú-ul-li-il***

ki-ma qá-né-e-e[m] ***ku-up-ra-aš-šu***

gi-mi-il-lam e-li-ia ***šu-ku-un***

[i-na] an-ni-tim (translate *annītu* as **this matter**) *at-hu-tam* ***ku-ul-li-im***

ru-ub-ṣa-am ***šu-ku-un-ši-na-t[i]*** (translate *šakānu* as **to provide s/o** (accusative) **with s/th** (accusative))

al-ku-nu ***ku-ṣí-ra***

ni-iš ^{d}*šu-bu-la* (indeclinable name) *i-li be-li-šu i-na pí-šu* ***šu-ku-un***

ta-ap-hu-ri i-na iš-ri-im a-na ^{d}asaru (indeclinable name) ***šu-uk-na-a****-ma* (*-ma* **and**) *i-la-am* ***su-ul-li-ma***

Exercise 20.3, Standard Babylonian

a-ma-ti-ia ***li-im-d***[***a***]

ši-ra ki-ma ši-ri-šú da-ma ki-ma da-me-šú ***i-din***

i-na pa-an ṣal-tim-ma ***pu-ṭur***

nap-lis-ma (do not translate *-ma*) *be-lum šu-nu-hu* arad-*ka*

id-nam-ma (do not translate *-ma*) *šam-ma šá a-la-di* (*alādu* **conception**) ***kul-li-man-ni*** *šam-ma šá a-la-di*

pil-ti ***ú-suh-ma*** (*-ma* **and**) *šu-ma* ***šuk-na-an-ni***

The most important things to remember

1. Negative 2nd person commands (i.e. commands *not* to do something) are issued with *lā* + present.
2. Positive 2nd person commands are issued with a special form. The 2nd m. sg. forms for *parāsu* **to separate** are G *purus* N *napris* D *purris* Š *šupris.*
3. 2nd f. sg. and 2nd pl. forms are created by adding the suffixes *-ī* and *-ā* to the 2nd m. sg. form. (Vowel elision ensues in the G system, as per to the rule stated in Unit 47.4.)
4. When the first root letter is *n*, this is lost in positive commands in the G system.
5. Babylonian can also address commands to the 1st and 3rd person; these are done in a different way (see next unit).

SELF CHECK

	I can ...
	... issue a command to one or more people
	... explain the difference in form between positive and negative commands
	... explain how the imperative is used
	... explain how its forms differ from those of other tenses
	... (in time:) recall the forms of the imperative.

21 *The precative: commands to third parties and oneself*

In this unit you will learn:

- **the forms of the 'precative', i.e.**
- **how to express commands and wishes for third parties or oneself.**

In the previous unit we saw how Babylonian addresses commands to interlocutors (i.e. **you**, singular or plural). Unlike English, Babylonian also has forms for addressing commands (and wishes) to a third party, or to oneself. These are known as 'precative' forms.

An example of English trying to cope with commands to a third party occurs in the Lord's Prayer: **Our father which art in heaven, hallowed be thy name, thy kingdom come, thy will be done ...** Considered in isolation, the clause **thy kingdom come** is grammatically odd, even 'wrong' in modern English: if we constructed an analogous clause such as **your vision expand** and said it to someone, it would not at all be clear that we meant **let your vision expand**, with the **vision** as subject. They would probably think we had spoken an ungrammatical jumble of words. This is because the King James translation is using an archaic construction which no longer survives in modern English: to express commands to a third party, Modern English requires a helping verb (**let**).

Babylonian does this much more neatly, with a special form of the verb: the 'precative'. This is the tense used in blessings and curses (as well as in other contexts).

Since the precative stands in a complementary relationship to the imperative, it is useful to think of the basic sense of the precative as being a command (to oneself, or to a third party). However, as we saw in Unit 14.19, wishes and commands can be quite hard to disentangle, and this is even truer of Babylonian than of English. Accordingly, translations of the precative often blur into a wish, and it is only context which shows which nuance is better: **Let me become rich/May I become rich**; **Let it really happen/May it really happen**; **Let her arrive tomorrow/May she arrive tomorrow**; **Let their days be long/May their days be long**.

In the first person singular, the precative often denotes an intention. In the first person plural, it often translates as **Let's ...**.

When a clause containing a precative follows another clause, the precative can assume nuances of purpose, concession and result. This will be discussed in Unit 32.1.

The precative is formed differently for actions ('precatives of action') and states ('precatives of state'). Like other verbal tenses, the precative can take ventive, accusative, and/or dative suffixes.

LANGUAGE TIP

In a formal linguistic description of Babylonian grammar, the precative would be analysed in terms of 'mood'. For the purposes of learning to translate, however, one can simply think of the precative as a tense with a wish-related meaning.

21.1 Precatives of action: forms in the G, N, D and Š systems

All forms of the precative of action are in various ways derived from the preterite. Using the system explained in Unit 5, the precative forms of strong verbs conform to the following patterns. Positive forms (**may I ..., may you ...**, etc.) are shown in Table 15. Negative forms (**may I not ..., may you not ...**, etc.) are shown in Table 16. Sometimes, *lā* + present is also used as a negative precative, so that *lā iparras* has a meaning very similar to that of *ay iprus*.

Table 15 Positive forms

	G	N	D	Š
1st	*luPRvS*	*luPPaRvS*	*luPaRRiS*	*lušaPRiS*
2nd m.	*lū taPRvS*	*lū taPPaRvS*	*lū tuPaRRiS*	*lū tušaPRiS*
2nd f.	*lū taPRvSī*	*lū taPPaRSī*	*lū tuPaRRiSī*	*lū tušaPRiSī*
3rd	*liPRvS*	*liPPaRvS*	*liPaRRiS*	*lišaPRiS*
1st	*ī niPRvS*	*ī niPPaRvS*	*ī nuPaRRiS*	*ī nušaPRiS*
2nd	*lū taPRvSā*	*lū taPPaRSā*	*lū tuPaRRiSā*	*lū tušaPRiSā*
3rd m.	*liPRvSū*	*liPPaRSū*	*liPaRRiSū*	*lišaPRiSū*
3rd f.	*liPRvSā*	*liPPaRSā*	*liPaRRiSā*	*lišaPRiSā*

'*v*' means: the same vowel as in the preterite of the same system.

Table 16 Negative forms

	G	N	D	Š
1st	*ay aPRvS*	*ay aPPaRvS*	*ay uPaRRiS*	*ay ušaPRiS*
2nd m.	*ē taPRvS*	*ē taPPaRvS*	*ē tuPaRRiS*	*ē tušaPRiS*
2nd f.	*ē taPRvSī*	*ē taPPaRSī*	*ē tuPaRRiSī*	*ē tušaPRiSī*
3rd	*ay iPRvS*	*ay iPPaRvS*	*ay uPaRRiS*	*ay ušaPRiS*
1st	*(ē niPRvS ?)*	*(ē niPPaRvS ?)*	*(ē nuPaRRiS ?)*	*(ē nušaPRiS ?)*
2nd	*ē taPRvSā*	*ē taPPaRSā*	*ē tuPaRRiSā*	*ē tušaPRiSā*
3rd m.	*ay iPRvSū*	*ay iPPaRSū*	*ay uPaRRiSū*	*ay ušaPRiSū*
3rd f.	*ay iPRvSā*	*ay iPPaRSā*	*ay uPaRRiSā*	*ay ušaPRiSā*

'*v*' means: the same vowel as in the preterite of the same system.

21.2 Comments on positive forms

LEARNING TIP

A verb form starting with an *l* is likely to be a precative (the alternative is that the *l* is the first root letter).

Positive forms (except 1st pl.) derive from *lū* + preterite. When the preterite begins with a vowel (*aPRvS*, *uPaRRiS*, etc.), contraction takes place. By convention, circumflex accents (^) are not written on the resulting vowel (e.g. *liPRvS* rather than *lîPRvS*).

taškunī **you** (f. sg.) **placed** → *lū taškunī* **may you** (f. sg.) **place**
iškun **he/she placed** → *liškun* **let him/her place**

In the 1st sg. precative of the G and N systems, unusually for a Babylonian contraction, it is the first vowel which wins (*lū aPRVS* → *luPRvS*; *lū aPPaRvS* → *luPPaRvS*).

aškun **I placed** → *luškun* **I will place**

CULTURE TIP

It is likely that many works of Babylonian literature were sung aloud. Indeed, several compositions open with the first person singular precative *luzmur* **I will sing of ....**

All 3rd pers. forms (sg., m. pl., f. pl.), in all four systems, begin with *li-*. (Some learners find this counter-intuitive for the D and Š systems!) The 1st sg. form begins with *lu-* in all four systems.

21.3 Comments on negative forms

Negative forms derive from original *ai* + preterite. Before a vowel, *ai* becomes *ay*; before a consonant, it becomes *ē*.

taškunī **you** (f. sg.) **placed** → *ē taškunī* **may you** (f. sg.) **not place**
iškun **he/she placed** → *ay iškun* **let him/her not place**

LANGUAGE TIP

As certain spellings show, *ay* was (at least sometimes) pronounced as part of the following word. Accordingly, it would be legitimate to normalize combinations of this type as a single word (*ay iškun* → *ayiškun*), but this course keeps them separate (for greater clarity).

21.4 Spellings of *ay*

In cuneiform, *ay* can be spelled *a*, *a-i*, *a-a*, *a-ia*, *ia*, and (on Old Babylonian tablets from the city of Mari) *a-wa*.

21.5 Precatives of state

Precatives of state are formed by putting *lū* before the stative.

lū šalmāta lū balṭāta **Be well, be healthy!** (m. sg.) or **May you be well, may you be healthy**

You have already met such formations in Unit 18.9, though the label 'precative of state' was not used there.

Exercise 21.1, Old Babylonian

a.šà *me-e* ***i ni-il-pu-ut***

bu-nu nam-ru-tum ša ^{d}amar.utu *i-li* (*ili*, irregular construct form of *ilu*) *a-li-ka* ***li-im-hu-ru-ka*** *ni-pa-ti-šu* ***li-wa-aš-še-ru***

i-la-a-tim a-na šu-ub-ti-ši-na ***li-ša-al-li-mu***

^{d}amar.utu *a-na e-pé-ši-ka an-ni-im* ***li-ik-ru-ub***

ṣa-al-mi-ka i-na a-hi-ia ***lu-uq-qú-ur*** (see Unit 16.5)

ú-ta-a-am i-na ba-bi-im ***li-iš-ku-un***

pi-ir-ṣa-am la-ma e-bu-ri-im ***li-ik-šu-ur***

^{d}utu *ù* ^{d}amar.utu *da-ri-iš* u_4*-mi* (*dāriš ūmī* **forever**) ***li-ba-al-li-ṭú-ka***

ba-ma-sú-nu ***lu wa-aš-bu*** *ba-ma-sú-nu* [***l***]***i-li-ku*** (*lillikū* = G prec. 3rd m. pl. of *alāku*) (see Unit 14.3)

Exercise 21.2, Old and Middle Babylonian

The last six sentences are MB.

[*a*]*t-ti* (*atti* **you** f. sg.) *qá-qá-di ku-ub-bi-ti-ma ù* (see Unit 30.6) *a-na-ku qá-qá-ad-ki* ***lu-ka-ab-bi-it***

be-el-ki ù be-le-et-ki ki-ma ki-si ša (see Unit 13.2) *qá-ti-šu-nu* ***li-iṣ-ṣú-ru-ki***

^{mf}*šu-bu-ul-tum* géme-*ka* ^{gi}pisan ***li-ša-ap-li-is-ka***

^{lú}*ma-aṣ-ṣa-ru* ***li-iṣ-ṣú-ru-ni-iš-šu***

am-tam ***li-di-kum***

dingir *na-a-am* (*nâm* **our**) ***i nu-ba-li-iṭ***

ú-ṣú-ra-ti-ia ***a ú-ša-si-ik***

^{d}utu *da-a-a-an di-na-ti e-le-nu* ***lí-né-er-šu*** *šap-la-nu a-ru-ta-šu* (see Unit 11.6, end) a^{meš} *ka-ṣu-ti* ***a-a ú-šam-hir***

a-ia iṣ-bat uru^{ki} ^{d}utu *qù-ra-a-dì* ***a-ia iš-lu-ul*** *šal-la-tam-ma* (*-ma* **and**) *li-ib-ba-šu* ***a-ia ib-lu-uṭ***

^{d}30 *na-an-nar* an-e kù^{meš} *sahar-šub-ba-a la te-ba-a gi-mir la-ni-šu* ***li-lab-biš***

^{d}utu di.kud an-*e u* ki-*tim pa-ni-šu* ***lim-haṣ***

^{d}nergal en *til-le-e u qa-ša-ti ka-ak-ki-šu* ***li-še-bir***

^{d}nergal en *qab-li u ta-ha-zi i-na* mè-*šu* ***liš-gi-is-su***

Exercise 21.3, Standard Babylonian

dan-nu ***lum-ha-aṣ-ma*** *a-ka-a* ***lu-pal-lih***

e ta-as-niq-šú

um-ma-nu ***lu-šá-as-hir***

bi-lat-su-nu ka-bit-tu ***liš-du-du*** *ana qé-reb šu-an-na*^{ki}

géme *ina* é ***e tu-kab-bit***

šam-na ši-ga-ri-ka gim a^{meš} ***li-šar-me-ek***

ùg^{meš} ***lip-la-ha-ma*** (*-ma* **and**) ***lit-qu-na*** *hu-bur-ši[n]*

Exercise 21.4

From The Epic of Erra. (*lišmû-ma* = **may they** (m.) **hear, and ...**)

dingir^{meš} *liš-mu-ma* ***lik-nu-šu*** *ana ni-ri-ka*

mu-ul-ki liš-mu-ma ***lik-mi-⸢su⸣*** *šu-pul-ku*

The most important things to remember

1 The basic function of the precative is to express commands, though these can blur into wishes. In the first person singular it can declare an intention.

2 Precatives referring to states ('precatives of state') are formed by putting *lū* before the stative. *lū* remains a separate word, and no contraction occurs.

3 Precatives referring to actions ('precatives of action') are formed by putting *lū* before the preterite. When the preterite form begins with a vowel, contractions occur.

4 For practical purposes, the positive 3rd person G precatives are formed by putting *l* in front of the preterite:

iprus **he/she separated** → *liprus* **let him/her separate, may he/she separate**
iprusā **they** (f.) **separated** → *liprusā* **let them** (f.) **separate, may they** (f.) **separate**

5 3rd person precatives in the D and Š systems begin with *li-* (not *lu-* !).

6 1st person singular precatives in all four systems begin with *lu-*.

SELF CHECK

	I can ...
	... express a command to a third party
	... express a wish
	... explain how the precative is used
	... explain how its forms differ from those of other tenses
	... (in time:) recall the forms of the precative
	... explain how the precative is negated
	... explain why it can be hard to translate the precative into a language (such as English) which does not have a form for commands to third parties.

22 *The infinitive*

In this unit you will learn:

- **that the Babylonian infinitive generally means '...-ing'**
- **what its forms are**
- **how it is used.**

The form of the verb known as the infinitive is that which the ancients used as the 'dictionary form': when they made lists of words, they cited verbs by what we call the infinitive. It is also the 'dictionary form' in modern dictionaries and glossaries (as at the end of this course).

Though it is a form of the verb, the Babylonian infinitive behaves like a noun: it declines (nominative, accusative, genitive) with the same endings as nouns, it can take possessive suffixes (not dative or accusative suffixes), and be put in the construct state.

The infinitive has no plural: it is used only in the singular.

In isolation, the Babylonian infinitive is usually translated as an English infinitive: *parāsu* **to separate**, *dummuqu* **to make good**, *šubšû* **to cause to exist**. However, when it appears in an actual Babylonian sentence, it is generally best translated not with an English infinitive (**to eat, to learn**) but with an English verbal noun (**eating, learning**).

OB <u>*paṭārī*</u> *qerub* **My departing** (i.e. **my departure**) **is close at hand** (AbB 9, 14: 8)

Sometimes the English translation requires a paraphrase.

OB *kīma lā* <u>*nazāqika*</u> *epuš* **Act in such a way that you will not be annoyed!** (lit. **Act in accordance with your not being annoyed!**) (*epuš* **act!**) (AbB 3, 2: 27)
OB *kīma lā* <u>*šuzzuqiya*</u> *epuš* **Act in a way which does not annoy me!** (lit. **Act in accordance with not annoying me**) (AbB 9, 14: 13–14)

The infinitive is negated by *lā* (not *ul*).

SB *lā balāssu* (from *balāṭšu*) *iqbi* **He decreed his not living**, i.e. **He condemned him to death** (AfO 17, 1: 19)

22.1 Forms in the G, N, D and Š systems

Using the system explained in Unit 5, the nominative forms of the infinitive are shown in Table 17. As with nouns, mimation is usually present in Old Babylonian and usually absent later (see Unit 6.11).

Table 17

	G	N	D	Š
strong	*PaRāSu(m)*	*naPRuSu(m)*	*PuRRuSu(m)*	*šuPRuSu(m)*
I-weak	*aRāSu(m)*	*nanRuSu(m)*	*uRRuSu(m)*	*šūRuSu(m)*
II-weak	*PâSu(m)*	*(unknown)*	*PuSSu(m)*	*šuPūSu(m)*
III-weak	*PaRû(m)*	*naPRû(m)*	*PuRRû(m)*	*šuPRû(m)*

In *e*-verbs, *a* changes to *e*: *qerēbu* **to approach**, *emēdu* **to come into contact with**, *ṭênu* **to grind**, *leqû* **to take**, etc. Examples of infinitives:

G *maqātu* **to fall** → Š *šumqutu* **to cause to fall**
G *lemēnu* **to be bad** → D *lummunu* **to make bad**
G *bašû* **to exist** → N *nabšû* **to come into being**
G *etēqu* **to pass** → Š *šūtuqu* **to cause to pass**
G *kânu* **to be firm** → D *kunnu* **to make firm**

22.2 Infinitives with subjects and objects

Though it behaves like a noun, the infinitive has not entirely given up its verbal nature: like ordinary verb forms, it can have a subject and/or an object. Grammatically, the subject and object's relation to the infinitive can manifest itself in several ways.

a) They can stand as entirely independent words, in which case the subject goes in the nominative, and (subject to Unit 22.5) the object in the accusative:

OB *dannum enšam ana lā habālim* **For the strong man not oppressing the weak man**, i.e. **So that the strong will/would not oppress the weak** (CH Prologue i.37–9)
OB *raggam u ṣēnam ana hulluqim* **For destroying the wicked man and the malevolent man**, i.e. **To destroy the wicked and the malevolent** (CH Prologue i.35–6)

CULTURE TIP
A stele bearing Hammurapi's laws, from which the two sentences above are taken, is now in the Louvre museum. It was excavated not in Mesopotamia, but in the city of Susa (Iran), where it was taken as booty by the Elamites.

b) The infinitive can be put in the construct state, with the subject or the object following in the genitive:

OB *ana lamād šāpiriya ašpuram* **I have written for my boss's being informed**, i.e. **I have written so that my boss would be informed** (AbB 13, 37: 30)

c) The subject or object can be represented by a possessive suffix:

OB *ana lamādika ašpuram* I **have written for your being informed**, i.e. **I have written so that you would be informed** (AbB 1, 9: 35)

The last two constructions are essentially the same, the difference being that in the first the subject or object is an independent word, while in the second it is represented by a possessive suffix.

The first of the three constructions can be combined with the second or third.

OB *ana nīš ilī šuzkurišu* **In order to make him swear an oath by the life of the gods** (ARM 26/2, 393: 5)

22.3 *ina* + infinitive

ina + infinitive, literally **upon ...-ing**, means **when ...**

OB *[tup]pī annī'am ina amārim* **Upon reading this my tablet**, i.e. **When (you) read this tablet of mine** (AbB 14, 11: 21)
MB *anu amāta annīta ina šemê[š]u ilsi* **Upon his hearing this word, Anu cried out**, i.e. **When he heard this word, Anu cried out** (Adapa 16: 12'–13')

CULTURE TIP
When reading cuneiform tablets inscribed on both sides, they should usually be turned not around the vertical axis (like the pages of a book), but around the horizontal axis.

22.4 *ana* + infinitive

ana + infinitive, literally **for ...-ing**, often means **so that ..., in order to ....**

SB *ana šubruq ulmēšu šērūti* **To cause his fierce axes to shine** (lit. **For the make-shine-ing of his fierce axes**) (Erra I 5)

A special case is *ana* + infinitive ... *nadānu*: in this construction, *nadānu* (literally **to give**) means **to allow someone to do something** (expressed by the infinitive).

OB *ašlam ana tarāṣim u sikkatam ana mahāṣī ul addiššum* **I did not allow him to stretch out the measuring line, (n)or to drive in the foundation peg** (AbB 3, 55: 22–3)

More rarely, *ana* is dropped and the infinitive goes in the accusative as an object of *nadānu*.

OB *ina māt atamrim hiṭītam nabšâm ul ninaddin* **We will not allow a crime to occur** (lit. **to come into being**) **in the land of Atamrum** (ARM 26/2, 427: 26–8)

22.5 Case attraction

When the object of an infinitive is placed between a preposition and the infinitive, it is 'attracted' into the genitive case (even though logically speaking it should be accusative):

OB *sîn–damiq ana ṭēmika lamādi išpura* **Sîn–damiq wrote to me to learn your news** (AbB 1, 79: 27–8)
OB *ana wardim naṣārim lā teggu* **Do not be remiss in guarding the slave!** (AbB 1, 133: 25–6)

22.6 The infinitive of emphasis

The infinitive is sometimes used to add emphasis to a verb from the same root and in the same system. In such cases it has the ending *-u(m)*, often followed by *-ma*.

OB *[h]alāqum-ma haliq* **He/it has well and truly vanished!** (AbB 13, 7: 13)

OB *ṭēmka šapārum-ma u[l t]ašpuram* **You jolly well didn't write your news to me!** (AbB 13, 19: 10–11)

Some grammars call this the 'paronomastic infinitive'.

Exercise 22.1, Old Babylonian

a-na íd ***pé-tem se-ke-ri-im*** *ša-ak-na-ku*

a-na e-pé-ri ***ša-pa-ki-im*** *qa-tam iš-ku-un*

a-na ṭe$_4$-mi-šu ***la-ma-di-im*** *aš-pu-ra-ak-kum*

a-na ṭe$_4$-mi-ka ***la-ma-di*** *iš-pu-ra*

^{giš}*ma-ga-ri-ka* ***ra-ka-bu-um*** *ú-ul ar-ka-ab*

a-na (translate *ana* as **in**) ***ša-pa-ri-im*** *la te-e-gi$_4$* (*teggi* **you are being remiss**, present)

a-na (translate *ana* as **in**) áb $^{gu_4 hi.a}$ *ù anše*$^{h[i.a]}$ ***bu-ul-lu-ṭi-im*** *la te-gi* (*teggi* **you are being negligent**, present)

a-la-ka-a-am *a-na ṣe-e-ri-ka ú-la ni-le-e* (*nile''e* **we are able to** + acc. inf.)

a-na (*ana* **regarding**) erim dusu *šu-a-[t]u* (*šuātu* **that same**) *la* ***du-ub-bu-ub-šu-nu*** *šar-rum iq-bi* (*iqbi* **he decreed**)

[i-na (*ina* **through**) *la]* ***a-ka-lim*** *ù* ***ša-te-em*** *ma-ṭì-a-ku* (*maṭiāku* **I am wasting away**) *ù la-ba-šum-ma ú-ul la-ab-ša-a-ku*

an *ù* ^{d}en.líl *a-na ši-ir ni-ši* ***ṭú-ub-bi-im*** *šu-mi ib-bu-ú* (*ibbû* **they called out**)

a-la-ki *qù-ru-ub*

ga-gu-um a-na ma-ša-i-im ***ša-ki-in*** (question)

Exercise 22.2, Standard Babylonian

a-na ***ub-bu-bi-ka*** *iš-pu-ra-an-[ni]*

i-ris-su-ma (*īrissu-ma* **it demanded of him**) *lìb-ba-šú* ***e-peš*** *ta-ha-zi*

[a-n]a ***šá-kan*** *a-bu-bi ub-la* (*ubla* **it brought**, i.e. **it induced**) *lìb-ba-šú-nu* dingir^{meš} gal^{meš}

Exercise 22.3

From The Epic of Gilgameš. (The goddess Bēlet-ilī regrets her part in bringing about the Deluge.)

ki-i (*kī* **how (could I ...)?**) *aq-bi* (*aqbi* **I spoke**) *ma-har* dingir.dingir ^{munus}hul

ana ***hul-lu-uq*** ùg^{meš}*-ia qab-la aq-bi-ma* (*aqbi-ma* **I declared**)

The most important things to remember

1 In isolation, the Babylonian infinitive is conventionally translated as an English infinitive (**to do**, **to eat**).

2 In the context of an actual sentence, a Babylonian infinitive usually translates as an English noun in **-ing.**

3 Possessive suffixes (but not dative or accusative suffixes) can attach to the infinitive. They represent the subject or the object (context shows which).

4 *ina* + infinitive usually translates into English as **when ....**

5 *ana* + infinitive usually translates into English as **in order to ....**

6 When the object of an infinitive is a noun sandwiched between a preposition on the left and an infinitive on the right, it is 'attracted' into the genitive case (instead of the accusative), e.g. *ana ṭēmika lamādi* **in order to learn your news**.

7 The infinitive is sometimes used to reinforce a verb from the same root and in the same system. In this function it ends in *-u(m)*, and is often followed by *-ma*.

SELF CHECK

	I can ...
	... explain what the infinitive is and how it is used
	... recall what *ina* and *ana* plus infinitive means.

Part four

Weak and irregular verbs

23 *III-weak verbs*

In this unit you will learn:

- **the forms of 'third weak' verbs**
- **how they differ from strong verbs.**

III-weak ('third weak') verbs are ones which behave as if they had no third root letter. (Originally, they did have third root letters, but for the purposes of learning how to inflect them it is useful to pretend that they do not. Some books would say that you can think of the third root letter as being a vowel.)

III-weak verbs are inflected with the same prefixes and suffixes as strong verbs. They also undergo the same sound changes as strong verbs (with some additional ones).

23.1 The dictionary form

For most III-weak verbs (as for most verbs of any type), the dictionary form is the G infinitive. The G infinitive of III-weak verbs follows the pattern *PaRû* (*PeRû* for *e*-verbs), contracted from *PaRāu* (*PeRēu* for *e*-verbs).

banû(m) **to build**, *leqû(m)* **to take**, *malû(m)* **to be full**, *manû(m)* **to count**, *zenû(m)* **to be angry**

LANGUAGE TIP

Sometimes, Babylonian and English display parallel shifts in meaning. Just as in English **to recount** (events) comes from **to count** (numerically), the Babylonian verb *manû* **to count** (numerically) can also mean **to recount** (events) (also **to recite** (incantations)).

The dictionary form of verbs which are not attested in the G system is the infinitive of the system in which they are attested most frequently.

zummû(m) **to be deprived of** (D system)

23.2 The theme vowel

Every III-weak verb has one theme vowel (whereas strong verbs can have two, e.g. *a/u* for *šakānu*). This vowel can be *a*, *i*, *e*, or *u*. Each verb's theme vowel is supplied in the Glossary. The theme vowel *e* occurs only in *e*-verbs. It was originally *a*, but turned to *e* through *e*-colouring (see Units 14.13 and 47.7). A III-weak *e*-verb does not necessarily have *e* as theme vowel (e.g. *zenû* **to be angry** has *i*).

23.3 General principles of inflection

The chief difference between III-weak and strong verbs is that where a strong verb has a third root letter, the corresponding form of a III-weak verb has nothing.

ipaqqid **he/she/it entrusts**
ipqid **he/she/it entrusted**
paqid **he/she/it is entrusted**
udammaq **he/she/it makes good**
udammiq **he/she/it made good**
dummuq **he/she/it is made good**

ibanni **he/she/it builds**
ibni **he/she/it built**
bani **he/she/it is built**
umalla **he/she/it makes full/fills**
umalli **he/she/it made full/filled**
mullu **he/she/it is made full/filled**

When suffixes are added, the absence of a third root letter can lead to the occurrence of two adjacent vowels. When this occurs, the two adjacent vowels often contract (see Unit 47.1).

ibanniū **they** (m.) **build** → *ibannû* **they** (m.) **build**

liqeā **take!** (pl.) → *liqâ* **take!** (pl.)

When a III-weak verb without suffix was followed by *-ma*, its final vowel was probably long: *ilqe* vs. *ilqē-ma*. For simplicity's sake, however, in this course the vowel is normalized short.

LANGUAGE TIP

Because it goes back to original *PaRāi* (with contraction of *ā* and *i*; see Unit 47.1), the genitive of the G infinitive of III-weak verbs (whether *a*-verbs or *e*-verbs) normally ends in *ê* (not *î*), e.g. *ana lā mašê* **so as not to forget**.

23.4 Verbal 'cores' in the G, N, D and Š systems

Table 18 gives the verbal 'cores', to which the same prefixes and suffixes are added as for strong verbs. (In *e*-verbs, *a* usually turns to *e*; see section 23.6.)

Table 18

	G	N	D	Š
Pres.	*-PaRRv*	*-PPaRRv* (from **nPaRRv*)	*-PaRRa*	*-šaPRa*
Pret.	*-PRv*	*-PPaRi* (from **nPaRi*)	*-PaRRi*	*-šaPRi*
Perf.	*-PtaRv*	*-ttaPRi* (from **ntaPRi*)	*-PtaRRi*	*-štaPRi*
Stat.	*PaRv*	*naPRi*	*PuRRu*	*šuPRu*
Imp.	*PvRv*	*naPRi*	*PuRRi*	*šuPRi*
Inf.	*PaRû(m)*	*naPRû(m)*	*PuRRû(m)*	*šuPRû(m)*

v means: a short vowel (see section 23.5).

23.5 The vowel in the G and N systems

In the G and N systems it is necessary to insert a vowel which varies from verb to verb (and from tense to tense). This vowel is indicated by the symbol *v* in Table 18. In the present, preterite and perfect, all verbs insert their theme vowel. In the G stative, all verbs insert *i* except a few verbs with theme vowel *u*, which insert *u*:

malû **to be(come) full** (*a*) → *mali* **he is full**
hadû **to be(come) glad** (*u*) → *hadi* **he is glad**
zakû **to be(come) pure** (*u*) → *zaku* **he is pure**

In the G imperative, verbs with theme vowel *i* and *u* insert *i…i* and *u…u*.

banû **to build** (*i*) → *bini* **build!**
manû **to count** (*u*) → *munu* **count!**

Verbs with theme vowel *a* or *e* (which derives from original *a*) insert *i…a*, *i…e*.

kalû **to detain** (*a*) → *kila* **detain!**
leqû **to take** (*e*) → *liqe* **take!**
šemû **to hear** (*e*) → *šime* **hear!**

23.6 *e*-verbs

In III-weak *e*-verbs, *e*-colouring (see Unit 14.13) can extend from the core to prefixes. This happens especially often in Old Babylonian.

aleqqe or *eleqqe* **I take**; *taleqqe* or *teleqqe* **You** (m. sg.) **take**

Rarely, *e*-colouring can extend from the core to stative suffixes.

patietku **She/it is open for you** (m. sg.)

In Old Babylonian, the addition of a suffix with the vowel *a* (including the ventive suffix *-am*) sometimes undoes the *e*-colouring before the second root letter.

OB *šameāku* **I am hearing** (from *šeme* + *āku*)

Exercise 23.1, Old Babylonian

li-ib-bi ***li-ih-du***

li-ib-bi ú-ul ***ih-du***

ka-ṣú-tim me-e a-na ^{d}utu ***ta-na-qí***

ma-ti-ma bi-it-ni ú-ul ***i-le-qú-ú***

mu-ú ***i[ṭ]-ṭe$_4$-hu-ni-im***

it-ti-ka ***e-ze-en-ne***

šar-ru-um li-ib-ba-tim ***im-ta-la***

ze-nu-um za-ni-a-ta

ha-al-ṣú-um la ***in-na-ad-di***

[t]a-ap-ta-a *uz-ni-ia*

a-wa-tam ***i-qá-ab-bi*** *šu-a-ši-im* (*šuāšim* = **to him**)

ib-ki-i-ma *li-ib-ba-ša ú-na-ap-pí-iš*

Exercise 23.2, Old Babylonian

a-na né-me-li-ša i-in-ka la ***ta-na-ši***

ši-ṭú-ti ***le-qí-at***

lu ***ma-li*** *ka-ra-aš-ka*

ú-na-ti ***li-iš-šu-nim***

ni-zi-iq-tum i-na li-ib-bi-ki la ***i-ba-aš-ši-i*** (ignore the extra *i*)

la ***ik-ka-lu-nim***

šu-nu-ti (*šunūti* **those ones**, acc.) ***uh-ta-ap-pí-a-am*** *i-na uz-zi-šu*

šar-ru-um ku-nu-ka-tim ša hu-bu-lim ***ú-he-ep-pi***

a-mi-ni (*ammīni*, for *ana mīni*) ***ba-ri-a-nu***

mu-ur-ṣú-um iṣ-ba-ta-an-ni-ma i-na na-pí-iš-tim ***an-na-di***

a-na al-pi-im ú-ku-lu-ú la ***i-ma-ṭi***

i-na hu-bu-ri-ši-na ***ú-za-am-ma*** *ši-it-ta*

hu-di-i *ù* **é.gal**-*ki bu-us-si-ri*

CULTURE TIP

In Mesopotamian mythology, the gods brought about the Flood because they could not bear the noise which humans made.

Exercise 23.3, Middle Babylonian

u'-ur-ti man *dan-ni ki-ma a-le-e zu-mur-šu* ***ik-si***

uz-za ù ša-gal-ta ša tah-šu-hu ***nu-šab-ra*** *né-e-nu* (sp. *nīnu*)

ú-⌜šèr⌝-di im *a-bu-ba* ugu *ta-ha-zi-šu-nu* ^{d}iškur *ur-šá-an-nu*

ar-ki (*arki* **behind**) dingir^{meš} *tik-li-šu šar-ru ina pa-ni um-ma-ni* ***ú-šar-ri*** $murub_4$

i-na zi-qít mul-mul-li-ia a-di a.ab.ba *e-le-ni-te lu* ***ar-di-šu-nu-ti***

Exercise 23.4

From The Epic of Tukulti-Ninurta:

[*l*]*a-ab-bu-ma* ⌜*šàm*⌝*-ru ki-ma an-zi-i* ***ša-nu-ú*** *nab-ni-ta*

[*ka*]*d-ru ez-zi-iš a-na te-še-e ba-lu tah-li-pi*

Exercise 23.5, Standard Babylonian

a-sak-ku mar-ṣu ina zu-mur lú ***it-tab-ši*** lú *mut-tal-li-ka ki-ma ṣu-ba-ti ik-ta-tam*

ki-ma ti-bu-ut e-ri-bé-e ma-a-ta ***im-ta-lu-ú***

dingir ***al-si-ma*** (*alsi*, from *aššī*; *-ma* **but**) *ul id-di-na* (translate *nadānu* as **show**) *pa-ni-šú*
par-ṣi-ia ***ú-šal-qu-u*** *šá-nam-ma* (see Unit 30.7)
na-pi-ih-ta ***bul-li***
šap-la-a-nu (translate *šaplānu* as **deep down**) *lìb-ba-šu re-e-mu* ***ra-ši-šu***
i-naq-qa-nik-ka *ši-kar sa-bi-ʾi ta-mah-har*
kab-ta-at šu-*su ul* ***a-le-ʾi-i na-šá-šá***
ta-šem-me ᵈutu *su-up-pa-a su-la-a ù ka-ra-bi*
il-ta-qu-ú *har-ha-ru-ú a-na* (*anā* **I**) *at-taš-pil*
ši-pat ba-la-ṭi ***id-da-a***

The most important things to remember

1 III-weak verbs take the same prefixes and suffixes as strong verbs.
2 They differ from strong verbs in the formation of the 'core': where a strong verb has a third root letter, they have nothing.
3 When the vowel at the end of the core is followed by a suffix beginning with a vowel, the two vowels usually contract (but *ia* is usually left uncontracted in Old Babylonian).
4 You need to learn the 3rd person singular forms for the present, preterite, perfect, and stative, and 2nd sg. m. for the imperative, in all four systems. (This is a total of 20 forms, but they are very similar to the corresponding forms of strong verbs.)

SELF CHECK

	I can ...
	... explain what a III-weak verb is
	... describe the dictionary form of a III-weak verb (*a* or *e*)
	... look up a III-weak verb in the Glossary
	... explain how its forms can be deduced from those of strong verbs
	... explain why vowel contraction is important for III-weak verbs.

24 *I-weak verbs*

In this unit you will learn:

- **the forms of 'first weak' verbs**
- **how they differ from strong verbs.**

I-weak ('first weak') verbs are ones which have no visible first root letter in the G infinitive. (As comparison with cognate words in other languages shows, the first root letter was originally present, but got lost. In Old Babylonian, whether the verb is an *e*-verb or not depends on which sound was lost; later, *e*-colouring can spread to verbs which were *a*-verbs in Old Babylonian – see Unit 14.13.)

24.1 The dictionary form

For most I-weak verbs (as for most verbs of any type), the dictionary form is the G infinitive. The G infinitive of I-weak verbs follows the pattern *aRāSu* (*eRēSu* for *e*-verbs).

akālu **to eat**, *epēšu* **to make, to do**

LANGUAGE TIP

The general meaning of *epēšu(m)* can be thought of as being **to carry out the action appropriate to the noun**: **to build** a house, **to wage** war, **to use** a tool, **to perform** a ritual, **to cultivate** a field, etc.

Verbs which are not attested in the G system have as their dictionary form the infinitive of the system in which they appear most frequently.

uššušu **to renew** (D system)

24.2 Forms in the G, N, D and Š systems

Using the system explained in Unit 5, whereby R represents a verb's second root letter and S represents the third, the basic forms of I-weak verbs in the G, N, D and Š systems are as shown in Table 19. (By 'basic form' we mean 3rd m. sg. for the stative, 2nd m. sg. for the imperative, 3rd sg. for other tenses; they are considered basic because other forms can easily be derived from them by substituting the relevant prefixes and suffixes.) The prefixes and suffixes used for I-weak verbs are the same as for strong verbs, except that in some forms the vowel in the prefix is long.

Table 19

	G	N	D	Š
pres. 3rd sg.	OB *īRRvS (*later *iRRvS)*	*innaRRvS*	*uRRaS*	*ušaRRaS*
pret. 3rd sg.	*īRvS*	*innaRvS*	*uRRiS*	*ušāRiS*
perf. 3rd sg.	*ītaRvS*	*ittanRvS*	*ūtaRRiS*	*uštāRiS*
stat. 3rd m. sg.	*aRvS*	*nanRuS*	*uRRuS*	*šūRuS*
imp. m. sg.	*aRvS*	*nanRiS*	*uRRiS*	*šūRiS*
inf.	*aRāSu(m)*	*nanRuSu(m)*	*uRRuSu(m)*	*šūRuSu(m)*

'v' means: a short vowel which changes from verb to verb.

If the vowel in the prefix is long in Table 19, then the prefix vowel is long for all persons.

ākul, tākul, tākulī, īkul, nīkul, tākulā, īkulū, īkulā (**I ate**, etc.)

24.3 *e*-verbs

In *e*-verbs, *a/ā* changes to *e/ē* – except in the D present.

epēšu **to make** → D pres. *uppaš*

The G and N system prefixes of *e*-verbs are subject to *e*-colouring; likewise stative suffixes in the G and N systems.

ēpuš **I made**, *eppuš* **I will make**, *tennepuš* **you were made**, etc.; *epšēku* **I have been treated**

On Assyrian manuscripts of Standard Babylonian compositions, initial *ī*- is often spelled *ē*-, so a third person singular form can look like a first person singular form.

24.4 The vowel in the G system

As indicated in Table 19, in the G system it is necessary to insert a vowel which varies from verb to verb. The rules for determining the vowel are the same as for strong verbs. They can be recapitulated as follows.

In the present, preterite, perfect and imperative, insert the theme vowel. If the theme vowel is *a/u* (= *e/u* in *e*-verbs), insert *a* (= *e* in *e*-verbs) in the present and perfect, *u* in the preterite and imperative. The stative vowel is usually *i* regardless of the theme vowel, but a few verbs differ. (When the stative vowel is not *i*, it is given in the Glossary.)

agāgu **to be furious** (*a/u*) → *agug* **he is furious**
epēšu **to do, to make** (*e/u*; later *u/u*) → *epuš* **it is made**

As with all verbs, the stative vowel is the same as that in the verbal adjective. This is elided in the dictionary form (m. sg.), but visible in the f. sg.

24.5 The vowel in the N system

As indicated in Table 19, in the N system it is necessary to insert a vowel which varies from verb to verb. The rules for the vowel are the same as for strong verbs. They can be recapitulated as follows.

In the present and perfect, insert the theme vowel; if the theme vowel is *a/u* (= *e/u* in *e*-verbs), then insert *a* (= *e* in *e*-verbs). In the preterite, insert *u* if the theme vowel is *u*; insert *i* if the theme vowel is *i* or *a/u* (= *e/u* in *e*-verbs).

24.6 Why the long vowel?

In language learning it is not always practical to deduce everything from first principles, and with I-weak verbs there is much to be said for simply learning their forms through practice. Nonetheless, for interest's sake we mention that the reason why the long vowel arose in many forms (*īRuS*, *ītaRvS*, *ūtaRRis*, *ušāRiS*, *uštāRiS*, *šūRuS*, *šūRiS*, *šūRuSu*, etc.) is that 'compensatory lengthening' occurred (see Unit 47.2): *īkul* **he ate** from original *i'kul*.

24.7 Statives of verbs of being from *PRR* roots

Like strong verbs (see Unit 18.10), I-weak verbs of being from *PRR* roots (i.e. from roots which have identical second and third root letters) can form the 3rd m. sg. stative according to the pattern *v̄S*.

edēdu **to be sharp** → *ēd* **he/it is sharp**
ēmēmu **to be hot** → *ēm* **he/it is hot**

In the first millennium, they can also follow the pattern *aRvS*.

ezēzu **to be angry** → *eziz* **he/it is angry**
agāgu **to be angry** → *agug* **he/it is angry**

24.8 I-weak verbs as strong verbs

Occasionally, and not always predictably, I-weak verbs behave as if they were strong verbs whose first root letter is the glottal stop ('). You will meet an instance in Exercise 24.5: *na'durū* as the pattern *naPRuSū* for *adāru* **to be(come) dark**. When you come across a verbal form which seems to belong to a verb whose first root letter is the glottal stop, you will normally find that the Glossary and the dictionaries list the relevant verb as a I-weak verb (occasionally a I-*w* verb, see Unit 26).

Exercise 24.1, Old Babylonian

a-na-ku (*anāku* **Me, ...**) *le-em-ni-iš* ***ep-še-e-ku***

te-re-tim a-na (*ana* **about**) *šu-lum ma-ti-ia* ***lu-pu-úš***

te-re-e-tim ***nu-še-pí-iš***

ša-ap-ti-ia iš-ši-iq bi-ṣú-ri il-pu-ut ⸢*i-š*⸣*a-ar-šu a-na bi-ṣú-ri-i*[*a*] ⸢*ú*⸣*-ul* ***i-ru-ub***

ši-ta-am ša i-li a-na-ku (*anāku* **I**) ***ek-mé-ku***

i-na an-ni-tim at-hu-ut-ka ***lu-mu-ur***

ša-at-tam ^{giš}má$^{\text{hi.a}}$ *ú-ul* ***ni-pu-uš*** *pu-ul-lu-ha-a-ku ù le-em-ni-iš* ***ep-še$_{20}$-e-ku***

ša-at-ta-am a-na ša-at-ti-im na-am-da-at-ta-šu-nu ***e-bé-ṭú-um-ma i-bi-iṭ***

mi-na-am ***ni-ka-al***

a-na bi-ti-ia la ***i-ru-ba-am***

ki-ma ha-de-ia ***e-pu-uš***

i-na an-ni-tim a-hu-ut-ka ***lu-mu-ur***

Exercise 24.2, Old Babylonian

ka-ar-ṣí-ka a-na šar-rim ***i-ku-lu***

ma-ar-ti lu-ud-di-kum-ma (*-ma* **so**) ***a-hu-uz***

ša-pí-ir-ni mi-nam ***ni-ip-pa-al***

e-ru-ú ***i-ku-ul i-ku-lu*** *ma-ru-šu*

i-na tup-pí la-bi-ru-tim ša é ^{d}*nisaba ki-a-am* ***a-mu-ur***

a-na-ku-ú (*anāku* **I**) *mi-na-am* ***lu-pu-uš***

i-na é.gal-*lim a-wa-tu-šu* ***li-na-am-ra***

a-hu-ni ṣe-eh-rum aš-ša-tam ú-ul ***a-hi-iz***

se-bé-ta (*sebetta* **seven**) *ba-bu* ***ud-du-lu*** *e-lu da-ap-nim*

du-lu-um ki-ma hé-ri-ni-im ***i-te-ru-ub*** *a-na li-bi-ia*

aš-šum ki-a-am šu-ut-ta-a-am (ignore the extra *-a-*) ***ta-mu-ur***

it-ti-ia ***na-an-mi-ir***

Exercise 24.3, Old Babylonian

From a prayer, describing what the gods have done at nightfall. (The three lines make up a single sentence.)

i-li (for *ilū*) *ma-tim iš-ta-ra-at ma-a-tim*

^{d}utu ^{d}en.zu ^{d}iškur *ù* ^{d}inanna

i-te-er-bu-ú *a-na ú-tu-ul ša-me-e*

Exercise 24.4

From a letter sent by Hammurapi, who is suspicious of what he has heard about a field (quotation marks have been inserted to help you).

um-ma šu-ma

"$^{\mathrm{m.d}}$utu–*ha-zi-ir* a.šà é *a-bi-ia* ***i-ki-ma-an-ni-ma*** (*-ma* **and**) *a-na* aga.uš *it-ta-di-in*"

ki-a-am ú-lam-mi-da-an-ni

a.šà-*ú-um* (see Unit 44.9) *du-ru-um* (translate *eqlum dūrum* as **a permanently owned field**)
ma-ti-ma ***in-ne-ek-ki-im*** (question)
wa-ar-ka-tam pu-ru-ús

Exercise 24.5, Old and Middle Babylonian

The last sentence is MB.

$^{\text{m.d}}$utu–*ha-zi-ir ù tap-pu-šu* ***i-ki-mu-ni-a-ti***

ša-am-mi ka-lu-ma-ti-ia ***li-ša-ki-lu***

še-pa-am a-hi-tam a-na li-ib-bi a-lim la ***tu-še-er-re-ba***

i-na sà-ar-tim la ***te-né-mì-da***

a-na du-ri-im ***e-re-ba-am*** *ma-an-nu-um i-qá-ab-bi-kum*

ša ar-hi-iš bu-ul-lu-ṭi$_4$*-šu* ***e-pu-úš***

šu-up-ra-am-ma (*-ma* **and**) *ṣi-bu-ut-ka* ***lu-pu-ša-kum***

ib-ri ⸢***a***⸣***-ta-mar*** *šu-ut-tam am-mi-*⸢*nim*⸣ *la te-ed-ki-a-ni ma-di-*⸢*iš pa-al-ha*⸣*-*[*at*]

ki-ma la na-za-qí-ka ***e-ep-pu-uš***

mi-im-ma a-na-ku ú-ul [***š***]***u-hu-za-ku***

u$_4$*-ma-am* (*ūmam* **today**) *di-im-ma-sú* ***i-ta-ak-la-ni-a-ti***

a-n[*a-k*]*u* (*anāku* **I**) ***el-te-em-na-ki-im***

a-ia i-ku-ul ninda *bu-lu-uṭ li-ib-bi* ***a-ia i-ṣí-in*** [*ni-p*]*í-iš ši-i-ra-aš*

Exercise 24.6, Middle Babylonian

lugal ***i-bu-uk-šu-nu-ti***

e-pu-uš *ú-*⸢*sa*⸣*-a-ti a-na* en ^{uru}ká.dingir *gi-mil-ta iš-ku-un*

[*i*]*t-ti nu-ha-tim-mì nu-ha-tim-mu-ta* ***ip-pu-uš***

Nebuchadnezzar I (King of Babylon c. 1125–1104 BC) fights the king of Elam (Ancient Iran):

ur-ri-ih-ma lugal *dan-nu ik-ta-šad a-na* gú ^{íd}*ú-la-a (ulāya)*

in-nen-du-ma lugal^{meš} *ki-lal-la-an* ***ip-pu-šu*** mè

i-na bi-ri-šu-nu in-na-pi-ih i-šá-tu

i-na tur-bu-ú'-ti-šu-nu ***na-á'-du-ru*** igi (pl.) ^{d}utu-*ši*

(Ulāya is the name of a river in south-west Iran.)

Exercise 24.7, Standard Babylonian

ina pi-i lab-bi na-'i-r[*i*] *ul* ***ik-ki-mu*** *šá-lam-tú*

gal-*a* ^{d}amar.utu ***ú-šag-gag***

ki-i ú-lil-te ***an-na-bi-ik***

ú-ru-uh-ka ***te-ez-zib***

kal pag-ri-ia ***i-ta-haz*** *ri-mu-tú*

a-na ***šu-zu-ub*** zi-*tì-šú* ***in-na-bit*** *a-na qé-reb* ^{uru}*ni-i'* (*ni'* = Thebes, in Egypt)

te-te-né-ti-iq *gi-na-a šá-ma-mi* (said to the sun god)

pi-ti-ma ni-ṣir-ta-šú ***e-ru-ub*** *ana lìb-bi*

ik-kal (translate *akālu* as **to live off**) *le-'u-u ši-im i-di-šú ù la le-'u-u ši-im* [*šè*]*r-ri-šú*

šá-di-i bé-ru-ti ***e-ri-ma*** (sp. *irrima*) *šá-lum-mat-ka*

a-hu-uz *qát-su pu-ṭur a-ra-an-šú*

[*š*]*u-ut-bi-ma* (*-ma* **and**) *šèr-tuk-ka* (*šērtukka* **your punishment**, acc.) *ina na-ri-ṭi* ***eṭ-ra-áš-šú***

^{d}*iš-tar* ***ug-gu-gat***

su-un-qu i-na bi-ri-šú-un iš-šá-kin-ma a-na (translate *ana* as **in**) *bu-ri-šú-nu* ***e-ku-lu*** (Ass. sp.) uzu^{meš} dumu^{meš}-*šú-un*

ni-kis sag.du ^{m}*te-um-man* en-*šú-nu qé-reb* nina^{ki} ***e-mu-ru-u-ma*** (Ass. sp.) *šá-né-e* (see end of Unit 10.2) *ṭè-e-mi iṣ-bat-su-nu-ti*

The most important things to remember

1 I-weak verbs have no visible first root letter.

2 They have the same prefixes and suffixes as strong verbs, except that the vowels of prefixes are sometimes lengthened (*iprus* **he separated** vs. *īkul* **he ate**).

3 The 1st person singular G system prefix *a-/ā-* changes to *e-/ē-* in *e*-verbs.

4 You need to learn the 3rd person singular forms for the present, preterite, perfect, and stative (m.), and 2nd sg. m. for the imperative, in all four systems. (This is a total of 20 forms, but they are very similar to the corresponding forms of strong verbs.)

SELF CHECK

	I can ...
	... explain what a I-weak verb is
	... describe the dictionary form of a I-weak verb (*a* or *e*)
	... look up a I-weak verb in the Glossary
	... explain what 'compensatory lengthening' is
	... explain how forms of I-weak verbs can be deduced from those of strong verbs
	... (in time:) recite the forms of *akālu*(*m*)
	... (in time:) explain what is special about the Š present of I-weak verbs.

25 *II-weak verbs*

In this unit you will learn:
- **the forms of 'second weak' verbs**
- **how they differ from strong verbs.**

II-weak ('second weak') verbs are ones whose second root letter is not a consonant. They fall into two types: 'II-guttural verbs', whose second root letter was originally a guttural consonant, subsequently lost (see Unit 47.7); and 'II-vowel verbs', whose middle root letter is, and always was, a long vowel (*ī, ū, ā*). These two types sometimes inflect differently. II-weak *e*-verbs are only of the II-guttural type.

All II-weak verbs are inflected with the same prefixes and suffixes as strong verbs. The differences vis-à-vis strong verbs lie in the formation of the verbal 'core'.

25.1 The dictionary form

For most II-weak verbs (as for most verbs of any type), the dictionary form is the G infinitive. The G infinitive of II-weak verbs follows the pattern *PâSu* (*PêSu* for *e*-verbs). (For exceptions in Old Babylonian, see section 25.8 below.)

šâlu **to ask**, *bêlu* **to rule**, *kânu* **to be firm**, *mâtu* **to die**

Verbs which are not attested in the G system have as their dictionary form the infinitive of the system in which they appear most frequently.

kullu **to hold** (D system); *puqqu* **to pay attention** (D system); *šummu* **to ponder** (D system)

25.2 The theme vowel

Each II-weak verb has one theme vowel (whereas strong verbs can have two, e.g. *a/u* for *šakānu* **to put**). This vowel can be *a*, *i*, *e*, or *u*.

Each verb's theme vowel is supplied in the Glossary (in brackets after the infinitive). The theme vowel *e* occurs only in *e*-verbs, and all II-weak *e*-verbs have *e* as theme vowel. In II-vowel verbs, the theme vowel is the same as the vowel which constitutes the second root letter.

25.3 Doubling of the third root letter instead of the second

Before introducing the forms of II-weak verbs, it is necessary to present a general principle which underlies their behaviour. Where a form of a strong verb doubles the second root letter (e.g. *iparras*, *uparris*, etc.), the corresponding forms of II-weak verbs cannot do this, because they do not have a second consonantal root letter to double. In compensation for this, as it were, when possible they double the third root letter.

išammū **they buy** (= *iPaRRvSū* form of *šâmu* **to buy**)

This is only possible when the third root letter is followed by a vowel. Otherwise there would be two consonants at the end of a word (if there were no suffix), or three consonants in a row (if there were a suffix beginning with a consonant, e.g. *-šu*), and Babylonian allows neither (see Unit 47.13). Hence, in forms where strong verbs double their second root letter, suffixes beginning with a vowel (e.g. the ventive, or plural markers) enable the doubling of the third root letter in II-weak verbs.

An example of the ventive suffix enabling doubling is shown in Table 20: the strong verb *parāsu* doubles its second root letter in both cases, the II-weak verb *šâmu* doubles the third only with the ventive ending.

Table 20

	G present, 3rd sg.	
	non-ventive	**ventive**
parāsu **to separate**	*iparras*	*iparrasa(m)*
šâmu **to buy**	*išâm*	*išamma(m)*

An example of the m. pl. suffix enabling doubling is shown in Table 21: the strong verb *parāsu* doubles its second root letter in both cases, the II-weak verb *kânu* doubles the third only with the plural ending.

Table 21

	D preterite	
	3rd sg.	**3rd pl.**
parāsu **to separate**	*uparris*	*uparrisū*
kânu **to be firm**	*ukīn*	*ukinnū*

25.4 Forms in the G, N, D and Š systems

Using the system explained in Unit 5, whereby *P* represents a verb's first root letter and *S* represents the third, the basic forms of II-weak verbs in the G, N, D and Š systems are as shown in Table 22. (On 'basic forms' see Unit 24.2.) (Given the particularity of II-weak verbs with regard to doubling of the third root letter, for every combination of tense and system we will give two forms: one where doubling is not possible, and one where it is.)

Table 22

	G	**N**	**D**	**Š**
pres. 3rd sg.	*iPâS*	*iPPâS*	II-vowel: *uPāS* II-guttural: *uPâS*	II-vowel: *ušPāS* II-guttural: *ušPâS*
3rd m. pl.	*iPvSSū*	*iPPvSSū*	*uPaSSū*	II-vowel: *ušPāSū* II-guttural: *ušPâSū*
pret. 3rd sg.	*iPv̄S*	*iPPv̄S*	*uPīS*	*ušPīS*

3rd m. pl.	*iPv̄Sū*	*iPPv̄Sū*	*uPiSSū*	*ušPīSū*
perf. 3rd sg.	*iPtv̄S*	(unknown)	*uPtīS*	*uštaPīS*
3rd m. pl.	*iPtv̄Sū*	(unknown)	*uPtīSū*	*uštaPīSū*
stat. 3rd sg.	*Pv̄S*	(unknown)	*PūS*	*šuPūS*
3rd m. pl.	*Pv̄Sū*	(unknown)	*PuSSū*	*šuPūSū*
imp. m. sg.	*Pv̄S*	(unknown)	*PīS*	*šuPīS*
pl.	*Pv̄Sā*	(unknown)	*PiSSā*	(*šuPīSā*)
inf.	*PâSu(m)*	(unknown)	*PuSSu(m)*	*šuPūSu(m)*

'*v*' means: a short vowel which changes from verb to verb; '*v̄*' means: a long vowel which changes from verb to verb.

Some features of these forms should be noted. In the present and preterite of the Š system, the *š* is directly in contact with the first root letter. In strong verbs, they are separated by *a*: *ušmīt* **he killed** vs. *ušalmid* **he taught**. As in strong verbs, present and preterite in the D and Š systems are only distinguished by the vowel (*a* vs. *i*): *ukān*, *ukīn* like *uparras*, *uparris*; *ušmāt*, *ušmīt* like *ušalmad*, *ušalmid*.

25.5 The vowel in the G and N systems

In the G and N systems it is necessary to insert a vowel which varies from verb to verb, and from tense to tense. This vowel is indicated by the symbols *v* and *v̄* in Table 22. In the present, perfect, preterite and imperative, the vowel to be inserted is the verb's theme vowel.

In the G stative of II-vowel verbs, the vowel to be inserted is *ā* for II-*ā* verbs, and *ī* for II-*ū* and II-*ī* verbs (except that a few II-*ī* verbs of being insert *ā*).

dâṣu (*ā*) **to disrespect** → *dāṣ* **he/it is not respected**
dâku (*ū*) **to kill** → *dīk* **he/it has been killed**
qâšu (*ī*) **to give as a gift** → *qīš* **he/it has been given as a gift**

but

ṭâbu (*ī*) **to be good** → stative *ṭāb* **he/it is good**
sâmu (*ī*) **to be red** → stative *sām* **he/it is red**

For all II-weak verbs, the vowel between the first and third root letter in the G stative is the same as the vowel in the same position in the G system verbal adjective.

kīnu **firm**; *ṭābu* **good**; *dāṣtu* **disrespect** (f. adj. used as noun)

25.6 Why *â* in the G and N present?

A feature of II-weak verbs which learners of Babylonian tend to find counter-intuitive is the *â* in the present of the G and N systems when the third root letter is not doubled: why *â*? Why not simply the theme vowel?

A good way to think of this is to imagine II-weak verbs in the G and N present as desperately wanting to imitate the corresponding forms of strong verbs. So, let us put ourselves in the position of a II-weak verb: 'I want to imitate strong verbs. What is their most distinctive feature in the G and N present? Surely, the doubling of the second root letter. So, I will try to imitate this. I don't have a second root letter to double, but as the next best thing I will double my third, e.g. *ikunnū* **they are firm** and *išammū* **they buy**.' So far, so good.

'But oh dear, sometimes I can't double my third root letter because of the consonant clusters this would create. So, what to do? Doubling my first root letter is not an option – in the N system it is already doubled, and if I did it in the G system the resulting form would look like it belonged to the N system. Hmmm, I see that I am going to have to give up on doubling altogether. What is another distinctive feature of the G and N present of strong verbs which I can imitate?'

'Well, since the vast majority of strong verbs have theme vowels *a/u*, the vowel before the third root letter in the G and N present is usually *a*. So, it's perhaps not unduly stretching the truth to say that in strong verbs there is a significant association between the G and N present and the vowel *a* before the third root letter. For want of better, I will take this as my feature to imitate.'

'So, putting *a* before my third root letter, I get forms like *ikūan*, *iṭīab*, *īšāal*, etc. The adjacent vowels will then of course contract (except for *ia* in Old Babylonian), so my equivalent of *iparras* will be *ikân*, *iṭâb* (*iṭīab* in Old Babylonian), *išâl*, etc.'

25.7 II-guttural verbs: weak and strong

II-guttural verbs (but not II-vowel verbs) sometimes behave as if they were strong, with ' as their middle root letter. When this happens, ' behaves like a normal consonant (and so can double). Thus there can be two variants of the same verb form, one II-weak and one strong. Examples from *šâlu/ša'ālu* **to ask**:

inf.: *šâlu* (II-weak), *ša'ālu* (strong, like *parāsu*) **to ask**
pres. *išallū* (II-weak), *iša''alū* (strong, like *iparrasū*) **they ask**
prec.: *lišālū* (II-weak), *liš'alū* (strong, like *liprusū*) **may they ask**
imp.: *šāl* (II-weak), *ša'al* (strong, like *ṣabat* **seize!**) **ask!**

This unit deals with II-guttural verbs on the assumption they are behaving as II-weak verbs; when they behave as strong verbs, they follow the patterns presented in the units on strong verbs, and the present unit does not apply to them.

25.8 The G infinitive of II-*ī* verbs in Old Babylonian

Using *v* to represent the vocalic root letter, II-vowel verbs originally formed the G infinitive after the pattern *PvāSum*. By the Old Babylonian period, in most cases the two adjacent vowels had contracted, yielding the pattern *PâSum*. The exception is verbs whose vocalic root letter is *ī*, since the sequence *ia* was normally left uncontracted in Old Babylonian. Thus, for example, the Old Babylonian infinitive of the verb whose root is √*ṭīb* is *ṭiābum* (or perhaps *ṭīābum*), whereas the Old Babylonian infinitive of the verb whose root is √*kūn* is *kânum*.

The Concise Dictionary of Akkadian (and W. von Soden's *Akkadisches Handwörterbuch*, on which the *Concise Dictionary* is based) cite verbs by their Old Babylonian G infinitive (with mimation in brackets). Hence they cite the G infinitives of II-*ī* verbs in uncontracted form, i.e. *ṭiābu(m)* rather than *ṭâbu(m)*. (However, they provide cross-references from e.g. *ṭâbu(m)* to *ṭiābu(m)*.)

Exercise 25.1, Old Babylonian

da-ha-at-ni (sp. *da'atni*) *ú-ul* ***i-ša-al***

a-ma-at-ma ṭá-ab-ku-um

um-ma-ka ***im-tu-ut***

na-ga-ru la ***i-ri-qú***

aš-šu-mi-šu-nu ***re-ma-an-ni***

šum-ma (*šumma* **even if**) *at-ta* (*atta* **you** (m. sg.)) ***mi-ša-ta-an-ni*** *a-na-ku e-li-ka a-ha-ab-bu-ub*

i-mé-ri ***ša-am***

li-ib-ba-šu ***it-tu-uh***

mi-nu-ú-um ***ú-ba-ša-ka***

mu-ut-ni ***ta-ra-mi-ma*** *[b]a-la-aṭ-ni* ***te-ze-ri***

li-ib-bi ***ú-ṭi-ib***

ri-qú-sú (*rīqūssu* **empty-handed**) *la* ***i-tu-ra***

Exercise 25.2, Old Babylonian

ka-al-la-at-ki ***i-ze-er-ki***

^{d}utu *di-ni* ***li-di-in***

ú-ru-um ***se-er***

kù.babbar *ú-ul na-ši-a-ku-ma* (*-ma* **so**) *ú-ku-ul-tam ú-ul* ***a-ša-am***

ha-ar-ba-am a-na be-lí-šu ***te-er*** (sp. *tīr*; see Unit 47.14)

ša-du-um ***i-qù-pa-am****-ma i-si-ha-an-[ní]*

gi-ru-um ***ru-uq****-ma* (*-ma* **so**) *[m]a-am-ma-an a-na a-la-ki-im [ú-u]l i-ma-ga-ra-an-ni*

ša (translate *ša* as **with**) kù.babbar *šu-a-ti* (*šuāti* **that**) ku$_6^{hi.a}$ *dam-qú-tim* ***ša-ma-am-ma*** (*-ma* **and**) *a-na a-ka-li-ia šu-bi-lam* (*šūbilam* **have (it) sent to me!**)

kù.babbar *ma-hi-ir li-ba-šu* ***ṭa-ab***

ki-ma (see Unit 13.4) *ka-al-bi da-ah-ti* (sp. *da'tī*) *ú-ul* ***ta-ša-li***

ši-ir ni-ši ***ú-ṭi-ib***

ki-ma ša (*kīma ša* **just as if**) *a-[n]a-ku wa-aš-ba-[k]u li-ba-šu* **[ṭ]*ì-ib-ba***

Exercise 25.3, Old Babylonian

[hi]-ib-le-tu-ú-a i-na qá-ti (see Unit 12.1) ^{d}utu–*ha-zi-ir* (*šamaš–hāzir*, personal name) ***im-ti-da***

i-na ša-at-tim an-ni-tim ***ti-ri-in-ni-i****-ma* (*-ma* **and**) *na-ra-am šu-bi-ri-in-ni* *di-ni ú di-in-ka* ^{d}utu ***li-di-in***

gu$_4$$^{hi.a}$ *ú-ul ta-ap-ṭú-ur-ma* (*-ma* **and so**) *i-na da-an-na-at ku-uṣ-ṣi* ***tu-uš-ta-mi-is-sú-nu-ti***

[l]a-ma a-la-ki-ni [l]i-ib-ba-ka ***nu-ṭá-ab***

a-na hi-sà-ti-i-ki ***ru-uq***

le-mu-ut-ta ú-ul ***ú-ki-il*** (translate *kullu* as **to hold in store**) *a-na ib-ri-ia*

šum-ma i-na ki-na-a-tim ***ta-ra-am-ma-an-ni*** *a-na bi-ti-šu ma-am-ma-an la i-ša-ás-si*

i-na ma-ak aga.uš^{meš} *i-na* sag.da–in.pàd^{ki} (Bab. reading uncertain) *ha-al-ṣa-a[m] ma-am-ma-an ú-ul ú-ka-al*

a.šà-*am šu-a-ti* (*šuāti* **that**) *i-na qá-tim* ***ki-il-la-aš-šu****-ma la a-na-az-zi-iq*

a-na na-ah-la-ap-tim ú-sa-li-a-ki-ma ú-ul ***te-re-mi-ni***

2 (*šitta* **two**) kuš.ùsan *šu-uh-mi-ṭa-am* g[u]$_4$$^{hi.a}$ *i-na ma-ak* kuš.ùsan ***ri-qú***

a-na mi-ni-im ki-a-am ***te-mi-ša-an-ni***

da-aw-da-am ***du-uk-ma*** (*-ma* **and so**) *šu-ma-am na-aš-ki-in*

Exercise 25.4, Middle Babylonian

[am]-mi-ni šu-ú-tu iš-tu 7 (sebet) ú-mi a-na ma-a-ti la ***i-zi-qá***

a-na bi-it be-lí-ia i-na qá-ab-la-at ta-am-ti nu-ni ***a-ba-ar***

me-e mu-ú-ti ***ú-ka-lu-ni-ik-ku-ma*** (*-ma* **so**) *la ta-ša-at-ti*

mi-i-du *ar-nu-ia*

na-an-na-ru ^{d}30 ***ú-kín*** ugu-*šu-nu na-mu-un-ga-at* murub$_4$

CULTURE TIP

The number 30 was used as a sumerogram for the moon god (*Sîn*) because, in the lunar calendar, the ideal month has 30 days.

LANGUAGE TIP

It is very unusual to spell the word *ūmu* **day** using the sign *ú*. Normally *u*$_4$ is used, as this also is the sumerogram for **day**: *u*$_4$*-mu*, *u*$_4$*-mi*, etc. (or u$_4$*-mu*, u$_4$*-mi*, etc.) The manuscript with *ú-mi* (first sentence of Exercise 25.4) was found at Tell el-Amarna, in Egypt. Very likely, the person who inscribed the manuscript wanted to use as few signs and sign values as possible, for the sake of foreign learners. The same manuscript contains no sumerograms, probably for the same reason.

Exercise 25.5, Standard Babylonian

ina ru-ub-ṣi-ia ***a-bit*** *ki-i al-pi*

šar-ra-ha-ku-ma (*-ma* **but**) ***a-tur*** *ana re-e-ši*

a-na a-hi-i a-hi i-tu-ra a-na lem-ni u gal-le-e ***i-tu-ra*** *ib-ri*

ana gul-lul-ti-šú-nu ***ri-ib*** *dum-qí*

a-na e-piš le-mut-ti-ka sig$_5$ ***ri-ib-šú***

za-qì-qu a-bal-ma ul ú-pat-ti uz-ni

a-na kib-si a-he-e ú-zu-un-šá ***tur-rat***

Exercise 25.6, Standard Babylonian

From The Epic of Erra.

(Translate *-ma* as **and**.)

ma-ra ***uš-mat****-ma a-bu i-qa-ab-bir-šu*

ar-ka a-ba ***uš-ma-at****-ma qé-bi-ra ul i-ši*

qu-ra-du ^{d}*èr-ra ki-nam-ma* (see Unit 30.7) ***tuš-ta-mit***

la ki-nam-ma ***tuš-ta-mit***

Exercise 25.7

From The Epic of Gilgameš. Gilgameš reproves the goddess Ištar for how she treated her former lovers:

ta-ra-mi*-ma* ur.mah *ga-mi-ir e-mu-qí* (*gamir emūqī* **perfect in strength**)

tu-uh-tar-ri-iš-šú 7 u 7 (sebe u sebe) šu-ut-ta-a-ti

ta-ra-mi*-ma* anše.kur.ra *na-'i-id qab-li* (*na'id qabli* **devoted to battle**)

iš-tuh-ha ziq-ti u dir-ra-ta ***tal-ti-miš-šu***

The most important things to remember

1 II-weak verbs behave as if they had no second root letter.

2 They have the same prefixes and suffixes as strong verbs.

3 When strong verbs double their middle root letter, II-weak verbs double their third root letter if they can (i.e. if it is followed by a suffix beginning with a vowel).

4 You need to learn the 3rd person singular and plural forms for the present, preterite, perfect, and stative, and 2nd m. sg and 2nd pl. for the imperative, in all four systems. Other forms can be derived from these.

SELF CHECK

	I can ...
	... explain what a II-weak verb is
	... describe the dictionary form of a II-weak verb (*a* or *e*)
	... look up a II-weak verb in the Glossary
	... explain which of its forms can be deduced from those of strong verbs, and which can't
	... explain under what circumstances the third root letter doubles
	... (in time:) recite the forms of *kânu(m)*.

Reading B: The evils of Sennacherib

Sennacherib, King of Assyria 705–681 BC, is a very interesting figure. As well as having commissioned gardens in Nineveh which Greek tradition perhaps turned into the 'Hanging Gardens' of Babylon (see S. Dalley, *The Mystery of the Hanging Gardens of Babylon*, Oxford University Press 2015), he defeated Babylon militarily, and sacked the capital. This was an enormous blow to Babylonian morale, and the Babylonians must have derived great satisfaction from the fact he was later murdered by one of his own sons (see Reading C).

Here we read a passage from the 'Babylon Stele' of Nabonidus, the last native king of Babylonia before the conquest by the Persians (539 BC), which was prominently placed near the Ištar Gate. The extract tells of Sennacherib's sack of Babylon (after H.-P. Schaudig, *Die Inschriften Nabonids und Kyros' des Großen*, Ugarit-Verlag 2001, pp. 515–516). As a Neo-Babylonian king, and therefore a devotee of the Marduk (chief god of Babylon), Nabonidus presents the sack of Babylon not as an offence against Marduk (which would have involved admitting weakness on the god's part), but as something which Marduk allowed to happen, during an unfortunate lapse of his usual mercifulness.

The stele is inscribed in Monumental Old Babylonian script. Sennacherib is the subject of the extract. He is referred to as 'king of Subir' (i.e. king of Assyria).

Cuneiform

Spaces have not been inserted between words – note how much harder the script is to read when this happens, as it is less clear where words start and stop. You can generate a spaced version using the Cuneifyplus tool (http://cuneifyplus.arch.cam.ac.uk). For technical reasons, it is not possible to show damage to the signs (cf. square brackets in the transliteration).

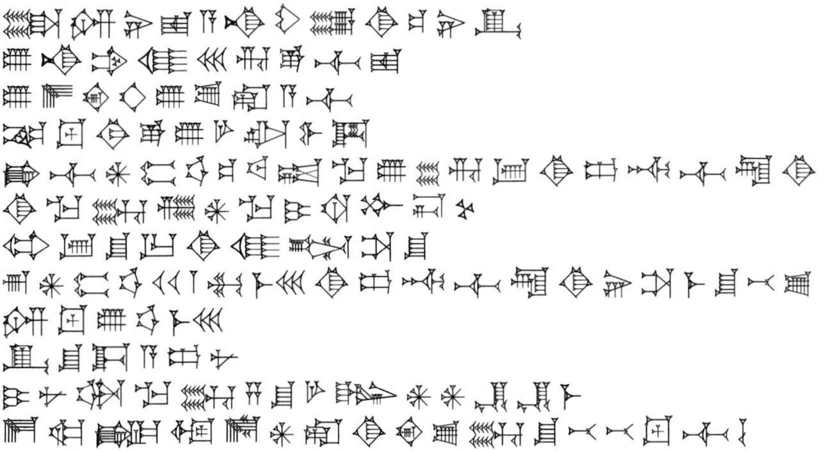

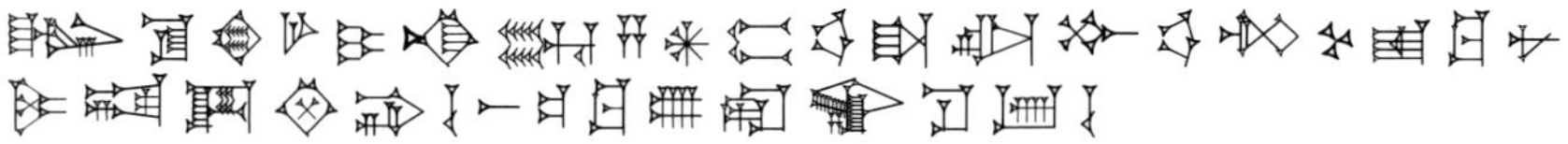

Transliteration

le-em-[ni-i]š a-na tin.tir[^{ki} *is-ni-i*]*q*

ú-na-am-mi eš-re-e-ti-iš

ú-sa-ah-hi ú-ṣú-ra-a-ti

pil-lu-de-e ú-šá-al-pi-it

qá-ti ^{d}amar.utu *iṣ-ba-at-ma ú-še-ri-ib qé-reb* bal.ti.la^{ki}

ki-ma uz-zi dingir*-ma i-te-pu-uš* kur

ul ip-šu-ur [k]i-mi-il-ta-šu

nun ^{d}amar.utu 21 (written 10, 10, 1) mu^{meš} *qé-reb* bal.ti.la^{ki} *ir-ta-mì šu-bat-su*

[*i*]*m-lu-ú* u$_{4}^{meš}$

ik-šu-da a-dan-nu

i-nu-úh-ma uz-za-šu šá (see Unit 30.2) lugal dingir.dingir en en^{méš}

é.sag.íl *ù* ká.dingir.ra^{ki} *ih-su-us šu-bat be-lu-ti-šú*

lugal su$_4$.bir *šá i-na uz-za* ^{d}amar.utu *ša-al-pu-ut-tì* kur *iš-ku-nu*

dumu *ṣi-it* šà*-bi-šú ina* ^{giš}tukul *ú-ra-as-si-ib-šú*

lem[ni]š ana bābili [isni]q

unammi ešrētiš (*-š* is for *-šu*)

usahhi uṣurāti

pilludê ušalpit

qāti marūtuk iṣbat-ma ušērib qereb (*q.* replaces expected *ana*) *aššur*

kīma uzzi ilim-ma ītepuš māta

ul ipšur [k]imiltašu

rubû marūtuk 21 šanāti qereb aššur irtami šubassu

[i]mlû ūmū

ikšuda adannu

inūh-ma uzzašu ša šar ilī bēl bēlī

esagil u bābili ihsus šubat bēlūtišu

šar subarti ša ina uzza marūtuk šalputti māti iškunu mār ṣīt libbišu urassibšu

Translation

Malevo[lentl]y he approached Babylon.

He laid waste to its shrines.

He destroyed the ordinances.

He ruined the cults.

He seized the hand of Marduk, and led him to (lit. **caused (him) to enter into**) **Assur.**

He treated the land as (with, see Unit 13.4) **the fury of a god.**

He did not ease his rage.

Prince Marduk remained at his dwelling in Assur for 21 years.

The days passed (lit. **filled**).

The appointed time arrived.

The wrath of the king of the gods, lord of lords, abated.

He became mindful of (lit. **remembered**) **Esagil and Baylon, his lordly dwelling** (lit. **dwelling of his lordship**).

The king of Subartu, who at the wrath of Marduk had brought about the ruin of the land – one of his (see Unit 11.12) **own sons smote him.**

26 *I-w verbs*

In this unit you will learn:

- **the forms of 'first doubleyou' verbs**
- **how they differ from strong verbs.**

I-*w* ('first doubleyou') verbs are ones whose first root letter is *w*. In the G system (also the Gtn and Gt systems, see Units 33 and 34), I-*w* verbs of being behave differently from I-*w* verbs of doing. In the N, D and Š systems (and their derived systems) the two types behave the same. The forms of I-*w* verbs change slightly from Old Babylonian to later periods.

> **LANGUAGE TIP**
> Nouns from I-*w* roots can lack the *w*, and start directly with the second root letter: *biltu* **tribute** from *(w)abālu* **to bring**, *šubtu* **dwelling** from *(w)ašābu* **to dwell**, etc.

26.1 I-*w* verbs of doing in Old Babylonian

Using the system explained in Unit 5, the basic forms of I-*w* verbs of doing conform in Old Babylonian to the patterns shown in Table 23. (On 'basic forms' see Unit 24.2.) The G preterite has two alternative forms.

Table 23

	G	N	D	Š
pres.	*ūbbal* (later *ubbal)*	*iPPaRRaS*	*uPaRRaS*	*ušaRRaS*
pret.	*ūRiS*, *uRiS*	*iPPaRiS*	*uPaRRiS*	*ušāRiS*
perf.	*ittaRaS*	(*ittaPRaS*)	*ūtaRRiS*	*uštāRiS*
stat.	*PaRiS*	(unknown)	*PuRRuS*	*šūRuS*
imp.	*RiS*	(unknown)	*PuRRiS*	*šūRiS*
inf.	*PaRāSu(m)*	(unknown)	*PuRRuSu(m)*	*šūRuSu(m)*

When suffixes beginning with a vowel (e.g. ventive *-am*) are added in the preterite, vowel elision happens if the *u* is short (see Unit 47.4).

ūbil **he brought** → *ūbilam* **he brought here**
ubil **he brought** → *ublam* **he brought here**

The 3rd sg. G precative begins with *lī-* (not *lū-*!), e.g. *līrid* **let him go down**; the 1st sg. G precative begins with *lū-*. The bracketed N form *ittaPRaS* is not attested in Old Babylonian, but can be reconstructed from the forms attested in later periods.

LANGUAGE TIP

N system forms of I-*w* verbs are rarely used.

26.2 Prefixes and suffixes

When a form in Table 23 begins with *i*-, to produce the forms for all persons use the same prefixes and suffixes as for strong verbs:

G perf. of *warādu* **to go down** (**I have gone down**, etc.)
sg. 1st *attarad*, 2nd m. *tattarad*, 2nd f. *tattardī*, 3rd *ittarad*
pl. 1st *nittarad*, 2nd *tattardā*, 3rd m. *ittardū*, 3rd f. *ittardā*

When a form in Table 23 begins with *u*- or *ū*-, to produce the forms for all persons use the prefixes and suffixes shown in Table 24.

Table 24

	for *u*-	for *ū*-
1st sg.	*u*-	*ū*-
2nd sg. m.	*tu*-	*tū*-
2nd sg. f.	*tu…ī*	*tū…ī*
3rd sg.	*u*-	*ū*-
1st pl.	*nu*-	*nū*-
2nd pl.	*tu…ā*	*tū…ā*
3rd m. pl.	*u…ū*	*ū…ū*
3rd f. pl.	*u…ā*	*ū…ā*

G pres. of *wabālu* **to bring** (**I bring**, etc.)
sg. 1st *ubbal*, 2nd m. *tubbal*, 2nd f. *tubbalī*, 3rd *ubbal*
pl. 1st *nubbal*, 2nd *tubbalā*, 3rd m. *ubbalū*, 3rd f. *ubbalā* (OB has *ūbbal, tūbbal*, etc.)

G pret. of *wabālu* **to bring** (**I brought**, etc.)
sg. 1st *ūbil*, 2nd m. *tūbil*, 2nd f. *tūbilī*-, 3rd *ūbil*
pl. 1st *nūbil*, 2nd *tūbilā*, 3rd m. *ūbilū*, 3rd f. *ūbilā* (also: *ubil*, *tubil*, etc.)

26.3 I-*w* verbs of being in Old Babylonian

In the G infinitive and stative, I-*w* verbs of being (e.g. (*w*)*aqāru* **to be precious**) behave like I-*w* verbs of doing. In other tenses of the G system, they behave instead like I-weak verbs with theme vowel *i*. Their 'basic forms' in the G system are shown in Table 25. (On 'basic forms' see Unit 24.2.) In the N, D and Š systems, I-*w* verbs of being behave like I-*w* verbs of doing.

Table 25

	I-*w* being	I-*w* doing	I-weak
pres. 3rd sg.	*īRRiS* (later *iRRiS*)	*ūRRaS* (later *uRRaS*)	*iRRvS*
pret. 3rd sg.	*īRiS*	*ūRiS, uRiS*	*īRvS*
perf. 3rd sg.	*ītaRiS*	*ittaRaS*	*ītaRvS*
stat. 3rd m. sg.	*PaRiS*	*PaRiS*	*aRvS*
imp. m. sg.	*aRiS*	*RiS*	*aRvS*
inf.	*PaRāSu(m)*	*PaRāSu(m)*	*aRāSu(m)*

'*v*' means: a short vowel which changes from verb to verb.

26.4 Changes from Old Babylonian to later periods

From the late Old Babylonian period onwards, *w* at the start of a word usually vanishes. (Since the *Chicago Assyrian Dictionary* lists words according to their Standard Babylonian forms, I-*w* verbs which occur in the G system should be sought in it under the letter *a*.)

OB *wašābum* **to dwell** (G inf.) → later *ašābu*
OB *wašib* **he dwells** (G stat.) → later *ašib*
OB *wuššurum* **to release** (D inf.) → later *uššuru*

After the Old Babylonian period, *w* inside a form is usually spelled in a way that is conventionally transliterated and normalized as *m* (but between vowels it probably continued to be pronounced *w*).

OB *uwaššer* he released (D pret.) → later *umaššer* (probably pronounced *uwaššer*).
(For *e* vs. *i* see Unit 47.14.)

Since *w* arises naturally between the vowels *a* and *u*, the sequence of sounds *uwa* was sometimes spelled *u'a* or *ua* (both pronounced *uwa*).

u'aššer, *uaššer* (pronounced *uwaššer*) **he/she released**
u'allad, *uallad* (pronounced *uwallad*) **he/she begets**

Rarely in the Old Babylonian period, but more often thereafter, the D present and preterite can follow the patterns *uRRaS* and *uRRiS* instead of *uPaRRaS* and *uPaRRiS*.

OB *uwaššer* **he released** → later *umaššer*, *uššer*
OB *uwattar* **he increases** → later *u'attar* (pronounced *uwattar*), *uttar*

In Standard Babylonian, in the Š system -*ā*- often appears as -*ē*-.

SB *ušēbil* (for earlier *ušābil*) **I/he/she got (s/o) to send (s/th)**
SB *uštēšib* (for earlier *uštāšib*) **I/he/she got (s/o) to dwell**

Exercise 26.1, Old Babylonian

Normalize and parse the following forms of *wašāru* **to be low**, *wašābu* **to dwell**, *warādu* **to go down**, *waqāru* **to be precious**, *walādu* **to give birth to**, and *wabālu* **to bring**.

1 *ul-la-ad* **2** *i-wa-al-du* **3** *i-wa-li-id* **4** *ú-li-id-ka* **5** *ú-ul-da-an-ni* **6** *ú-li-is-sí* **7** *tu-ul-di-in-ni* **8** *bi-lam* **9** *ub-ba-lam* **10** *tu-ub-ba-li-in-ni* **11** *li-ib-lu-ni-iš-šu* **12** *it-ta-ba-al* **13** *ú-ša-ab-ba-la-*

ak-kum **14** *uš-ta-bíl* **15** *ú-ta-aš-šar* **16** *ú-ta-aš-ša-ru* **17** *wu-uš-še-ra-am* (see Unit 47.14) **18** *tu-wa-ša-ar-šum* **19** *ú-wa-še-ru-šu* **20** *wa-aš-ra-a-ta* **21** *li-wa-še-ra-an-ni* **22** *šu-ši-ba-a-ma* **23** *ú-ša-ši-ib* **24** *ú-še-ši-im-ma* (see Unit 47.9) **25** *šu-ši-ba-an-ni* **26** *ur-da-am* **27** *li-ri-du-ú-ma* **28** *ur-du-nim* **29** *i-iq-qí-ir* **30** *wa-aq-ra-at*

Exercise 26.2, Old Babylonian

it-ti-šu a-na a.šà **ri-id**

a-*na mu-ti-ša* 2 (*šina* **two**) dumu^{meš} **al-da-at**

ma-ar-ti **aṣ-ba-at**

^{giš}tukul *ša* dingir *a-na* a.šà-*im* **li-ri-id**

Exercise 26.3, Standard Babylonian

Normalize and parse the following forms of *atāru* **to be much**, *ašāru* **to be low**, *ašābu* **to dwell**, *arāqu* **to be(come) green/yellow**, *arādu* **to go down**, *aqāru* **to be precious**, *alādu* **to give birth to**, and *abālu* **to bring**.

1 *at-ra-at* **2** *li-in-da-šer* (see Unit 47.10) **3** *ú-maš-šar-ki* **4** *ú-maš-ši-ru* **5** *uš-šèr* **6** *lu-maš-šèr* **7** *nu-maš-šèr* **8** *muš-šu-rat* **9** *un-da-šèr* **10** *tu-še-šib-šu* **11** *ul-te-ši-ba-an-ni* **12** *lu-še-ši-ib* **13** *tu-ur-ra-qí* **14** *ur-ru-uq* **15** *nu-ur-rad* **16** *ú-rid* **17** *at-tar-da* **18** *ú-ri-da-ním-ma* **19** *ri-da-ni* **20** *i-qir-šu* **21** *li-qir* **22** *aq-rat* **23** *it-ta-a'-lad* **24** *ta-at-tal-da* **25** *ul-da-áš-šum-ma* **26** *ú-al-lad-ka* **27** *lu-ub-la* **28** *ú-ša-bi-la* **29** *ul-te-bi-la*

Exercise 26.4, Standard Babylonian

pa-la-hu da-ma-qa **ul-la-ad** *ni-qu-u ba-la-ṭu* [*u*]*t-tar*

na-ši ^{giš}mar *al-li tup-šik-ki e-piš dul-li za-bil ku-dur-ri ina e-le-li ul-ṣi hu-ud lìb-bi nu-um-mur pa-ni* **ub-ba-lu₄** *u₄-um-šú-un*

[*a-n*]*a šá-kan a-bu-bi* **ub-la** *lìb-ba-šú-nu* dingir^{meš} gal^{meš}

il-qu-in-ni-ma (-*ma* **and**) *ina ru-qí ina ka* íd^{meš} **uš-te-ši-bu-in-ni** (see Unit 19.7)

ana šu-un-bu-uṭ zi-m[*í*]-*ia u ub-bu-ub ṣu-ba-ti-ia* ^dgìra **um-ta-'i-ir**

e-li (*eli* **to**) ^m*tar-qu-ú* (Taharka) lugal kur *ku-ú-si a-na šá-kan a-de-e u sa-li-me* **ú-ma-'e-e-ru** ^{lú}rak-*bé-e-šú-un*

The most important things to remember

1 In the G present and preterite, I-*w* verbs of doing use the prefixes which strong verbs use in the D and Š systems (*u*-, *tu*-, etc.), except that sometimes the *u* is lengthened (*ū*-, *tū*-, etc.).

2 I-*w* verbs of being behave like I-weak verbs in the G system (and its sub-systems), and like I-*w* verbs of doing in other systems.

3 After the Old Babylonian period, *w* between vowels is often spelled *m* (but probably still pronounced as *w*).

4 After the Old Babylonian period, *w* at the beginning of a word vanished.

5 Learn the G forms *ubbal* (OB *ūbbal*) **he/she/it brings**, *ūbil/ubil* **he/she/it brought**, *ittabal* **he/she/it has brought**, *bil* **bring!**.

6 Learn the Š forms *ušabbal* **he/she/it gets (s/o) to bring**, *ušābil/ušēbil* **he/she/it got (s/o) to bring**, *uštābil/uštēbil* **he/she/it has got (s/o) to bring**, *šūbil* **get (s/o) to bring!**.

SELF CHECK

	I can ...
	... explain what a I-*w* verb is
	... describe the dictionary form of a I-*w* verb
	... look up a I-*w* verb in the Glossary
	... explain how its forms differ from those of strong verbs
	... (in time:) explain how G forms of I-*w* verbs differ from D forms of strong verbs
	... (in time:) recite the forms of (*w*)*abālu*(*m*).

Reading C: The death of Sennacherib

Extract from the *Babylonian Chronicle* (column iii, lines 28–38), after A. K. Grayson, *Assyrian and Babylonian Chronicles* (J. J. Augustin, 1975), pp. 81–2.

A copy of an original cuneiform manuscript of the passage (in Neo-Babylonian script) can be consulted in L. Abel and H. Winckler, *Keilschrifttexte zum Gebrauch bei Vorlesungen* (Spemann, 1890), p. 48 – downloadable from either of

http://www.etana.org/node/837

http://digital.library.stonybrook.edu/cdm/ref/collection/iraqiarcheology/id/82

The *Babylonian Chronicle* is generally regarded as the most 'sober' of all historiographical writings from Ancient Mesopotamia. The following extract gives a good sense of its concise and matter-of-fact style.

Cuneiform

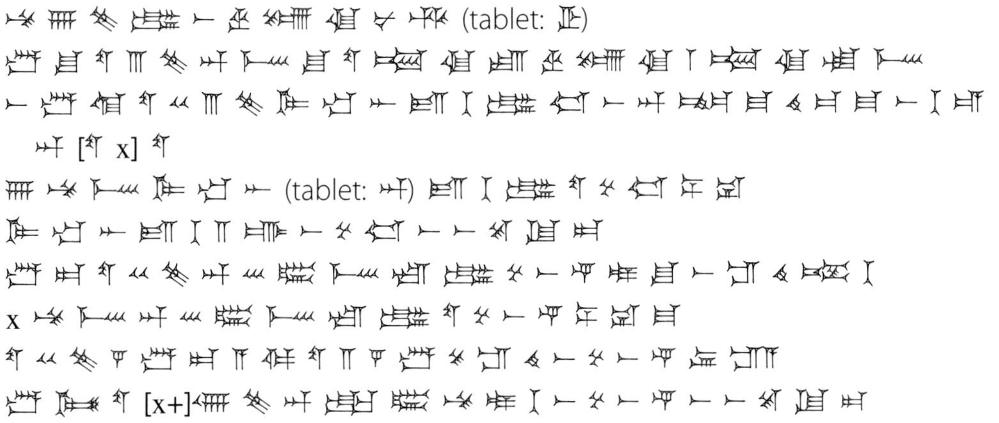

Transliteration

mu 8 kám lugal *ina* tin.tir^{ki} nu gál$^{!}$ (tablet: tuk)

^{iti}šu ud 3 kám dingir^{meš} *šu-ut* unug^{ki} ta [tin.ti]r^{ki} *ana* unug^{ki} ku$_4^{meš}$

ina ^{iti}du$_6$ ud 23 kám *hum-ba-[hal]-da-šú* lugal nim *ina* an.bar$_7$ *ma-hi-iṣ-ma ina* šú-e ^{d}[utu *x*]*-ut* (probably *imtūt* **he died**)

8 mu^{meš} *hum-ba-hal*(tablet: *an*)*-da-šú* lugal-*ut* kur nim dù-*uš*

hum-ba-hal-da-šú 2-*ú ina* kur nim *ina* aš.te tuš-*ab*

^{iti}ab ud 20 kám ^{d}30–šeš^{meš}–su lugal kur *aš-šur* dumu-*šu ina si-hi* gaz-[*šú*]

[x] mu^{meš} ^{d}30–šeš^{meš}–su lugal-*ut* kur *aš-šur* dù-*uš-ma*

ud 20 kám *šá* [iti]ab *a-di* ud 2 *šá* [iti]še *si-hi ina* kur *aš-šur sa-dir*

[iti]sig_4 ud [x?+]18 kám an.šar–šeš–mu dumu-*šú ina* kur *aš-šur ina* aš.te tuš-*ab*

Normalization

samānītu šattu šarru ina bābili ul ibašši

du'ūzu šalšu ūmu ilū šūt uruk ultu [bābil]i ana uruk īrubū

ina tašrīti 23rd *ūmi humba[hal]dašu šar elamti ina muṣlāli mahiṣ-ma ina rabê [šamši imt]ūt*

samāne šanāti humbahaldašu šarrūt māt elamti īpuš

humbahaldašu šanû ina māt elamti ina kussî ittašab

ṭebētu 20th (= *ešrû?*) *ūmu sîn–ahhê–erība šar māt aššur mārūšu* (Unit 11.9) *ina sīhi idūk[šu]*

[x] *šanāti sîn–ahhê–erība šarrūt māt aššur īpuš-ma*

20th *ūmu ša ṭebēti adi šanî ūmi ša addari sīh(u) ina māt aššur sadir*

simanu [x?+]18 *ūmu aššur–ahhê–iddina mārūšu ina māt aššur ina kussî ittašab*

Translation

Eighth year (that) there is no (lit. **not a**) **king in Babylon.**

(Month) Du'ūzu (June/July/August), third day: the gods of Uruk entered from Babylon into Uruk.

In (the month) Tašrītu (September/October/November), 23rd day, Humbahaldašu king of Elam was struck at siesta time and [di]ed at [sun]set.

For (Unit 36.5) **eight years Humbahaldašu exercised kingship over** (lit. **of**) **the land of Elam.**

Another Humbahaldašu sat on the throne (i.e. **became king**) **in the land of Elam.**

(Month) Ṭebētu (December/January/February), day 20: Sennacherib, king of Assyria – his son killed [him] in a rebellion.

For [x] years Sennacherib exercised kingship over (lit. **of**) **the land of Assur.**

(From) the twentieth day of Ṭebētu to the second day of Addaru (February/March/April) the rebellion continued in the land of Assur.

(Month) Simanu (May/June/July), 18+(?)th day: Esarhaddon, his son, sat on the throne in the land of Assur.

Notes

1 gál! (text: tuk) means that the manuscripts have *tuk* (Bab. *rašû* **to acquire**), but that this is very likely an error for the (in Neo-Babylonian script) similar sign *gál* (Bab. *bašû* **to exist**).
2 *si-hi ina* for expected *si-hu ina* may be a *sandhi* spelling (Unit 44.3), with the *i* of *ina* eliding the *u* of *sīhu*.

CULTURE TIP

The Babylonian months were: *nisannu* (I), *ayyaru* (II), *simanu* (III), *du'ūzu* (IV), *abu* (V), *elūlu* (VI), *tašrītu* (VII), *arahsamna* (VIII), *kislīmu* (IX), *ṭebētu* or *kinūnu* (X), *šabāṭu* (XI), *addaru* (XII). These cannot be correlated on a one-to-one basis with our months (**March**, **April**, etc.), because of the use of intercalary months: the part of a year which a given Babylonian month comprised varied with the year in question.

27 *Doubly weak verbs*

In this unit you will learn:
▸ the forms of 'doubly weak' verbs.

Doubly weak verbs are those whose first and third root letters are weak. These include four common verbs: *edû* **to know**, *išû* **to have**, *elû* **to go up** and *(w)aṣû* **to go out**.

In principle, it is possible for two consecutive root letters to be weak. However, in such cases one of the two weak root letters usually becomes a glottal stop (sometimes known as a 'strong aleph'), which behaves like a normal consonant (and so can double). Thus for practical purposes the verb ceases to be doubly weak, and is inflected like a I-weak or III-weak verb.

e'ēlu **to bind** (I-weak, like *emēdu*)   *še'û* **to seek** (III-weak, like *leqû*)

27.1 Forms in the G, N, D and Š systems

Doubly weak verbs inflect like a I-weak verb at the front (i.e. before the second root letter), and a III-weak verb at the rear (i.e. after the second root letter). Their forms can be constructed by taking the front part from a I-weak form in the same person, tense and system, and the rear part from a III-weak form in the same person, tense and system. The second root letter doubles if it doubles in these forms of the I-weak and III-weak verbs.

For example, for the 3rd sg. G present, 3rd sg. G preterite and m. sg. Š imperative of the doubly weak verb *elû* **to go up** (*i*), you take the corresponding forms of a I-weak verb (e.g. *emēdu*) and a III-weak verb (e.g. *zenû*). The part which *elû* 'borrows' from these verbs is marked in bold in Table 26.

Table 26

	3rd sg. G pres.		
	II root letter		
emēdu:	***i***	mm	id
zenû:	ize	nn	***i***
elû:	*i*	*ll*	*i*

illi 'he/she/it goes up'

	3rd sg. G pret.		
	II root letter		
ī	m	id
iz	n	***i***
ī	*l*	*i*

īli 'he/she/it went up'

	m. sg. Š imp.		
	II root letter		
šū	m	id
šuz	n	***i***
šū	*l*	*i*

šūli 'make (s/o) go up!'

When the first root letter of the doubly weak verb is *w*, one takes a I-*w* verb and a III-weak verb. For example, for the 3rd sg. G present, 3rd sg. G preterite and m. sg. Š imperative of *waṣû* **to go out** (*i*), you can take the corresponding forms of *wabālu* and *banû*, as shown in Table 27.

Table 27

	3rd sg. G pres.			3rd m.sg. G pret.			m. sg. Š imp.		
		II root letter			II root letter			II root letter	
wabālu:	***u***	*bb*	*al*	***ū***	*b*	*il*	***šū***	*b*	*il*
banû:	*iba*	*nn*	***i***	*ib*	*n*	***i***	*šub*	*n*	***i***
waṣû:	*u*	*ṣṣ*	*i*	*ū*	*ṣ*	*i*	*šū*	*ṣ*	*i*
	uṣṣī 'he/she/it goes out'			*ūṣī* 'he/she/it went out'			'*šūṣī* make (s/o) go out!'		

27.2 Particularities of *išû* **to have** and *edû* **to know**

The two verbs *išû* **to have** and *edû* **to know** are used only in a small number of forms. In the G system they inflect like preterites, but they can refer to both the present and the past.

In both verbs the first person singular G is identical with the third person singular, and begins with *ī-*. The second person begins with *tī-*.

īde **I/he/she/it knows/knew**, *īšu/īši* **I/he/she/it have/has/had** (*īšu* is the older form)

For the imperative, both verbs use what is formally a precative:

lū tīde **Be aware (that ...)!** *lū tīši* **Have (... ready)!**

The 3rd sg. prec. of *edû* is *lū īde* **Let him be aware!**.

Both *išû* and *edû* can form statives, but these are rarely used. (The stative of *edû* can begin with *i* or *e*.)

MB *išâku* **I have**
OB *idâta* **You** (m. sg.) **know**
SB *lū edânikka* **May they** (f. pl.) **be known to you** (for *-ka* instead of *-ku* see Unit 19.4)

The 2nd f. sg. of *edû* is *tīdê* (from original *tīda'ī* – see Unit 47.1).

> **LANGUAGE TIP**
> In their ability to refer to both the present and the past, and also in the fact that *lū* does not contract with the following vowel, the forms of *išû* **to have** and *edû* **to know** which look like preterites actually behave like statives.

Exercise 27.1, Old and Middle Babylonian

The last two sentences are MB.

pi-i-ka la ***te-e-ni*** (sp. *tenni*)

ki-ma a-na ka-ši-im-m[a] ta-ak-la-a-k[u] at-ta (*atta* **you** m. sg.) *ú-ul* ***ti-de-e*** (question, see Unit 44.9)

^{d}utu ù ^{d}amar.utu *iq-bu-ma* (*-ma* **so**) *ke-er-rum ši-i ú-ul* ***ú-ṣí***

di-ib-ba-tum ma-at-tum ***i-li-a-am***

ma-tum ka-lu-ša a-na e-re-ši-im ***it-ta-ṣí***

ṣé-he-er-ni ù ṣé-he-er-ta-ni ká é.gal *ú-ul* ***ú-ṣí*** (see Unit 14.3) *ni-pa-ti-ka i-na nu-úr-pa-ri-im* ***šu-ṣí-a-am***

a-bu-ul-la ***a-ṣa-am*** *ú-ul e-le-i* (*ele"i*)

a-wi-le-e a-na ṣe-ri-ia ***šu-ri-a-nim***

an-ni-a-ti gu-ul-lu-la-ti-ka lu ***ti-de***

ri-ik-sa-ti-ia ú-ul ***e-en-ni***

i-du-ú *qar-ra-du-ut-ka* man^{meš} *i-ta-na-da-ru* (*ītanaddarū* **they constantly fear**) *qa-bal-k*⸢*a*⸣

ú-uṭ-ṭí *e-en* (sp. *īn*) *um-ma-na-at* kur *šu-me-ri u* uri^{ki} ^{d}*šá-maš* en *de-e-né* (sp. *dīni*)

Exercise 27.2, Standard Babylonian

qé-reb mur-⸢*ṣi*⸣*-šú mam-ma ul* ***i-de***

qu-ra-du ^{d}*èr-ra* ***ṣi-i-ma*** (do not translate *-ma*) *a-na* edin

The most important things to remember

1 The forms of doubly weak verbs can be created by taking the front part of a I-weak (or I-*w*) verb and the rear part of a III-weak verb.

2 *edû* **to know** and *išû* **to have** are unusual:

3 the first person singular is identical to the third person singular (*īde*, *īšu/īši*);

4 the same form can refer to past or present;

5 in the precative, *lū* does not contract with an initial vowel (*lū īde* **let him know**).

SELF CHECK

	I can ...
	... explain what 'doubly weak' verbs are
	... explain how to produce their forms by blending I-weak and III-weak forms
	... explain what is unusual about the forms of *išû*(*m*) and *edû*(*m*)
	... (in time): recite the forms of *išû*(*m*) and *edû*(*m*).

Reading D: Hammurapi laws 3–5

Hammurapi (the name is sometimes read Hammurabi) was a king who brought Babylon to prominence in the 18th century BC. He conquered a large area, which extended as far as the city of Mari, in Syria. Those interested in him may be pointed to the excellent book *Hammurabi of Babylon* by Dominique Charpin (London: I.B. Tauris, 2012).

At some point in his reign, Hammurapi (or authorities acting in his name) issued a collection of laws, with an elaborate prologue and epilogue. This was not the first collection of laws from Ancient Mesopotamia: there had already been some in Sumerian and at least one in Babylonian (the Codex Ešnunna). However, Hammurapi's is by far the best preserved.

The grammar of Hammurapi's laws is highly regular – especially as regards mimation (in terms of spelling, by contrast, it is sparing in its use of plene spellings). Also, the structures of the laws are predictable: the 'if' part is usually composed of a string of preterites followed by a perfect, all connected by *-ma*; the 'then' part is in the present. Impersonal 3rd masculine plurals (Unit 14.16) are common. Its linguistic consistency has made Hammurapi's laws a staple of Babylonian courses all over the world.

The stele is inscribed in Monumental Old Babylonian script (see Unit 1.5). Extremely high-quality photographs of the inscription on the stele can be found in Volume 4 of the *Mémoires de la Délegation en Perse* (by V. Scheil; Paris, 1902), freely available online (https://archive.org/details/mmoires04franuoft), pp. 212ff.

A highly faithful scale drawing of the signs (which it is instructive to compare with the electronically generated version) by Robert Francis Harper is available at: https://archive.org/stream/cu31924074445523. Law 3 starts at column V line 57 (Plate VIII).

LAWS 3 AND 4

This pair of laws pertains to false testimony. The first *šumma* **if** introduces the scenario as a whole; the next two *šummas* introduce sub-scenarios, whereby the case is a capital trial or a trial for goods.

Cuneiform

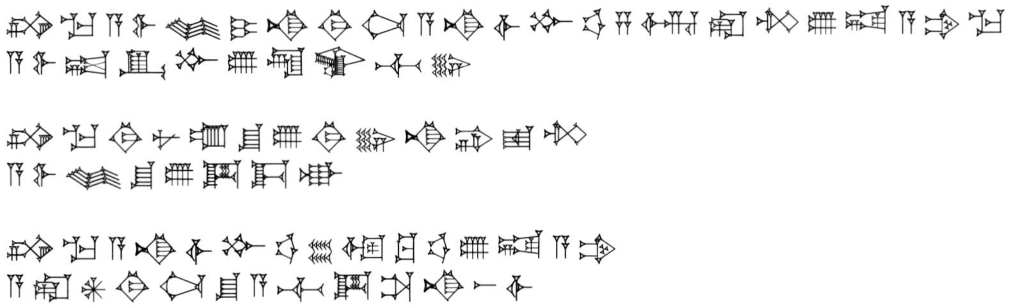

Transliteration

šum-ma a-wi-lum i-na di-nim a-na ši-bu-ut sà-ar-ra-tim ú-ṣi-a-am-ma
a-wa-at iq-bu-ú la uk-ti-in
šum-ma di-nu-um šu-ú di-in na-pí-iš-tim
a-wi-lum šu-ú id-da-ak

šum-ma a-na ši-bu-ut še ù ku.babbar *ú-ṣi-a-am*
a-ra-an di-nim šu-a-ti it-ta-na-aš-ši

Normalization

šumma awīlum ina dīnim ana šībūt sarrātim ūṣi'am-ma
awāt (or pl. *awât*) *iqbû* **(the utterance(s) which he spoke)** *lā uktīn*

šumma dīnum šū dīn napištim
awīlum šū iddâk

šumma ana šībūt îm u kaspim ūṣi'am
aran dīnim šuāti ittanašši **(he will bear)**

Translation

If a man came forth in a trial for (i.e. **to give**) **a testimony of lies** (i.e. **false testimony**)**, and**
he could not prove the word(s) he spoke,

If this trial is a trial of life (i.e. **a capital case**),
this man shall be put to death.

If (instead) he came forward for a testimony of (i.e. **pertaining to**) **grain or silver,**
he will bear the penalty of (i.e. **attaching to**) **this trial.**

LAW 5

This law pertains to a crooked judge.

Cuneiform

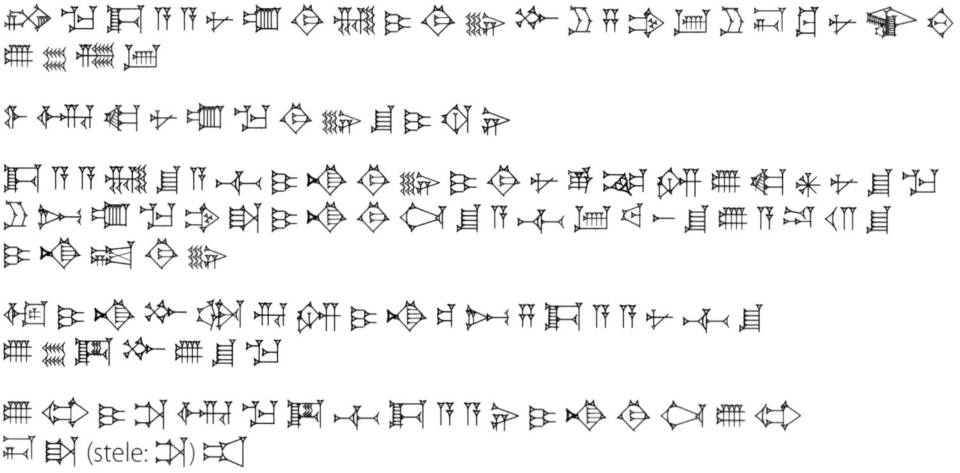

Transliteration

šum-ma da-a-a-nu-um di-nam i-di-in pu-ru-sà-am ip-ru-ús ku-nu-uk-kam ú-še-zi-ib

wa-ar-ka-nu-um-ma di-in-šu i-te-ni

da-a-a-nam šu-a-ti i-na di-in i-di-nu e-ne-em ú-ka-an-nu-šu-ma
ru-gu-um-ma-am ša i-na di-nim šu-a-ti ib-ba-aš-šu-ú a.rá 12-*šu i-na-ad-di-in*

ù i-na pu-úh-ri-im i-na gišgu.za *da-a-a-nu-ti-šu ú-še-et-bu-ú-šu-ma*

ú-ul i-ta-ar-ma it-ti da-a-a-ni i-na di-nim ú-ul uš-ša(stele:*ta!*)*-ab*

> **CULTURE TIP**
> It is far from certain that Ancient Mesopotamia had people employed full-time as judges, as we do today. Quite possibly, this was a role adopted as and when necessary by officials whose primary activities lay elsewhere.

Normalization

šumma dayyānum dīnam idīn purussâm iprus kunukkam ušēzib

warkānum-ma dīnšu īteni

dayyānam šuāti ina dīn idīnu enêm ukannūšu-ma
rugummâm ša ina dīnim šuāti ibbaššû adi 12-šu inaddin

u ina puhrim ina kussi dayyānūtišu ušetbûšu-ma

ul itâr-ma (see Unit 32.4) *itti dayyānī ina dīnim ul uššab*

Translation

If a judge gave (lit. **judged**) **a judgment, rendered** (lit. **decided**) **a verdict, had a sealed document issued,**

(but) subsequently changed his judgment,

'they' (see Unit 14.16) **will prove that judge (guilty) of** (lit. **in**) **changing the judgment which he gave** (lit. **judged**)**, and**

he will pay twelvefold the claim which arises in that lawsuit,

and in the assembly 'they' will evict him from the seat of his judgeship, and

he will never again sit in judgment with the judges.

28 *Three irregular verbs: alāku, izuzzu and itūlu*

In this unit you will learn:

- **the main forms of the only three properly irregular verbs in Babylonian.**

So far, you have met many different types of Babylonian verbs: strong, I-weak, II-weak, III-weak, doubly weak. In this unit you will be introduced to three irregular verbs: *alāku* **to go**, *izuzzu* **to stand** and *itūlu* **to lie down**. *alāku* occurs quite frequently; *izuzzu* is rarer, and *itūlu* is rarer still. *alāku* is slightly irregular, *izuzzu* ridiculously so.

28.1 The forms of *alāku(m)*

alāku occurs only in the G and Š systems (and their derived systems) – see Table 28. In the Š system, *alāku* behaves like a normal I-weak verb. The Š perfect is only attested in the assimilated form *ultālik*.

In the G system, present and preterite are distinguished only by the vowel alternation *a/i*. (Cf. the D and Š present and preterite of strong verbs and the G present and preterite of I-*w* verbs.)

Table 28

	G	Š
3rd sg. pres.	OB *īllak*, SB *illak*	*ušallak*
3rd sg. pret.	*illik*	*ušālik*
3rd sg. perf.	*ittalak*	*(uštālik)*
3rd sg. stat.	*alik*	*šūluk*
m. sg. imp.	*alik*	*šūlik*
inf.	*alāku(m)*	*šūluku(m)*

28.2 The forms of *izūzzu(m)*

It is not necessary to learn all the forms in Table 29. (Some are extremely rare.) Initially, just learn *izuzzu* (G inf.), *izzâz* (G pres.) and *izzīz* (G pret.), and whenever you come across a puzzling verb form that contains a *z*, come back to Table 29 to see if it might be a form of *izuzzu*. *izuzzu* is not attested in the D system. Its occurrences in the N system are extremely rare, and not taught here. (You can find the forms by consulting the dictionaries.) The basic forms in the G and Š systems are shown in Table 29. Prefixes and suffixes are the same as for strong verbs. When suffixes beginning with a vowel are added, the *z* in contact with the suffix doubles.

izzâz **he stands** → *izzazzū* **they** (m.) **stand**

Table 29

	G	Š
3rd sg. pres.	*izzâz*	*ušzaz* (1st mill. also *ušazzaz*)
3rd sg. pret.	*izzīz*	*ušziz* (1st mill. also *ušazziz*)
3rd sg. perf.	*ittaziz, ittašiz*	1st mill. *uštazziz*
3rd m. sg. stat.	*nazuz, nanzuz, ušaz, uzuz*	*šuzzuz*
m. sg. imp.	*iziz, išiz*	*šuziz* (1st mill. also *šuzziz*)
inf.	*izuzzu, uzuzzu, ušuzzu*	*šuzuzzu* (1st mill. also *šuzzuzzu*)

In the G system, present and preterite are distinguished only by the vowel alternation *a/i*. This recalls the D and Š present and preterite of strong verbs. Another similarity between the G system of *izuzzu* and the D and Š systems of strong verbs is that the perfect has the same vowel as the preterite rather than the present.

The G present is often used with stative meaning, instead of the stative.

28.3 The forms of *itūlu(m)*

Most of the forms in Table 30 are very rare. Forms in brackets are attested only after the Old Babylonian period. The forms of *itūlu* can be very difficult to separate from Gt forms of *nâlu* **to lie down**. Indeed, a strong case can be made that no verb *itūlu* exists, and that all the forms it is alleged to have actually belong to *nâlu*.

Table 30

	Gt	Gtn	D	Š
3rd sg. pres.	*ittâl, ittêl*			
3rd sg. pret.	*ittīl*	*(ittatīl)*	*uttīl*	*(ultīl)*
3rd sg. perf.	*ittatīl*			
3rd m. sg. stat.	*(utūl)*			
m. sg. imp.	*(itīl)*			
inf.	*itūlu, utūlu*			

Exercise 28.1, Old and Middle Babylonian

The last sentence is MB.

i-na i-di-šu ***i-zi-iz***

a-na-ku a-na i-si-in-na[ki] (*isinna* **Isin**) ***a-la-kam***

[giš]*di-im-tam* ***uš-zi-iz***

a-na a-wa-ti-šu ki-ma a-wa-ti-ni ***i-z[i]-iz***

il-li-ik-ma *a-na ši-ma-tu a-wi-lu-tim*

di-im-ti ù di-ma-ti e-li-ki ***li-li-ik*** (see Unit 14.3)

a-na ká.dingir.ra[ki] ***al-lik-kam****-ma* (see Unit 44.7) *ú-ul a-mu-ur-ki ma-di-iš az-zi-iq*

a-na ba-ab ga-gi-im ***a-li-ik***

pu-ul-lu-sa-ku-ma a-na ma-har a-bi-ia ú-ul ***al-li-kam***

i-nu-ma (*inūma* **when**) *uš-tu* ud.kib.nun^{ki} *a-na* ká.dingir.ra$^{k[i]}$ ***al-li-kam*** *i*[*t*]-[*t*]*i a-*[*w*]*i-lim ú-túl–ištar an-na-me-er*

a-***lik*** *ur-ha e-tiq šá-da-a*

a-na pa-ni ^{d}*a-ni i-na* ***ú-zu-zi-ka*** *a-ka-la ša mu-ti ú-ka-lu-ni-ik-ku-ma la-a ta-ka-al*

Exercise 28.2, Standard Babylonian

ga-na e ***ta-at-til*** 6 (*šeššet*) *ur-ri ù* 7 (*sebe*) *mu-šá-a-ti*

a-dak-ka-ma pa-na-tú-u-a (*panātuya* **ahead of me**) ***ú-šal-lak-ka*** (add **to the netherworld**)

nam-ri-ri an.šár *u* ^{d}*iš-tar is-hu-pu-šú-ma* ***il-li-ka*** *mah-hu-tíš*

The most important things to remember

1. Prefixes and suffixes for *alāku*, *izuzzu* and *itūlu* are the same as for strong verbs.
2. *illak* = **he/she/it goes**
3. *illik* = **he/she/it went**
4. *izzâz* = **he/she/it stands**; m. pl. *izzazzū* **they stand**
5. *izzīz* = **he/she/it stood**; m. pl. *izzizzū* **they stood**

SELF CHECK

	I can ...
	... recognise forms of *alāku*(*m*), *izuzzu*(*m*) and *itūlu*(*m*)
	... (in time:) recite the forms of *alāku*(*m*).

Part five

Clauses and sentences

29 *Verbless clauses*

In this unit you will learn:

- **more about how Babylonian expresses 'to be'**
- **when the stative can and cannot be used for this**
- **what verbless clauses are and how they work.**

For the English language, a useful definition of 'clause' is: a group of words which cluster around a verb. Some Babylonian clauses lack a verb, and hence are known as 'verbless clauses'.

Babylonian verbless clauses consist of a subject and 'predicate' (i.e. information which the clause supplies about the subject). The subject must be a noun (or a genitive construction) or pronoun. The predicate may be various things, including a noun or a prepositional phrase (see Unit 36.1). In English translation, the subject and predicate of Babylonian verbless clauses are linked by a form of the verb **to be**. (Thus, in translation, verbless clauses become verbal, and conform to the notion of 'clause' which English speakers are used to.)

29.1 To be in Babylonian

Babylonian does not employ a verb **to be** in the same way that English does. Occasionally, the verb *bašû* can be translated with English **to be**.

OB *kīma ilim tabašši* **You** (m. sg.) **are like a god** (Gilg. II 53)
OB *ana mīnim kī'am tabašši* **Why are you like this?** (AbB 9, 264: 28–29)
OB *ibrī naplis mātu kī mīn[i] ibašši* **My friend, look at the land – what is it like?** (Etana-Epos 198: 39)

However, such uses of *bašû* are rare. Usually, where English would use **to be**, Babylonian does not use *bašû*. Rather, it does two other things: one is to use the stative (e.g. *lemnētunu* **you** (m. pl.) **are evil**; see Unit 18); the other is to use 'verbless clauses'. Generally, if a stative can be used, it is. (Though occasionally a verbless clause is used where a stative could have been used.) However, there are some grammatical situations where the stative cannot be used, so verbless clauses have to be used there instead.

29.2 Situations where the stative cannot be used

Grammatical situations in which the stative cannot be used include the following:

- It is not possible to form the stative of a word which bears a possessive suffix, e.g. *šarrakunu* **your** (m. pl.) **king**.

- It is not possible to form the stative of a genitive construction, e.g. *šar māti* **king of the land**.
- It is not possible to form the stative of a noun qualified by an adjective, e.g. *šarru damqu* **good king**. (Note: the stative combination *šarrāku damqāku* does not mean **I am a good king** but **I am a king**, **I am good**.)
- It is not possible to form the stative of a prepositional phrase, e.g. *ina ēkalli*.

LEARNING TIP

The last three bullet points could be amalgamated by saying that it is impossible to form the stative of a group of words which belong together.

In situations like these, Babylonian uses verbless clauses instead of the stative. These make it possible to say things like **I am your king**, **I am a good king**, **I am king of the land**, and **I am in the palace**; also **Am I your king?**, **Am I a good king?**, **Am I king of the land?**, and **Am I in the palace?**. (The word order in Babylonian does not change from statement to question.)

29.3 Subject and predicate of verbless clauses

Like English clauses with the verb **to be**, Babylonian verbless clauses consist of a subject and a predicate. These can be identified by thinking of the equivalent English sentence: the subject in the Babylonian sentence = the subject of the verb **to be** in the English sentence; the predicate = what follows the verb **to be** in the English sentence. Usually, the subject precedes the predicate, but in poetic language the opposite can happen.

If the subject of a verbless sentence is an independent pronoun (see Unit 37), this usually goes at the end of the clause; unless it is followed by *-ma*, in which case it goes at the beginning.

ina aššur anāku **I am in Assur** (AbB 12, 58: 6)
anāku-ma rē'ûm mušallimum ša haṭṭašu išarat **I am a protective** (lit. **protector**) **shepherd whose staff is straight** (CH xlii.42–5)

The subject stands in the nominative case (though this is not always visible). The predicate may consist of a prepositional phrase, or a noun by itself, or a genitive construction, or a noun with possessive suffix (+ adjective), or a noun + adjective. The predicate also (when possible) stands in the nominative, and is often marked with *-ma*, though this is not obligatory.

29.4 Examples of verbless clauses

1 With prepositional phrases as predicate:

OB *tūša ṣābum mādum ittišu* **For sure a great army is with him** (i.e. **For sure there is a great army with him**) (ARM 26/2, 323: 4–5)

SB *ibrūtum ša ūmakk[al] kinātūtu ša darât[i]* **Friendship is for** (lit. **of**) **a single day, being colleagues is forever** (lit. **of eternity**) (BWL 259: 9–11)

2 With a noun or adjective standing by itself as predicate – the noun goes in the nominative case:

SB *annûm-ma simat ilūti suppû sullû u labān appi* **That which befits divinity is this: prayer, supplication and prostration** (BWL 104: 138–9)

(Usually, in this situation the stative is used instead.)

3 With a genitive construction as predicate – the first word of the genitive construction stands in the nominative (though this is usually not visible):

OB *awīlum šū bēl arnim* **This man is a criminal** (lit. **possessor of a sin**)**!** (ARM 26/2, 413: 11)
OB *šūt abnim-ma gilgameš mušēbirūya* **Those who enabled me to cross, O Gilgamesh, were the stone ones** (lit. **those of stone**) (Gilg. VA+BM: iv.22)

4 With a noun with possessive suffix as predicate – the noun goes in the nominative (though the case is not always visible):

OB *annûtum dayyānūya* **These (men) are my judges** (AbB 2, 106: 10)
OB *[ṣu]hārum šū mārūka-ma* **This boy is your son** (ARM 10, 104: r.8′)

5 With a noun + adjective as predicate – both go in the nominative:

OB *anāku-ma šarrum rabûm* **I am a great king**

29.5 Which tense in translation?

Which tense of the verb **to be** to use in translation is determined by context. Thus *awīltum-ma šī* (AbB 4, 147: 16) could mean **she was a lady**, **she is a lady**, or (more rarely) **she will be a lady**.

LANGUAGE TIP

In their non-specificity of tense, verbless sentences resemble the stative (to which they are also similar in meaning).

29.6 Negating verbless clauses

The same rules apply as for verbal clauses (see Unit 14.18): verbless clauses which make statements are negated by *ul*; verbless clauses which ask a question are negated by *lā* if there is a question word, and by *ul* if there is not. Sometimes in translation it is necessary to insert **it** as subject.

OB *ul awātī* **It is not my matter**, i.e. **It is nothing to do with me** (AbB 5, 26: 7′)

29.7 Verbless clauses with *lū*

If *lū* precedes the predicate, a verbless clause expresses a command or wish.

OB *lū awīlum atta* **Be a man!** (AbB 12, 58: 15)

SB *šillatum magrītum lū ikkibūka* **Let sacrilege and slander be things you abhor** (lit. **your abominations**) (BWL 100: 28)

29.8 Verbless clauses as questions

Verbless clauses can be used to ask questions. Like verbal clauses, they may or may not contain a question word.

OB *mannum–kīma–adad* **Who is like Adad?** (= personal name) (AbB 7, 175: 7)
OB *maruštī ula maruštaká u pištī ula pišatká* **Is your distress not my distress, and is an insult to you not an insult to me?** (lit. **... is my insult not your insult?**) (AbB 10, 207: 4–7)

29.9 Verbs within verbless clauses!

The basic structure of a verbless clause is 'X Y', or 'X Y-*ma*', or 'Y-*ma* X'. Sure enough, this structure involves no verb. It is possible, however, for a verb to be included *within* the entities X and/or Y, without affecting the overall structure.

OB *ša iqtanabbûkum sarrātum-ma* **What they keep on saying to you** (m. sg.) **is lies!** (AbB 5, 157: 12′–13′)

Here, the overarching structure follows the model 'X Y-*ma*', where X = **What they keep on saying to you** and Y = **lies**. Thus, at the level of overarching structure, this is a verbless clause. This does not stop it from containing a verb (*iqtanabbûkum*).

More will be said in the following unit about verbs being subsumed into larger entities and not affecting the overall structure.

Exercise 29.1, Old and Middle Babylonian

The last sentence is MB.

*šar-rum–ki-ma–*dingir

šum-gu-rum ù qá-bu-um it-ti-ka-ma

lu-ú lú *at-ta*

ma-an-nu-um (English would say **what?**) *šu-um-ka*

bi-ti bi-it-ka ù ki-si ki-is-ka

iš-tu pa-a-na (*ištu pana* **since previous times**) *bi-it-ni ù bi-it-k[a] iš-te-en-ma*

ši-ip-ru-um e-li ta-ši-im-ti-ka

ṣíl-lí–^{d}amar.utu

ú-ul [a]h-hu-ka-a ni-i-nu bi-ta-t[u]-ni ú-ul bi-it-ka-a (question, see Unit 44.9)

bi-tum šu-ú ú-u[l b]i-it aga.uš *bi-it* lú *èš-nun-na*^{ki}

ú-ul bi-it-ku-nu-ú (question)

šu-ú-ma ṣa-lam ^{d}bad *da-ru-ú*

Exercise 29.2, Standard Babylonian

da-bi-ib nu-ul-la-ti-ia dingir *re-ṣu-šú*

a-mur gul-gul-le-e šá egir^{meš} *u pa-nu-u-ti* (translate *(w)arkû* and *panû* as **low** and **high**) *a-a-u* (sp. *ayyû*) *be-el le-mut-tim-ma* (*-ma* **and**) *a-a-u* (sp. *ayyû*) *be-el ú-sa-ti*

a-ta (*atta* **you** (m. sg.)) *di-pa-ru-um-ma i-na-aṭ-ṭa-lu nu-úr-ka* (*nūrka* **by your light**) *na-pis-su-nu mu-tùm-ma*

at-ta (*atta* **you** (m. sg.)) *nam-ṣa-ru-um-ma*

The most important things to remember

1 Verbless clauses translate into English as clauses with a form of the verb **to be**.

2 Which tense of **to be** to use in translation is determined by context.

3 The subject and predicate both stand in the nominative case (unless the predicate is a prepositional phrase).

4 Verbless clauses follow the same rules for negation as verbal clauses.

5 The stative can also be used to express the idea of **to be**, but there are situations where a stative cannot be used, while a verbless clause can.

6 The notion of 'verblessness' means that there is no verb linking subject and predicate; verbs can appear within the subject and/or predicate, when these consist of a group of words.

SELF CHECK

	I can ...
	... explain how a Babylonian verbless clause works
	... translate a Babylonian verbless clause
	... explain how a verb might sneak its way into a verbless clause
	... negate a verbless clause.

Reading E: An anti-witchcraft incantation

Extract from the anti-witchcraft work *Maqlû* (Tablet, i.e. chapter, III lines 146–53). The speaker addresses the witch (hence 2nd f. sg. forms!), magically identifying him or herself with things in the natural world that are immune to sorcery. This shows the witch that the speaker is immune to her evil-doing.

The lines are cited after the composite text produced by Tzvi Abusch in his edition *The Magical Ceremony* Maqlû (Brill, 2015). The line divisions are original.

Cuneiform

The same remarks apply as for the cuneiform in Reading B.

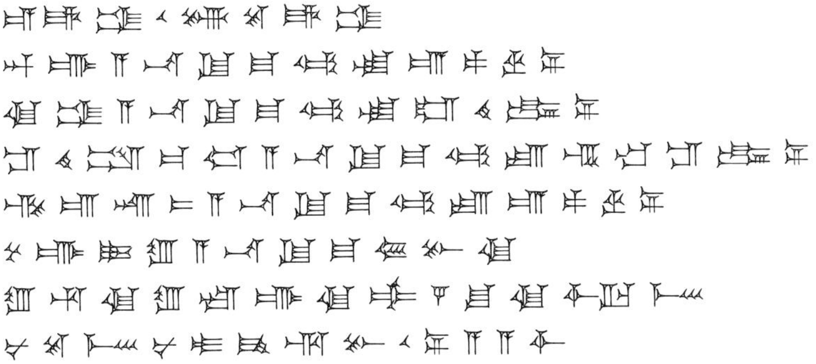

Transliteration

e-piš-tu$_4$ *u muš-te-piš-t[u*$_4$*]*

an-*ú a-na-ku-ma ul tu-lap-pa-tin-ni*

ki-*tu*$_4$ *a-na-ku-ma ul tu-ra-hi-in-ni*

si-hi-il ^{giš}nim *[a-n]a-ku-ma ul ta-kab-ba-si-in-ni*

zi-qit gír.tab *a-na-ku-ma ul ta-lap-pa-tin-ni*

kur-*ú zaq-ru a-na-ku-ma kiš-pu-ki*

ru-hu-ki ru-su-ú-ki up-šá-šu-ki hul^{meš}

nu te^{meš} nu *i-qar-[r]i-bu-u-ni a-a-ši*

Normalization

epištu u muštēpištu

šamû anāku-ma ul tulappatīnni

erṣetu anāku-ma ul turahhînni

sihil balti anāku-ma ul takabbasīnni

ziqit zuqāqīpi anāku-ma ul talappatīnni

šadû zaqru anāku-ma kišpūki

ruhûki rusûki upšāšūki lemnūti

ul iṭehhûni ul iqarribūni ayyâši (= *ana yâši* **to me**)

Translation

O sorceress and bewitcher,

I am heaven, so *(-ma)* **you cannot touch me.**

I am the earth, so you cannot seep over me.

I am thorn of *bāltu*-**bush, so you cannot tread on me.**

I am scorpion sting, so you cannot touch me.

I am a lofty mountain, so your magic,

your spells, your witchcraft, your evil machinations,

cannot approach me, cannot come near me.

Notes

1 *ū* **and** could also be **or**; **2** *-mā* means **so** here; **3** *erṣetu* **earth** could also mean **underworld**; **4** *turahhînni* and *iqarribūni* (without e-colouring) are Assyrianizing forms, corresponding to Babylonian *turehhînni* and *iqarribūni*; **5** unlike English **approach**, which takes a direct object, both *ṭehû* and *qerēbu* take *ana*: **to draw close <u>to</u>**; **6** *lemnūti* **evil** (m. pl.) could go with all of the preceding nouns, so the translation could also run **your evil magic, spells, witchcraft (and) machinations**; **7** the exact nuances of the magic-related words (*ēpištu*, *muštēpištu*, *kišpū*, *ruhû*, *rusû*, *upšāšū*) are difficult, so the translations are very approximate.

LANGUAGE TIP

ēpištu and *muštēpištu*, both participles (see Unit 35) from *epēšu* **to do**, super-literally mean **female doer** and **female get-(someone-else)-to-do-er**. Compare our use of **to do s/o in**, using **to do** in a sinister way.

30 *Clauses and sentences*

In this unit you will learn:

- **more about how clauses are put together**
- **what a subordinate clause is**
- **how the 'subordinative suffix' is used**
- **how Babylonian links clauses into sentences.**

You have already met quite a number of Babylonian clauses, and indeed sentences, in the examples and exercises. Nonetheless, what you have formally been taught so far has mostly been on a 'one-word-at-a-time' basis. In this unit we consider larger units of speech, first in terms of what happens within a clause, then in terms of how clauses can be joined into sentences, and placed one within the other ('subordination').

30.1 Recapitulation of clause structure

In prose, the verb goes at the end of the clause; in poetry it can go in other positions, most often antepenultimate.

The subject usually goes at the beginning of the clause.

In English translation, the Babylonian infinitive can give rise to additional clauses.

30.2 Reverse and anticipatory genitival constructions

You have already met three ways of forming genitival expressions:

1 *kaspum ša āli(m)*

2 *kasap āli(m)*

3 *ša āli(m) ... kasapšu*, all meaning **the city's silver**

A further permutation is possible:

4 *kasapšu ša āli(m)* **its silver of the city**, again meaning **the city's silver**

Construction **3)** is known as a 'reverse genitival construction (or: syntagm)' because, though the overall meaning is the same as in **1)**, the elements have been swapped round.

Construction **4)** may be termed 'anticipatory genitival construction' on the basis that the possessive suffix (-*šu*) anticipates the *ša*-phrase.

30.3 Choosing between genitival constructions

Babylonian is not alone in having multiple ways of expressing genitival relations (i.e. the notion **of**): English has two, **the parrot's beak** and **the beak of the parrot**. Sometimes one sounds more natural than the other (though it would not always be easy to say why), sometimes they can be used interchangeably.

The situation in Babylonian would seem to be similar: *bītu* **house(hold)**, for example, almost never takes *ša*. Thus *bīt awīli* **the man's house** would have sounded a lot more natural to a Babylonian ear than *bītu ša awīli*. Other words are more flexible. The overall patterns are still being worked out.

There is also an element of change over time, whereby *ša* is used more (and the construct state less) as the language evolves. In the second millennium, participles (see Unit 35) and infinitives (Unit 22) as first members of a genitival expression would normally take the construct state rather than *ša*, but in the first millennium *ša* is possible too. Construction **4)** is mostly used for family relations (e.g. *mārūšu ša awīli* **his son of the man**, i.e. **the son of the man**), and mostly in the first millennium.

30.4 Predicative complements

Consider the English sentence **Blueberries make most people happy**. The subject is **blueberries**. The verb is **make**. The direct object is **most people**. But what about **happy**? At some underlying level, the sentence basically means **Blueberries produce an effect such that people are happy** – here, **happy** is the predicate of the clause **people are happy**. Such expressions, which qualify the direct object but indirectly, are known as 'predicative complements'.

Another English example is **I pronounce you man and wife**: **man and wife** is predicative complement to **you**.

Predicative complements occasionally arise in Babylonian, and usually it is best to translate them with **as**:

OB *warhum ša īrrubam ulūlum šanûm l[i]ššaṭer* **The next month** (lit. **the month which is entering**) **should be registered** (lit. **written**) **(as) a second** *Ulūlu'* (AbB II 14, 15–16)
SB *adanna šamaš iškunamma* **(As) a deadline he set me Šamaš** (the sun god) (Gilg. XI 87)

Note how, the grammatical case of Šamaš not being marked by an ending, this could also be translated **Šamaš set me a deadline** – it is only context which allows one to decide.

SB *esagil u bābili ihsus šubassu* **He remembered Esagil and Babylon (as) his dwelling**, i.e. **He remembered that his (proper) dwelling was Esagil and Babylon** (AOAT 256 p. 516: i.32'–4')

30.5 The connective particle *-ma*

One of Babylonian's favourite ways of joining clauses into a sentence is to link them with the particle *-ma*. In prose, this goes on the verb. In poetry, it usually goes at whatever stands at the end of the clause (which may or may not be the verb).

Connective *-ma* indicates that the clause it is in and the following clause are closely connected. Some scholars think that, rather than linking two entities on an equal footing, it puts more emphasis on the second clause, presenting it as the outcome of the first. This is hard to prove.

In poetry, verbs at the start of a poetic line quite often have *-ma*, but apparently without connective meaning. Again in poetry *-ma* can move from the verb to another part of the clause, taking the connective function with it. Much about the functions of *-ma* in poetry still very likely has to be elucidated.

LANGUAGE TIP

In this course, a hyphen appears before *-ma* in normalization: *išpuram-ma* **He wrote to me, and ...**. This is simply for convenience. It would be perfectly reasonable to omit the hyphen, and indeed some Assyriologists do this.

In translation, clause-connective *-ma* can be rendered in several ways, and one is usually guided by the context. Sometimes it does not seem necessary to translate it at all. Sometimes **and** or **so** (more rarely: **but**) do the job. Here are some examples:

OB *murṣum iṣbatanni-<u>ma</u> ana mahar šāpiriya ul allikam* **A disease seized me, <u>so</u> I could not come into the presence of my master** (AbB 9, 42: 10–11)

OB *amtam ina bītiya rēdûm ikla-<u>ma</u> ina bītim ihliq* **The soldier locked the slave girl up in my house, <u>but</u> she escaped from the house** (AbB 6, 48: 5–6)

Sometimes, a free translation is called for:

OB *amši-<u>ma</u> ṣubātam ula addiššum* **I forgot to give him the garment** (lit. **I forgot, <u>and</u> I did not give him the garment**) (AbB 10, 185: 8–9)

Sometimes, *-ma* links clauses in a way that changes their meaning. These cases are discussed in the following unit.

-ma can also have non-connective functions, discussed in Unit 30.7.

30.6 The conjunction *u*

Babylonian clauses can be linked by the conjunction *u*, which is usually translated as **and** or **but** according to the context. This is used much less often than *-ma*. The precise nuances of *u* (and how it differs in meaning from *-ma*) are still being worked out, but it is generally thought that it establishes a looser connection between clauses than *-ma*. For the purposes of translation, in most cases *u* can be rendered as **and** or **but**. Be guided by the context.

SB *lipâ lā takkal* <u>*u*</u> *dāma lā teteṣṣi* **Do not eat fat, <u>and</u> you will not excrete blood** (BWL 240: 9–10)

Sometimes, *-ma* and *u* occur together (in that order), as in the first sentence of Exercise 20.2. The nuance of this is uncertain.

30.7 Non-connective *-ma*

As well as the clause-connective function just described, *-ma* can have the following non-connective functions:

1 Emphasis:

OB *ana bēltiya-ma taklāku* **I trust in <u>my lady</u>** (AbB 1, 53: 24–5)

Here, the emphasis could be rendered in translation by rephrasing, e.g. **It is in my lady that I trust**.

2 Cross-reference to something previously said, translating as **equally**, **likewise**, **also**.

In this function it is very common after *šanû* **(an)other**: the idea of 'another' inherently presupposes that we have already mentioned something, so it has an in-built cross-reference function, which therefore attracts *-ma*.

It is also common when a king's ancestors are noted as having the same epithets he does. An example appears in Reading A:

Assurnaṣirpal, great king, strong king, king of the Universe
the son of Tukultī-Ninurta, great king, strong king, king of the Universe,
the son of Adad-Nērārī, great king, strong king, king of the Universe-*ma*.

In English, the *-ma* can best be rendered as **who was likewise ...**

2a Sometimes, it seems that two *-mas* work together in this function:

ki-nam-ma tuš-ta-mit la ki-nam-ma tuš-ta-mit **Just as** (*-ma*) **you have killed the righteous one, so** (*-ma*) **you have killed the non-righteous one** (Erra IV 104–5).

3 In poetry *-ma* often occurs after prepositional phrases. Those introduced by *kīma* **like** may have it because of function 2.

4 On *-ma* in verbless clauses see Unit 29.3.

30.8 Subordinate clauses

So far we have been discussing how to link clauses in ways which, so to speak, keep them on a par with each other. However, as in English, it is possible for Babylonian clauses to be linked in such a way that one 'absorbs', or 'includes', the other: the 'absorbed' clause might function as the direct object of the verb in the 'absorbing' clause, or it might qualify a noun in the 'absorbing' clause, or the entire 'absorbed' clause might function as an adverb within the architecture of the 'absorbing' clause. This 'absorption' is made possible by particular words which introduce the clause to be 'absorbed'.

Here are some English examples of 'absorbed' clauses. The 'absorbed' clause is underlined, and the word which triggers the 'absorption' is marked in italics (many grammarians would say that the words in italics are themselves part of the 'absorbed' clause):

Did you know *that* <u>Nebuchadnezzar had a big beard</u>? (absorbed clause is direct object of 'know')
The flower pot *which* <u>sits on the shelf</u> is made of terracotta (absorbed clause qualifies 'flower pot')
***Where* <u>angels fear to tread</u>, devils make merry** (absorbed clause acts as adverb)

CULTURE TIP
At the Neo-Assyrian court, the phrase *ša ziqni* **one with** (lit. **of**) **a beard** was used to mean **non-eunuch**.

What we have been calling the 'absorbed' clause is generally known as a 'subordinate' clause; what we have been calling the 'absorbing' clause is generally known as a 'main' clause. Words which cause a clause to become subordinate (i.e. to be 'absorbed' by another clause) are known as 'subordinators'. Babylonian subordinators (to be discussed in the following sections) include:

- the word *šumma* **if**;
- words otherwise used as prepositions;
- nouns in the construct state.

Subordinate clauses in Babylonian are negated by *lā* (not *ul*).

30.9 *šumma* if

This is the simplest of all subordinators: it goes at the beginning of its clause, which precedes the main clause. Apart from the use of *lā* rather than *ul* for negation, the grammar of the subordinate clause is not affected by the presence of *šumma*. In other words, if *šumma* were removed, its clause would (discounting *lā* for *ul*) look exactly like a non-subordinate clause.

OB <u>*šumma awīlum makkūr ilim u ēkallim išriq*</u> *awīlum šū iddâk* **<u>If a man stole property from</u>** (lit. **of**) **<u>the temple</u>** (lit. **the god**) **<u>or the palace</u>, this man will be put to death** (CH § 6)
OB *aššum ê[m] ša tašpura[m]* <u>*šumma bulālu[m] haših*</u> *ana bulālum mudud* <u>*šumma itūr–salim haših*</u> *ana itūr–salim mudud-ma kanīkam liqe* **Regarding the grain which you wrote to me (about): <u>if Bulalum wants</u> (some), measure (some) out for Bulalum; <u>if Itur-salim wants</u> (some), measure (some) out for Itur-salim, and take a sealed document (as receipt)** (AbB 9, 84: 15–24)
SB *šumma* <u>*amīlu šārat lētīšu magal išahhuh*</u> *amīlu šū ilšu ištaršu ittišu zenû* **<u>If the hair on a man's cheeks is very loose</u>, that man's god (and) goddess** (lit. **that man, his god (and) goddess**) **are angry with him** (JMC 5, p. 13: 181')

30.10 Prepositions as subordinators

All (or nearly all) Babylonian prepositions can be used as subordinators. Thus the words which so far you have met as prepositions can be used in two different ways: as prepositions, in which case they introduce a noun in the genitive; or as subordinators, in which case they introduce a clause, causing it to become subordinate. Compare the following two sentences. The word *kīma* **like, as** functions as preposition in the first, and as subordinator in the second. The part introduced by *kīma* is highlighted in each case.

OB *kīma* **amtim** *ina bīt mutiša uššab* **She shall abide in her husband's household as a (female) slave** (CH § 141: 57–9)

OB *kīma* **udammiqakkunūši** *dummiqānim* **Do good to me, as I did good to you** (m. pl.)**!** (AbB 9, 53: 5–6)

The meanings attaching to the prepositional and subordinating uses of a given word are usually very similar, e.g. *aššu* **because of** (preposition), **because** (subordinator). The chief exceptions (from the point of view of an English speaker) are that as a preposition *ša* means **of**, while as a subordinator it means **which, who, whom** (i.e. it is a 'relative pronoun'); and that *kīma* as subordinator can mean **that** (as in **I know that ...**).

When a subordinate clause is introduced by a word which doubles as a preposition, the verb in the clause may take the suffix *-u* (see 30.12).

30.11 Nouns in the construct state as subordinators

In Unit 10 you learned that a noun in the construct state introduces a noun in the genitive. It is also, however, possible for a noun in the construct state to introduce a clause. When this happens, the noun in the construct state is functioning as a subordinator, so that the clause which it introduces is subordinate.

When a noun in the construct state acts as a subordinator, the English translation requires a word such as **which, who, whom, that** (i.e. a relative pronoun) between the subordinator and the clause. For example, compare the following two sentences. The word *qibīt* (construct state of *qibītu* **utterance, command**) introduces a genitive noun in the first, and an entire clause in the second:

OB *ina qibīt šarri mušēpiš[ūt]a ēpuš* **I acted as overseer by order of the king** (AbB 11, 83: r. 5'–6")
OB *qibīt ina mahrišin magrat dubub* **Speak an utterance which is pleasing to them** (lit. **... which is pleasing in their presence**)**!** (AbB 2, 83: 35–6)

Sometimes in translation it is necessary to insert a preposition before **which**.

OB *ina ereš nadâku dikianni* **Rouse me from the bed (in) which I lie!** (AbB 12, 99: 14)

Sentences in which a noun in the construct state acts as subordinator can be reformulated by introducing *ša* **which**. If this is done, the noun ceases to act as subordinator (this function being taken over by *ša*), and so ceases to be in the construct state. The translation stays the same. For example, the previous sentence *qibīt ina mahrišin magrat dubub* could be reformulated as *qibītam ša ina mahrišin magrat dubub* (same translation).

When a subordinate clause is introduced by a noun in the construct state, the verb in the clause may take the suffix *-u* (see below).

30.12 The verbal suffix *-u*

We have seen that prepositions, prepositional phrases and nouns in the construct state can all function as subordinators. Something these three categories have in common is that they can all introduce a noun in the genitive. Accordingly, when they introduce a clause, one could say that the clause occupies a 'slot' in a sentence which could otherwise be occupied by a noun in the genitive.

In these situations (i.e. when a subordinate clause occupies a 'slot' in a sentence which could otherwise be occupied by a noun in the genitive), a suffix *-u* attempts to attach itself to the verb in the subordinate clause. A good way to think of this is to regard the suffix *-u* as turning the entire clause into a noun: only then can the clause be introduced by words which want to be followed by a noun in the genitive; the subordinator *šumma* **if** does not have this requirement, so subordinate clauses introduced by *šumma* do not display the suffix *-u*, because they do not need to be turned into nouns. (This explanation is not necessarily the correct one, but it is a good way to think about the suffix *-u*.)

Some grammars call the suffix *-u* the 'subjunctive' suffix, others the 'subordinative' suffix. The latter term is better than the former (which unhelpfully puts one in mind of unrelated phenomena in other languages), but is itself not free of problems: *šumma* clauses are subordinate clauses, but the suffix does not appear in them. This course will simply call it 'the (verbal) suffix *-u*'.

In first millennium vernacular language, the suffix *-u* was lost at the end of strong and I-weak verbal forms (see Unit 47.6), but it was often still written.

30.13 The verbal suffix *-u*: where and when

The suffix *-u* attempts to position itself directly after the verb's third root letter (or, in the case of III-weak verbs, where the third root letter would be). Whether it is successful or not depends on what, if anything, directly follows the verbal form's third root letter:

- If nothing follows the third root letter (e.g. *tašpur* **you sent**), then the suffix *-u* successfully appears (*tašpuru*).
- If the third root letter is followed by a vowel (e.g. *tašpurī* **you** (f. sg.) **sent**, *tašpuram* **you** (m. sg.) **sent to me**, *išpurū* **they** (m.) **sent**), then the suffix *-u* is unsuccessful, and the form does not change.
- If the third root letter is in direct contact with a suffix pronoun beginning with a consonant (e.g. *tašpuršu* **you sent him**), the suffix *-u* successfully appears, positioning itself between the third root letter and suffix pronoun (*tašpurušu*).

- If the third root letter is in direct contact with the particle *-ma* (e.g. *tašpurma* **you sent, and …**), the suffix *-u* successfully appears, positioning itself between the third root letter and *-ma* (*tašpuru-ma*).

Some generalizations which follow from these rules are that:

- The suffix *-u* never appears in any form which has a ventive suffix;
- In the plural, in any combination of tense and system, the suffix *-u* only appears in the first person (but even here it can be ousted by the ventive and stative suffixes);
- In the stative, the suffix *-u* only appears in the third masculine singular (but even here it can be ousted by the ventive suffix).

Some examples in which *-u* successfully appears:

OB *kīma tuppī annī'am tāmmaru* **When you read this tablet of mine** (lit. **this my tablet**), **…** (AbB 14, 7: 8–9)

OB *inūma marūtuk šumka izkuru mādiš ahdu* **When Marduk mentioned your name, I was mightily glad** (AbB 10, 1: 7–8)

Some examples in which *-u* cannot appear:

OB *ṭēm bēlī išapparam ašapparakkum* **I will send you the report which** (see 30.11) **my lord sends me** (AbB 8, 11: 11–12)

OB *kīma ana marūtuk taklāku ana kâšu[m t]aklāku* **I trust in** (lit. **to**) **you as I trust in Marduk** (AbB 8, 99: 7–8)

LANGUAGE TIP

Since cuneiform spelling does not distinguish the suffix *-u* from the 3rd masculine plural suffix *-ū*, many cuneiform spellings (hence many transliterations) of third person forms are ambiguous: *ip-ru-su* could be *iprusu* or *iprusū* (3rd m. pl.).

30.14 Changes induced by the verbal suffix *-u*

Depending on the verbal form's syllabic structure, the addition of the suffix *-u* may induce vowel elision (see Unit 47.4).

iptaras **he has separated** → *iptarsu* (from *iptarasu*)
paris **he/it is separated** → *parsu* (from *parisu*)
OB *kīma ina tuppi ēkallim šaṭru* **As is written on the tablet of the palace …** (from *šaṭir* **it is written** + *u*) (AbB 14, 1: 36)

In III-weak verbs, when the suffix *-u* appears, it usually contracts with the immediately preceding vowel.

nibni **we built** → *nibnû* (from *nibniu*)
bani **it is built** → *banû* (from *baniu*)

In cuneiform, if the contracted *u*-vowel occurs at the end of a word, it is usually spelled *plene* (see Unit 44.2).

30.15 Verbless clauses as subordinate clauses

Like verbal clauses, verbless clauses can also be made subordinate. This is usually done by *šumma* and prepositions (very rarely, if ever, by nouns in the construct state). Like all subordinate clauses, verbless subordinate clauses are negated by *lā* (not *ul*). Apart from this, the grammar of verbless clauses is not affected by their being made subordinate. In other words, if its subordinator were removed, a subordinate verbless clause would (discounting *lā* for *ul*) look exactly like a non-subordinate verbless clause.

OB *šumma ina kīnātim abī atta* **If in truth you are my father** (AbB 5, 76: r.9')

> **CULTURE TIP**
> In Old Babylonian letters, **father** is used as an honorific term, and **brother** as a term of familiarity or endearment: they do not always literally mean that the correspondents are parent and offspring, or siblings.

OB *kīma napišti māti eqlum-ma ul tīdê* **Do you** (f. sg.) **not know that the life of the land is the field?** (AbB 9, 48: 14–15)
The ending *-u* does not appear in subordinate verbless clauses, because it only attaches to verb forms. (NB statives of nouns count as verbs, and make the clause verbal.)

30.16 Subordinate clauses within verbless clauses

As noted in Unit 29.9, though the overall structure of verbless clauses is something like 'X Y-*ma*', it is possible for the two entities X or Y to incorporate subordinate clauses which include verbs.

OB *itti ṣ̣ābī ša imuttū napištaka* **Your life will be with the troops who will die** (AbB 10, 66: 13–14)
SB *sinništu patri* (for earlier *patar*) *parzilli šēlu ša ikkisu kišād eṭl[i]* **Woman is a sharp iron dagger which slits** (lit. **slit**) **a man['s] throat** (BWL 146: 52)
SB *mīnum ṣābum [š]a anāku aṭarradu* **What is the troop which I shall dispatch?** (i.e. **Which troop am I supposed to dispatch?**) (ARM 26/2, 404: 68–9)

Exercise 30.1, Old Babylonian

ki-ma ***a-ša-ap-pa-ra-kum*** *e-pu-uš*

i-nu-ú-ma a-na-ku i-na da-na-tim ša be-li-ia ***ka-li-a-ku*** *re-du-ú bi-ti i-ma-ša-ú (imaššaʾū)*

iš-tu i-na a-li-ni ***wa-aš-bu*** *i-na* (translate *ina* as **in connection with**) *sà-ar-tim ma-ti-ma* (*matīma … ul* **never**) *šu-um-š[u] ú-ul ha-si-is*

nar *a-na* [lú]*su-ti-i* (*sutû* = **the Suteans**) ***ta-aṭ-ru-dam*** *ma-di-iš na-zi-iq*

ki-ma ki-na-ti ***a-da-ab-bu-bu*** *ma-ru-ús-si*

ki-ma ša (*kīma ša* **just as if … were**) *be-lí* ***ba-al-ṭú*** *a-na be-el-ti-ia-ma ta-ak-la-a-ku*

šum-ma lu-ú i-na a-hi-ia lu-ú (*lū … lū* **either … or**) *i-na ma-ar a-hi a-bi-ia ma-ma-an bi-tam* ***ú-da-ba-ab*** *ṭe$_4$-ma-am ga-am-r[a-am] šu-up-ra-am*

a-di ṣé-[e]h-ru la ***na-am-ru*** *i-na ú-ba-[n]e l[a] ta-la-pa-at* *a-di la* ***na-am-ra-at*** *ù ṣé-eh-r[e-e]t i-na ú-ba-ne la ta-la-pa-at*

ki-ma en-šum a-na da-an-nim ma-har be-lí-ia la ***iš-ša-ar-ra-ku*** ud.kib.nun^{ki} *ka-lu-šu li-mu-u[r]*

Exercise 30.2, Old Babylonian

a-šar ***i-qá-ab-bu-ú*** kù.babbar *lu-di-in*

ma-am-ma-an ša i-na i-di-šu ***iz-za-az-zu*** *ú-la i-ba-aš-ši*

ša-ap-ta-ka lu-ú ṭà-ba ki-ma i-na mu-uh-hi-ša ***ta-az-za-zu***

ki-ma a-wa-a-at ha-am-mu-ra-pí ***tu-um-mu-ra*** *i-na pa-ni-tim-ma a-na ṣe-er be-lí-ia áš-tap-ra-am*

érin$^{hi.a}$ *ša a-di a-na* larsam^{ki} ***a-al-la-ka-am*** *ù* ***a-tu-úr-ra-am*** *a-lam* ***ú-ša-al-la-mu*** *i-šu*

ma-li dingir^{meš} ***ú-ka-la-mu-ka*** *e-pu-úš*

ki-ma ***ta-qá-ab-bu-ú*** *in-ne-ep-pu-uš*

ki-ma ***ta-qá-ab-bi-i*** *li-in-ne-pu-uš*

šum-ma at-ti (*atti* **you** f. sg.) *te-ri-ši at-ti-i-ma* (*atti-ma* **so you** f. sg.) *ep-ši*

a-na ṣe-ru-ma (*ana ṣērum-ma* **furthermore**) *a-da-nam ša* ***iš-ša-ak-nu*** *tu-uš-te-ti-qá-ni-in-ni*

Exercise 30.3, Old Babylonian

i-nu-ma dingir^{meš} ***ib-nu-ú*** *a-wi-lu-tam mu-tam iš-ku-nu a-na a-wi-lu-tim ba-la-ṭám i-na qa-ti-šu-nu iṣ-ṣa-ab-tu*

a-di ***wa-aš-ba-a-ku*** *ṣi-bu-ut-ka li-pu-uš*

e-pe-šum ša ***te-pu-šu*** *da-mi-iq*

ia-a-ši-im (*yâšim* **to me**) *ma-ag-ri-a-tim ša a-na e-ṣé-nim la* ***na-ṭa-a*** *id-bu-ub*

a-šar wa-aš-ba-a-ku ^{uzu}*ú-ku-ul-tum a-na a-ka-li-ia ú-ul i-ba-aš-ši*

i-na a.šà*-lim ša* ***id-di-nu-ni-a-ši-im*** *ba-ma-as-sú mu-ú it-ba-lu ù ni-nu* (*nīnu* **we**) *ba-ri-a-nu*

be-lí at-ta (*atta* **you** m. sg.) *i-na qí-bi-it* ^{d}amar.utu *ba-n[i]-i-ka a-šar* ***ta-qá-ab-bu-ú*** *ta-am-ma-ag-ga-ar*

^{še}*a-am ša-ni-a-am ša um-ma-šu a-na ka-ši-im* (*kâšim* **you**, m. sg.) *ba-ba-lam* ***iq-bu-šum*** *a-na sà-bi-ti-šu im-ta-da-ad*

i-nu-ma kù.babbar ***im-ta-aq-ta*** *ú-ša-ba-la-ki-im*

Exercise 30.4, Old Babylonian

aš-šum ṣú-ha-ra-am a-na ti-nu-r[i-i]m [***i***]***d-du-ú*** [*a*]*t-tu-nu* (*attunu* **you** (m. pl.)) $^{[s]ag}$arad *a-na ú-tu-nim i-di-a* (see Unit 20.5)

ma-ru-um ša a-na a-bi la ***ú-ga-la-lu*** *ú-ul i-ba-aš-ši*

i-nu-ma wa-ar-du-um i-na bi-tim ***iṣ-ṣa-ab-tu*** *a-lu-um i-ša-al-šu-ma* dumu *nu-úr*–dingir.mah-*ma* (*nūr*–dingir.mah, personal name) *ih-sú-us* dumu a.zu *ú-ul ih-su-us* *a-di ṭe*$_4$*-e-em-ni* ***nu-ta-ra-kum*** é.gal-*lam la tu-la-ma-ad*

aš-šum (*aššum* **regarding**) gu$_4$ *ša* ***ša-a-ma-am*** *aq-bu-kum šum-ma* ***ta-áš-ta-a-ma*** gu$_4$ *šu-ri-a-am-ma* kù.babbar-*am lu-ša-bi-la-ku[m]*

túg *a-na pa-ni-ia ša-a-am-ma* (in translation insert **(if)** here) *a-na pa-ni-ia ú-ul ta-ša-am mi-im-ma ú-ul ra-i-mi* (*rā'imī* **one who loves me**) *at-ta it-ti-ka ú-ul a-da-bu-ub*

la-ma a-na ṣe-er bé-li-šu ***il-li-ka-am-ma*** *bé-el-šu* ***ú-lam-mi-du*** *li-ib-ba-šu ṭi-i-ib*

am-ši-i-ma ú-ul aq-bi-kum

šum-ma ***ṭà-ba-ak-kum*** *it-ti-ia li-il-li-ik*

Exercise 30.5, Middle Babylonian

ma-an-nu i-lu še-na (*šina* **two**, follows referent) *ša i-na ma-a-ti* ***ha-al-qú***

a-ma-ta ša ***aq-ba-ku*** *lu ṣa-ab-ta-ta* (translate *ṣabātu* as **to take on board**)

ṭe-e-ma ša ***áš-ku-nu-ka*** *la te-mé-ek-ki* (translate *ṭēmu* as **instructions**)

a-na sik-kàt hur-ša-ni ša-qu-ti ù gi-sal-lat kur-*i pa-áš-qa-a-te ša a-na ki-bi-is* lú *la-a* ***na-ṭu-ú*** egir-*šu-nu lu e-li*

ina murub$_4$ *šá la-lu-ka* ***iṣ-ru-pu*** *qé-reb-ka nu-up-piš*

an-nu-ú u$_4$*-mu šá da-am* ùg^{meš}-*ka* (see Unit 36.5) ***ú-ma-ka-ru*** *na-me-e qer-be-ti*

ul-tu ^{m}šeš–*da-ru-ú* (*ahu–darû*, personal name) ***i-mu-tu*** $^{m.d}$amar.utu–níg.du–ùru (*marūtuk–kudurrī–uṣur*, personal name) *ṭè-em-šu a-na* lugal *me-li–*^{d}*ši-pak ú-tir*

lú *ša-a-šu* (*šâšu* **that** m. acc. sg.) dingir^{meš} gal^{meš} *ma-la i-na* an-*e u* ki-*tim* (traditional spelling, normalize without mimation) mu-*šú-nu* ***zak-ru*** *ag-giš li-ru-ru-šu* (see Unit 19.9)

é ***ip-pu-šu*** *li-bé-el* (translate *bêlu* as **to be master in**) *ša-nu-um-ma* (see Unit 30.7)

a-di an *u* ki ***ba-šu-ú*** numun-*šu* (*zēru* **progeny** is from a III-weak root, see Unit 11.9) *li-ih-liq*

Exercise 30.6, Standard Babylonian

ge-er-ri an-nu-tu-ú ***i-ku-šu*** *a-la-ka tah-ši-ih* (question)

dingir^{meš} kur *šá* ***iz-nu-u*** *tu-šal-lam ana šub-ti-šu-nu*

a-me-lu ša sar-tam ***ip-pu-uš*** *šum-ma di-i-ku šum-ma* ⌜*ki*⌝*-ṣi šum-ma nu-up-pu-lu šum-ma ṣa-bit šum-ma ina* é *kil-lu na-di* (on the strength of *ṣa-bit* and *na-di*, take the other spellings as statives and normalise *dīk, kīṣ, nuppul*)

šá ***ih-ṭu-ka****-ma tuš-ta-mit šá la* ***ih-ṭu-ka****-ma tuš-ta-mit* (see Unit 30.7)

lugal *šá šu-mi* ***ú-šar-bu-ú*** *li-be-el kib-ra-a-ti*

a-mat ^{d}*èr-ra* ***iq-bu-ú*** ugu-*šú i-ṭib man-nu i-de ki-i* ***šak-na-ku*** *še-ret-ka*

mim-mu-ú ina ṣur-ri-ku-un ***ib-šu-u*** *li-in-né-pu-uš*

a-šar ***tal-la-ki*** *it-ti-ki lu-ul-lik*

Exercise 30.7, Standard Babylonian

A scene from the love life of equids:

anše.kur.ra *ti-bu-ú* (sp. *tebû* or *tēbû*) *ina* u[g]u *a-ta-ni* (sp. *atān*) *pa-re-e ki-i*⌜***e-lu-ú***⌝

ki-i šá (*kī ša* **while**) ***ra-ak-bu-ú-ma*** *ina uz-ni-šá ú-làh-ha-áš* (translate as past tense)

u[*m-ma m*]*u-ú-ru šá*⌜***tu-ul-li***⌝***-di*** (see Unit 47.8) *ki ia-ti* (*yâti* **me**) *lu la-si-im*

Advice on choosing a wife

e ta-hu-uz ha-rim-tum š[*á*] *šá-a-ri mu-tu-šá*

iš-ta-ri-tu šá a-na dingir ***zak-***⌜***rat***⌝

kul-ma-ši-tu šá qé-reb-ša ***ma-a'-d***[***a***]

ina ma-ru-uš-ti-ka-ma ul i-na-áš-ši-ka

ina ṣal-ti-ka-ma e-li-ka šá-an-ṣa-at

pa-la-hu u ka-na-ša ul i-ba-áš-ši it-ti-šá

On demons

a-lu-u lem-nu šá ki-ma bìr-qí ***it-ta-nab-ri-qu***

e-ṭém-mu lem-nu šá lú ***ih-ha-zu***

gal-lu-u lem-nu šá lú *im-tú* ***i-šá-qu-u***

šú-nu dumu *šip-ri lem-nu-t*[u_4] *šú-nu*

(translate *šunu* ... *šunu* as **they are ..., they are**)

The most important things to remember

1. Main clauses are most often joined by *-ma* **and, but, so**, less frequently by *u* **and, but**.
2. Subordinate clauses can be introduced (i.e. made subordinate) by *šumma* **if**, by prepositions (and prepositional phrases), and by nouns in the construct state.
3. In all subordinate clauses except those introduced by *šumma*, a suffix *-u* attempts to position itself after the third root letter, but it is thwarted (i.e. does not appear) if another vowel occupies that position.
4. In III-weak verbs, the suffix *-u* contracts with the vowel at the end of the 'core'.
5. The suffix *-u* can induce vowel elision (as per the rule in Unit 47.4).

SELF CHECK

	I can ...
	... translate *-ma*
	... explain what a subordinator is
	... explain what happens to the verb in subordinate clauses (except those introduced by *šumma*).

Reading F: A failed rebellion

This is the short sad story of a would-be rebel, as recounted in an inscription of Adad-Nērāri I, king of Assyria c. 1300 BC (RIMA 1, p. 136). Having failed to secure the support of the Hittites, the rebel goes on to meet a sticky end. You can read Kirk Grayson's edition of the full inscription online: http://oracc.museum.upenn.edu/riao/Q005740 (lines 4–20).

Cuneiform

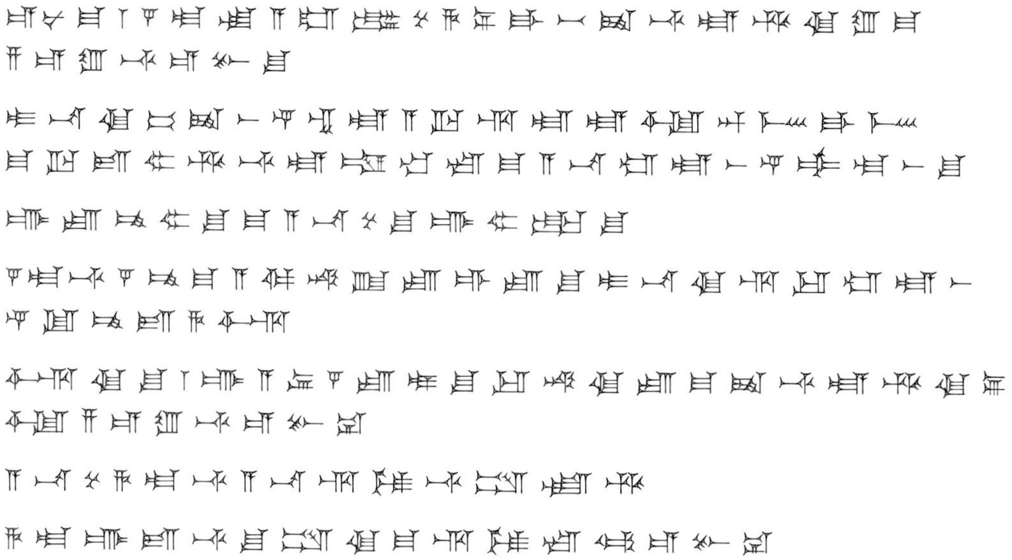

Transliteration

e-nu-ma ^{m}*šá-at-tu-a-ra* lugal kur *ha-ni-gal-bat it-ti-ia ik-ki-ru-ma za-e-ru-ti e-pu-šu*

i-na qí-bi-it aš-šur en-*ia a-lik re-ṣi-ia ù* dingir^{meš} gal^{meš} *ma-lik da-mi-iq-ti-ia aṣ-ba-su-ma a-na* uru-*ia aš-šur ub-la-aš-šu*

ú-ta-am-mi-šu-ma a-na kur-*šu ú-mé-šìr-šu*

šá-at-ti-šá-am-ma a-di bal-ṭu ta-mar-ta-šu i-na qé-re-eb uru-*ia aš-šur lu am-da-ha-ar*

ar-ki-šu ^{m}*ú-a-sa-šá-ta* dumu-*šu ib-bal-ki-ta-ma it-ti-ia ik-ki-ir ù za-e-ru-ti e-pu-uš*

a-na kur *ha-at-ti a-na re-ṣu-ti il-li-ik*

ha-at-<tu>-ú ṭa-ti-šu il-qé-ma re-ṣu-su ul e-pu-uš

Normalization

enūma šattuara šar māt hanigalbat ittiya ikkir-ma zā'erūtī ēpušu

ina qibīt aššur bēliya ālik rēṣiya u ilī rabûti mālik damiqtiya aṣbassu-ma ana āliya aššur ublaššu utammišu-ma ana mātišu umešširšu

šattišam-ma adi balṭu tāmartašu ina qereb āliya aššur lū amdahhar (= **I received regularly**)

arkišu uasašata mārūšu ibbalkitam-ma (see Unit 38) *ittiya ikkir u zā'erūtī ēpuš*

ana māt hatti ana rēṣūti illik hattû ṭâtišu ilqe-ma (*-ma* = **but**) *rēṣūssu ūl ēpuš*

Translation

When Šattuara, the king of the land of Hanigalbat, became enmitous to me and committed hostilities against me (lit. **my hostility**),

at the command of Assur, my lord, my helper, and the great gods who advise my favour, I seized him and brought him to my city, Assur.

I made him swear an oath (of loyalty) and released him to his land.

Year after year, so long as he was alive, I did regularly receive his audience gift in the middle of my city, Assur.

After him (i.e. **after he died**) **Uasašata** (or **Wasašata), his son, rebelled against me and became enmitous to me, and committed hostilities against me** (lit. **my hostility**).

He went for help (i.e. **to seek help**) **to the land of Hatti. The Hattian** (i.e. **Hittite**) **(king) accepted his bribes, but did not help him.**

31 *Particularities of relative clauses with ša*

In this unit you will learn:
- **how to say 'whose'**
- **other uses of *ša*.**

As noted in the previous unit, *ša* can act as a subordinator, i.e. make a clause subordinative. When it acts as subordinator, *ša* can have various meanings. These include **although**, **because** and **who/which**. This unit is about how to use *ša* with the meaning **who/which** (i.e. when it acts as a relative pronoun).

31.1 How to say **whose**

Babylonian does not have a word for **whose**. Instead, one uses a construction which literally would translate as **which/who … its/his/her/their**.

SB *kuppu ibrī libbaka ša lā iqattû naqab[šu]* **Your mind, my friend, is a spring whose water does not run out** (lit. **… a spring which – [its] water does not run out**) (BWL 70: 23)

31.2 *ša* the person who …, the thing which …

In English, words such as **which** and **who** (i.e. relative pronouns) always need a word before them, to which they refer (an 'antecedent'): **the bank which you want to rob**, **the guard who will try to stop you**. In Babylonian, clauses introduced by *ša* do not need an antecedent. When there is no antecedent, *ša* means (**the**) **one(s) who(m) …**, **the/a thing(s) which ….**

SB *ša naqba īmuru išdī māti* **The one who saw the deep, the foundations** (lit. **the two roots**) **of the land** (Gilg. I 1)

> **CULTURE TIP**
> In Babylonian mythology, deep below the surface of the earth were cosmic waters known as the *apsû*. The god of wisdom (Enki/Ea) dwelled there, and other deities originated in it. Some incantations were said to be 'from the *apsû*', implying they were invented by the god of wisdom.

SB *ša lamûšināti dannu agû tušezzeb atta* **You save the ones whom a mighty wave has surrounded** (BWL 136: 159)

SB *ša etelliš attallaku halāla almad* **I, who used to walk about like a lord, learned to creep** (lit. **learned creeping**) (BWL 34: 77)

Within the structure of the sentence, *ša* clauses without an antecedent occupy 'slots' which could otherwise be filled by nouns or pronouns. Thus a clause (or clauses) dependent on *ša* can be governed by a preposition.

SB *ana ša imhû bēlšu imšû nīš ilišu kabti qalliš izkuru anāku amšal* **I was identical to one who had become frenzied, forgotten his master, (and) lightly sworn a solemn oath on the life of his god** (BWL 38: 21–2a)
OB 10 (= *ešret*) *šiqil* (see Unit 40) *kaspam ana ša tuppātim ubbalakkum kaspam ṣarpam damqam idin* **Give ten shekels of silver – refined, good silver – to the one who brings you the tablets!** (AbB 7, 123: 15–19)

A *ša* clause without antecedent can act as subject or predicate in a verbless clause.

OB *mannum ša salīma[m] u damqātim lā hašhu* **Who is the one who does not want peace and good deeds?** (i.e. **Who does not want ...?**) (ARM 10, 140: 8–9)

A *ša* clause without antecedent can be used in the 'dangling construction' (see Unit 11.12).

OB *ša lā īšû šarram u šarratam bēlšu mannum* **One who does not have king or queen, who is his master?** (i.e. **Who is the master of one who ...?**) (BWL 277: 13–14)

31.3 *ša* which and prepositions

When *ša* has an antecedent (i.e. when it means **which** or **who** as opposed to **the person who ..., the thing which ...**), it cannot be governed by a preposition. In other words, Babylonian does not literally say **in which**, **like which**, etc. Often, the preposition is simply dropped.

OB *ālum ša wašbāk[u]* lit. **The city which I lived**, i.e. **The city in which I lived** (AbB 1, 26: 13)
OB *ištu ūmi ša abul sippir ūṣû nazqāku* **Since the day which he went through the gate of Sippar, I have been worried**, i.e. **Since the day on which ...** (AbB 2, 162: 14–26)

Exercise 31.1, Old Babylonian

mi-iq-tum im-qú-tam-[m]a **ša a-na a-si-im a-na-di-nu** *ú-ul i-šu-ú*

be-lí **ša e-li-šu ṭà-bu** *li-pu-úš*

ša ta-qá-ab-bu-ú *lu-pu-ša-ak-kum*

ša e-li-šu ki-iš-pí id-du-ú *id-da-ak*

ša šu-úr-qá-am i-na qá-ti-šu im-hu-ru *id-da-ak*

é **ša ka-li-a-ku** é *da-an-na-tim*

Exercise 31.2, Standard Babylonian

a-lu **šá kak-ka-šú la dan-nu** *na-ak-ru ina pa-an a-bu-ul-li-šú ul ip-paṭ-ṭar*

šá šuk-ṣu-ru *ta-paṭ-ṭar*

ša ana **man^{meš} ad^{meš}*-ia i-šu-ṭu-ma e-tap-pa-lu ze-ra-ti*** *ina qí-bit* ^{d}*aš-šur en-ia ina* šu^{2}*-ia im-ma-nu-ú*

man^{meš}*-ni a-ši-bu-te* (sp. *āšibūt*) *tam-tim* ***ša*** **bàd^{meš}*-šú-nu tam-tim-ma*** (see Unit 44.11) ***e-du-u šal-hu-šú-un ša ki-ma*** ^{giš}**gigir** ^{giš}**má** ***rak-bu ku-um*** **anše.kur.ra^{meš}*-e ṣa-an-du*** (assimilated from *ṣamdū*) ***par-ri-sa-ni*** *pal-hiš ul-ta-nap-šá-qu* (translate as past tense)

^{m}*ab-di–mi-il-ku-ut-ti* (*Abdi–milkutti*, personal name) lugal ^{uru}*ṣi-dun-ni la pa-lih be-lu-ti-ia la še-mu-u zi-kir šap-ti-ia* ***ša*** **ugu *tam-tim gal-la-tim it-tak-lu-ma iṣ-lu-u*** ^{giš}**šudun** ^{d}***aš-šur*** ^{uru}*ṣi-du-un-nu* uru *tuk-la-a-ti-šú ša qé-reb tam-tim na-du-ú a-bu-biš as-pu-un*

šá igi-gál-la-šu ^{giš}**tukul*-šú*** **érin *šu-a-tu*** (*šuātu* **this**) ***ik-mu-ú ik-šu-du i-na-ru*** *ina* ^{na4}na.dù.a *ul* sar (sar is a sumerogram for the 3rd sg. G pret. of *šaṭāru*)

The following poetic description of a mountain is taken from an inscription of Sargon II, king of Assyria from 721 to 705 BC. All verbs in lines 19–21 are dependent on the *ša* in line 19.

18 ^{kur}*si-mir-ri-a* (indeclinable name of a mountain) šu.si kur*-i* gal*-tu ša ki-ma še-lu-ut šu-kur-ri* ***zaq-pat-ma*** ugu *hur-šá-a-ni šu-bat* ^{d}*be-let–*dingir^{meš} ***šá-qa-at*** *re-e-ši*

19 *ša e-liš re-šá-a-šá šá-ma-mi* ***en-da-ma*** (*nd* is assimilated from *md*) *šap-la-nu šur-šu-šá* ***šuk-šud-du*** (ignore the *d* being doubled) *qé-reb a-ra-al-li*

20 *ù ki-ma* edin *nu-ú-ni i-di a-na i-di me-te-qa la* ***i-šá-at-ma*** *pa-niš ù ar-kiš* ***šum-ru-ṣu*** *mu-lu-ú-šá*

21 *i-na a-hi-šá* (dual!) *har-ri na-at-ba-ak* kur^{meš}*-e* ***iq-du-du-ú-ma*** *a-na i-tap-lu-us ni-ṭil* igi^{2} ***šit-pu-rat*** *pu-luh-tu*

In line **18** *ubān šadî* is in apposition to *simirria*; there is no main verb. In lines **18** and **19** *rēšu* **top** is dual but has sg. meaning; in line **19** the double *d* is an Assyrianism; in line **20** *idi ana idi* means **(from) side to side** and *i-šá-at-ma* is a stative of *isû* **to have** (see Unit 27.2).

CULTURE TIP

Sargon is a Biblical (Isaiah 20:1) modification of the original Assyrian name, which was probably *šarru-ukīn* **He (a god) made the king legitimate**. That Sargon II of Assyria should have chosen this as his throne name is suggestive, for his inscriptions never refer to his parentage, and he was probably a usurper.

The most important things to remember

1 The Babylonian for **whose** is literally **which ... its**, **who ... his/her/their**.

2 As well as just **which/who**, *ša* can mean **the thing which ...**, **the person/people who ...**.

3 In translating clauses introduced by *ša* **which**, it is sometimes necessary to add a preposition: **(in) which**, **(on) which**, etc.

SELF CHECK

	I can ...
	... explain the various meanings of *ša*
	... explain how to say 'whose' in Babylonian.

32 *The interrelation of clauses*

In this unit you will learn:
- **how clauses can change in meaning when they are joined together**
- **how to express purpose and result**
- **what 'verbal couples' are.**

When two Babylonian clauses are joined into a single sentence, it sometimes happens that the overall meaning is slightly different from that of the sum of its parts.

32.1 Precatives expressing purpose or result

When a clause containing a precative stands alone, the meaning of the precative is **let such-and-such happen**, **such-and-such should happen** (see Unit 21). However, when a clause containing a precative follows another clause, the clause containing the precative may have a nuance of purpose (**in order that, in order to**) or result (**with the effect that**). This applies both to precatives of action (*liprus*) and to precatives of state (*lū paris*). In most such cases the two clauses are linked by *-ma*.

Sometimes it can be difficult to decide between the nuances of purpose and result. In such cases it is useful to translate with the English phrase **so that**: this can also express both purpose and result, and so maintains the ambiguity of the Babylonian.

OB *šībī mūdi awātišunu ana bābilim ṭurdam-ma warkatum lipparis* **Send (some) witnesses who know their matter to Babylon, so that the facts can be established** (AbB 7, 108: r.6′–8′)
OB *[ma]har bēliki kurbī-ma [ašš]umiki lū šalmāku* **Pray [be]fore your** (f. sg.) **lord, so that for your sake I will be well!** (AbB 1, 31: 20–1)

Sometimes a loose translation is called for:

OB *mamman ša šakānika šukun-ma ina panī ummānim lillik* **Appoint anyone you want** (lit. **anyone of your appointing**) **to lead the army** (lit. **so that he will go before the army**) (AbB 9, 217: 19–23)

32.2 *-ma* expressing purpose or result

A nuance of purpose or result can arise in a clause when it is joined to the previous clause by *-ma*.

OB *mīnum arnī-ma nārī īkimanni-ma ana etellim [i]ddin* **What was my fault** (i.e. **what fault had I committed**), **that he stole my canal from me and gave it to Etellum?** (AbB 9, 252: 4–8)

SB *ila tulammassu-ma* <u>*kī kalbi arkika ittanallak*</u> **You can train** (lit. **teach**) **a god** <u>**so that he will follow you about**</u> (lit. **walk about behind you**) **like a dog** (BWL 148: 60)

In such cases, a present in the clause following *-ma* is usually negated by *lā*.

OB *ṭēm sili'tiša šupram-ma lā anakkud* **Send me a report about** (lit. **of**) **her illness, so that I will not be afraid!** (AbB 10, 210: 11–13)
OB *kaspam šūbilam-ma alpum ina qātini lā uṣṣi* **Send me some silver, so that the ox will not leave our possession** (lit. **hands**)**!** (AbB 8, 78: 40–2)

32.3 *-ma* expressing **if**

When two clauses are joined by *-ma*, the sense of the first clause can be **if ...**. Usually in such cases the verbs in both clauses are in the present.

OB <u>*rīqūssu illakam-ma*</u> *kalbū īkkalūninni* <u>**If he comes back empty-handed**</u>**, dogs will eat me** (AbB 2, 83: 27–8)
OB <u>*ul tušeppešanni-ma*</u> *ittika ezenne* <u>**If you do not allow me to do (it)**</u>**, I will be angry with you** (AbB 3, 2: 49–50)

This is analogous to certain English usages: **Touch my stamp collection, and I'll see you in court** really means **If you touch my stamp collection, I'll sue you**. However, in English such constructions are usually only employed when the first part is a command. In Babylonian, this need not be the case.

32.4 Verbal couples

Sometimes, given a sequence of two verbs in the same tense, one verb does not have the meaning it would if standing alone, but effectively functions as a modifier of the other verb.

In German Assyriology, such a construction is known as a *Koppelung*. English-speaking scholarship often terms it 'hendiadys' (as did the first edition of this course), but strictly speaking this is a misnomer: 'hendiadys' comes from the Ancient Greek for **one through two** (*hen dia duoin*), and it denotes cases where two entities mentioned by the speaker are supposed to coalesce in the hearer's mind into a single entity, which is distinct from the sum of the two. An English example is **law and order**: this is often not used to mean **law** *and* **order**, but to represent a more general idea of peaceful civil society, which does not otherwise have its own name. This course will therefore eschew the term 'hendiadys' for the behaviour of Babylonian verbs, and instead speak of 'verbal couples', inspired by the German term.

The two verbs in a verbal couple are usually (but not always) linked by *-ma*. In English translation, the verb which functions as a modifier is often rendered with an adverb or adverbial phrase, while the other verb retains the meaning it would have if standing alone.

OB *ul* <u>*itâr*</u>*-ma itti dayyānī ina dīnim ul uššab* **He will not sit in judgment with the judges** <u>**again**</u> (lit. **He will not return and he will not sit in judgment with the judges**) (CH § 5: 27)

OB *aššum eqlim šâti atūr ašpurakkum-ma* **I wrote to you again about that field** (lit. **About that field I returned and wrote to you**) (ARM 10, 108: 9–10)
OB *ašhiṭ awīlam* [*š*]*âtu aṣbat* **I hurriedly seized that man** (lit. **I jumped, I seized that man**) (ARM 2, 129: 24–5)
OB *awātam īniš-ma ana šarrim iqbi* **He spoke the word to the king in a moment of weakness** (lit. **The word, he became weak and spoke (it) to the king**) (AbB 10, 32: 5)

Dictionaries (and the Glossary at the end of this course) indicate how to translate a given verb when it is used as a modifier in verbal couples.

Exercise 32.1, Old and Middle Babylonian

The last two sentences are MB.

šu-up-ra-ma ar-ka-tam li-ip-ru-su-ni-ku-nu-ši-im

él-qé-ma a-na ši-bu-ut a-wa-tim ṣú-ba-ti aš-ru-uṭ

ša pa-ni-ni (*ša panīni* **that which is before us**) *i ni-ip-pa-li-is-ma*

ṭe$_4$*-ma-am ga-am-ra i ni-iš-pu-ra-ak-ku*

iš-tu i-na-an-na-ma da-ba-ba du-um-mu-qá-am it-ti-šu du-bu-um-ma (see Unit 47.9) *la i-ta-ar-ma ṣe-eh-ri la i-ṣa-ba-at*

ki-ma ṣuhārtum(^{munus}tur) *ši-i mi-ta-at qí-bí-šum-ma* (or *-bé-*) *lu-ú i-de*

a-na (translate *ana* as **beyond**) *a-da-an iš-ša-ap-ra-ak-kum tu-la-ba-da-am-ma* (sp. *tulappatam-ma*) *pa-nu-ka ú-ul ib-ba-*[*a*]*b-ba-lu*

ar-hi-iš a-pu-ul-šu-ma né-me-tam e-li-ka la i-ra-aš-ši

mi-nam te-pu-ša-an-ni-ma ṭa-ap-la-ti-ka a-da-ab-bu-ub

ú-ul a-ta-ar-ma ú-ul a-ša-ap-pa-ra-ku

a-na a-ii-i (*ayyî*, goes with *namrāṣi*) *ta-at-ták-kal nam-ra-ṣi-ma* (do not translate *-ma*) ùg^{meš}*-ka ti-ṭe-er* (sp. *teṭṭer*)

^{d}*gu-la a-zu-gal-la-tu be-el-tu* gal-*tu si-im-ma la-az-za i-na* su-*šu li-šab-ši-ma* lugud ù múd *ki-ma* a^{meš} *li-ir-tam-muk*

LANGUAGE TIP

In Babylonian similes, the verb is usually chosen to match the source of the comparison: a sentence such as **He flew to the top of the mountain like a bird** does not actually mean that anyone flew; **to fly** is simply used to match **bird**. The sentence could be translated **He (went) to the top of the mountain as (fast as) a bird flies**.

The most important things to remember

1 When clauses are joined into sentences, they do not always have exactly the same meaning they would if they stood on their own.

2 When they follow another clause (especially if linked to it by *-ma*), clauses containing precatives or presents may acquire a nuance of purpose or result.

3 When two clauses are linked by *-ma*, the sense of the first clause can be **if ...**.

4 Some verbs can give up their normal meaning, and function in such a way that they are translated as adverbs modifying other verbs. This course calls such constructions 'verbal couples'. A verb commonly used in verbal couples is *târu* **to (re)turn**: it has the meaning **again**.

SELF CHECK

	I can ...
	... explain how the meanings of clauses can change when they are put side by side
	... explain how a 'verbal couple' works, and how to translate it
	... explain what meanings precative clauses (i.e. clauses containing a precative) can take on when tagged onto a main clause.

Part six

Further topics

33 *The Gtn, Ntn, Dtn and Štn systems*

In this unit you will learn:

- **what the '*-tan-*' systems mean**
- **how to form them.**

So far you have studied the verbal G, N, D and Š systems. From these are derived four more verbal systems, known as the Gtn ('gee tee en'), Ntn, Dtn and Štn ('sheen tee en') systems.

It is convenient to think of the Gtn, Ntn, Dtn and Štn systems as having been created from their parent system by the insertion of an infix *-tan-* (though some scholars question whether this is historically accurate). The *-tan-* infix is visible in its entirety only in present forms. In other forms one can think of the *n* as either having assimilated to a following consonant, or having been removed to avoid a sequence of three consonants, which Babylonian does not tolerate (see Unit 47.13). In *e*-verbs, the *a* of the *-tan-* infix changes to *e*.

> **LANGUAGE TIP**
> The longest (or equal longest) Babylonian word was probably *tattanablakkatāniššunūšim* **You** (pl.) **will constantly revolt against them** (m.), Ntn present of the quadriliteral verb *nabalkutu(m)*. This form is not actually attested, but what it would have looked like can be deduced from attested forms.

33.1 The meaning of the Gtn, Ntn, Dtn and Štn systems

The Gtn, Ntn, Dtn and Štn systems normally have the same meaning as their parent systems (i.e. G, N, D, Š), with the addition of a nuance of repetition (so-called 'iterative' meaning) and/or graduality. In translation this is often conveyed with phrases such as **continually, constantly, bit by bit, gradually**.

OB *ilū mātim iptanahhurū ana ṭēmim* **The gods of the land came** (super-lit. **come**) **together for counsel, one by one** (SEAL 1.1.1.1: 6, Anzû)
SB *šumma amīlu mušaršu sinništa uštanaṣbat* **If a man is forever getting a woman to take hold of his penis, ...** (CT 39, 45: 28)

For some verbs, more specific translations are meet: the Gtn of *alāku* **to go** can be rendered as **to go back and forth, to go to and fro**. To decide how to translate the *-tan-* systems for a given verb, consult the Glossary at the end of this course (and later on the dictionaries).

It is not always necessary to preserve the nuance of the *-tan-* infix in translation. For example, in the phrase *šattišam amdahhar* (*amdahhar* = Gtn pret. of *mahāru* **to receive**) **I received (the tribute) year by year** (RIMA 3, 19: 29), the notion of repetition is already inherent in the English phrase **year by year**. To translate **I received (the tribute) on a regular basis year by year** or similar would arguably sound unnaturally heavy.

33.2 Forms in the Gtn, Ntn, Dtn and Štn systems

As in the G, N, D and Š systems, each verbal form consists in a 'core', determined by tense and system, to which prefixes and suffixes are added in accordance with the person, gender, and number of the subject.

LANGUAGE TIP

The tenses which are most frequently used in the *-tan-* systems are the present, preterite, imperative and infinitive. The perfect and stative are quite rare. The Ntn system is rarely used in any tense.

For strong verbs we give the 'cores' (most of which never stand alone), for weak verbs the 'basic forms' (see Unit 24.2). The system explained in Unit 5 is followed. Brackets indicate surmise: the form is not attested, but what is given in brackets is what it probably looked like.

Two exceptions (verbs with *n* as first root letter; verbs with *t*, *d*, *z*, *s* and *ṣ* as first root letter) are discussed later.

Strong verbs (core forms) are given in Table 31. The prefixes and suffixes are the same as for the G, N, D, and Š systems (see Unit 45). In place of *v*, insert the verb's theme vowel. For verbs with the two theme vowels *a/u* (e.g. *šakānu* **to put**), insert the first of these (*a*).

Table 31

	Gtn	Ntn	Dtn	Štn
pres.	*-PtanaRRvS*	*-ttanaPRvS*	*-PtanaRRaS*	*-štanaPRaS*
pret.	*-PtaRRvS*	*-ttaPRvS*	*-PtaRRiS*	*-štaPRiS*
perf.	*-PtataRRvS*	*(-ttataPRvS)*	*-PtataRRiS*	*-štataPRiS*
stat.	*PitaRRuS*	*itaPRuS*	*PutaRRuS*	*šutaPRuS*
imp.	*PitaRRvS*	*itaPRvS*	*PutaRRiS*	*šutaPRiS*
inf.	*PitaRRuSu(m)*	*itaPRuSu(m)*	*PutaRRuSu(m)*	*šutaPRuSu(m)*

v means: a short vowel which changes from verb to verb.

III-weak verbs (basic forms) are given in Table 32. In place of *v*, insert the verb's theme vowel.

Table 32

	Gtn	Ntn	Dtn	Štn
pres.	*iPtanaRRv*	*ittanaPRv*	*uPtanaRRa*	*uštanaPRa*
pret.	*iPtaRRv*	*ittaPRv*	*uPtaRRi*	*uštaPRi*
perf.	*iPtataRRv*	*(ittataPRv)*	*uPtataRRi*	*uštataPRi*
stat.	*PitaRRu*	*itaPRu*	*PutaRRu*	*šutaPRu*
imp.	*PitaRRv*	*itaPRv*	*PutaRRi*	*šutaPRi*
inf.	*PitaRRû(m)*	*itaPRû(m)*	*PutaRRû(m)*	*šutaPRû(m)*

v means: a short vowel which changes from verb to verb.

LEARNING TIP

Whereas in the D and Š systems present and preterite are distinguished only by vowel (pres. *a* vs pret. *i*), this is not so in the Dtn and Štn.

I-weak verbs (basic forms) are given in Table 33. In place of *v*, insert the verb's theme vowel. For verbs with the two theme vowels *a/u* (e.g. *šakānu* **to put**), insert the first of these (*a*).

Table 33

	Gtn	Ntn	Dtn	Štn
3rd sg. pres.	*ītanaRRvS*	*ittanaRRvS*	(*ūtanaRRaS*)	*uštanaRRaS*
3rd sg. pret.	*ītaRRvS*	*ittaRRvS*	*ūtaRRiS*	*uštaRRiS*
3rd sg. perf.	*ītataRRvS*	(unknown)	(*ūtataRRiS*)	(*uštataRRiS*)
3rd sg. m. stat.	(*ataRRuS*)	(unknown)	(*utaRRuS*)	*šutaRRuS*
m. sg. imp.	*ataRRvS*	(unknown)	*utaRRiS*	*šutaRRiS*
inf.	*ataRRuSu(m)*	(unknown)	(*utaRRuSu(m)*)	*šutaRRuSu(m)*

v means: a short vowel which changes from verb to verb.

II-weak verbs (basic forms) are given in Table 34. (The Štn and Ntn systems are not attested.) In place of *v* and *v̄*, insert the verb's theme vowel (respectively short and long).

Table 34

	Gtn	Dtn
pres. 3rd sg. 3rd pl.	*iPtanâS* *iPtanvSSū*	*uPtanāS* *uPtanaSSū*
pret. 3rd sg. 3rd pl.	*iPtv̄S* *iPtvSSū*	*uPtīS* *uPtiSSū*
perf. 3rd sg.	(unknown)	(*uPtatīS*)
stat. 3rd sg. 3rd pl.	(unknown) (unknown)	*PutūS* *PutuSSū*
imp.	(unknown)	(unknown)
inf.	*PitayyuSu(m)*	*PutuSSu(m)*

v and *v̄* mean: a short or long vowel which changes from verb to verb.

I-*w* verbs of doing are given in Table 35. (The Ntn system is not attested.)

Table 35

	Gtn	Dtn	Štn
3rd sg. pres.	*ittanaRRaS*	(*ūtanaRRaS*)	*uštanaRRaS*
3rd sg. pret.	*ittaRRaS*	(*ūtataRRiS*)	(*uštaRRiS*)
3rd sg. perf.	(*ittataRRaS*)	(*ūtaRRiS*)	(*uštataRRiS*)
3rd sg. m. stat.	(*itaRRuS*)	(*utaRRuS*)	(*šutaRRuS*)
m. sg. imp.	*itaRRaS*	*utaRRiS*	(unknown)
inf.	*itaRRuSu(m)*	*utaRRuSu(m)*	(*šutaRRuSu(m)*)

33.3 Examples of *-tan-* forms

Gtn present and preterite of *parāsu* **to separate** (*a/u*) (**I separate(d) again and again**, **I constantly separate(d)**, etc.) are given in Table 36.

Table 36

	pres.	pret.
1st sg.	*aptanarras*	*aptarras*
2nd sg. m.	*taptanarras*	*taptarras*
2nd sg. f.	*taptanarrasī*	*taptarrasī*
3rd sg.	*iptanarras*	*iptarras*
1st pl.	*niptanarras*	*niptarras*
2nd pl.	*taptanarrasā*	*taptarrasā*
3rd pl. m.	*iptanarrasū*	*iptarrasū*
3rd f. pl.	*iptanarrasā*	*iptarrasā*

Gtn present and preterite of *maqātu* **to fall** (*u*) (**I fall/fell again and again, I constantly fall/fell**, etc.) are given in Table 37.

Table 37

	pres.	pret.
1st sg.	*amtanaqqut*	*amtaqqut*
2nd sg. m.	*tamtanaqqut*	*tamtaqqut*
2nd sg. f.	*tamtanaqqutī*	*tamtaqqutī*
3rd sg.	*imtanaqqut*	*imtaqqut*
1st pl.	*nimtanaqqut*	*nimtaqqut*
2nd pl.	*tamtanaqqutā*	*tamtaqqutā*
3rd pl. m.	*imtanaqqutū*	*imtaqqutū*
3rd pl. f.	*imtanaqqutā*	*imtaqqutā*

33.4 Assimilations

When the *t* of the *-tan-* infix is directly preceded by a consonant, assimilations take place with certain consonants. These are the same as for the perfect (see Unit 17.4).

33.5 *n* as first root letter

Verbs with *n* as first root letter lose this in all Gtn and Dtn forms where the first root letter *n* would appear at the start of the word).

33.6 *t, d, z, s* and *ṣ* as first root letter

In Gtn forms without prefix (i.e. stative, imperative, infinitive) of verbs with *t, d, z, s, ṣ* as first root letter, the infixed *t* and the first root letter change places. (Such instances are rare.)

Exercise 33.1, Old Babylonian

at-ti (*atti* **You, ...**) *li-ba-ki* [***i***]***m-ta-na-ra-aṣ***

u_4-mi-ša-am ***ab-ta-na-ak-ki***

an-ni-a-tim ***ta-aš-ta-na-pa-ri***

u_4-mi-ša-am i-na é-sag-íl (name of temple) ***ak-ta-na-ra-ba-ak-kum***

ki-ma ***ta-ag-da-na-am-mi-la-an-ni*** *gi-im-la-an-ni*

at-tu-nu (*attunu* **you** (m. pl.)) *a-wa-tim* ***tu-uk-ta-na-ta-ma****-ma a-na ṣe-ri-ia ú-ul ta-ša-pa-ra-nim*

at-ta-na-ag-gi-iš *ki-ma ha-bi-lim qá-bal-tu* (see Unit 10.9) *ṣe-ri*

a-wa-tu-ka dam-qá-a-tum ***ik-ta-na-aš-ša-da-ni-in-ni***

a-na ṭe$_4$-mi ša ta-aš-pu-ri-im ma-di-iš ah-du

ma-ha-ar ištar ù ^{d}taš-me-tum ***ak-ta-na-ra-ba-ak-ki-im*** *ù a-lum ka-lu-šu ṭe-ma-am šu-a-ti* (*šuāti* **this**) *iš-me-ma i-ka-ar-ra-ba-ak-ki-im*

ma-ha-ar a-wi-le-e [*s*]*à-bi-i ṭa-ap-la-ti-ia* ***ta-ad-da-na-bu-bi***

CULTURE TIP

By age-old tradition, Mesopotamian temples always had Sumerian (not Babylonian or Assyrian) names.

Exercise 33.2, Old and Middle Babylonian

The last two sentences are MB.

mu-tam ša ***a-ta-na-ad-da-ru*** *a-ia* (see Unit 21.4) *a-mu-ur*

iš-tu u_4-mi-im ša ṭe$_4$-ma-am ša-a-tu (*šâtu* **this**) ***eš-mu-ú*** *ia-am-ṣí-ha-at-nu i-na* é.gal-*lim-ma ib-ta-na-ia-at* (translate as **has been ...**)

ša ***te-te-né-ep-pu-ši*** *šu-na-tu-ia it-ta-na-ab-ba-la-nim*

na-p[*í*]*-iš-ti* ***ta-ta-ak-ki-is***

iš-tu mu 3 kam (**for the last three years**; Bab. reading uncertain) *aš-šum* gú.un$^{hi.a}$ a.šà-*ia u* ka.kešda é-*ti-ia* ***aš-ta-na-ap-pa-ra-ak-kum-ma*** (translate **I have been ...**) *ú-ul ^{še}am ú-ul* kù.babbar *tu-ša-ab-ba-la-am*

é [*a*]*n-tum* (*antum* = name of goddess) ***ta-ah-ta-na-sà-ás***

a.šà-*ka ù bi-it-ka ú-ha-al-la-aq a-na bi-ti-ia-a-*[*ma*] *a-na* ***ši-ta-ar-ru-qí-im*** *qá-tam ta-aš-ta-ka-an*

a-na ***i-ta-az-zu-uz-zi*** *a-na ša-ši-im a-ah-ka la-a ta-na-an-di*

a-wi-il-tum a-wa-tim ma-di-iš uk-ta-ab-bi-it a-na ṣe-ru-ma (*ana ṣērumma* **in addition to**) *u_4-mi-ša-am* ***ri-ta-qú-di-im*** *i-na* ***ru-te-eš-ši-im*** *qá-qá-ad-ni ma-di-iš uq-ta-li-il*

ki-ma ^{d}nin-urta a-na ni-iš ^{giš}tukul^{meš}-*šu* ***ul-ta-nap-šá-qa*** *ka-liš* (*kalîš* **altogether**) ub^{meš}

ki-ma ur.gi$_7$ ***li-ib-ta-'i-i-ta*** *i-na re-bi-it* uru-*šu*

Exercise 33.3, Standard Babylonian

ep-šet ina kur.kur *nak-ra-a-ti* ***e-tep-pu-šú*** *ina ši-pir* ^{lú}*ur-ra-ku-ti e-si-qa qé-reb-šá* (*qerebša* **inside it**)

mi-qi-it-ti bu-li ***iš-ta-nak-ka-a***[***n***]

ina šá-ha-a-ti la ***ta-at-ta-na-áš-šá-ab-šú*** (translate *-šu* as **next to him**)

te-te-né-bir *ta-ma-tum* dagal-*tum šá-dil-ta*

[*at*]-*ta* (*atta* **you** (m. sg.)) *a-na* dingir-*ma su-pe-e* ***šu-taq-rib***

u$_4$*-mì-šam-ma* ***im-da-na-ha-ra*** ⌜^{d}utu⌝

šat-ta a-na šat-ti (year by year) ***bi-tak-ka-a*** *tal-ti-míš-šú*

šá u$_4$*-mi* (translate *ūmu* as **weather**) ***at-ta-ṭal*** *bu-na-šu* (see Unit 11.13)

^{d}*e-ta-na u-mì-šam-ma* ***im-ta-ah-ha-ra*** ^{d}utu

up-tah-hi-ir ^{d}*iš-tar ke-ez-re-e-ti* ^{munus}*šam-ha-a-ti u* ^{munus}kar.kid^{meš}

The most important things to remember

1. The *-tan-* systems have the same meaning as the parent stems, but with a nuance of repetition or graduality.
2. The same assimilations affect the *t* of the *-tan-* infix as affect the *t* of the perfect infix *-ta-*.
3. It is essential that you learn the G present and preterite (3rd sg. = *iptanarras* and *iptarras*); other forms are rarer.

SELF CHECK

	I can ...
	... explain the meaning of the *-tan-* infix
	... (in time): recite the *-tan-* forms
	... explain the sound changes undergone by *-tan-* forms.

Reading G: A Mari letter

The following letter was sent to Zimrī-Līm, king of Mari from c. 1775 to 1761 BC, when he was overthrown by Hammurapi of Babylon. It gives different accounts of the death of Zuzû (indeclinable), who had previously been king of the land of Apum but by this point had already been defeated. The Hanaeans are a group or tribe of nomadic pastoralists.

The letter is a fascinating case study in ancient communications, and in how an administrator might try to make sense of conflicting reports and establish facts.

The letter was edited by Dominique Charpin in J.-M. Durand (ed.), *Tell Mohammed Diyab – Campagnes* 1987 et 1988 (Paris, Sepoa: 1990), 120–2. The line divisions have been rearranged here, to provide grammatically complete units.

Cuneiform

The original tablet is written in Cursive (not Monumental) Old Babylonian. You can generate an electronic version in Cursive Old Babylonian using the Cuneifyplus tool, which will also enable you to insert spaces between words. For technical reasons, it is not possible to show damage to the signs (cf. square brackets in the transliteration). The *x* in the cuneiform indicates a sign which is hard to read (perhaps, as suggested in the transliteration, Ú). It may well have been erased by the ancient writer.

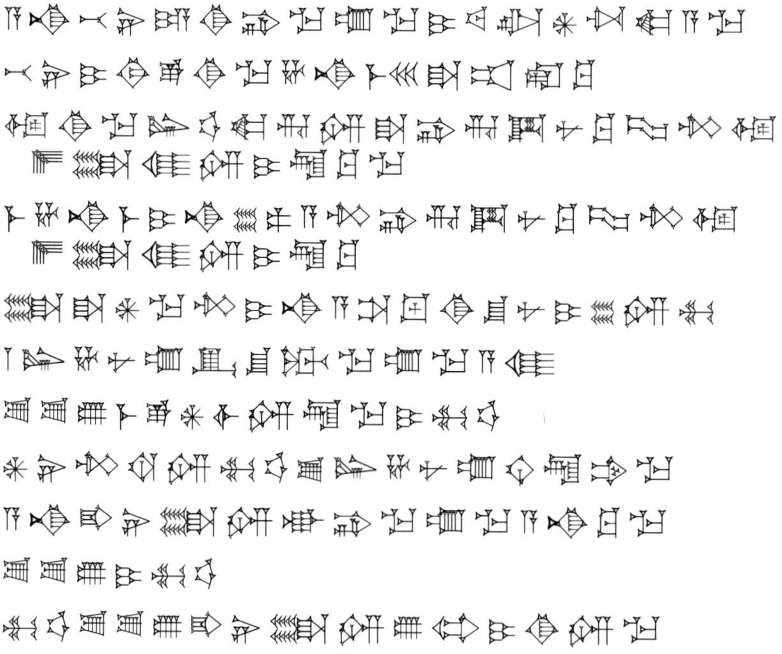

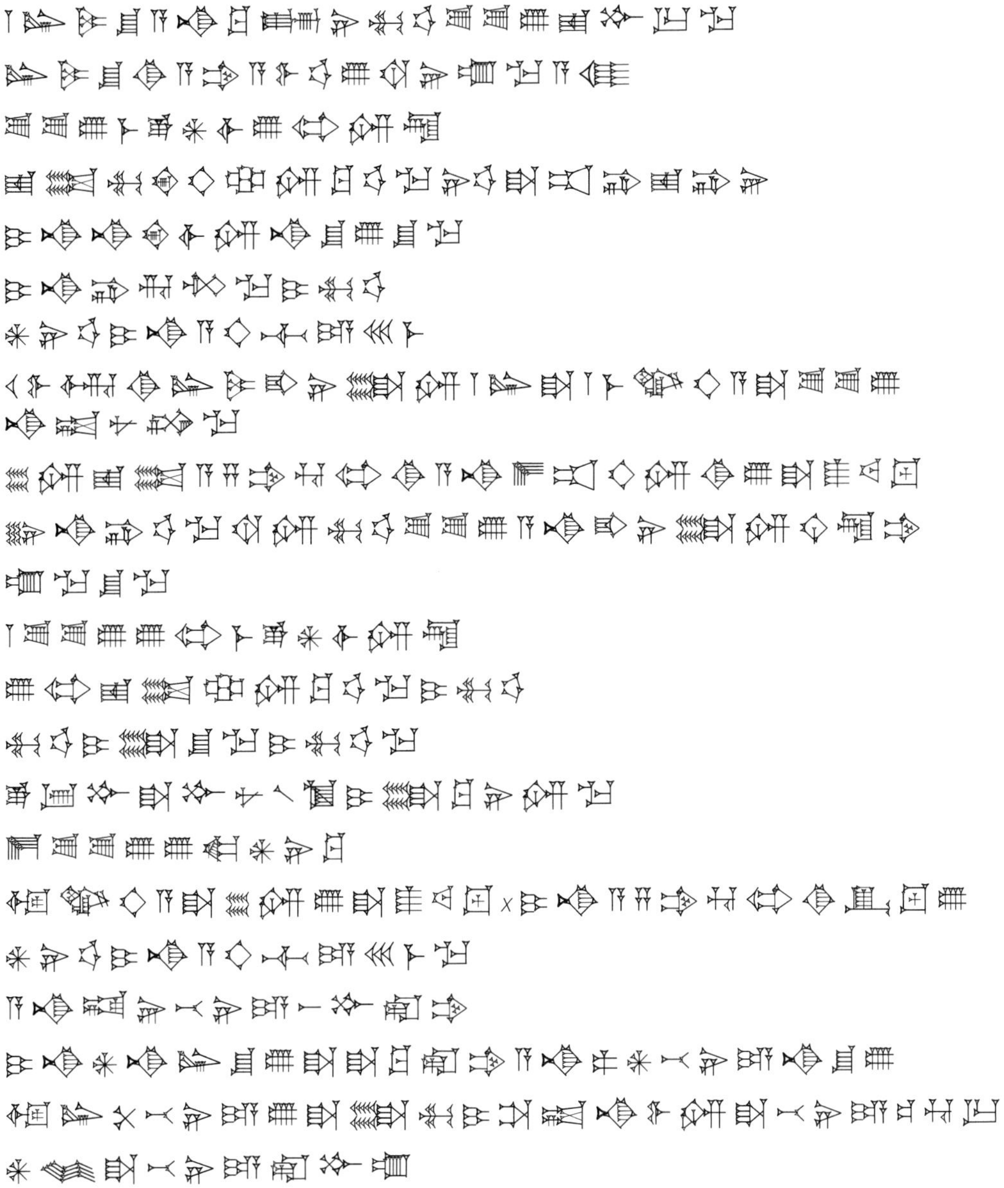

[2–3 line break]

[...] 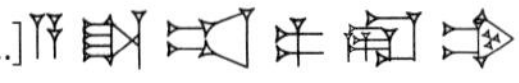

Transliteration

Quotation marks (which cuneiform does not use) have been inserted to mark direct speech as such.

*[a-n]a be-lí-i[a qí-bi-ma um]-ma i-ba-al–*dingir(*el*) ìr-*ka-a-[ma]*

be-lí i-de-e ki-ma ha.na^{meš} *ša-a[p-ra-ku]*

ù ki-ma ^{lú}*tam-ka-ri-im ša bi-r[i]-i[t] nu-ku-úr-tim ù sa-li-[mi-im] i-la-ku-ma* «*me*» ha.na^{méš} *i-na še-pa-a-t[im bi-ri-it] nu-ku-úr-tim ù sa-li-mi-im i-la-[ku]*

li-ša-an ma-tim i-na a-ta-lu-ki-šu-n[u í]-še-em-mu

1 ^{lú}*ha-nu-um ik-šu-dam-ma um-ma-a-mi*

"*[zu]-zu-ú me-e* dingir-*lim im-la-ma i-mu-ut*"

an-né-tim ṭe$_4$-em mu-ut-su (see note) ^{lú}*ha-nu-um ub-la-am-ma*

a-na qar-ni–li-im [a]q-bi-ma um-ma a-na-ku-ma

"*zu-zu-ú i-mu-ut*"

[mu-u]t zu-zu-ú qar-ni-li-im ú-ul i-qí-im-ma (assimilated from *i-qí-ip-ma*)

1 ^{lú}tur-*šu a-na ku-un-ni mu-ut zu-zu-[ú] i[š-p]u-⸢ur-ma⸣*

^{lú}tur-*šu ki-a-am a-wa-tam [ú-te-er um]-ma-a-mi*

"*zu-zu-ú [me-e* dingir-*lim ú-ul i]m-la*

iš-tu mu-uh-hi bàd *[im-q]ú-ut-ma* ⸢na$_4$⸣ *ša ap-pí iš-bi-ir*

[i-na] na-ah-ši-im na-šu-ú-šu-ma

[i-na] bi-ri-tim-ma i-mu-ut"

an-ni-tam i-na a-hi-ti-ia eš-me

⸢*u*⸣ *wa-ar-ki* ^{lú}tur *qar-ni-li-im* 1 lú *ša* 1 me anše$^{hi.a}$ *ša zu-zu-ú na-ad-nu-šum-ma*

^{še}*em iš-tu a-za-am-hu-ul*^{ki} *a-na sa-ap-hi-im*^{ki} *ú-ša-áz-ba-lu*

in-na-bi-tam-ma ṭe$_4$-em mu-ut zu-zu-ú ⸢*a-na*⸣ *qar-ni-li-im ub-la-am*

um-ma šu-ma

"^{I}*zu-zu-ú ú-ul me-e* dingir-*lim im-la*

ú-ul [i]š-tu bàd *im-qú-ut-ma i-mu-ut*

mu-ut i-li-šu-ma i-mu-ut-ma"

e-eb-bu ša bu-nu–iš$_8$-tár i-li-ku-ni-im-ma

é *zu-zu-ú ú-ka-an-ni-ku*

ù anše$^{hi.a}$ *ša* ^{še}*em ú-ša-áz-ba-lu* «*ú?*» *i-na a-za-am-hu-ul*^{ki} *ik-lu-ú*

an-ni-tam i-na a-hi-ti-ia eš-me-ma

[a]-na ṣe-er be-lí-ia aš-pu-ra-am

i-na-an-na lú *šu-ú ša ša-ku-ra-am a-na pa-an be-lí-ia [n]a-šu-ú*

ù ^{lú}kúr *be-lí-ia ú-ša-l[i-mu] [i-t]a-at na-we-em ša be-lí-[ia] [is-hu-ur]*

[din]gir-*lum ša be-lí-ia r[a-bu-um]*

[2–3 line break]

[…] *a-ša-ap-pa-ra-am*

Normalization

See comment to transliteration re quotation marks.

[an]a bēliy[a qibima um]ma ibāl–el waradka[ma]

bēlī īdé kīma hanê(?) ša[prāku]

u kīma tamkārim ša birī[t] nukurtim u salī[mim] illakū-ma

«me» hanû ina šēpāt[im birīt] nukurtim u salīmim illa[kū]

lišān mātim ina atallukišun[u (Gtn inf. *alākum*) *i]šemmû*

istēn hanûm ikšudam-ma umma-mi

"[zu]zû mê ilim imla-ma imūt"

annêtim (for *anniātim*, see Unit 47.1) *ṭēm mūtsu hanûm ublam-ma*

ana qarni–lim [a]qbi-ma umma anāku-ma

"zuzû imūt"

[mū]t zuzû qarnī–līm ul iqīm-ma

ištēn ṣuhāršu ana kunni mūt zuz[û] i[š-p]u⌜r-ma⌝

ṣuhāršu kī'am awātam [utēr um]ma-mi

"zuzû [mê ilim ul i]mla

ištu muhhi dūri [imq]ut-ma ⌜abnum⌝ ša appi išbir

[ina] nahšim našûšu-ma

[ina] birītim-ma imūt"

annītam ina ahītiya ešme

⌜u⌝ warki ṣuhār qarnī-līm ištēn awīlum ša (ištēn) meat imērī ša zuzû nadnūšum-ma

âm ištu azamhul ana saphim ušazbalu

innabitam-ma ṭēm mūt zuzû ⌜ana⌝ qarnī–līm ublam

umma šū-ma

"zuzû ul mê ilim imla

ul [i]štu dūrī imqut-ma imūt

mūt ilišu-ma imūt-ma"

ebbū ša būnū–ištar illikūnim-ma

bīt zuzû ukannikū

u imērī ša êm ušazbalu «ú?» ina azamhul iklû

annītam ina ahītiya ešme-ma

[a]na ṣēr bēliya ašpuram

inanna awīlum šū ša šakurram ana pan bēliya [n]ašû

u nakur bēliya ušall[imu] [it]ât nawêm ša be-lí-[ia] [ishur]

[i]lum ša bēliya r[abûm]

[2-3 line break]

[…] *ašapparam*

CULTURE TIP

Crime novelist Agatha Christie's second husband was the archaeologist Max Mallowan, so she was often to be found on excavations in the Middle East. Some of these experiences rubbed off onto her writing. One of the characters in *They Came to Baghdad* is said to have 'allowed his mind to dwell pleasantly on some aspects of the Mari letters'.

Translation

Say to my lord, thus your servant Ibāl–el

My lord knows that I am in charge of the Hanaeans,

and (that), like a merchant who goes between hostility and peace (perhaps meaning: **between hostile country and friendly country**),

the Hanaeans go on foot (lit. **feet) between hostile and friendly (country),**

(and) in their wanderings they hear the 'tongue of the land'.

One Hanaean came up to me, saying:

'Zuzû filled with god's water and died'

In these (words) the Hanaean brought me the report of his death, so

I spoke to Qarnī–līm as follows:

"Zuzû has died"

(But) Qarnī–lim didn't trust (the report of) Zuzû's death, so

he sent a servant of his to confirm Zuzû's death, and

his servant sent back a word thus:

"Zuzû did not fill with god's water and die (i.e. **did not die by filling with god's water**),

he fell from the top of the city wall, and the stone broke 'that of his nose' (i.e. **his nasal region**).

They carried him [in] *našhim*, but
he died in the meantime."

This (is what) I heard secondhand (lit. **around me**).

And after Qarnī–līm's servant, a man to whom a hundred donkeys belonging to Zuzû had been given,

and who should get (them) to carry barley from Azamhul to Saphum,

ran off and brought a report of Zuzû's death to Qarnī–līm.

Thus he:

"Zuzû did not fill with god's water and die (i.e. **did not die by filling with god's water**),

he did not fall from the city wall and die (i.e. **did not die by falling from the city wall**),

he died the death of his god (i.e. **a natural death**)'.

The emissaries of Būnū–Ištar came and

sealed Zuzû's house,

and held in Azamlû the donkeys which he was supposed to get to carry the barley.

This (is what) I heard secondhand (lit. **around me**),

and I have written to my lord.

Now this man, who holds a lance against my lord

and protects my lord's enemy, [has threatened] my lord's pasturelands.

The god of my lord is great,

I will send [my lord a full report as soon as I have received confirmation].

Notes

The letter includes several instances of the Mari phenomenon whereby *i+a* contracts to *ê* (including *êm* as the accusative of *ûm* **barley**).

The double chevrons around «*me*» indicate that it is not understood and was probably written in error.

ṭēm mu-ut-su **the report of his death** is grammatically odd: one expects *ṭēm mūtišu*. Since *-su* is written round the edge of the tablet, quite possibly the writer first intended to write *ṭēm mūt zuzû*, but having written *mu-ut,* which got to the end of the line, decided there would be not enough space for *zuzû*, and so compromised by adding an ungrammatical *-su*, trusting that the sense would be clear (as indeed it is).

The phrase [*i-na*] *na-ah-ši-im* is not clear. Jack Sasson (https://discoverarchive.vanderbilt.edu/bitstream/handle/1803/4005/OnReadingTheDiplomatic.pdf?sequence=1) amends it to [*i*]*-na mu!-ši-im* **at night**.

The translation indicates how the letter is likely to have ended.

34 *The Gt, Dt and Št systems*

In this unit you will learn:

- **what the '*-t-*' systems mean**
- **how to form them.**

The G, D and Š systems give rise to sub-systems created through the addition of the infix *-t-* (which often appears as *-ta-*). Unlike the *-tan-* infix, which has the same meanings across all four systems, the meaning of the *-t-* infix changes from one system to another.

34.1 Forms in the Gt, Dt and Št systems

The forms of the Gt, Dt and Št (pronounced 'gee tee, dee tee, sheen tee') systems for strong, III-weak, I-weak and II-weak verbs are given in the following tables, using the system explained in Unit 5. Two exceptions (verbs with *n* as first root letter; verbs with *t, d, z, s* and *ṣ* as first root letter) are discussed. Some comments relevant to all verbs, strong and weak, appear after the tables. For $Št_1$ and $Št_2$ see 34.7.

Strong verbs are given in Table 38; III-weak verbs in Table 39; I-weak verbs in Table 40. (After the Old Babylonian period, the pattern *atRvS* is sometimes replaced with *itRvS*, by analogy with strong verbs.) II-weak verbs are given in Table 41.

The following comments apply to all verbs, strong and weak:

- Forms with prefixes (present, preterite, perfect) have the infix *-ta-* (*-te-* in *e*-verbs); forms without prefix (imperative, stative, infinitive) have the infix *-it-*.

Table 38 – Strong

	Gt	Dt	Št
3rd sg. pres.	*iPtaRRvS*	*uPtaRRaS*	$Št_1$: *uštaPRaS* $Št_2$: *uštaPaRRaS*
3rd sg. pret.	*iPtaRvS*	*uPtaRRiS*	*uštaPRiS*
3rd sg. perf.	(*iPtatRvS* ?)	*uPtataRRiS*	*uštataPRiS*
3rd m. sg. stat.	*PitRuS*	(unknown)	(unknown)
m. sg. imp.	*PitRvS*	*PutaRRiS*	*šutaPRiS*
inf.	*PitRuSu(m)*	(*PutaRRuSu(m)*)	*šutaPRuSu(m)*

v means: a short vowel which changes from verb to verb.

Table 39 – III-weak

	Gt	Dt	Št
3rd sg. pres.	*iPtaRRv*	*uPtaRRa*	$Št_1$: *uštaPRa* $Št_2$: *uštaPaRRa*
3rd sg. pret.	*iPtaRv*	*uPtaRRi*	*uštaPRi*
3rd sg. perf.	(*iPtatRv ?*)	*uPtataRRi*	(*uštataPRi*)
3rd m. sg. stat.	*PitRu*	(unknown)	(*šutaPRu*)
m. sg. imp.	*PitRv*	*PutaRRi*	*šutaPRi*
inf.	*PitRû(m)*	(*PutaRRû(m)*)	*šutaPRû(m)*

v means: a short vowel which changes from verb to verb.

Table 40 – I-weak

	Gt	Dt	Št
3rd sg. pres.	*ītaRRvS*	*ūtaRRaS*	*uštaRRas*
3rd sg. pret.	*ītaRvS*	*ūtaRRiS*	*uštāRiS*
3rd sg. perf.	(*ītatRvS ?*)	*ūtataRRiS*	*uštatāRiS*
3rd m. sg. stat.	*atRvS*	(unknown)	*šutāRuS*
m. sg. imp.	*atRvS*	(unknown)	*šutāRiS*
inf.	*atRvSu(m)*	(*utaRRuSu(m)*)	*šutāRuSu(m)*

v means: a short vowel which changes from verb to verb.

Table 41 – II-weak

	Gt	Dt	Št
pres. 3rd sg.	*iPtâS*	*uPtāS*	$Št_1$: *uštaPāS* ($Št_2$ unknown)
3rd pl.	*iPtvSSū*	*uPtaSSū*	*uštaPaSSū*
pret.	*iPtāS*	*uPtīS*	*uštaPīS*
3rd pl.	*iPtāSū*	*uPtiSSū*	*uštaPīSū*
perf.	(*iPtatāS ?*)	(*uPtatīS*)	(unknown)
3rd pl.	(*iPtatāSū ?*)	*uPtatiSSū*	(unknown)
stat.	(*PitūS*)	(*PutuSSu(m) ?*)	(unknown)
3rd pl.	*PitūSu*	(*PutuSSu(m)*)	(unknown)
imp.	*PitāS*	(unknown)	(unknown)
2nd pl.	*PitāSā*	(unknown)	(unknown)
inf.	*PitūSu(m)*	(*PutuSSu(m) ?*)	(unknown)

v means: a short vowel which changes from verb to verb.

- The vowel which changes from verb to verb (symbol *v* in the tables) is the theme vowel; *a* for verbs with the theme vowels *a/u*).
- The stative and infinitive always have *u* between the second and the third root letter (in II- and III-weak verbs: in between where these two root letters would be).
- The Gt, Dt and Št preterite is always the same as the G, D and Š perfect.
- Apart from the present (Dtn *uPtanaRRaS*, Dt *uPtaRRaS*), all Dt forms are the same as the corresponding Dtn forms. The same probably applies for Št and Štn. (For Dtn and Štn forms, see Unit 33.2.)

- The existence of a Gt perfect is disputed. Dt and Št perfects are extremely rare, and not taught here.

34.2 *n* as first root letter

Verbs with *n* as first root letter lose this in all Gt and Dt forms where the first root letter *n* would appear at the start of the word.

34.3 *t, d, z, s* and *ṣ* as first root letter

In Gt forms without prefix (i.e. stative (hence also verbal adjective), imperative, infinitive) of verbs with *t, d, z, s, ṣ* as first root letter, the infixed *t* and the first root letter change places.

G *ṣabātu* **to seize** → Gt *tiṣbutu* **to seize each other**

34.4 Assimilations

When the *t* of the *-t-* infix is directly preceded by a consonant, assimilations take place with certain consonants. These are the same as for the perfect (see Unit 17.4).

34.5 The meanings of the Gt system

The meaning of the Gt system varies from verb to verb. The most common meanings are reciprocal, reflexive and separative; they respectively add **each other**, **oneself** and **away** to the meaning of the G system. (For a given verb, the Gt system usually has only one of these meanings, but see *šâlu* Gt: both reciprocal and reflexive.)

1 Reciprocal Gt

nakāpu **to butt (like an ox)**	→	*itkupu* (see section 34.2) **to butt each other, to fight**
rakābu **to ride**	→	*ritkubu* **(to ride each other**, i.e.**) to copulate**
awû **to talk**	→	*atwû* **to talk with each other**
malāku **to advise**	→	*mitluku* **to advise each other, to take counsel together**
šâlu **to ask**	→	*šitūlu* **to ask each other, to confer**

2 Reflexive Gt

šâlu **to ask**	→	Gt *šitūlu* **(to ask oneself**, i.e.**) to reflect**
pašāšu **to anoint**	→	*piššušu* **to anoint oneself** (from *pitšušu*)

CULTURE TIP

Did you know? In Ancient Mesopotamia, anointing did not just serve ritual and symbolic purposes. It was also a way of keeping warm – soldiers were issued with oil for this.

3 Separative Gt (verbs of motion and, more rarely, a few verbs that imply motion)

alāku G **to go** → Gt *atluku* **to go away**

elû G **to go up** → Gt *etlû* **to go up and away**
(w)aṣû **to go out** → Gt (infinitive form uncertain) **to go out and away**

For many verbs (e.g. *karābu* **to pray, to bless**) it is not clear how the meaning in the Gt system differs from the meaning in the G system. With rarer forms, there is often disagreement over whether they should be parsed as Gt (rather than G perfect or Gtn preterite).

34.6 The meanings of the Dt system

The Dt system is usually the passive counterpart to the D system.

šebēru D **to smash** → Dt *šitebburu* **to be smashed**

More rarely, the Dt system has a reciprocal function, adding **each other** to the meaning of the D system.

34.7 The two Št systems and their meanings

There are two Št systems, with different forms for the present tense but identical forms for other tenses. They are known as $Št_1$ and $Št_2$. The $Št_1$ system is usually the passive counterpart to the Š system.

lapātu Š **to destroy** → $Št_1$ *šutalputu* **to be destroyed**

The $Št_2$ system has meanings which vary from verb to verb. These meanings are not derived from the meaning of the Š system, and indeed verbs used in the $Št_2$ system are not necessarily used in the Š system at all. Rather, they tend to be related to the meaning of the Gt. The meanings of the $Št_2$ system should be sought in the dictionaries (and in the Glossary at the end of this course).

Exercise 34.1, Old and Middle Babylonian

The last three sentences are MB.

a-wi-lu-ú šu-nu (*šunu* **those**) *la* ***ud-da-ab-ba-bu***

i-ti-šu ***ti-iṣ-bu-ta-ku***

šuku-*ti* ***šu-ta-am-ṭa-a-at***

qa-aq-qa-da-ti-ku-nu ***šu-te$_9$-mi-da***

a-na-ku-ú ù ah-hu-ia a-na zi-it-tim ***ti-iṣ-bu-ta-nu***

ka-al-ba-tum i-na (*ina* **through**) ***šu-te-pu-ri-ša*** *hu-up-pu-du-tim ú-li-id*

bi-tam a-na pa-ni-ia (*ana panīya* **before my arrival**) ***šu-ta-as-sí-iq***

u⌜l i⌝b-ba-aš-ši ṭu-ub-tu ba-lu ***ši-it-nu-ni***

lu-ú-ba-ra (see Tip box) *ú-ka-lu-ni-ik-ku-ma* ***⌜li⌝-it-ba-aš*** *ša-am-na ú-ka-lu-ni-ku-ma* ***pí-iš-ša-aš***

LANGUAGE TIP

Sometimes, cuneiform signs are not inserted to be read in their own right, but to help the reader read the signs nearby ('aids to reading'). *lu-ú-ba-ra* (in Exercise 34.1) may be such a case: because the sign *LU* can also be read *dib*; upon seeing *LU-ba* the reader might have been tempted to read *dib-ba*. The otherwise redundant *-ú-* may be showing that *LU* is to be read *lu*, and not *dib*.

Exercise 34.2, Standard Babylonian

lit-pa-tu *i-mut mu-ti*

ub-tal-lil *ki-i* udu.níta *ina ta-ba-áš-ta-ni-ia*

u_4-mi-šam-ma dingir-*ka* ***kit-rab***

a-bi e ***tu-uš-ta-ni-ih***

a-na bu-ú-li ***kit-pad*** *e-re-šá* ***hi-is-sa-as***

lem-né-e-ti e ***ta-ta-me*** *da-me-eq-ta* ***ti-iz-kàr***

ge-er bu-li la-ba šá tah-su-su ga-na ***bi-it-ru*** *gi-il-lat* ur.mah *i-pu-šu pe-ta-as-su haš-tum*

liš-tap-ši-ih *šèr-ta-ka ka-bit-ta*

ur-ra ***ú-tak-ka-ak*** *mu-šá i-na-ah-hi-[is] ina ṣe-ri-šú* (*ina ṣērišu* **from him**) ***it-ku-šú*** *re-e-mu un-ni-[nu]*

^{d}amar.utu *e-li ma-aq-tu-ti* ***taš-ta-kan*** *gi-mil-la*

a-mur šu-ut-ta-tu qé-reb-šá ***bit-ri***

lu-ú ***mìn-du-da*** (see Unit 47.10–11) *mi-na-tu-šá* (*-ša* refers to a boat)

Exercise 34.3, Standard Babylonian

From an inscription of Assurbanipal, narrating the grisly end of an enemy king. (Translate *panuššu* as **in his eyes**).

ik-ku-ud lìb-ba-šú ir-šá-a na-qut-tu

na-piš-ta-šú pa-nu-uš-šú ul i-qir-ma

ih-šu-ha mi-tu-tu

a-na ^{lú}*ki-ze-e ra-ma-ni-šú iq-bi-ma*

um-ma ra-as-si-ban-ni (Ass. for *russibanni*) *ina* ^{giš}tukul

šu-u ^{lú}*ki-zu-šú ina* gír.an.bar *šib-bi-šú-nu* ***up-ta-at-ti-hu*** *a-ha-míš*

CULTURE TIP

A relief from the palace of the Assyrian king Assurbanipal depicts the king and his wife merrily banqueting in the garden. The head of the defeated Elamite king hangs from a nearby tree.

The most important things to remember

1. The Gt system has several meanings, including reflexive, reciprocal and separative.
2. The Dt system usually forms the passive of the D system.
3. The Št system forms the passive of the Š system. The meanings of the Št system vary from one verb to another.
4. The forms of the $Št_1$ and $Št_2$ systems differ only in the present ($Št_1$ *uštapras*, $Št_2$ *uštaparras*).
5. Whenever a form looks like a perfect, ask yourself whether it might in fact belong to the Gt, Dt or Št systems.

SELF CHECK

	I can ...
	... explain the meaning of the Gt, Dt and Št systems
	... (in time): recite the forms of the Gt, Dt and Št systems.

35 *Participles*

In this unit you will learn:

- **what 'participle' means in the context of Babylonian grammar**
- **how participles are formed**
- **how they are used.**

In Babylonian grammar, participles are words which mean 'person or thing who performs the action of the corresponding verb'. They occur in all the systems of the verb, and have separate forms for masculine and feminine. In the plural they can take noun endings, or adjective endings.

Feminine participles are formed by adding *-t-* or *-at-* to the masculine stem.

Participles often translate into English as relative clauses (**who ..., which ...**).

OB *šarrum nādin napištim ana utab* lit. **King, giver of life to Adab**, i.e. **The king who gives life to Adab** (CH Prologue iii.65–7)
OB *rīmum kadrum munakkip zā'irī* **Wild bull who butts the enemies** (CH Prologue iii.7–9)
OB *būnū namrūtum ša marūtuk rā'imika u adad bānîka limhurūka* **May the friendly faces of Marduk, who loves you, and Adad, who built you, meet you** (AbB 11, 119: 29–30)
OB *munawwir panī tišpak* **The one who brightens the face of Tišpak** (CH Prologue iv.34–5)

All participles except those in the G system begin with *mu-*.

35.1 Forms of masculine participles for strong verbs

Using the system explained in Unit 5, the masculine participles of strong verbs conform to the patterns shown in Table 42.

Table 42

G	N	D	Š
PāRiSu(m)	*muPPaRSu(m)*	*muPaRRiSu(m)*	*mušaPRiSu(m)*
Gtn	**Ntn**	**Dtn**	**Štn**
muPtaRRiSu(m)	*muttaPRiSu(m)*	*muPtaRRiSu(m)*	*muštaPRiSu(m)*
Gt		**Dt**	**Št**
muPtaRSu(m)		*muPtaRRiSu(m)*	*muštaPRiSu(m)*

35.2 Forms of masculine participles for III-weak verbs

Using the system explained in Unit 5, the participles of III-weak verbs conform to the patterns shown in Table 43.

Table 43

G	N	D	Š
PāRû(m)	*(muPPaRû(m))*	*muPaRRû(m)*	*mušaPRû(m)*
Gtn	**Ntn**	**Dtn**	**Štn**
muPtaRRû(m)	*muttaPRû(m)*	*muPtaRRû(m)*	*muštaPRû(m)*
Gt		**Dt**	**Št**
muPtaRû(m)		*muPtaRRû(m)*	*muštaPRû(m)*

35.3 Forms of masculine participles for I-weak verbs

Using the system explained in Unit 5, the masculine participles of I-weak verbs conform to the patterns shown in Table 44.

Table 44

G	N	D	Š
āRiSu(m)	*munnaRSu(m)*	*muRRiSu(m)*	*mušāRiSu(m)*
Gtn	**Ntn**	**Dtn**	**Štn**
mūtaRRiSu(m)	(unknown)	(unknown)	*muštaRRiSu(m)*
Gt		**Dt**	**Št**
(unknown)		(unknown)	*muštāRiSu(m)*

35.4 Forms of masculine participles for II-weak verbs

Using the system explained in Unit 5, whereby P and S represent a verb's first and third root letters, the masculine participles of II-weak verbs conform to the patterns shown in Table 45.

Table 45

G	N	D	Š
Pā'iSu(m)	(unknown)	*muPiSSu(m)*	*mušPīSu(m)*
Gtn	**Ntn**	**Dtn**	**Štn**
(unknown)	(unknown)	*muPtiSSu(m)?*	*muštaRRiSu(m)*
Gt		**Dt**	**Št**
muPtāSu(m)		*muPtiSSu(m)?*	*muštaPīSu(m)*

35.5 Plural endings

Masculine plural participles may take noun or adjective endings. (For feminine ones there is no difference.)

35.6 Unusual participles

A small number of weak verbs form G participles in *mu-*:

šâmu **to decree a destiny** → *mušīmu* **one who decrees a destiny**
dâku **to kill** → *mudīku* **one who kills**
idû **to know** → *mūdû* **one who knows**

35.7 A particularity of participle usage

When a participle is the subject of a verb from the same root and in the same system, it translates as **someone**.

OB *nādinānummi iddinam* **someone sold it to me** (super-lit. **a seller sold it to me**; ignoring *-mi*, which in elevated OB marks direct speech)

35.8 Participles in the stative

Grammatical tables of Babylonian verbs often present the participle as a form of the verb, in which case (somewhat stretching the notion of 'tense') it is a 'tense': it stands in a mutually exclusive relationship to other tenses such as the infinitive, the present, the imperative, etc.

In this scheme, the participle ought also to be in a mutually exclusive relationship with the stative. However, one can form the stative of a participle. This is because the participle is part-noun (as well as being part-adjective and part-verb), and so one can put it into the stative thanks to the principle that one can form the stative of nouns (Unit 18.8).

ina būlim māhiṣaku **Among the cattle I am one who strikes (them) down** (lit. **I am a striker**) (Erra I 112, see Exercise 18.6)

The most important things to remember

1. Babylonian participles have the meaning 'person or thing who performs the action of the corresponding verb'.
2. They have different forms for masculine and feminine.
3. In free English translation they are often best rendered as relative clauses (**who ...**).
4. Any word beginning with *mu-* is likely to be a participle.
5. The masculine participles of *parāsu* in the G, N, D and Š systems are *pārisu*, *mupparsu*, *muparrisu* and *mušaprisu*.
6. Like nouns, participles can be put in different states (basic, construct, possessive, etc.). Thus they can take case endings and possessive suffixes.

SELF CHECK

	I can ...
	... explain what a 'participle' is in the context of Babylonian grammar
	... (in time): recite the forms of participles for all systems.

36 *Adverbs*

In this unit you will learn:

- **how Babylonian forms adverbs**
- **how adverbs relate to adverbial phrases**
- **how adverbial phrases relate to prepositional phrases**
- **how Babylonian forms the 'locative'.**

An adverb is a word which answers questions such as **how?**, **when?**, **where?**, **how much?**. English examples are **thus**, **slowly**, **tomorrow**, **here**, **somewhere**, **enough**, **much**, **very**, **too**. Whilst understanding adverbs will deepen your knowledge of Babylonian and its structures, much of the information presented here is not essential to translation because you can simply look most adverbs up in the Glossary (later, in the dictionaries).

36.1 Adverbial phrases

When the questions **how?**, **when?**, **where?**, **how much?** are answered by a group of words rather than a single word (e.g. **like that** rather than **thus**; **in the house** rather than **there**; **at the beginning of the second millennium** BC rather than **then**) one speaks of an adverbial phrase (i.e. a phrase which has the same function as an adverb). Babylonian adverbs are often translated with English adverbial phrases, e.g. *šaddaqdi(m)* **last year**.

> **LANGUAGE TIP**
> The word *šaddaqdi(m)* **last year** is a compound (with some phonetic modification) of *šattu* **year** and *qadmu* **previous**. However, the word's origin was forgotten: the final *m* (a root letter from √*qdm*) was reinterpreted as mimation (see Unit 6.11), and so it was dropped in late Old Babylonian.

Many adverbial phrases are also prepositional phrases, and vice versa: the label depends on how one classifies them. The criterion for deciding whether a phrase is prepositional considers only the phrase itself: whether it is introduced by a preposition. To decide whether a phrase is adverbial, one needs to consider whether it is performing a function in the clause which could be occupied by an adverb.

36.2 Adverbs in *-iš* and *-āniš*

One way to transform Babylonian nouns and adjectives into adverbs is to add the suffix *-iš* to the stem.

abūbu **flood** → *abūbiš* **like a flood, like the Flood**
aggu **furious** → *aggiš* **furiously**

ayyābu **enemy** → *ayyābiš* **in a hostile manner**
danānu **power, might** → *danāniš* **violently, by strength**
elu **upperside** → *eliš* **above**
halāqu **to flee** → *halāqiš* **into flight**
išaru **correct** → *išariš* **correctly**
ištēn **one** → *ištēniš* **together** (lit. **one-ly**, **as one**)
kamâtu **the outside** → *kamâtiš* **to the outside**
mādu **much, many** → *mādiš* **greatly**
šalālu **to creep** → *šalāliš* **surreptitiously**
šallatu **booty** → *šallatiš* **as booty**
šuršu **root** → *šuršiš* **by the roots**

Sometimes, *-ān-* is inserted before *-iš*, producing the adverbial ending *-āniš*.

abūbu **flood** → *abūbāniš* **like a flood**
dūru **wall** → *dūrāniš* **over the wall**
zuqaqīpu **scorpion** → *zuqaqīpāniš* **like a scorpion**

The feminine *t* is removed before *-āniš* (but not before *-iš*).

aptu **window** → *apāniš* **through the window**
karpatu **pot** → *karpāniš* **like a pot**
sinništu **woman** → *sinnišāniš* **into a woman** (as in **to turn into a woman**)

There is no significant difference in meaning between the endings *-iš* and *-āniš*. They are both characteristic of elevated language, and mostly appear in literature. However, the adverbs *mādiš* **much** and *arhiš* **quickly** were common in everyday language.

36.3 Adverbs in *-iš* and *-āniš* followed by genitives and possessive suffixes

Adverbs in *-iš* and *-āniš* can be followed by a noun in the genitive, as if the adverb were a noun in the construct state. (But, unlike nouns, the adverb does not change in any way.)

dāriš ūmī **for** (-iš) **an eternity of days**, i.e. **for ever and ever**

Adverbs in *-iš* can be followed by a possessive suffix.

OB *bābiška* **at** (-iš) **your gate** (AH 48: 114)

When a suffix beginning with *š* is added to an adverb ending in *š*, despite what happens in nouns and verbs (see Units 11.7 and 19.3) *š* + *š* does not change to *ss*.

OB *šukkalliššu* **to** (-iš) **his** (-šu) **vizier** (Akkade 184: 13)

36.4 Adverbs in *-išam*

Another way of forming adverbs from nouns is to add *-išam* to the stem. The sense is usually **X by X**, **X after X**.

ūmišam **day by day**; **day after day**; *ugārišam* **meadow by meadow**; *ālišam* **town by town**; *šattišam* **year by year**, **year after year**; *(w)arhišam* **month by month**

Occasionally, there is a different meaning.

dārišam **for ever**; *eššišam* **anew**

In Standard Babylonian, *-išam* is often followed by *-ma* (*ūmišam-ma*, etc.), with no discernible change in meaning.

36.5 The accusative used as an adverb

Nouns in the accusative (singular or plural) can be used as adverbs ('adverbial accusatives'). They are usually rendered into English with adverbial phrases. Which preposition to use in English is suggested by context. If an accusative functions as an adverbial accusative, it cannot at the same time be the clause's direct object: the two functions (adverb vs direct object) are mutually exclusive.

OB *ina niziqtika mušiātim ul aṣallal* **Through worry for you I cannot sleep at night** (lit. **nights**) (AbB 14, 206: 33–5)
OB *huwawa maṣṣaram inēr-ma kaqqaram* **He smote Huwawa the guardian to the ground** (Gilg. Ishch. 26')
OB *mušītam allakam* **I will come during the night** (AbB 3, 66: 19)
OB *mūšī u urrī aktanarrabakku* **I pray constantly for you, day and night** (lit. **days and nights**) (AbB 7, 28: 14–16) (or see 36.6)

Adverbial accusatives of abstract nouns in *-ūt-* with possessive suffixes translate literally as **in my/your**, etc. **…-ness**.

ūmūssu (*ūmūt+šu*) **in its day(li)ness,** i.e. **every day**
OB *rīqūssu* (*rīqūt+šu*) *lā taṭarradaššu* **Do not send him in his emptiness** (i.e. **empty-handed**) (AbB 7, 173: 20)
OB *marṣūtī iṭrudūninni* **They sent me in my illness** (i.e. **while I was ill**) (AbB 7, 166: 3)
OB *[b]alṭūtka u šalmūtk[a] alkam* **Come in your healthiness and wellness** (i.e. **well and healthy**) (AbB 13, 140: r.6'–7')

Some accusatives have taken on a special adverbial meaning of their own, and are listed in dictionaries as words in their own right.

ūmu **day** → *ūma(m)* **today**; *urru* **day** → *urra(m)* **tomorrow**

The adverbial accusative is the origin of many prepositions and subordinators. For example, *qereb* can effectively be used as a preposition meaning **in**, and probably was perceived thus. But in origin it is the noun *qerbu* **middle**, in the construct state and (adverbial) accusative case: *qereb X* **in the middle of X**, coming just to mean **in X**.

Similarly, the subordinator *ašar* **where** is in origin the construct state, and (adverbial) accusative case, of the noun *ašru* **place**. The construct state is used to introduce a relative clause (see Unit 30.11), so *ašar* originally means **in the place which …**, whence it was a brief step to **where**.

36.6 Adverbs in *-ī*

A number of adverbs are formed with the ending *ī*, but at the end of a word this probably shortened to *i*.

bārārī or *bārāri* **at dusk**; *amšālī* or *amšāli* **yesterday**; *timālī* or *timāli* **yesterday**; *matīma* (*matī* + *ma*) **ever**

36.7 Adverbs in *-ī-* followed by possessive suffixes

Some adverbs are formed by adding *-ī-* followed by possessive suffix to a noun stem. They often translate literally as **in my/your**, etc. **…-ness**.

ērīššīya **in my nakedness**
OB *ištu <u>ṣuhrīya</u> ana bābilim ilqûninni-ma ina bābilim warad ēkallim anāku* **(Ever) since they took me to Babylon <u>in my youth</u>, I was a palace servant in Babylon** (AbB 4, 118: 7–8)

For *mahru*, the sense is **in the presence of**.

OB *urram <u>mahrīkunu</u> anāku* **Tomorrow I will be with you** (lit. **<u>in your presence</u>**) (AbB 10, 10: 16)

36.8 Adverbs in *-atta(m)*, *-atti*

Some adverbs can be formed by adding *-attam* (Old Babylonian), *-atta* (Middle and Standard Babylonian), or *-atti* (Standard Babylonian) to the word stem.

kurkâtta **like a goose**; *ahlamâtti* **in Aramaic**; *pašālatti* **crawling**; *pašīratti* **secretly**; *sartatti* **fraudulently**

36.9 The locative in *-um*

Adverb-like expressions can be produced by adding *-um* to the noun stem. This ending usually has a locative (place-related) meaning.

The 'locative' is a case of the noun (alongside nominative, accusative, genitive, vocative), but, like the vocative (Unit 6.4) it is easier to think of it as an isolated oddity.

In the basic state, the locative looks like the nominative (though there is a tendency for the *m* of the locative to be kept long after it has disappeared for the nominative). In the construct and possessive states, the forms differ (see next section).

36.10 Locatives followed by genitives and possessive suffixes

Like adverbs in *-iš* and *-āniš*, locatives can be followed by genitives and possessive suffixes. When they are followed by possessive suffixes, the *m* assimilates to the initial consonant of the suffix.

qātukka **in your** (m. sg.) **hand** (from *qātum* + *ka*)
SB *adi atta tadekkûšu ṣalil uršuššu* **Until you** (m. sg.) **wake him up, he will lie in his bed** (Erra I 19)

-um followed by the first person singular suffix becomes *uwwa* or *uwa*.

qa-tu-ú-a (sp. *qātuwwa* or *qātuwa*) **in my hand**

Some prepositions also behave like this:

OB *ullânukka hāsisam ul īšu* **Apart from you, I have no one who thinks (of me)** (AbB 7, 28: 6–8)
OB *elênukka ana manniya uznāya ibaššiā* **On whom of mine other than you is my attention (focused)?** (AbB 11, 106: 11′–12′)
šap$_5$*-lu-u-a* (sp. *šapluwwa* or *šapluwa*) **under me**

36.11 Adverbs after prepositions and nouns in the construct state

Some adverbs can follow prepositions and nouns in the construct state. They are indeclinable, and so do not display a genitive ending.

OB *adi inanna* **until now**
OB *ebūr šaddaqdam* **The harvest of last year**, i.e. **Last year's harvest** (AbB 7, 168: r.2′)

The most important things to remember

1 Adverbs (mostly of manner) can be formed with the endings *-iš* and *-āniš*.

2 Accusatives can be used as adverbs. Translate them according to the context.

3 Adverbs (mostly of place) can be formed with the 'locative' ending *-um*. They are usually followed by possessive suffixes, and the *m* assimilates to the initial consonant of the suffix. (For the first person, *-umya* → *-uwwa* or *-uwa*.)

4 Adverbs can be formed with the ending *-iša(m)*, meaning **X by X** (e.g. *ūmišam* **day by day**).

SELF CHECK

	I can ...
	... explain what an adverb is
	... explain the main ways in which adverbs are formed in Babylonian
	... explain how adverbial phrases relate to prepositional phrases
	... give the forms of the locative, with and without possessive suffixes.

37 Independent pronouns

In this unit you will learn:

- **what independent pronouns are**
- **what forms they take.**

So far, you have learned that Babylonian can render English pronouns (**I**, **me**, **you**, **he**, **him**, **she**, **her**, **we**, **us**, etc.) with prefixes and suffixes. It can also, however, do this with independent words, as in English: see Table 46.

Table 46

	nom.	**acc./gen.**	**dat.**
1st	*anāku*	*yâti*	*yâši(m)*
2nd m.	*atta*	*kâta*	*kâši(m)*
2nd f.	*atti*	*kâti*	*kâši(m)*
3rd m.	*šū*	*šuātu, šâtu, šâti*	*šuāši(m), šâšu(m), šâši(m)*
3rd f.	*šī*	*šuāti, šiāti, šâti*	*šuāšim, šiāšim, šâši(m)*
1st	*nīnu*	*niāti*	*niāši(m)*
2nd m.	*attunu*	*kunūti*	*kunūši(m)*
2nd f.	*attina*	*kināti*	*(kināši(m))*
3rd m.	*šunu*	*šunūti*	*šunūši(m)*
3rd f.	*šina*	*šināti*	*(šināši(m))*

The nominative pronouns are used as subjects of verbless clauses (see Unit 29.3) and sometimes, though they are not grammatically necessary, as subjects of verbs (see Unit 14.2).

Accusative/genitive pronouns are so called because they have the same form for accusative and genitive. It is quite rare for them to be used as accusatives: usually, accusative suffixes (see Unit 19.1) are used for this. They are used as genitives after prepositions (but not after the construct state).

SB *kī yâti-ma atta* **You** (m. sg.) **are like me** (Gilg. XI 3) (on *-ma* see Unit 30.7)

Dative pronouns mean **to**, **for**. Sometimes they are preceded by *ana*. Strictly speaking, one would expect *ana* to be followed by genitive forms, but since its meaning is inherently datival (i.e. **to**, **for**), dative pronouns are compatible with it.

OB *ana kâšim taklāku* **I trust you** (lit. **to you**) (m. sg.) (AbB 4, 161: 39)

Mimation in the dative pronouns is usually present in Old Babylonian, and usually absent later (see Unit 6.11).

anāku has an occasional by-form *ana* (or *anā?*), which can look like the preposition.

SELF CHECK

	I can ...
	... explain what independent pronouns are, and how they relate to suffix pronouns
	... (in time): recite the independent pronouns.

38 *Quadriliteral verbs*

In this unit you will learn:
- **what quadriliteral verbs are**
- **some of their main forms.**

A minority of Babylonian verbs have four root letters, rather than the usual three. Some occur chiefly in the N system, and so have dictionary forms beginning with *na-* (*ne-* in *e*-verbs). Those whose first root letter is *š* originally took the prefixes of the G system, but were subsequently reassigned the prefixes of the Š system. The following are the most common:

šuharruru(m) **to be deathly still** (pres. *ušharrar*, pret. *ušharrir*, stat. *šahur* and *šuharrur*)
šuqammumu(m) **to be utterly silent** (pres. *ušqammam* – Old Bab. also *išqammam*, pret. *ušqammim*, stat. *šuqammum*)
šuqallulu(m) **to be hanging down** (pres. *išqallal* and *ušqallal*, pret. *ušqallil*, stat. *šuqallul*)
šupêlu(m) **to exchange** (pres. *ušpêl*, pret. *ušpēl*)
šukênu(m) **to bow down** (pres. *uškên*, pret. *uškēn* and *uškīn*)
nabalkutu(m) **to cross over, to turn over** (pres. *ibbalakkat*, pret. *ibbalkit*, perf. *ittabalkat*)
naharmuṭu(m) **to dissolve** (pret. *ihharmiṭ*)
naparšudu(m) **to flee** (pret. *ipparšid*)
naparkû **to shirk** (pres. *ipparakku*, pret. *ipparku*)
negeltû(m) **to wake up** (pret. *iggeltu* and *iggelti*)
nekelmû(m) **to look at with anger (or malice)** (pres. *ikkelemme*, pret. *ikkelme*)
neqelpû(m) **to float, to glide (along)** (pres. *iqqeleppu*, pret. *iqqelpu*)

Other forms of these verbs are rare. You can find them online in the *Chicago Assyrian Dictionary* (see Unit 42.2).

SELF CHECK

	I can ...
	... recognise forms of quadriliteral verbs
	... look them up in the Glossary.

39 *Numbers*

In this unit you will learn:

- **the basics of Babylonian numbers.**

Babylonians overwhelmingly wrote numbers as sumerograms (which modern editors transliterate directly into Arabic numerals). Accordingly, there is often uncertainty about how the numbers were actually pronounced.

For the purposes of translation it is not really necessary to know Babylonian numbers: on the rare occasions when you encounter a number spelled syllabically, you can look it up. Nonetheless, for interest's sake, we give here the numbers from one to ten.

Each number has both a masculine and a feminine form.

	m.	f.		m.	f.
1	*ištēn*	*išteat*	**6**	*šediš*	*šeššet*
2	*šina*	*šitta*	**7**	*sebe*	*sebet*
3	*šalāš*	*šalāšat*	**8**	*samāne*	*samānat*
4	*erba*	*erbet*	**9**	*tiše*	*tišīt*
5	*hamiš*	*hamšat*	**10**	*ešer*	*ešret, ešeret*

Up to and including two, cardinal numbers agree with the gender of the noun they refer to. Above two, cardinal numbers take the opposite gender (this is known as 'gender polarity').

SB *šeššet* (f.) *ūmī* (m.) *sebe* (m.) *mūšāti* (f.) *enkidu tebi-ma šamhat irhi* **For six days and seven nights Enkidu was erect and coupled with Šamhat** (Gilg. I 194)

Ordinal numbers are adjectives, and always agree with the gender of the noun they refer to. They precede the noun they qualify.

SB *ina mahrê gerriya* **during my first campaign** (Chic. i.20)

SELF CHECK

	I can ...
	... explain the basics of Babylonian numbers
	... explain 'gender polarity'
	... (in time): count from one to ten.

40 *The endingless state*

In this unit you will learn:

- **what the 'endingless state' is**
- **how it is used.**

As noted in Unit 10.4, in addition to the basic, construct, possessive and predicative states, the Babylonian noun can go into the 'endingless state'. (Some books call it the 'absolute' state, 'absolute' in this context being an old term roughly tantamount to 'endingless'.)

As per its name, the 'endingless state' is formed by removing the case vowel and (if present) the feminine *t* and (if present) a preceding short vowel.

LANGUAGE TIP

The notion of an 'endingless state' (and even more its fearsome Latin name, *status absolutus*) is really a grammarian's fig leaf meaning: 'a noun which lacks an ending, for reasons we don't understand'.

Its two most important uses are:

1 it is used after *lā*, to mean **without**, e.g. *lā šanān* **without compare**,

2 it is used in phrases like **two jars of grain**, which have units of measurement preceded by a number: in Babylonian, such constructions are non-genitival (there is no **of**). The commodity measured (grain in this instance) goes in whatever case the sentence requires, and the unit is singular and goes in the endingless state (not the construct state, though often they look the same).

OB *šina šiqil kaspam inaddinšum* **He will pay him two shekels of silver** (super-lit. **two shekel silver**)

The endingless state is also used in certain prepositional expressions, e.g. *ana dūr dār* **forever and ever**, and in some adverbs, e.g. *zamar* **quickly**.

Assyrian royal inscriptions often describe enemy captives with the phrase (and variants thereof) *ṣeher rabi zikar u sinniš* **young** (lit. **small**), **old** (lit. **big**), **male and female**. These are all in the endingless state.

Note how *sinniš* **female**, from *sinništu* **woman**, is different from the construct form of the same word (which would be *sinništi*).

SELF CHECK

	I can ...
	... explain how the 'endingless state' is used.

Reading H: The Poor Man of Nippur

Most of surviving Babylonian narrative literature is concerned with gods. Rather than reflecting a salient fact about 'the Babylonian mind' per se, this may well have to do with what got written down and what did not; and also with the fact that surviving libraries tend to be linked to temples or other institutions.

Be that as it may, *The Poor Man of Nippur* is one of a small number of works firmly rooted in the world of menfolk. It gives us a hint of the sort of things which must have existed in larger numbers, and may yet be found.

In June 2017, members of the University of Cambridge's Mesopotamian community filmed a dramatization of the story in the original language, which is freely accessible at https://tinyurl.com/y9wzcwdv.

The story was first edited by Oliver Gurney in 1956, in volume 6 of the journal *Anatolian Studies* (https://www.jstor.org/stable/3642407). Improvements to Gurney's edition were made by Gurney himself, Wilfred Lambert, Wolfram von Soden, Bill Moran, Jerrold Cooper and Andrew George. The story was re-edited online in 2010 by Greta van Buylaere (http://oracc.museum.upenn.edu/cams/gkab/P338355), and again in 2016 in a book by Baruch Ottervanger, as volume XII in the series *State Archives of Assyria*. The text below uses readings from all these sources. In many places where the tablet is broken there is uncertainty about which sign is present (some of these cases might be resolved by re-examination of the tablet). Nonetheless, the general shape of the story is clear.

Cuneiform

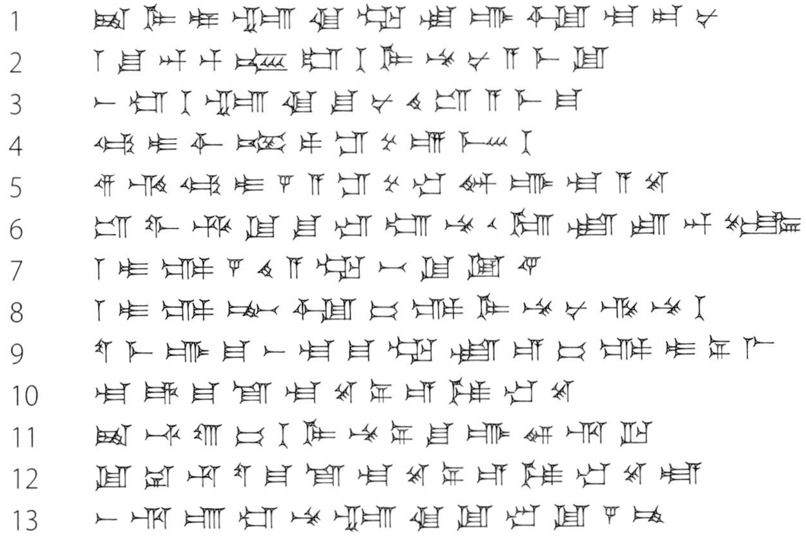

15.
16.
17.
18.
19.
20.
21.
22.
23.
24.
25.
26.
27.
28.
29.
30.
31.
32. xx[xxx]x
33.
34.
35.
36.
37.
38.
39.
40.
41.
42.
43.
44.
45.
46.
47.
48.
49.

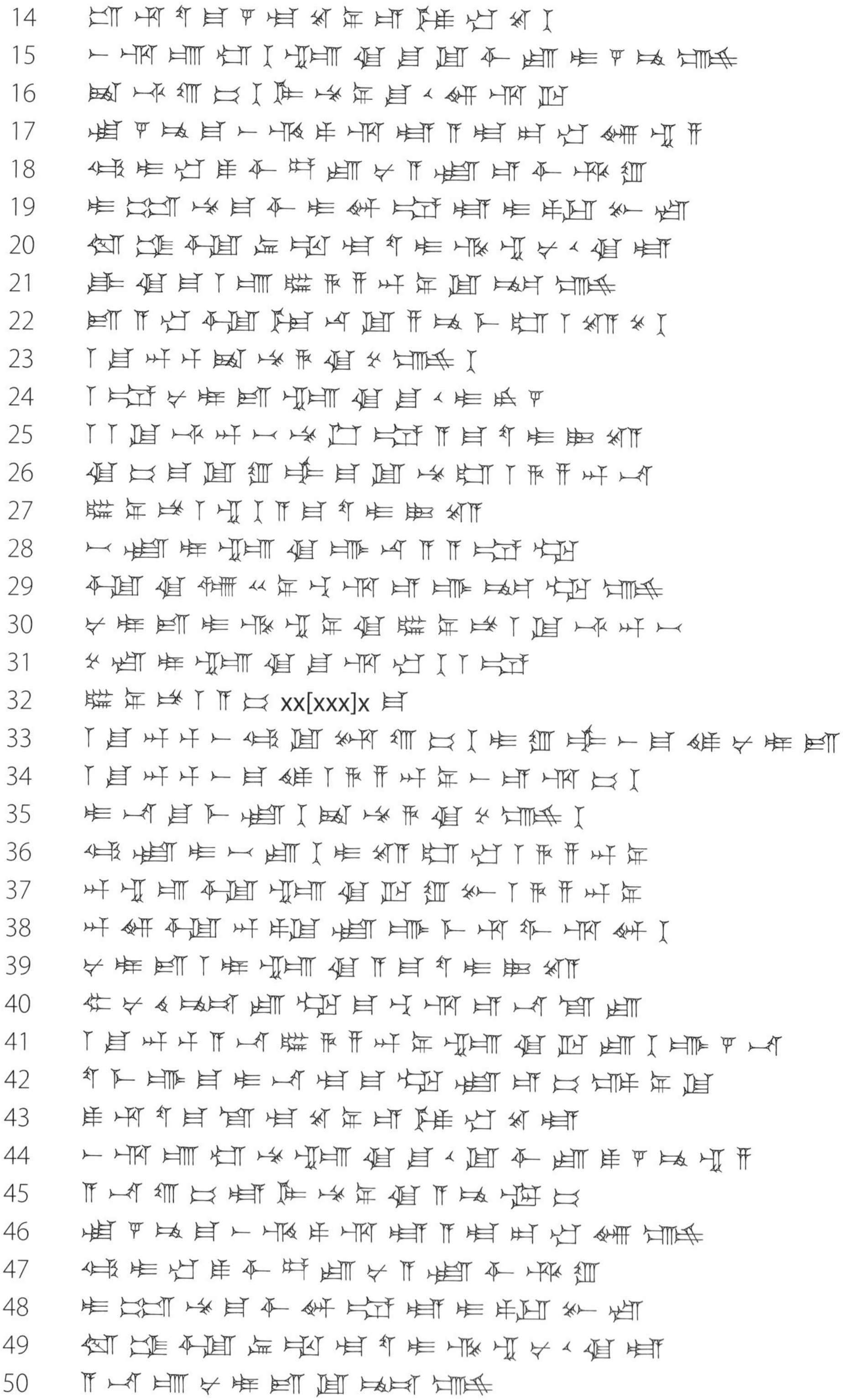

52 [...]x

53 [...]x

54 [...]x xx

55 [...]x

56 [...]x

57 [...]

58

59

60

61

62

63

64

65

66

67

68

69

70

71

72

73

74

75

76

77

78

79

80

81

82 x[xxx]

83

84 xx

85

86

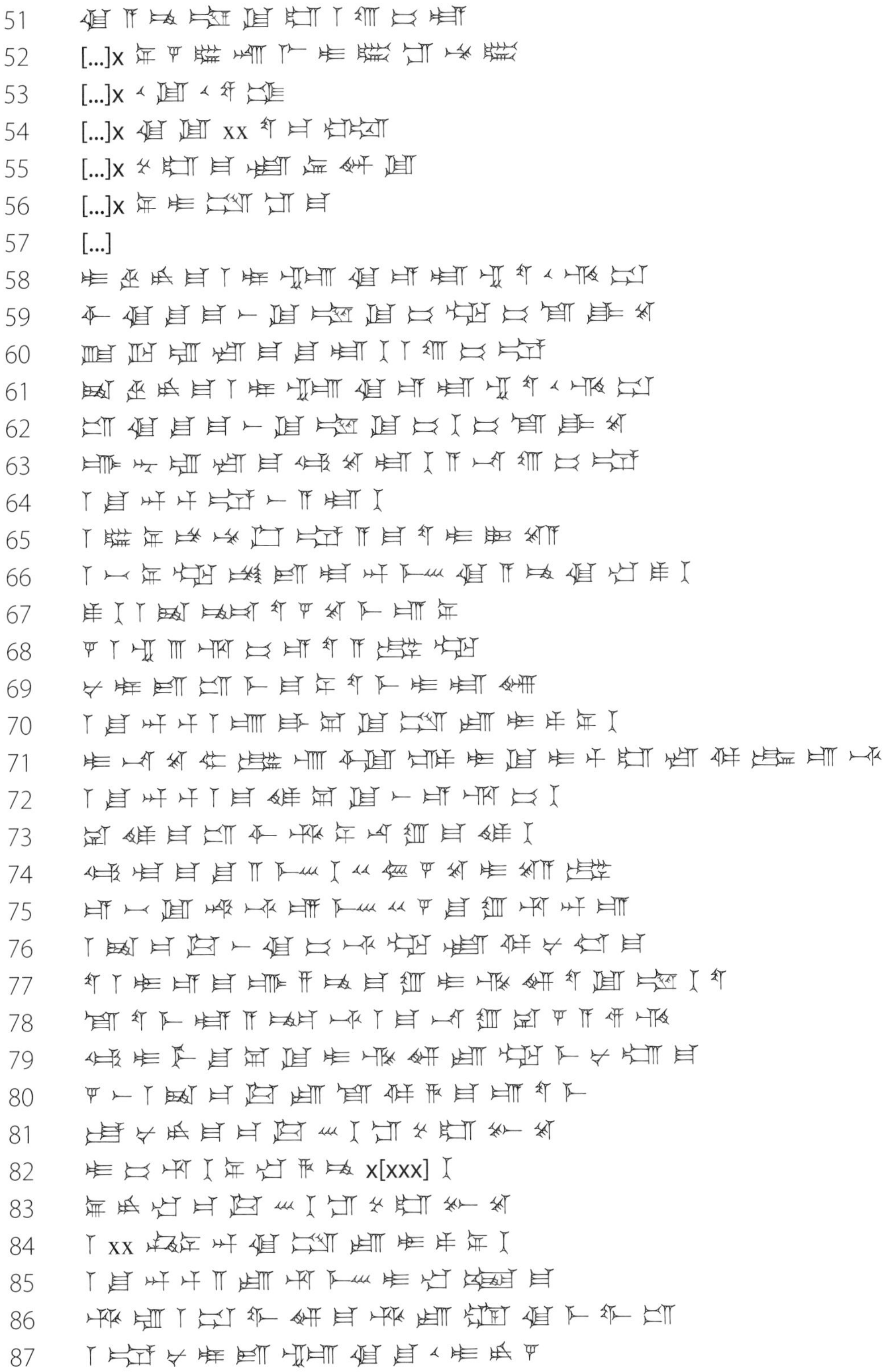

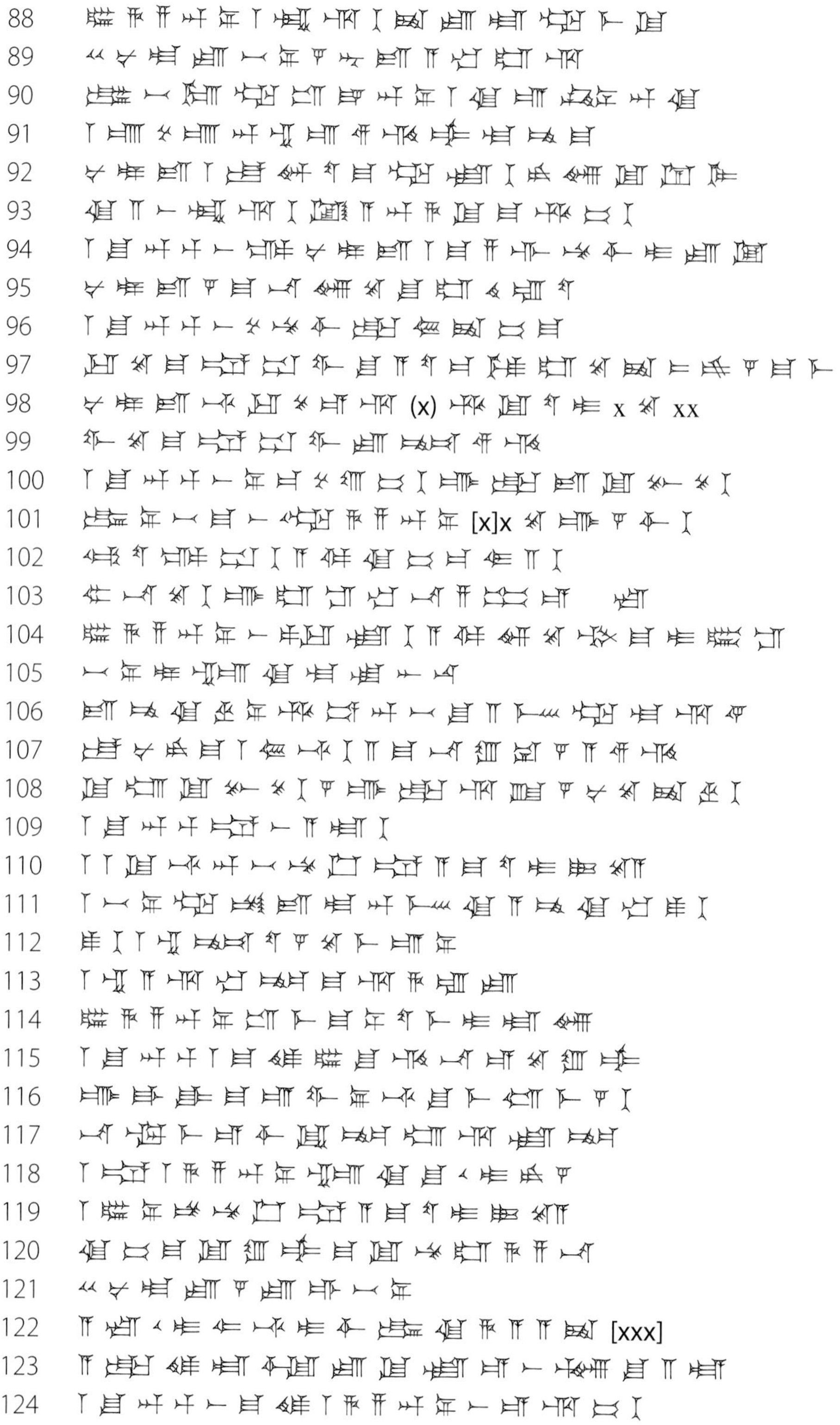
88
89
90
91
92
93
94
95
96
97
98 (x) x xx
99
100
101 [x]x
102
103
104
105
106
107
108
109
110
111
112
113
114
115
116
117
118
119
120
121
122 [xxx]
123
124

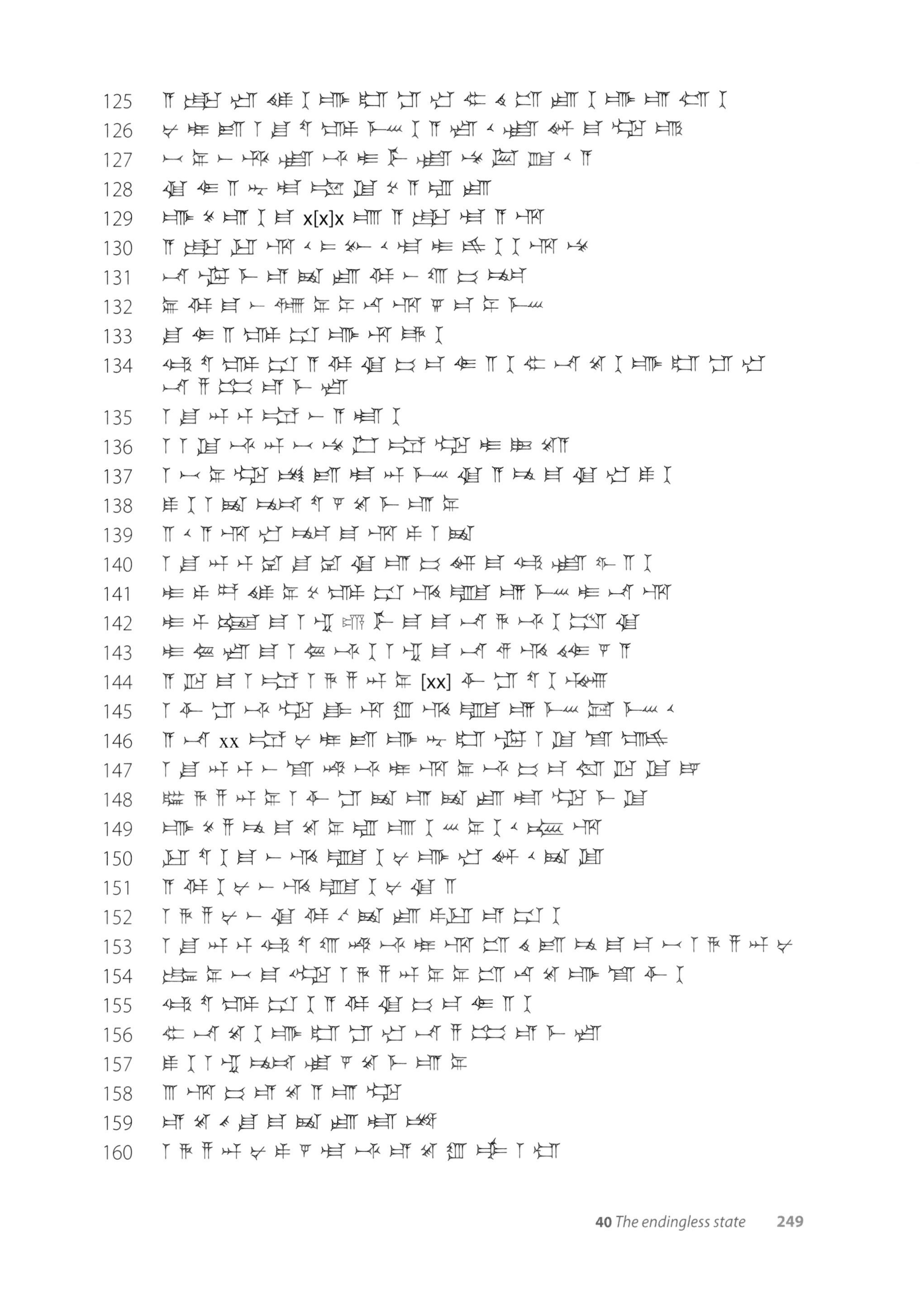

125 [illegible]
126 [illegible]
127 [illegible]
128 [illegible]
129 [illegible] x[x]x [illegible]
130 [illegible]
131 [illegible]
132 [illegible]
133 [illegible]
134 [illegible]
135 [illegible]
136 [illegible]
137 [illegible]
138 [illegible]
139 [illegible]
140 [illegible]
141 [illegible]
142 [illegible]
143 [illegible]
144 [illegible] [xx] [illegible]
145 [illegible]
146 [illegible] xx [illegible]
147 [illegible]
148 [illegible]
149 [illegible]
150 [illegible]
151 [illegible]
152 [illegible]
153 [illegible]
154 [illegible]
155 [illegible]
156 [illegible]
157 [illegible]
158 [illegible]
159 [illegible]
160 [illegible]

Transliteration

1 *eṭ-lum* dumu nibru(EN.LÍL)^{ki} *ka-tu-ú ù la-ap-nu*
2 ^{m}šu–^{d}maš *zik-ra-šú lum-mu-nu a-mì-lu*
3 *ina* uru-*šú* nibru^{ki} *šu-nu-hi-iš a-šib-ma*
4 *ul [i]-ši kàs-pa si-mat* ùg^{meš}-*šú*
5 kù.gi *ul i-šá-a si-mat ba-ʾu-ú-la-a-t*⌞*e*⌟
6 *iš-pi-ik-ku-šu zu!-um-mu-u el-le-ta* ^{d}nisaba
7 *ana i-riš* ninda$^{hi.a}$ *ka-bat-tuš ṣar-*⸢*pat*⸣
8 *ana i-riš* uzu ù kaš.sag *lum-mu-nu zi-mu-šú*
9 *u$_4$-mì-šam-ma ina la ma-ka-le-[e] bé-riš i-ṣal-lal*
10 *la-biš-ma ša la te-né-[e] ṣu-ba-te*$^{!}$*-<šú>*
11 *it-ti lìb-bi-šú lum-mu-ni šu-ú im-tal-lik*
12 *lu-uš-hu-uṭ-ma ša*$^{!}$ *la te-né-[e] [ṣ]u-ba-te*$^{!}$*-ia*
13 *ina re-bit* uru-*ia*$_5$ nibru^{ki} udu.níta *[l]u-šá-am*
14 *iš-hu-uṭ-ma šá la te-né-e ṣu-b[a-t]e-šú*
15 *ina re-bit* uru-*šú* nibru^{ki} ⸢*šu-lu*⸣*-ši-ta [i]-[š]á-am* ùz
16 *it-ti lìb-bi-šú lum-mu-ni šu-u im-t[al]-lik*
17 *tu-šá-am-ma ina gi-pa-ri-ia a-aṭ-ab-ba-ah en-[z]a*
18 *ul i-ba-áš-ši nap-ta-nu a-le-e ši-ik-*⌞*ru*⌟
19 *i-šem-mu-ma ši-i-ʾi* ká-*ia i-šab-bu-s[u]*
20 *kim-tum* ⸢*ù*⸣ *sa-al-la-tú i-ze-en-nu-*⸢*ú*⸣ ki *-ia*
21 *lul-qé-ma ana* é ^{lú}*ha-za-an-ni lu-bil* ùz
22 *ṭa-a-ba ù dam-qa lu-ṣa-am-me-ra ana kar-še*$^{!}$*-[šú]*
23 ^{m}šu–^{d}maš *it-mu-ha ki-šad* ⸢ùz⸣ -[*šú*]
24 *ana* ká nu.bàn.da nibru^{ki} *šu-u [i]-[tak-šá]*
25 *ana* ^{m}*tukul-ti–*^{d}bad *mu-kil* ká *a-ma-tam [i]-za[k-kar]*
26 *qí-bi-ma lu-ru-ub-ma lu-mu-ra* ^{m}*ha-za-[an-na]*
27 ^{lú}ì.du$_8$ *ana* en-*šú a-*⌞*m*⌟*a-tam i-zak-[kar]*
28 *be-li* dumu nibru^{ki} ⌞*ú-qa-a*⌟*-a* ká-⸢*ka*⸣
29 *ù*$^{!}$ *ki [š]ul-man-ni* ⸢*kad*⸣*-[re-e] ú-bil-ka* ùz
30 nu.bàn.da *i-ze-e[n-ni* ki ^{lú}ì.du$_8$ ^{m}*tuk]ul-ti–*^{d}bad
31 kur$^{?}$-*su* dumu nibru^{ki} [*šu-ri-ba-šú*] *ana* ká
32 ^{lú}ì.du$_8$$^{!}$ *ana a-*⸢*bi*⸣*x x[xxx]x-ma*
33 ^{m}šu–^{d}maš *ina ul-lu-uṣ lìb-bi-šú [i-ru-ub ina ma-h]ar* nu.bàn.⌞da⌟
34 ^{m}šu–^{d}maš *ina ma-har* ^{m}*ha-za-an-n[i ina]* ⸢*e-re*⸣ *-b[i]-šú*
35 *[i]-na šu-me-li-šú it-mu-ha ki-šad* ⸢ùz⸣ *-šú*
36 *[u]l-li*$^{!}$ *i-mit-ta-šú i-kar-ra-*⌞*ba*⌟ *ana ha-za-an-ni*
37 $^{[d]}$en-líl *ù* nibru$^{!ki}$ *lik-ru-bu ana ha-za-an-ni*
38 [^{d}ad]ad *ù* ^{d}nusku *li-šam-mì-hu [pe]-re-eʾ-šú*
39 [nu].bàn.da *ana* dumu nibru$^{!ki}$ *a-ma-*⸢*tam*⸣ *i-z[a]k-k[ar]*

40 *[mi-n]u hi-bíl-ta-ka-ma kad-re-e na-ša-ta*
41 [^{m}šu–]^{d}maš *a-na* ^{lú}*ha-za-an-ni* nibru$^{!ki}$ *ur-⸢t⸣a-šú ú-šá-na*
42 *[u*$_4$*-mì-š]am-ma i-na la ma-ka-le-e bé-riš ṣala-⸤ku⸥*
43 *[áš-hu-u]ṭ-ma ša la te-né-e ṣu-ba-te-ia*
44 *[ina re-bit]* uru-*ia*$_5$ nibru$^{!ki}$ *šu-u-lu-[š]i-ta áš-šá-am en-za*
45 *[a-na lìb]-bi-ia lum-mu-ni ki-a-a⸢m aq⸣-[b]i*
46 *[tu-šá-am-m]a ina gi-pa-ri-ia a-aṭ-ab-ba-a⸢h* ù⸣z
47 *[ul i-ba-áš-š]i ⸤nap⸥-ta-nu a-le ši-ik-ru*
48 *[i-šem-mu-ma š]i-⸢ʾ⸣i* ká-*ia i-šab-bu-su*
49 *[kim-tu*$_4$ *ù sa]-al-la-tú i-ze-en-nu-u* ki-*ia*
50 *[a-na* é nu.bà]n.da *lu-bíl* ùz
51 *[ki-a-am az-k]u-ra ana*$^{!}$ *lìb-bi-ia*
52 [. . .]*x-⸢ni*$^{?}$*⸣ šá* ^{lú}gír.lá *i-šas-si mu-šiš*
53 [. . .]*x-u lu-u ṣab-tu*$_4$
54 [. . .]*x ki lu x[x] tú* ^{giš}banšur
55 [. . .]*x kur-ra-ma li-sa-aʾ-lu*
56 *x-⸢ni⸣ i-il-si-ma*
57 [. . .]
58 *i-din-šum-ma ana* dumu ⸢nibru^{k}[^{i} *e-ṣ]e-en-tú u gi-du*
59 *ši-qí-šu-ma ina ku-uk-ku-bi-k[a* kaš *š]a-lul-te*
60 *ṭu-ur-rid-su-ma šu-ṣi-šú an[a lìb-b]i* ká
61 *id-din-šum-ma ana* dumu nibru$^{!ki}$ *[e]-[ṣe-en-t]ú u gi-du*
62 *iš-qí-šu-ma ina ku-uk-ku-bi-š[ú* kaš *ša-l]ul-t[e]*
63 *ú-ṭar-rid-su-ma ul-te-ṣi-[šú a-na lìb-bi]* ká
64 ^{m}šu–^{d}maš ká *ina [a]-ṣe-šú*
65 *ana* ^{lú}ì.du$_8$ *mu-kil* ká *a-ma-tam [i]-zak-kar*
66 *ana be-lí-ka tah-da-at* dingir^{m}[^{eš} *k]i-a-am qí-ba-áš-šú*
67 *áš-šú* 1^{et} *píl-tú šá te-m[ì-d]an-ni*
68 *šá* 1^{en} 3 *ri-bé-[e]-⸤tú⸥ a-rab-ka*
69 nu.bàn.da *iš-me-[m]a kàl u*$_4$*-me i-ṣi-ih*
70 ^{m}šu–^{d}maš *ana* [é].gal *mal-ku il-ta-kan pa-ni-šú*
71 *i-na ⸢ṭ⸣e*$_4$*-mi [(šá)]* lugal nun *ù šak-kana-ku i-pár-ra-su di-in kit-ti*
72 ^{m}šu–^{d}⸢maš⸣ *ana ma-har mal-ku ina e-re-bi-šú*
73 *uš*$^{!}$*-kín*$^{!}$*-[m]a*$^{!}$ *iš-ši-iq qaq-qa-ru ma-har-šú*
74 *u ⸢l⸣-⸤l⸥a-[m]a* šu^{2meš}-*šú* man *kiš-šá-te i-kar-rab*
75 *e-tel-l[u b]al-ti* ùg^{meš} man *šá šu-ru-hu* ^{d}lamma
76 1^{et} ⸢^{giš}gigir⸣ *ina qí-bi-ti-ka li-di-nu-nim-ma*
77 ud 1 kám *e-ma ú-ṣa-am-ma-ru i-z⸤i⸥-im-tú l⸤u⸥-uk-šú-ud*

78 [š]a u$_4$-mì-ia a-⸢pil⸣-[t]i 1 ma-na ⸢r⸣u-uš-šá-a k[ù].gi
79 [u]l i-šal-šu mal-ku [i]-⸤zi⸥-im-ta-ka mì-nu-[u]m-ma
80 šá ina 1^{et} ^{giš}gigir ta-š[a$^?$-di$^?$]-⸢ha$^?$-ma$^?$⸣ kal [u$_4$]-me
81 ⸤šúm⸥-nu-šum-ma ^{giš}gigir eš-šú ⸢si⸣-m[at ra]-⸤bu-t⸥e
82 i-[bí]-hu-šú né-ba-ha-am x[xxx]-šú
83 ⸤i⸥r-[ta]k-ba ^{giš}gigir ⸤eš⸥-šú si-mat [r]a-bu-⸤te⸥
84 ana xx dur-an-ki il-ta-kan pa-ni-šú
85 ^{m}⸢šu⸣–$^{[d]}$[ma]š 2ta mušen^{meš} i-ba-ram-ma
86 ⸤ik-mis⸥ ⸤ana⸥ q[u]p-pi-im-ma ik-ta-nak ki-šip-pi-⸤iš⸥
87 ana ká nu.bàn.da nibru$^{!ki}$ šu-u i-ta[k-šá]
88 ^{lú}ha-za-an-ni ana mah-ri-šú it-ta-ṣi k[a-me-tuš]
89 man-nu at-ta be-lí šá tara-da-a ba-r[a-ri]
90 lugal be-el-ka iš-pur-an-ni ana q[é-re]b d[ur-an-ki]
91 ana é.kur é ^{d}en.líl kù.gi u[b]-la-a[m-ma]
92 nu.bàn.da ana ⸤šúm⸥-'u-ud ma-ka-li-šú šum-uh ^{udu}as$_4$-[lum]
93 ki.min ina mah-ri-šú u$_8$-a an-ha-ku-ma iq$^!$-b[i-šú]
94 ^{m}šu–^{d}maš ina sag nu.bàn.da 1 ma-ṣa-rat mu-⸢ši⸣ [i]-[t]a-ṣ[ar]
95 nu.bàn.da šá ma-⸢na⸣-ah-[t]e-šu ra-hi šit-⸤tú⸥
96 ^{m}šu–^{d}maš ina šat mu-ši ša[r-q]iš it-bé-ma
97 ip-te-ma ká qup-pi šu$^!$-a$^!$-tú iṣ-ṣu-ra-te it-tap-r[aša$^?$ šá]-ma-méš
98 nu.bàn.da ti-ib ⸢še-e-ri⸣ (x) ⸢ig-l⸣u-ud i-x-te xx
99 pe-te-⸤ma k⸥á qup-pi ta-bíl kù.gi
100 ^{m}⸢šu–^{d}maš⸣ [ina] n[i-i]s-sat lìb-bi-šú ú-[ša]ra-ṭa lu-bu-še-šú
101 in-né-m[i]d-ma ⸢ina ugu⸣ ha-za-a[n-ni ni-iš q]a-te ú-šá-lim-šu
102 ul-tú sag.du-šú a-di ki-bi-is gìr^2-šú
103 mi-na-te-⸤šú⸥ ú-ra-si-ba na-za-qu e-mid-su
104 ^{lú}ha-za-an-ni ina šap-li-šú a-di ní.te-⸢tim⸣-ma i-šas-si
105 [b]e-lí dumu nibru^{ki} la tu-hala-qa
106 da-am ki-[di]n-ni ik-kib ^{d}bad šu^{2meš}-[k]a la t[a]la-pat
107 šúm-nu-šu[m-m]a ana qiš-ti-šú 2 ma-na ru-uš-šá-⸢a kù⸣.gi
108 ku-um lu-bu-še-šú šá ú-šar-ri-ṭu š[á-n]u-te id-din-šú
109 ^{m}šu–^{d}maš ká ina ⸢a⸣-ṣe-šú
110 ana ^{m}tukul-ti–^{d}[b]ad mu-kil ká a-ma-tam [i]-zak-k[ar]
111 ana be-lí-k[a t]ah-da-at dingir^{m}[^{eš} k]i-a-am qí-ba-á[š-šú]
112 áš-šú 1^{en} píl-tú šá [te-mì-dan-ni]
113 1^{en} a-ri-ba-kúm-ma [re-ha šit-ta]
114 ^{lú}ha-za-an-ni iš-me-ma ⸤kàl⸥ u$_4$-m[i i-ṣi-ih]
115 ^{m}šu–^{d}maš ana ma-har ^{lú}⸢šu⸣.[g]i.na [e-te-ru-ub]

116 *ú-gal-lib-ma kal pe-*⸢*er*⸣*-ti(-*$^{?}$*)šu me-la*[*m-me* gar-*šu*]

117 *na-ak-me-e ši-kin* izi *um-tal-*[*li* dè]

118 *ana* ká ^{m}*ha-za-an-ni* nibru^{ki} *šu-u* [*i-tak-ša ?*]

119 *ana* ^{lú}ì.du$_{8}$ *mu-kil* ká *a-ma-tam* [*i-zak-kar*]

120 *qí-bi-ma lu-ru-ub-ma lu-mu-ra* [*ha-za-na ?*]

121 *man-nu at-ta šá ta-mar* [*be-lí*]

122 *a-su-u i-lit-ti i-ši-in*^{ki} *ha-a-*[*a*]*-*[*iṭ* xxx]

123 *a-*[*š*]*ar mur-ṣi ù ta-ku-le-e aš-ku*[*n*$^{?}$ šu^{2}*-ia*$^{?}$]

124 ^{m}šu–[^{d}ma]š *ina ma-har* ^{m}*ha-za-an-ni ina e-re-bi-*⸢*šú*⸣

125 *a-šar z*[*u-mu*]*r-šú ú-ra-si-ba mi-hi-iš-ta-šú ú-kal-l*⸢*am*⸣*-šú*

126 nu.bàn.[da *ana š*]*u-ut* sag^{meš}*-šú a-su-u le-'i-ma* du$_{11}$.ga

127 *be-lí ina ek-l*[*e*$^{?}$*-t*]*i i-šal-li-mu bul-ṭu-u-a*

128 ki gìr^{2} tar-*at* [*u*]*k-ku-lat a-lak-ta*

129 *ú-še-rib-šú-ma x*[*x*]*x* é *a-šar la a-ri*

130 *a-šar ib-ri u tap-pu-u* ⸢*la*⸣ *i-raš-šú-šú re-mu*

131 *na-ak-me-e it-ta-di ina lìb-bi* izi

132 *ir-ṭi-ma ina dun-ni qaq-qa-ri* 5 ^{giš}gag^{m}[^{eš}]

133 šu gìr^{2} [s]ag.du *ú-pak-kir-šú*

134 *ul-tú* sag.[d]u *a-di ki-bi-is* gìr^{2}*-šú mi-na-te-šú ú-ra-si-ba na-za-qu e-mì-su*

135 ^{m}šu–^{d}maš ká *ina a-ṣe-šú*

136 *ana* ^{m}*tukul-ti–*^{d}bad *mu-kil* ká inim *i-zak-kar*

137 *ana be-lí-ka tah-da-at* dingir^{meš} *ki-a-am-ma qí-ba-áš-šú*

138 *á*[*š*]*-šú* 1^{et} *píl-tú šá te-mì-dan-ni*

139 [2]^{u} [*a*]*-ri-ba-kúm-*⸢*ma*⸣ *re-hat* 1^{et}

140 ^{m}šu–^{d}maš *uš-šu-uš ki* ⸢*kal*⸣$^{!}$*-bi-im-ma ul-l*[*i*] ⸢geštu^{2}*-šú*⸣

141 *i-haṭ na*[*p-h*]*ar ṣal-mat* sag.du *gi-m*[*i*]*r* ùg$^{!m}$[^{eš} *i-n*]*a*$^{!?}$*-ṭal*

142 *i-bar-r*[*a*]*m*$^{!?}$*-ma 1*^{en} guruš *mim-ma ma-*⸤*na*⸥*!-ha-*[*ti-šú il*]*-qé*

143 *i-*[*q*]*is-su-ma ana qiš-t*[*i-šú* 1^{en} *ma-na* kù.gi *ruš-šá*]*-a*

144 *a-lik-ma ana* ká $^{[m]}$⸢*ha-za-an-ni*⸣ [*xx*] *ši-si-tú šú-kun*

145 *ana ši-*⸤*si-ti-k*⸥[*a*] *lip-hu-ru gi-mir* [ùg]^{meš} dagal^{meš} *« u »*

146 *a-n*[*a? xx* k]á nu.bàn.da *ú-tar-r*[*a-a*]*k ana-ku ša* ùz

147 ^{m}[šu–^{d}maš *ina ša-pa*]*l ti-tur-ri ir-t*[*i*]*-bi-iṣ* gim ur.gi$_{7}^{!}$*(text:*bur*)*

148 ⸢^{lú}*ha-za-an*⸣*-ni ana ši-si-it* guruš *i*[*t*]*-ta-ṣi ka-me-tuš*

149 *ú-še-ṣa-am-ma te-<né>-*[*š*]*et* é*-šú sin-*⸢*ni*⸣*-šú u zik-ri*

150 *ip-par-šú-ma ina gi-m*[*i*]*r-šú-nu ú-ba-'u-u eṭ-lu*

151 *a-di šú-nu ina* [*g*]*i-mir-š*⸤*ú*⸥*-nu* ki.min

152 ^{m}*ha-za-nu ina ki-di : i*[*t*$^{?}$*-ta*$^{?}$*-šab*$^{?}$] *e*$^{?}$*-du-šú*

153 ^{m}šu–^{d}maš *ul-tú šà-pal ti-tur-ri i*[*š-hi-ṭa-a*]*m-ma iṣ-bat* ^{m}[*ha-za-an*]*-nu*

154 *in-né-mid-ma* ugu ^{m}*ha-za-an-ni ni-i*[*š qa-te ú-š*]*a-lim-šú*

155 *ul-tú* sag.du*-šú a-di ki-bi-is* gìr[^{2}*-šú*]

156 *[mi-na-te-šú ú-ra-si-ba na-za-qu e]-mì-su*
157 *[áš-šú* 1^{ent} *píl-tu šá te-mì]-dan-ni*
158 [3 *ri-b*]*é-*⸢*e*⸣-[*te*] *a-rib-ka*
159 [*e-te-zib*]-*šu-ma it-ta-ṣi* edin
160 [^{m}*ha-za-an-n*]*u pa-šá-la-ti e-te-ru-ub ana* uru

Translation

1 **(There was) a young man, a citizen (**lit. **son) of Nippur, needy and poor**
2 **Gimil-Ninurta was his name, a truly wretched man.**
3 **He eked out a living (**lit. **dwelled with great difficulty) in his city, Nippur.**
4 **He had no silver, as would befit his people,**
5 **gold, the mark of people, he had none.**
6 **His grain bins were bereft of Nisaba the pure.**
7 **His liver burned for want of food,**
8 **his face was wretched for want of meat and beer.**
9 **Day after day he lay (there) hungrily for want of food,**
10 **clad in his one garment.**
11 **This man communed with his wretched heart:**
12 **'I'll strip off my one garment,**
13 **I'll buy a sheep in the square of my city, Nippur.'**
14 **He stripped off his one garment,**
15 **in the square of Nippur, his city, he bought a three-year old nanny goat.**
16 **This man communed with his wretched heart:**
17 **'Suppose I butcher the goat in my shed:**
18 **there would be no feast; where would the ale be?**
19 **Word would get round, and those who visit my gate would be angry.**
20 **Friends and family would be furious with me.**
21 **I'll take the goat and deliver it to the house of the Mayor,**
22 **I'll strive to sweeten his stomach** (or: **mood**)**.'**
23 **Gimil-Ninurta grasped the neck of his goat.**
24 **Away he went to the gate of the Mayor of Nippur.**
25 **To Tukultī-Illil the doorkeeper he spoke a word:**
26 **'Say you, I would enter and see the Mayor.'**
27 **The doorman spoke a word to his master:**
28 **'My lord, a citizen of Nippur waits at your gate,**
29 **and as a greeting gift he has brought you a goat.'**
30 **The Mayor was angry with the doorman Tukultī-Ellil**
31 **'Go to the citizen of Nippur! [Bring him in] through the gate!'**
33 **Gimil-Ninurta, his heart a-swelling, went before the Mayor.**
34 **When Gimil-Ninurta came before the Mayor**
35 **in his left hand he held his goat by the neck,**

36 he raised his right to greet the Mayor.
37 'May Enlil and Nippur bless the Mayor,
38 May Adad and Nusku make his offspring flourish.'
39 The Mayor spoke a word to the man of Nippur:
40 'What is your crime, that you bring me a present?'
41 Gimil-Ninurta repeated his mission to the Mayor of Nippur.
42 'Day after day through want of food I lay awake in hunger.
43 I ripped off my one garment,
44 I bought a three-year old goat in the square of my city, Nippur.
45 I spoke thus to my wretched heart:
46 'Suppose I slaughter the goat in my shed,
47 there would be no feast; where would the ale be?
48 Word would get round, and those who visit my gate would be angry.
49 Friends and family would be furious with me.
50 I'll take the goat to the house of the Mayor.
51 Thus I spoke to my heart.'
[six lines fragmentary; a butcher and tables are mentioned; the goat is presumably slaughtered and eaten]
58 'Give the man of Nippur the bone and gristle,
59 have him drink third-rate beer from your can,
60 drive him away and throw him out of the gate!'
61 He gave the man of Nippur the bone and gristle,
62 he had him drink third-rate beer from his can,
63 he drove him away and threw him out of the gate.
64 As Gimil-Ninurta exited the gate,
65 he spoke a word to the doorman at the gate:
66 'Tell your master thus about the blessings of the gods:
67 for one insult which you imposed on me –
68 for that one, I shall repay you thrice.'
69 The Mayor heard, and laughed all day.
70 Gimil-Ninurta set out for the palace of the king:
71 'Prince and governor judge aright by order of the king.'
72 When Gimil-Ninurta came before the king,
73 he did obeisance and kissed the ground before the king,
74 he lifted his hands to greet the king of all.
75 'Noble one, pride of the people, sovereign glorified by the winged bull,
76 at your command may I be given a chariot,
77 so that for one day I achieve whatever I aspire to.
78 My payment (to you) for my day will be a mina of red gold.'
79 The king did not ask him: 'What desire of yours is this,
80 that you would parade about in a chariot for a whole day?'

81 They gave him a brand new chariot, befitting a nobleman,
82 they girt him with a sash and gave him [the king's seal].
83 He mounted the brand new chariot befitting a nobleman.
84 He headed for Nippur, bond of heaven and earth.
85 Gimil-Ninurta caught two birds,
86 packed them into a box, and sealed it.
87 Off he went to the gate of the Mayor of Nippur.
88 The Mayor went out to receive him:
89 'Who are you, my lord, who rides here at dusk?'
90 'The king your master has sent me to the bond of heaven and earth.
91 I have brought gold to the Ekur, the house of Enlil.'
92 To give him a sumptuous meal the Mayor butchered a sheep
93 The Mayor said to him 'Ohh, I'm tired.'
94 Gimil-Ninurta kept watch by the Mayor for the first watch.
95 The Mayor, in his weariness, was overcome by sleep.
96 In the middle of the night, Gimil-Ninurta got up furtively.
97 He opened that box, and the birds flew heavenwards.
98 In the morning, the Mayor grew fearful [...]
99 The box was open, the gold had been taken!
100 Gimil-Ninurta rent his clothes in the grief of his heart,
101 he jumped on the Mayor and repaid him with raised hand.
102 From his head to the soles of his feet
103 he smote his limbs and made him squeak.
104 Underneath him, the Mayor cried out in terror:
105 'My Lord, do not destroy a man of Nippur,
106 don't soil your hands with the blood of a *kidinnu*, sacred to Enlil!'
107 As his compensation they gave him two minas of red gold,
108 in place of the garments he had rent they gave him others.
109 As Gimil-Ninurta exited the gate,
110 he spoke a word to Tukultī-Ellil the gatekeeper:
111 'Tell your master thus about the blessings of the gods:
112 for one insult which you imposed on me –
113 I have repaid you one, and two remain.'
114 The Mayor heard, and laughed all day.
115 Gimil-Ninurta went before the barber.
116 He shaved all of his hair, and [made him look] awe-[inspiring].
117 He filled a roasting pot with [embers].
118 Off he went to the gate of the Mayor of Nippur.
119 To the doorman he spoke a word:
120 'Say you, I would enter and see the Mayor.'
121 'Who are you who would see my master?'

122 **'A doctor born in Isin, who inspects [the sick]**
123 **I have placed my hands on spots of hurt and pain.'**
124 **When Gimil-Ninurta came before the Mayor,**
125 **he (GN) showed him (Mayor) the bruise where he had smitten his body.**
126 **'The doctor is very** (*-ma*) **skilful' said the Mayor to his attendants.**
127 **'My lord, my cures work best in darkness,**
128 **where access is blocked, and darkens the course.'**
129 **He sent him ..., the house, an inaccessible place**
130 **where no friend or companion could help him.**
131 **He cast the roasting pot into the fire(place),**
132 **he drove five pegs into the ground,**
133 **he immobilized him hand, head and foot.**
134 **From his head to the soles of his feet he smote his limbs and made him squeak.**
135 **As Gimil-Ninurta exited the gate,**
136 **he spoke a word to Tukultī-Ellil the gatekeeper:**
137 **'Tell your master thus about the blessings of the gods:**
138 **for one insult which you imposed on me –**
139 **I have repaid you twice, and one remains.'**
140 **Gimil-Ninurta was as menacing as a dog. He pricked up his ears,**
141 **he looked at all the people, scrutinized all of the folk.**
142 **He fired up a young man, undertaking to reward his services in full.**
143 **As his payment he gave him [a mina of red gold]**
144 **'Go to the gate of the Mayor of Nippur! Give out a shout,**
145 **so that all the people gather at your shouting.'**
146 **He knocked at the gate of the Mayor: 'I'm the man with the goat.'**
147 **Gimil-Ninurta lay below the way like a dog.**
148 **At the man's shout, the Mayor went out.**
149 **He likewise brought out all the occupants of his house, male and female.**
150 **All of them together flew off to catch the man.**
151 **While all of them were catching the man,**
152 **the Mayor sat down alone outside the city.**
153 **Gimil-Ninurta sprang out from under the way and seized the Mayor,**
154 **he jumped on the Mayor and** [...]
155 **From his head to the soles of his feet,**
156 **he smote his limbs and made him squeak.**
157 **'For the one insult which you imposed on me,**
158 **I have repaid you thrice.'**
159 **He left him and went out into the country.**
160 **The Mayor entered the city crawling.**

See notes at end of book.

41 *The main features of Assyrian*

In this unit you will learn:

- **the basics of how Assyrian differs from Babylonian**
- **something of the history of Assyrian.**

Assyria sits in the north of Iraq, separated from Babylonia by a natural boundary of mountains (their Arabic name is *Jebel Hamrin*). Its landscape is very different from Babylonia's: it has more natural resources (stone, wood) and it was dependent on rainfall rather than inundation. Those interested in the culture and history of Assyria can be pointed to the excellent *A Companion to Assyria* edited by Eckart Frahm (Wiley, 2017).

Assyrian is a language extremely similar to Babylonian – so much so, that the two are often regarded as 'dialects' of a single language, Akkadian. The extent to which they were mutually comprehensible is unclear, and probably lessened over time. Like Babylonian, Assyrian underwent developmental stages: Old (early second millennium BC), Middle (later second millennium BC) and Neo- (first millennium BC).

Babylonian and Assyrian appear to have evolved in parallel in several respects (such as loss of mimation and the change *št* > *lt*), presumably owing to mutual influence. Assyrian has a shorter history than Babylonian, however: after the collapse of the Neo-Assyrian empire (Nineveh fell in 612 BC), writings in Assyrian all but cease to exist, whereas Babylonian went on being written (albeit by increasingly small groups of people) into the Common Era. An excellent introduction to their comparative history is the article 'Babylonian and Assyrian: A History of Akkadian' by Andrew George, published in 2007 and freely downloadable from https://eprints.soas.ac.uk/3139/.

Old Assyrian is chiefly known from the Assyrian merchants' colony in central Turkey (ancient Kaneš, modern Kültepe). A highly readable overview of the Old Assyrian merchants and their activities is *Ancient Kaneš: A Merchant Colony in Bronze Age Anatolia* by M. T. Larsen (Cambridge University Press, 2015).

From at least the Middle Assyrian period, Assyrians were great admirers of Babylonian culture, and collected (but also recopied and reorganized) works of Babylonian scholarship and literature. Assyrian kings wrote inscriptions and prayed to gods in Babylonian, probably for reasons of cultural prestige.

Writings surviving in Assyrian are largely utilitarian (e.g. letters and legal records). We have very little literature (and even less scholarship) in Assyrian (as opposed to Babylonian), although linguistic Assyrianisms can creep into Babylonian works when Assyrians copy them.

Being great admirers of Babylonian culture, the Assyrians were keen to get their hands on tablets bearing Babylonian scholarship. Indeed, our single-best source for Babylonian intellectual culture are the Nineveh libraries of the Assyrian king Assurbanipal.

CULTURE TIP

The Epic of the Assyrian king Tukulti-Ninurta I (c. 1243–1207 BC) says (presumably with some exaggeration) that he plundered so many tablets from Babylonia that not one was left there.

The way most people today study Assyrian, even in university courses, is to start off thinking of it as a series of modifications to what they already know about Babylonian. This is of course unfair to the Assyrians, but it is nonetheless didactically expedient in several respects (esp. vowel assimilation, see 41.1 number 5). Therefore, you should assume that what previous units said about Babylonian also applies to Assyrian, except in so far as it is modified by the present unit.

The following information should go some way to helping you to read Assyrian, but it is not a full description of all the differences between Babylonian and Assyrian (many details of which still have to be clarified), nor of Assyrian *per se*. To learn more about Assyrian, you might start with *A Sketch of Neo-Assyrian Grammar* by J. Hämeen-Anttila (Helsinki, 2000). There is also the (much more detailed and much more expensive) book *A Grammar of Old Assyrian* by N. J. C. Kouwenberg (Brill, 2017).

In the following, each Assyrian feature is numbered, for convenience of cross-reference in the extracts at the end of the unit.

41.1 Vowels

1 Assyrian often writes *e/ē* where Babylonian writes *i/ī*. For Old and Middle Assyrian, patterns can be found. In Neo-Assyrian, *i* and *e* are largely interchangeable in writing.

2 In Assyrian, *e*-colouring is confined to the position in the word where the guttural was lost, and does not spread to the rest of the word: Bab. *epēšu* = Ass. *epāšu*. (If no guttural was lost, Assyrian has *a* throughout: Bab. *qerēbu* = Ass. *qarābu*.)

3 Assyrian is much less prone to vowel contraction than Babylonian.

4 Whereas in Babylonian *w-* at the beginning of a verb is lost after the Old Babylonian period, in Middle Assyrian word-initial *wa-* turns to *u-*. Hence Middle (and later) Bab. *abālu* = Middle (and later) Ass. *ubālu* (both from earlier *wabālum*).

5 Short *a* at the end of a syllable assimilates to (becomes identical to) the vowel in the next syllable:

Bab. *šarratu*, *šarrata*, *šarrati* **queen** = Ass. *šarrutu*, *šarrata*, *šarrete*
Bab. *imtaqut*, pl. *imtaqtū* **he has fallen, they have fallen** = Ass. *imtuqut*, pl. *imtaqtū/imtuqtū*

This does not happen with infinitives of III-weak verbs (Bab. *leqû* = Ass. *laqû* **to take**).

6 Given two successive syllables containing the vowel *u*, the first often turns to *a*. (This is widely believed to be a result of stress patterns.) Bab. *ša* … *iškunu* = Ass. *ša* … *iškanuni* **which … he placed**. (For *-ni* see item 11.)

7 Compensatory lengthening (Unit 47.2) seems not to occur in Assyrian nouns. Nouns from third weak roots can use a 'strong aleph' as third root letter. Thus Bab. *māru* **son** (long *ā* arisen through compensatory lengthening) is Assyrian *mer'u* or *mar'u*, with strong aleph as third root letter (why *e* instead of *a* is unclear). Cf. item 18.

41.2 Consonants

8 The Babylonian abstract ending *-ūtu* (see Unit 46.1) is *-uttu*: Bab. *šarrūtu* = Ass. *šarruttu* **kingship**.

9 In Neo-Assyrian, *lt* → *ss* (e.g. *assapar* from *altapar*, from earlier *aštapar* **I have sent**); *qt* → *qṭ* (*aqṭirib* **I approached** = Bab. *aqterib*) – this happens already in Middle Assyrian; *tt* sometimes → *ss* (*ma'assu* **much** (f.) = Bab. *ma'attu*); in some verbs, *m* + *t*-infix → *tt* (*attahar* **I received** = Bab. *amtahar*, *amdahar*).

10 From a Babylonian viewpoint, Assyrian spellings often invert *š* and *s*. This is probably because Assyrian inverted the two sounds.

41.3 Verbs

11 The Babylonian verbal suffix *-u* (Unit 30.11) is usually *-u* ... *ni* in Assyrian (though *-u* alone occurs too). *-u* goes where it would in Babylonian; *-ni* goes at the end of the verbal form, after suffixes (if present) but before *-ma* (if present).

Beware that, in Assyrian, *-anni* need not be the first person accusative suffix: it can be ventive/first person dative + the *ni* of *-u* ... *ni*. Furthermore, Assyrian can have *-annini* (accusative *-anni* + the *ni* of *-u* ... *ni*) and even *-ninnini*: *nim+ni* (forming the first person accusative suffix after e.g. the m. pl. ending *-ū*) + the *ni* of *-u* ... *ni*.

12 Some verbs have different theme vowels and/or different stative vowels in Babylonian and Assyrian (e.g. Bab. *maruṣ* vs Ass. *mariṣ* **he is ill**). In such cases the dictionaries give both, specifying which is which.

13 Neo-Assyrian uses the perfect (not the preterite) in positive main clauses, and the preterite (not the perfect) in negated main clauses.

14 Assyrian can (but does not always) distinguish masculine and feminine verbal prefixes in the third person singular: *i-* (m.) vs. *ta-* (f.); *u-* (m.) vs. *tu-* (f.).

She gave = Bab. *iddin*, Ass. *taddin* (or *iddin*).

15 In D system forms where Babylonian has *u* between the first and second root letter (e.g. imp. *PuRRiS*, inf. *PuRRuSu*), Assyrian has *a* (imp. *PaRRiS*, inf. *PaRRuSu*).

Similarly, in Š system forms where Babylonian has *šuPRuS*, Assyrian has *šaPRuS*.

16 The first person G precative (*luprus* in Babylonian) is *laprus* in Assyrian.

uṣulti parzilli bilāni <u>labtuq</u> ina qinniti [*ša*] *pāhiti <u>laškun</u>* **Bring me an iron knife <u>so I can cut</u> (it) <u>off</u> (and) <u>stick</u> (it) up (**lit. **in) the governor's ass!** (SAA XVI 63: 24-25)

17 The Assyrian 3rd m. sg. precative prefix in the D and Š systems is *lu-* (Bab. *li-*).

18 Assyrian II-weak and III-weak verbs often inflect as if they had a 'strong aleph' (i.e. a glottal stop) as second or third root letter. Cf. item 7.

41.4 Nouns and adjectives

19 In Old and Middle Assyrian, noun and adjective endings are the same as in Old and Middle Babylonian, except that: **a)** Assyrian usually has *-e* instead of *-i* in the basic state (*-i-* is retained in the possessive state); **b)** accusatives in *-u(m)* can appear.

20 The Neo-Assyrian basic case endings in the singular are as follows:

nom.: *-u*; acc.: *-u*; gen.: *-i/e*

This case system is sometimes used on Standard Babylonian manuscripts inscribed by Assyrians.

41.5 Specifically Assyrian or Babylonian words

Most Babylonian words are (subject to phonetic changes) also Assyrian words, and vice versa, but occasionally one has a word which the other does not, or a word is common in one which is rare in the other.

21 An example: in the first millennium, *ummu* is a specifically Babylonian word for **fever**, the Assyrian equivalent being *hunṭu* (from *hamāṭu* **to burn**). More generally, Assyrian has a word *laššu* **there is/are not**, which is rare in Babylonian.

22 An example of a specifically Old Assyrian usage is that *lapātum* means **to write**.

Probably we are currently failing to recognize many words as specifically Babylonian or Assyrian because they are not attested often enough to reveal the pattern.

41.6 Suffixes

Possessive suffixes are the same as in Babylonian.

23 Plural accusative suffixes of the 2nd and 3rd person are the same as corresponding possessive suffixes (i.e. *-šunu* rather than *-šunūti* **them**, etc.).

24 Neo-Assyrian has given up dative suffixes (except for the first person singular *-a*), and uses accusative suffixes instead.

laddinak<u>ka</u> **I will give <u>you</u>** (i.e. **to you**)

The same development has taken place in English, where pronouns no longer have a dative form, and use accusative ones (me, you, her, etc.) instead.

41.7 Other

25 Middle and Neo-Assyrian negate only with *lā*, not *ul*. In Old Assyrian, Babylonian *ul* has the form *ula* (both probably go back to an original two-word expression *u lā* **and not**).

26 Neo-Assyrian does not use *-ma* to link clauses.

27 The Babylonian pronouns *šū* and *šī* (**he**, **that one**, **she**, **that one**) are *šūt* and *šīt* in Assyrian.

41.8 Practice passage: an Old Assyrian letter

This letter is written by one Lamassī, who lives in Assur, to her husband the merchant Pûšu–kēn, who spends most of his time in faraway Kanesh, in central Anatolia. As is typical of the Old Assyrian merchants in Kanesh, Lamassī arranges for her husband to receive textiles, which they sell to Anatolian populations, sending some of the money back to Assur. Here Lamassī is complaining that she still has to receive the money due for a previous shipment. Quite a large dossier of letters from this family survives.

The Old Assyrian syllabary is different from that in other varieties of Babylonian and Assyrian. For example, it normally represents the syllable *la* using the sign *lá*; the syllable *tu* with the sign *tù* (= *du*); the syllable *ab* with the sign *áb*; and so on. This does not make it harder to read in transliteration, but it is a bit of a shock if you start to read Old Assyrian in cuneiform, when you are used to other syllabaries.

On the other hand, Old Assyrian seems to use as few signs as possible, probably because the merchants and their families were practically-minded individuals who wanted to facilitate written communication. Its repertoire of signs and readings is, therefore, the quickest to learn.

The tablet was published in cuneiform by F. J. Stephens, *Old Assyrian Letters and Business Documents* (= Babylonian Inscriptions in the Collection of James B. Nies, Yale University, Vol. VI; New Haven, 1944) as number 7 (plate 11). The entire volume has been transliterated by Karl Hecker: https://www.hethport.uni-wuerzburg.de/altass/pdfsrc/BIN6.pdf.

Cuneiform

(Using Neo-Assyrian script for an Old Assyrian letter is, of course, anachronistic. So far, no Old Assyrian font exists.)

Old Assyrian uses a single vertical wedge as 'word divider' (transliterated with a colon), though not consistently.

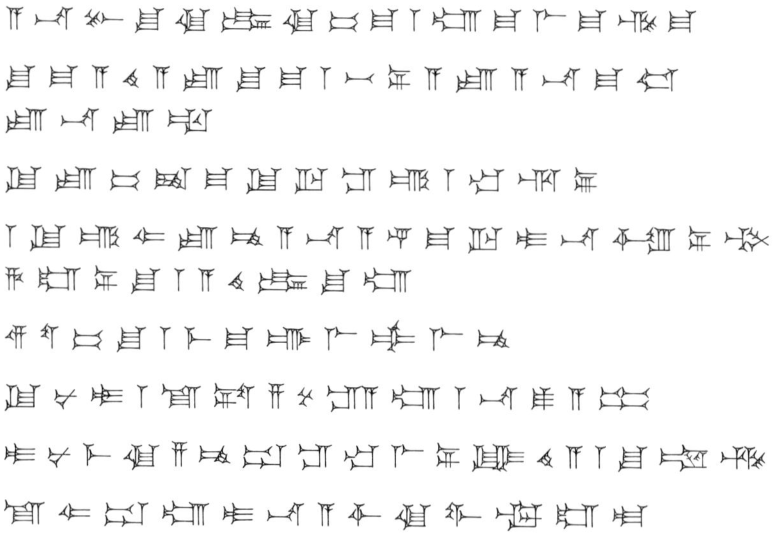

Transliteration

Note how Old Assyrian rarely writes double consonants as such.

[1] *a-na pu-šu–ke-en*$_6$ [2] *qí-bi-ma : um-ma* [3] *lá-ma-sí-ma*

šu-ma a-hi a-ta [4] *šu-ma : be-lí a-ta a-na ma-nem* [5] *ta-na-ṭá-al*

[6] *ku-ta-bi-it-ma* [7] *ku-ur-si-kà : pá-re-er*

[8] 1 túg *kà-áb-ta-am* [9] *a-na A-šur–ma-lik* [10] *i-na pà-ni-tem* [11] *ha-ra-ni-šu : a-dí-[í]n-[š]u-um*

[12] kù.babbar-*pí-šu : mì-ma* [13] *ú-lá ub-lá-am*

[14] *ku-nu-kam : ša* $^{\text{na4}}$za.gìn [15] diri-*um : na-áš-a-kum*

[16] *i-nu-mì ki-sà-am* [17] *tù-šé-ba-lá-ni* [18] síg$^{\text{hi.a}}$ *: šu-uk-nam*

[19] *ša-áp-tù-um* [20] *i-na a-lem*^{ki} [21] *wa-aq-ra-at*

Normalization

Assyrianisms are highlighted in bold.

*ana pûšu-k**ē**n qibi-ma umma lamassī-ma*

*šumma ahī atta šumma bēlī atta ana mann**e**m tanaṭṭal*

*kutabbit-ma kursīka p**a**rrir*

1 *ṣubātam kabtam ana Aššur–malik ina panīt**e**m harrānišu addin[š]um*

*kaspīšu mimma **ulā** ublam*

*kunukkam ša uqnîm watarum na**š'**akkum*

*inūmi kīsam tušebbalan**ni** šāptam šuknam*

*šāptum ina āl**e**m waqrat*

> **CULTURE TIP**
>
> This letter follows the convention of many Babylonian and Assyrian letters, which is to write as if one were addressing someone other than the addressee, such as a secretary or a public scribe: instead of writing **Dear Alex, ... Yours, Martin**, one writes **Tell Alex that Martin says ....** The convention very likely originated out of the real-world situation of addressees getting people to read to them, but once it had established itself it could well have persisted even when the addressee was expected to read the letter directly.

Translation

Say to Pûšu-kēn: thus (speaks) Lamassī:

If you are my brother, if you are my lord, make an effort(?) and break your fetters!

I gave one heavy textile to Aššur-malik in his previous journey.

He has absolutely not brought me its money (i.e. the money deriving from it).

Moreover, he is bringing you a seal of lapis-lazuli.

When you send me the money-bag, put (some) wool (in it).

Wool is expensive in the City!

Notes

Note that, though Lamassī is addressing her husband, she metaphorically calls him **brother** to rhetorically reinforce his obligations to her. The nuance of *kutabbit* is unclear. The translation **make an effort** is a guess based on the context, following the *Chicago Assyrian Dictionary*.

Assyrianisms (numbered by the list in Unit 41.7): *kēn* (1); *parrir* (15); *naš'akkum* (18); *tušebbalanni* (11); *ula* (25).

41.9 Practice passage: two Middle Assyrian laws

The Middle Assyrian laws are known from clay tablets rather than monuments (such as Hammurapi's stele). One manuscript of them was found in a city gate at Assur. This being a site of trials, the tablet was probably used in practice. The Middle Assyrian Laws often prescribe horrendously elaborate physical punishments, though there is doubt over whether they were supposed to be understood literally.

You can see Otto Schroeder's hand drawing of a cuneiform manuscript of the Laws (no. 1 in *Keilschrifttexte aus Assur verschiedenen Inhalts*; Leipzig, 1920) at: http://etana.org/sites/default/files/coretexts/14877.pdf (first page of cuneiform in the book; Law 2 starts at line 14). Schroeder's manuscript is in Cursive Middle Assyrian, which you will see is not very different from Cursive Neo-Assyrian.

LAW 2

Note: in Middle Assyrian, **man** is *a'īlu* (Bab. *awīlu*)

Transliteration

šum-[*ma*] munus *lu-ú* dam-*at* lú *lu-ú* dumu.munus lú *ši-il-la-ta taq-ṭì-bi*

lu-ú mi-qí-it pe-e ta-ar-ti-i-ši

munus *ši-i-it a-ra-an-ša ta-na-áš-ši*

a-na mu-ti-ša dumu^{meš}-*ša* dumu.munus^{meš}-*ša la-a i-qar-ri-i-bu*

Normalization

šum[*ma*] *sinniltu lū aššat a'īle lū mārat a'īle šillata* ***ta****q****ṭi****bi*

lū miqit pê ***ta****rt****i****ši*

sinniltu ***šīt*** *aranša tanašši*

ana mutiša mar'īša mar'ātiša ***lā*** *iqarribū*

Translation

If a woman, whether married or unmarried (lit. **either a man's wife or a man's daughter), said something untoward or became verbally offensive** (lit. **acquired a falling of the mouth), this woman shall (herself) bear her penalty. There shall be no claim on** (lit. **'they' shall not have a claim on ...**; impersonal, see Unit 14.16) **her husband, her sons (or) her daughters.**

Assyrianisms: *a'īlu* for Bab. *awīlu* (see note above); *taqṭibi* for Bab. *iqtabi* (5, 9, 14); *tartiši* for Bab. *irtaši* and *tanašši* for Bab. *inašši* (5, 14); *šīt* for Bab. *šī* (27); *mar'īša mar'ātiša* for Bab. *mārīša mārātiša* (7); *lā* for Bab. *ul* (25).

LAW 3

Transliteration

šum-ma lú *lu-ú ma-ri-iṣ lu-ú me-et* dam-*su i-na* é-*šu mi-im-ma tal-ti-ri-iq*

lu-ú a-na lú *lu-ú a-na* munus *ù lu-ú a-na ma-am-ma ša-ni-em-ma ta-ti-din*

dam-*at* lú *ù ma-he-ra-nu-te-ma i-du-uk-ku-šu-nu*

ù šum-ma dam-*at* lú *ša mu-us-sa bal-ṭu-ú-ni i-na* é *mu-ti-ša tal-ti-ri-iq*

lu-ú a-na lú *lu-ú a-na* munus *ù lu-ú a-na ma-am-ma ša-né-em-ma ta-at-ti-din*

lú dam-*su ú-ba-ar ù hi-i-ṭa e-em-mì-id* (ignore the extra *e*)

ù ma-he-ra-a-nu ša i-na qa-at dam-*at* lú *im-hu-ru-ú-ni šur-qa i-id-da-an*

ù hi-i-ṭa ki-i ša-a lú dam-*su e-mi-du-ú-ni ma-he-ra-a-na e-em-mi-du*

Normalization (with Assyrianisms highlighted in bold)

*šumma a’īlu lū mar***iṣ** *lū m***ē***t aššassu ina b***ē***tišu mimma* **ta***lt***i***riq*

*lū ana a’īle lū ana sinnilte u lū ana mamma šan***īe***mma* **ta***tt***i***din*

aššat a’īle u māherānūtemma idukkūšunu

*u šumma aššat a’īle ša mussa balṭu***ni** *ina b***ē***t mutiša* **ta***lt***i***riq*

*lū ana a’īle lū ana sinnilte u lū ana mamma šan***īe***mma* **ta***tt***i***din*

a’īlu aššassu ubār u hīṭa **e***mmid*

*u māherānu ša ina qāt aššat a’īle imhuru***ni** *šurqa iddan*

u hīṭa kī ša a’īlu aššassu **ē***midu***ni** *māherāna* **e***mmidū*

Literal translation

If a man – either he being sick or he being dead – , his wife ('dangling construction', see Unit 11.12) **stole something from his house (and) gave it either to a man, or to a woman, or to anyone else: the man's wife and likewise** (*-ma*) **the receivers, 'they'** (impersonal, see Unit 14.16) **shall kill them** (redundant suffix, see Unit 19.9).

And/but if a man's wife whose husband is healthy stole from her husband's house, (and) gave it either to a man, or to a woman, or to anyone else: the man shall denounce his wife, and impose the penalty. And the receiver who received (see Unit 35.7) **from the hand of the man's wife shall give the stolen goods, and 'they' shall impose on the receiver a penalty like the man imposed on his wife.**

Freer translation

If the wife of a sick or dead man stole something from his house (and) gave it either to a man, or to a woman, or to anyone else, the man's wife and likewise the receivers shall be put to death.

If however a married woman whose husband is healthy steals from her husband's house, (then) the man shall denounce his wife, and decide the penalty. Whoever

received (them) from the man's wife shall give (back) the stolen goods, and he will be subject to a penalty equal to that which the man imposed on his wife.

Assyrianisms: *a'īlu* for Bab. *amīlu*; *mariṣ* for Bab. *maruṣ* (12); *mēt* for Bab. *mīt* and *bētišu* for Bab. *bītišu* (1); *taltiriq* for Bab. *iltariq* (from earlier *ištariq*) (5, 14); *šanīem-ma* for Bab. *šanîm-ma* (3, 1); *tattidin* for Bab. *ittadin* (5, 14); *balṭuni* for Bab. *balṭu* (11); *emmid* for Bab. *immid* and *emmidū* for Bab. *immidū* (1); *imhuruni* for Bab. *imhuru* (11); *ēmiduni* for Bab. *īmidu* (1, 11). See also note to previous law, on *a'īlu* (Bab. *awīlu*).

The basic state gen. sg. endings are also Middle Assyrian: *sinnilte* for Bab. *sinnilti*, etc. (19).

41.10 Practice passage: a Neo-Assyrian letter about a stolen statue

Like many cuneiform tablets, this one is broken: the first lines are lost. With a work surviving on multiple manuscripts, it would be possible to piece together a composite text. Here we have only a single manuscript, and very likely only one ever existed, so the beginning cannot be restored. The letter is a good example of how, though Mesopotamian sources can be understood on a sentence-by-sentence basis, it is often difficult (not least because of the breaks) to work out exactly what is happening, and exactly what each word means.

What survives, however, gives us enough information to reconstruct the general context: a stolen statue was found, and the culprit killed. The letter is probably written by an administrator, who appears to be citing reports from different sources – one from the servant of Nabû-šallim–ahhê, and one from the temple stewardess. There may have been previous ones, lost in the break.

The letter was edited by Cole and Machinist as number 157 in volume XIII of the series State Archives of Assyria. Their edition is also available online, at http://oracc.museum.upenn.edu/saao/P334870.

Cuneiform

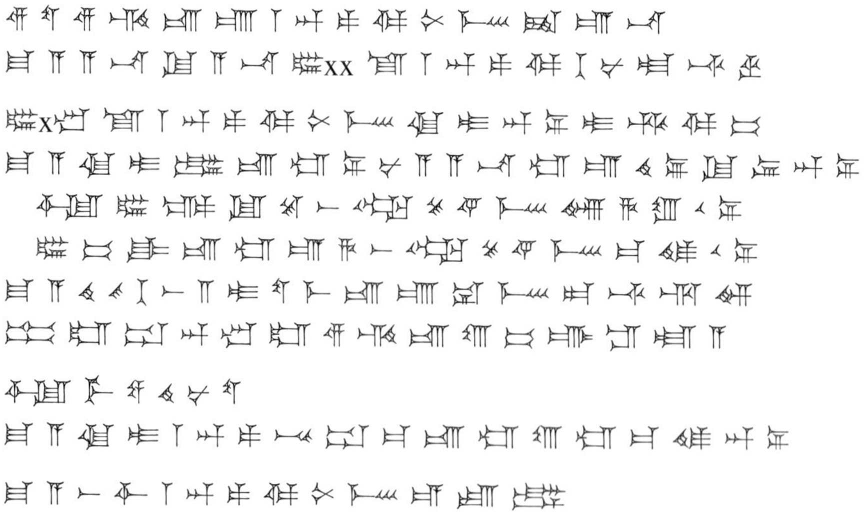

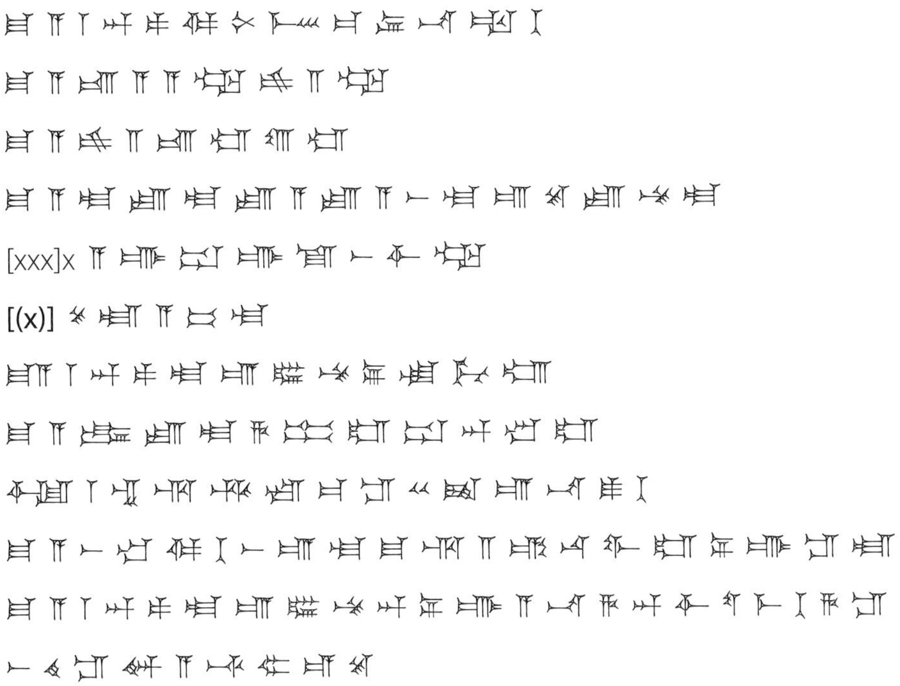

Transliteration

ta^{v} means: a particular form of the cuneiform sign TA:  (TA^{V}) rather than  (TA).
[kug].ud kug.gi ta^{v} é ^{md}pa–di–[pab^{meš}] *it-tan-na*

ma-a a-na-ku a-na ^{lú}.[xx] ⸢*ša*⸣ ^{md}pa–di-*šú-nu at-ti-din*

^{lú}*x* arad *ša* ^{md}pa–di–pab^{meš} *ki-i an-ni-i iq-ṭi-bi*

ma-a ki-i lugal ta^{v} ^{uru}*ni-nu-a a-na* ^{uru}*kal-hi ir-ku-sa-an-ni*

ù ^{lú}*šag-lu-te ina* ugu še.pad^{meš} *ih-ha-ru-u-ni*

^{lú}kaš.lul ta^{v} ^{uru}*kal-ha ina* ugu še.pad^{meš} *is-har-u-ni*

ma-a hi-ṣib-šú ina 2-*i* ud-*me* ta$^{\text{v*}}$ é uš^{meš} *ab-ti-ri-im*

qu-ra-du ^{d}ìr.ra kug.gi ta^{v} šà-*bi ú-se-ṣi-a*

ù ^{munus}*láh-hi-nu-tú*

ma-a ki-i ^{md}pa–numun–gin–giš ta^{v} ^{uru}šà–uru *is-hur-an-ni*

ma-a ina igi ^{md}pa–di–pab^{meš} *e-ta-rab*

ma-a ^{md}pa–di–pab^{meš} ⸢*is?*⸣-*sa-na-al-šú*

ma-a ta^{v} *a-a-ka* kaskal^{2}-*ka*

[*ma-a* kaskal]^{2} ta^{v} ^{uru}*šà*–uru

ma-a at-ta at-ta [*a?*]-⸢*ta*⸣-*a ina la ket-te ta-mu-at*

[x x x] ⸢x⸣ *a? ú-du-ú ša ina* igi-⸢*ka**⸣

[(x)] *še-ṣi-a bi-la*
ma-a ^{md}pa–ad–kalag ^{lú}mu *ir-tu-gu-um*
ma-a in-ta-at-ha qu-ra-du ^{d}ìr.ra
ù 1-*en ri-ik-su is-se-niš it-tan-na-áš-šú*
ma-a ina ba-di-šú ina kal-la-ma-ri 2 ^{dug}*qa-pi-ra-ni ú-se-ṣi*
ma-a ^{md}pa–ad–kalag ^{lú}mu *an-ni-ú a-na ha-an-ši* ud-*me-šú ha-si*
ina hi-si-ʾa-a-ti mé-e-te

Normalization

*kaspu hurāṣu **issu** b**ē**t nabû–š**a**llim–[ahhê] ittanna*
*mā anāku ana [...] ša nabû–š**a**llim**šunu** att**i**din*

*x **u**rdu ša nabû–š**a**llim–ahhê kī ann**ii** iq**ṭi**bi*
*mā kī šarru **issu** ninua ana kalhi irkusan**ni***
*u šaglūte ina muhhi kurummāte ihh**a**rū**ni***
*šāq**iu** **issu** kalha ina muhhi kurummāte ish**a**runi*
*mā hiṣibšu ina šan**ii** ūme **issu** bēt ridûti abt**i**rim*
*qurādu erra hurāṣu **issu** libbi u**ss**ēṣ**ia***

*ù lahhin**u**tu*
*mā kī nabû–zēr–kītti–lēšir **issu** libbi–āli ishuran**ni***
*mā ina pan nabû–š**a**llim–ahhê ēt**a**r**a**b*
*mā nabû–š**a**llim–ahhê* ⌜*is*⌝*sana”alšu*
*mā **issu** ayyika hūlka* (or *harrānka*)
[*mā hūlī* (or *harrānī*)] *issu libbi–āli*
*mā atta atta [a]tá ina lā kētte tam**ua**t*
[x x x] ⌜x⌝ x *udû ša ina pani*⌜*ka*⌝

[(x)] *š**ē**ṣ**ia** bila*
*mā nabû–abu–d**a**”in nuhatimmu irt**u**gum*
mā intatha qurādu erra
*u i**ss**ēn riksu i**ss**ēniš ittannaššu*
*mā ina bādišu ina kallamāri šina qapīrānī u**ss**ēṣi*
*mā nabû–abu–d**a**”in nuhatimmu ann**īu** ana hanši ūmišu hasi*
*ina hisi**ʾā**ti m**ē**t*

Translation

From the house of Nabû-šallim-ahhê ('Nabû, preserve the brothers!') he gave silver and gold,

saying (*mā*) **'I gave (it) to the [...] of Nabû-šallimšunu ('Nabû, preserve them!')'.**

The x, servant of Nabû-šallim-ahhê spoke thus:

When the king transferred me from Nineveh to Kalhu,

and the deportees demanded (barley) rations,

(and) the cup-bearer came back from Kalhu for the (barley) rations,

Two days after the (ceremony in) the succession house (lit. **on the second day since the succession house**; notwithstanding Unit 13.2) **I sealed his produce.**

I brought out Warrior Erra (of) gold (i.e. a golden statue of the god Erra)**.**

So the temple stewardess said (*mā*)**:**

'When Nabû–zēr–kītti–lēšir came back from the Inner City (lit. **middle of the city**),

he entered into the presence of Nabû-šallim-ahhê.

Nabû-šallim-ahhê questioned him,

saying (*mā*) **'Where have you come from?'** (lit. **from which (place) is your path?**)

(Nabû–zēr–kītti–lēšir) replied (*mā*) **'my path] is from the Inner City.'**

(Nabû-šallim-ahhê) said (*mā*) **'You – you – why would you die in non-truth?!'**

[...] get out and bring me the utensils that are with you.

He summoned Nabû-abu-da"in ('Nabû, strengthen the father!') the cook,

saying (*mā*) **'He removed Warrior Erra and at the same time (***issēniš***) gave him (i.e. the above-mentioned servant?) a** *riksu*.'

That evening (and) in the morning he brought out two *qapīru*-pots.

Nabû-abu-da"in, this cook, was beaten on the fifth day. He died of his beatings.

Assyrian features

issu (Bab. *ištu*, later *ultu*); *bēt* (Bab. *bīt*); *šallim* (Bab. *šullim*); *-šunu* for Bab. *-šunūti*; *urdu* (Bab. *wardu(m)*, later *ardu*); *annīi* (Bab. *annî*); *iqṭibi* (Bab *iqtabi*); *irkusanni* (Bab *irkusa*); *ihharūni* (Bab *imhurū*); *šāqiu* (Bab. *šāqû*); *isharuni* (Bab. *ishuru*); *šanīi* (Bab. *šanî*); *abtirim* (Bab. *abtarim*); *ussēṣia* (Bab. *uštēṣâ*, later *ultēṣâ*); *lahhinutu* (Bab. *lahhinatu*); *ishuranni* (Bab. *ishura*); *ētarab* (Bab. *īterub*); *tamūat* (Bab. *tamât*); *šēṣia* (Bab. *šūṣâ*); *da"in* (Bab. *dunnin*); *irtugum* (Bab. *irtagum*); *issēn(iš)* (Bab. *ištēn(iš)*, later *iltēn(iš)*); *ussēṣi* for Bab. *ultēṣi* (OB *uštēṣi*); *annīu* (Bab. *annû*); *hisi'āti* (Bab. *hisâti*); *mēt* (Bab. *mīt*).

Notes

1 *Nabû-šallim-ahhê* (**'Nabû, preserve the brothers!'**) and *Nabû-šallimšunu* (**'Nabû, preserve them!'**) may be variants of the same name, referring to the same person. **2** *The Chicago Assyrian Dictionary* (vol. Q, p. 91) sees *udû* **utensils** as meaning the two *qapīru*-pots referred to later.

SELF CHECK

	I can ...
	... explain the main ways in which Assyrian is different from Babylonian.

42 *Taking things further*

In this unit you will learn:

- **how to expand your study of Babylonian and Assyrian beyond this book**
- **about some important online tools.**

The best way to continue learning Babylonian and Assyrian (for, as with any language, one never stops ...) is to read widely. Initially, you can be satisfied with understanding how the editor's translation corresponds to the transliteration (no mean achievement!). Subsequently, you can start to translate for yourself.

42.1 Things to read

Depending on your interests, you might start with:

- *The Law Code of Hammurapi* (king of Babylonia, c. 1792–1750 BC). This is Old Babylonian grammar 'at its best', with mimation used consistently. A transliteration by Walter Sommerfeld can be found here: https://www.uni-marburg.de/cnms/forschung/dnms/apps/ast/ob/kh_transliteration.pdf (the Code starts off with a lengthy prologue. The laws themselves begin on page 8). There is not at present a freely available English translation online. Among paper books, you can consult the (sometimes quite free) rendition in M. Roth's *Law Collections from Mesopotamia and Asia Minor* (Society of Biblical Literature 1995). *The Babylonian Laws* by G. R. Driver and C. J. Miles (Clarendon Press, 1952) is also still fairly reliable.
- Assyrian royal inscriptions, which are usually in Babylonian (the most heavily Assyrianized ones are those of Assurnaṣirpal II). Their style tends to be quite repetitive, which is excellent for beginners. Prepare for an inundation of place names, many of which cannot yet be matched to modern ones. Editions are being put online at http://oracc.museum.upenn.edu/riao/ (click 'Browse').
  Good ones to tackle first would be: **a)** the Prism Inscription of Tiglath-Pileser I (the one used in the experiment of 1857, see 'In a nutshell'). This is in Middle Babylonian, and so uses triptotic case endings (i.e. *-u*, *-a*, *-i/e*) but not mimation. The composite text assembled by Kirk Grayson is accessible online at http://oracc.iaas.upenn.edu/riao/Q005926. **b)** the 'Rassam Prism' of Assurbanipal, which uses Neo-Assyrian case endings (sg. *-u*, *-u*, *-i/e*) but is otherwise in Standard Babylonian. The scale drawing by Theophilus Pinches can be found in Volume 5 of the *Cuneiform Inscriptions of Western Asia* (London, 1909; plates I-X; freely downloadable from http://etana.org/sites/default/files/coretexts/20376.pdf);

a transliteration and translation by Jamie Novotny and Joshua Jeffers are accessible at http://oracc.museum.upenn.edu/rinap/rinap5/Q003710.

- Standard Babylonian *Gilgameš*, Tablets I and XI – a great story, and linguistically not too complicated. The critical edition by A.R. George (Oxford University Press, 2003) is freely accessible at http://eprints.soas.ac.uk/1603/. (See also http://www.soas.ac.uk/nme/research/gilgamesh/standard/.) Some ideas on *Gilgameš* Tablet I by the author of this book can be found at https://www.jstor.org/stable/pdf/41490042.
- For Assyrian, one can recommend Old Assyrian and Neo-Assyrian letters. At present editions are easier to find online for the latter than the former, but this is likely to even out.

42.2 Dictionaries

You are strongly recommended to equip yourself with a copy of *A Concise Dictionary of Akkadian* (Wiesbaden: Harrassowitz Verlag). (Make sure to use the list of roots at the front, which is very helpful in parsing verbal forms.) Note the online addenda and corrigenda at https://www.soas.ac.uk/cda-archive/lemmata/.

Additionally, you can consult the multi-volume *Chicago Assyrian Dictionary* (available for free online at http://oi.uchicago.edu/research/pubs/catalog/cad). Some of the earlier volumes are now rather out of date. Note that CAD does not use 'G, D, Š and N' as names for the verbal systems: instead it calls them I, II, III and IV (respectively). The sub-systems are indicated by /2 (the *t* series) and /3 (the *tan* series). Thus II = D; III/3 = Štn; I/2 = Gt; and so on.

Particularly when making your way through longer CAD entries (which can be *very* long, and initially quite confusing), it may be useful to bear in mind that they are generally structured according to the principles 'from older to newer', and 'from concrete to abstract' (where these two principles conflict, some sort of compromise is made).

For readers of German there is also W. von Soden's stupendous *Akkadisches Handwörterbuch*, though this is very expensive and not user-friendly for beginners.

It is a real problem that the existing dictionaries of Babylonian and Assyrian are going out of date with every day that passes. This would not happen to an appreciable extent with a modern language, but in a field as fast-evolving as Assyriology, new words are being found all the time, and old passages being reinterpreted. This will not concern you as a beginner, as the basic vocabulary is unlikely to change much. But you will notice it if you continue your studies.

42.3 Sign lists

As you become proficient in Babylonian, you will start wondering how else a given cuneiform sign can be read. For this, you turn to a comprehensive sign list (which the ones at the end of this course are not). The most up-to-date of these is R. Borger's *Mesopotamisches Zeichenlexikon* (Münster, 2003). Once you get the hang of it, you can use it without knowing German, but it is an intimidating book for non-specialists. Less up to date, but somewhat more user-friendly, is R. Labat and F. Malbran-Labat's *Manuel d'épigraphie akkadienne* (6th ed. Paris, 1982).

42.4 List of sumerograms

W. Schramm's book *Akkadische Logogramme* (Göttingen, 2016), freely available online (www.oapen.org/download?type=document&docid=610357), offers a list of sumerograms in transliteration, each with its Babylonian equivalent(s), a German translation of the Babylonian words, and a bibliographical reference. In terms of this course, it is a massive expansion of the list of sumerograms provided here.

42.5 Babylonian and Assyrian on the internet

The amount of Babylonian and Assyrian online is huge, and growing fast.

The largest portals of editions are:

- The Open Richly Annotated Cuneiform Corpus (ORACC), which incorporates many different sub-projects: http://oracc.museum.upenn.edu/projectlist.html. To actually get to see transliterations and transliterations, click 'browse'. It is worth pointing out that the Royal Inscriptions of Assyria Online (RIAo) sub-project gives you the option to convert the transliteration into elecronically generated cuneiform.
- The Cuneiform Digital Library Initiative (CDLI), with many sources, often with photographs of the tablet: http://cdli.ucla.edu.
- Sources of Early Akkadian Literature (SEAL): editions (including bespoke glossaries) for Old and Middle Babylonian and Assyrian literature, including incantations: http://www.seal.uni-leipzig.de/
- Archives Babyloniennes (ARCHIBAB), with transliterations and French translations of thousands of documents in Old Babylonian: http://www.archibab.fr/en/accueil.htm. Having clicked 'I agree' to enter the site, click on 'Text(s)' then enter ARM into the first search box. This will bring up the more than 5000 letters published in the series Archives Royales de Mari.

The following websites are also very useful:

- Transliterations of all manuscripts of Standard Babylonian *Gilgamesh*: http://www.soas.ac.uk/nme/research/gilgamesh/standard/
- ETANA project (scans of out-of-copyright books, including many volumes of cuneiform copies): http://www.etana.org/coretexts.shtml
- Free PDFs of publications by the Oriental Institute of the University of Chicago: http://oi.uchicago.edu/research/pubs/catalog/
- Several volumes of the *Revue d'assyriologie et d'archéologie orientale* are available online for free (this includes editions of tablets and articles – sometimes in English – about Mesopotamian history, languages and culture): http://www.cairn.info/revue-d-assyriologie.htm
- If you have access to *JSTOR* (http://www.jstor.org/), many other specialist journals are available to you. Note especially *IRAQ*, *Orientalia*, the *Journal of the American Oriental Society*, the *Journal of Cuneiform Studies*, and the *Journal of Near Eastern Studies*.

42.6 Reference grammars

The information in this course should be enough to help you understand the workings of most sources in Babylonian and Assyrian. Nonetheless, you may wish to explore the languages in more detail than it was possible to present them here.

The last attempt to produce a full grammar of all periods of Babylonian and Assyrian was W. von Soden's *Grundriss der akkadischen Grammatik* (3rd ed; Rome, 1995). Any reference grammar of Babylonian and Assyrian is bound to become outdated fairly quickly: while the basics are unlikely to change much, all sorts of refinements are being made all the time. An update to von Soden's grammar was published by W. R. Mayer in the journal *Orientalia* in 2016.

A recent work which goes quite some way towards being a full grammar of Babylonian and Assyrian is N. J. C. Kouwenberg's *The Akkadian Verb and its Semitic Background* (Eisenbrauns, 2010). While reading the whole thing cover to cover would be quite heavy-going, anyone interested in languages is likely to find it a fascinating book to dip in and out of.

43 *Tricks of the trade*

In this unit you will learn:

- **a bit about Sumerian**
- **a bit about Babylonian poetry**
- **a bit about mistakes by ancient writers.**

This unit gives you some information which is not strictly about Babylonian as a language, but will help you make better sense of things you have learned, and/or help you understand how Assyriologists interpret original Babylonian sources.

43.1 How cuneiform signs acquired their readings

Cuneiform signs accrued readings over time, and the proliferation of readings in Standard Babylonian can become truly disorienting. Ultimately, many of them simply have to be learned, but understanding how they came into being can be a big help in remembering them (and also intellectually satisfying).

1 Cuneiform signs all started out as pictures, and represented the Sumerian word for the thing depicted. For example, a picture of three drops of water was used to represent *a*, the Sumerian word for **water**. Babylonians therefore used the same sign for the sound *a*, borrowing the Sumerian value. Similarly, a picture of mountains was used to represent *kur*, the Sumerian word for **mountain**.

2 The Sumerians themselves started giving signs multiple readings. Thus, for obvious reasons, they used the same sign that wrote *a* **water** to write $duru_5$ **wet**. Babylonians therefore used this sign to write *dur*, so the sign is today said to have the Babylonian reading dur_5. Again they are essentially borrowing the Sumerian value, with little modification.

   Similarly, in Sumerian there is a complex religious entity known as *me*, written with the sign ME. The cultic functionary responsible for attending to the *me* was known as the *išib*. Since there was such a close connection between the *išib* and the *me*, Sumerians used the sign ME to write both *me* and *išib*. Babylonian speakers then adapted the latter reading, using ME to write *me* and *šib*.

3 As discussed in Unit 4.1, Babylonians used cuneiform signs as sumerograms, to represent entire words. Thus, using the examples from **1**, they used *a* to represent their word for **water** (Bab. *mû*) and *kur* to represent their word for **mountain** (Bab. *šadû*).

Syllabic readings arose from the Babylonian equivalents of Sumerian words which signs represented. For example, since Sumerian *kur* **mountain** translates into Babylonian as *šadû*, Babylonians used this sign for the syllable *šad*. Equally, Sumerian *úš* means **to die**, so since the Babylonian for **dead** is *mītu*, the sign acquired the reading *mit*.

Readings of this kind arise often, but not consistently. For example, the sign *a* is not normally used to write *mu* (though it could have been), presumably because there was already a sign with the reading *mu* in Sumerian.

4 More readings still evolved by slight modification of existing readings. Thus once the sign ÚŠ had acquired the Babylonian reading *mit*, it was also given the readings *mid*, *miṭ*, *met*, *med*, and *meṭ*. Since the sign KUR had the reading *kur*, it was also given the readings *gur* (which modern Assyriologists call gur_{16}) and *qur* (which modern Assyriologists call *qúr*). And so on, for many different signs.

General principles in **4** are that: any CVC (consonant-vowel-consonant) sign with the vowel *i* could also have *e*; and families of similar-sounding consonants became interchangeable at the end of sign readings. This happened with *p* and *b*; *t*, *d* and *ṭ*; *k*, *g* and *q*. Thus IP is the same sign as IB, AP is the same sign as AB, ŠUP is the same sign as ŠUB, etc. By contrast, PA and BA, KU and GU, TI and DI, are two different signs (the consonant is at the start of the syllable, not the end).

43.2 How sumerograms work

Users of this course encounter a number of sumerograms. Sometimes they are only one word long, e.g. *anše* (Bab. *imēru*) **donkey**. In such cases no explanation is required: *anše* is simply the Sumerian word for **donkey**. But sometimes a single Babylonian word is represented by a sumerogram several signs long, and in such cases you might well be curious as to how it works.

For this, a smattering of Sumerian grammar is useful, which is provided below. Once the super-literal meaning of the sumerogram is apprehended, it will transpire that it does not always match exactly what the sumerogram represents in Akkadian.

43.3 How Sumerian expresses *of*

In principle, Sumerian expresses **X of Y** as *X Y-ak*, using a suffix *-ak*. There are, however, three particularities:

a the Sumerian *-ak* morpheme is never (neither in sumerograms nor in connected Sumerian) written with the sign AK: rather, *a* and *k*, if present, must be written as part of different signs, one ending in *a* and one starting with *k*;

b either or both of *a* and *k* may vanish; in particular, the *k* vanishes unless it is 'protected' by a following vowel ending;

c if the Y-word ends in a consonant, this is often written again, together with the *a* of the morpheme *ak*, yielding a *Ca* (consonant-plus-*a* sign).

Thus *anše.kur.ra* **horse** super-literally means **donkey** (*anše*) **of the mountain** (*kur*). The morpheme *ak* has been added after *kur*. The *r* of *kur* has been doubled, and put into a sign with the *a* of *ak*, yielding RA. The *k* has been lost because there is no vowel ending to 'protect' it (there might be such an ending in a proper Sumerian sentence, but sumerograms are usually endingless).

The same explanation applies to *a.ab.ba* (Bab. *tâmtu*) **sea**: super-literally, this means **water** (*a*) **of the sea** (*ab*).

The same phenomenon features in the sumerogram for **Babylon**. In Babylonian, the word for **Babylon** is *bābili*, which (whether correctly or not is hard to say) was understood in antiquity as *bāb ili* **gate of the god**. The Sumerian for **gate** being *ká*, and **god** being *dingir*, **gate of the god** is *ká.dingir.ra*. This (which is very likely a back-translation from Babylonian) is often used as sumerogram for Babylon, often with the place determinative ^{ki}.

43.4 Sumerian adjectives

Several sumerograms are made up of noun+adjective. As in Babylonian, Sumerian adjectives follow the noun they qualify.

Thus: *kù* being the Sumerian word for **metal** and *babbar* **bright**, *kù.babbar* (Bab. *kaspu*) **silver** is super-literally **bright metal**; *ur* being **dog** and *mah* (Bab. *ṣīru*) **great**, the sumerogram *ur.mah* (Bab. *nēšu*) **lion** super-literally means **great dog**; *gi*$_7$ meaning something like **noble**, and *ur* being the same word as in *ur.mah* **lion**, *ur.gi*$_7$ (Bab. *kalbu*) super-literally means something like **noble dog**; *é.gal* (Bab. *ēkallu*) **palace** is super-literally **big house**.

43.5 Sumerian compound nouns

English very often puts two nouns together, so that the first one qualifies the second and together they form a so-called 'compound noun': **table leg**, **toy gun**, **garden fence**, **cellar door**. (The expression **compound noun** is itself a compound noun.) Sometimes, the relation between them becomes so close that they get written as one, e.g. **toothpaste**.

Sumerian does exactly the same, except that things work the other way round: the second noun qualifies the first. As it happens, a subset of English expressions works in the same way. These are British government titles which include the word **Lord**: **Lord Chancellor**, **Lord Privy Seal**, **Lord Keeper of the Great Seal**, etc. In the same way that a **table leg** is (grammatically speaking) a kind of **leg**, and the Lord Chancellor is (grammatically speaking) a kind of **Lord**, according to normal English grammar we would expect **Chancellor Lord** rather than **Lord Chancellor**. Quite possibly, such titles were influenced by French, which in respect of compound nouns behaves like Sumerian (e.g. *les rois jardineurs* switches round in English translation: **the gardener kings**).

An example of a sumerogram consisting in a compound noun is *am.si* (Bab. *pīru*) **elephant**. This is made up of *am* **aurochs** and *si* **horn** (here probably meaning **tusk**): super-literally, **horn aurochs** or **tusk aurochs**, i.e. **aurochs with horns**, **aurochs with a tusk**.

Another example is *ì.giš* (Bab. *šamnu*) **oil**. By itself, *ì* can be any sort of creamy or fatty substance, so let's translate it **fattiness/creaminess**; *giš* (Bab. *iṣu*) is **wood**. Hence *ì.giš* is super-literally **wood fattiness/creaminess**, i.e. **oil of vegetable origin** (as opposed to animal fat).

The same construction probably applies to *ì.nun* (Bab. *himētu*) **ghee**, super-literally **prince fattiness/creaminess**. But one could also interpret *nun* as an adjective **princely**, which would place it in Unit 43.4. (Many details of Sumerian are quite slippery, even when one is not dealing with oil!)

43.6 Sumerian participles

The Sumerian verb without prefixes or suffixes can be used to indicate the person or thing which performs the action (like a Babylonian participle). Thus *gu*$_7$ (Bab. *akālu*) **to eat** can also mean **eater**. (It can have further meanings too, but these do not concern us here.) This is one of various types of participles which Sumerian can form. Such a participle can have a direct object, which precedes it.

A nice example of a sumerogram formed with one of these participles and foregoing direct object *is zú.lum* (Bab. *suluppu*) **date** (i.e. the fruit): *lum* means **to delight**, so used as a participle it is **thing which delights**; *zú* means **tooth** (Bab. *šinnu*), and is the direct object of *lum*. The expression therefore super-literally means **thing which delights the tooth** (showing, incidentally, that our notion of a sweet tooth goes back a long way!).

Similarly, *aga* being **axe** and *úš* **to bring (something) into contact (with something)**, *aga.úš* is literally **the one who brings the axe into contact (with something)**, i.e. **the one who wields the axe**. Small surprise that this represents Bab. *rēdû* **soldier**.

43.7 Babylonian poetry

Babylonian poems do not usually rhyme, nor do they have the regular rhythms which are characteristic of much English verse. (Both these features can be found – though not systematically – in incantations, perhaps suggesting that they partook of a 'popular' style which was different to that of mainstream written poetry.) The easiest way to identify a Babylonian composition as poetical is that it is arranged in lines which are syntactically complete – i.e. the end of the line coincides with the end of a clause or sentence.

The vast majority of poetic lines have a 'heavy' (long or stressed) penultimate syllable, though in the view of the author of this course the jury is still out over whether this is accident or design.

Most lines fall into four or three parts, conventionally termed 'beats': each 'beat' is a major word plus any adjacent minor words (prepositions, conjunctions, particles, negations). Genitive constructions can count as one beat or two, and adjectives can be a beat in their own right or form one beat with the headword.

Many four-beat lines seem to fall naturally into two halves, and the hiatus arising between them is termed a 'caesura'. Using the symbol | to mark a division between beats, and || to mark the caesura, the first four lines of *Enūma eliš* (often called the **Epic of Creation**) can be analysed thus:

enūma | eliš || lā nabû | šamāmū

šapliš | ammatum || šuma | lā zakrat

apsû-ma | rēštû | zārûšun

mummu | tiāmtu || mu'allidat | gimrišun

When, | above, || the heavens | were not (yet) named,

(and), below, | the earth || had not been called | a name,

there was Apsû | their first | begetter

(and) *mummu* Tiāmtu || bearer | of them all.

(*mummu* is a difficult word; English word order required moving some beats round.)

LANGUAGE (AND CULTURE) TIP

The name *Tiāmtu* often appears as *Tiāmat* in modern editions, going back to a nineteenth-century idea that Babylonian names did not have case endings. While this may well apply to some names (one can especially imagine endings being omitted in vernacular language), in syllabic spelling *Tiāmtu* always has a case ending. Her name literally means **sea**, and she is the personification of salt water, while her consort *Apsû* is the personification of freshwater. According to *Enūma eliš*, it is from their union that the world is born.

The fourth line could also be taken as a three-beater:

mummu | tiāmtu | mu'allidat gimrišun

(and) *mummu* | Tiāmtu | bearer of them all.

Such uncertainties are common, and very hard to resolve. You can experience this for yourself if you try dividing *The Poor Man of Nippur* into beats: most lines fall nicely into four beats, but some could have three. Should we expect regularity? Should we expect variability? It is hard to know.

While this division into 'beats' works very well on the page, it is difficult to translate into recitation. Possibly the salient difference is between lines which fall naturally into two halves, and lines which do not.

In studying Babylonian poetry, it is an interesting exercise to see what steps were taken to avoid straddling the caesura with words which belonged closely together (such as noun and adjective, or a genitive construction).

A general stylistic feature is that Babylonian poetry is very fond of parallelism, both within the two halves of a line and across adjacent lines (couplets).

43.8 What if they got it wrong?

Babylonian tablets were written by human beings every bit as fallible as ourselves. They could miss words out, write signs incorrectly, use the wrong readings for signs, and perpetrate all sort of other distortions to what they were supposed to be writing.

Deciding that an ancient manuscript contains an error is no easy matter, and there are doubtless cases where our perception of an error will be shown by future researchers to be erroneous itself. That said, we are increasingly confident in our ability to 'correct' Babylonian manuscripts.

The most frequent error seems to have been the careless omission of a sign (lipography). Thus modern editors have to be on the lookout for cases where a sign might have been omitted. When they propose an insertion, this is indicated by diamond brackets, e.g. *ik-<ta>-šad* **he has conquered**.

Sometimes, writers realized part-way through writing a word that they had made a mistake, but went on to correct themselves – without however erasing the wrong signs they had just written ('soft auto-correction'). This can lead to odd-looking spellings such as *ma-ti-a-ti* **lands**, which mixes the singular *māti* with the plural *mātāti*.

Writers could also inadvertently swap words of opposite meaning (**hot** for **cold**), or words of opposite gender.

For a more detailed discussion of error types in Babylonian, I refer the interested reader to my *Principles of Akkadian Textual Criticism* (De Gruyter, 2012).

43.9 Case endings and the sign *UD*

Taken at face value, manuscripts in Neo-Assyrian script (which constitute a very large share of first-millennium scholarship and literature) often have *-tú* where one would expect *-te*. This is, however, an oddity which arises purely at the graphic level: in Neo-Assyrian script, the sign UD (= *tú*) is very similar to the sign TE. So much so, that they are effectively used interchangeably (this usually happens at the end of words).

Therefore, when you encounter *-tú* for expected *-te* in a transliteration deriving from a manuscript in Neo-Assyrian script, in normalization you can switch from one to the other.

SB *áš-šú 1-et píl-tú* normalized *aššu ištēt pilte* **because of the one insult** (*Poor Man of Nippur*, line 67).

Part seven

Reference

44 *The main features of syllabic spellings*

In this unit you will learn:

▸ **complexities attaching to syllabic spellings of Babylonian words.**

We summarize here the main features of cuneiform syllabic spellings. Unlike Modern English, the cuneiform script does not distinguish upper case and lower case. Scribes could choose whether to write double consonants double, and long vowels long (but see section 44.2).

LANGUAGE TIP

The first root letter in the N pres. and pret. is usually spelled double.

44.1 Ambiguous spellings

Many syllabic spellings are ambiguous. For example, there are two ways of interpreting the spelling *iš-pu-ra-ku-nu-ti*:

išpurākunūti (= *išpurā* + *kunūti*) **They** (f.) **sent you** (m. pl.)

išpurakkunūti (= *išpur* + *am* + *kunūti*) **He/she sent you** (m. pl.)

Such ambiguities are usually resolved by context. By contrast, the spelling *iš-pu-ra-ak-ku-nu-ti* would not have been ambiguous. (It can only be *išpur* + *am* + *kunūti* **He/she sent you** (m. pl).)

Spellings of nouns can be ambiguous as to whether they are singular or plural.

šar-ru = *šarru* (nom. sg.) or *šarrū* (nom. pl.) **king(s)**
šar-ra-ti = *šarrati* (gen. sg.) or *šarrāti* (acc. or gen. pl.) **queen(s)**

In feminine nouns and adjectives, a spelling such as *šar-ra-a-tu* (with 'extra' *-a-*) is a strong indication that the form is plural.

44.2 Contracted vowels at the end of words

Contracted vowels at the end of words are usually written with an 'extra' vowel ('plene spelling'): *iq-bu-ú* = *iqbû* **they said** (from *iqbiū*).

Conversely, if a word is written with an 'extra' vowel at the end of the word the vowel is probably contracted. Other possibilities are: interrogative intonation (section 44.9), 'orthographic bulk' (section 44.14), or simply manuscript idiosyncrasy.

44.3 Sandhi spellings

'Sandhi spellings' are spellings in which a single cuneiform sign straddles two words. (The term 'sandhi' is borrowed, somewhat improperly, from Sanskrit grammar.)

OB *ú-li-le-qè* for *ul ileqqe* **He will not take** (AbB 11, 27: 13)

Sometimes vowel elision across words (see Unit 47.3) has occurred:

OB *a-na šu-ul-mi-ka-aš-pu-ra-am* for *ana šulmiki ašpuram* **I wrote (about) your** (f. sg.) **well-being** (AbB 10, 170: 10)
SB *šu-bat ne-eh-tu-ú-še-šib for šubat nēhti ušēšib* **I caused (them) to dwell (in) a dwelling of peace** (Khorsabad 76: 9)

Whenever you see a word ending in a vowel you don't expect, it is worth looking at the next word: if it starts with the same vowel, you are probably looking at a sandhi spelling.

44.4 Spellings of the glottal stop

The glottal stop can be written in several ways:

- in Standard Babylonian: with the sign transliterated as ';
- in Old Babylonian: with *h*, e.g. *re-hu-ú* for *rē'û* **shepherd**;
- in all periods: with a hiatus between syllables, e.g. *teš-e* for *teš'e* **you sought**;
- with a repeated vowel sign, e.g. *ra-bi-a-am* for *rabi'am* **great** (acc. sg.) – this is especially common in Old Babylonian.

44.5 Morpho-graphemic spellings

Writers of Babylonian did not always write words as they were pronounced. Often they wrote the form which, so to speak, underlay the spoken form. For example, it is likely that already in the Old Babylonian period *iškun* + *ma* was pronounced *iškumma*. However, it is usually written with *nm* rather than *mm*. Spellings such as these, which prioritize etymology over pronunciation, are known as 'morpho-graphemic spellings'.

44.6 Morpho-phonological spellings

Writers of Babylonian sometimes wrote a hiatus between different morphemes within a word: *iš-pur-am* (instead of *iš-pu-ram*, which would follow the syllable division). These are known as 'morpho-phonological' spellings. It is not necessary to suppose a hiatus in pronunciation in such cases.

44.7 Purely orthographic consonantal doubling

Sometimes consonants were written double but, it is suspected, pronounced non-double. This is known as '(purely) orthographic consonantal doubling'. It is especially common at morpheme boundaries, and where the first of the two signs is a consonant + vowel + consonant sign (e.g. *pur*): *iš-pur-ra* **he wrote to me** (probably pronounced *išpura*). This happens already in Old Babylonian, but becomes more frequent in Standard Babylonian.

DID YOU KNOW?

A letter from the Assyrian king Sargon II (721–705 BC) instructs the recipient to write in Babylonian or Assyrian rather than Aramaic. The reason may have been pride in cultural heritage, or the fact that, being harder to read than Aramaic (which was written alphabetically), Babylonian and Assyrian (which were written in cuneiform) were a more secure means of communication. You can read the letter at http://oracc.museum.upenn.edu/saao/saa17/P237990.

44.8 Vowel-indifference

In the first millennium BC, scribes who wrote Babylonian often had Aramaic as their mother tongue. Under the influence of Aramaic (whose script includes only consonants), they sometimes used cuneiform signs for their consonants alone.

44.9 Plene spellings marking questions

Plene spellings (i.e. 'extra' vowel signs) are sometimes used to show that a sentence is a question: *atta ul* <u>*ti-de-e*</u> **Do you** (m. sg.) **not know?** The relevant syllable was probably pronounced with interrogative intonation of some kind.

There is no established convention for how to normalize such spellings. One possibility is to use an accent (*tīdé*). Such spellings are not used systematically, so their absence does not prove that a sentence is *not* a question.

44.10 The sign sequence *a-a*

The sign sequence *a-a* can represent *āy* or *ayy* + any long or short vowel (e.g. *āyu*, *ayyī*): *da-a-a-nu* = *dayyānu* **judge**.

44.11 Fossilized spellings

In the first millennium, some spellings which originated as syllabic spellings became fossilized, and were used (like sumerograms) to write a word regardless of the actual form which it assumed. (Some books call these 'semi-logographic' spellings.) Thus the word *tâmtu(m)* is often spelled *tam-tim*, but on manuscripts which distinguish case vowels this should sometimes be normalized *tâmtu*. In some books, fossilization is indicated by small capitals: TAM-TIM.

44.12 *CV-CV* representing *CVC*

In the first millennium, particularly on manuscripts written by Assyrians, two consecutive CV (consonant+vowel) signs with the same vowel can in fact represent CVC (consonant+vowel+consonant), so that the final vowel is a purely written phenomenon, and was not pronounced. For example:

la-ka could represent *laka* or just *lak*
mi-di could represent *midi* or just *mid*
ru-bu could represent *rubu* or just *rub*

This trait can generate ambiguities. For example, if *il-la-ka* truly represents *illaka* or *illakā*, the form has an ending *-a* (ventive) or *-ā* (3rd f. pl.); but if it represents *illak*, there is no ending. The difference impinges on translation: *illaka* **he/she comes**, *illakā* **they** (f.) **go**, *illak* **he/she goes**.

This phenomenon probably originated from the wish to disambiguate which consonant occurred at the end of a syllable. Cuneiform signs don't distinguish between related sounds in syllable-final position (see end of Unit 43.1). Thus the same cuneiform sign represents *ut*, *ud* and *uṭ*, and a spelling such as *i-ma-qu-ut* could, in principle, represent *imaqqut*, *imaqquṭ*, or *imaqqud*. If considered in isolation, this does not seem a big problem, because only the first of the three is a real Babylonian form. But to someone puzzling their way through a cuneiform tablet, and grappling with questions such as which signs are written, how they should be read, and where words start and stop, any help is welcome. Since the sign TU normally represents *tu* but not *ṭu* or *du*, changing the standard spelling *i-ma-qu-ut* into *i-ma-qu-tu* eliminates at least one ambiguity.

The principle of CV-CV for CVC apparently went on to be generalized so that it was used even when there was no ambiguity.

44.13 *CVC* for *CVCV*

In the first millennium, it seems that CVC signs (consonant-vowel-consonant signs, e.g. *lam*) could be used as CVCV.

tar-bak representing *tarabbak* **You decoct**

There may even be cases where the CVC signs represents two different vowels, but these are very hard to pin down.

44.14 Orthographic bulk

Writers of Babylonian generally prefer for a syllabic spelling to be more than one sign long. For this reason plene spellings are sometimes inserted not to indicate that the vowel has any special phonetic property (length, stress, etc.), but simply to 'flesh out' the spelling. This happens e.g. in the Middle Assyrian laws: *ša-a* for the word *ša* **of/which**; earlier *ki-i* for later *ki*, both representing the preposition *kī* **like**.

45 Summary of strong verbs' cores and suffixes

This unit provides you with a summary of the 'cores' and suffixes in strong verbs.

As noted in Unit 14.2, Babylonian verbal forms consist of a 'core' (determined by tense and system), to which prefixes and suffixes (determined by the grammatical characteristics of the subject) are added.

Here we provide an overview of cores for strong verbs in the different combinations of tense and system. The overview is provided so that from time to time you can remind yourself how what you are learning fits into the overall mosaic of Babylonian verb forms.

Most of the cores never stand alone, but only appear with prefixes and suffixes. When a core must take a prefix or a suffix, this is indicated by a hyphen.

45.1 Overview of cores for strong verbs

Brackets mean: this is what we imagine the core looked like, but it is not yet attested. A cell with nothing but a hyphen means: this form seems not to have been used.

Tables 47–9 apply to *a*-verbs. In *e*-verbs, *a* changes to *e*. The cores for the G, N, D and Š systems are shown in Table 47; those for the Gtn, Ntn, Dtn and Štn systems are shown in Table 48; and those for the Gt, Dt and Št and Št systems are shown in Table 49.

Table 47

	G	N	D	Š
Present	*-PaRRvS*	*-PPaRRvS*	*-PaRRaS*	*-šaPRas*
Preterite	*-PRvS*	*-PPaRvS*	*-PaRRiS*	*-šaPRis*
Perfect	*-PtaRvS*	*-ttaPRvS*	*-PtaRRiS*	*-štaPRiS*
Stative	*PaRiS*	*naPRuS*	*PuRRuS*	*šuPRuS*
Imperative	*PvRvS*	*naPRiS*	*PuRRiS*	*šuPRiS*
Infinitive	*PaRāSu(m)*	*naPRuSu(m)*	*PuRRuSu(m)*	*šuPRuSu(m)*

v means: a short vowel which changes from verb to verb.

Table 48

	Gtn	Ntn	Dtn	Štn
Present	*-PtanaRRvS*	*-ttanaPRvS*	*-PtanaRRaS*	*-štanaPRaS*
Preterite	*-PtaRRvS*	*-ttaPRvS*	*-PtaRRiS*	*-štaPRiS*
Perfect	*-PtataRRvS*	*(-ttataPRvS)*	*-PtataRRiS*	*-štataPRiS*
Stative	*PitaRRuS*	*itaPRuS*	*PutaRRuS*	*šutaPRuS*
Imperative	*PitaRRvS*	*itaPRaS*	*PutaRRiS*	*šutaPRiS*
Infinitive	*PitaRRuSu(m)*	*itaPRuSu(m)*	*PutaRRuSu(m)*	*šutaPRuSu(m)*

v means: a short vowel which changes from verb to verb.

Table 49

	Gt	Dt	Št$_1$	Št$_2$
Present	*-PtaRRvS*	*-PtaRRaS*	*-štaPRaS*	*-štaPaRRaS*
Preterite	*-PtaRvS*	*-PtaRRiS*	*-štaPRiS*	*-štaPRiS*
Perfect	(*-PtatRvS ?*)	*-PtataRRiS*	*-štataPRiS*	*-štataPRiS*
Stative	*PitRuS*	-	-	*šutaPRuS*
Imperative	*PitRvS*	*PutaRRiS*	*šutaPRiS*	*šutaPRiS*
Infinitive	*PitRuSu(m)*	(*PutaRRuSu(m)*)	(*šutaPRuSu(m)*)	*šutaPRuSu(m)*

v means: a short vowel which changes from verb to verb.

45.2 Overview of prefixes and suffixes

Prefixes and suffixes in different tenses in different systems are shown in Table 50. The stative and imperative tenses use the same suffixes in all four systems. The present, preterite and perfect have two different sets of prefixes, one for the G and N systems (and their derived systems) and another for the D and Š systems (and their derived systems).

Table 50

<table>
<tr><th></th><th>G, Gtn, Gt   N, Ntn</th><th>D, Dtn, Dt   Š, Štn, Št</th></tr>
<tr><td>Present</td><td rowspan="3">sg. a-, ta-, ta…ī, i-
pl. ni-, ta…ā, i…ū, i…ā</td><td rowspan="3">sg. u-, tu-, tu…ī, u-
pl. nu-, tu…ā, u…ū, u…ā</td></tr>
<tr><td>Preterite</td></tr>
<tr><td>Perfect</td></tr>
<tr><td>Stative</td><td colspan="2">sg. -āku, -āta, -āti, -Ø, -at, pl. -ānu, -ātunu, -ātina, -ū, -ā</td></tr>
<tr><td>Imperative</td><td colspan="2">sg. -Ø, -ī, pl. -ā</td></tr>
</table>

The symbol 'Ø' means 'nothing'.

The *a*-vowels in bold are not normally subject to *e*-colouring. The other *a*-vowels may undergo it, depending on the variety of Babylonian involved. For example, *elqe* **I took** (G preterite; prefix *a-*) would usually be an Old Babylonian form, whose Standard Babylonian equivalent is *alqe*.

46 *Forming nouns and adjectives*

In this unit you will learn:

- **some patterns by which Babylonian nouns and adjectives are formed**
- **about the '*nisbe*' ending**
- **about the 'gentilic' ending.**

As mentioned in Unit 5, most Babylonian words are formed according to regular patterns. Though one can learn to translate simply by looking words up as necessary, one will develop a much more refined appreciation of the language by understanding how they are formed. Accordingly, this unit presents some of the most important patterns in the formation of nouns and adjectives. We use the system explained in Unit 5, whereby PRS represent the three root letters. Two preliminary points:

- In nouns and adjectives related to *e*-verbs (see Unit 14.13), *a* and *ā* change to *e* and *ē*.
- In nouns related to weak verbs, one or more of the consonants will be missing, as in the parent verb.

LANGUAGE TIP

As a convenient way of speaking about relations between nouns and verbs, the phrase 'parent verb' is used: *pahāru* **to come together** for *puhru* **assembly**, *bêlu* **to rule** for *bēlu* **lord**, *awû* **to speak** for *awātu* **word**, etc. (This does not necessarily imply that the verb originated before the noun.)

46.1 Patterns

PāRiS-: someone who performs the action of the parent verb in the G system (see Unit 35).

PaRRāS-: someone who performs the action of the parent verb in the G system; for most such nouns there is the extra nuance of performing the action on a regular basis.

šarāqu **to steal**	→	*šarrāqu* **thief**
dânu **to give judgment**	→	*dayyānu* **judge**

PaRS-: (verbal) adjectives (see Unit 18.1). (Exceptions: *kalbu* **dog**, *eṭlu* **young man**, *halṣu* **district**.)

PuRS-: mostly abstract nouns, mostly derived from verbs of being.

damāqu **to be good**	→	*dumqu* **goodness**
ṭâbu **to be good**	→	*ṭūbu* **goodness**
lemēnu **to be evil**	→	*lumnu* **evil(ness)**

ekēlu **to be dark** → *uklu* **darkness**
kânu **to be firm** → *kūnu* **firmness**
pahāru **to come together** → *puhru* **assembly**

PiRS- and *PiRiSt-*: nouns of action, and of the product resulting from the action.

kalû **to detain** → *kīlu* **confinement**
gapāšu **to swell** → *gipšu* **welling up, mass**
patālu **to twist** → *pitiltu* **string, cord**
mesû **to wash** → *mīsu* **(the action of) washing**

CULTURE TIP

Deities were installed in their statues through a ritual called *mīs pî* **washing of the mouth**. Afterwards, statues were treated as if the gods lived inside them: they were fed, taken on trips, and put into bed with each other.

maPRaS(t)- and *maPRāS-*: places where the parent verb occurs, or instruments with which the action of the parent verb is performed.

nâlu **to lie down** → *mayyālu* **bed** (from *manyālu*)
etēqu **to pass by** → *mētequ* **route** (for *ē* see Unit 47.2)
erēbu **to enter** → *nēreb(t)u* **entrance** (for *ē* see Unit 47.2)
marāṣu **to be difficult** → *namrāṣu* **difficult territory** (for *na-* see Unit 47.12)
rakābu **to ride** → *narkabtu* **chariot** (for *na-* see Unit 47.12)

PuRuSSā-: mostly produces legal terms.

nadānu **to give** → *nudunnû* **dowry**
parāsu **to separate** → *purussû* **legal decision**

taPRīS- and *taPRīSt-* (or *taPRiSt-*, see Unit 47.14): nouns related to the meaning of the verb in the D system (more rarely the Gt system).

halāpu D **to clothe** → *tahlīpu* **armour**
rabû D **to bring up** → *tarbītu* **upbringing** (in CH also: **person brought up**)
šummu **to ponder** → *tašīmtu* **reckoning**

The suffix *-ūtu* produces abstract nouns of f. gender.

šarru **king** → *šarrūtu* **kingship**
ṣīru **exalted** → *ṣīrūtu* **exaltedness**
awīlu **man** → *awīlūtu* **humanity, humankind**

46.2 'Nisbe' adjectives

Adjectives can be formed by adding *-ī-* (known as the 'nisbe' morpheme, a term borrowed from Arabic grammar) to a pre-existing word. In masculine adjectives it goes before the case vowel (with which it usually contracts), in feminine adjectives before the 'feminine *t*'.

aššurû (from *aššur* + *ī* + *u*) **Assyrian** (m.)

aššurītu (from *aššur* + *ī* + *tu*) **Assyrian** (f.)

Thus also: *mahrû*, f. *mahrītu* **previous** (from *mahru* **front**) *ahû*, f. *ahītu* **strange, foreign** (from *ahu* **side**)

> **LANGUAGE TIP**
> By coincidence, the nisbe ending has a neat parallel in English: English nouns can be turned into adjectives by adding **y** (**mud → muddy**). A difference, however, is that in English no case vowel or 'feminine *t*' follows **y**.

The nisbe morpheme is not used with all nouns (in fact, it is only used with a few). It cannot, for example, be used with *šarru* **king** or *bēlu* **lord**. To convey the idea of something being **kingly**, **lordly**, etc., abstract nouns in *-ūtu* can be used.

SB *narkabat šarrūtiya* **The chariot of my kingship**, i.e. **My kingly chariot**

46.3 Gentilic adjectives

The ending *-āy(a)* forms 'gentilic' adjectives, i.e. adjectives for a people. The ending is spelled the same way for singular and plural, in all grammatical cases (see Unit 44.10).

man-na-a-a or *man-na-a* (both for *mannāya*) **Mannean(s)**

Owing to the ambiguities of cuneiform spelling, it is uncertain whether the final vowel was uniformly *a*, or whether, as seems likely, it changed with grammatical case (i.e. *-āyu*, *-āya*, *-āyi*).

[a]na mitatti zi-kir-ta-a-a (*zikirtāya* or *zikirtāyi* ?) *ittaklū* **They trusted to Mitattu the Zikirtean** (Khorsabad 90: 60)

māt ma-da-a-a (*madāya* or *madāyī* ?) *rūqūti* **The land of the distant Medes** (Khorsabad 77: 23)

46.4 The importance of parent verbs

When words from weak roots had a parent verb, this helped Babylonian speakers to 'remember' where the weakness was.

In words from III-weak roots which have the 'feminine *t*', whether or not the feminine *t* comes into contact with the second root letter depends on whether it was 'remembered' that the root was III-weak. When the word had a parent verb, the III-weakness was 'remembered', and a vowel always interposed between the second root letter and the feminine *t*, e.g. *rabītu* **great** (f. sg.).

When the word had no parent verb, it could be 'forgotten' that it came from a III-weak root, so the feminine *t* could be in contact with the second root letter, e.g. *pērtu* **hair**, *tūltu* **worm**. In such cases, one only knows that the word comes from a III-weak root from looking at related languages where the third root letter is preserved.

47 *Some sound changes*

In this unit you will learn:

- **some of the sound changes which take place in Babylonian, especially:**
- **vowel contraction**
- **vowel elision**
- **loss of guttural consonants**
- **assimilations.**

This unit gathers together the principal sound changes which occur in Old, Middle and Standard Babylonian.

47.1 Vowel contraction

Two adjacent vowels within a word usually contract. When contraction occurs, the resulting contracted vowel has the quality of the second vowel (for an exception see Unit 21.2). In normalization, contracted vowels bear a circumflex accent.

rabiūtu → *rabûtu* **great** (m. pl. nom.)
ibaššiā → *ibaššâ* **they** (f.) **exist**

a (long or short) + *i* (long or short) contract to *ê*.

šamû **sky** (from *šamāū*) → acc./gen. pl. *šamê* (from *šamāī*)
rubû **nobleman** (from *rubāu*) → gen. sg. *rubê* (from *rubāi*), acc./gen. pl. *rubê* (from *rubāī*)
šemû to hear (from *šemēu*, from original *šamāʿu*) → gen. sg. *šemê* (from *šemēi*, from original *šamāʿi*)

i+a (either vowel long or short) normally stays uncontracted in Old Babylonian.

qibiam **tell me!**
rabû **great** → acc. sg. *rabiam*

On Old Babylonian tablets from the city of Mari (more rarely elsewhere in the OB period), *i+a* (either vowel long or short) contracts to *ê*.

iqbiam **he/she told me** → *iqbêm*
rabûm **great** → acc. sg. *rabêm* (from *rabiam*)
ûm **barley** → acc. sg. *êm* (from *īam*)

Contracted vowels at the end of a word are overwhelmingly spelled *plene* in cuneiform (e.g. *ra-bu-ú*).

When adjacent vowels have not contracted, some books uniformly normalize them with a glottal stop (') in between, e.g. *annī'am* instead of *annīam*, *rabi'ūtim* instead of *rabiūtim*. This does not affect the meaning. The practice adopted in this course is to insert the glottal stop only if its presence is implied in the relevant cuneiform spelling (see Unit 44.4). Thus *an-ni-a-am* is normalized *annī'am* and *an-ni-am* is normalized *annīam*, though they represent the same word. It is uncertain whether in such cases the two spellings reflect different pronunciations.

47.2 Compensatory lengthening

When a guttural consonant was lost (this usually happened before the Old Babylonian period), the preceding vowel was lengthened, so as to maintain each syllable's length invaried. For example, using ' to represent the root letter which disappeared, the 3rd sg. G preterite of the verb *akālu* was originally *i'kul*. When ' was lost, the *i* was lengthened in compensation. Similarly, *mīlu* **flood** from earlier *mil'u* (related to *malû* **to be full**); *nērebu* **entrance** from earlier *ne'rebu* (related to *erēbu* **to enter**).

47.3 Vowel elision across words (crasis)

When a word ending in a vowel was followed by a word beginning with a vowel, one vowel could elide the other (usually the vowel at the start of the word elided the one at the end). This probably happened more often in speech than is recorded in writing (examples in Unit 44.3).

47.4 Vowel elision within words

Babylonian words obey the following rule: 'Within a word, two consecutive syllables ending in a short vowel can only appear at the end of the word; in other positions, the vowel in the second of the two syllables (which need not be the same as the second syllable in the word) is lost'.

The rule is especially important in the behaviour of the G perfect, the G stative, the N preterite, and feminine plural nouns.

taštaknī **You** (f. sg.) **have placed** (from *taštakanī*, syllabified *taš–ta–ka–nī*)

Sometimes the vowel to be elided is 'protected' by following *r*.

nakarāta **You** (m. sg.) **are foreign**
zikaru **man**

The rule of vowel elision does not apply to possessive suffixes.

libbašunu **their heart**

(Forms such as *libbašnu* are however found in Old Assyrian, and may have been more widespread in everyday language than is visible in writing.)

47.5 Division into syllables

The rules for dividing a Babylonian word into syllables are as follows (note that the rules for English are different):

1 A single consonant between vowels must begin a new syllable, so for example *amāt* is syllabified *a-māt* (not *am-āt*) and *mētequ* is syllabified *mē-te-qu* (not *mē-teq-u*).

2 A syllable can begin and end with no more than one consonant. Thus, given two adjacent consonants, the first closes one syllable, the second opens a new one. For example, *ištakan* is syllabified as *iš-ta-kan* (not *i-šta-kan*), and *ītaklū* as *ī-tak-lū* (not *ī-ta-klū*).

3 Two adjacent vowels belong to separate syllables, e.g. *anniam* is syllabified *an-ni-am*. (When vowels are separated by a glottal stop, this is treated like any other consonant: *annī'am* is syllabified *an-nī-'am*.)

Whether the vowels in a word are short (e.g. *a*) or long (e.g. *ā*) does not affect where the syllable boundaries are drawn. It is possible that contracted vowels at the end of a word (e.g. *â*) sometimes counted as two syllables. Double consonants (*kk*, *mm*, etc.) are treated like any other group of two adjacent consonants.

Examples of Babylonian words divided into syllables: *purkullūtu*: *pur-kul-lū-tu*; *mātāti*: *mā-tā-ti*; *rabûti*: *ra-bû-ti*; *da'ummatu*: *da-'um-ma-tu*; *iparras*: *i-par-ras*; *iprus*: *ip-rus*; *iptaras*: *ip-ta-ras*; *iptarsū*: *ip-tar-sū*; *na'dum*: *na'-dum*.

47.6 The loss of short vowels at the end of words

Around 1000 BC, short vowels at the end of words ceased to be pronounced distinctly in the spoken language, probably collapsing into sounds like the first **a** in **banana** (so-called 'schwa' sounds) or vanishing altogether. An effect of this was that cases were no longer distinguished in the singular basic state and feminine plural basic state, and that the verbal ending *-u* (Unit 30.11) vanished when it stood at the end of a word (though it often continued to be written).

47.7 The loss of guttural consonants

Semitic languages are rich in guttural sounds, but Babylonian gave up several of these early in its history, before the Old Babylonian period. The loss of a guttural which was not between vowels usually caused compensatory lengthening (see section 47.2).

orig. *nahrum* → Bab. *nārum* **river**

Depending on which consonant was lost, a shift from *a* to *e* might occur. This (which could also occur for other reasons, see Unit 14.13) is known as *e*-colouring.

orig. *ṭaḥānum* → *ṭeēnum* → *ṭênum* **to grind**

47.8 Long vowels inducing consonant doubling

After the Old Babylonian period, it sometimes happens that a single consonant following a long vowel doubles. It is likely that the vowel shortened.

kīlu **confinement** → *killu*

LANGUAGE TIP

In linguistic jargon, this is known as 'metathesis of length'.

47.9 Assimilation of consonants

Given two adjacent consonants, it can happen that they assimilate (i.e. change so as to become more similar or identical). The combinations of consonants which result in assimilation, and the forms which the assimilation takes, change from one variety of Babylonian to another. We give the main ones here.

- *nC* (i.e. *n* followed by any consonant) → *CC* (i.e. the consonant is doubled). This happens in all periods of Babylonian: *addin* **I gave** (from *andin*); *šukuttu* **jewellery** (from *šukuntu*).
- Sibilant (*š*, *s*, *ṣ*, *z*) or dental (*t*, *d*, *ṭ*) + *š* → *ss*. This happens in all periods: *bīssu* **his house** (from *bītšu*); *mihissu* **strike him!** (from *mihiṣšu*) (for an exception see Unit 36.3).
- *št* → *lt* and *šd* → *ld*. This occurs very rarely in Old Babylonian, but is frequent in later periods: *ištapar* → *iltapar* **he/she has sent**; *iktašdā* → *iktaldā* **they** (f.) **have arrived**; *napšaštu* → *napšaltu* **salve, ointment.**
- *b* sometimes assimilates to *m* before *-ma*: *i-ru-um-ma* (= *īrub-ma*) **he entered, and ...**
- *d* + feminine *t* → *tt*: *lidtu* → *littu* **progeny**. This happens in all periods.
- *ṣ* + feminine *t* → *št*: *maruṣtu* → *maruštu* **ill** (f. sg.). This happens in all periods.

47.10 Assimilations involving the verbal -t- infix

The *-t-* infix in verbs (*-ta-*, *-tan-*) obeys the relevant rules above (*nt* → *tt*; *št* → *lt*). Additionally:

- *it* assimilates to first root letter *s*, *ṣ*, *d*, *z* (e.g. *iṣṣabat* **he has seized**, from *iṣtabat*); this happens in all periods.
- *gt* → *gd* (e.g. *igdapuš* **he has become proud**, from *igtapuš*); this can happen in all periods.
- *mt* → *md* or *nd* (e.g. *amdahhar* **I received regularly**, Gtn pret., from *amtahhar*); this happens after the Old Babylonian period.

47.11 Nasalization of double consonants

Double voiced 'stop' consonants (*bb*, *dd*, *gg*) sometimes nasalized. This (which mostly happens after the Old Babylonian period) appears in writing as *n* or *m*:

inaddin **he will give** → *inamdin*
imaggur **he agrees** → *imangur*

iddi **he threw** → *indi*
aštaddih **I sped across** → *aštamdih*
ibbi **he named** → *imbi*

LANGUAGE TIP

Usually, *bb* nasalizes to *mb* and *dd* to *nd*. But if there is an *m* earlier in the word, the nasalization appears as *n*, and vice versa.

47.12 The change of *ma-* to *na-*

The prefix *ma-*, used (among other functions) to form nouns of place and instrument (see Unit 46), changes to *na-* (*ne-* in nouns related to *e*-verbs) if the root includes *b, p, w* or *m* ('bilabial sounds'). This has already happened by the Old Babylonian period.

orig. *markabtum* → *narkabtu(m)* **chariot**
orig. *maghrabum* → *nērebu(m)* **entrance**

This is known as Barth's Law.

47.13 Sound sequences which Babylonian does not allow

Babylonian never allowed a sequence of three consecutive consonants. Also, at least until the first millennium BC, it never allowed a sequence of two consonants at the beginning or end of a word (unless the following word began with a vowel, in which case the two words could be spoken as one).

Babylonian does not usually allow a word to contain two 'emphatic' consonants (*q, ṣ, ṭ*). When this would arise (e.g. because Babylonian inherited such a word from an ancestor language), one changes to the non-emphatic equivalent (*k, s, t*). This is known as Geers' Law.

An example is the root √*qtr* (**smoke**): other Semitic languages show that the root was originally √*qṭr*, but in Babylonian the emphatic *ṭ* has become non-emphatic *t*, e.g. *qutāru* **fumigation**.

47.14 *i* to *e* before *r* or *h*

Many spellings suggest a change *i* to *e* before *r* or *h*.

ú-te-er (utīr) **I/he/she turned**
ú-maš-še-er (umaššir) **I/he/she released**

However, many spellings are ambiguous (*gi-ir-ru* or *ge-er-ru* **campaign**), and exceptions can be found (e.g. *wu-uš-ši-ir* at the end of Exercise 8.1 and *na-an-mi-ir* at the end of Exercise 24.2). It is not clear if the variability arose in pronunciation, or in spelling.

Assyriologists vary in whether they apply this change to their normalizations, particularly for ambiguous spellings.

47.15 A hypothesis

Some scholars believe that long vowels were shortened when they occurred in closed syllables (i.e. syllables ending in a consonant).

m. *kaššāpu* **sorcerer** vs. f. *kaššaptu* **sorceress**
f. sg. *kittu* **truth** vs. f. pl. *kīnātu*

This seems to have happened in Neo-Assyrian, but it has yet to be proven for Babylonian. Being aware of the idea will help you to understand the normalizations produced by scholars who subscribe to it.

This book normalizes the vowels long, to make the etymologies more transparent. For example, *kīttu/kittu* **truth** is simply the feminine equivalent of the masculine adjective *kīnu* **firm, true**, used as a noun (see Unit 6.10). If it is normalized *kittu*, the connection to *kīnu* becomes less obvious.

48 Babylonian's relation to Hebrew and Arabic

In this unit you will learn:

▶ **how Babylonian words compare to their relatives in Hebrew and Arabic.**

Babylonian (like Assyrian) died without issue, but as a member of the Semitic language family it has lots of living nephews and nieces, including Hebrew and Arabic. Like Babylonian, they build their words around (usually three-letter) roots.

48.1 Sounds

The sounds of the Semitic family being quite stable, Babylonian words closely resemble many modern Hebrew and Arabic ones, to whom they are related through – mostly quite regular – patterns of sound correspondences. This does not work for all words (not all Semitic words occur in every Semitic language; and Babylonian has many words which are not of Semitic origin), but it does for much of the basic vocabulary.

For instance, once one knows that *y* at the start of a Hebrew word can correspond to Babylonian *w*, and that Hebrew *v* matches Babylonian *b*, it becomes apparent that Hebrew *yāšav* **he sat** is related to Babylonian *wašābu* **to sit**. Equally, once one knows that ʿ (*ayin*) disappears in Babylonian, giving rise to *e*-colouring, and that original *ay* becomes Babylonian *ī*, it is clear why the Arabic preposition *ʿalā* (originally *ʿalay*) matches Babylonian *eli* (originally *elī* **over, upon**).

Of course, even in the basic vocabulary there could be shifts in meaning from one language to another. For example, Hebrew *ʿāmadh* **he stood** is etymologically the same verb as Babylonian *emēdu* **to come into contact with**. Their meanings have diverged, but not so far as to hide the relation.

48.2 Consonants

Table 51, excerpted (with cosmetic changes) from the chart by L. Kogan in *The Semitic Languages: An International Handbook* (De Gruyter, 2011), p. 55, illustrates regular relations between consonants across Babylonian, Hebrew and Arabic, and how they derive from those which have been reconstructed for the ancestor language, 'Proto-Semitic'.

The sound which in this course has been represented by *h* should, strictly speaking, be represented by *ḫ* (see Unit 3.1). When talking about Babylonian alone, there is no danger of confusion, because (at least in writing) it had only one *h*-like sound. However, when enlarging the picture to other members of the Semitic family it is important to distinguish *h*, *ḫ* and *ḥ*, as these are all different sounds which undergo different fates: in Babylonian *h* is lost with no *e*-colouring, *ḫ* stays the same (this course represents it as *h*), and *ḥ* is lost with *e*-colouring.

Table 51

Proto-Semitic	Babylonian	Hebrew	Arabic
b	*b*	*b/v* (ב)	*b* (ب)
d	*d*	*d/dh* (ד)	*d* (د)
g	*g*	*g* (ג)	*j* (as in 'jam') (ج)
ḫ	*ḫ*	*ḥ* (ח)	*ḫ* (خ)
k	*k*	*k/kh* (כ)	*k* (ك)
l	*l*	*l* (ל)	*l* (ل)
m	*m*	*m* (מ)	*m* (م)
n	*n*	*n* (נ)	*n* (ن)
p	*p*	*p/f* (פ)	*f* (ف)
q (some books use *ḳ*)	*q*	*q* (some books use *ḳ*) (ק)	*q* (ق)
r	*r*	*r* (ר)	*r* (ر)
s	*s*	*s* (ס)	*s* (س)
ṣ	*ṣ*	*ṣ* (צ)	*ṣ* (ص)
ṣ̂	*ṣ*	*ṣ* (צ)	*ḍ* (ض)
ṯ̣	*ṣ*	*ṣ* (צ)	*ḏ̣* (some books use *ẓ*) (ظ)
ṯ	*š*	*š*	*ṯ* (some books use *th*) (ث)
š	*š*	*š* (שׁ)	*s* (س)
ŝ	*š*	*ŝ* (שׂ)	*š* (ش)
t	*t* feminine *t*:	*t/th* (ת) fem. ה	*t* (ت) fem. ة
ṭ	*ṭ*	*ṭ* (ט)	*ṭ* (ط)
w	*w*	*w* (ו); at the start of a word: *y* (י)	*w* (و)
y	*y*, can also disappear	*y* (י)	*y* (ي)
z	*z*	*z* (ז)	*z* (ز)
ḏ	*z*	*z* (ז)	*ḏ* (some books use *dh*) (ذ)
ḥ	(lost, with *e*-colouring)	*ḥ* (ח)	*ḥ* (ح)
ʿ (ʿ*ayin*)	(lost, with *e*-colouring)	ʿ (ע)	ʿ (ع)
gh (*ghayin*)	(lost, with *e*-colouring)	ʿ (ע)	*gh* (غ)
ʾ	(lost, without *e*-colouring)	ʾ (א)	ʾ (*hamza*)
h	(lost, without *e*-colouring)	*h* (ה)	*h* (ه)

The table shows why e.g. Babylonian *ṣ* matches three different sounds in Arabic: they go back to three different sounds in Proto-Semitic, which Arabic had kept distinct, while Babylonian (as far as we can tell from our written sources) merged them into one.

48.3 Vowels

Arabic vowels and vowel patterns are quite similar to those of Babylonian (except that Arabic does not, formally, have *e* or *ē*; though this can arise in vernacular pronunciation).

Hebrew vowels are more subject to change, and so more complicated. A general pattern is that Babylonian long *ā* usually shows up in Hebrew as *ō*. Thus Bab. *anāku* vs Heb. *anōchi* **I**, and Bab. *-āt-* vs Heb. *-ōt* for the feminine plural morpheme.

As for dipthongs, Arabic (and Proto-Semitic) *aw* and *ay* become Babylonian *ū* and *ī* respectively. Thus Arabic *bayt* **house** shows up in Babylonian as *bītu*.

48.4 Word formation

Hebrew and Arabic mostly use the same patterns of word formation as Babylonian: *PuRS-*, *PaRS-*, *PiRS-*, *maPRaS-*, *taPRīS*, *PāRiS-* (which serves as the G participle in all three languages; in Hebrew, with the change of *ā* to *ō* mentioned above, it shows up as *PōRēS-*), *muPaRRiS-*, etc. The same patterns are not, however, always used in the same way across the three languages – for details you need to consult a grammar of Arabic or Hebrew. These languages also have patterns not attested in Babylonian, e.g. Arabic *muPaRRaS* (corresponding in meaning to the Babylonian D verbal adjective *PuRRuS-*).

48.5 Verbal forms

There is no space here for anything like a full discussion of the Hebrew and Arabic verbal system, and how it differs from the Babylonian one. That said, if you examine a grammar of Hebrew or Arabic, you will see that the organization into systems is very similar; that the D system (called *pi'el* in Hebrew; II in Arabic) is alive and well, with its double consonant.

Pointers that you may find useful:

- neither Hebrew or Arabic have sub-systems (Gt, Gtn, etc.) in the way that Babylonian does. However, some of the Babylonian sub-systems show up as fully-fledged systems (NB the *-t-* infixes show up *before* the three root letters, i.e. they become prefixes)
- the past tense in Hebrew and Arabic corresponds etymologically to the Babylonian stative (no prefixes; similar suffixes)
- the present tense in Hebrew and Arabic corresponds etymologically to the Babylonian preterite
- the Babylonian present and perfect tenses have no etymological counterparts in Hebrew or Arabic
- the *š* of the Š system shows up as *h* in Hebrew and *s* in Arabic
- the verbal prefixes *i-* and *u-* go back to Proto-Semitic *ya-* and *yu-*. Arabic keeps these unchanged, Hebrew modified them into *yi-* and *ye-*.

49 *Some common words*

This unit contains 160 common Babylonian words, arranged in groups of ten. You may want to use them as a way of monitoring your acquisition of vocabulary from time to time, and/or as suggestions for words to learn. Very roughly speaking, they are arranged in order of increasing frequency, but since statistics of lexical frequency have yet to be produced for Babylonian, the arrangement is somewhat impressionistic.

It should also be noted that many items of Babylonian vocabulary are rather genre-specific. Thus many words (and phrases) which appear frequently in one genre (e.g. royal inscriptions, letters, etc.) may be rare outside that genre. (To some extent this is true also of English, but with Babylonian it is more noticeable.)

Not all the words are equally common in all periods of the language; for example, *anumma* **now** is common in Old Babylonian, but hardly used thereafter (the later equivalent being *eninna/inanna*).

All the words are cited in their dictionary form (= nom. sing. for nouns and adjectives, infinitive for verbs). Variant forms of a word are separated by a diagonal slash. The *m* in brackets at the end of a word ('mimation') and *w* in brackets at the beginning of a word are usually present in Old Babylonian, and usually absent in later periods (see Units 6.11 and 26.4).

In learning words by heart (best done aloud), it is most practical to pronounce initial *w* (if present), to remind oneself it is there; and to omit mimation. Also, in the early stages of learning it is useful to really lengthen the contracted vowel in III-weak verbs and II-weak verbs: *raaaaaaamu* **to love** vs *ramuuuuuuu* **to sit**. This helps one to remember which type of verb it is. The same goes for nouns ending in a contracted vowel: *šaduuuuuuu* **mountain**.

CULTURE TIP

The first dictionary of Babylonian and Assyrian was Edwin Norris' three-volume Assyrian Dictionary (London, 1868–1872), freely accessible via the HathiTrust digital library (https://babel.hathitrust.org/cgi/pt?id=njp.32101058864388 for volume 1). It is fascinating to see what was already known, and what has been revised.

List of common words (and phrases)

bītu(m) house (m.)
awātu(m)/amātu(m) utterance, matter (f.)
ilu(m) god
šarru(m) king
mātu(m) land (f.)
ālu(m) town, city
ina in, at, from, by means of, among
ana to, for, against
awīlu(m)/amīlu(m) man
ṭēmu(m) message, plan, report

šapāru(m) to send, to send a letter, to write
ina libbi in, within, into
kīma like, as, in accordance with
ul not
lā not
u and, or
ša of, who/which, the one of, the one who/which
bēlu(m) lord, master
alāku(m) to go
qabû(m) to speak

epēšu(m) to do, to make
šumma if
(w)ardu(m) male slave
abu(m) father
leqû(m) to take
māru(m) son
annû(m) this
adi until
ina muhhi on, onto, on top of
šanû(m) second, other

qātu(m) hand (f.)
rabû(m) big, great
(w)abālu to bring
nadānu(m) to give
itti together with
kī'am thus
eli over, above, than
edû(m) to know
šakānu(m) to put
amāru(m) to see

ūmu(m) day
ana mīni(m) why? (lit. for what?)
umma (introduces direct speech)
našû(m) to carry
ēkallu(m) palace
šemû(m) to hear
anumma now
šumu(m) name
mannu(m) who?
(w)ašābu(m) to sit, to dwell

bašû(m) to exist
palāhu(m) to be afraid
amtu(m) female slave (f.)
ṣehru(m) small
nadû(m) to throw
ummānātu(m) (f. pl. only) troops
mīnu(m) what?
ištu since
(w)arhu(m) month
mūšu(m) night

damqu(m) good
lemnu(m) evil
šīmtu(m) fate (f.)
dannu(m) strong
sinništu(m) woman (f.)
šadû(m) mountain
tuppu(m) cuneiform tablet
šattu(m) year (from *šantu(m)*) (f.)
aššu(m) because of, about (a topic), for the sake of
ahu(m) brother

mahāru(m) to receive
râmu(m) to love
hurāṣu(m) gold
qablu(m) battle
ṣēru(m) open country, steppe
mārtu(m) daughter (f.)
ummu(m) mother
mû water
mati, immati when?, ever
šalāmu(m) to be well

balāṭu(m) to be alive, to be healthy
marāṣu(m) to be ill
pû(m) mouth
kabtu(m) heavy, important (m.)
mādu(m) sg.: much, pl.: many
mahar before
(w)arka/(w)arki after
šasû(m) to call out, to read aloud
elû(m) to go up
išû(m) to have

uznu(m) ear (f.)
qaqqadu(m)/kaqqadu(m) head
le'û(m) to be able (I can, you can, etc.)
kakku(m) weapon
rēšu(m) head
kī how?, like
gerru(m) campaign, caravan
akālu(m) to eat
ana … erēbu(m) to enter
târu(m) to turn, to return

halāqu(m) to vanish
malû(m) to be full (of)
izuzzu(m) to stand
rašû(m) to acquire
damu(m) blood
dayyānu(m) judge
etēqu(m) to pass
(w)u''uru(m) to give a task to
apālu(m) to answer
šâlu(m) to ask

zumru(m) body
šammu(m) plant
kaspu(m) silver
ebēru(m) to cross
ṣuhāru(m) boy, young man
zenû(m) to be angry (*itti* with)
narkabtu(m) chariot (f.)
(w)uššuru(m) to let go
ṣabātu(m) to seize
kirû(m) garden

šību(m) old (said of people)
tāhāzu(m) battle
dūru(m) city wall
kalbu(m) dog
šatû(m) to drink
dâku(m) to kill
tabāku(m) to pour
šaṭāru(m) to incise, to write
(w)arādu(m) to go down
rakāsu(m) to bind

pagru(m) body
inanna/eninna now
labīru(m) old (said of things)
šarrāqu(m) thief
rubû(m) nobleman
nakru(m) enemy
mašku(m) skin, leather
šēpu(m) foot (f.)
īnu(m) eye (f.)
šīru(m) flesh

alpu(m) ox
balu(m) without
ūmišam/ūmišamma day by day, every day
sisû(m) horse
imēru(m) donkey
eqlu(m) field
murṣu(m) disease
eleppu(m) ship (f.)
nūru(m) light
bābu(m) gate

nūnu(m) fish
iṣṣūru(m) bird
ahātu(m) sister (f.)
šarrūtu(m) kingship (f.)
amšāli yesterday
ūma(m) today
nāru(m) river
eššu(m) new
tamkāru(m) merchant
nakāsu(m) to cut

Sumerograms and their Babylonian equivalents

We here give the sumerograms used in this course, with the Babylonian equivalents you need to know to do the exercises. It is not a complete list of sumerograms, nor of the Babylonian words they represent. For this, see the references in Unit 42.3.

1 Determinatives

Determinatives are an aid to reading: their function is to indicate what kind of word is at hand. They can be used in conjunction with both sumerograms and syllabic spelling. Some precede the relevant word, some follow it. Some words are (almost) always spelled with determinatives, for others it is optional.

In transliteration, determinatives are printed in superscript. In normalization they are usually omitted.

PRECEDING

d – names of gods and goddesses

dug – pot-types

f – female personal names (*f* is a conventional modern reading; the cuneiform sign is *munus*, sumerogram for **woman**)

gi – objects made of reed

giš – wooden objects

I – personal names, usually male (*I* is a conventional modern reading, reflecting the shape of the sign, which is a single vertical wedge)

íd – names of rivers

kur – names of mountains, countries and peoples

lú – nouns denoting male humans

m – personal names, usually male (*m* is a conventional modern reading; the cuneiform sign is a single vertical wedge; can also be transcribed *I*)

mí – see *munus*

munus – nouns denoting female humans; or shows that the Babylonian word represented by a sumerogram is grammatically feminine

na_4 – stone objects

še – grains

uru – names of cities

uzu – appears before nouns denoting body parts and edibles

CULTURE TIP

By tradition, the sumerogram *tukul* (Bab. *kakku* **weapon**) continued to be written with the *giš* determinative long after weapons had come to be made of metal rather than wood.

FOLLOWING

há – see hi.a

hi.a – indicates that the word is plural; in the first millennium also simply used to indicate that the preceding sign(s) should be read as a sumerogram

ki – names of places

meš – indicates that the word is plural; in the first millennium also simply indicates that the preceding sign(s) should be read as a sumerogram; in scholarly writings, when used with verbs spelled sumerographically it is often a clue to a form other than the G system (usually, D or Gtn)

2 – indicates that the word is dual; in the first millennium also simply used to indicate that the preceding sign(s) should be read as a sumerogram

2 Sumerograms

The following list gives the dictionary form of the Babylonian word represented by the sumerogram. In the context of a sentence, sumerograms often represent forms other than the dictionary form, and when normalizing you have to put the word into the appropriate form in accordance with your knowledge of the language.

The list does not count determinatives (in upper case) for the purpose of alphabetization.

Occasionally, it is not certain how a sumerogram was read. In such cases, a conventional reading is employed, and many books (including this one) transliterate the relevant sumerogram in small capitals. (See *dbad*, *dgiš* and *ka.kešda*.)

^{d}15	*ištar* **Ištar** (goddess of sex and war)
^{d}30	*sîn* **Sîn** (moon god)
a^{meš}	*mû* **water**
a	*aplu(m)* **heir, son**
a.ab.ba	*tâmtu(m)* **sea** (see Unit 43.3)
a.šà	*eqlu(m)* **field**
a.zu	*asû(m)* **physician**
^{iti}ab	*abu(m)* (the fifth Babylonian month)
áb	*lītu(m)* **cow**
^{d}adad	*addu(m)* (the weather god)
aga	*agû(m)* **crown**

aga.uš	*rēdû(m)* **soldier**
^{d}amar.utu	*marūtuk* **Marduk** (chief god of Babylon)
am.si	*pīru(m)* **elephant** (see Unit 43.5)
an	*šamû* **heaven**, *anu(m)* **Anu** (sky god)
an.bar$_7$	*muṣlālu(m)* **siesta time**
anše	*imēru(m)* **donkey**
anše.kur.ra	*sisû(m)* **horse**
arad	*(w)ardu(m)* **slave**
aš.te	*kussû(m)* **throne**
^{d}BAD	*enlil* (a god)
bàd	*dūru(m)* city wall
bal.ti.la^{ki}	*aššur* **Assur**
^{giš}banšur	*paššūru(m)* **table**
dagal	*rapšu(m)* **broad**
di.kud	*dayyānu(m)* **judge**
dingir	*ilu(m)* **god**
dingir.dingir	ilū/ilī (SB also *ilānī*) **gods**
du	*alāku(m)* **to go** (du.du = Gtn)
dù	*epēšu(m)* **to do, to make**; *kalû(m)* **all**
^{iti}du$_6$	*tašrītu(m)* (the seventh Babylonian month)
du$_{11}$.ga	*qabû(m)* **to say**
dumu	*māru(m)* **son**
dusu	*tupšikku(m)* **earth basket, toil**
é	*bītu(m)* **house**
é.gal	*ēkallu(m)* **palace**
é.sag.íl	*esagil* **Esagil**
edin	*ṣēru(m)* **back, steppe**
^{d}en.zu	*sîn* **Sîn** (moon god)
^{munus}ensi	*šailtu(m)* **female dream interpreter**
erim	*ṣābu(m)* **troop(s)**, *ummānu(m)* **army** (erim and érin are two readings of the same cuneiform sign)
erim.tah (or érin.tah)	*nērāru(m)* **help**
érin	*ṣābu(m)* **troop(s)**, *ummānu(m)* **army** (erim and érin are two readings of the same cuneiform sign)
ga	*šizbu(m)* **milk**
gag	*sikkatu(m)* **peg**
gal	*rabû(m)* **great**

gál	*bašû(m)* **to exist**
gar	*šakānu(m)* **to put**
garza	*parṣu(m)* **rite**
géme	*amtu(m)* **slave girl**
geštin	*karānu(m)* **wine**
geštu	*uznu(m)* **ear**
gim	*kīma* **like, as, when**
^{giš}gigir	*narkabtu(m)* **chariot**
gír.an.bar	*patru(m)* **sword**
^{lú}gír.lá	*ṭābihu(m)* **butcher**
gír.tab	*zuqāqīpu(m)* **scorpion**
gìr	*šēpu(m)* **foot**
gìr.pad.du	*eṣemtu(m)* **bone**
^{d}gìra	*girra* (the fire god)
^{d}GIŠ(.gím.maš)	*gilgameš* **Gilgameš** (mythical hero)
gú	*kišādu(m)* **neck, bank (of river)**
gu_4	*alpu(m)* **ox**
gú.un	*biltu(m)* **tribute**
^{giš}gu.za	*kussû(m)* **throne**
gun	*biltu(m)* **tribute**
ha.na	*hanû(m)* **Hanean**
hé.gál	*hegallu(m)* **abundance**
hul	*lemnu(m)* **evil**
^{munus}hul	*lemuttu(m)* **evil**
^{lú}ì.du_8	*atû(m)* doorman
ì.giš	*šamnu(m)* **oil** (see Unit 43.5)
ì.nun	*himētu(m)* **butter, ghee** (see Unit 43.5)
íd	*nāru(m)* **river**
^{d}im	*adad, addu* **Adad** (storm god)
igi	*panu(m)* **front** (pl. **face**)
igi.gál	*igigallu(m)* **wise one**
im	*šāru(m)* **wind**
^{d}inanna	*ištar* **Ištar** (goddess of sex and war)
inim	*awātu(m)*, later *amātu(m)* **utterance**
^{d}iškur	*adad, addu* **Adad** (storm god)
izi	*išātu(m)* **fire**
ka	*pû(m)* **mouth, utterance**

ká	*bābu(m)* **gate**
^{uru}ká.dingir	*bābili(m)* **Babylon**
ká.dingir.ra^{ki}	*babili(m)* **Babylon**
KA.kešda	*riksu(m)* **knot, bond**
kalam	*mātu(m)* **land**
kam, kám	This often appears after numbers, almost like a determinative for them. In most cases it probably did not correspond to a spoken Babylonian word. It can usually be ignored in translation.
kar.kid	*harimtu(m)* **harlot**
kaš, kaš.sag	*šikaru(m)* **beer**
ki	*erṣetu(m)* **earth, netherworld**
ki.min	(reading uncertain) **ditto** (is sporadically used as an abbreviation, to avoid repeating neighbouring stretches of text)
ki.sì.ga	*kispu(m)* **funerary ritual**
ki.sikil	*(w)ardatu(m)* **girl, young woman**
^{giš}kiri$_6$	*kirû(m)* **garden, orchard**
kù	*ellu(m)* **pure**
kù.babbar	*kaspu(m)* **silver**
kù.gi	*hurāṣu(m)* **gold**
ku$_4$	*erēbu(m)* **to enter**
ku$_6$	*nūnu(m)* **fish**
kur	*šadû(m)* **mountain**, *mātu(m)* **land**; kur.kur = *mātātu/i(m)* **lands**
kúr	*nakru(m)* **enemy**
kuš	*mašku(m)* **skin, leather**
kuš.ùsan	*qinnāzu(m)* **whip, work team**
^{giš}lal	*tuquntu(m)* **battle**
larsam^{ki}	*larsa* **Larsa** (a city)
lú	*awīlu(m), amīlu(m)* **man**
lugal	*šarru(m)* **king**
lugud	*šarku(m)* **pus**
ma.da	*mātu(m)* **land**; ma.da.ma.da = *mātātu/i(m)* **lands**
^{giš}má	*eleppu(m)* **boat, ship**
man	*šarru(m)* **king**
^{giš}mar	*marru(m)* **spade**

^{d}maš	*ninurta* (a warrior god)
^{lú}maš.maš	*mašmaššu(m)* **incantation priest** (this translation is conventional)
máš	*urīṣu(m)* **male goat**
me	*meat* **a hundred**
mu	*šattu(m)* **year**; in names: *nadānu(m)* **to give**
múd	*damu(m)* **blood**
mun	*ṭābtu(m)* **salt**
munus	*sinništu(m)* **woman**
murub$_4$	*qablu(m)* **battle, middle**
muš	*ṣerru(m)* **snake**
mušen	*iṣṣūru(m)* **bird**
na.ru	*narû(m)* **stele**
na$_4$	*abnu(m)* **stone**
nar	*nāru(m)* **singer**
^{iti}ne.ne.gar	*abu(m)* **Abu** (a month, ≈ **August**)
^{d}nergal	*nergal* **Nergal** (the god of plague)
ní.te	*puluhtu(m)* **fear**
nibru	*nippur* (a city in Northern Babylonia)
nim	*elamtu(m)* **Elam**; ^{giš}nim *baltu(m)* **(a thorny bush)**
nina$^{(ki)}$	*ninua* **Nineveh**
ninda	*ak(a)lu(m)* **bread, food**
^{d}nisaba	*nisaba* (the grain goddess)
níta	*zikaru(m)* **man**
nu	*ul, lā* **not**
nu.bàn.da	*hazannu(m)* **mayor**
numun	*zēru(m)* **seed, progeny**
nun	*rubû(m)* **nobleman**
^{d}nusku	*nusku* (god of the night)
^{gi}pisan	*pišannu(m)* **wooden chest**
sag	*rēšu(m)* **head**, *ašarēdu(m)* **foremost**
sag.du	*qaqqadu(m)* **head**
síg	*šīpātu(m)* **wool** (Old Assyrian *šāptum*)
^{iti}sig$_4$	*simanu(m)* (the third Babylonian month)
sig$_5$	*damqu(m)* **good**
^{lú}sipa	*rē'û(m)* **shepherd**
su$_4$.bir	*subartu(m)* **Assyria**

šà	*libbu(m)* **heart, centre**
še	*û(m)* **barley**
^{iti}še	*addaru(m)* (the twelfth Babylonian month)
šid	*iššiakku(m)* **(a type of ruler)**
šu	*qātu(m)* **hand**; *gimillu(m)* **requital, favour**
^{iti}šu	*du'ūzu(m)* (the fourth Babylonian month)
^{lú}šu.gi.na	*gallābu(m)* **barber**
šu.si	*ubānu(m)* **finger**
šú	*kiššatu(m)* **entirety, Universe**; *rabû(m)* **to set** (of heavenly bodies)
šuku	*kurummatu(m)* **food ration**
šum	*ṭabāhu(m)* **to butcher**
šúm	*nadānu(m)* **to give**
ta	*ištu, ultu* **from, since**
tar	*parāsu(m)* **to separate**
te	*ṭehû(m)* **to approach**
tin.tir^{ki}	*bābili(m)* **Babylon**
túg	*ṣubātu(m)* **garment**
tuku	*rašû(m)* **to acquire**
^{giš}tukul	*kakku(m)* **weapon**
tur	*ṣehru(m)* **small, youngster**; *ṣuhāru(m)* **boy** (also in the sense **servant**)
^{munus}tur	*ṣuhārtu(m)* **girl**
tuš	*(w)ašābu(m)* **to sit, to stay**
ub	*kibru(m)* **edge**
ud.kib.nun^{ki}	*sippir* **Sippar** (a city)
udu.níta	*immeru(m)* **sheep**
ùg^{meš}	*nišū* **people** (pl. only, f.)
ugu	*eli* **on, above, over**; *muhhu(m)* **top**
ukkin	*puhru(m)* **assembly**
unug^{ki}	*uruk* **Uruk** (a city)
ur.gi$_7$	*kalbu(m)* **dog**
ur.mah	*nēšu(m)* **lion**
uri^{ki}	*akkadû(m)* **Akkadian** (in the first millennium BC this means **Babylonian**)
uru$^{(ki)}$	*ālu(m)* **city**
urudu	*erû(m)* **copper**

^{d}utu	*šamaš* **Šamaš** (sun god)
ùz	*enzu(m)* **female goat**
uzu	*šīru(m)* **flesh**
za.gìn	*uqnû(m)* **lapis lazuli**
zi	*napištu(m)* **life**
zú	*šinnu(m)* **tooth**
zú.lum	*suluppu(m)* **date** (the fruit)

The exercises in cuneiform

Cuneiform does not normally put spaces between words. Indeed, the calligraphy of many scholarly manuscripts demands that the end of each sign just touch the beginning of the next, leaving no 'empty space'. But also, spaces can appear between signs in ways that to us look random, and for this reason spacing between signs is ignored in transliteration. Here, for ease of learning, spaces have been inserted between words – including between prepositions and the noun they govern, though this may go against Babylonian linguistic instincts (see Unit 13, Tip). Where a name consists of different words (joined by – in Roman script), space has been inserted between them. The script runs left to right.

7.1

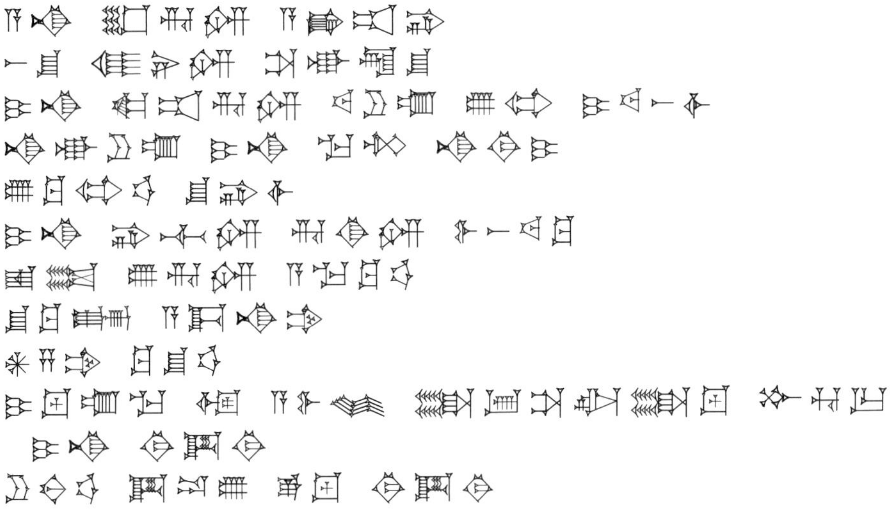

7.2

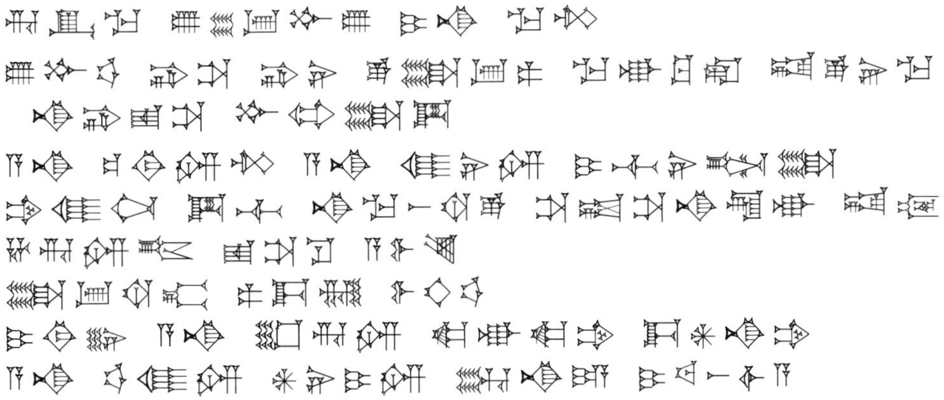

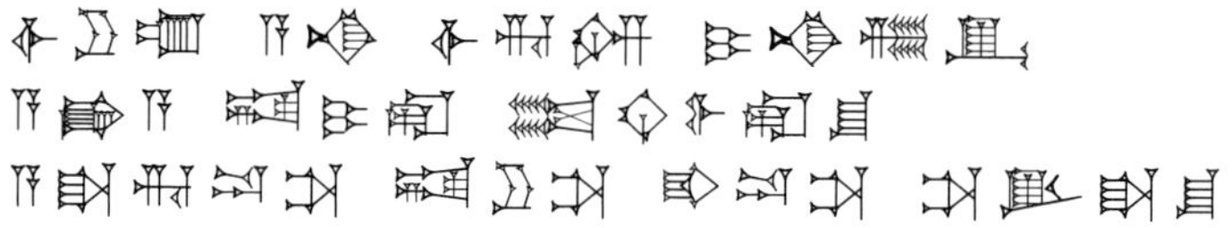

7.3

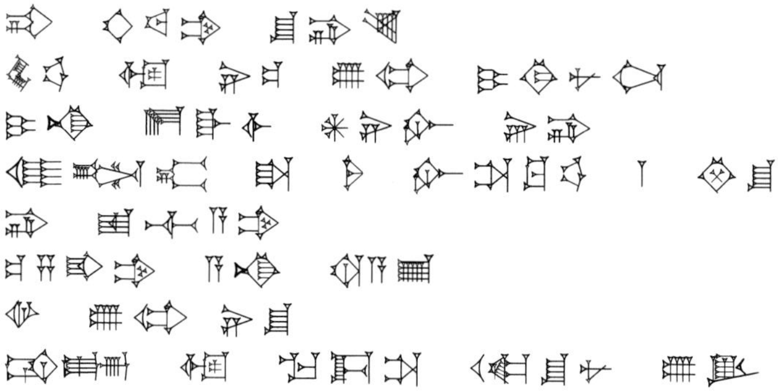

7.4

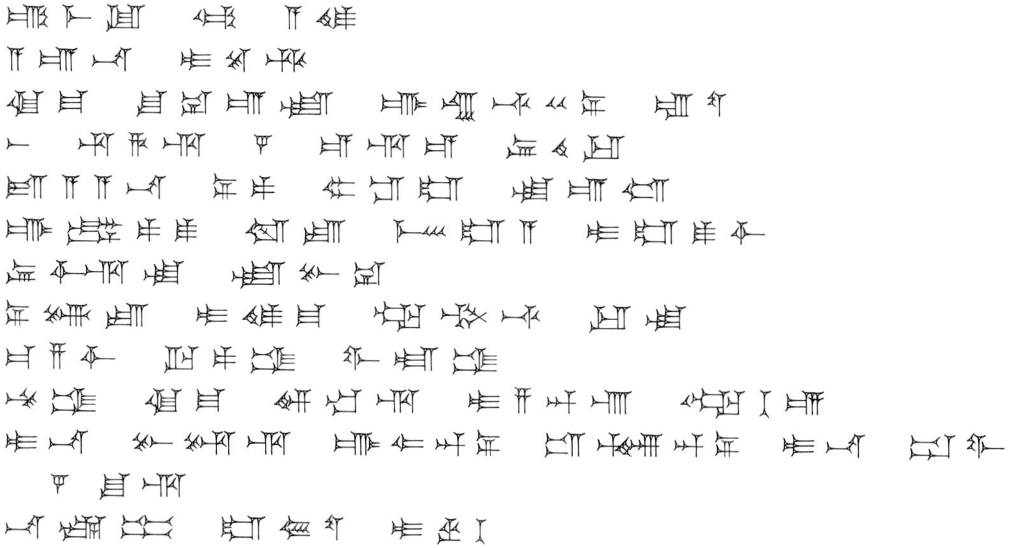

8.1

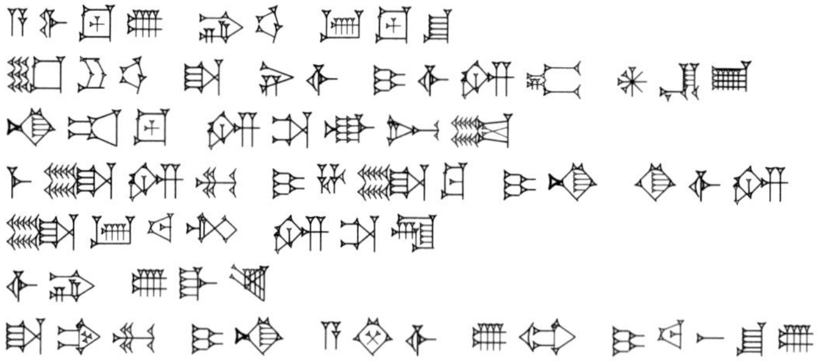

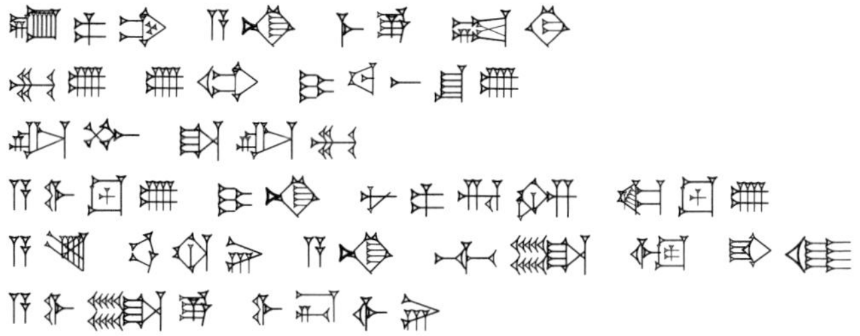

8.2

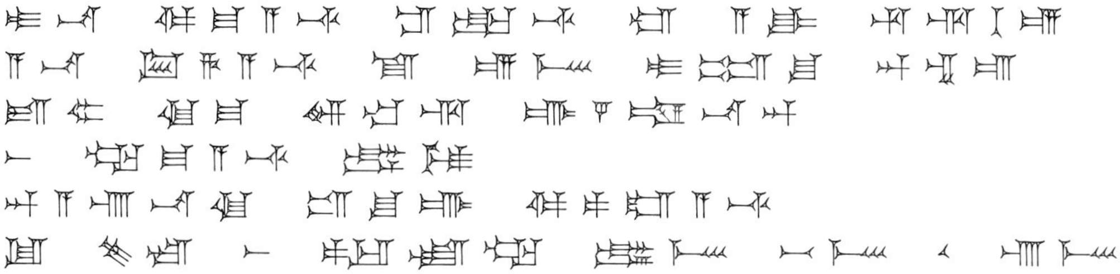

9.1

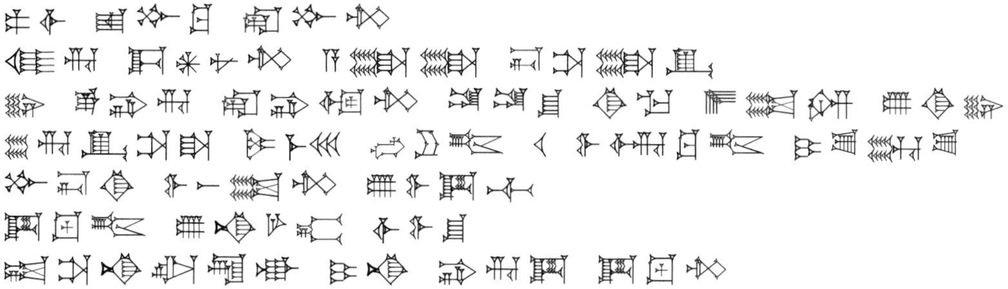

9.2

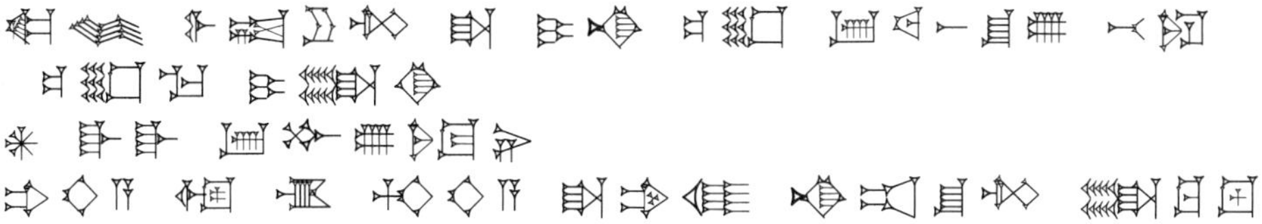

9.3

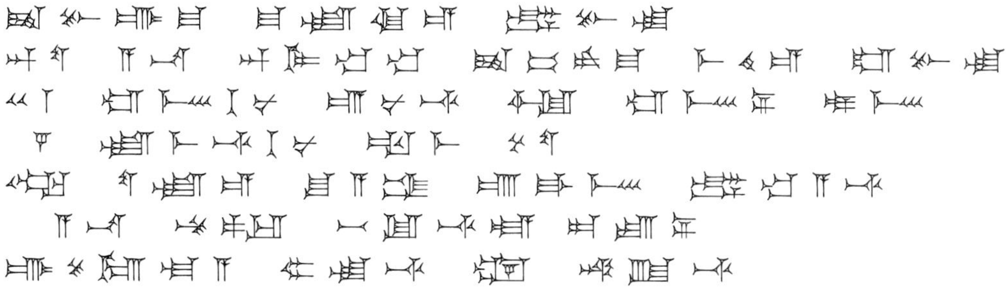

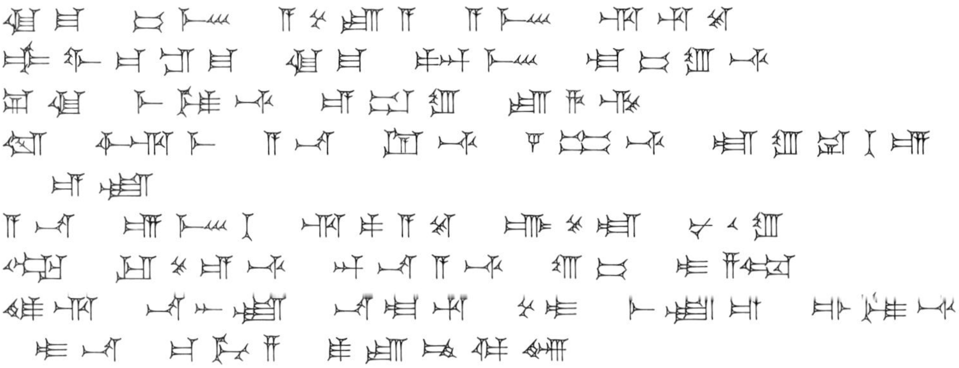

10.1

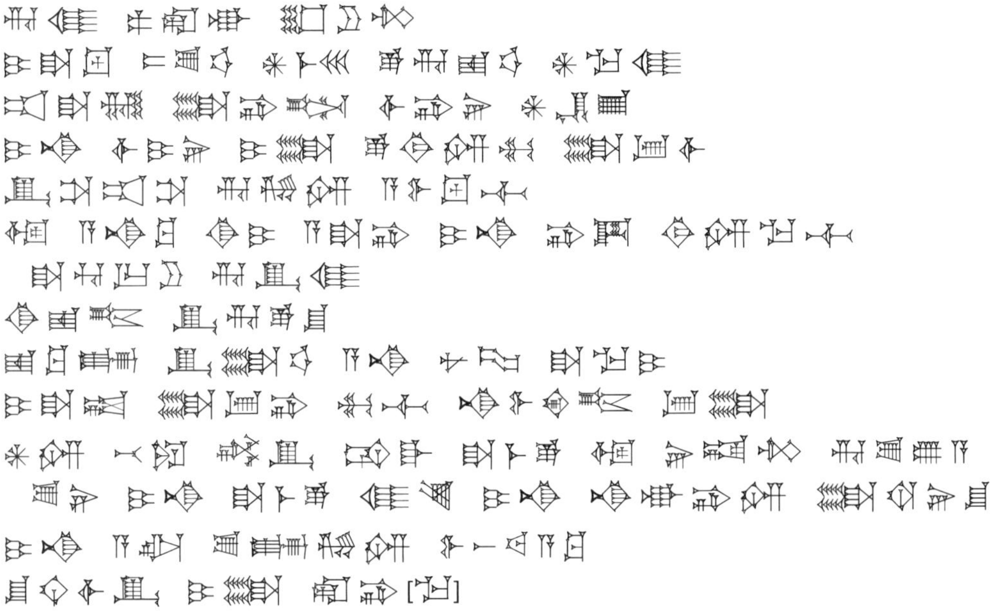

10.2

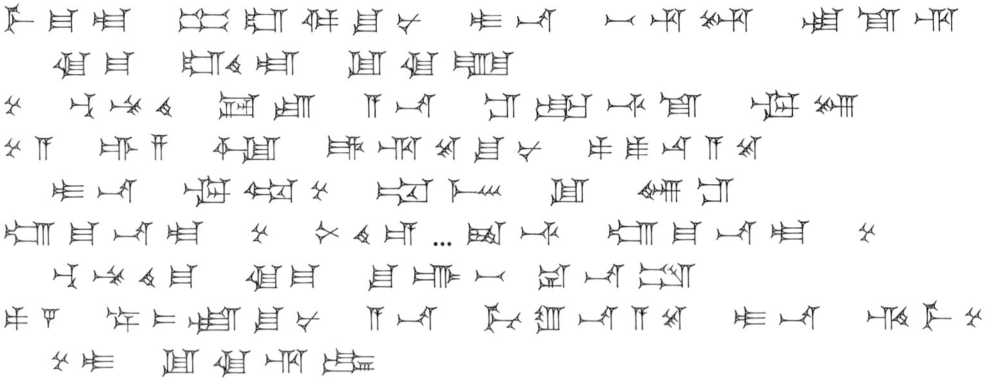

10.3

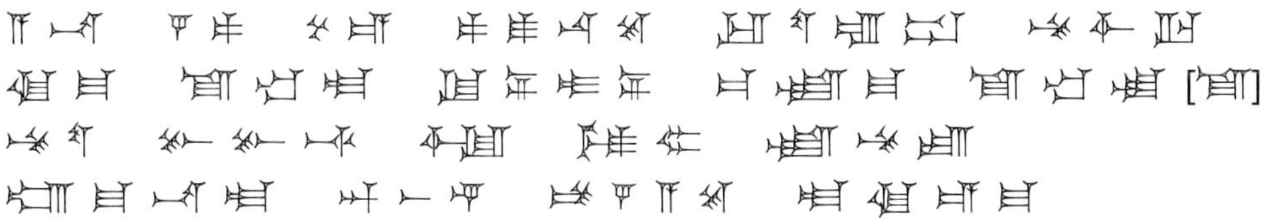

11.1

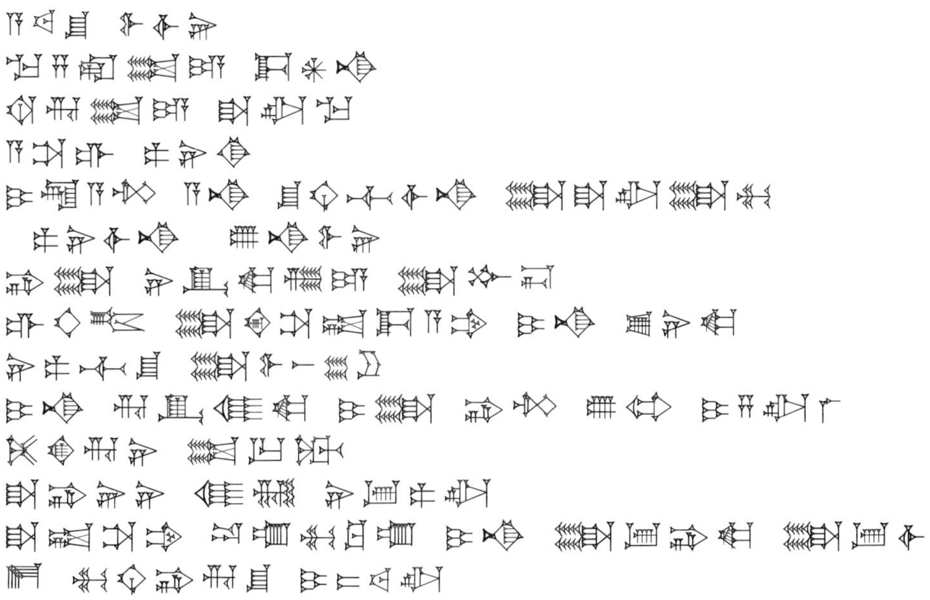

11.2

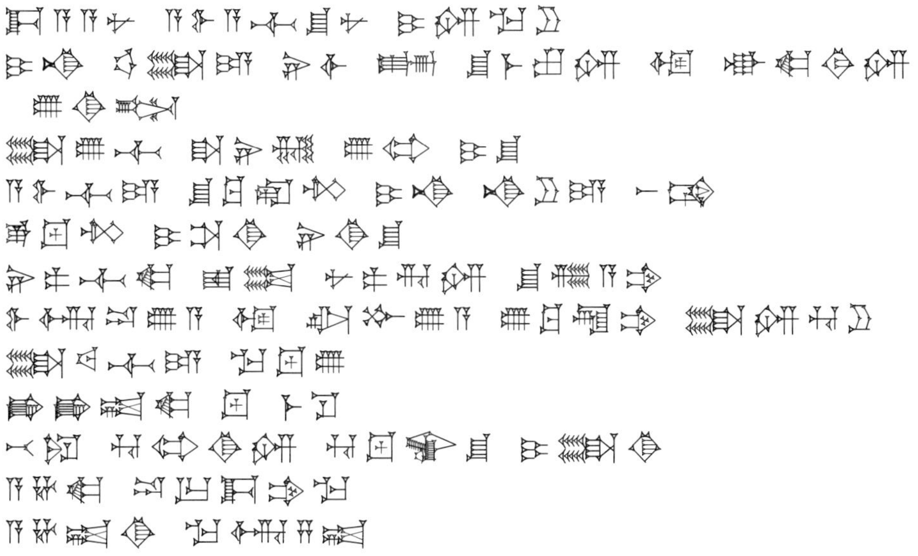

11.3

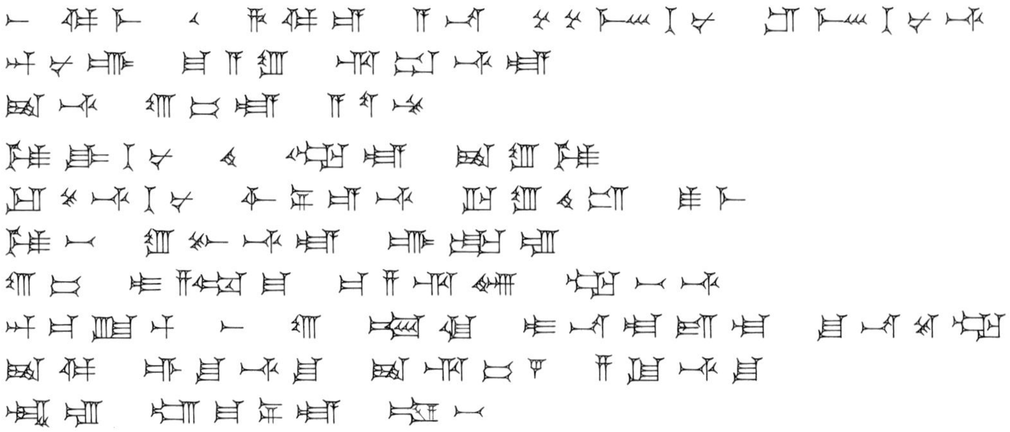

11.4

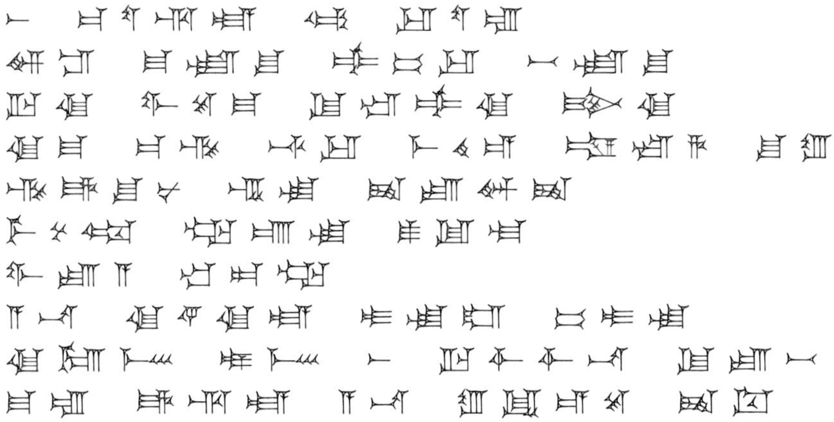

15.1

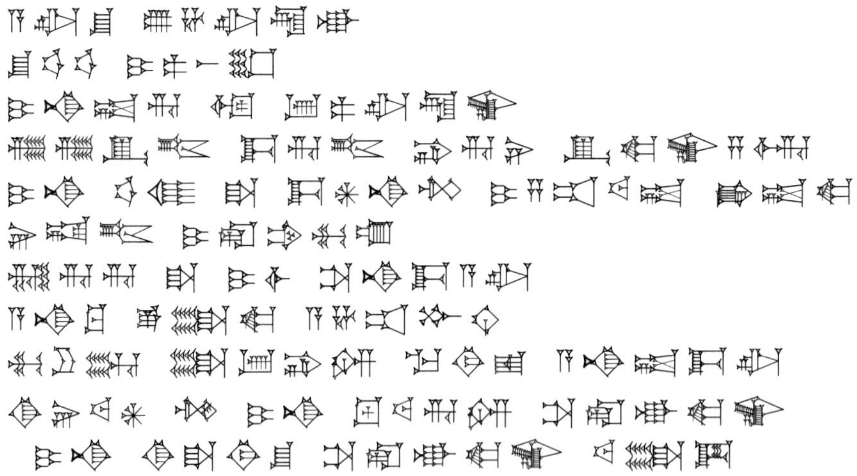

15.2

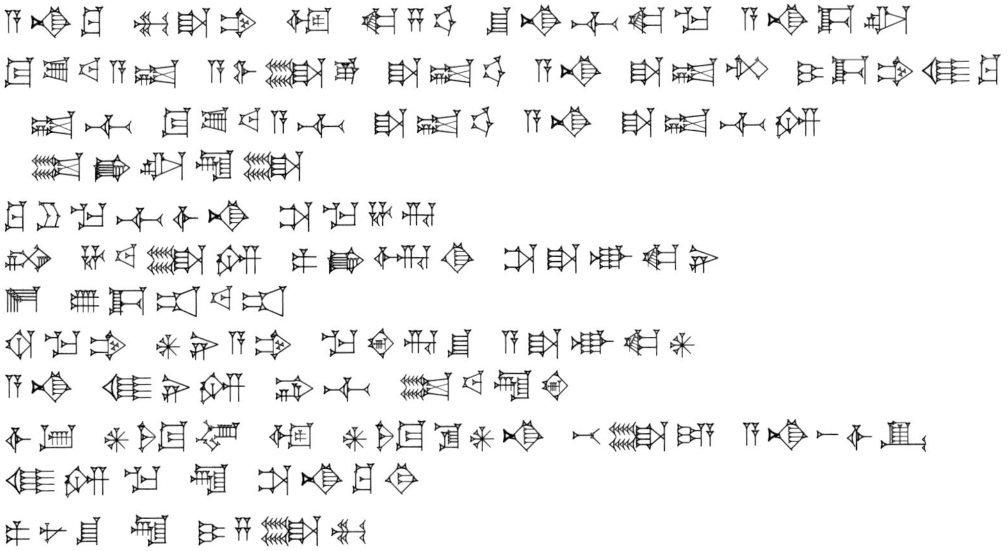

15.3

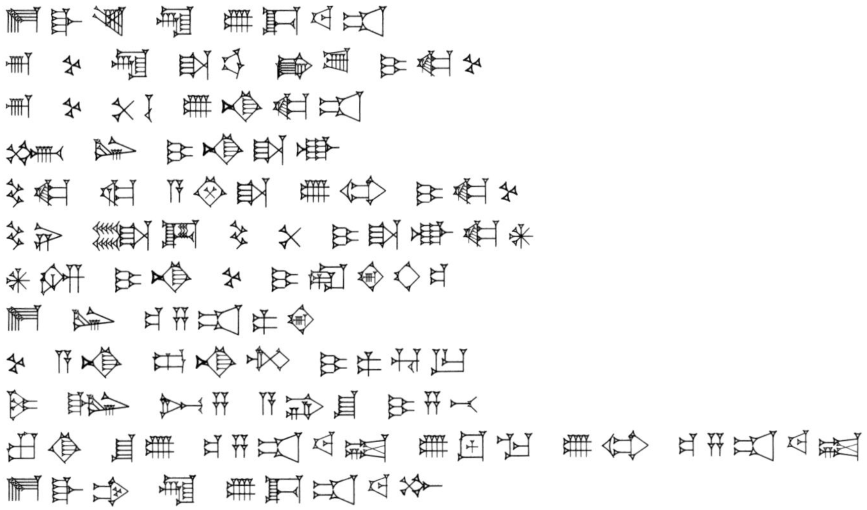

15.4

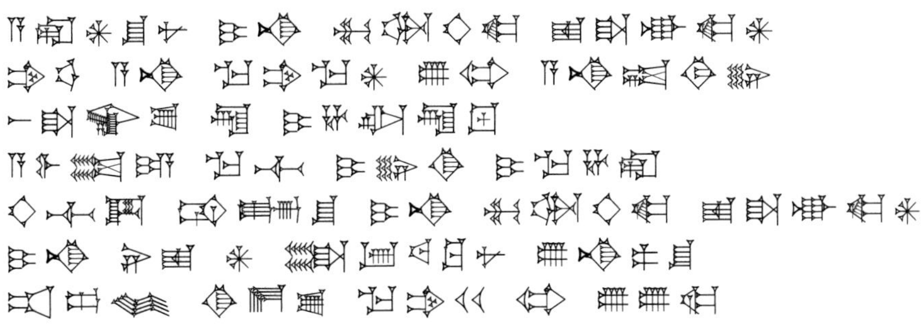

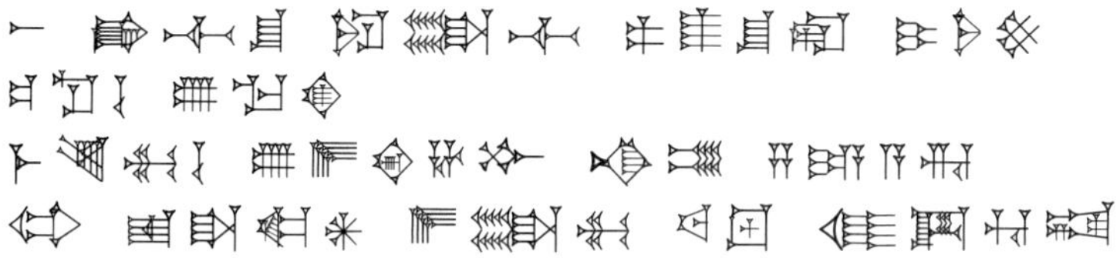

15.5

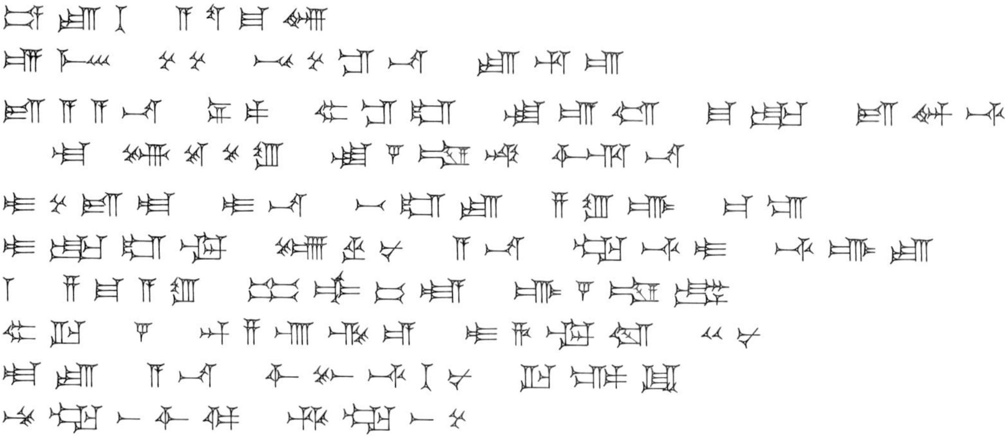

16.1

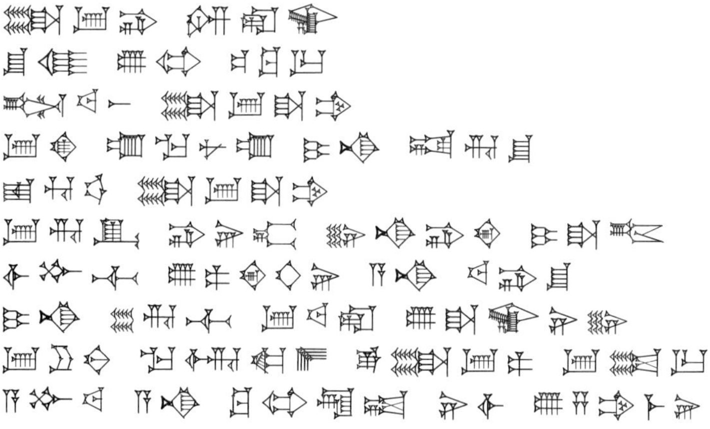

16.2

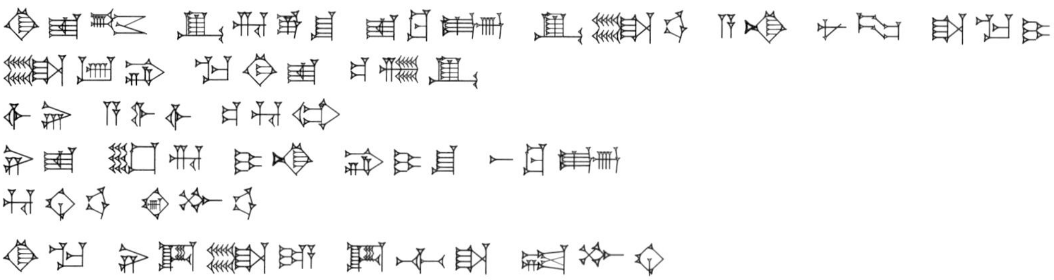

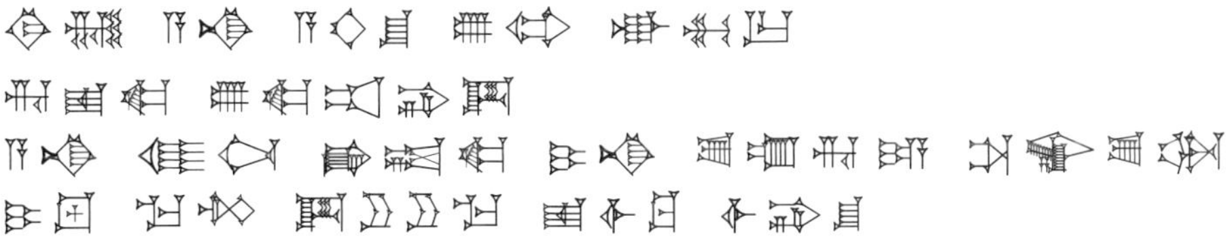

16.3

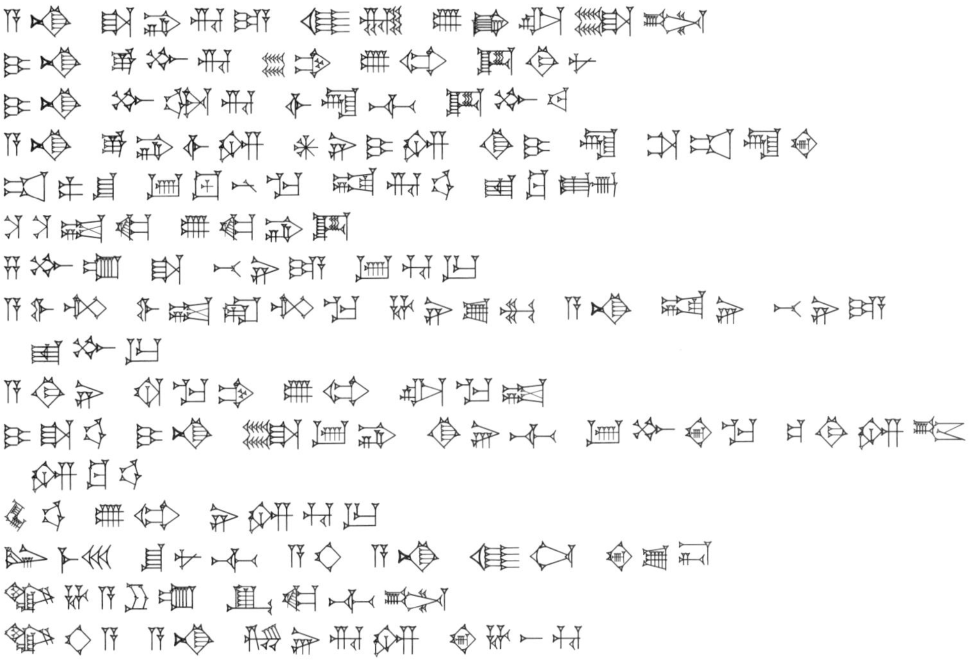

16.4

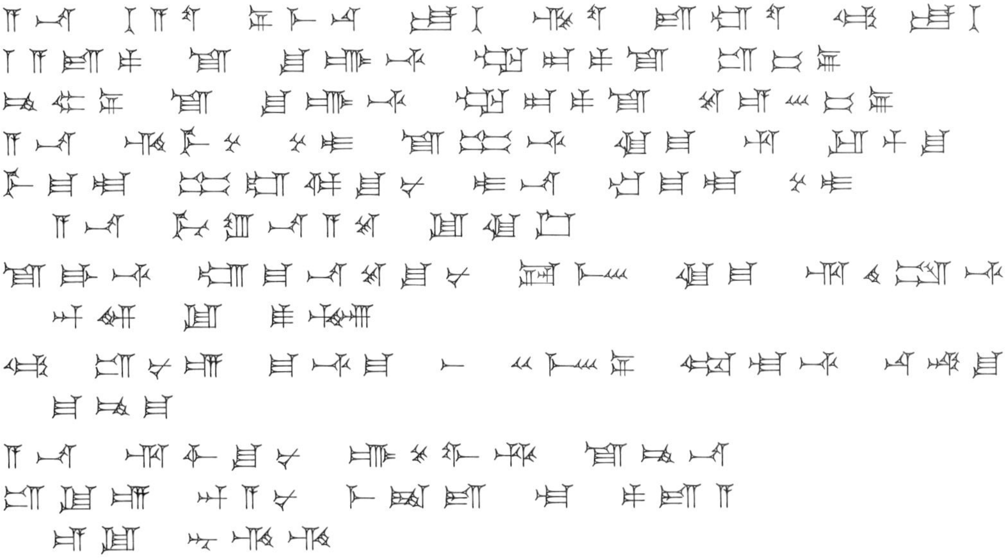

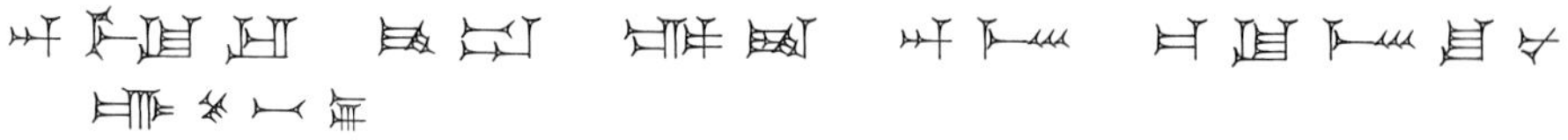

16.5

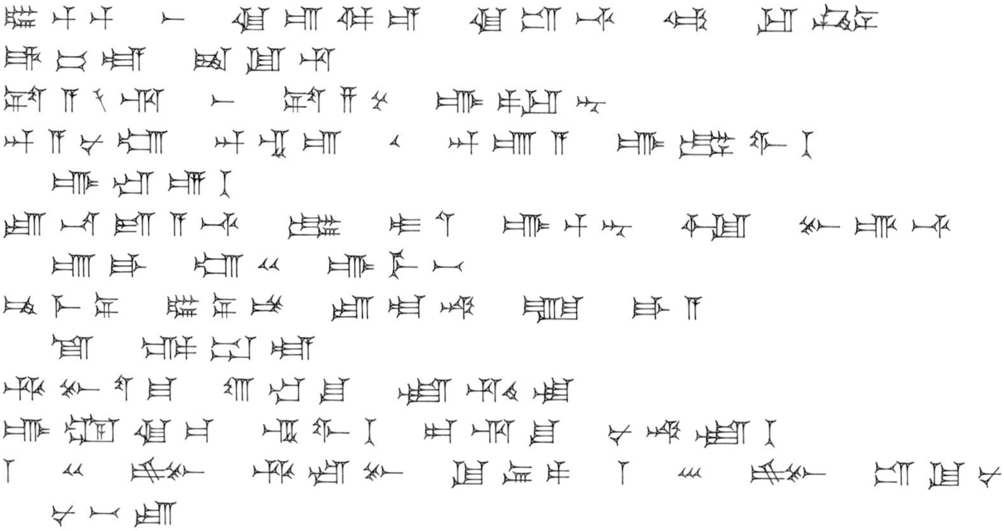

16.6

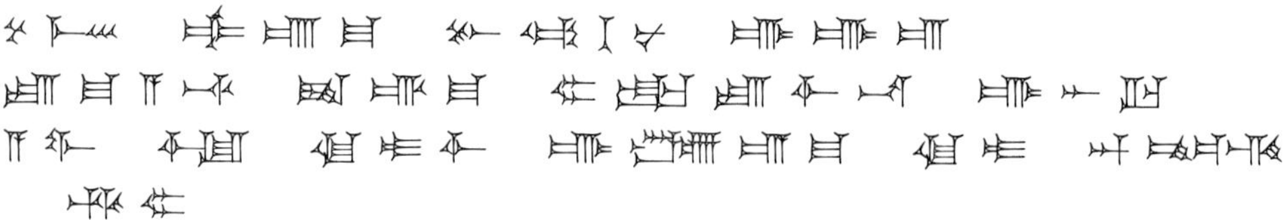

17.1

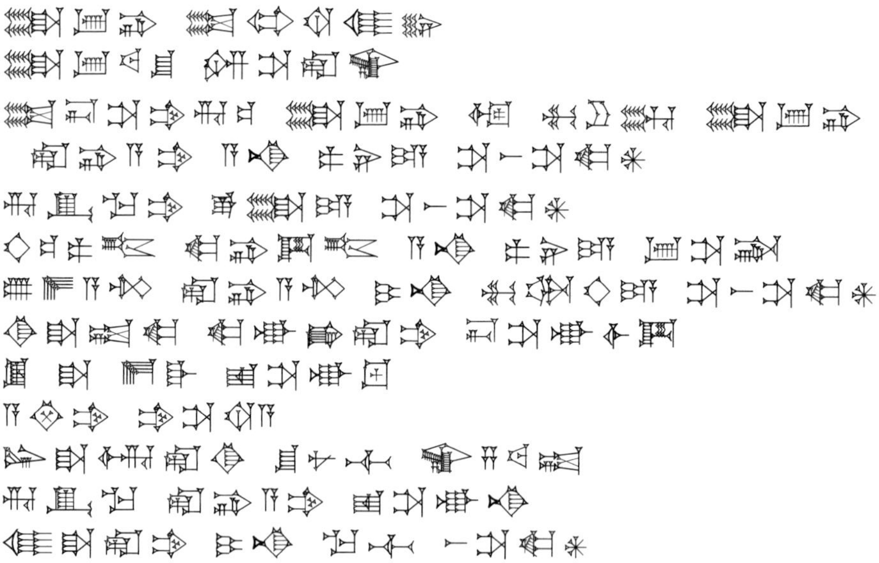

17.2

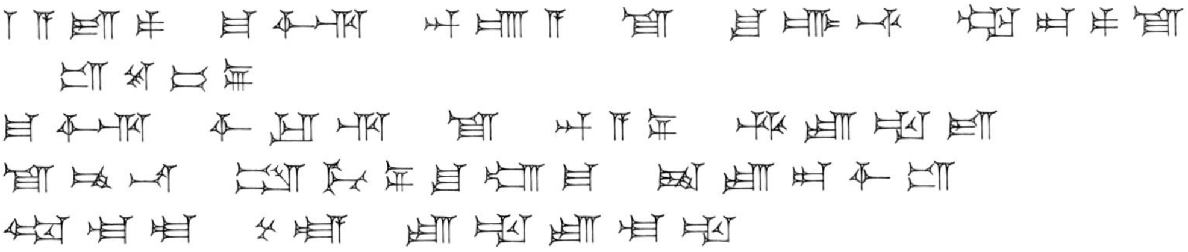

17.3

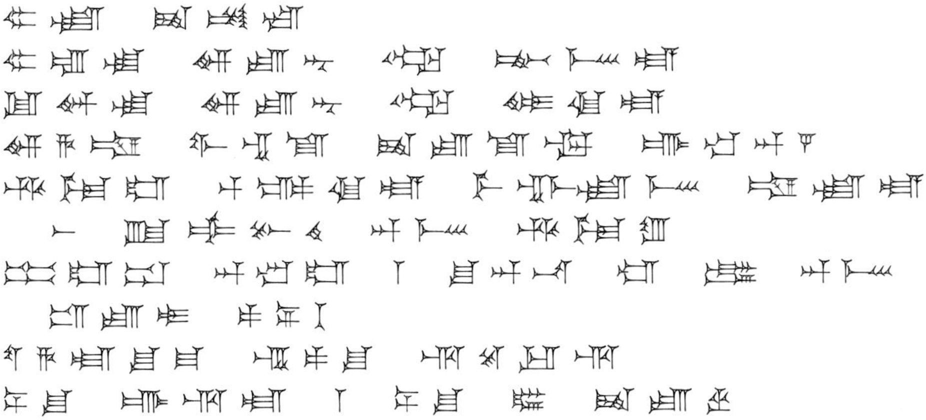

18.1

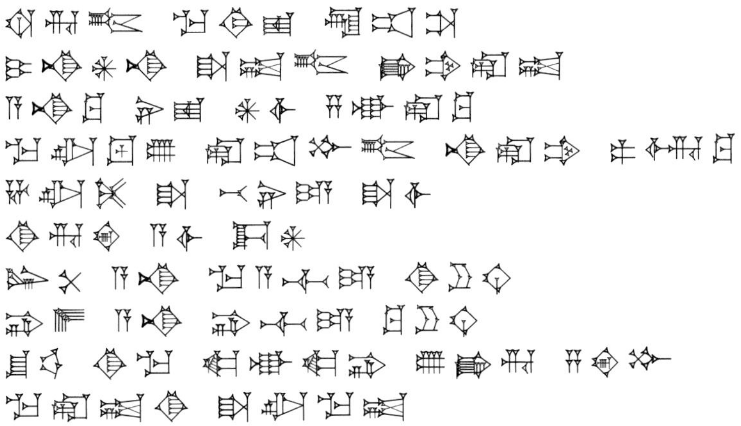

18.2

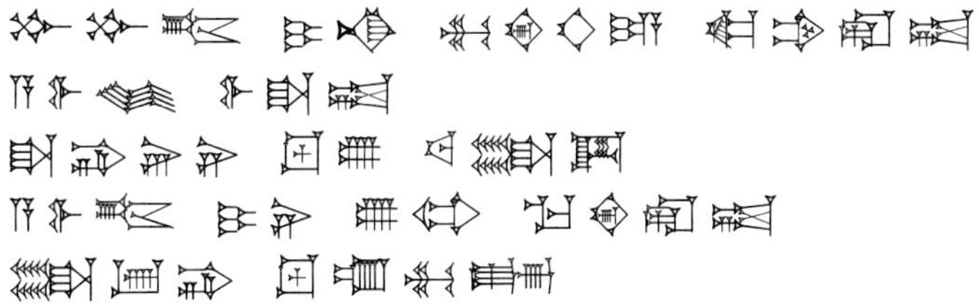

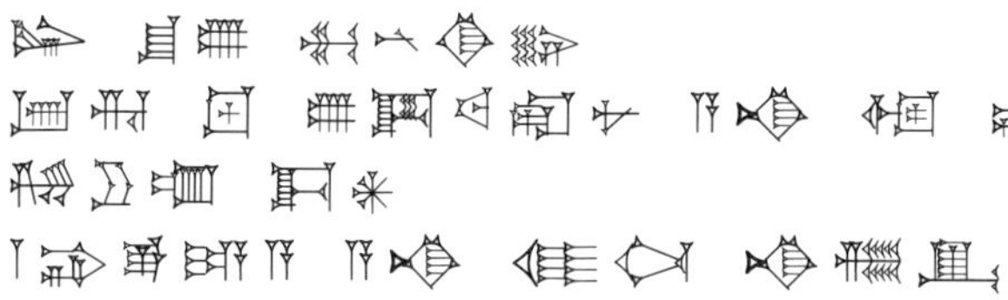

18.3

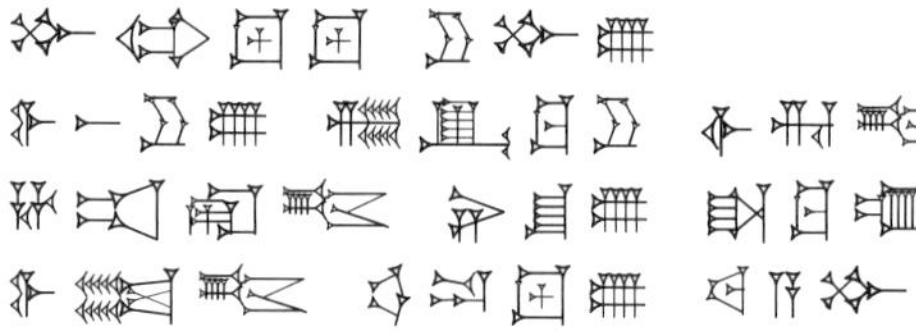

18.4

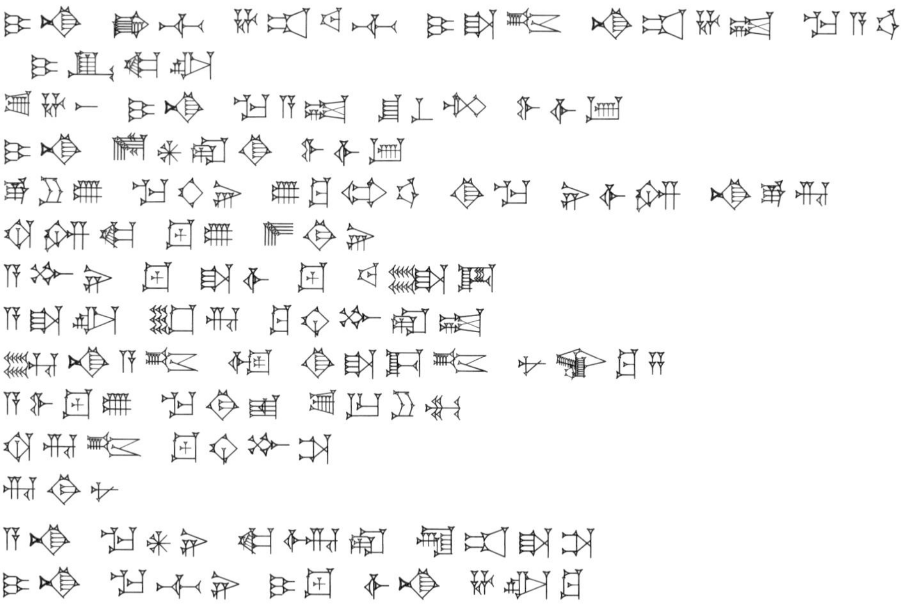

18.5

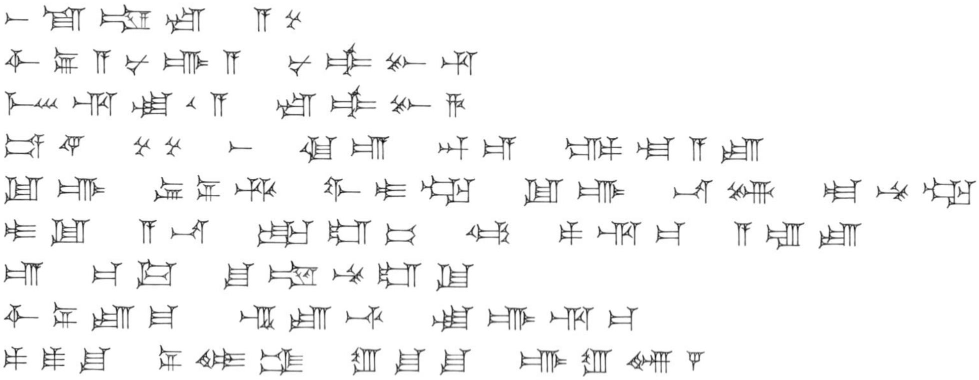

18.6

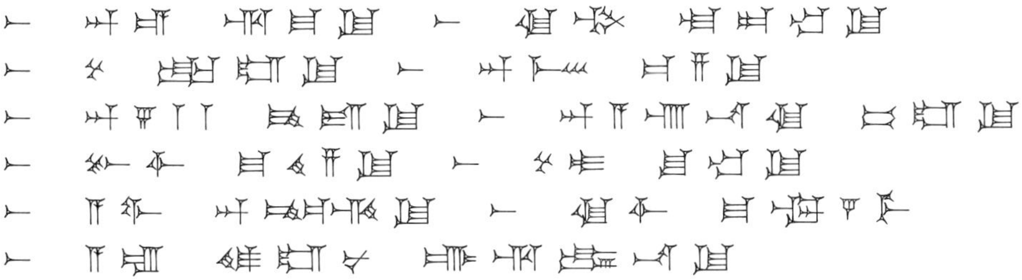

18.7

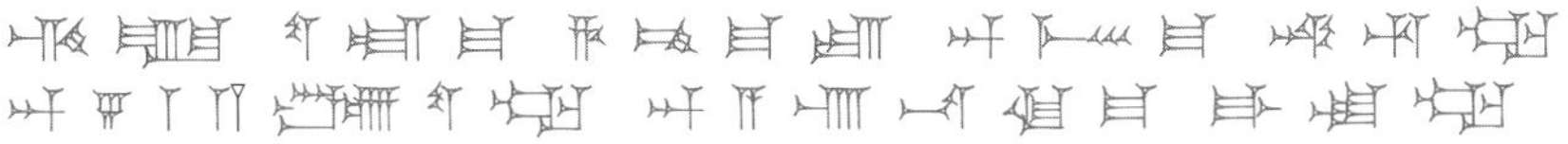

19.1

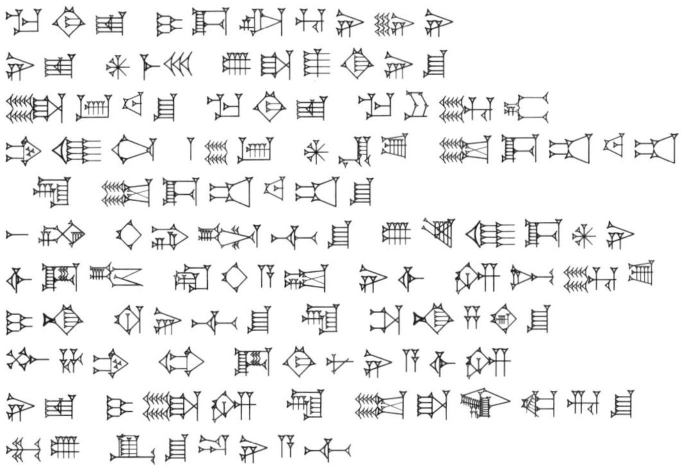

19.2

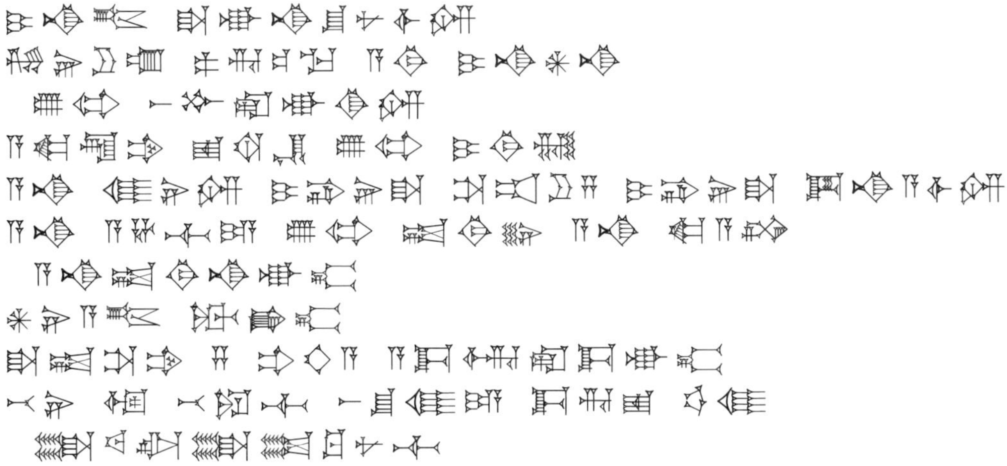

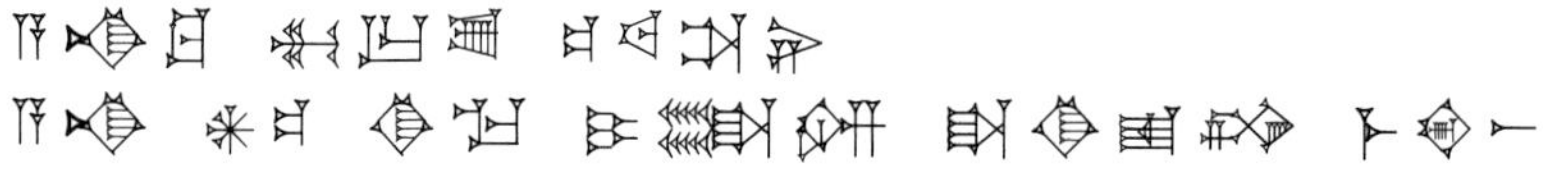

19.3

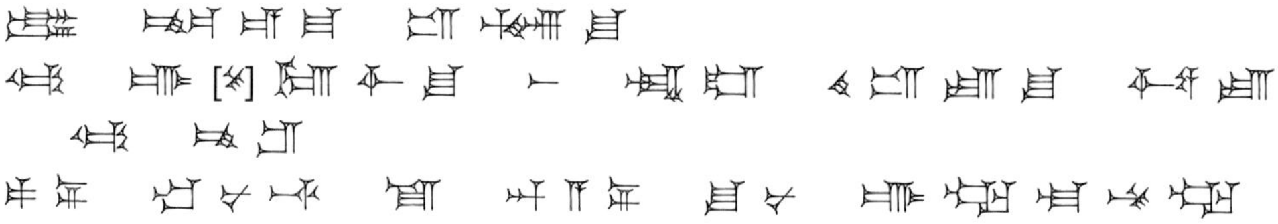

19.4

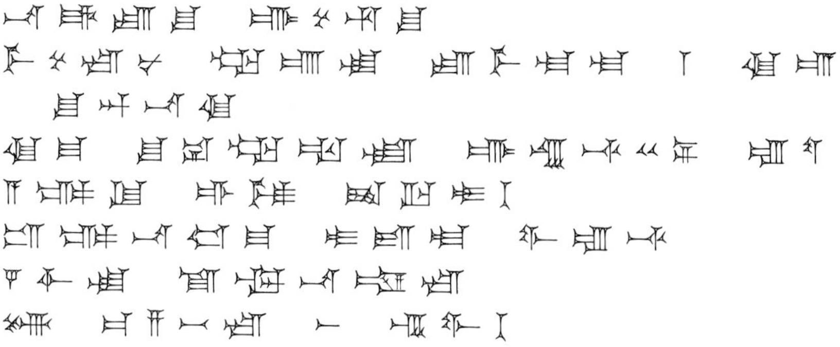

20.1

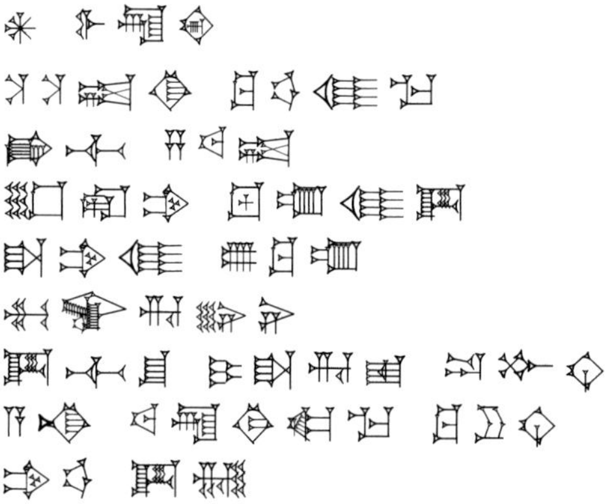

20.2

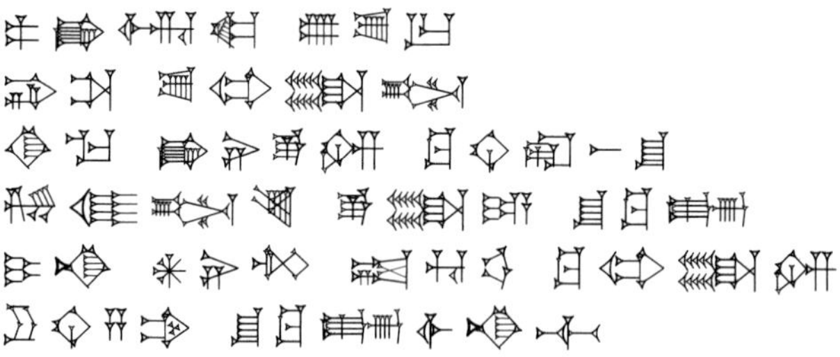

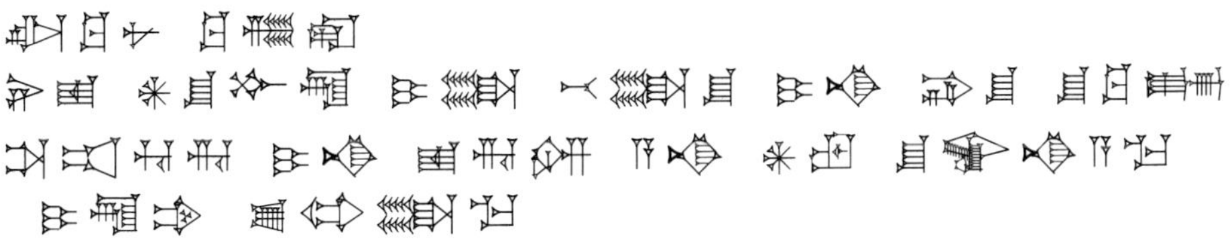

20.3

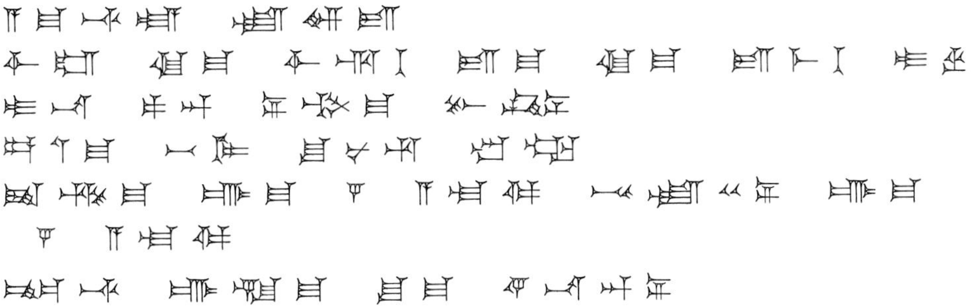

21.1

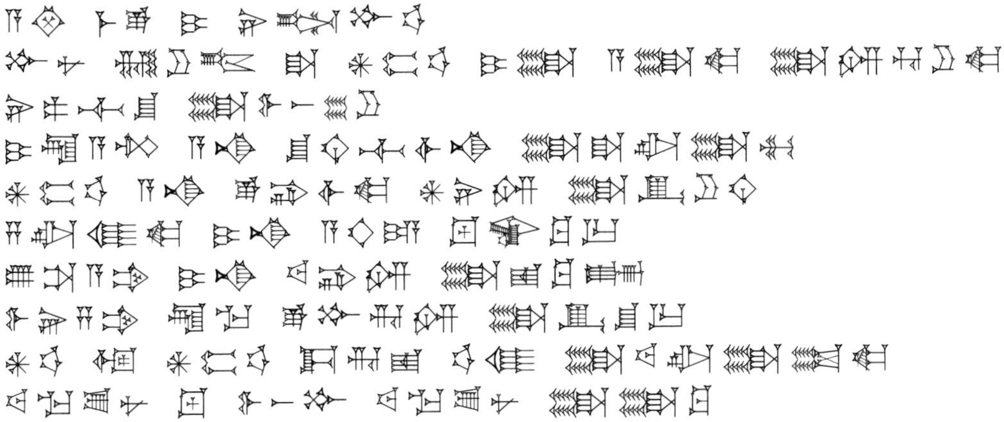

21.2

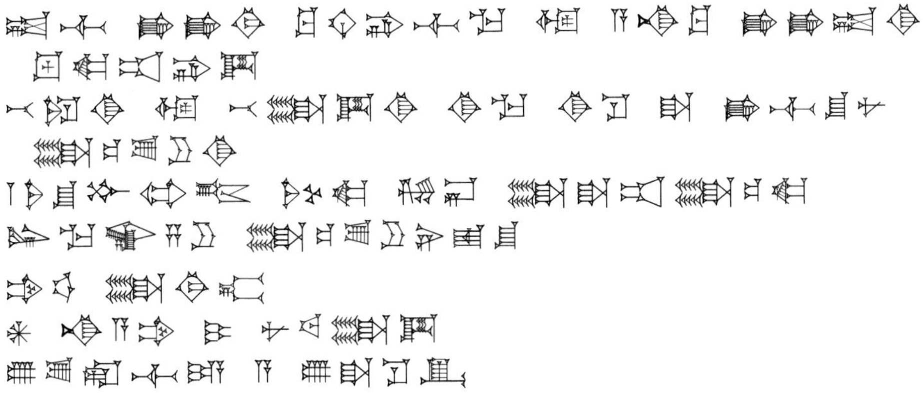

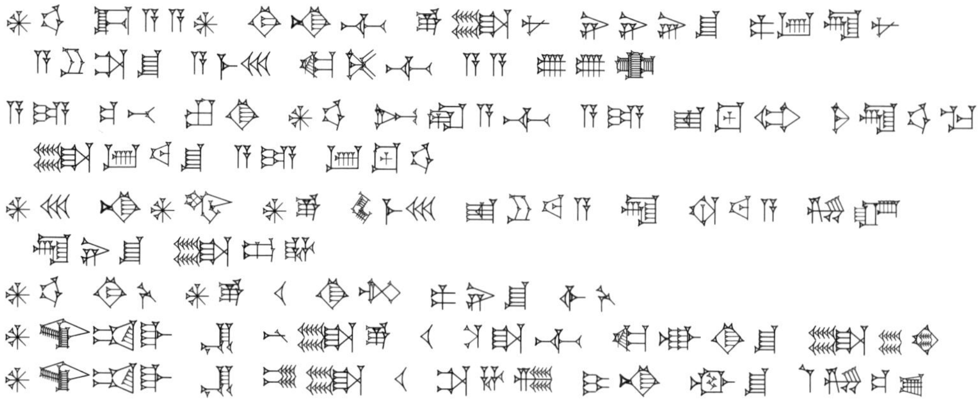

21.3

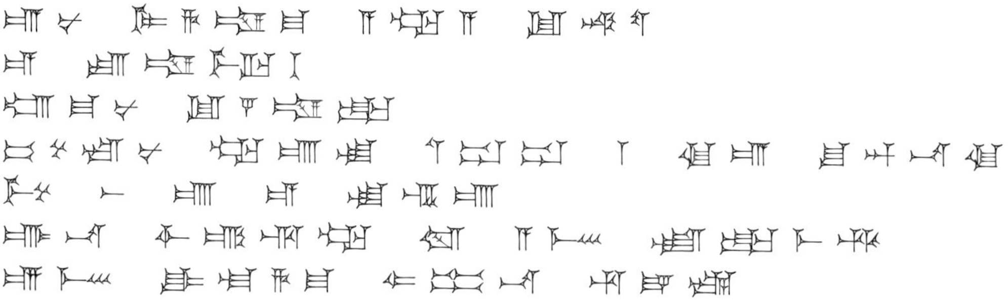

21.4

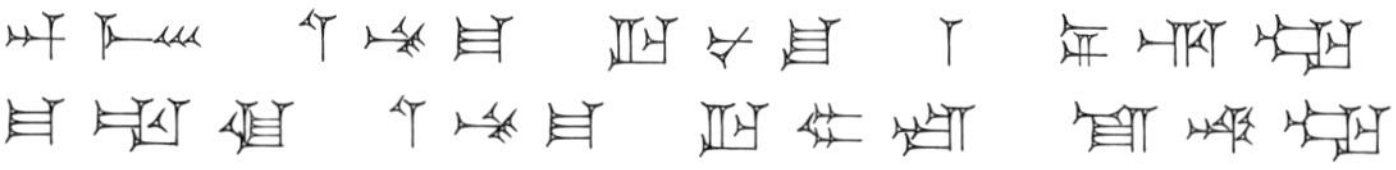

22.1

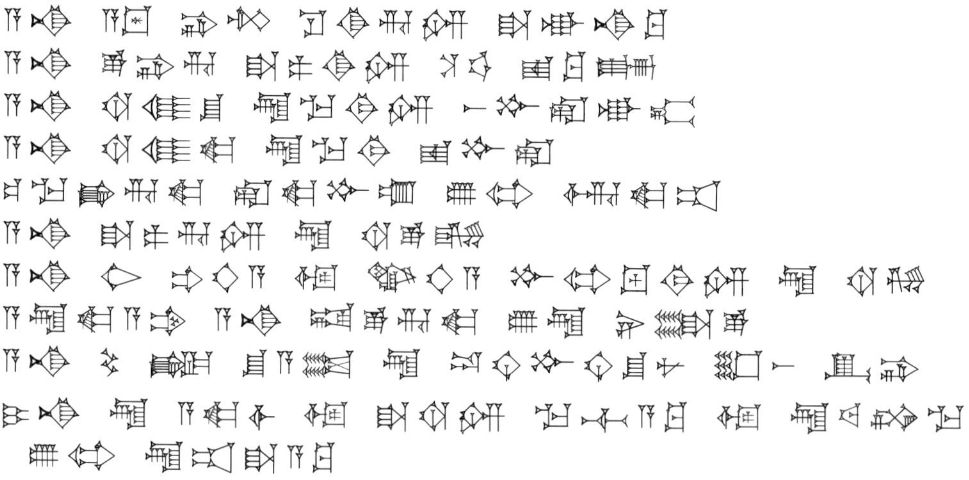

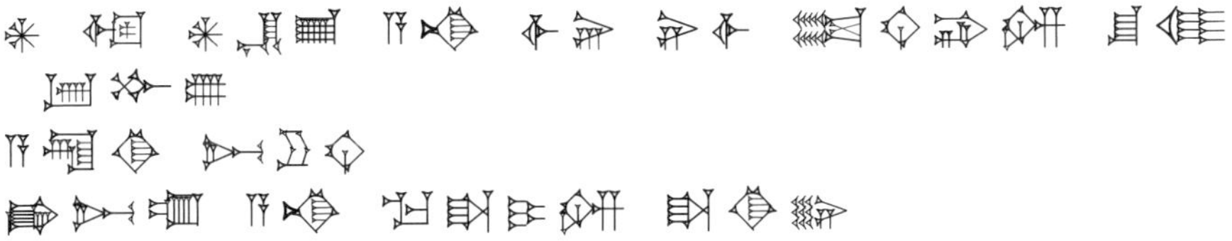

22.2

22.3

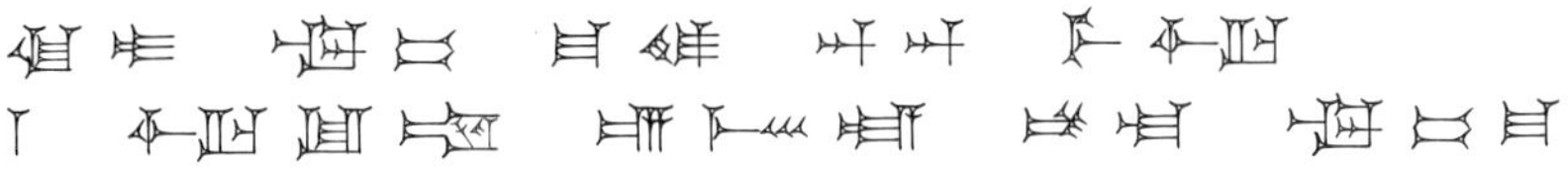

23.1

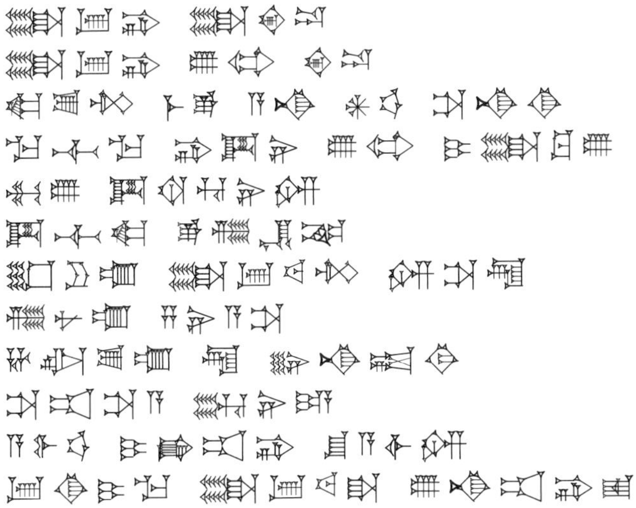

23.2

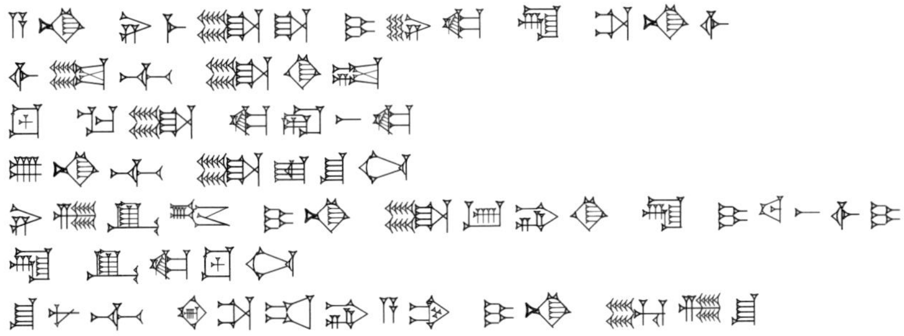

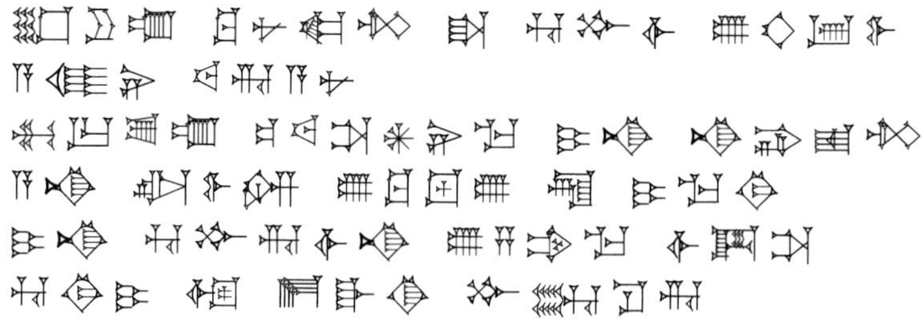

23.3

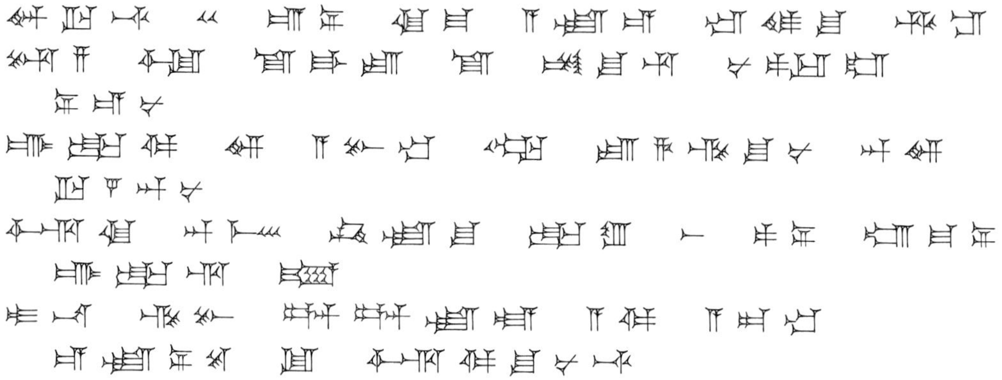

23.4

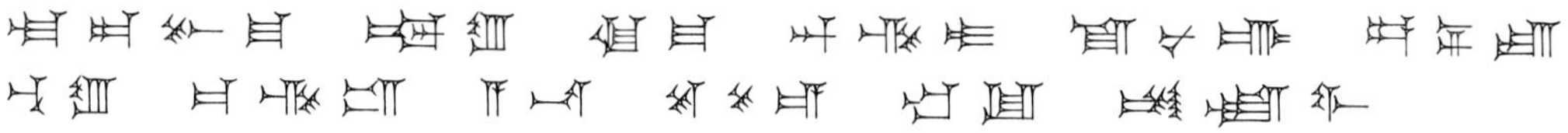

23.5

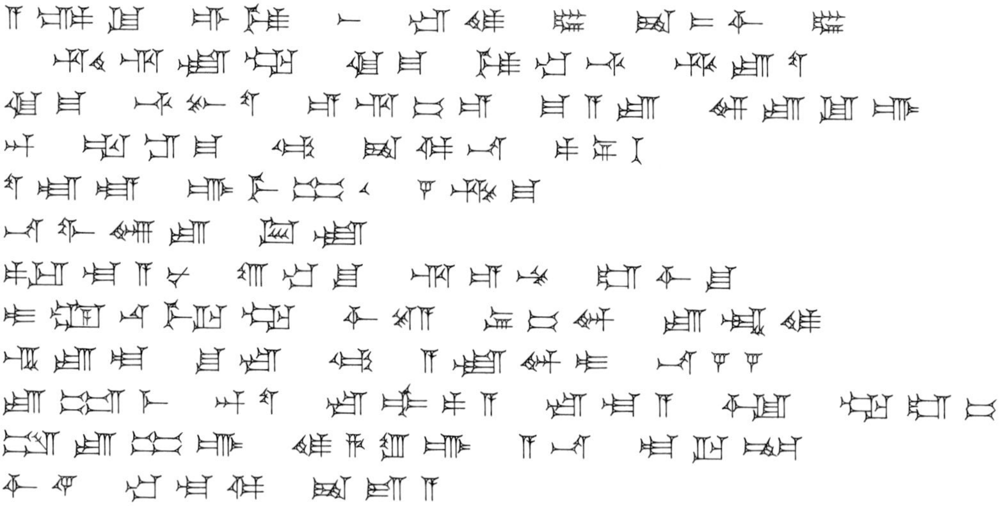

24.1

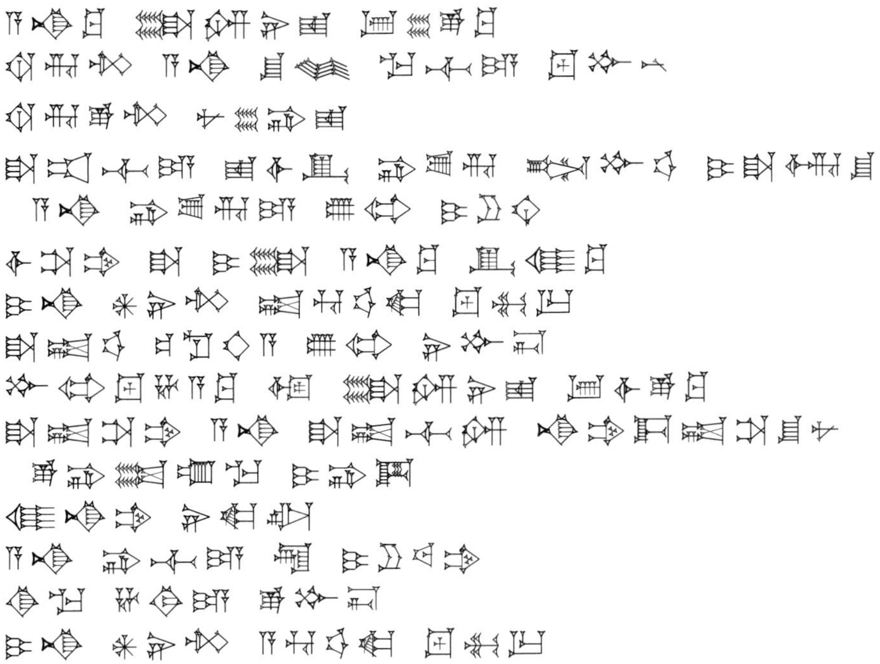

24.2

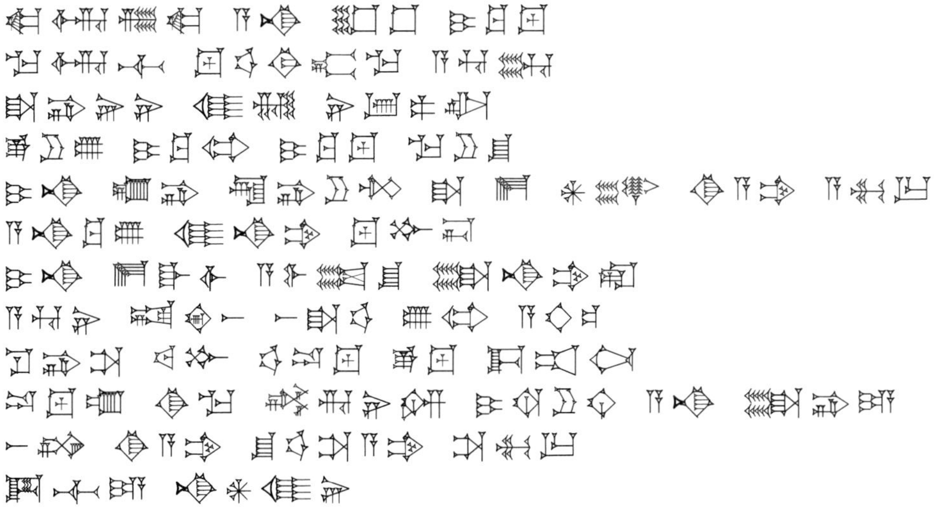

24.3

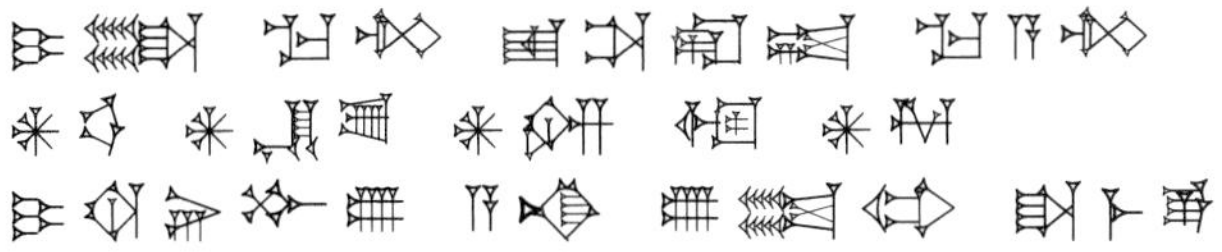

24.4

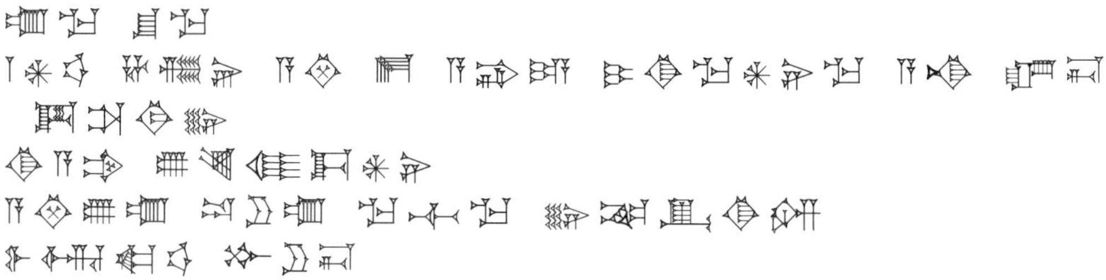

24.5

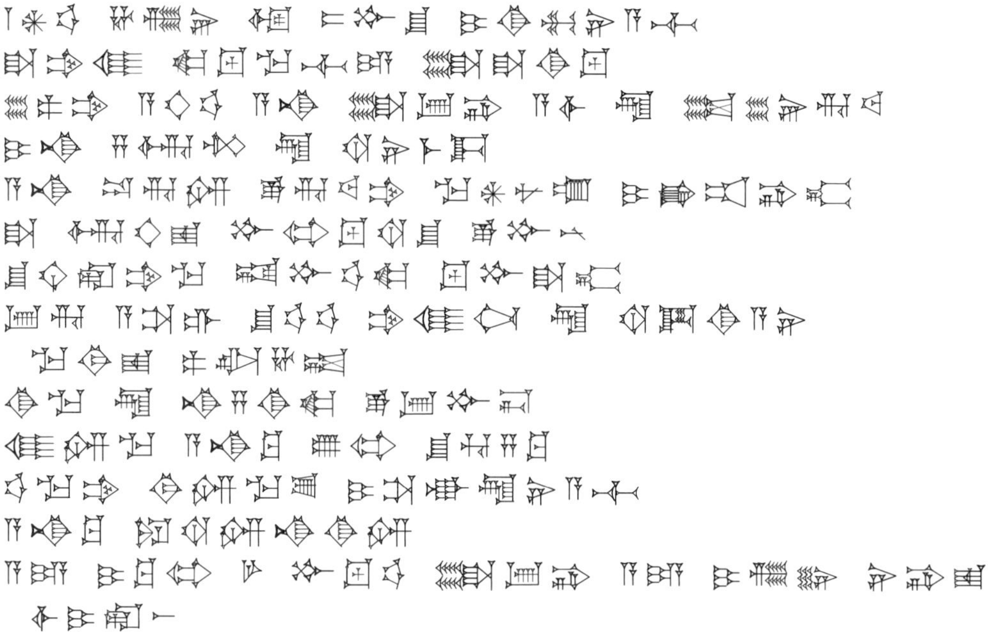

24.6

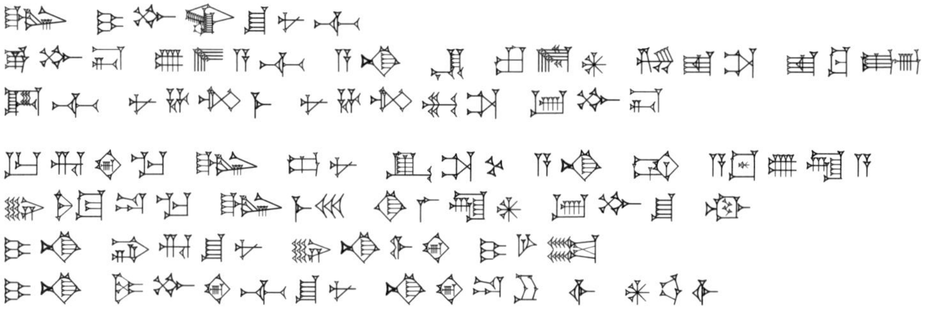

24.7

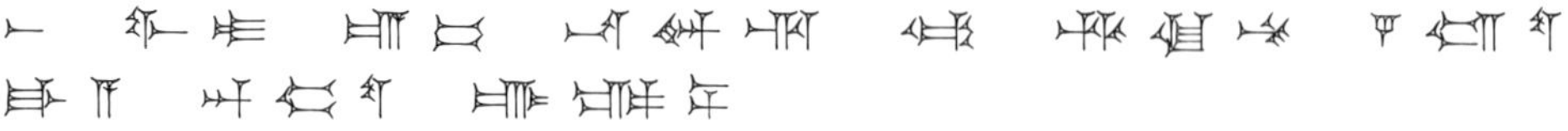

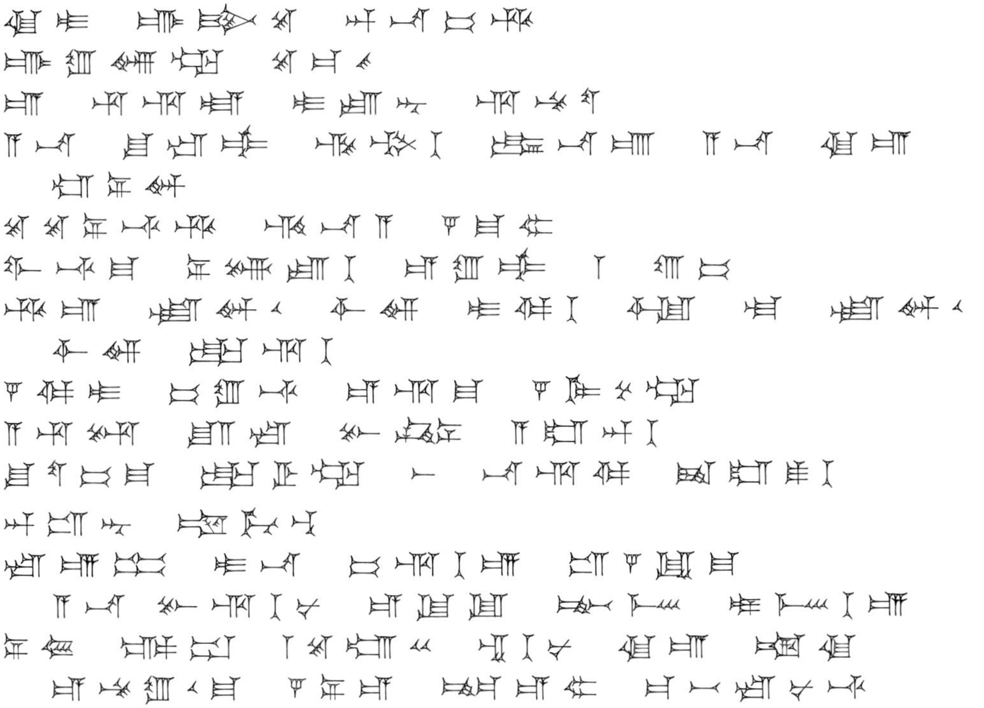

25.1

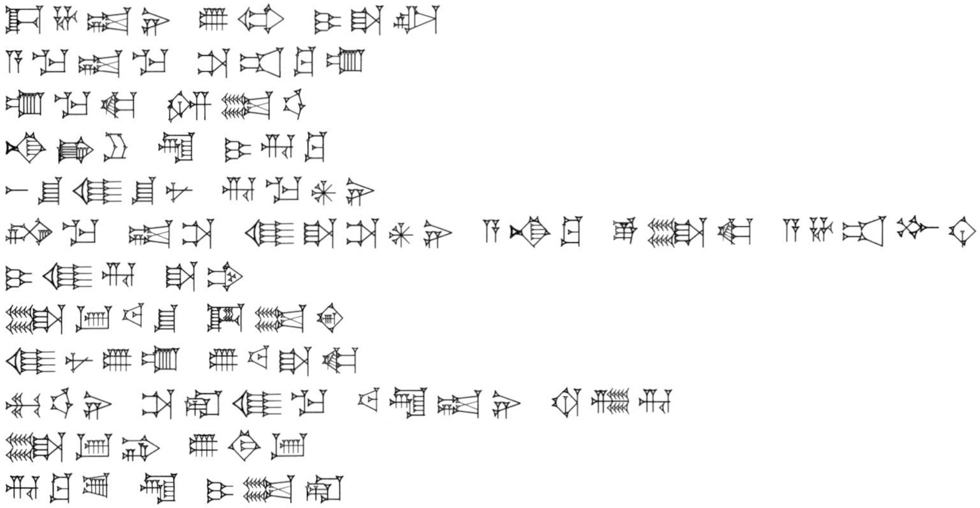

25.2

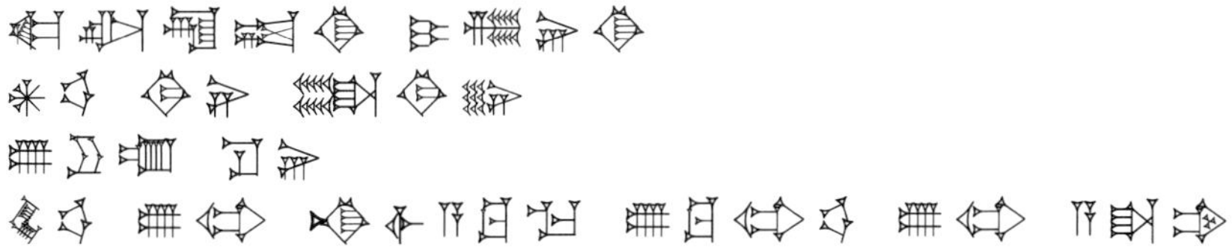

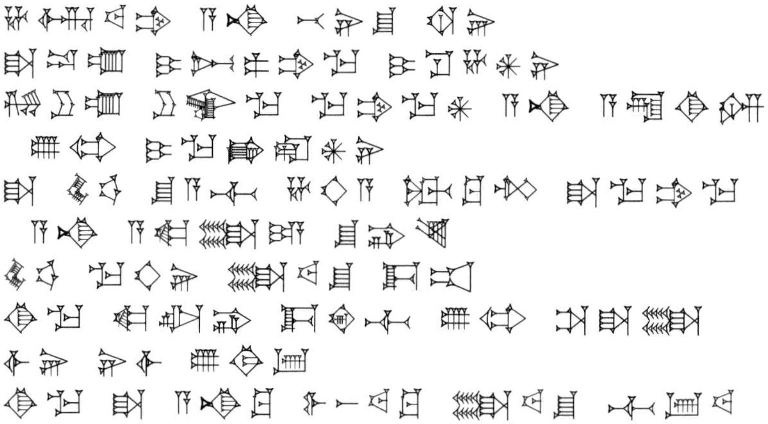

25.3

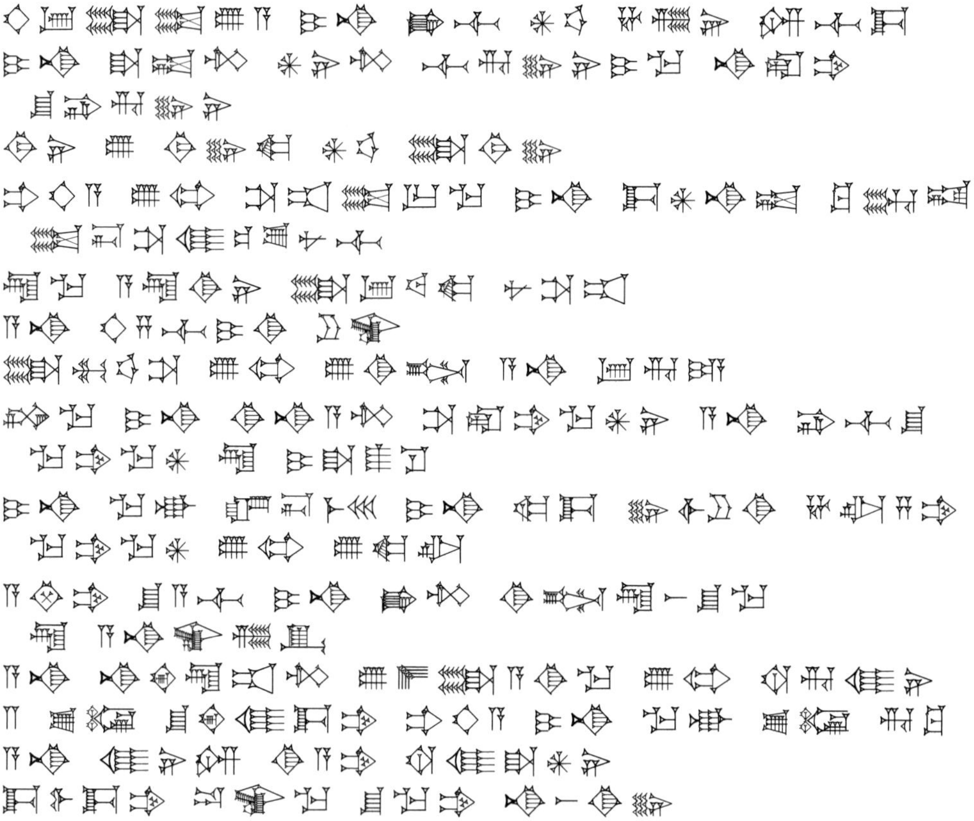

25.4

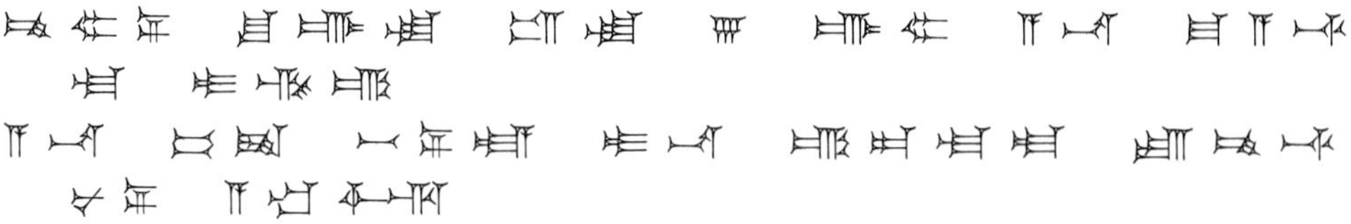

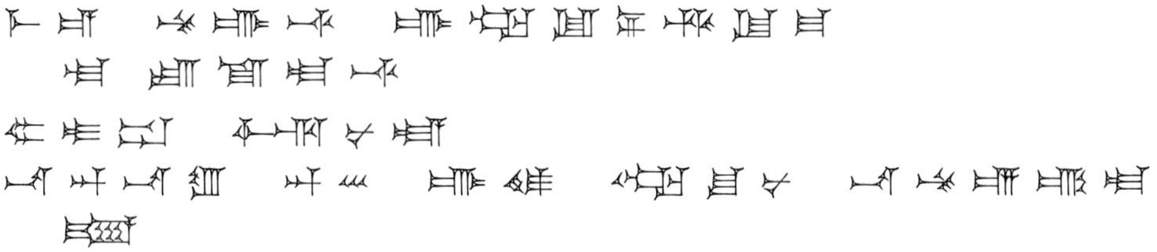

25.5

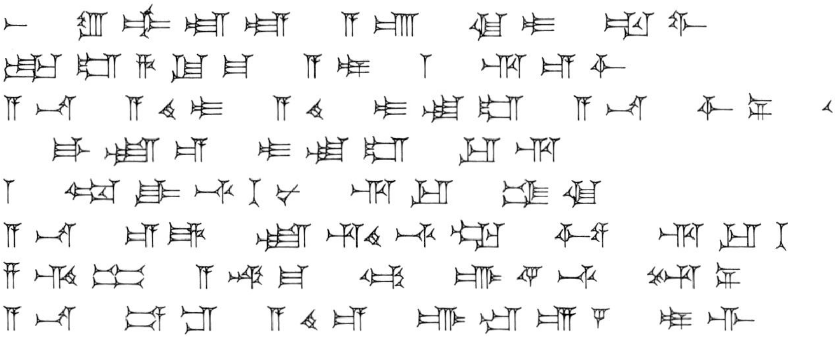

25.6

25.7

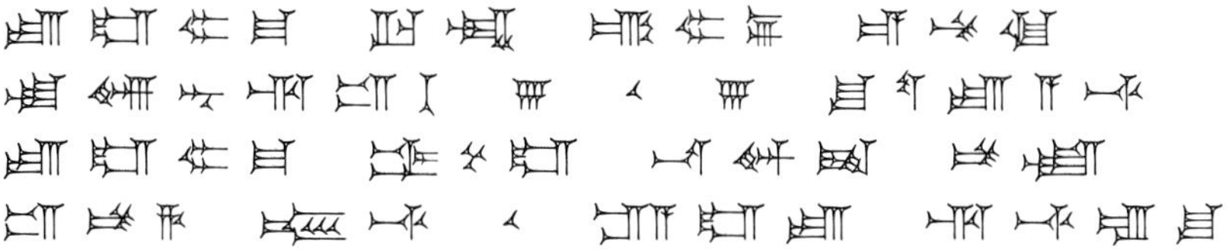

26.1

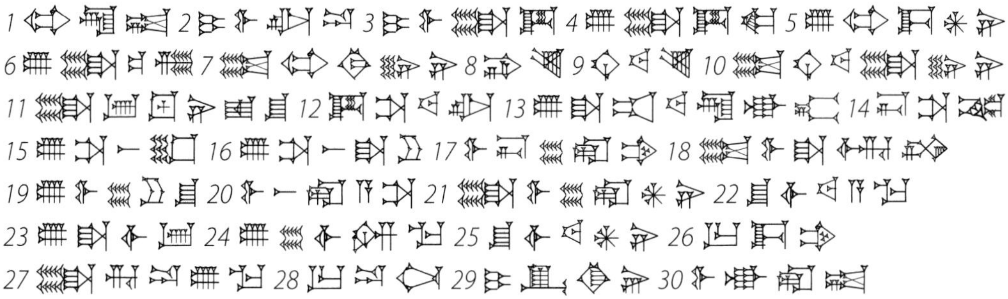

26.2

26.3

1 ... 2 ... 3 ... 4 ...
5 ... 6 ... 7 ... 8 ... 9 ...
10 ... 11 ... 12 ... 13 ...
14 ... 15 ... 16 ... 17 ...
18 ... 19 ... 20 ...
21 ... 22 ... 23 ... 24 ...
25 ... 26 ... 27 ...
28 ... 29 ...

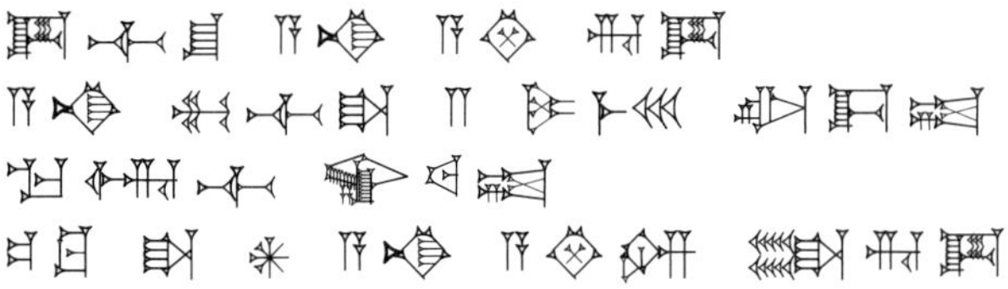

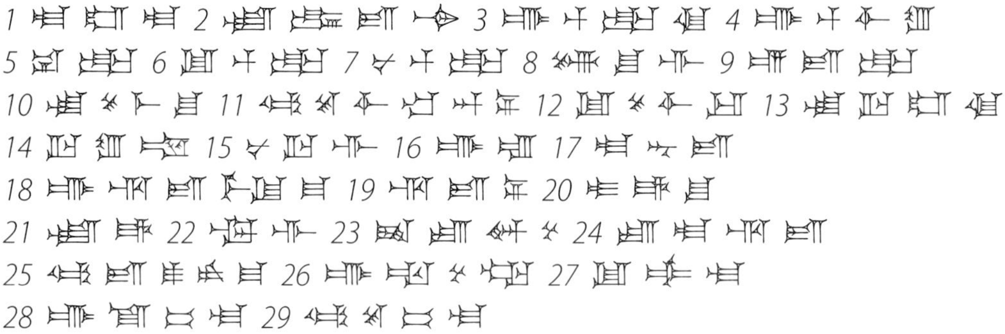

26.4

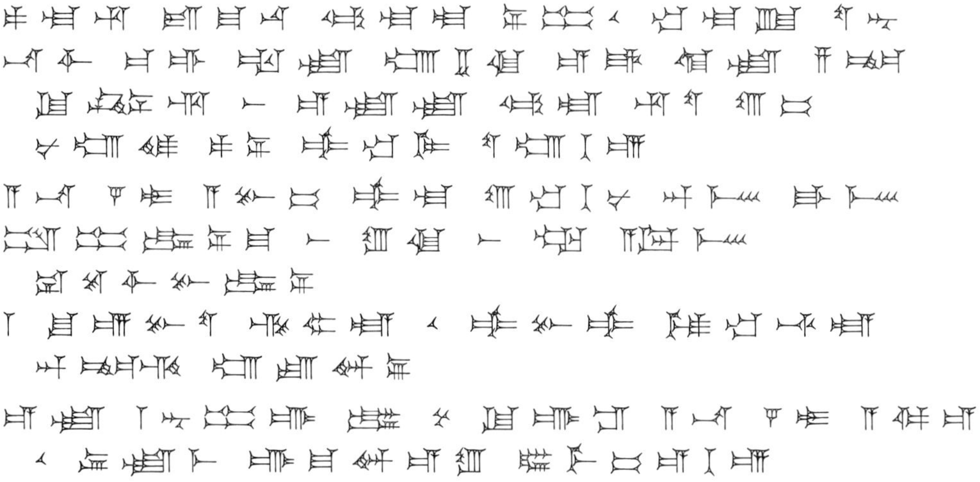

27.1

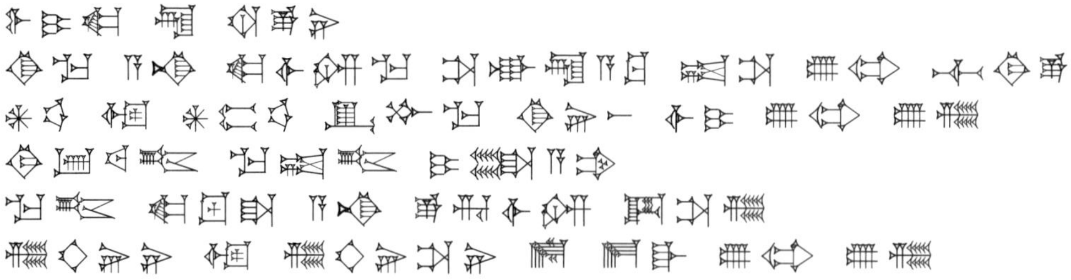

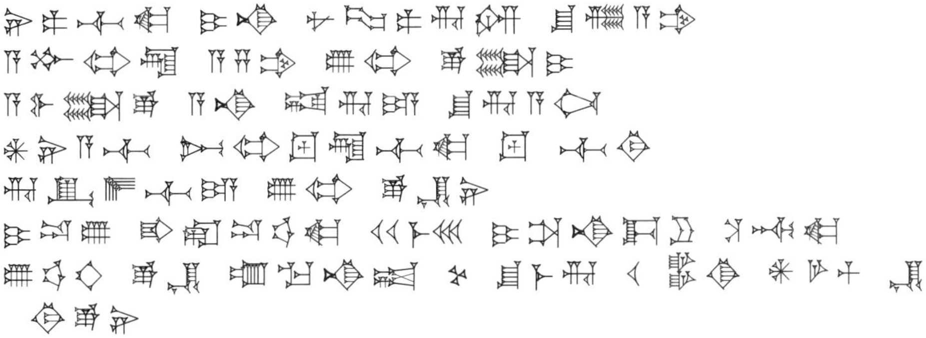

27.2

28.1

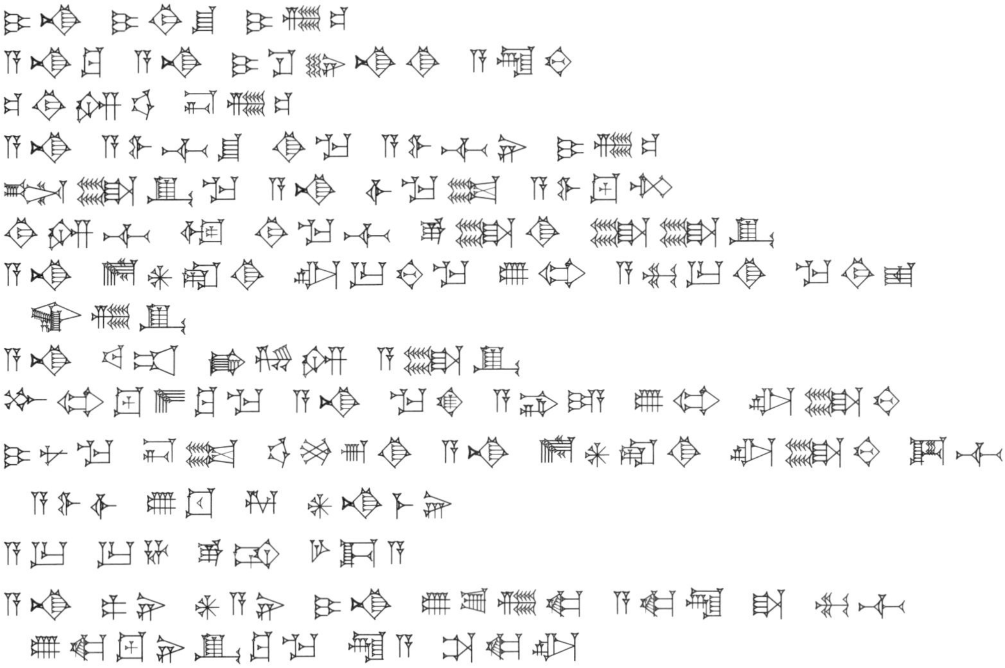

28.2

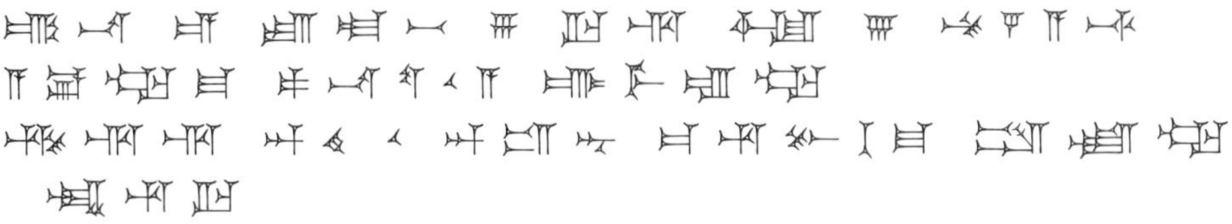

29.1

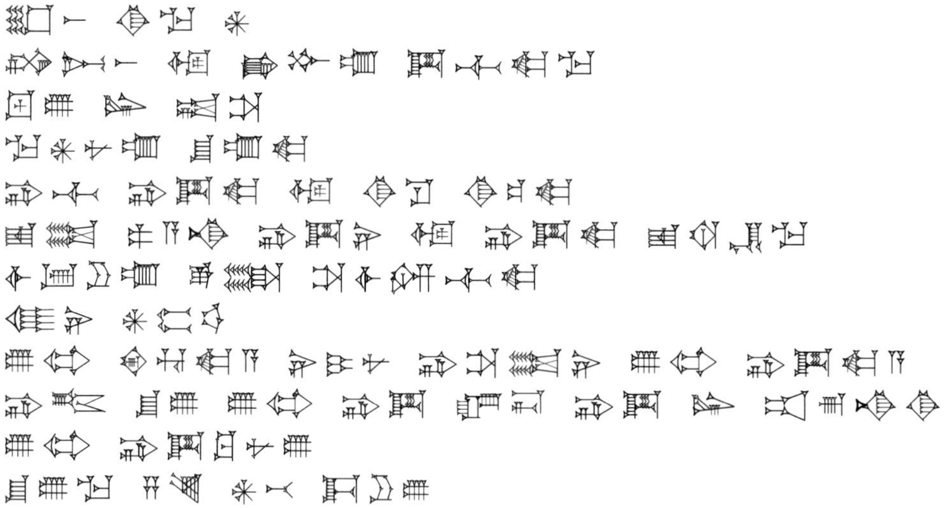

29.2

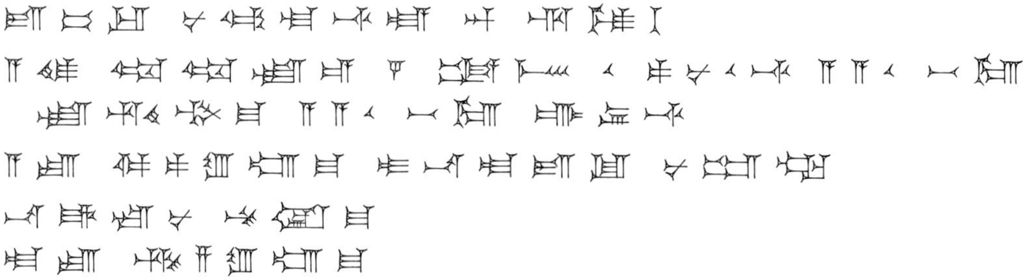

30.1

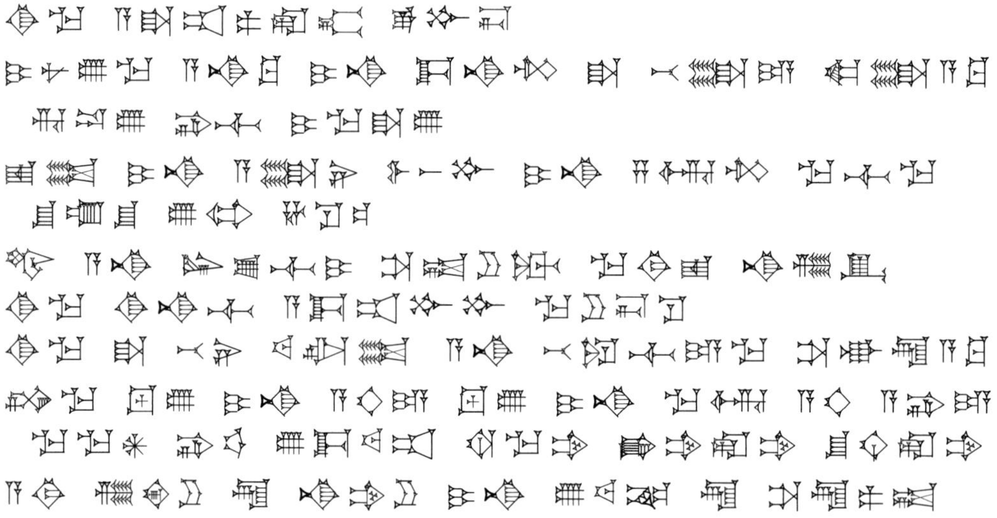

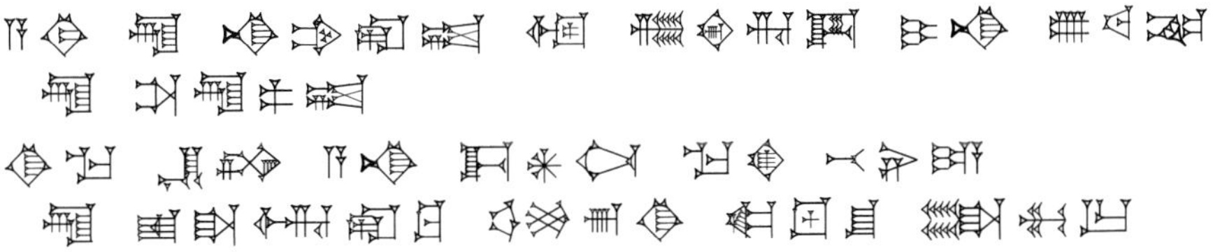

30.2

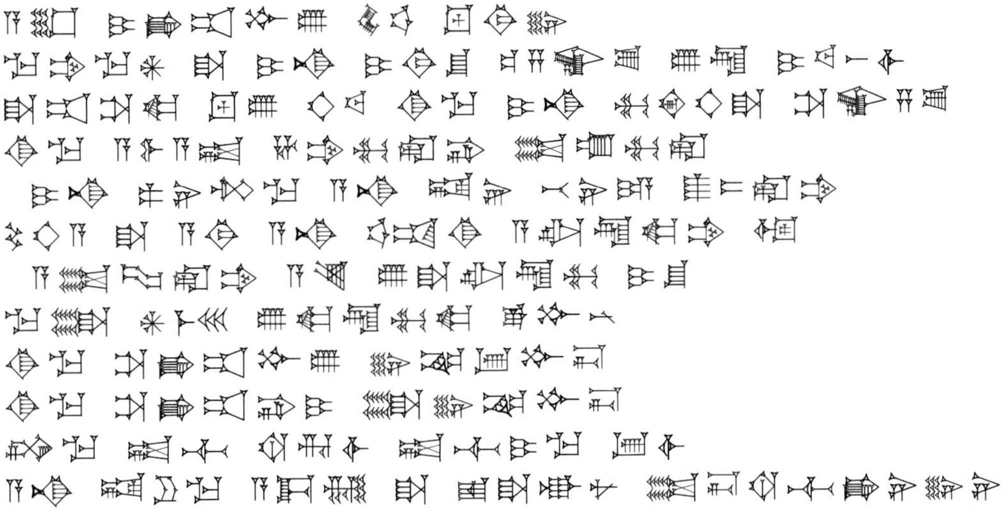

30.3

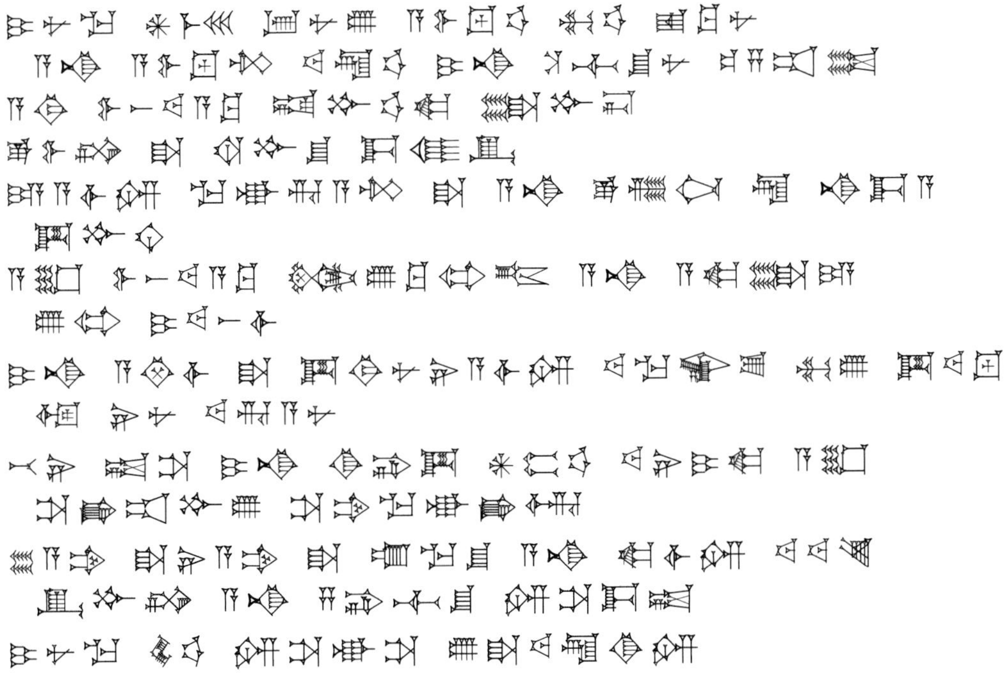

30.4

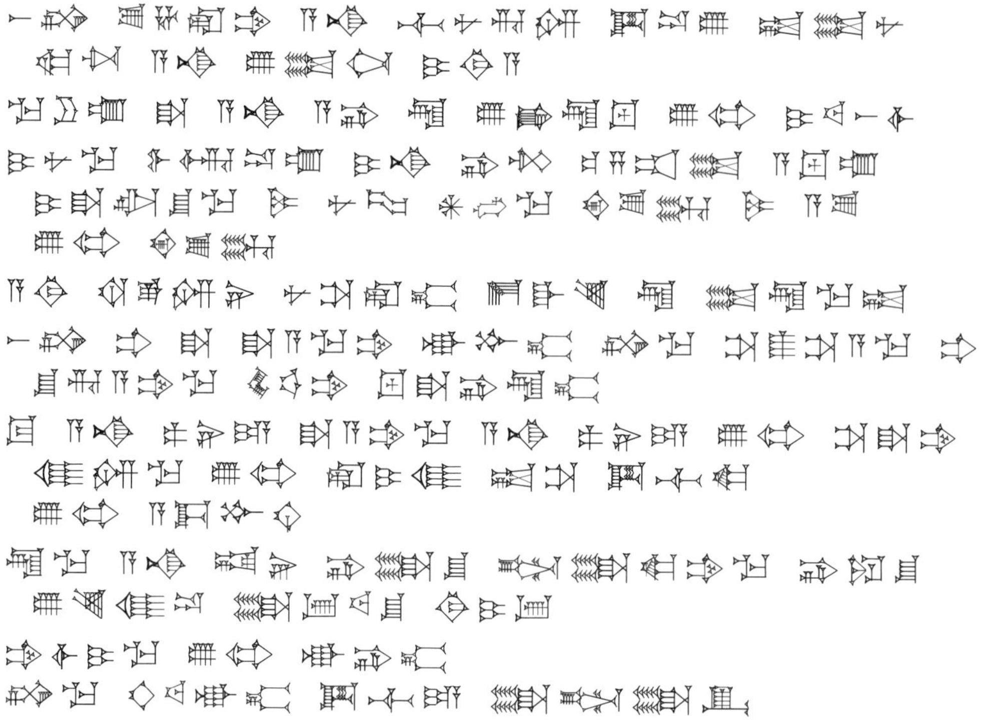

30.5

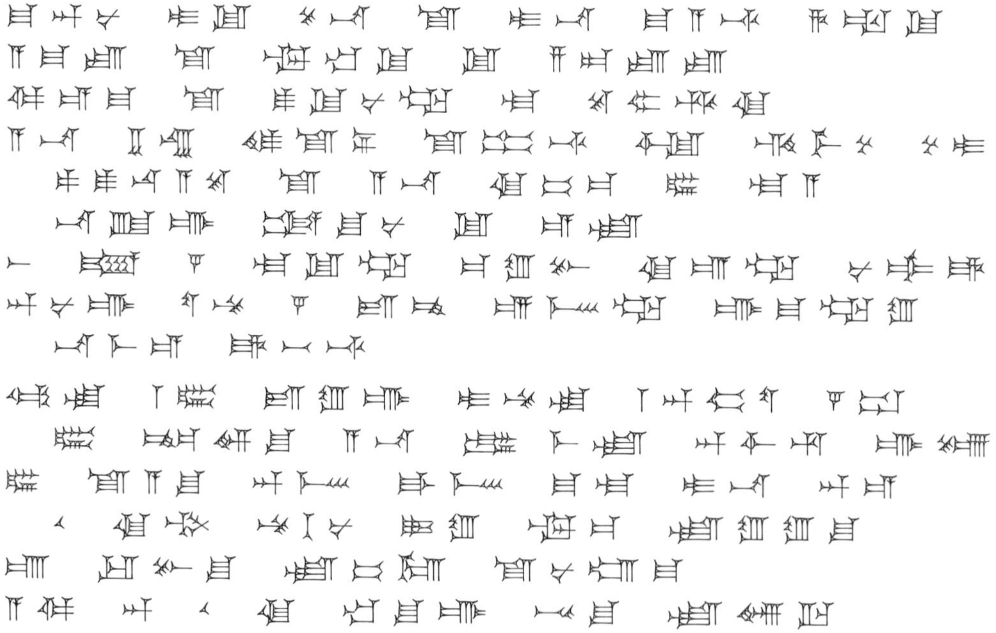

30.6

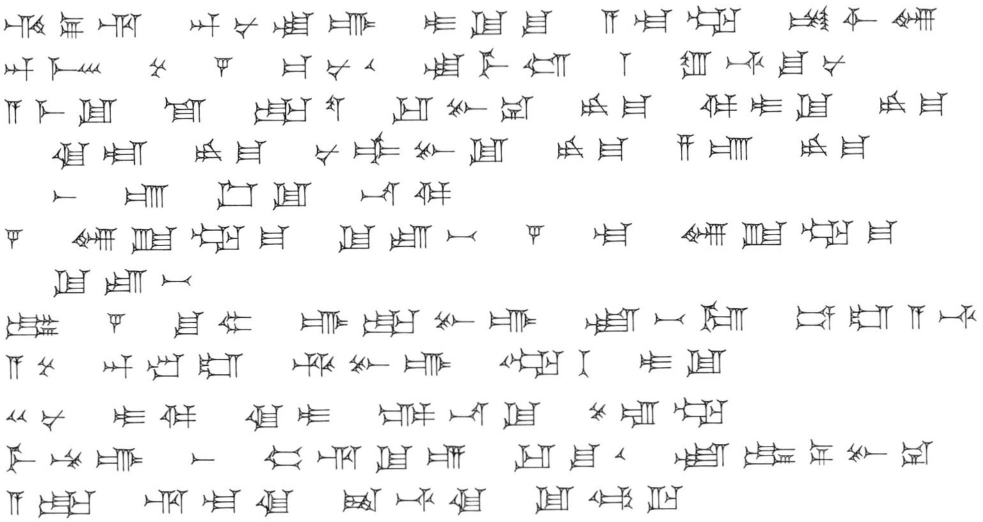

30.7

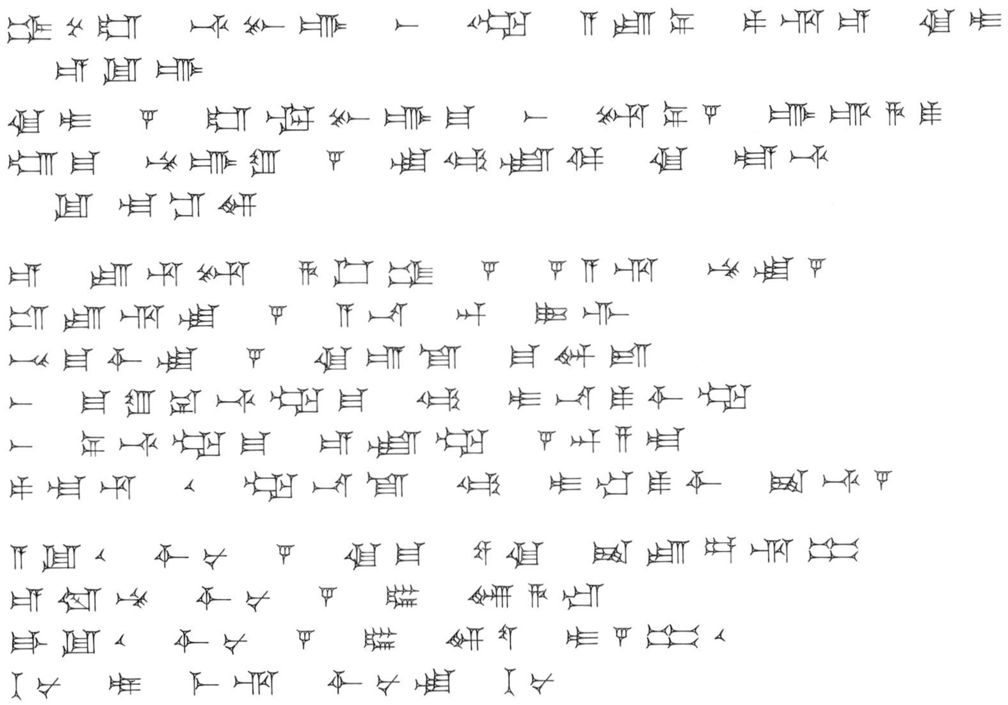

31.1

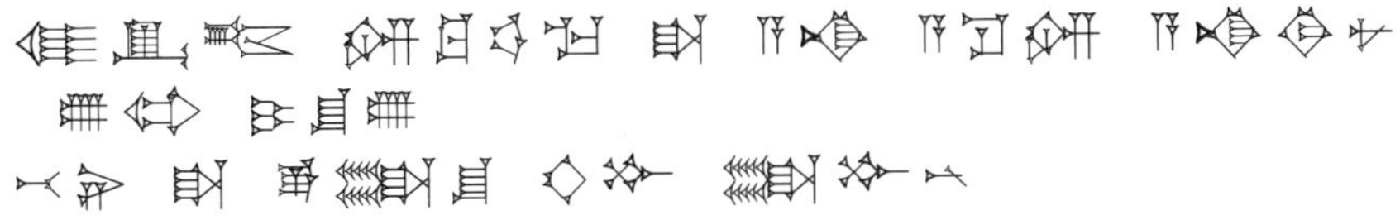

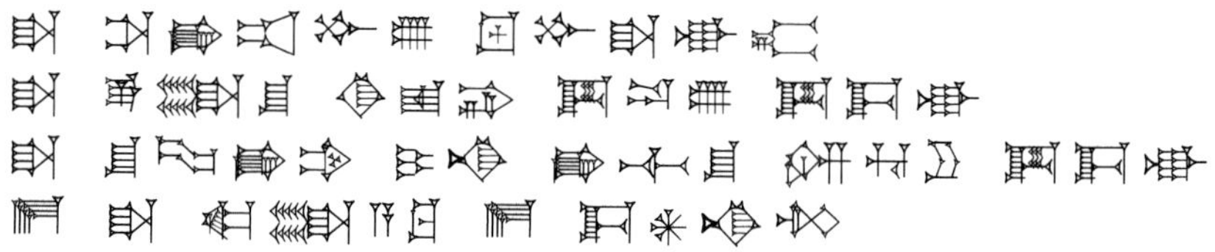

31.2

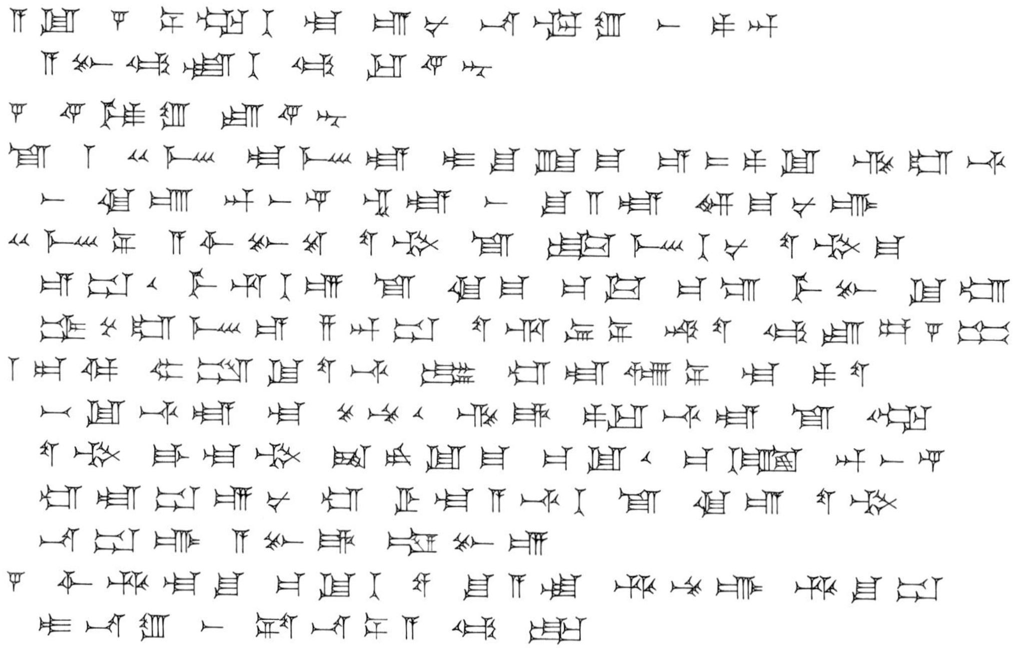

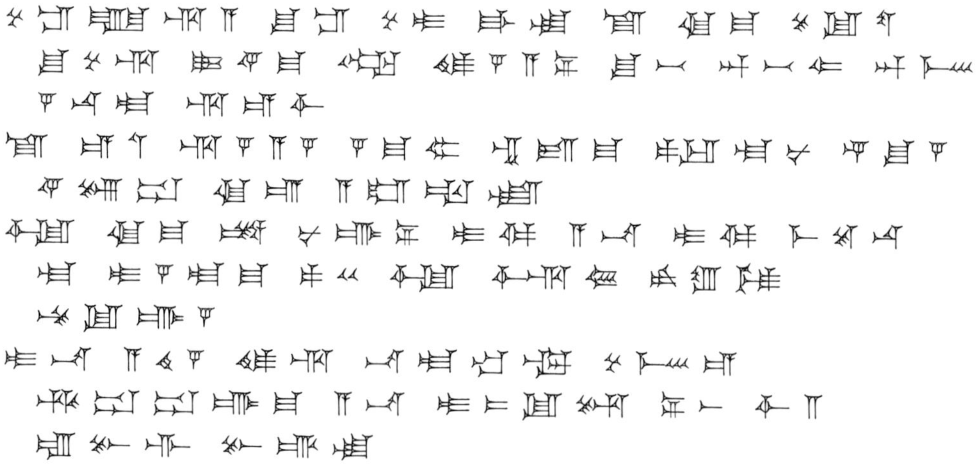

32.1

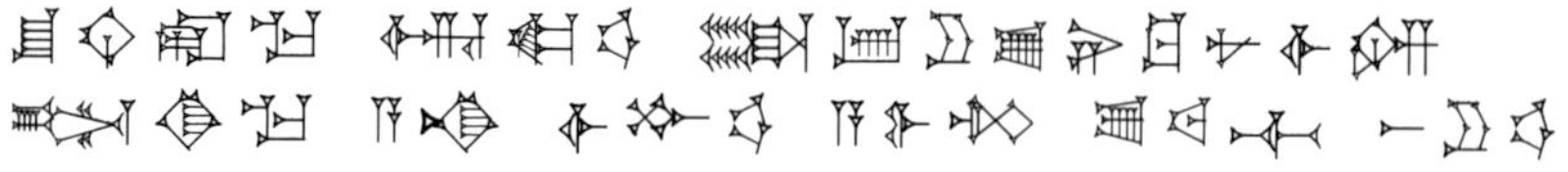

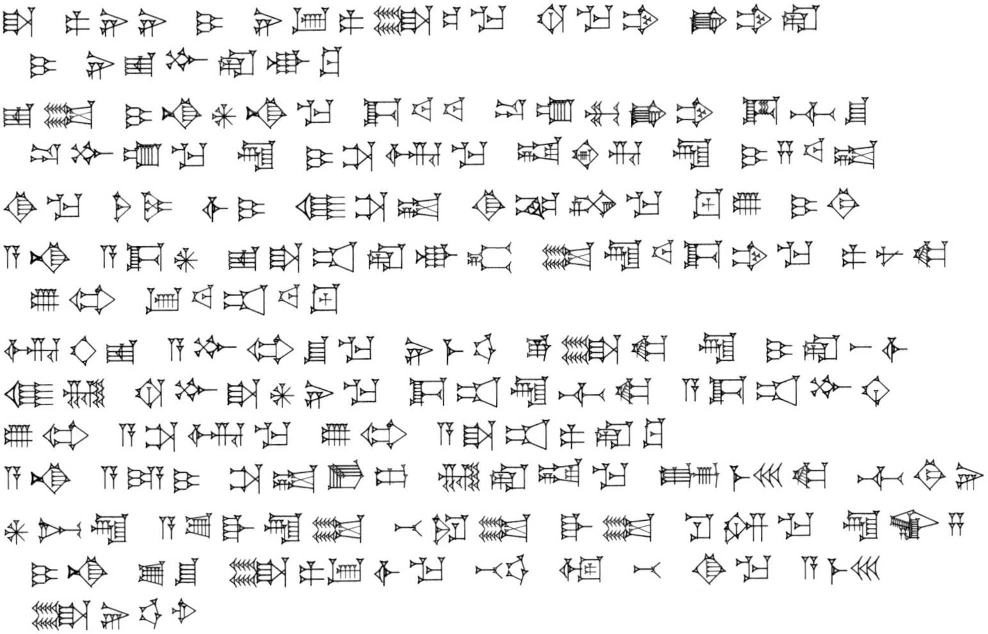

33.1

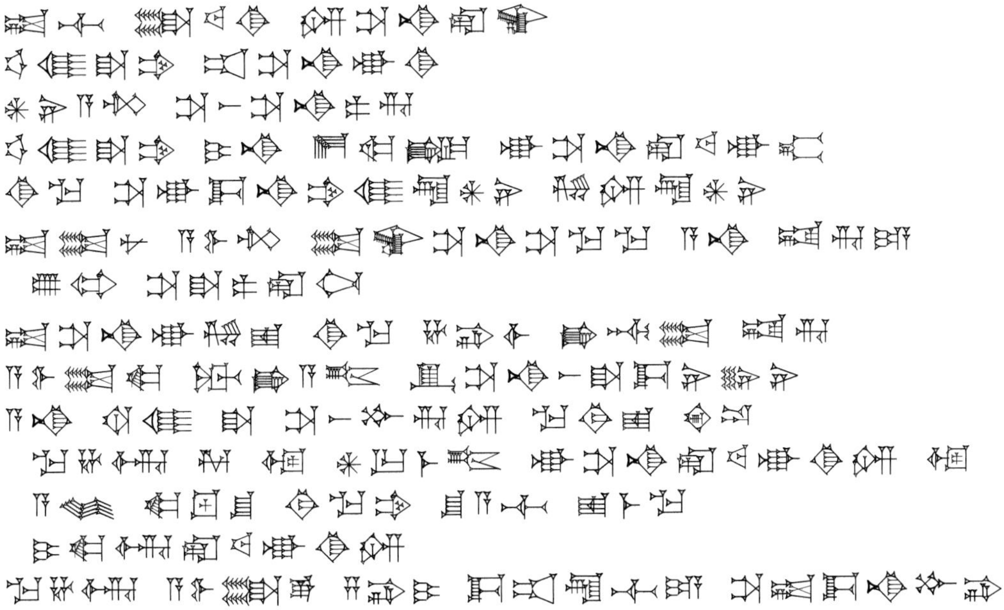

33.2

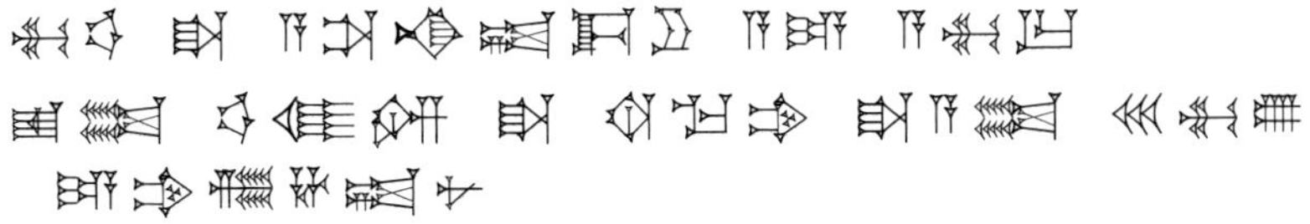

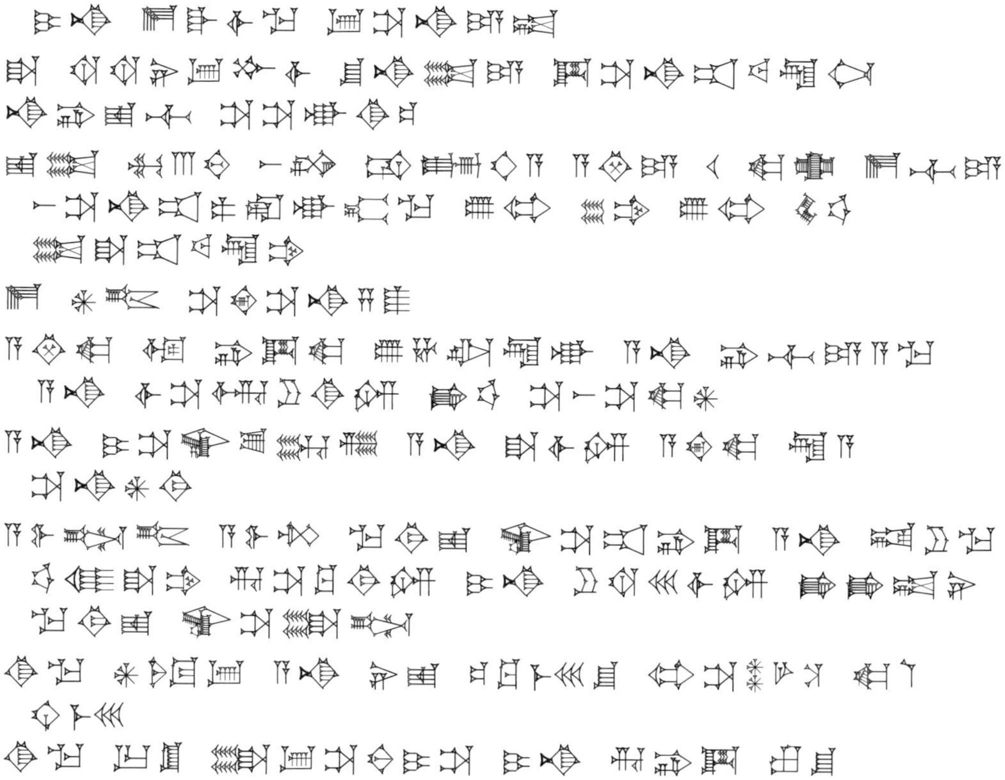

33.3

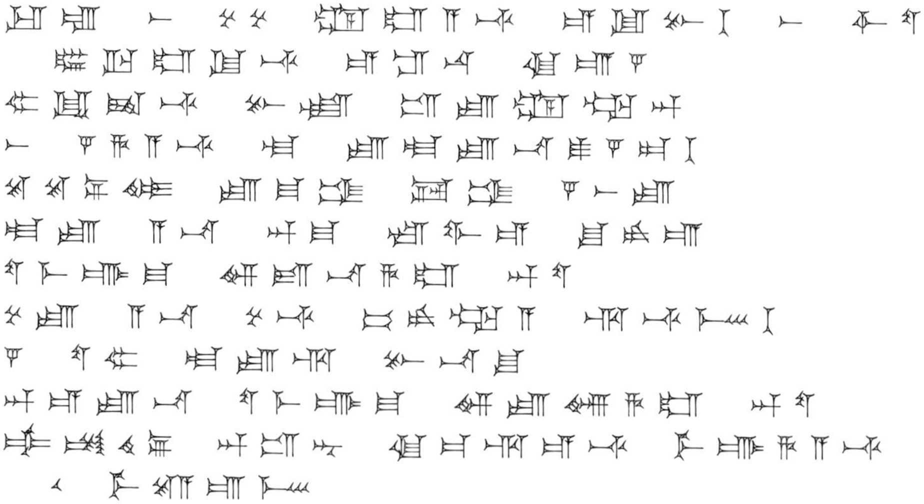

34.1

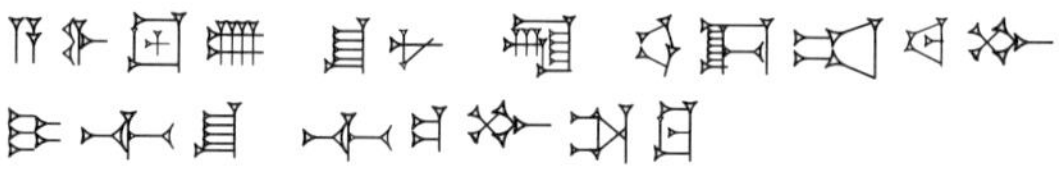

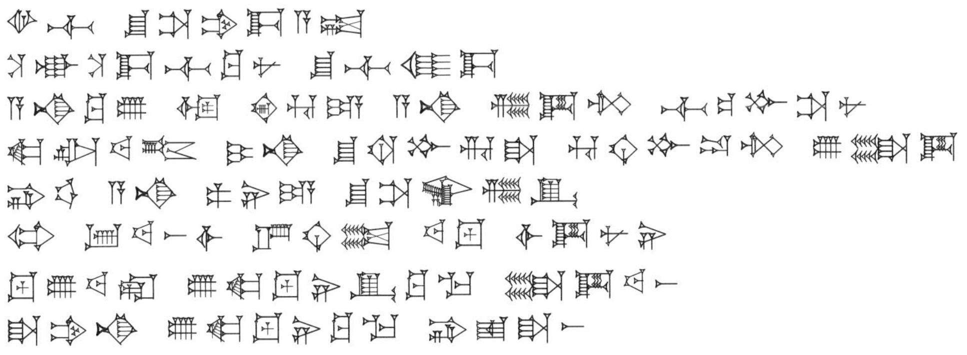

34.2

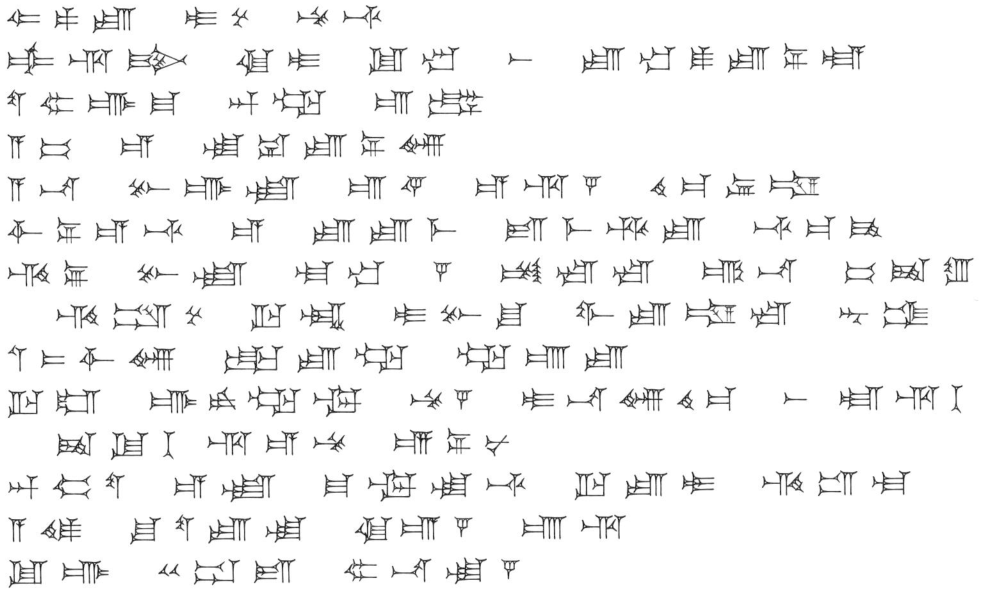

34.3

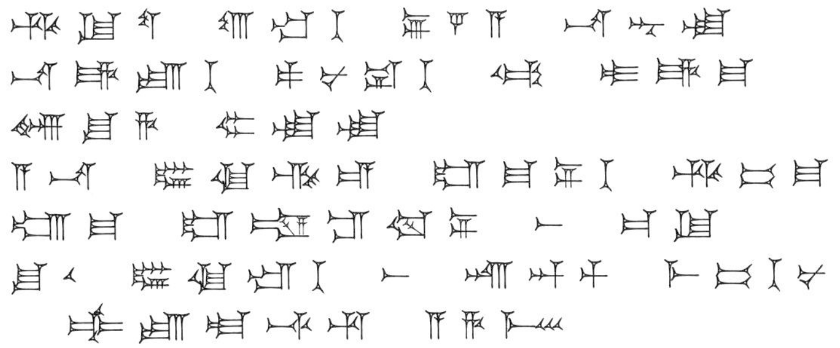

Sign list – Monumental Old Babylonian signs

The following list gives the 205 Monumental Old Babylonian signs used in this course, together with the readings which they have in this course. Many of them have other readings, which happen not to be used here. And of course signs exist beyond those listed here.

For a full survey of all cuneiform signs, and their readings and shapes in different periods, you need to turn to a comprehensive book-length signs list (see Unit 42.3).

There is not a conventional order for listing Monumental Old Babylonian signs, so one has been created *ad hoc* here, according to the following criteria:

- **1** Starts with one horizontal
  - **1.1** at top of sign
  - **1.2** in middle of sign
    - **1.2.1** followed by horizontal
    - **1.2.3** followed by vertical
    - **1.2.4** followed by diverging wedges
    - **1.2.5** followed by *Winkelhaken**
    - **1.2.6** followed by other
  - **1.3** at bottom of sign
- **2** Starts with two large horizontals
- **3** Starts with two small horizontals
- **4** Starts with three or more horizontals
- **5** Starts with tall vertical
  - **5.1** followed by vertical
  - **5.2** followed by horizontal(s)
  - **5.3** forming triangle
  - **5.4** followed by other
- **6** Starts with two verticals
- **7** Starts with small vertical
- **8** Starts with converging wedges
- **9** Starts with diverging wedges
  - **9.1** Starts with diamond shape
- **10** Starts with one *Winkelhaken**
- **11** Starts with two *Winkelhaken**

* a *Winkelhaken* (German for **corner hook**) is a triangular wedge (𒌋).

12 Starts with three *Winkelhaken**

13 Starts with double signs

14 Starts in other ways

The criteria were applied to the signs *as they appear in the font used in this course* ('CuneiformOB'). Other Monumental Old Babylonian fonts, and especially real clay tablets, might have small differences that would lead to signs moving to another section.

For your convenience, each sign has been given its Neo-Assyrian form in brackets. There is not always a one-to-one correspondence between Monumental Old Babylonian and Neo-Assyrian sign forms. For example, Monumental Old Babylonian BAD and ÚŠ converge into a single sign in Neo-Assyrian.

1 Starts with one horizontal

1.1 AT TOP OF SIGN

𒋛	(𒋛)	*si, se*
𒋜	(𒋜)	*si*$_4$, SU$_4$
𒈣	(𒈣)	MÁ
𒈠	(𒈠)	*ma*
𒋻	(𒋻)	*tár*

1.2 IN MIDDLE OF SIGN

𒀸	(𒀸)	*aš, ina, rum*

1.2.1 Followed by horizontal(s)

𒀝	(𒀝)	*ak, ag, aq*
𒁄	(𒁄)	*bal*, BAL
𒁺	(𒁺)	*du, ṭù*, RÁ
𒋢	(𒋢)	SUHUŠ

1.2.3 Followed by vertical

𒈦	(𒈦)	*maš*
𒈧	(𒈧)	MÁŠ
𒀭	(𒀭)	*an*, ^{D}, DINGIR, AN
𒉡	(𒉡)	*nu*
𒄷	(𒄷)	*hu*
𒋥	(𒋥)	*rat, rad*
𒊑	(𒊑)	*ri, re, ṭal, tal*
𒄀	(𒄀)	*gi, qì, ge*, GI
𒈹	(𒈹)	INANNA
𒍣	(𒍣)	*zi, sí, ṣí, ze, ṣé*
𒉣	(𒉣)	*nun*, NUN
𒉆	(𒉆)	*nam*

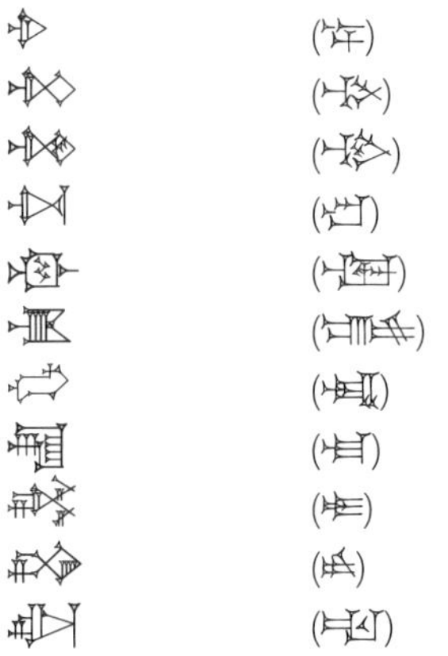

muk
tim, tem, tì
mun
ARAD, ÌR
MÈ
ÙZ
mah, MAH
la, LA
hé, HÉ
šum
al

1.2.4 Followed by diverging wedges

na, NA
šubur
šer

1.2.5 Followed by *Winkelhaken*

be, bat, BAD, MÚD
ti, ṭì, dì, te_9, TI
LUGUD
mu, MU

1.2.6 Followed by other

an, ^{D}, DINGIR, AN
úš, til

1.3 AT BOTTOM OF SIGN

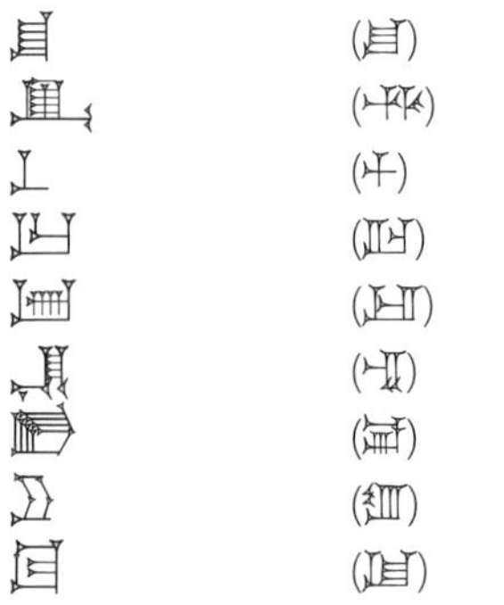

šu
ik, ek, ig, iq, GÁL
bar
ur, lik, taš, UR
ip, ep, ib, eb, urta
en, EN
ták
ru, šub
TÚG

2 Starts with two large horizontals

tap, tab
is, iṣ, iz, giš, GIŠ
mar
pa

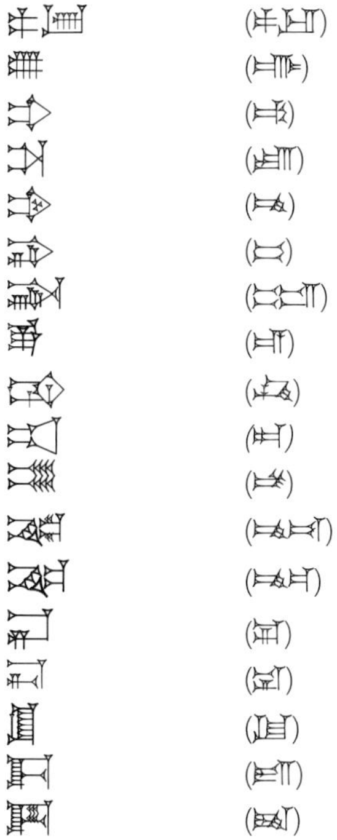

- *šap, šab*
- *ú, šam*
- GU_4
- *ta, ṭá* (compare )
- *am*, AM
- *bi, pí, pé, bé*
- *rik*
- *e*
- *gú, tiq*, GÚ
- *ap, ab, èš*
- *gab, qab*
- *bíl*
- *ne, bí, pil*
- PISAN
- *uš, ús*, UŠ
- GI_7
- *da, ṭa*
- *it, et, id, ed, iṭ, eṭ*

3 Starts with two small horizontals

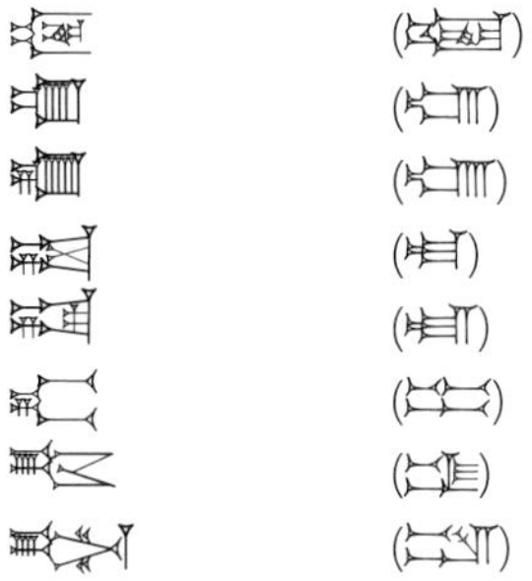

- *ram*
- *um*
- *tup*
- *at, ad, aṭ*
- *ṣi, ṣe, zé*
- *qu, qum, kum*
- *tum*
- *il, él*

(for  and  see 1.2.3)

4 Starts with three or more horizontals

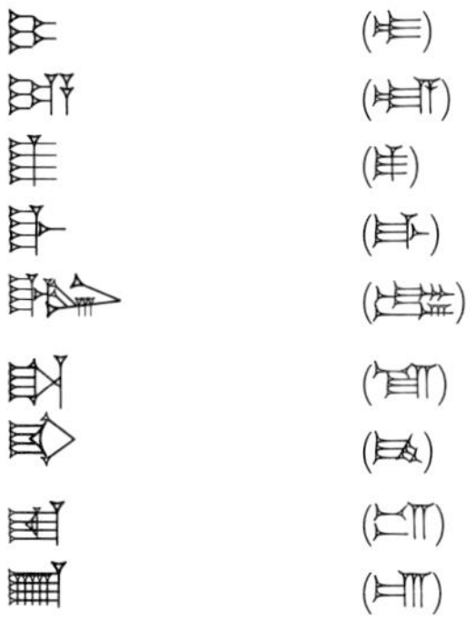

- *i*, I
- *ia, ii*
- *áš, áz, ás*
- *gal, kál*, GAL
- LUGAL
- *ša* (compare )
- *qar, kàr*
- *iš*, $eš_{15}$, *sahar, mil*
- *líl*

mir, AGA
gi$_4$
biš, *qir*

5 Starts with tall vertical

^{M}, 1
šú

5.1 FOLLOWED BY VERTICAL

2
3
a, A
ÍD
šá, NINDA

5.2 FOLLOWED BY HORIZONTAL(S)

me, *mì*, *šib*, ME, MÉŠ
MEŠ
lal
úr

5.3 FORMING TRIANGLE

rak, *šal*, ^{F}, MUNUS
el
nin, *nen*, *ním*
ṣu, *ṣum*
dam
GÉME

5.4 FOLLOWED BY OTHER

LÚ
tur, DUMU, TUR
sa
é, *bit*, É
KÁ

6 Starts with two verticals

za, *ṣa*, *sà*, 4, ZA
ha, KU$_6$, HA

7 Starts with small vertical

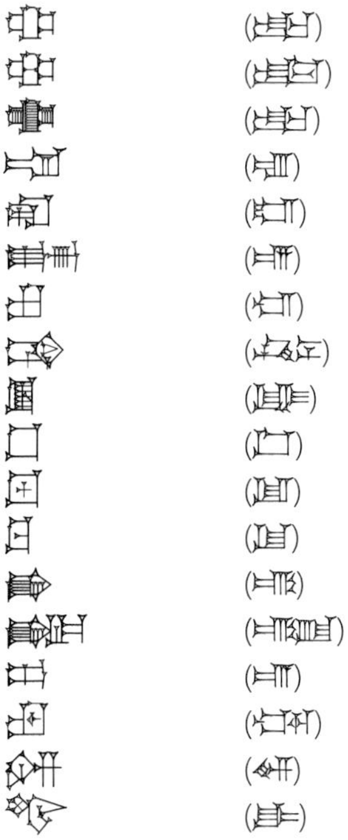

šèr
BÀD
hir, KEŠDA
rid
ra, RA
un, KALAM, UN, ÙG
rí, URU
ṭur
SÍG
rim
lu
ku, *qú*, TUKUL, KU
ga, *qá*
íl, DUSU, ÍL
dan, *kal*, *lap/b*, *rib*, *reb*
ASARU
im, *em*, IŠKUR
nar, NAR

8 Starts with converging wedges

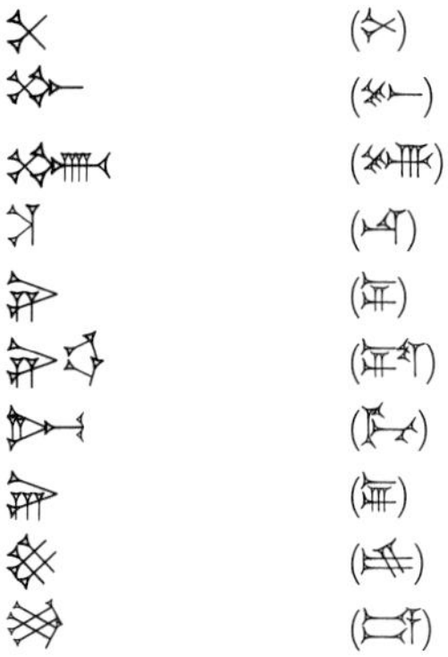

kúr, KÚR
pu, *bu*
muš
qa
ni, *né*, *lí*, *ià*
NA_4
gu, *qù*, GU
ir, *er*
kas
KIB

9 Starts with diverging wedges

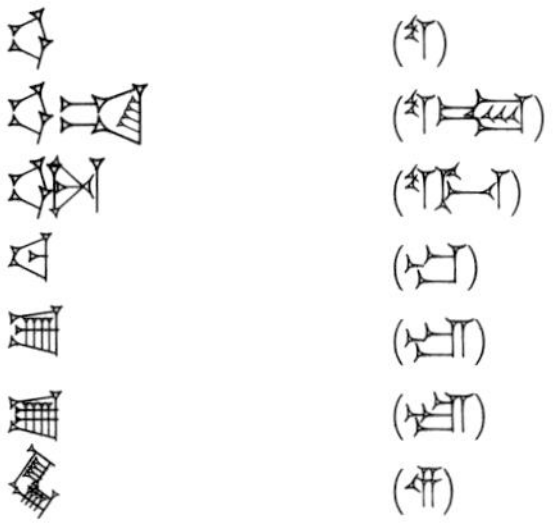

ut, *ud*, *uṭ*, u_4, *tam*, *ṭám*, U_4, UD, UTU, BABBAR
LARSAM (UD.UNUG)
úh
ba, *pá*
zu, *sú*, *ṣú*, ZU
su, KUŠ, SU
KÙ

	(⟨symbol⟩)	UZU
	(⟨symbol⟩)	*sag, sak*, SAG
	(⟨symbol⟩)	*ka, qà*, KA, ZÚ
	(⟨symbol⟩)	ANŠE
	(⟨symbol⟩)	NERGAL
	(⟨symbol⟩)	*uq, uk, ug*
	(⟨symbol⟩)	*as, aṣ, az*

9.1 STARTS WITH DIAMOND SHAPE

	(⟨symbol⟩)	*hi, he, ṭí, ṭà*, HI
	(⟨symbol⟩)	*u', a', e', i'* (these readings are simplified)
	(⟨symbol⟩)	*kam*, KAM
	(⟨symbol⟩)	*up/b*
	(⟨symbol⟩)	*bir*, BIR
	(⟨symbol⟩)	*har, hur*
	(⟨symbol⟩)	*ih, ah, uh, eh, ú', á', é', i'*

(for ⟨symbol⟩ see 13)

	(⟨symbol⟩)	*te, ṭe$_4$, ṭi$_4$*
	(⟨symbol⟩)	*kar*

(for ⟨symbol⟩, ⟨symbol⟩ and ⟨symbol⟩ see 14, because the diagonals diverge from the top, not from the left)

10 Starts with one *Winkelhaken*

	(⟨symbol⟩)	*u*, 10, 60
	(⟨symbol⟩)	*man*, MAN
	(⟨symbol⟩)	30, *eš*
	(⟨symbol⟩)	*ul*
	(⟨symbol⟩)	*ši, še$_{20}$, lim*, IGI
	(⟨symbol⟩)	*ù*
	(⟨symbol⟩)	*ar*
	(⟨symbol⟩)	PÀD
	(⟨symbol⟩)	ÁB
	(⟨symbol⟩)	*nim*
	(⟨symbol⟩)	*kur, šad, lad*, KUR
	(⟨symbol⟩)	*mi, mé, ṣíl*
	(⟨symbol⟩)	ŠUKU

11 Starts with two *Winkelhaken*

	(⟨symbol⟩)	TIN
	(⟨symbol⟩)	*wa, wi, wu, we, pi, pe, aw*
	(⟨symbol⟩)	AMAR

- NISABA
- *tu, ṭú*
- *us, uz, uṣ*
- *še*, ŠE, ŠE
- *li, le*
- *TIR*

12 Starts with three *Winkelhaken*

- *in, en*$_6$
- *šar*, KIRI$_6$

13 Starts with double signs

- ÉRIN, ERIM
- ÙSAN
- URI
- *nap/b*

14 Starts in other ways

- ŠÀ (the left-hand diagonals diverge from the top, not from the left; hence not in 9.1)
- *di, de, ṭi, ṭe*
- *ki, ke, qí, qé*
- *iš*$_8$
- *liš*
- *haṣ, tar*, KUD
- *lam*
- *lum*
- *qi*

Sign list – Neo-Assyrian signs

The following list gives the 287 cursive Neo-Assyrian signs used in this course, together with the readings which they have in this course. Many of them have other readings, which happen not to be used here. And of course signs exist beyond those listed here.

For a full survey of all cuneiform signs, and their readings and shapes in different periods, you need to turn to a comprehensive book-length list of signs (see Unit 42.3).

Comparison with the Monumental Old Babylonian list will show you that Neo-Assyrian signs tend to be used with more readings than Monumental Old Babylonian ones. In particular, they are used with more CVC (consonant-vowel-consonant) readings.

The signs are listed here according to the order in Borger's *Mesopotamisches Zeichenlexikon*, whose number for each sign is reproduced here.

- **1** starts with horizontal(s)
  - **1.1** at top of sign
  - **1.2** in middle of sign
    - **1.2.1** followed by horizontal
    - **1.2.2** followed by two aligned horizontals
    - **1.2.3** followed by two non-aligned horizontals
    - **1.2.4** followed by three horizontals
    - **1.2.5** followed by vertical
    - **1.2.6** followed by one or more *Winkelhaken*
    - **1.2.7** followed by other
  - **1.3** at bottom of sign
  - **1.4** at top and bottom of sign
  - **1.5** starts with two short horizontals in middle of sign
  - **1.6** starts with two long horizontals in middle of sign
  - **1.7** starts with GIŠ (𒄑)
  - **1.8** starts with two horizontals at top of sign
  - **1.9** starts with two horizontals at bottom of sign
  - **1.10** starts with three horizontals
- **2** starts with a *Winkelhaken**
  - **2.2** starts with a *Winkelhaken**, followed by a vertical
  - **2.3** starts with two *Winkelhaken**
  - **2.4** starts with ŠE (𒊺)
  - **2.5** starts with HI (𒄭)
- **3** starts with vertical
  - **3.1** starts with ŠÚ (𒋙)
- **4** starts with other

* a *Winkelhaken* (German for **corner hook**) is a triangular wedge (𒌋).

The above criteria were applied to the signs *as they appear in the font used in this book* ("Assurbanipal"). Other Neo-Assyrian fonts, and especially sign forms in original cuneiform inscriptions, might have small differences that would lead to signs migrating to another section.

1 Starts with one horizontal

1.1 AT TOP OF SIGN

𒈮	*muq*	*12*
𒋛	*si, se,* SI	*181*
𒊕	*šak, šag, šaq, sak, ris, riš,* SAG	*184*
𒈣	MÁ	*201*
𒍚	ÙZ	*203*
𒁇	*dir*	*207*
𒊭	*ša*	*566*

1.2 IN MIDDLE OF SIGN

𒀸	*ina, aš, dil, ṭil,* AŠ	*1*

1.2.1 Followed by horizontal

𒄬	*hal*	*2*
𒁄	*pal, bal*	*5*
𒄈	GÍR	*6*
𒋻	*tar, ṭar, šil, qut, haz, haš,* TAR	*9*
𒀭	*an,* ᵈ, DINGIR, AN	*10*

1.2.2 Followed by two aligned horizontals

𒅗	*ka,* KA, DU_{11}, INIM	*24*
𒅘	*nak, nag, naq*	*64*
𒅥	GU_7	*65*
𒌷	*rí,* URU	*71*
𒁲	BANŠUR	*75*

1.2.3 Followed by two non-aligned horizontals

𒁀	*ba, pá,* BA	*14*
𒍪	*zu*	*15*
𒋢	*su,* SU	*16*
𒋤	*ruq, šin*	*17*
𒀴	*ìr, èr,* ARAD, NÍTA	*18*
𒌗	ITI	*20*
𒋚	*šah*	*23*

1.2.4 Followed by three horizontals

𒇷	*li, le*	*85*
𒌅	*tu,* KU_4	*86*

	la	*89*
	mah, meh, MAH	*91*

1.2.5 Followed by vertical

	maš, MAŠ	*120*
	bar, pár, BAR	*121*
	ak, aq, ag	*127*
	kun	*131*
	hu, pak, pag, paq, bak, MUŠEN	*132*
	nam	*134*
	ik, ek, ig, eg, iq, eq, GÁL	*136*
	mut	*137*
	rat	*139*
	zi, ze, ZI	*140*
	gi, ge, qì, GI	*141*
	ri, re, dal, ṭal, tal	*142*
	nun, NUN	*143*
	kap, kab	*148*
	kat, kad, gat	*157*
	tim, tì	*167*
	en, EN	*164*
	ENSI(=EN.ME.LI)	
	NIBRU(=EN.LÍL)	
	qa	*99*
	kàt	*109*

1.2.6 Followed by one or more *Winkelhaken*

	mu, ia_5, MU	*98*
	bat, be, mit, mid, miṭ, til, tel, BAD, IDIM	*113*
	kul, NUMUN	*117*
	ti	*118*
	na, NA	*110*

1.2.7 Followed by other

	nu, NU	*112*
	šur	*151*
	suh	*152*

1.3 STARTS WITH HORIZONTAL AT BOTTOM OF SIGN

	tin, din, TIN	*119*
	sa	*172*
	tik, GÚ	*176*
	ṭur, dur	*178*
	GUN(=GÚ.UN)	*179*

gur, GUR	*180*
GEŠTIN	*212*
šu, qat, qad, qaṭ, ŠU	*567*
qát	*567*
lip, lib, lul	*570*
tuk, TUKU, TUK	*827*
ur, taš, tíš, lik, liq, UR	*828*
ṭu, gím, GÍN	*836*

1.4 STARTS WITH HORIZONTALS AT TOP AND BOTTOM OF SIGN

il	*348*
du, qup, DU	*350*
ANŠE	*353*
tum, dum, tu_4	*354*
EGIR	*356*
iš, mil	*357*
bi, bé, kaš, gaš, KAŠ	*358*
šim, šem	*362*
kip, kib, qip	*378*
qaq, gag, kak, kàl, GAG, DÙ	*379*
ni, né, ṣal, lí, ì, Ì	*380*
ir, er	*437*
uš	*381*
NA_4	*385*
mal	*387*
DAGAL	*392*
dak	*438*
qu, kum	*339*
úr	*341*

1.5 STARTS WITH TWO SHORT HORIZONTALS IN MIDDLE OF SIGN

um	*238*
tup	*242*
i	*252*
kan, gan, kám, KÁM	*253*
tur, TUR, DUMU, BÀN	*255*
at, ad, aṭ, AD	*258*
ṣi, ṣe	*259*
ia	*260*
ap, ab, AB	*223*
šum, tak, tag, taq, ŠUM	*221*
tap, tab, TAB	*209*

1.6 STARTS WITH TWO LONG HORIZONTALS IN MIDDLE OF SIGN

KÁ	*222*
URUDU	*230*
uk, ug, uq	*296*
as, az, aṣ	*297*
UNUG	*232*
NINA	*236*
ram	*326*
šàm	*320*
zik, zig, ziq	*336*
kàs, GAZ	*340*
gab, gap, qab, tuh, TÁH, DU$_8$	*298*
EDIN	*300*
tah	*301*
raš	*302*
DANNA (=KASKAL.BU)	*305*
am	*309*
UZU	*311*
bíl, píl	*312*
ṭè, pil, bil, kúm, IZI, BAR$_7$	*313*
GÌRA (=IZI.GI)	
pa, hat, had, haṭ	*464*
GARZA(=PA.AN)	*464a*
šap, šab	*466*
NUSKU	*467*
SIPA	*468*

1.7 STARTS WITH *GIŠ*

giš, is, iṣ, iz, es, eṣ, ez, GIŠ	*469*
e	*498*
dan, kal, rib, reb, lab, lap, LAMMA, GURUŠ	*496*
mar, MAR	*483*
líl, kit, kid, kiṭ, qit, qid, qiṭ, LÍL	*484*
ú, šam	*490*
luh, làh	*494*
ga, qá	*491*
bit, é, É	*495*
un, ÙG, UN	*501*
al	*474*
šit, šid, šiṭ, šet, šed, šeṭ, lak, rit, rid, riṭ, ret, miš, mis, ŠID	*485–486*
up, ub	*504*

1.8 STARTS WITH TWO HORIZONTALS AT TOP OF SIGN

	*nab, nap*	*246*
	*mul*	*247*

1.9 STARTS WITH TWO HORIZONTALS AT BOTTOM OF SIGN

	*ta,* TA	*248*
	*in*	*261*
	*rab, rap*	*262*
	LUGAL	*266*
	*hir, šir, šèr, šar, sar,* SAR, ŠAR	*271/541*
	BÀD	*275*
	*šúm,* ŠÚM	*292*

1.10 STARTS WITH THREE HORIZONTALS

	*qar, kàr*	*543*
	*lil*	*544*
	MURUB_4	*545*
	*áš*	*548*
	*ma*	*552*
	*gal,* GAL	*553*
	*mir,* AGA	*556*
	*kir, ker, gir, ger, qir, qer, piš, peš, pis, pes, biš, beš*	*558*
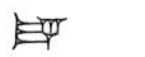	*pur, bur,* BUR	*559*
	*it, et, id, ed, iṭ, eṭ*	*560*
	*da, ṭa*	*561*
	*ra,* RA	*511*
	LÚ	*514*
	*šeš, šiš, šas,* ŠEŠ, ÙRU	*535*
	*zak, zag, zaq*	*540*

2.1 STARTS WITH A *WINKELHAKEN*

	u, 10	*661*
	*man, mam, mìn, niš,* MAN, 20	*708*
	21	
	23	
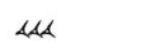	*eš, sin,* 30	*711*
	18	
	*eli,* UGU	*663*
	*lit, liṭ, lid, let, leṭ, led*	*672*
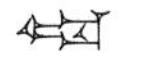	*gul, qúl, kúl, sún*	*682*
	*ul*	*698*
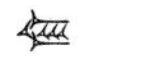	*kis, kiš, qiš, qis*	*678*

	mi, mé	*681*
	ṣur, AMAR	*695*
	nim, NIM	*690*
	ban	*685*
	kim, ṭém, GIM	*686*
	tùm	*691*
	lam	*693*
	GÌR	*701*
	ki, ke, qí, qé, KI	*737*
	DU$_6$, dul	*721*

2.2 STARTS WITH A *WINKELHAKEN*, FOLLOWED BY A VERTICAL

	ši, lim, lem, igi, IGI, ŠI	*724*
	ar	*726*
	SIG$_5$	*729*
	ù	*731*
	hul, HUL	*733*
	di, de, ṭi, ṭe, šùl	*736*
	dun, šul	*744*
	KÙ, KUG	*745*
	pat, pad, paṭ, šuk, ŠUKU	*746*

2.3 STARTS WITH TWO *WINKELHAKEN*

	ut, ud, uṭ, tú, tam, par, pir, lih, u$_4$, hiš, U$_4$, UD, UT, UTU, BABBAR	*596*
	pi, pe, GEŠTU	*598*
	šà, lìb, ŠÀ	*599*
	ṣab, bìr, ÉRIN, ERIM	*612*

2.4 STARTS WITH *ŠE*

	še, ŠE	*579*
	NISABA (=ŠE.NAGA)	
	pu, bu, qít	*580*
	us, uṣ, uz	*583*
	šud	*584*
	ṣir, muš, MUŠ	*585*
	tir, ter, TIR	*587*
	te, ṭe$_4$, TE	*589*
	kar (=TE.A)	*590*

2.5 STARTS WITH *HI*

	hi, he, ṭà, ṭí, HI, DU$_{10}$, ŠÁR	*631*
	ah, uh, eh, ih	*636*

	’, a’, ’a, u’, ’u, i’, ’i, e’, ’e	*635*
	im, em, IM, IŠKUR, ADAD, NÍ	*641*
	bir, ber	*643*
	mur, hur, har, kín	*644*

3 Starts with vertical

	ana, gì, ^{m}, 1	*748*
	lal, LAL, LÁ	*750*
	me, mì, šip, šep, šib, šeb, méš	*753*
	meš, míš, meš	*754*
	rin, rim, kil	*755*
	GIGIR	*760*
	u_8	*766*
	ṣar	*767*
	ṭul	*786*
	pul, bul	*788*
	zuq, AS_4	*795*
	ip, ep, ib, eb, urta	*807*
	ku, qú, tuš, tukul, TUKUL, TUŠ	*808*
	lu, ṭib, tep, UDU	*812*
	qi, qe, kin	*815*
	2, MIN	*825*
	3	
	a, A	*839*
	ÍD	*839c*
	za, ṣa, sà, 4	*851–852*
	ha	*856*
	gug	*858*
	6	
	7	
	8	
	šá, gar, ŠÁ, NINDA, NÍG	*859*
	í, 5	*861*

3.1 STARTS WITH *ŠÚ*

	šú, ŠÚ	*869*
	šik, sik	*881*
	ŠUDUN	*876*
	šal, sal, rak, mim, MUNUS	*883*
	ṣu	*884*
	nin	*887*
	dam	*889*

	GÉME	*890*
	*gu, qù,* GU	*891*
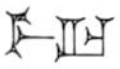	*nik, nig, niq*	*898*
	*el,* SIKIL	*899*
	*hum, lum,* lu_4, LUM	*900*
	SIG_4	*905*

4 Starts with other

	*pap,* KÚR, PAP	*92*
	*gúr*	*576*
	*liš, lis*	*591*
	*zib*	*628*
	*šat, šad, sat, lat, mat, kur,* KUR, GÌN	*578*
	*ru, šup, šub*	*111*

Key to the exercises

The bracketed sigla following the translations indicate where the sentence was taken from. (Abbreviations are explained at the end of the course, before the Index.)

5.1: *rakbāku, rakbāta, rakbāti, rakib, rakbat, rakbānu, rakbātunu, rakbātina, rakbū, rakbā.*
šarqāku, šarqāta, šarqāti, šariq, šarqat, šarqānu, šarqātunu, šarqātina, šarqū, šarqā.
habšāku, habšāta, habšāti, habiš, habšat, habšānu, habšātunu, habšātina, habšū, habšā.

5.2: *unakkis, tunakkis, tunakkisī, unakkis, nunakkis, tunakkisā, unakkisū, unakkisā.*
upaššiš, tupaššiš, tupaššišī, upaššiš, nupaššiš, tupaššišā, upaššišū, upaššišā.
upaṭṭir, tupaṭṭir, tupaṭṭirī, upaṭṭir, nupaṭṭir, tupaṭṭirā, upaṭṭirū, upaṭṭirā.
ubaqqim, tubaqqim, tubaqqimī, ubaqqim, nubaqqim, tubaqqimā, ubaqqimū, ubaqqimā.

7.1: *ana šarrim aqabbi* **I will speak to the king** (AbB 13, 177: r.5′)
aššu mīnim taklašu **What did you detain him for?** (lit. **Because of what did you detain him?**) (AbB 6, 10: 7–8)
ina kaprim bārûm ul ibašši **There is no (**lit. **not a) diviner in the village** (AbB 6, 22: 28–9)
nakrum ina mātim nadi **The enemy has settled in the country** (AbB 14, 81: 6)
ukultam šūbilīm **Send me (some) food!** (AbB 2, 150: 19)
ina bītim rīqim wašbāku **I am living in an empty house** (AbB 12, 89: 18–19)
ištu ūrim amaqqut **I will jump down from the roof** (ARM 10, 33: 9)
šukun adannam **Set a time limit!** (SEAL 1.1.1.1: 52)
anzâm kušud **Defeat the anzû-bird!** (SEAL 1.1.1.1: 56)
ilum-ma u awīlum libtallilū puhur ina ṭiṭṭi **May god and man be thoroughly mixed together in clay** (AH I 212–13)
ru'tam iddû elu ṭiṭṭi **They spat** (lit. **threw spittle**) **upon the clay** (AH I 234)

7.2: *rigma ušebbû ina mātim* **They made a cry resound in the land** (AH II ii.22)
ubut bīta bini eleppa makkūra zēr-ma napišta bulliṭ **Destroy the house, build a boat, spurn property, and preserve life** (AH III i.22–4)
ana dimtim ana mīnim ītenelli **Why does he constantly go up the wooden siege tower?** (ARM 10, 51: 14–15)
ammīnim itti nammaštê tattanallak ṣēram **Why do you roam through the open country with the wild beasts?** (Gilg. II 54–5)
harimtum ištasi awīlam **The harlot called out to the man** (Gilg. II 143)
liptekum padānam pehītam **May he open for you a closed path** (Gilg. III 259)
idin ana šarrim kakkam dannam **Give the king a mighty weapon!** (Akkade 198: 65)
ana ūmim annîm uznāya ibaššiā **My attention is focused on this day** (AbB 5, 239: 34–5)
šīrum ana šīri[m] inazziq **Flesh worries about flesh (i.e. one living being worries about another)** (AbB 5, 42: r.2′–3′)
agâ ṣīra tuppirāšu **You** (pl.) **crowned him with a majestic crown** (RIMA 2, 13 i.21)
ašarēdūta ṣīrūta qardūta taqīšāšu **You bestowed upon him pre-eminence, exaltedness (and) heroism** (RIMA 2, 13 i.23–4)

7.3: *karānam ṭābam šūbilam* **Send me (some) good wine!** (AbB 6, 52: 17)
kaspam u šamnam ul iddinūnim **They did not give me silver or oil** (ARM 10, 39: 23–4)
ina ēkallim annîm irbi **He grew up in this palace** (ARM 10, 57: 6)
milkum ša sinništim imtaqut ana libbišu **The counsel of the woman fell into his heart (i.e. struck him profoundly)** (Gilg. II 67–8)

šikaram išti'am **He drank the beer** (Gilg. II 101)
issaqqaram ana harimtim **He spoke to the harlot** (Gilg. II 139)
kurummatam ul nīšu **We do not have a food ration** (AbB 7, 104: 27)
bilta u maddatta elišunu ukīn **I imposed upon them *biltu*-tribute and *maddattu*-tribute** (RIMA 2, 20 iv.29–30)

7.4: *gāmilu ul āmur* **I could not find a helper** (BWL 34: 98)
adanna īteq **The appointed time passed;** also possible: **He/she overstepped the appointed time** (BWL 38: 1)
kīma šuškalli ukattimanni šittu **Sleep enveloped me like a net** (BWL 42: 72)
ina huhāri ša erê sahip **He is caught in a bird-snare of copper** (BWL 130: 94)
dayyāna ṣalpa mēsera tukallam **You make a crooked judge experience imprisonment** (BWL 132: 97)
urappaš kimta mešrâ irašši **He will enlarge (his,** lit. **the) family, he will acquire wealth** (BWL 132: 120)
sartu lēpuš **I will commit a crime** (BWL 146: 40)
[ni]ṣirta īmur-ma katimti iptu **He saw the [se]cret and opened what was hidden** (Gilg. I 7)
iṣṣalim urpatum peṣītum **A white cloud turned black** (Gilg. V 135)
mūtum kīma imbari izannun elišun **Death was raining down upon them like fog** (Gilg. V 136)
ina puzri ūlidanni iškunanni ina quppi ša šūri **She gave birth to me in secret, placed me in a basket of reed** (Akkade 40: 5–6)
naruqqu rakistu idinšu **Give him a bound leather bag!** (GBAO 2, 48: 43)

8.1: *awīlû bītam iplušu* **The** (or: **some**) **men broke into a** (or: **the**) **house** (AbB 3, 70: 8)
šarrūtam ša nišī išīmkum enlil **Enlil destined you for the kingship over** (lit. **of**) **the people** (Gilg. II 239–40)
nablū imtaqqutū **The flames gradually died down** (Gilg. Schøyen$_2$ 41)
melemmū ihalliqū ina qīšim **The auras are escaping into the wood** (Gilg. Ishch. 12')
libbātim imtala **He has become full of anger** (AbB 5, 48: 6'–7')
šībī ukallam **He will display witnesses** (CH § 122)
šammū ina eqlim ul ibaššû **There are no** (lit. **not**) **plants in the field** (AbB 14, 92: 9–10)
ṭuppam ana mê addi **I threw the tablet into the water** (AbB 3, 21: 31–2)
mû ul ibaššû **There is no** (lit. **not**) **water** (Bab. is plural!) (AbB 10, 177: 30)
alpū šalmū **The oxen are healthy** (AbB 5, 151: 4')
awīlû ina nupārim kalû **The men are detained in prison** (AbB 7, 58: 6–7)
ālam uttēr ana tīlī u karmī **He turned the city into tells and ruin mounds** (Akkade 70: 71)
awīlê wuššir **Release the men!** (AbB 5, 32: 3')

8.2: *ina dimāti sihirti āli ālul pagrīšun* **I hung their corpses on towers round the town** (Chic. iii.9–10)
ana pulhāti ša nišī išīmšu enlil **Enlil solemnly appointed him as the terror of the people** (Gilg. II 228)
dāmī kīma imbari ušazna[n] **He makes blood rain down like fog** (GBAO 2, 34: 22)
ina kamâti rabṣū **They were sitting in the open** (Gilg. XI 116)
anunnakī iššû dipārāti **The Anunnaki-gods carried torches** (Gilg. XI 104)
lū kamsū ina šaplika šarrū kabtūtu u rubû **May kings, magnates and nobles bow down beneath you** (m. sg.) (Gilg. VI 16)

9.1: *pāšī išpukū rabûtim* **They cast great axes** (Gilg. III 165)
mīrī dannūtim alīlī uš[tālik] **He sent forth the strong bulls, the powerful ones** (Akkade 66: 44)
in eperī rabi'ūtim išdīšu kīma šadîm ukīn **With great earthworks he made its roots as firm as (those of) a mountain** (Les. 53: 137–9)

šeriktaša mārū mahrûtum u warkûtum izuzzū **Her previous and later sons (i.e. her sons from the previous and subsequent marriages) shall divide her dowry** (CH § 173)
pušqī waštūtim u[p]etti **I found ways out of dire straits** (CH ep. xlvii.19–20)
eṭlūtum unaššaqū šēpīšu **The young men kiss his feet** (Gilg. II 21)
attanallak ina birīt eṭlūtim **I was walking about among the young men** (Gilg. II 4–5)

9.2: *suluppī watrūtim ša ina kirîm ibbaššû bēl kirîm-ma ile[qqe]* **It is the owner of the orchard who will receive the surplus dates which grew in the orchard** (CH § 66)
ilū rabbûtum ibbûninni **The great gods called me** (CH ep. xlvii.40–1)
alpū u enzētum urīṣū šammī napšūtim līkulū **The oxen (and) the nanny goats (and) billy goats should eat grass in abundance** (lit. **abundant grass**) (AbB 3, 11: 36–7)

9.3: *itbû-ma mālikē rabbûtu* **The great counsellors arose** (Gilg. II 287)
šamaš ana humbaba idkâššum-ma mehê rab(b)ûtu **Šamaš roused great storm-winds against Humbaba** (Gilg. V 137)
21 *ālānīšunu dannūti u ālānī ṣehrūti* (or *ṣehherūti*) *ša limētišunu alme akšud* **I besieged (and) conquered their 21 large cities and the small cities in their environs** (Asar. 51: 52–3)
eli tamlê šuātu ēkallāti rabbâti ana mūšab bēlūtiya abtani **On that terrace I built great palaces as my lordly residence(s)** (Asar. 61: 2–4)
ušellâ mītūti ikkalū balṭūti **I will bring up the dead, (and) they will eat the living**; also possible: **I will bring up the dead, and the living will eat** (ID Nin. 19)
kīma šikari ašattâ mê dalhūte **Instead of beer I will drink muddy water** (ID Ass. Vs. 35)
uppissi-ma kīma parṣī labīrūt[i] **Treat her in accordance with the ancient rites!** (ID Nin. 38)
malkī šepṣūti ēdurū tāhāzī **The obdurate rulers feared doing battle with me (**lit. **my battle)** (Chic. i.16)
kīma arme ana zuqtī ša(q)qûti ṣēruššun ēli **Like a mountain goat I went up against them onto lofty peaks** (Chic. iv.6–7)
ana nišīšu dalpāte ušēṣi nūru **I provided light for his wearied people** (TCL 3, 155)
eli epšēti annâti libbī īgug **At these deeds my heart became furious** (BIWA 18: A i.63–4)
harrī nahallī natbāk šadî mēlê marṣūti ina kussî aštamdih **On a sedan chair I sped across channels, wadis, mountain gulleys, (and) difficult heights** (Chic. iv.3–4)

10.1: *rimi parak šarrūtim* **Sit on the dais of kingship!** (Akkade 196: 27)
išālū tabsūt ilī erištam mami **They asked the midwife of the gods, wise Mami** (AH I 192–3)
abšānam lībil šipir enlil **Let him bear (as) a yoke the work of (i.e. assigned by) Enlil** (AH I 196)
ina šīr ili eṭemmu libši **Let a spirit come into being from the god's flesh**; also possible: **ilī the gods' flesh** (AH I 215)
iktabta rigim awīlūti **The noise of mankind has become burdensome for me** (AH II 7)
u anāku kī aššābi ina bīt dimmati šahurru rigmī **As for me, like one who dwells in a house of mourning, my cry is silent** (AH III iii.46–7)
qištum igrešu iškun ekletam ana nūr šamā'ī **The forest attacked him, it brought darkness on the light of the heavens** (Akkade 70: 59–61)
išāt libbi muti napihtum ibli **The blazing fire within the man (**lit. **burning fire-of-the-inside-of-the-man) became extinguished** (Akkade 184: 11)
adad bēl hegallim gugal šamê u erṣetim rēṣūya zunnī ina šamê mīlam ina nagbim līṭeršu **May Adad, lord of plenty, irrigation supervisor of heaven and earth, my helper, deprive him of rain in heaven and flood (water) in the depths below** (CH ep. l.64–71)
ina āl sunqim wašbāku **I am living in a town beset by** (lit. **of**) **famine** (AbB 9, 240: 9–10)
šupšik ilī rabi-[m]a **The toil of the gods was great** (AH I 3)

10.2: *šalmat qurādīšunu ina mithuṣ tūšari kīma rāhiṣi lukemmir* **Like the storm god in full flood, in a pitched battle I truly piled up the corpses** (lit. **corpse**; see Unit 6.13) **of their warriors** (RIMA 2, 14 i.77–9)

māt katmuhi rapašta ana sihirtiša akšud **I conquered the vast land of Katmuhu in its entirety** (RIMA 2, 16 ii.56–7)

šadâ marṣa u gerrētešunu pašqāte ina aqqullāt erî lū ahsi **I truly hewed my way through the difficult mountain range and their (the mountains') troublesome paths with axes of copper** (RIMA 2, 14–15 ii.7–9)

ummānāt māt paphê . . . itti ummānāt māt katmuhi-ma kīma šūbē ušna''il **The troops of the land of the Papheans . . . together with the troops of the land of Katmuhu I laid low like rushes** (RIMA 2, 15 ii.16–20)

pagar muqtablīšunu ana gurunnāte ina gisallât šadî luqerrin **I truly stacked the bodies of their warriors into piles in the mountain ledges** (RIMA 2, 15 ii.21–2)

10.3: *ana šahāt šadê pašqāte ipparšiddū mūšītiš* **They fled by night to difficult mountain flanks** (TCL 3, 214)

kīma šapat kunīni iṣlimā šapātuš[a] **Her lips turned dark like the rim of a *kunīnu*-bowl** (ID Ass. Vs. 30)

mūt bubūti u ṣūmi limūta **May he/she die a death of hunger and thirst** (Etana-Epos 180: 86)

ummānāt aššur gapšāte adke-ma **I called up the vast armies of Assur** (Khorsabad 91: 62)

11.1: *abāšu wuššir* **Let his father go!** (AbB 1, 50: 19)

maṣṣārātuya dannā **My guards are strong** (ARM 26/2, 346: 5)

[t]êrētuya šalmā **My omens are in good order** (ARM 26/2, 394: 11)

ātamar panīki **I have seen your** (f. sg.) **face** (Gilg. VA+BM ii.12′)

ilātim ana šubtišina lišallimū **They** (m.) **should safely deliver the goddesses to their dwellings** (lit. **dwelling**, see Unit 6.13) (or see Unit 14.16) (AbB 5, 135: 11–13)

panīšina unawwir **I brightened their** (f.) **faces** (AbB 1, 139: r.5)

bēlī nikkassīya līpuš **My lord should do my accounts** (AbB 5, 218: r.4′–5′)

marhītum lihtaddâm ina sūnika **Let the wife enjoy herself in your lap** (Gilg. VA+BM iii.13)

nipâtišu (from *nipūtu*) *liwaššerū* **They should release his debt slaves** (or see Unit 14.16) (AbB 5, 130: r.2′–3′)

ina rigmika ili bītim ul iṣallal **Owing to your noise the house god cannot sleep** (Schlaf, 36: 11–12)

ṣuhārêni [ṭ]urda[m] **Send me our boys!** (AbB 5, 58: 7–8)

šāpirni mīnam nippal **What will we answer our boss?** (AbB 5, 262: 9′)

šattam dummuqum ina libbika libši **Let there be great goodness in your** (m. sg.) **heart this year** (AbB 1, 108: 16–17)

bīt mubbirišu itabbal **He shall take the house of his accuser** (CH § 2)

11.2: *dayyānū awâtišunu immarū* **The judges will inspect their words** (CH § 9)

ina utliya nišī māt šumerim u akkadim ukīl **I held the people of the land of Sumer and Akkad in my lap** (CH ep. xlvii.49–52)

lē'ûtī šāninam ul īšu **My power is unrivalled** (lit. **has no rival**) (CH ep. xlvii.82–3)

awâtiya šūqurātim ina narîya ašṭur **I inscribed my precious words on my stele** (CH ep. xlvii.74–5)

ellūtim ittaqqi niqīšu **He poured his pure libations** (Akkade 82: 14′)

nipâtika ištu nupārim šūṣi'am **Release your** (m. sg.) **debt slaves from prison!** (AbB 5, 228: 19–20)

wardūya u alpūya ukullâm limhurū **My slaves and my oxen should receive food!** (AbB 9, 236: 9–12)

libbātiya malû **They** (m.) **are full of anger at me** (lit. **my anger**) (AbB 9, 232: 6–7)
qaqqadka lū mesi **Let your** (m. sg.) **head be washed** (Gilg. VAT+BM iii.11)
bēl hulqim huluqšu ileqqe **The owner of the lost property will take his lost property (back)** (CH § 9)
ahāka ṭurdam-ma **Send me your** (m. sg.) **brother!** (AbB 9, 106: 6)
ahātki marṣat **Your** (f. sg.) **sister is ill** (AbB 10, 169: 20)

11.3: *ina šulme u hadê ana mātātišunu utīršunūti* **I sent them back to their lands in peace and joy** (RIMA 2, 293: 153–4)
annû māru ridûtiya **This is my crown prince** (Asar. 40: 12)
itti libbiya atammu **I communed with my heart** (Asar. 42: 32)
ṣulūlšunu ṭāba eliya itruṣū **They spread their kindly protection over me** (Asar. 42: 39–40)
epšētišunu lemnēti urruhiš ašme **I heard of their evil deeds very quickly** (Asar. 43: 55)
ṣubāt rubûtiya ušarriṭ **I tore my lordly garment** (lit. **my garment of lordliness**) (Asar. 43: 51)
libbī īgug-ma iṣṣarih kabattī **My heart became furious, and my liver became hot (with rage)** (Asar. 47: 57)
gilgameš ina libbi uruk inaṭṭala šunāteka **In Uruk, Gilgameš was seeing dreams about you** (m. sg.) (Gilg. I 244)
iddi maršūtišu ittalbiša zakûtišu **He flung off his dirty (garments), he clad himself in his clean (garments)** (Gilg. VI 3)
mehret ummāniya aṣbat **I seized the front of my army** (TCL 3: 25)

11.4: *ina gišparriya ul ipparšid* **He could not escape from my snare** (Asar. 58: 11)
imsi malêšu ubbib tillêšu **He washed his filthy hair, he cleansed his tools** (Gilg. VI 1)
ūrki pitê-ma kuzubki lilqe **Open your vulva, so he can take your sexiness** (Gilg. I 181)
kīma ezzi tīb mehê assuha šurussun **I tore out their root like the furious onslaught of a storm** (Asar. 58: 16)
zikiršunu kabtu itta'id **He strictly observed their grave command** (Asar. 40: 15)
šallassun kabittu ašlula **I plundered their weighty plunder (i.e. I plundered their belongings in ample measure)** (Asar. 55: 52)
pitâ bābka **Open your** (m. sg.) **gate for me!** (ID Nin. 14)
ana kišukkiya itūra bītu **The house turned into my prison** (lit. **my captivity**) (BWL 44: 96)
ardāti ṣehherēti (or *ṣehrēti*) *ina uršišina tuštamīt* **You** (m. sg.) **have killed the young girls in their beds** (lit. **bed**, see Unit 6.13) (Erra IV 111)
mālak girriya ana rūqēte iṭṭul **He/she observed the course of my campaign from afar** (TCL 3: 82)

15.1: *ālšu uhallaq* **I/he/she will destroy his city** (ARM 10, 80: 16)
šuttam ipaššar **He/she interprets a dream** (Gilg. Schøyen$_2$ 13)
inaṭṭal u ippallas **He/she watches and gazes** (Gilg. 88–9)
sissiktum darītum birīni ikkaṣṣar **An eternal alliance will be established** (lit. **knotted**) **between us** (ARM 26/2, 449: 55)
ina ūmī ša dannatim iṣabbat qātka **In times** (lit. **days**) **of hardship he/she will seize your hand** (Gilg. Schøyen$_2$ 22)
erṣetum irammum **The earth rumbles** (Gilg. Schøyen$_2$ 34)
namrīrī ša ilim tanaṭṭal **You** (m. sg.) **will behold the radiant auras of the god** (Gilg. Nippur 3)
anāku elika ahabbub **Me, I will croon over you** (ARM 10, 8: 10–11)
muruṣ libbim mādiš anaṭṭal **I will experience great sorrow** (ARM 10, 74: 11–12)
kirbān ṭābtim ina lubārim tarakkas ina kišādišu tarakka[s] baliṭ **You** (m. sg.) **tie a lump of salt in a rag, tie (it) onto his neck, (and) he will be well** (SEAL 5.1.26.2: 6–9)

15.2: *anāku mūšam u kaṣâtam šunātika-ma anaṭṭal* **I see dreams about you** (lit. **your** (m. sg.) **dreams**) **day and night** (AbB 14, 154: 8–9)

ṣubāt awīlê šattam ana šattim idammiqū atti ṣubātī šattam ana šattim tuqallalī **Year by year, the (other) men's garment(s) get better, (but) you** (f. sg.), **you make my garment shabbier year by year!** (AbB 14, 165: 7–12)

kurummātišin[a] tamahhar[ī] **You** (f. sg.) **will receive their** (f. pl.) **food rations** (AbB 1, 26: 11–12)

šum habālim pagarki tašakkanī **You will establish a bad name** (lit. **a name of wrongdoing**) **for yourself** (lit. **(as) your body**) (AbB 1, 115: r.4′)

bītam udabbab **He/she is pestering the household** (AbB 1, 67: r.11)

ṭēmam annī'am mahrīšu ašakkan **I shall place this matter before him** (AbB 3, 2: 29)

ana m[ī]nim bītī tupallah **Why are you intimidating my household?** (AbB 9, 260: 4–6)

šēp ninšubur u ninsianna bēlīya anaššiq **I will kiss the feet** (lit. **the foot**) **of Ninšubur and Ninsianna, my lords** (AbB 5, 172: 16–17)

mimma lā tanakkudī **Do not be at all worried** (AbB 5, 255: 17)

panūšu lā iṣallimū **His face must not turn black** (AbB 1, 79: 17)

15.3: *ēkallam lā udabbab* **He/she must not pester the palace!** (AbB 4, 64: 19)

rubûm mātam lā šâtam qāssu ikaššad **The ruler will by his hand conquer a land other than his own** (OBE 98: 9′)

rubûm māt nakrišu unakkap **The ruler will gore the land of his enemy** (OBE 99: 19′)

ṣerrum awīlam inaššak **A snake will bite a man** (OBE 99: 22′)

ummānka rēš eqliša ul ikaššad **Your army will not reach its destination** (lit. **the head of its field**) (OBE 150: r.9′)

ummānī līt ummān nakrim išakkan **My army will bring about a victory over** (lit. **of**) **the army of the enemy** (OBE 156: 6)

adad ina mātim irahhiṣ **Adad** (= the storm god) **will be in full flood in the land** (OBE 158: 44)

bīt awīlim issappah **The man's household will be dispersed** (OBE 158: 5′)

mātum ana dannatim ipahhur **The land (i.e. the land's inhabitants) will assemble in the fortress**; also possible: *dannātim* **fortresses** (OBE 159: 8′)

mār šarrim kussi abīšu iṣabbat **The** (or: **A**) **king's son will seize his father's throne** (OBE 171: 16′)

ālu šū iṣṣabbat ūlū-ma ul iṣṣabbat **Will this city be seized, or will it not be seized?** (ARM 10, 120: 15–16)

ēkallam lā udabbabū **They must not pester the palace!** (or see Unit 14.16) (AbB 4, 83: 11–12)

15.4: *aranšunu ina muhhik[a] iššakkan* **Their punishment will be imposed** (lit. **placed**) **on you** (AbB 9, 192: 16–17)

amtam ana mamman ul anaddin **I will not give the slave girl to anyone** (AbB 9, 149: 20–1)

aššassu lā ihallalū **They** (m.) **must not shut his wife away** (AbB 9, 215: 23–24)

awâtuya mati īnki imahharā **When will my words please you** (lit. **meet your** (f. sg.) **eye**)**?** (AbB 3, 15: 20–1)

hiṭīt biltišu ina muhhika iššakkan **The outstanding payment of his rent will be imposed on you (i.e. You will be held responsible for payments outstanding in his rent)** (AbB 4, 18: 23–5)

ina nīš ilim libbakunu unappašū **They will ease your heart through (i.e. by swearing) an oath on the life of the god** (or see Unit 14.16) (AbB 13, 34: 26′–8′)

apkallum qibīssu mamman ul ušamsak **No one will consider a sage's utterance bad** (see Unit 11.12) (Adapa 9: 7′)

[in]a qātišu elleti (or dual: *qātīšu ellēti*) *paššūra irakkas* **He lays the table with his pure hand** (or: **hands**) (Adapa 9: 13′)

eleppašu umahhar **He steers his boat upstream** (Adapa 9: 21′)

melammūšu usahhapū nagab zayyārī **His auras overwhelm all foes** (lit. **the entirety of the foes**) (TN 66: 12′)

ul [i]ššakkan salīmu balu mithuṣi **Peace cannot be achieved** (lit. **set in place**) without strife (TN 90: 15′)

15.5: *qīptašu atammah* **I will seize his position** (BWL 32: 61)

nišī mātāti kullassina tapaqqid **You care for the people of the lands in their entirety** (BWL 126: 23)

dayyāna ṣalpa mēsera tukallam māhir ṭa'ti lā muštēširu tušazbal arna **You give the crooked judge experience of imprisonment, an unjust bribe-taker you make bear punishment** (BWL 132: 97–8)

išaddad ina miṭrata zārû eleppa **A father drags a boat along the canal** (BWL 84: 245)

išarrak terdinnu ana katî tiûta **The second son gives food to a pauper** (BWL 84: 250)

[ana za]māru qubbîya ušaṣrap **[For a s]ong I make my laments resound** (BWL 36: 108)

milik ša anzanunzê ihakkim mannu **Who understands the plan of the underworld gods?** (BWL 40: 37)

atta ana šībūtišunu taššakkan **You will be appointed as their witness** (lit. **to their witness-hood**) (BWL 100: 34)

mukaššidī ikkaššad **My pursuer is being** (or: **will be**) **pursued** (BWL 241: iii.1–2)

16.1: *libbī imraṣ* **My heart became sore** (ARM 10, 44: 6)

šumī ul izkur **He/she did not utter my name** (ARM 10, 39: 32–3)

ilbaš libšam **He/she donned clothing** (Gilg. II 110)

iphur ummānum ina ṣērišu **The populace gathered round him** (Gilg. II 178)

išhuṭ libšam **He/she tore off the garment** (Gilg. II 69)

ibriq birqum innapih išātum **Lightning flashed, fire broke out** (Gilg. Schøyen$_2$ 36)

šībūti upahhir ana bābišu **He gathered the elders to his gate** (AH I 386)

ina šērēti ibbara ušaznin **In the morning hours he caused a fog to rain down** (AH II ii.30)

ipru' markasa eleppa ipṭur **He severed the rope (and) released the boat** (AH III ii.55)

abūba ana kullat nišī uzammer **I/he/she sang of the flood to all** (lit. **all of**) **the people** (AH III viii.18–19)

16.2: *qištum igrešu iškun ekletam ana nūr šamā'ī* **The forest attacked him, it set darkness in place of the light of the heavens** (Akkade 70: 59–61) (For another possibility see Ex. 10.1.)

libbī mādiš izziq **My heart was very vexed** (ARM 10, 114: 12–13)

šīr awīlim ishul **He/she/it pierced the** (or: **a**) **man's flesh** (AbB 3, 85: 4)

nīš šarri ina pîšu aškun **I placed in his mouth an oath sworn on the life of the king** (AbB 3, 55: 21)

hubtam ihbut **He/she carried off the plunder** (AbB 14, 146: 8)

kīma niṭliya ittiša adbub **I spoke with her according to my judgment** (lit. **gaze**) (AbB 3, 2: 9)

dīnam an[a] ahīšu ul agmur **I have not completed a judgment (i.e. not yet reached a full judgment) about his brother** (AbB 3, 21: 23–4)

rēška ukabbit **I/he/she honoured you** (m. sg.) (lit. **made your head heavy**) (SEAL 1.1.5.1 Susa rev.13′)

ana mīnim qātka ina zumriya tassuh **Why did you** (m. sg.) **wrench your hand away from me** (lit. **my body**, see Unit 13.1)**?** (AbB 10, 52: 4–5)

ilū mātim itrurū-ma iššiqū šēpīšu **The gods of the land trembled and kissed his feet** (SEAL 1.1.1.1 42)

16.3: *ana šāpiriya mīnam ugallil* **What sin have I** (or: **has he/she**) **committed against my boss?** (AbB 1, 16: 9)

ina ebūri (or *ebūrī*) *âm ul idd[i]nū* **They did not give out grain during the harvest** (or: **harvests**) (or see Unit 14.16) (AbB 1, 4: r.7')
ina puhri šillāti idbubā **They** (f. pl.) **spoke slander in the assembly** (AbB 6, 124: 16–17)
ana epēšim annîm kī lā taplah **How come you** (m. sg.) **were not afraid of this undertaking?** (AbB 2, 53: 17–18)
appašu ipluš-ma [ṣe]rretam iškun **He/she perforated his nose and installed a nose rope** (ARM 26/2, 434: 36–7)
qaqqadka ukabbit **I/he/she honoured you** (m. sg.) (lit. **made your head heavy**) (ARM 26/2, 449: 28)
ṣābum ša bēliya iphur **My lord's troops assembled** (Bab. is singular!) (ARM 26/2, 408: 9)
awâtim watrātim-ma hayasumu ana ṣēr bēliya išpur **Hayasumu wrote additional words to my lord** (ARM 26/2, 409: 22)
adīni ṭēmam ul almad **Up till now I have heard** (lit. **learned**) **no news** (ARM 26/2, 404: 92)
išātam ina libbi qīrti ippuh-ma dimtum imqut **He kindled a fire in** (or: **with**) **the bitumen, and the siege tower collapsed** (lit. **fell**) (ARM 26/2, 318: 11–12)
kaspam ul nimhur **We received no silver** (lit. **We did not receive silver**) (AbB 12, 95: 8)
awīlê šunūti ahī ana mīnim ihsus **Why did my brother think of those men?** (ARM 26/2, 408: 50)
hârum iqqaṭil **The sacrificial donkey was killed** (ARM 26/2, 404: 61–2)
imērū ana gerrim ihhašhū **Donkeys were needed for the caravan** (AbB 13, 52: 5)

16.4: *ana šuātu nēmeqa iddinšu* (or *iddinaššu*) *napištam darītam ul iddinšu* **To that one he gave wisdom, (but) not** (lit. **he did not give**) **eternal life** (Adapa 9: 4')
adapa ša šūti [k]appaša išbir **Adapa broke the south wind's wing** (Adapa 18: 35'–6')
ammīni ša šūti kappaša tešbir **Why did you break the south wind's wing?** (Adapa 18: 48'–9')
ana gisallât šadî šaqûti kīma iṣṣūrāti ipparšū **Like birds they flew to the ledges of lofty mountains** (RIMA 2, 15: ii.41–2)
šalmat (pl. *šalmāt* also possible, see Unit 6.13) *qurādīšunu ina bamāt šadî ana qurunnāte lū uqerrin* **I truly heaped up the corpses of their warriors into piles on the mountain slopes** (RIMA 2, 18: iii.53–4)
šagalti ummānātešunu rapšāti kīma rihilti adad lū aškun **I truly accomplished the slaughter of their vast armies like a flood of the storm god** (RIMA 2, 21: iii.89–91)
ul išnun mati-ma ina šarrānī kullati qabalšu mamma **None among the kings of the entire earth ever matched his onslaught** (lit. **any … did not match**) (TN 70: 22')
ana rēšišunu ušeppik šamna **He poured oil onto their heads** (lit. **head**, see Unit 6.13) (TN 74: 10')
iškun anu miṭṭa lā pādâ elu targīgī **Anu brought down** (lit. **set**) **the merciless *miṭṭu*-weapon on the evildoers** (TN 118: 35')
ninurta qardu ašarēd ilānī kakkīšunu ušebber **Heroic Ninurta, foremost of the gods, smashed their weapons** (TN 118: 39')

16.5: *mašmaššu ina kikiṭṭê kimiltī ul ipṭur* **The incantation priest could not dissolve the (divine) wrath against me with a ritual;** also possible to interpret *ki-mil-ti* as a basic state accusative: **the (divine) wrath** (BWL 38: 9)
qerbīya idluhū **They stirred up my insides** (BWL 42: 65)
agurrī ina uqnî ušabšil **I glazed the bricks with lapis lazuli** (RIMA 2, 290: 32)
anum enlil u ea urappišū uzunšu **The gods Anu, Enlil and Ea broadened his wisdom** (Gilg. I 242)
tanādāt(i) šarri iliš umaššil u puluhti ēkalli ummān ušalmid **I made the praises of the king equal to (those of) a god, and I taught the populace reverence for the palace** (BWL 40: 31–2)

ammīni ata tatbal agâ rabâ ša qaqqadiya **Why, O doorman, did you remove the great crown on** (lit. **of**, see Unit 13.2) **my head?** (ID Nin. 43)
ikpud-ma libbašu lemuttu **His heart plotted evil** (Etana-Epos 174: 38)
unakkis kappīšu abrīšu nuballīšu (duals!) **He cut off its *kappu*-wings, its *abru*-wings, (and) its *nuballu*-wings** (Etana-Epos 184: 117)
ana ešrā bīrī iksupū kusāpa ana šalāšā bīrī iškunū nubatta **At 20 leagues they broke bread, at 30 leagues they stopped for the night** (Gilg. XI 319–20)

16.6: *šadê ubbit-ma būlšunu ušamqit / tâmāti idluh-ma miširtašina uhalliq / apī u qīšī ušahrib-ma kī girra iqmi* **He annihilated mountains and felled their cattle, he stirred up seas and destroyed their produce, he laid reed beds and forests to waste and burned (them) like Girra** (= the fire god) (Erra IV 147–9)

17.1: *libbī tultemmin* **You** (m. sg.) **have troubled my heart** (AbB 7, 61: 20)
[l]ibbašu imtaraṣ **His heart has become sore (i.e. He is worried)** (AbB 5, 42: r.11′)
tuštamriṣ libbī u muruṣ libbi rabi'am ana panīya taštakan **You** (m. sg.) **have made my heart sore and brought about great soreness of heart for me (i.e. You have made me very worried)** (AbB 14, 18: 6–8)
rigmam eliya taštaka[n] **You** (m. sg.) **have raised a complaint against me!** (AbB 3, 26: 7)
hiṣpatum kabittum ana panīya iptarik **Grave insolence has lain in the way of my face (i.e. in my way)** (AbB 1, 128: r.13′–14′)
usātim rabiātim ina muhhiya taštakan **You** (m. sg.) **have rendered me** (lit. **placed onto me**) **great assistance** (AbB 9, 174: 1–2)
kišādka kaqqaram uštakšid **I have** (or: **he/she has**) **made your neck reach the ground, i.e. I have** (or: **he/she has**) **trampled you down** (AbB 7, 187: 6–7)
šīpātim ša ēkallim ištaqlū **They** (m. pl.) **have weighed out the wool for** (lit. **of**) **the palace** (or see Unit 14.16) (AbB 7, 160: 1)
eqlam amtakar **I have watered the field** (AbB 7, 55: 19)
šarrāqī šunūti aṣṣabat **I have caught those thieves** (AbB 13, 12: 14–15)
rigma rabi'am ištaknā **They** (f. pl.) **have raised a big complaint** (AbB 6, 193: 12–13)
mīšaram ina māti aštakan **I have established justice in the land** (AbB 14, 130: 15–16)

17.2: *adapa mār ea ša šūti kappaša ištebir* **Adapa, son of Ea, has broken the wing of the south wind** (lit. **of the south wind … its wing**) (Adapa 16: 11′–12′)
mār šipri ša ani iktalda (from *kašādu*) **Anu's messenger has arrived** (Adapa 18: 34′–5′)
šamna [ilq]ûniššum-ma ittapšiš **They brought him oil, and he was anointed** (Adapa 20: 64′–5′)
[k]ullat mātiya taltalal (from *šalālu*) **You** (m. sg.) **have plundered all of my land** (TN 88: 5′)

17.3: *mīlī ittahsū* **The floods have subsided** (Erra I 136)
mišittu imtaqut eli šīrīya **Paralysis has fallen upon my flesh** (BWL 42: 76)
lu'tu imtaqut eli birkīya (du.) **Debility has fallen upon my loins** (BWL 42: 78)
imhaṣ pēnša ittašak ubānša **She** (also possible: **he**) **struck her thigh, bit her finger** (ID Ass. Rs. 17)
igdamrā maššakkīya šā'ilātu aslīya ina ṭubbuhi ilū igdamrū **The female dream interpreters have used up my incense, the gods have used up my sheep through slaughter (for sacrifices)** (Etana-Epos 188: 135–6)
qurādu erra ana šuanna āl šar ilī ištakan panīšu **Erra the warrior set his face towards Šuanna, city of the king of gods** (Erra I 124)
tamhaṣīšu-ma kappašu talteb[ri] **You** (f. sg.) **struck him, and broke his wing** (Gilg. VI 49)
qaqqad urīṣi ana qaqqad amīli ittadin **He has given the head of a male goat in place of the head of a man** (GBAO 2, 40: 22)

18.1: *têrētum mādiš laptā* **The omens are very unfavourable** (ARM 26/2, 411: 64)
inanna šattum gamrat **Now the year is complete** (AbB 10, 96: r.1)
anāku nīš ilim zakrāku **I myself have sworn an oath on the life of the god** (ARM 10, 32: 11)
mallû rabbûtum nāram parkū **Big *mallû*-boats are blocking the river** (ARM 10, 10: 7–8)
halṣum ša bēliya šalim **My lord's district is well** (ARM 26/2, 481: r.12')
kirih ālim dān **The town's enclosure wall is strong** (ARM 26/2, 424: 29)
nakrum ana mātiya qerub **The enemy is close to my country** (ARM 26/2, 416: 8)
bīssa ana bītiya qurrub **Her house is very close to my house** (AbB 3, 18: 17)
šūt kīma kakkabī ugārī sahpū **They covered the meadows** (or: **my meadow**) **like stars (cover the sky)** (Akkade 68: 55–6)
māratki šal[m]at **Your** (f. sg.) **daughter is well** (AbB 1, 26: 5)

18.2: *bubūtum ina muhhiya kamrat* **Hunger is heaped up upon me** (AbB 14, 37: 18–19)
awīlum wašaṭ **The man is difficult** (AbB 3, 81: 9–10)
šāpirni lū baliṭ **May our boss be in good health!** (AbB 1, 45: 6)
awātum īnī ul mahrat **The matter does not please me** (lit. **meet my eye**) (AbB 8, 61: 7)
libbī lummun **My heart is very wretched** (AbB 11, 14: 15)
awīlum šū muškēn **This man is a wretch** (ARM 26/2, 377: 11)
ibrī lū itbārānu anā u atta **My friend, let us be partners, you** (m. sg.) **and I** (SEAL 1.1.5.1 Morgan vi.6')
gerrum dān **The journey is difficult** (AbB 2, 87: 25)
bēyā ana mīnim naziq **What is Beya annoyed about?** or **Why is Beya annoyed?** (AbB 11, 14: 19–20)

18.3: *pullulū rubû / wašrū sikkūrū šērētum šaknā / habrātum nišū šaqummā / petûtum uddulū bābū* **The nobles are seen to, bolts are lowered (and) bars are set in place, the noisy people are utterly silent, (previously) open gates are shut** (SEAL 2.1.3.1: 1–4)

18.4: *ina qātī habbā[tī] išātum naphat mātam ikka[l]* **A fire has arisen through the doings** (lit. **hands**, dual) **of the robbers, (and) it is consuming the land** (AbB 8, 28: 8–10)
ṣuhārum ina māt šubartim wašib **The young man is living in the land of Šubartu** (AbB 12, 60: 11–12)
ina bābilim wašib **He lives in Babylon** (AbB 7, 4: 26)
erû mahir ukultam kīma nēšim nā'eri **The eagle was receiving the food like a roaring lion** (SEAL 1.1.5.1 Morgan vi.3')
ṭēmka lū sadir **May your report be regular** i.e. **Please report on a regular basis** (AbB 3, 12: 21)
abūni lū šalim lū baliṭ **May our father be well, may he be healthy** (AbB 1, 131: 6)
ašal šarri kubburat **The king's measuring rope is very thick** (AbB 3, 55: 25)
uznātum u kišādāt[um] nukkusā **Ears and necks are being cut (off) in great numbers** (AbB 9, 264: 9–11)
awīlû mādiš ṣurrumū **The men are striving hard** (lit. **greatly**) (AbB 3, 55: 26)
têrētum lupputā **The omens are very unfavourable** (ARM 10, 87: 7)
rēdênu (from *rēdû*) **We are soldiers** (AbB 7, 125: r.17)
ana manni karra labšāta **For whom are you wearing a mourning garment?** (Adapa 18: 22'–3')
ina mātini ilū šina hal[q]ū **Two gods have vanished from our land** (Adapa 18: 23')

18.5: *aššassu amat* (from *amtu*) **His wife is a slave girl** (BWL 236: iii.4)
šir'ānū'a nuppuhū **My sinews were/are inflamed** (BWL 44: 94)
mešrêtu'a suppuhā **My limbs are/were splayed** (BWL 44: 105)

kippat mātāti ina qereb šamê šaqlāta **You suspend the orb of the lands from the middle of heaven** (BWL 126: 22)

lū saniq pīka lū naṣir atmûka **May your mouth be controlled, may your speech be guarded** (BWL 100: 26)

ilu ana šarrābi ul paris alakta **The god has not blocked the way of** (lit. **interrupted the way for**) **the *šarrābu*-demon** (BWL 84: 244)

kal narkabti šugmurāku **I am in complete control of the entire** (lit. **all of the**) **chariot** (BWL 178 r.10)

lemnēta-ma kabtatī tušamriṣ **You** (m. sg.) **are evil, and you have made my liver sore (with anger)** (Etana-Epos 186: 127)

pašqat nēbertum šupšuqat uruhša **The crossing is difficult, its path is extremely difficult** (Gilg. X 83)

18.6: *ina ša[m]ê rīmāku ina erṣetim labbāku / ina māti šarrāku ina ilī ezzāku / ina igigī qardāku ina anunnakī gašrāku / ina [b]ūlim māhiṣāku ina šadî šubâku / ina apī girrā[ku] ina qīšī ma[g]šarāk / ina alāk harrāni urinnāku* **In heaven I am a wild bull, on earth I am a lion. In the land I am king, among the gods I am furious. Among the *Igigū*-gods I am a warrior, among the *Anunnakū*-gods I am powerful, among the cattle I am a striker, on mountains I am a battering ram. In crane thickets I am fire, in forests I am an axe. On campaign** (lit. **in the going of the journey**) **I am a standard** (Erra I 109–114) (Could also be rendered **I am most furious**, etc. see Unit 6.14)

18.7: *gimir parṣī-ma hammāta ilū-ma palhūka / igigī šahtūka anunnakī-ma galtūka* **You concentrate all** (lit. **all of**) **the rites in yourself, the gods fear you. The *Igigū*-gods revere you, the *Anunnakū*-gods tremble at you** (Erra III D 9–10)

19.1: *mādiš iddalhūninni* **They have greatly disturbed me** (AbB 4, 152: 11)

nīš ilī ušazkiršu **I/he/she got him to swear an oath by the life of the gods** (ARM 26/2, 401: 7)

libbašu mādiš maruṣkum **His heart is very sore (i.e. He is very angry) at you** (m. sg.) (AbB 5, 32: 1′–2′)

ammīnim šēp–sîn tudabbab lā tudabbabšu **Why are you** (m. sg.) **harassing Šep–Sîn? Do not harass him!** (AbB 9, 105: 23–5)

aššum hibiltīšu ulammidanni **He informed me about his crime (i.e. the crime done to him)** (AbB 10, 161: 2′–3′)

šittum rāhi'at nišī imqussu **Sleep, which seeps over people** (lit. **the seeper of people**)**, fell upon him** (Gilg. Schøyen$_2$ 30)

ina têrtišu lā tanassahšu **Do not remove him from his office!** (AbB 14, 66: 23)

pūham ul iddinūniāši[m] **They did not give us a substitute**, or **We were not given a substitute** (see Unit 14.16) (AbB 14, 1: 8)

nīš ilim [l]ā tušazkarīšu **Do not get him to swear an oath on the life of the god!** f. sg. addressee (AbB 13, 87: 10–11)

mû ikšudūniāti **The water** (Bab. is plural!) **reached us** (AbB 4, 148: 14)

19.2: *īnātum šaknāšunūšim* **Eyes are** (lit. **are placed**) **upon them** (m.) (ARM 26/2, 370: tl. i.3″)

gerrum paris-ma adi inanna ul ašpurakki[m] **The way was cut off, so I could not write to you** (f. sg.) **until now** (AbB 6, 64: 10–11)

akalam ištēn ul iddinam **He/she did not give me one loaf of bread** (AbB 7, 36: 22–3)

ana mīnim ipirša taprusā ipirša idnāšim **Why did you** (pl.) **discontinue her food allowance? Give her her food allowance!** (AbB 2, 117: 17–21)

ana ahātiya ul addin ana kâšum anaddinakkum **I did not give (it) to my sister, (but) I will give (it) to you** (AbB 1, 51: 34–6)

anniātum damqāk[u]m **These things are good for you** (m. sg.) (AbB 5, 193: 10′)

šattam erbet alpī aṭarradakkum **This year I will send you four oxen** (AbB 1, 123: 5–6) *bēlī u bēltī aššumiya dāriš ūmī liballiṭūkunūti* **For my sake may my lord and my lady keep you** (m. pl.) **alive forever**; grammatically also possible: **My lord and my lady, for my sake may they keep you alive forever** (or see Unit 14.16) (AbB 7, 100: 4–5)

anāku murṣu iṣbatanni **Me, a disease has seized me** (AbB 7, 144: 14′)

ana gilgameš kīma ilim šakiššum (*šakin* + *šum*, see Unit 47.9) *mehrum* **For Gilgameš, like a god, a counterpart has/had been appointed** (Gilg. II 194–5)

19.3: *šarru ṭēma iškunšu* **The king gave him instructions** (BBSt. 13: 8)

ul u[š]ellimšu ina mahra himiltašu damiqta (or: *damqata*) *ul amgur* **I did not make it good to him previously, I did not agree to his excellent plan** (TN 92: 26′)

panī banûti ša ani šunu ukallamūka **Those ones will show you the friendly face of Anu** (Adapa 18: 27′–8′)

19.4: *napištašu ušatbakšu* **I** (or: **he**) **will make him shed his life** (BWL 32: 59)

šallassunu kabittu tašallala ana qereb šuanna **You** (m. sg.) **will carry off their** (m.) **weighty tribute into Šuanna** (i.e. **Babylon**) (Erra V 30)

kīma šuškalli ukattimanni šittu **Sleep covered me like** (i.e. **as thoroughly as**) **a net** (BWL 42: 72)

asakku marṣu ittaškanšu (N perf.) **A grievous *asakku*-demon has been assigned to him** (GBAO 2, 46: 20)

iššaknānim-ma idāt (from *ittu*) *piritti* **Omens of terror** (i.e. **terrifying omens**) **were assigned to me** (BWL 32: 49)

šalimtu šaknassu **Good fortune is decreed for him**; also possible: **She has decreed good fortune for him** (Erra V 58)

ṣerru iṣṣabassu ina kappīšu (dual!) **The snake has seized him/it by his/its wings** (Etana-Epos 184: 109)

20.1: *ilam–pilah* **Fear the god!** m. sg. (AbB 1, 91: 1)

qaqqadki kutmī-ma **Cover your** (f. sg.) **head!** (ARM 10, 76: 8)

qātī ṣabat **Seize my hand!** m. sg. (AbB 14, 177: 19)

šarram lummid **Inform the king!** m. sg. (AbB 10, 57: 24)

šammī ukum **Heap up the plants!** m. sg. (AbB 3, 11: 47)

mugrīnni **Agree with me!** f. sg. (AbB 3, 15: 25)

ittišu išariš dubub **Talk straight with him!** m. sg. (AbB 12, 144: 20–1)

ana balāṭika-ma kurub **Pray for your life!** m. sg. (AbB 14, 115: 28–9)

amtam idnam **Give me a slave girl!** m. sg. (AbB 9, 149: 15)

Negated:

ilam–lā–tapallah **Do not fear the god!**

qaqqadki lā takattamī-ma **Do not cover your head!**

qātī lā taṣabbat **Do not seize my hand!**

šarram lā tulammad **Do not inform the king!**

šammī lā tanakkam **Do not heap up the plants!**

lā tamaggurīnni **Do not agree with me!**

ittišu išariš lā tadabbub **Do not talk straight with him!**

ana balāṭika-ma lā takarrab **Do not pray for your life!**

amtam lā tanaddinam **Do not give me a slave girl!**

20.2: *pagarka uṣur* **Protect yourself** (lit. **your body**)**!** m. sg. (AbB 1, 71: 21)

bīta ṣullil **Roof the house over!** m. sg. (AbB 10, 145: 23)

kīma qanê[m] kupraššu **Cut him down to size like a reed for me!** m. sg. (AbB 9, 206: 10–11)

gimillam eliya šukun **Do me a favour!** m. sg. (AbB 10, 82: r.10′–11′)

[ina] annītim athûtam kullim **Show partnership [in] this matter!** m. sg. (AbB 1, 13: 23–4)
rubṣam šukunšināt[i] **Provide them** (f.) **with a bed place!** m. sg. (AbB 9, 76: 7)
ālkunu kuṣṣirā **Fortify your** (pl.) **town!** pl. (ARM 26/2, 409: 60)
nīš šubula ili bēlišu ina pîšu šukun **Place in his mouth an oath sworn on the life of Šubula, the god his lord!** m. sg. (AbB 6, 189: 20–2)
taphūrī ina išrim ana asaru šuknā-ma ilam sullimā **Hold assemblies for Asaru in the village, and appease the god!** pl. (AbB 2, 118: 15–19)

Negated:

pagarka lā tanaṣṣar **Do not protect yourself!**
bīta lā tuṣallal **Do not roof the house over!**
kīma qanêm lā takapparaššu **Do not cut him down to size like a reed for me!**
gimillam eliya lā tašakkan **Do not do me a favour!**
ina annītim athûtam lā tukallam **Do not show partnership in this matter!**
rubṣam lā tašakkanšināti **Do not provide them** (f. pl.) **with a bed place!**
ālkunu lā tukaṣṣarā **Do not fortify your town!**
nīš šubula ili bēlišu ina pîšu lā tašakkan **Do not place in his mouth an oath sworn on the life of Šubula, the god his lord!**
taphūrī ina išrim ana asaru lā tašakkanā-ma ilam lā tusallamā **Do not hold assemblies for Asaru in the village, and do not appease the god!**

20.3: *amâtiya limd[ā]* (pl. ; or *limd[a]*, m. sg. + vent.) **Mark** (lit. **learn**) **my words!** (Erra V 5)
šīra kīma šīrišu dāma kīma dāmišu idin **Give flesh instead of his flesh, blood instead of his blood** m. sg. (GBAO 2, 36: 69)
ina pan ṣāltim-ma puṭur **In the face of a quarrel, go away!** (BWL 100: 36)
naplis-ma bēlum šūnuhu aradka **Look, lord, at your exhausted servant** m. sg. (AfO 19, 57: 57)
idnam-ma (from *nadānu*) *šamma ša alādi kullimanni šamma ša alādi* **Give me the plant of conception! Show me the plant of conception!** m. sg. (Etana-Epos 188: 138–9)
piltī (from *pištu*) *usuh-ma* (from *nasāhu*) *šuma šuknanni* **Wipe out my insult, and gain me** (lit. **equip me with**) **a name!** m. sg. (Etana-Epos 188: 140)

21.1: *eqlam mê ī nilput* **Let's sprinkle the field with water** (AbB 10, 42: 34)
būnū namrūtum ša marūtuk ili ālika limhurūka **May the bright face of Marduk, the god of your town, greet** (lit. **meet**) **you** (m. sg.) (AbB 13, 140: r.4′–5′)
nipâtišu liwaššerū **They** (m.) **should release his debt slaves** (or see Unit 14.16) (AbB 5, 130: r.2′–3′)
ilātim ana šubtišina lišallimū **They should lead the goddesses to their dwellings** (lit. **dwelling**, see Unit 6.13) **safely** (or see Unit 14.16) (AbB 5, 135: 11–13)
marūtuk ana epēšika (inf. used as noun) *annîm likrub* **May Marduk bless (you) for this deed of yours** (m. sg.) (AbB 9, 174: 3–4)
ṣalmīka ina ahiya luqqur **I will destroy your** (m. sg.) **statues with my arm**; also possible: *ahīya* **arms**, du. (AbB 3, 22: 9)
utâm ina bābim liškun **He/she should appoint a doorman at** (lit. **in**) **the gate** (AbB 6, 189: 24)
pirṣam lāma ebūrim likšur **He/she should repair the breach before the harvest** (AbB 14, 180: 19–20)
šamaš u marūtuk dāriš ūmī liballiṭūka **May Šamaš and Marduk keep you** (m. sg.) **alive forever** (AbB 1, 3: 4–5)
bāmassunu lū wašbū bāmassunu [l]illikū **Half of them should stay, half of them should go** (AbB 13, 104: 5′–6′)

21.2: *[a]tti qaqqadī kubbitī-ma* (D imp. 2nd sg. f.) *u anāku qaqqadki lukabbit* **You** (f. sg.) **honour me** (lit. **make my head heavy**), **and I will honour you** (f. sg.) (AbB 7, 151: 4′–6′)

bēlki u bēletki kīma kīsi ša qātišunu liṣṣurūki **May your** (f. sg.) **lord and your lady protect you like the money bag in their hand** (see Unit 13.2) (AbB 6, 1: 11–12)
šubultum amatka pišannam lišapliska **Šubultum, your** (m. sg.) **slave-girl, should show you the chest** (AbB 1, 105: 7–8)
maṣṣarū liṣṣurūniššu **The guards should protect him** (AbB 13, 40: 9–10)
amtam liddikkum (*liddin* + *kum*) **He/she should give you** (m. sg.) **a slave girl!** (AbB 9, 149: 9)
ilam nâm ī nuballiṭ **Let's provide for our god!** (AbB 3, 73: 23)
uṣurātiya ay ušassik **May he/she not allow (anyone) to repeal my ordinances** (CH ep. xlviii. 73–4)
šamaš dayyān dīnāti elēnu linēršu šaplānu arūtašu mê kaṣûti ay ušamhir **May Šamaš, the decider of verdicts, kill him (here) above (i.e. on earth), (and) not allow his libation pipe to receive cold water below (i.e. in the netherworld)** (BBSt. 6: 19–20)
ay iṣbat āl šamši qurādi ay išlul šallatam-ma libbašu ay ibluṭ **May he/she not seize the city of Šamaš, the warrior, may he/she not carry off (its) plunder, and may his/her heart not be healthy** (Akkade 286: 20′–1′)
sîn nannār šamê ellūti saharšubbâ lā tēbâ gimir lānišu lilabbiš **May Sîn, light of the pure heavens, clothe all his body with incurable *saharšubbû*-disease** (BBSt. 7: ii.16–17)
šamaš dayyān šamê u erṣetim panīšu limhaṣ **May Šamaš, the judge of heaven and earth, smite his face** (BBSt. 7: ii.19)
nergal bēl tillê u qašāti kakkīšu lišebbir **May Nergal, lord of trappings and bows, smash his weapons** (BBSt. 8: iv.21–2)
nergal bēl qabli u tāhāzi ina tāhāzišu lišgissu (*lišgiš* + *-šu*) **May Nergal, lord of battle and combat, slaughter him as he fights** (lit. **in his combat**) (BBSt. 9: ii.3–5)

21.3: *dannu lumhaṣ-ma akâ lupallih* **I will strike the strong (one) and terrify the weak (one)** (Erra IV 115)
ē tasniqšu **Do not approach him!** (or: **Do not test him!**) m. sg. (Akkade 365: 167)
ummānu lušashir **I will cause the army to turn about**, i.e. **I will put the arm to flight** (Erra IV 116)
bilassunu kabittu lišdudū ana qereb šuanna **May they drag their heavy tribute into Šuanna** (i.e. **Babylon**) (Erra V 35)
amta ina bīti ē tukabbit **Do not treat a slave girl as important in (your) house** m. sg. (BWL 102: 66)
šamna šigarīka kīma mê lišarmik **May he bathe your** (m. sg.) **bolts with oil (as plentifully) as water** (AfO 19, 59: 163)
nišū liplahā-ma litquna hubūrši[n] **May the people be afraid, and may their din subside** (Erra I 73)

21.4: *ilū lišmû-ma liknušū ana nīrika / malkī lišmû-ma likmisū šapalka* **May the gods hear, and may they bow down to your** (m. sg.) **yoke. May the kings hear, and may they kneel down beneath you** (Erra I 64–5)

22.1: *ana nārim petêm sekērim šaknāku* **I have been appointed to open up (and) block the river** (lit. **for opening (and) blocking the river**) (AbB 5, 224: 10–12)
ana eperī (or *eperi*) *šapākim qātam iškun* **He/she set (his/her) hand to heaping up the soil** (ARM 26/2, 416: 5–6)
ana ṭēmišu lamādim ašpurakkum **I wrote to you** (m. sg.) **to learn his news** (AbB 2, 92: 27)
ana ṭēmika lamādi išpura (or *išpurā*) **He/she wrote to me** (or: **they** (f.) **wrote**) **to learn your** (m. sg.) **news** (AbB 1, 79: 28)
magarrīka rakābum ul arkab **I jolly well didn't ride your** (m. sg.) **waggons!** (AbB 8, 5: 16–17)
ana šapārim lā teggi **Do not be remiss in writing!** m. sg. (AbB 5, 159: r.16′)

ana līātim alpī u imērī bulluṭim lā teggi **Do not be remiss in keeping the cows, oxen and asses alive!** m. sg. (AbB 3, 38: 14–15)

alākám ana ṣērika ula nile"e **We are not able to come to you** (m. sg.) (AbB 9, 88: 9–11)

ana ṣāb tupšikkim šuā[t]u lā dubbubšunu šarrum iqbi **Regarding that same troop of corvée workers, the king decreed that they should not be hassled** (lit. **the king decreed their non-hassling**) (AbB 10, 13: 17–18)

[ina lā] akālim u šatêm maṭiāku u labāšum-ma ul labšāku **I am wasting away through want of food and drink** (lit. **through not eating and drinking**), **and I do not even have anything to put on** (lit. **am not even clothed**) (AbB 5, 160: r.2′–4′)

anum u enlil ana šīr nišī ṭubbim šumī ibbû **Anu and Enlil called out** (lit. **named**) **my name** (i.e. **appointed me**) **to secure the bodily wellbeing of the people** (CH i.45–9)

alākī qurrub **My coming** (or: **my going**) **is very close at hand** (AbB 7, 64: 9)

gagûm ana mašā'im šakin **Is the convent placed for plundering?** i.e. **Is the convent there to be plundered?** (AbB 1, 129: 20–1)

22.2: *ana ubbubika išpuran[ni]* **He/she sent me to purify you** (m. sg.) (BWL 48: 26)

īrissu-ma libbašu epēš tāhāzi **His heart demanded of him to do battle** (Erra I 6)

[an]a šakān abūbi ubla libbašunu ilī (or *ilānī*) *rabûti* **Their heart induced the great gods [t]o bring about the flood** (Gilg. XI 14)

22.3: *kī aqbi mahar ilī* (or *ilānī*) *lemutta / ana hulluq nišīya qabla aqbi* **How could I speak evil before the gods (and) declare battle to destroy my people?** (Gilg. XI 121–2)

23.1: *libbī lihdu* **May my heart rejoice** (ARM 10, 64: 18)

libbī ul ihdu **My heart did not rejoice** (ARM 10, 65: 13)

kaṣûtim mê ana šamšim tanaqqi **You** (m. sg.) **shall pour cold water** (as a libation) **to Šamaš** (Gilg. III 270)

matīma bītni ul ileqqû **They** (m.) **will never take our house** (AbB 3, 48: 20)

mû i[t]ṭehûnim **The water has come close** (Bab. is pl.!) (AbB 9, 35: 5)

ittika ezenne **I will be angry with you** (m. sg.) (AbB 3, 2: 50)

šarrum libbātim imtala **The king has become full of anger** (AbB 11, 147: 7′–8′)

zenûm (see Unit 22.6) *zaniāta* **You** (m. sg.) **are well and truly angry!** (AbB 14, 31: 5)

halṣum lā innaddi **The district must not be abandoned!** (AbB 9, 140: 22–3)

[t]aptâ (*tapte* + *ā*) *uznīya* (dual) **You** (pl.) **enlightened me**; also possible: *tapte* + vent.: **You** (m. sg.) **enlightened me** (Akkade 62: 3)

awātam iqabbi šuāšim **He/she says a word to him** (Gilg. VA+BM iv.20)

ibki-ma libbaša unappiš **She wept and eased her feelings** (AH III iv.12)

23.2: *ana nēmeliša īnka lā tanašši* **Do not covet** (lit. **raise your eye at**) **her profit** m. sg. (AbB 5, 44: 8′–9′)

šīṭūtī leqiat **I have been scorned** (AbB 5, 160: r.10′)

lū mali karaška **May your** (m. sg.) **belly be full** (Gilg. VA+BM: iii.6)

unâti liššûnim **They** (m.) **should bring the equipment** (AbB 10, 45: 12)

niziqtum ina libbiki lā ibašši **There must be no worry in your** (f. sg.) **heart** (AbB 3, 68: 14–15)

lā ikkallûnim **They** (m.) **must not be detained!** (Could also be taken as G present of *akālum: lā ikkalūnim* **They** (m.) **must not eat!**) (AbB 10, 15: 36)

šunūti uhtappi'am ina uzzišu **He smashed those ones in his anger** (Gilg. VA+BM: iv.1)

šarrum kunukkātim ša hubullim uheppi **The king smashed the sealed documents pertaining to** (lit. **of**) **the debt** (AbB 14, 15: 18–19)

ammīni bariānu (from *berû*) **Why are we starving?** (AbB 7, 59: 12)

murṣum iṣbatanni-ma ina napištim annadi (*nadû* N) **A disease seized me, and I was thrown out of life** (AbB 14, 43: 17–18)

ana alpim ukullû lā imaṭṭi **The fodder must not diminish for the ox!** (AbB 9, 67: 10–11) *ina hubūrišina uzamma šitta* **Through their** (f.) **noise I am** (or: **he/she is**) **deprived of sleep** (AH II i.8)

hudî u ēkallaki bussirī **Rejoice and inform your** (f. sg.) **palace of the good news!** (MARI 5, p. 622: 17–18)

23.3: *u"urti šarri danni kīma alê zumuršu iksi* **The command of the mighty king bound his body like an alû-demon** (TN 92: 24′)

uzza u šagalta ša tahšuhu nušabra nīnu **We will get (you) to experience the fury and slaughter which you** (m. sg.) **wanted** (TN 106: 20′)

ušerdi šāra abūba eli tāhāzišunu adad uršannu **Adad the warrior made wind and flood flow over their** (m.) **battle** (TN 118: 37′)

arki ilī tiklīšu (or: *tiklišu*) *šarru ina panī ummāni ušarri qabla* **Behind the gods, his trust(s), the king commenced battle at the head of the army** (TN 120: 41′)

ina ziqit mulmulliya adi tâmti elēnīte lū ardišunūti **With my pointed arrow I truly chased them** (m.) **to the upper sea** (RIMA 2, 22: iv.99–100)

23.4 *labbū-ma šamrū kīma anzî šanû nabnīta / [ka]drū ezziš ana tēšê balu tahlīpi* **They were raging and furious, (as) different in form as an anzû-bird, [rea]ring up angrily into the mêlée without armour** (TN 120: 45′–6′)

23.5: *asakku marṣu ina zumur amīli ittabši amīla muttallika kīma ṣubāti iktatam* **The grievous asakku-demon has come into being in a man's body, he has covered the restless man like a garment** (GBAO 2, 40: 2–4)

kīma tibût eribê māta imtalû **They** (m.) **have filled the land like a swarm of locusts** (GBAO 2, 46: 18)

ila alsi-ma ul iddina panīšu **I called out to the god, but he did not show me his face** (BWL 38: 4)

parṣīya ušalqû šanâm-ma **They allowed someone else** (lit. **another**) **to take my offices** (BWL 36: 103)

napihta bulli (*belû D*) **Extinguish the blazing fire!** m. sg. (BWL 100: 37)

šaplānu libbašu rēmu rašīšu **Deep down, his heart has taken** (lit. **acquired**) **pity on** (lit. **to**) **him** (Asar. 42: 30)

inaqqânikka (see Unit 19.4) *šikar sābi'i tamahhar* **They** (f.) **pour out brewer's beer for you, (and) you** (m. sg.) **receive (it)** (BWL 136: 158)

kabtat qāssu ul ale"i našâša **His hand is heavy, I cannot lift it** (BWL 48: 1)

tašemme šamaš suppâ sullâ u karābi **You will hear, O Šamaš, supplication, entreaty and prayer**; also possible: *suppāya sullāya karābī* **my supplication, my entreaty and my prayer** (BWL 134: 130)

iltaqû harharū anā attašpil **Villains have risen** (i.e. **been successful**)**, I have been cast down** (BWL 76: 77)

šipat balāṭi iddâ **He/she cast a life-giving spell for me**, or **They** (f. pl.) **cast a life-giving spell** (BWL 48: 28)

24.1: *anāku lemniš epšēku* **Me, I have been treated badly** (AbB 1, 67: r.4–5)

têrētim ana šulum mātiya lūpuš **I will take omens about the well-being of my land** (ARM 26/2, 411: 23–4)

têrētim nušēpiš **We had omens taken** (ARM 26/2, 427: 22)

šaptīya (dual) *iššiq biṣṣūrī ilput išaršu ana biṣṣūriy[a] ul īrub* **He kissed my lips (and) stroked my vulva, (but) his penis did not enter my vulva** (ARM 26/2, 488: 34–7)

šittam ša ilī anāku ekmēku **I have been robbed of** (lit. **with respect to**, see Unit 18.5) **the sleep of the gods** (Gilg. Harmal 2)

ina annītim athûtka lūmur **May I see your** (m. sg.) **partnership in this (matter)** (AbB 1, 3: 22–3) *šattam eleppētim ul nīpuš* **This year we made no** (lit. **we did not make**) **boats** (AbB 14, 37: 5–6)

pulluhāku u lemniš epšēku **I have been intimidated and treated badly** (AbB 14, 149: 25–7)

šattam ana šattim namdattašunu ebēṭum-ma (see Unit 22.6) *ībiṭ* **Year by year, the amount they pay** (lit. **their** (m.) **paid amount**) **has well and truly increased** (lit. **swollen**) (AbB 1, 125: 4–8)

mīnam nikkal **What are we going to eat?** (AbB 3, 37: 17)

ana bītiya lā irrubam **He/she must not enter my house!** (AbB 10, 56: 34)

kīma hadêya (see the introduction to Unit 22) *epuš* **Act in such a way that I will rejoice** m. sg.; also possible: *ēpuš* **I acted in such a way that I would rejoice** (AbB 14, 65: 21)

ina annītim ahhūtka lūmur **May I see your brotherliness in this (matter)** (AbB 3, 62: 21–2)

24.2: *karṣīka ana šarrim īkulū* **They** (m.) **slandered you to the king** (AbB 5, 234: 10–12)

mārtī luddikkum-ma (*luddin + kum + -ma*) *ahuz* **I will give you my daughter, so marry her!** (AbB 14, 110: 40)

šāpirni mīnam nippal **What will we answer our boss?** (AbB 5, 262: r.9′)

erû īkul īkulū mārūšu **The eagle ate, its children ate** (SEAL 1.1.5.1 Susa obv.9′)

ina tuppī labīrūtim ša bīt nisaba kī'am āmur **I read as follows** (lit. **thus**) **on the old tablets from the temple of Nisaba**; also possible: *amur* **read!** m. sg. (AbB 4, 118: 11–12)

anākú mīnam lūpuš **What am I to do?** (AbB 8, 130: 8′)

ina ēkallim awâtušu linnamrā **His words should be checked in the palace** (AbB 10, 19: 16–17)

ahūni ṣehrum aššatam ul ahiz **Our little brother is not married** (lit. **He has not married a wife**) (AbB 3, 2: 11)

sebetta bābū uddulū elu dapnim **Seven gates are** (or: **were**) **barred against the aggressive one** (SEAL 1.1.5.1 Morgan i.10)

dullum kīma herīnim īterub ana libbiya **Misery has entered my heart like grass seeds** (grass seeds are used to convey the idea of pricking) (AbB 14, 9: 8′–9′)

aššum kī'am šuttám tāmur **That is why you** (m. sg.) **had** (lit. **saw**) **a dream** (AbB 9, 263: 8–10)

ittiya nanmir **Meet with me!** m. sg. (AbB 6, 52: 19–20)

24.3: *ilū mātim ištarāt mātim / šamaš sîn adad u ištar / īterbū ana utul šamê* **The gods of the land (and) the goddesses of the land have entered the interior** (lit. **lap**) **of heaven** (SEAL 2.1.3.1: 5–7).

24.4 *umma šū-ma šamaš–hāzir eqel bīt abiya īkimanni-ma ana rēdîm ittadin kī'am ulammidanni eqlúm dūrum matīma innekkim warkatam purus* **Thus he (said): 'Šamaš–hāzir stole the field of my father's household from me, and sold it to a soldier'. Thus he informed me. (But) is a permanently owned field ever stolen? Establish the facts!** (m. sg.) (AbB 4, 16: 7–14)

24.5: *šamaš–hāzir u tappûšu īkimūniāti* **Šamaš–hāzir and his associate** (or: **associates**) **robbed us** (AbB 4, 37: 10–11)

šammī kalūmātiya lišākilū **They should get/allow my lambs to eat grass** (or see Unit 14.16) (AbB 10, 117: r.1–2)

šēpam ahītam ana libbi ālim lā tušerrebā **Do not allow a foreigner** (lit. **a foreign foot**) **to enter the city!** pl.; also possible: *tušerreba* (m. sg. + vent.) (AbB 7, 50: 12′–14′)

ina sartim lā tennemmidā **Do not seek refuge in lies!** pl.; also possible: *tennemmida* (m. sg. + vent.) (AbB 2, 130: 18–19)

ana dūrim erēbam mannum iqabbikum **Who will tell you** (m. sg.) **to enter the city wall?** (AbB 9, 40: 13–14)

ša arhiš bulluṭīšu epuš **Do that-of-curing-him-quickly** m. sg., i.e. **Do whatever is necessary to cure him quickly!**; also possible: *ēpuš* **I did …** (AbB 8, 95: 12–14)

šupram-ma ṣibûtka lūpušakkum **Write to me, and I will do your** (m. sg.) **wish** (i.e. **as you wish**) (AbB 1, 40: 12–13) *ibrī ātamar šuttam ammīnim lā tedkianni mādiš palha[t]* **My friend, I have seen a dream. Why did you** (m. sg) **not wake me? It** (= the dream) **was very frightening!** (Gilg. Schøyen$_2$ 4)

kīma lā nazāqika eppuš **I will act in such a way that you** (m. sg.) **will not be annoyed** (lit. **in accordance with your not being annoyed**) (AbB 3, 2: 27)

mimma anāku ul [š]ūhuzāku **I have not been informed at all** (ARM 26/2, 404: 75)

ūmam dimmassu ītaklanniāti **Today his wailing has eaten us up!** (AbB 14, 83: 22)

an[āk]u eltemnakkim (*eltemin* + *am* + *kim*) **I have become angry at you** (f. sg.) (AbB 6, 188: 38′)

ay īkul akla buluṭ libbi ay īṣin [nip]iš šīrāš **May he/she not eat bread, the life of the heart, (and) may he/she not smell the [sce]nt of beer** (Akkade 286: 22′–3′)

24.6: *šarru ībukšunūti* **The king led them away** (BBSt. 11: 32)

ēpuš usāti ana bēl bābili gimilta iškun **To the lord of Babylon he/she rendered assistance, he/she did a favour** (TN 74: 8′)

[i]tti nuhatimmī (or: *nuhatimmi*) *nuhatimmūta ippuš* **He/she does duty as cook together with the cooks** (or: **cook**) (Adapa 9: 10′)

urrih-ma šarru dannu iktašad ana kišād ulāya / innendū-ma šarrū kilallān ippušū tāhāza / ina birišunu innapih išātu / ina turbu'tišunu na'durū panū šamši **The mighty king hastened, (and) arrived at the bank of the Euphrates. The two kings came together, (and) did battle. In between them, fire broke out. Through their dust storm** (i.e. **through the dust storm which they raised**) **the face of the sun was darkened** (BBSt. 32: 28–31)

24.7: *ina pî labbi nā'ir[i] ul ikkimū šalamtu* **They** (m.) **cannot snatch** (lit. **steal**) **a body from the mouth of a roaring lion** (or see Unit 14.16) (Erra V 11)

rabâ marūtuk ušaggag **I/he/she will anger Marduk the great** (Erra I 123)

kī ulilte annabik **I was thrown down like a dried fig** (BWL 42: 70)

uruhka tezzib **You** (m. sg.) **will abandon your path** (BWL 99: 24)

kāl pagriya ītahaz rimûtu **Paralysis has taken hold of my whole body**; also possible: **My whole body has taken paralysis on board** (BWL 42: 75)

ana šūzub napištišu innabit ana qereb ni' **To save his life he fled into Thebes** (BIWA 25: A ii.31)

tētenettiq ginâ šamāmī **You** (m. sg.) **regularly pass across the sky** (BWL 126: 27)

pite-ma niṣirtašu erub ana libbi **Open his treasure house and go inside!** m. sg. (BWL 102: 83)

ikkal lē'û šīm idišu (or dual *idīšu*) *u lā le'û šīm [še]rrīšu* **An able individual lives off the price of his arm(s)** (i.e. **off his wages**), **but a weak** (lit. **non-able**) **individual off the price of his children** (i.e. **by selling them**) (BWL 242: 7–10)

šadî bērūti irrima šalummatka **Your** (m. sg.) **radiance covers distant mountains**; also possible *īrima* **covered** (BWL 126: 19)

ahuz qāssu puṭur aranšu **Take his hand, undo his punishment!** m. sg. (AfO 19, 59: 151)

[š]utbi-ma šērtukka ina nāriṭi eṭraššu **Remove your** (m. sg.) **punishment, and save him from the swamp!** (AfO 19, 59: 154)

ištar uggugat **Ištar is/was utterly furious** (Gilg. VI 81)

sunqu ina birišun iššakin-ma ana būrišunu īkulū šīr mārīšun **Famine occurred in their midst, and in their hunger they** (m.) **ate the flesh of their children** (lit. **sons**) (BIWA 114: B viii.25–6)

nikis qaqqad teumman bēlišunu qereb ninua ēmurū-ma šanê (inf. construct state) *ṭēmi iṣbassunūti* **They** (m.) **saw the severed head of Teumman, their lord, in Nineveh, and madness seized them** (BIWA 106–107: B vi.62–3)

25.1: *da'atni ul išāl* **He/she did not ask after us** (also possible: *išâl* **he/she will not ask**) (AbB 1, 134: 24)

amât-ma ṭābkum **I'm going to die, and it is good for you** (m. sg.)! (perhaps meaning … **and you're happy with that!**) (AbB 9, 232: 22)

ummaka imtūt **Your** (m. sg.) **mother has died** (AbB 8, 100: 17)
nagārū lā iriqqū **The carpenters must not be without work!** (AbB 13, 86: 22)
aššumišunu rēmanni **For their sake, have mercy on me!** m. sg.; also possible **For their sake, he is having / has had mercy on me** (AbB 9, 141: 16–17)
šumma atta mīšātânni (*mīšāta + anni*) *anāku elika ahabbub* **(Even) if you** (m. sg.) **despise me, I will croon over you** (ARM 10, 8: 9–11)
imērī šām **Buy donkeys!** m. sg., also possible: **My donkey has been bought** or **Buy my donkey!** m. sg. (AbB 2, 176: 20)
libbašu ittūh **His heart has become calm** (ARM 26/2, 413: 24)
mīnúm ubaššakka **What can/will dishonour you** (m. sg.)**?** (Gilg. IM obv. 21)
mūtni tarammī-ma [b]alāṭni tezerrī **You** (f. sg.) **love our death** (i.e. **the idea of us dying**), **and hate our life** (i.e. **the idea of us being alive**); also possible: *tarāmī … tezērī* **you** (f. sg.) **loved … you hated** (AbB 12, 63: 26–7)
libbī uṭīb **He/she/it satisfied me** (AbB 6, 126: 21)
rīqūssu lā iturra **He must not come back empty-handed** (*lā* rather than *ul* shows cannot be *itūra*) (AbB 13, 146: 9)

25.2: *kallātki izêrki* **Your** (f. sg.) **daughter-in-law hates you**, also possible: *izērki* **hated you** or *izzērki* **has hated you** (AbB 2, 150: 14)
šamaš dīnī lidīn **May Šamaš render my judgment**, also possible: **May Šamaš render judgments** (AbB 5, 159: r.8′)
ūrum sēr **The roof has been plastered** (AbB 2, 140: 13)
kaspam ul našiāku-ma ukultam ul ašâm **I am carrying no silver, so I cannot buy (any) food**; also possible: *ašām* **I was carrying no silver, so I could not buy (any) food**; also possible: *našiakkum-ma* **He was carrying no silver for you, so …** (AbB 1, 132: 7–8)
harbam ana bēlīšu tīr **Return the plough to its owner!** (D imp.) m. sg. (AbB 10, 165: 26)
šadûm iqūpam-ma īsihan[ni] **The mountain collapsed upon me** (*-am*)**, and begirt me**; also possible: *iquppam-ma issihan[ni]* **… will collapse upon me and begirt me** (Gilg. Schøyen$_2$ 6)
girrum rūq-ma [m]amman ana alākim [u]l imaggaranni **The journey is long, so nobody agrees with me about going**, i.e. **The journey is so long that …** (AbB 7, 144: 5′–7′)
ša kaspim šuāti nūnī damqūtim šāmam-ma ana akāliya šūbilam **With that silver buy (some) good quality fish** (pl.)**, and have (them) sent to me so that I can eat them** (lit. **for my eating**)**!** m. sg. (AbB 5, 224: 20–4)
kaspam mahir libbašu ṭāb **He has received the silver, he is satisfied** (lit. **his heart is good**) (AbB 1, 139: 7′)
kīma kalbi da'tī ul tašālī **As if (for) a dog, you** (f. sg.) **did not enquire after me**, also possible: *ul tašallī* **you will not enquire** (AbB 5, 160: r.6′)
šīr nišī uṭīb **I/he/she gave bodily well-being to the people** (CH v.24)
kīma ša a[n]āku wašbā[k]u libbašu [ṭ]ibbā **Satisfy him just as if I were present!** (D imp. pl.; also possible: *ṭibba*, imp. m. sg. with ventive suffix) (AbB 13, 58: 27–30)

25.3: *[h]iblētuya ina qātī* (also possible: sg. *qāti*) *šamaš–hāzir imtīdā* **Through the doings** (lit. **hand(s)**) **of Šamaš–hazir, the wrongs done to me** (lit. **my wrongs**) **have become numerous** (AbB 4, 134: 9–10)
ina šattim annītim tirrīnni-ma (*tirrī*, D imp. sg. f. *târu*, + *m* + *ni* + *-ma*) *nāram šūbirīnni* (*šūbirī*, Š imp. sg. f. *ebēru*, + *m* + *ni*) **Send me back and allow me to cross the river this year** (addressee f. sg.); *ina šattim annītim* applies to both verbs (AbB 9, 63: 8–10)
dīnī u dīnka šamaš lidīn **May Šamaš render my judgment and your** (m. sg.) **judgment** (AbB 1, 135: 35)

alpī ul tapṭur-ma ina dannat kuṣṣi tuštamīssunūti **You** (f. sg.) **did not release the oxen (from the yoke), and so you have allowed them to die through the harshness of winter** (AbB 10, 96: r. 2–3)

[l]āma alākini [l]ibbaka nuṭāb **We will satisfy you** (m. sg.) **before we leave** (lit. **before our going**) (AbB 10, 114: 10–12)

ana hissatíki rūq **He is far away for thought of you** (f. sg.), i.e. **He is too far away to think of you** (AbB 9, 230: 9–10)

lemutta ul ukīl ana ibriya **I/he/she did not hold evil in store for my friend** (SEAL 1.1.5.1 Susa rev.14′)

šumma ina kīnātim tarammanni ana bītišu mamman lā išassi **If you** (m. sg.) **really** (lit. **in truth**) **love me, nobody must state a claim against his household** (AbB 10, 1: 32–5)

ina māk rēdî ina sag.da–in.pàd halṣa[m] mamman ul ukāl **Owing to** (lit. **through**) **a lack of soldiers in Sagda–inpad, nobody can hold the district** (AbB 9, 140: 9–13)

eqlam šuāti ina qātim killaššu-ma (*kīl*, D imp., + *am* + *šu*; *šu* = the field, see Unit 19.9) *lā anazziq* **Hold that field in hand for me, so that I will not be annoyed** m. sg.; also possible: *killašum-ma* (*kīl*, D imp., + *am* + *šum*) **Hold that field in hand for him, so that I will not be annoyed** m. sg. (AbB 3, 2: 53–4)

ana nahlaptim usalliakki-ma (from *sullû*) *ul terēmīnni* **I beseeched you for** (f. sg.) **a garment, but you did not take pity on me** (AbB 5, 160: r.4′–5′)

šitta qinnāzī (also possible: *qinnāzīn*, dual) *šuhmiṭam alpū ina māk qinnāzim rīqū* **Get two teams of workmen to hasten to me! Through want of a team of workmen, the oxen are inactive** imp. m. sg. (AbB 9, 116: 7–9)

ana mīnim kī'am temiššanni (or: *temīšanni*) **Why do** (or: **did**) **you** (m. sg.) **scorn me so?** (AbB 14, 73: 9)

dawdâm dūk-ma šumam naškin **Bring about a defeat, and so be equipped with a name** (i.e. **make a name for yourself**)**!** m. sg. (ARM 10, 107: 23–5)

25.4: *[am]mīni šūtu ištu sebet ūmī ana māti lā izīqa* **Why has the south wind not been blowing over** (lit. **at**) **the land for the past seven days?**; also possible: *izzīqa* (pf.), *iziqqa* (pres.) (Adapa 16: 9′)

ana bīt bēliya ina qablat tâmti nūnī abār **I caught fish for my lord's household in the middle of the sea**; also possible: *abâr* **I am catching, I will catch** (Adapa 18: 50′–1′)

mê mūti ukallūnikkum-ma (*ukallū* + *nim* + *kum* + *ma*) *lā tašatti* **They will offer you** (lit. **hold towards you** (m. sg.)) **water of death, but do not drink!** (Adapa 18: 30′–1′)

mīdū arnūya **Many are my misdeeds** (TN 94: 37′)

nannāru sîn ukīn elišunu namungat qabli **Luminous Sîn** (lit. **Sîn, the light of the sky**) **fixed upon them the paralysis of battle** (TN 118: 36′)

25.5: *ina rubṣiya abīt kī alpi* **I spent the night in my dung, like an ox** (BWL 44: 106)

šarrahāku-ma atūr ana rēši **I had been magnificent, but I turned into a slave** (BWL 34: 78)

ana ahî ahī itūra ana lemni u gallê itūra ibrī **My brother turned into a stranger, my friend turned into an evil being and a *gallû*-demon** (also possible: *iturra* **will turn**) (BWL 34: 84–5)

ana gullultišunu rīb dumqī **Requite their misdeed with good deeds!** m. sg. (Akkade 366: 172)

ana ēpiš lemuttika damiqta rībšu **To one who does evil to you** (lit. **to your** (m. sg.) **evildoer**), **requite goodness!** (BWL 100: 42)

zazīqu abāl-ma ul upatti uznī **I supplicated a dream spirit, but it did not enlighten me**; also possible: *abâl*, pres., same translation (BWL 38: 8)

ana kibsī ahê uzunša turrat **Her attention is turned to the tracks of a stranger**; also possible: **She has turned her attention to the tracks of a stranger** (BWL 102: 79)

25.6: *māra ušmāt-ma abu iqabbiršu / arka aba ušmāt-ma qēbira ul īši* **I will kill the son, and the father will bury him. Then I will kill the father, and he will have not one to bury him** (lit. **he will not have a burier**) (Erra IV 97–8)

qurādu erra kīnam-ma tuštamīt / lā kīnam-ma tuštamīt **O warrior Erra, you have killed the righteous one, you have killed the unrighteous one** (Erra IV 104–5) (see also Unit 30.7)

tarāmī-ma nēša gamir emūqi / tuhtarrîššu sebe u sebe šuttāti / tarāmī-ma sīsâ na'id qabli / ištuhha ziqtī (dual) *u dirrata taltīmīššu* **You** (f. sg.) **loved the lion, perfect in strength, / (but) you dug seven and seven pits for him. / You loved the horse, devoted to battle, / (but) for him you decreed as destiny crop, spurs and lash** (Gilg. VI 51–4)

26.1: **1** *ullad* G pres. 1st/3rd sg. **2** *iwwaldū* N pret. 3rd m. pl. **3** *iwwalid* N pret. 3rd sg. **4** *ūlidka* or *ulidka* G pret. 1st/3rd sg. + *ka* **5** *uldanni* G pret. 3rd sg. + *anni* **6** *ūlissi* or *ulissi* G pret. 1st/3rd sg. + *ši* **7** *tuldīnni* G pret. 2nd f. sg. + *(a)nni* **8** *bilam* imp. m. sg. + vent. **9** *ubbalam* G pres. 1st/3rd sg. + vent. **10** *tubbalīnni* G pres. 2nd f. sg. + *(a)nni* **11** *liblūniššu* G prec. 3rd m. pl. + vent. + *šu* **12** *ittabal* G perf. 3rd sg. **13** *ušabbalakkum* Š pres. 1st/3rd sg. + vent. + *kum* **14** *uštābil* Š perf. 1st/3rd sg. **15** *ūtaššar* D perf. 1st/3rd sg. **16** *ūtaššarū* D perf. 3rd m. pl. **17** *wuššeram* D imp. 2nd m. sg. + vent. **18** *tuwaššaršum* D pres. 2nd m. sg. + *šum* **19** *uwaššerūšu* D pret. 3rd m. pl. + *šu* **20** *wašrāta* G stat. 2nd m. sg. **21** *liwaššeranni* D prec. 3rd sg. + *anni* **22** *šūšibā-ma* Š imp. pl. + *ma* (theoretically possible: *šūšibam-ma* Š imp. m. sg. + vent. + *ma*, but the spelling would be odd) **23** *ušāšib* Š pret. 1st/3rd sg. **24** *ušēšim-ma* Š pret. 1st/3rd sg. + *-ma* **25** *šūšibanni* Š imp. m. sg. + *anni* **26** *urdam* G pret. 1st/3rd sg. + vent. **27** *līridū-ma* G prec. 3rd m. pl. + *ma* **28** *urdūnim* G pret. 3rd m. pl. + vent. **29** *iqqir* G pres. 3rd sg. **30** *waqrat* G stat. 3rd f. sg.

26.2: *ittišu ana eqlim rid* **Go down to the field with him!** m. sg. (AbB 1, 102: 11)

ana mutiša šina mārī (or dual: *mārīn*) *aldat* **She has given birth to two sons for her husband** (AbB 7, 106: 20–1)

martī aṣbat (3rd f. stat. *waṣābu*) **My gall bladder is enlarged**, i.e. **I am angry** (AbB 9, 260: 19–20)

kakkum ša ilim ana eqlim līrid **The weapon of the god should go down to the field** (AbB 4, 40: 32)

26.3: **1** *atrat* G stat. 3rd sg. f. **2** *lindaššer* D prec. 3rd sg. **3** *umaššarki* D pres. 1st/3rd sg. + *ki* **4** *umašširū* D pret. 3rd m. pl. **5** *uššer* D pret. 1st/3rd sg. or D imp. m. sg. **6** *lumaššer* D prec. 1st sg. **7** *numaššer* D pret. 1st pl. **8** *muššurat* D stat. 3rd sg. **9** *undaššer* D perf. 1st/3rd sg. (see Unit 47.10) **10** *tušēšibšu* D pret. 2nd m. sg. + *šu* or *tušeššebšu* D pres. 2nd m. sg. + *šu* **11** *ultešibanni* Š perf. 3rd sg. + *anni* **12** *lušēšib* Š prec. 1st sg. **13** *turraqī* D pres. 2nd sg. f. **14** *urruq* D stat. 3rd m. sg. **15** *nurrad* G pres. 1st pl. (also theoretically possible: D pres 1st pl., but this verb does not appear in the D system) **16** *ūrid* G pret. 1st/3rd sg. (also theoretically possible: *urrid* D pret. 1st/3rd sg., but this verb does not appear in the D system) **17** *attarda* G perf. 1st sg. + vent. **18** *ūridānim-ma* G pret. 3rd f. pl. + vent. + *ma* **19** *ridāni* G imp. pl. + vent. **20** *īqiršu* G pret. 3rd sg. + *šu* or *iqqiršu* G pres. 3rd sg. + *šu* **21** *līqir* G prec. 3rd sg. **22** *aqrat* G stat. 3rd f. sg. **23** *itta'lad* G perf. 3rd sg. **24** *tattalda* G perf. 2nd m. sg. + vent. or *tattaldā* G perf. 2nd pl. **25** *uldaššum-ma* G pret. 1st/3rd sg. + *šum* + *ma* **26** *u'alladka* G pres. 1st/3rd sg. + *ka* **27** *lubla* G prec. 1st sg. + vent. **28** *ušābila* Š pret. 1st/3rd sg. or *ušābilā* Š pret. 3rd f. pl. **29** *ultēbila* Š perf. 1st/3rd sg. or *ultēbilā* Š perf. 3rd f. pl.

26.4: *palāhu damāqa ullad niqû balāṭu [u]ttar* **Reverence** (lit. **being reverent**) **begets goodness** (lit. **being good**), **a sacrifice (to the gods) prolongs** (lit. **increases**) **life** (BWL 104: 143–4)

nāši marri alli tupšikki ēpiš dulli zābil kudurri ina elēli ulṣi hūd libbi nummur panī ubbalū ūmšun **The bearer of spade, hoe (and) earth basket, the worker** (lit. **the doer of work**) **(and) the hod carrier spend their day in song, delight, gladness of heart (and) brightness of face** (Asar. 62: 38–40) *[an]a šakān abūbi ubla libbašunu ilī rabûti* **The great gods, their hearts** (lit. **heart**, see Unit 6.13) **induced them to bring about the flood** (Gilg. XI 14)

ilqûinni-ma ina rūqi ina pî nārāti uštēšibūinni **They** (m.) **took me, and settled me far away, at the mouth of rivers** (Gilg. XI 206)

ana šunbuṭ zīm[ī]ya u ubbub ṣubātiya girra umta''ir **I have instructed the fire god to make my features shine, and to purify my garment** (Erra I 141)

eli tarqû šar māt kūsi ana šakān adê u salīmi uma''erū rakbêšun **To Taharka, king of the land of Kush, they** (m.) **sent their messengers on horseback to establish a treaty and peace** (BIWA 22: A i.123–4)

27.1: *pīka lā tenni* **Do not alter your** (m. sg.) **utterance!** (AbB 5, 2: r.2')

kīma ana kâšim-m[a] taklāk[u] atta ul tīdé **Do you** (m. sg.) **not know that it is to you whom I trust?** (AbB 5, 173: 6–8)

šamaš u marūtuk iqbû-ma kerrum šī ul ūṣi **Šamaš and Marduk spoke (through divination), so that caravan did not leave** (AbB 5, 232: 26–7)

dibbatum māttum īli'am **A lot of chatter came up to me (i.e. reached me)** (AbB 3, 2: 6)

mātum kalūša ana erēšim ittaṣi **The whole land has gone out to do the sowing** (ARM 26/2, 491: 42–3)

ṣeherni u ṣehertani bāb ēkalli ul ūṣi **Our little boy and little girl did not go out through the palace gate** (AbB 1, 134: 10–11)

nipâtika ina nurpārim šūṣi'am **Allow your** (m. sg.) **debt slaves to come out of prison!** (AbB 2, 114: 15–16)

abulla aṣâm (inf. *(w)aṣû*) *ul ele''i* **I cannot leave through the gate** (AbB 9, 146: 16–17)

awīlê ana ṣēriya šūriānim **Direct (some) men to me!** pl. (AbB 9, 113: 17–18)

anniāti gullulātika lū tīde **You** (m. sg.) **should be aware of these sins of yours** (lit. **these your sins**)**!** (AbB 11, 94: 32)

riksātiya ul enni **I will not change my contract** (AbB 12, 5: 28)

īdû qarrādūtka šarrānū ītanaddarū qabalka **The kings know your** (m. sg.) **valour (and) are constantly fearful of your onslaught**; *qabalka* could also mean **(doing) battle with you** (TN 116: 19')

uṭṭi (D pret. *eṭû*) *īn ummānāt māt šumeri u akkadi šamaš bēl dīni* **Šamaš, lord of judgment, darkened the eye of the troops of the land of Sumer and Akkad** (TN 118: 38')

27.2: *qereb murṣišu mamma ul īde* **No one understands** (lit. **anyone does not understand**) **the nature** (lit. **the inside**) **of his illness** (GBAO 2, 44: 8)

qurādu erra ṣi-ma ana ṣēri **Warrior Erra, go out to the steppe!** (Erra I 60)

28.1: *ina idišu iziz* **Stand at his side!** m. sg.; also possible: *izzīz* **He/ she stood …** (AbB 9, 219: 7–8)

anāku ana isinna allakam **I will come to Isin** (AbB 7, 77: 17–18)

dimtam ušzīz **I/he/she set up the wooden siege tower** (lit. **caused … to stand**) (ARM 26/2, 416: 5)

ana awātišu kīma awātini iziz **Assist in his matter as (in) our matter** m. sg.; also possible: *izzīz* **He/she assisted …** (AbB 4, 146: 20–1)

illik-ma ana šīmatu awīlūtim **He/she went to the destiny of mankind**, i.e. **He/she died** (Gilg. VA+BM ii.4')

dimtī u dimmatī eliki lillik **May my weeping** (lit. **tear**) **and lamenting** (lit. **lament**) **go over you** (f. sg.) (AbB 5, 160: r.7'–8')

ana bābilim allikam-ma ul āmurki mādiš azziq **I came to Babylon, but I did not see you** (f. sg.). **I was very worried** (AbB 5, 225: 9–12)

ana bāb gagîm alik **Go to the cloister gate!** m. sg.; also possible: *allik* **I went** (AbB 1, 137: 13–14) *pullusāku-ma ana mahar abiya ul allikam* **I was concerned, and so could not come to my father** (AbB 1, 100: 31–2)

inūma uštu sippir ana bābilim allikam i[tt]i a[w]īlim utul–ištar annamer **When I came from Sippar to Babylon I met Mr** (lit. **the man**) **Utul–Ištar** (AbB 7, 93: 10–12)

alik urha etiq šadâ **Go along the path, cross the mountain!** m. sg.; also possible: *allik urha ētiq šadâ* **I went along the path, I crossed the mountain** (Etana-Epos 188: 142)

ana panī ani ina uzuzzika akala ša mūti ukallūnikkum-ma lā takkal **When you** (m. sg.) **stand before Anu they will offer you** (lit. **hold to you**) **bread of death, but do not eat (it)!** (Adapa 18: 28′–30′)

28.2: *gana ē tattīl šeššet urrī u sebe mušâti* **Come, do not sleep for six days and seven nights!** m. sg. (Gilg. XI 209)

adâkka-ma panātu'a ušallakka **I will kill you** (m. sg.) **and make you** (m. sg.) **go (to the netherworld) ahead of me** (BWL 148: 85)

namrīrī aššur u ištar ishupūšu-ma illika mahhûtiš **The radiant auras of Assur and Ištar covered him, and he went berserk** (BIWA 20: A i.84)

29.1: *šarrum–kīma–ilim* **The king is like a god** (AbB 9, 95: 6)

šumgurum u qabûm ittika-ma **Persuading and talking** (i.e. **the negotiations**) **are up to** (lit. **with**) **you** (m. sg.) (AbB 11, 53: 19–20)

lū awīlum atta **Be a man!** (AbB 12, 54: 19)

mannum šumka **What** (lit. **who**) **is your name?** (Gilg. VA+BM: iv.5)

bītī bītka u kīsī kīska **My house is your** (m. sg.) **house, and my purse is your purse** (AbB 4, 152: 20)

ištu pana bītni u bītk[a] ištēn-ma **Since previous times, our house and yo[ur]** (m. sg.) **house are one** (AbB 1, 82: 5–7)

šiprum eli tašīmtika **The task is above your** (m. sg.) **reckoning** (i.e. **more than you thought**) (AbB 9, 202: 4–6)

ṣillī–marūtuk **Marduk is my protection** (AbB 8, 24: 1)

ul [a]hhūká nīnu bītāt[u]ni ul bītká **Are we not your** (m. sg.) **brothers? Are our houses not your house?** (AbB 7, 104: 12–13)

bītum šū u[l b]īt rēdîm bīt awīl ešnunna **That house is not the house of a soldier, (it) is the house of a man from** (lit. **of**) **Ešnunna** (AbB 10, 3: 9–11)

ul bītkunú **Is it not your** (m. pl.) **house?** (AbB 2, 154: 21)

šū-ma ṣalam enlil darû **The eternal image of Enlil is he** (TN 68: 18′)

29.2: *dābib nullâtiya ilu rēṣūšu* **The speaker of my calumny** (i.e. **the person who slandered me**), **god was his helper** (BWL 34: 95)

amur gulgullē ša arkûti u panûti ayyû bēl lemuttim-ma ayyû bēl usāti **Behold the skulls of low and high – which was a doer of evil and which was a doer of good?** m. sg. (BWL 148: 77–78)

atta dipārum-ma inaṭṭalū nūrka **You** (m. sg.) **are a/the torch, they see by your light** (Erra I 10)

napīssunu mūtum-ma **Their** (m.) **breath is death** (Erra I 25)

atta namṣarum-ma **You** (m. sg.) **are a sword** (Erra I 12)

30.1: *kīma ašapparakkum epuš* **Do as I will write to you** (m. sg.)**!** (AbB 3, 11: 50–1)

inūma anāku ina dannatim ša bēliya kaliāku rēdû bītī imašša'ū **While I am detained on my lord's harsh instructions, the soldiers are plundering my house** (AbB 8, 18: 4–7)

ištu ina ālini wašbu ina sartim matīma šumš[u] ul hasis **Since he has been living in our town, his name has never been mentioned in connection with a crime** (AbB 14, 144: 26–8) *nār ana sutî taṭrudam mādiš naziq* **The singer whom you** (m. sg.) **sent to the Suteans is very worried** or **He is very worried about the singer whom you sent to the Suteans** (AbB 5, 230: 7–8)

kīma kīnāti adabbubu marussi (from *maruṣ-šī*) **That I speak the truth is painful to her**, i.e. **It is painful to her that I speak the truth** (AbB 1, 28: 8–9)

kīma ša bēlī balṭu ana bēltiya-ma taklāku **I trust to my lady, just as if my lord were still alive** (AbB 1, 53: 24–5)

šumma lū ina ahhīya lū ina mār ahhī abīya mamman bītam udabbab ṭēmam gamr[am] šupram **If anyone among my brothers or my cousins** (lit. **the son(s) of the brothers of my father**) **bothers the house, write me a full[l] report!** m. sg. (AbB 14, 73: 24–8)

adi ṣehru lā namru ina ubā[n]i l[ā] talappat **As long as he is young and not (yet) fleshed out, do not touch (him) with a finger!** m. sg. (AbB 1, 139: 12′–13′)

adi lā namrat u ṣehr[e]t ina ubāni lā talappat **As long as she is not (yet) fleshed out and (still) young, do not touch (her) with a finger!** m. sg. (AbB 1, 139: 14′–15′)

kīma enšum ana dannim mahar bēliya lā iššarraku sippir kalūšu līmu[r] **May the whole of Sippar see that no weak man is given in gift to a strong man before my lord** (AbB 7, 153: 50–2)

30.2: *ašar iqabbû (iqabbi + u* or *iqabbi + ū) kaspam luddin* **I will give the silver where he/she says** or … **where they** (m. pl.) **say** (AbB 2, 105: 12–13)

mamman ša ina idišu izzazzu ula ibašši **There is no one to** (lit. **there is not anyone who can**) **stand at his side** (AbB 11, 167: 9–10)

šaptāka (dual!) *lū ṭābā kīma ina muhhiša tazzazzu* **May your** (m. sg.) **lips (i.e. your words) be sweet when you stand in her presence** (AbB 2, 141: 13–14)

kīma awât hammurapi tummurā ina panītim-ma ana ṣēr bēliya aštapram **I have written to my lord previously that Hammurapi's words are covered** (i.e. **disingenuous**) (ARM 26/2, 373: 3–4)

ṣābī ša adi ana larsa allakam u aturram ālam ušallamū īšu **I have troops which will keep the city safe until I come to Larsa and (then) return here** (AbB 8, 23: 17–20)

mali ilū ukallamūka epuš **Do everything that the gods show you!** m. sg. (ARM 10, 31: r.12′–13′)

kīma taqabbû inneppuš **It shall be done as you** (m. sg.) **command** (AbB 1, 7: 26–7)

kīma taqabbî linnepuš **May it be done as you** (f. sg.) **command** (AbB 1, 70: 20–1)

šumma atti terrišī atti-ma epšī **If you** (f. sg.) **yourself want (it), you yourself do it!** (AbB 3, 71: 6–7)

ana ṣērum-ma adannam ša iššaknu tuštētiqāninni **What is more, you** (pl.) **have caused me to pass** (i.e. **to miss**) **the deadline which had been set** (AbB 9, 19: 15–16)

30.3: *inūma ilū ibnû awīlūtam mūtam iškunū ana awīlūtim balāṭam ina qātīšunu* (dual) *iṣṣabtū* **When the gods made mankind, they apportioned death to mankind. Life they have kept** (lit. **seized**) **in their (own) hands** (Gilg. VA+BM: iii.3–5)

adi wašbāku ṣibûtka līpuš **So long as I am present, he/she should carry out your** (m. sg.) **wish** (AbB 12, 28: 13–15)

epēšum ša tēpušu damiq **The deed which you** (m. sg.) **did is/was good** (AbB 1, 56: 4)

yâšim magriātim ša ana eṣēnim lā naṭâ idbub **He/she spoke words of malice to me which were unpleasant to smell** (lit. **not fit for smelling**) (AbB 2, 115: 11–14)

ašar wašbāku ukultum ana akāliya ul ibašši **Where I am dwelling, there is no food for me to eat** (lit. **for my eating**) (AbB 5, 224: 13–16)

ina eqlim ša iddinūniāšim bāmassu mû itbalū u nīnu bariānu **In the field which they** (m.) **gave us, the (flood) water carried off half of it, and we are starving** (AbB 4, 131: 8–10)

bēlī atta ina qibīt marūtuk bānîka ašar taqabbû tammaggar **You, my lord, by the command of Marduk, your begetter, will be agreed with whatever you command** (AbB 2, 86: 14–15) *âm šani'am ša ummašu ana kâšim babālam iqbûšum ana sābītišu imtadad* **He has measured out for his female tavern keeper the other grain which his mother ordered him to bring to you** (AbB 7, 53: 11–14)

inūma kaspum imtaqta ušabbalakkim **When the silver has come to me** (lit. **fallen to me**), **I will send (it) to you** (f. sg.) (AbB 7, 36: 30–1)

30.4: *aššum ṣuhāram ana tinūr[i]m [i]ddû [a]ttunu wardam ana utūnim idiā* **Since he/she threw the boy into the oven, throw the slave into the kiln!** m. pl. (AbB 9, 197: 7–10)

mārum ša ana abi lā ugallalu ul ibašši **There is no son** (lit. **A son does not exist**) **who does not sin against his father** (AbB 6, 15: 17–19)

inūma wardum ina bītim iṣṣabtu (iṣṣabit + u) ālum išālšu-ma mār nūr–dingir-mah-ma ihsus mār asîm ul ihsus **When the slave was caught in the house the city questioned him, and he mentioned Nur–Dingir-mah, he did not mention the son of the doctor** (AbB 14, 144: 6–9)

adi ṭēmni nutarrakkum ēkallam lā tulammad **Until we send you** (m. sg.) **back our full report, do not inform the palace!** (AbB 9, 224: 10–11)

aššum alpim ša šâmam aqbûkum šumma taštāma alpam šūri'am-ma kaspam lušābilakku[m] **Regarding the ox which I told you to buy, if you** (m. sg.) **have (already) bought (it) for me** (*-a*), **have the ox sent to me, and I will have the silver brought to you** (AbB 9, 84: 25–30)

ṣubātam ana panīya šām-ma ana panīya ul tašâm mimma ul rā'imī atta ittika ul adabbub **Buy me a dress! (If) you** (m. sg.) **do not buy it for me, you do not love me at all** (lit. **you are not at all one who loves me**), **(and) I will not talk to you!** (AbB 8, 93: 18–21)

lāma ana ṣēr bēlišu illikam-ma bēlšu ulammidu libbašu ṭīb **Satisfy him before he gets to his lord and informs his lord!** m. sg. (AbB 4, 134: 19–22)

amši-ma ul aqbikum **I forgot to tell you** (m. sg.) (AbB 10, 8: 21)

šumma ṭābakkum (ṭāb + am + kum) ittiya lillik **If it's OK by** (lit. **good for**) **you** (m. sg.), **he should come with me** (AbB 14, 80: 19–20)

30.5: *mannu ilū šina ša ina māti halqū* **Who are the two gods who disappeared from the land?** (Adapa 18: 24'–5')

amāta ša aqbâkku (aqbi + am + ku) lū ṣabtāta **You should take on board the word which I said to you** (m. sg.)**!** (Adapa 18: 33'–4')

ṭēma ša aškunuka (aškun + u + ka) lā temekki **Do not neglect the instruction I imparted to you** (lit. **placed (on) you** (m. sg.))**!** (Adapa 18: 33')

ana sikkat (see Unit 6.13; pl. *sikkāt* also possible) *huršānī šaqûti u gisallât šadî pašqāte ša ana kibis amīli lā naṭû arkašunu lū ēli* **Truly, I went up after them** (m.) **(on)to the pinnacles of high tors and difficult ledges of mountains which are not suited to the tread of man** (RIMA 2, 17: iii.18–21)

ina qabli ša lalûka iṣrupu qerebka nuppiš **Ease your heart in the battle which you** (m. sg.) **so ardently wanted** (lit. **which your desire desired**) (TN 108: 28')

annû ūmu ša dām nišīka umakkaru namê qerbēti **This is the day (on) which I will drench deserts (and) fields with the blood of your** (m. sg.) **people** or **This is the day on which the blood of your people will drench deserts (and) meadows** (TN 108: 32')

ultu ahu–darû imūtu marūtuk–kudurrī–uṣur ṭēmšu ana šarri meli–šipak utīr **After Ahu–darû died, Marduk–kudurrī–uṣur returned his report to king Meli–šipak** (BBSt. 16–17: 7–11)

amīla šâšu ilū rab(b)ûtu mala ina šamê u erṣeti šumšunu zakrū aggiš līrurūšu **That man, may the great gods, as many as whose** (lit. **their**) **names are uttered** (i.e. **as many as exist**) **in heaven and earth, curse him angrily** (BBSt. 6: ii.37–8)

bīt ippušu libēl šanûm-ma **May another be master in the house which he/she builds** (BBSt. 36: 53) *adi šamû u erṣetu bašû zērūšu* (see Unit 11.9) *lihliq* **May his progeny be destroyed for as long as heaven and earth exist** (BBSt. 6: ii.60)

30.6: *gerri* (construct state of *gerru*) *annûtú īkušū alāka tahših* **Did you** (m. sg.) **need to go (by) the road (that) those ones went along?** (BWL 74: 65) (one could also read *taha-ših* (see Unit 44.13), and make the form present)

ilānī (or: *ilī*) *māti ša iznû tušallam ana šubtišunu* (see Unit 6.13) **You** (m. sg.) **shall lead the gods of the land who were angry back to their dwellings** (lit. **dwelling**) **safely** (Erra V 31)

amīlu ša sartam ippuš (for earlier *ippušu*) *šumma dīk šumma kīṣ šumma nuppul šumma ṣabit šumma ina bīt killu nadi* **The man who commits a crime is either killed, or flayed, or blinded, or caught, or thrown into jail** (BWL 146: 44–5)

ša ihṭûka-ma tuštamīt ša lā ihṭûka-ma tuštamīt **You** (m. sg.) **have killed the one who sinned against you, you have killed the one who did not sin against you** (Erra IV 106–7)

šarru ša šumī ušarbû libēl kibrāti **May the king who makes my name great rule the whole world** (Erra V 51)

amāt erra iqbû elišu iṭīb **The word which Erra spoke was pleasing to him** (Erra I 191)

mannu īdi kī šaknāku šēretka **Who knows that I bear your** (m. sg.) **punishment?** (lit. **...that I have been imposed in respect of your punishment?**) (Etana-Epos 186: 123)

mimmû ina ṣurrikun ibšû linnepuš **May whatever you wish for** (lit. **whatever came into being in your** (m. pl.) **mind**) **be done** (Asar. 82: 17)

ašar tallakī ittiki lullik **Wherever you** (f. sg.) **go, I will go with you** (BIWA 100: B v.61–2)

30.7: *sīsû tebû/tēbû ina mu[hh]i atān parê kī ēlû / kī ša rakbu-ma ina uzniša ulahhaš / u[mma m]ūru ša tullidī* (for earlier *tūlidī*) *kī yâti lū lāsim* **When a rutting stallion was mounting a she-mule** (lit. **the jenny of a mule**)**, while it was riding (her) it whispered in her ear: 'May the foal which you will have given birth to be as swift as** (lit. **a runner like**) **me'** (BWL 218: 15–17)

ē tāhuz harimtum š[ā] šāri mutūša / ištarītu ša ana ili zakrat / kulmašītu ša qerēbša ma'd[a] / ina maruštika-ma (see *marṣu(m)*) *ul inaššika / ina ṣāltika-ma elika šanṣat / palāhu u kanāša ul ibašši ittiša* **Do not marry a harlot, whose husbands are thousands, (or) a hierodule, who has been sworn to the god, (or) a *kulmašītu*-prostitute, who is often approached for sex** (lit. **whose approaching is much**)**: she will not carry you when you are distressed** (lit. **in your distress**)**, she will sneer at you when you are quarrelling** (lit. **in your quarrel**)**, reverence and submission do** (lit. **does**, see Unit 14.3) **not exist with her** (BWL 102: 72–7)

alû lemnu ša kīma birqi ittanabriqu / eṭemmu lemnu ša amīla ihhazu / gallû lemnu ša amīla imtu išaqqû / šunu mār šiprī lemnūt[u] šunu **The evil *alû*-demon who again and again flares up like lightning, the evil ghost who takes hold of a man, the evil *gallû*-demon who gives a man poison to drink – they are evil messengers, they are!** (GBAO 2, 46: 4–10)

31.1: *miqtum imqutam-[m]a ša ana asîm anaddinu ul īšu* ***miqtu*-disease has fallen on me, and I do not have that which I can give the doctor**, i.e. ***miqtu*-disease has befallen me, and I have nothing to give the doctor** (AbB 10, 55: 15–17)

bēlī ša elišu ṭābu līpuš **May my lord do that which is pleasing to** (lit. **good upon**) **him, i.e. My lord should do as he pleases** (ARM 26/2, 479: 23–4)

ša taqabbû lūpušakkum **I shall do for you** (m. sg.) **what** (lit. **that which**) **you** (m. sg.) **command** (AbB 7, 171: 17)

ša elišu kišpī iddû iddâk (N pres. *dâku*) **The one who accused him of sorcery** (lit. **the one who threw sorcery upon him**) shall be put to death; also possible: **The one who was accused of sorcery** (lit. **the one upon whom 'they' threw sorcery**) **shall be put to death** (CH § 2)

ša šurqam ina qātišu (or *qātīšu*, dual) *imhuru iddâk* **The one who received the stolen goods in his hands (or hands) shall be put to death** (CH § 6) *bītum ša kaliāku bīt dannatim* **The house where** (lit. **(in) which**) **I am detained is a house of hardship** (AbB 2, 83: 8)

31.2: *ālu ša kakkašu lā dannu nakru ina pan abullišu ul ippaṭṭar* **A city whose weapon is not strong – the enemy will not be dispelled from its gate** (BWL 245: 53–7)

ša šukṣuru (Š stat. + *-u*) *tapaṭṭar* **You** (m. sg.) **release the one who was tightly bound** (BWL 134: 129)

ša ana šarrānī abbīya išūṭū-ma ētappalū (Gtn pret. *apālu*) *zērāti ina qibīt aššur bēliya ina qātīya immanû* **By command of Assur, my lord, the ones who had despised the kings my fathers and replied (to them) in hostile fashion were delivered into my hands** (Asar. 57: v.3–4)

šarrānī āšibūt tâmti ša dūrānīšunu tâmtum-ma edû šalhûšun ša kīma narkabti eleppa rakbū kūm sīsê ṣandū parrisānī palhiš ultanapšaqū **The kings who dwell in the sea, whose fortification walls are the sea, and whose outer walls are waves, who ride the ship instead of the chariot (and) harness boatmen instead of horses, were fearfully suffering constant anguish** (Asar. 57: iv.82–5)

abdī–milkuttī šar ṣidunni lā pālih bēlūtiya lā šēmû zikir šaptīya (dual) *ša eli tâmtim gallatim ittaklu-ma* (N preterite) *iṣlû nīr aššur ṣidunnu āl tuklātišu ša qereb tâmtim nadû abūbiš aspun* **Abdī–milkuttī, king of Sidon, non-fearer of my lordship, non-listener of the utterance of my lips** (i.e. **who did not fear my lordship, who did not heed the utterance of my lips**), **who trusted to the rolling sea and threw off the yoke of Assur – Sidon, the city of his trust, which is situated in the middle of the sea, I flattened like the Flood** (Asar. 48: 65–9)

ša igigallašu kakkašu ṣāba šuātu ikmû ikšudu ināru ina narê ul išṭur **The one whose wisdom (and) weapon captured, defeated and killed that army did not inscribe (his victory) on a stele** (Akkade 306 and 337–8: 28–9)

simirria ubān šadî rabītu ša kīma šēlūt šukurri zaqpat-ma eli huršāni šubat bēlet–ilī šaqât rēšī
ša eliš rēšāša šamāmi endā-ma šaplānu šuršūša šukšuddū qereb aralli
u kīma ṣēr nūni idi ana idi mēteqa lā išât-ma (stative of *išû*) *paniš u arkiš šumruṣu mūlûša*
ina ahīša harrī natbāk šadê iqdudū-ma ana itaplus (Ntn inf. *palāsu*, construct state) *niṭil īnī šitpurat puluhtu* (The following translation is fairly literal, and does not aim to do justice to the passage's beauty) **Simirria – the great mountain pinnacle which sticks up like a spear blade and which is higher at** (lit. **in respect of**) **the top than the mountains (which are) home to** (lit. **of**) **Belet–ili, whose peak presses into the heavens above, and whose roots are driven right into the netherworld below, and (which) like the back of a fish has no passage (from) side to side, and whose ascent is very difficult afore and aback, on whose two sides channels and mountain waterways plunge down, and (which) at the repeated inspecting of the gaze of the eyes is shrouded in fearsomeness** (TCL 3: 18–21)

32.1: *šuprā-ma arkatam liprusūnikkunūšim* (*liprusū* + *nim* + *kunūšim*) **Write, so that they** (m.) **will establish the facts for you** (m. pl.)**!** (or Unit 14.16) (AbB 9, 111: 11′–12′)

elqe-ma (*leqû* in verbal couple) *ana šībūt awātim ṣubātī ašruṭ* **I undertook to tear my garment in testimony of the matter** (ARM 26/2, 323: 21–2)

ša panīni ī nippalis-ma ṭēmam gamra ī nišpurakku (*nišpur* + *am* + *ku*) **We will see what is before us, so we can send you** (m. sg.) **a full report** (AbB 7, 167: 11–12)

ištu inanna-ma dabāba dummuqam ittišu dubum-ma (*dubub* + *ma*) *lā itâr-ma ṣehrī lā iṣabbat* **From now on speak nicely** (lit. **speak a very nice speaking**) **to** (lit. **with**) **him, so that he will not seize my child again!** m. sg. (AbB 10, 181: 17–21)

kīma ṣuhārtum šī mītat qibišum-ma (or *qibêššumma*, *qibi* + *am* + *šum* + *ma*; the letter is from Mari; see Unit 47.1) *lū īde* **Tell him that that girl has died, so that he will know** (ARM 10, 106: 18–19) *ana adan iššaprakkum tulappatam-ma panūka ul ibbabbalū* **If you** (m. sg.) **are delayed beyond the time limit he/she wrote to you, you will not be forgiven** (AbB 1, 84: 25–7)

arhiš apulšu-ma nēmettam elika lā iraššī **Answer him quickly, so that he will not complain about you** (lit. **acquire a cause for complaint against you**) m. sg. (AbB 4, 54: 19–20)

mīnam tēpušanni-ma ṭaplātika adabbub **What did you** (m. sg.) **do to me, that I should slander you** (lit. **speak your slander**)**?** (AbB 5, 138: 12′–14′)

ul atâr-ma ul ašapparakku **I will not write to you** (m. sg.) **again** (AbB 14, 105: 28–9)

ana ayyî tattakkal (N pres. *takālu*) *namrāṣi-ma nišīka teṭṭer* **In which difficult terrain will you** (m. sg.) **trust to save** (lit. **so that you can save**) **your people?** (TN 108: 24′)

gula azugallatu bēltu rabītu simma lazza ina zumrišu lišabši-ma šarka u dāma kīma mê lirtammuk **May Gula, the great physician, the great lady, bring a persistent wound into being in his body, so that he is constantly covered in pus and blood as if he were bathing in water** (lit. **so that he constantly bathes in pus and blood like** (**in**, see Unit 13.4) **water**) (BBSt. 7: ii.29–31)

33.1: *atti libbaki [i]mtanarraṣ* **You** (f. sg.)**, your heart is always sore!** (AbB 7, 22: 6)

ūmišam abtanakki **I weep every day** (AbB 11, 14: 18)

anniātim taštanapparī **You** (f. sg.) **keep on writing these things to me** (AbB 9, 61: 13)

ūmišam ina esagil aktanarrabakkum **I pray for you** (m. sg.) **in the Esagil temple on a daily basis** (AbB 2, 89: 9–10)

kīma tagdanammilanni gimlanni **Be kind to me, as you** (m. sg.) **are so often kind to me!** (AbB 13, 149: 25–6)

attunu awâtim tuktanattamā-ma ana ṣēriya ul tašapparānim **You** (m. pl.) **are always covering matters up, and do not write (them) to me** (AbB 9, 113: 12–14)

attanaggiš kīma hābilim qabaltu ṣēri **I wandered like a trapper through the midst of the wild** (Gilg. VA+BM ii.11′)

awâtuka damqātum iktanaššadāninni **Your** (m. sg.) **good words are forever reaching me** (AbB 9, 174: 22–3)

ana ṭēmi ša tašpurīm mādiš ahdu mahar ištar u tašmētum aktanarrabakkim u ālum kalûšu ṭēmam šuāti išme-ma ikarrabakkim **I rejoiced greatly at the news which you** (f. sg.) **wrote me. I constantly pray before Ištar and Tašmetum for you, and the whole city heard this news and is praying for you** (AbB 7, 129: 5′–12′)

mahar awīlê [s]ābî ṭaplātiya taddanabbubī **You** (f. sg.) **are forever slandering me** (lit. **speaking my slander**) **before the gentlemen (and) brewers** (AbB 5, 138: 4′–5′)

33.2: *mūtam ša ātanaddaru ay āmur* **May I not see the death which I am always fearing**; also possible: *mutam* **the husband whom …** (Gilg. VA+BM: ii.13′)

ištu ūmim ša ṭēmam šâtu ešmû yamṣihatnu ina ēkallim-ma ibtanayyat (Gtn *bâtu*) **Since the day** (**on**, see Unit 31.3) **which I heard this news, Yamṣihatnu has been spending the night in the palace!** (ARM 26/2, 495: 15–17)

ša tēteneppušī šunātuya ittanabbalānim **My dreams keep on bringing me what you** (f. sg.) **are doing** (AbB 14, 53: 27–28)

napištī tattakkis **You** (m. sg.) **kept on slitting my throat** (AbB 3, 38: 21)

ištu mu 3 kam (Bab. reading uncertain; *šalāš šanātim?*) *aššum bilat eqliya u rikis bītiya aštanapparakkum-ma ul âm ul kaspam tušabbalam* **For the last three years I have been writing to you** (m. sg.) **again and again about the yield of my field and the contract on** (lit. **of**) **my house, but you have neither grain nor silver brought to me** (AbB 7, 155: 1–6)

bīt [a]ntum tahtanassas **You** (m. sg.) **are always reminiscing about the temple of [A]ntum** (AbB 8, 5: 7) *eqelka u bītka uhallaq ana bītiya-[ma]* (-ma is emphatic) *ana šitarruqim qātam taštakan* **I** (or: **he/she**) **will destroy your** (m. sg.) **house and your field. (For) you have set (your) hand to repeatedly robbing my house** (AbB 10, 178: 6–10)

ana itazzuzzi ana šâšim ahka lā tanandi (from *tanaddi*, with nasalization) **Do not neglect to stand by him from time to time** m. sg. (AbB 9, 1: 12–13)

awīltum awâtim mādiš uktabbit ana ṣērum-ma ūmišam ritaqqudim ina rutešším qaqqadni mādiš uqtallil **The lady has greatly aggravated matters. In addition to prancing about daily, she has greatly dishonoured us through repeated inconsiderateness** (AbB 14, 189: 10–15)

kīma ninurta ana nīš kakkīšu ultanapšaqā kalîš kibrātu **At the raising of his weapons (i.e. when he raises his weapons), the world is altogether convulsed again and again as at Ninurta('s)** (TN 68: 15′)

kīma kalbi libta"ita ina rebīt ālišu **May he/she spend night after night in his town square, like a dog**; also possible: *libta"itā* **May they** (f.) **spend night after night in his town square, like dog(s)** (BBSt. 7: ii.24)

33.3: *epšēt ina mātāti nakrāti ēteppušu ina šipir urrakūti ēsiqa qerebša* **Inside it, with sculptor's craft, I carved (reports of) the deeds which I accomplished in foreign lands** (Asar. 62: 28–9)

miqitti būli ištanakka[n] **Again and again he/she brings about deaths among** (lit. **death of**) **cattle** (GBAO 2, 34: 24)

ina šahāti lā tattanaššabšu **Do not sit next to him in the corner on a regular basis!** m. sg. (GBAO 2, 84: 32)

tētenebbir tâmatum rapaštum šadilta **You** (m. sg.) **keep on crossing the broad wide sea** (BWL 128: 35)

[at]ta ana ilim-ma suppê šutaqrib **[Y]ou, present prayers to the god on a regular basis!** m. sg. (BWL 108: 11)

ūmišamma imdanahhara šamaš **Day after day he/she appeals to Šamaš** (Etana-Epos 186: 121) (or 3 f. pl.)

šatta ana šatti bitakkâ taltīmīššu **You** (f. sg.) **have determined as his destiny constant weeping, year by year** (Gilg. VI 47)

ša ūmi attaṭṭal būnāšu **I studied** (lit. **looked repeatedly at**) **the weather's appearance** (Gilg. XI 92)

etana ūmišamma imtahhara šamaš **Day after day, Etana appealed to Šamaš** (Etana-Epos 186: 131)

uptahhir ištar kezrēti šamhāti u harmāti **Ištar gradually assembled the *kezertu*-prostitutes, the voluptuous ones, and the harlots** (Gilg. VI 158)

34.1: *awīlû šunu lā uddabbabū* **Those men should not be harassed!** (AbB 10, 13: 22)

ittišu tiṣbutāku **I am having a lawsuit with him** (AbB 14, 140: 43)

kurummatī šutamṭât (Št stat. *maṭû*) **My food ration has been diminished** (AbB 9, 160: 19)

qaqqadātikunu šutēmidā **Put your heads together!** pl. (ARM 26/2, 394: 13–14)

anāku u ahhūya ana zittim tiṣbutānu **My brothers and I are locked in litigation about the division (of our parents' estate)** (AbB 5, 223: 7–9)

kalbatum ina šutēpuriša huppudūtim ūlid **Through her hurrying about, the bitch gave birth to blind ones** (i.e. **blind puppies**) (ARM 1, 5: 11–13)

bītam ana panīya šutassiq **Get the house in order before my arrival!** m. sg. (AbB 9, 137: 29)

ul ibbašši ṭūbtu balu šitnuni **Peace does not come into being without strife** (TN 90: 16′)

lubāra ukallūnikkum-ma litbaš **They will offer you** (m. sg.) **a garment, so clothe yourself (with it)!** (Adapa 18: 31′–2′)

šamna ukallūnikkum-ma piššaš **They will offer you** (m. sg.) **oil, so anoint yourself (with it)!** (Adapa 18: 32′)

34.2: *litpatā* (or *litpata*) *imat mūti* **Smear yourselves** (or: **yourself**, m. sg. + vent.) **with deadly poison!** (Erra I 7)

ubtallil kī immeri ina tabāštaniya **I was smeared with my (own) excrement like a sheep** (BWL 44: 107)

ūmišamma ilka kitrab **Pray to your** (m. sg.) **god every day!** (BWL 104: 135)

abī ē tuštānih **My father, do not weary yourself!** (En. el. II 115)

ana būli kitpad erēša hissas **Be assiduously mindful of the cattle, and ponder sowing!** m. sg. (BWL 108: 14)

lemnēti ē tātami damiqta tizkar **Do not speak evil things, say something good!** m. sg. (BWL 104: 128)

gēr būli labba ša tahsusu gana bitru gillat nēšu īpušu petâssu haštum **Come, look carefully at the enemy of the cattle, the lion, whom you mentioned – the sin which the lion committed has opened a pit for him** m. sg. (BWL 74: 61–2)

lištapših šērtaka kabitta **May your** (m. sg.) **heavy punishment be alleviated** (AfO 19, 57: 59)

urra ūtakkak mūša inahhi[s] ina ṣērišu itkušū (Gt stat. *akāšu*) *rēmu unnī[nu]* **By day he scratches himself, by night he collapses, mercy and prayer have gone away from him** (AfO 19, 52: 148–9)

marūtuk eli maqtūti taštakkan gimilla **Marduk, you grant favour to the fallen** (AfO 19, 65: 15)

amur šuttatu qerebša bitri **Look at the pit, inspect its inside!** m. sg. (Etana-Epos 188: 143)

lū mindudā (*mitdudā* → *middudā* → *mindudā*) *minâtuša* **Her measurements should be commensurate with each other** (Gilg. XI 29)

34.3: *ikkud libbašu iršâ naquttu / napištašu panuššu ul īqir-ma / ihšuha mītūtu / ana kizê ramanišu iqbi-ma / umma rassibanni ina kakki / šū kizûšu ina patar šibbišunu / uptattihū ahāmiš* **His heart throbbed (with fear), he got desperate** (lit. **he acquired a critical condition**)**, and his life was worthless in his eyes. He desired death. To his own groom he said 'Smite me with a weapon!'. He (and) his groom stabbed each other with the swords from** (lit. **of**) **their belts** (BIWA 59: vii.31–7)

Glossary

This glossary is as an aid to translating the examples and exercises, not a guide to all the meanings and usages of the words listed. (In particular, no indications are given of the periods in which the words occur; many verbs are attested in more systems than are indicated here; and some words have more meanings than are given here.) For more detailed information about Babylonian and Assyrian vocabulary, the reader is referred to the dictionaries (see Unit 42).

Thanks are expressed to the editors of *A Concise Dictionary of Akkadian* and the *Chicago Assyrian Dictionary*, from whom many felicitous renderings of Babylonian words into English were borrowed.

Notes

For the bracketed *m* ('mimation') see Unit 6.11. Words which are listed without mimation never display it.

Some words which begin with *a* in Middle and Standard Babylonian are listed under *(w)*, because they begin with *w* in Old Babylonian.

s, *ṣ*, *š*, *t* and *ṭ* are all different letters.

For the purposes of alphabetical ordering it does not matter whether a vowel is short, long or contracted; the glottal stop (ʾ) is disregarded altogether.

abāku(m) 1 *(a/u)* **G** to lead away
abāku(m) 2 *(a/u)* **N** to be thrown down
abāru(m) *(i)* **G** to embrace **D** to accuse
abātu(m) 1 *(a/u)* **G** to destroy, **D** to annihilate
abātu(m) 2 *(a/u)* **G** to run away from **N** to run away
abnu(m) m. and f. stone
abru(m) (part or type of) wing
abšānu(m) yoke
abu(m) 1, pl. *abbū* or *abbû* father
abu(m) 2 (the fifth Babylonian month); see Reading C, Tip
abūbu(m) flood, deluge
abullu(m) f. gateway, (city) gate
adad, addu(m) (name of the storm god)
adannu(m) deadline, appointed time
adāru(m) 1 *(a/u)* **G** to be(come) dark **N** to become dark
adāru(m) 2 *(a/u)* **G** to fear **Gtn** iter.
addaru(m) (the twelfth Babylonian month); see Reading C, Tip
adi until, so long as, for as long as (prep. and subordinator)
adīni until now
ādiru(m) one who fears, fearer
adû pl. only: treaty
agāgu(m) *(a/u)* **G** to be(come) furious (stat. *agug*) **D** stat. to be utterly furious **Š** caus.
aggiš angrily
agû(m) 1 crown
agû(m) 2 wave
agurru(m) brick
ahāmiš each other (this word originated as an adverb in *-iš*, but can be used as a noun; it has no case ending)
ahātu(m) f. sister
ahāzu(m) *(a/u)* **G** to take on board, to take possession of, to marry **Š** stat. to be informed of (acc.)
ahhūtu(m) f. brotherhood, brotherliness
ahītu(m) surroundings
ahu(m) 1 arm; *a. nadû(m)* to throw down the arm, i.e. to be idle, to be negligent *ana* about
ahu(m) 2, pl. *ahhū* or *ahhû* brother
ahû, f. *ahītu(m)* foreign
akalu(m) (loaf of) bread
akālu(m) *(a/u)* **G** to eat
akāšu(m) *(u)* **G** to go (along) **Gt** to go away
akkadû(m) Akkad (*māt a.* 'land of Akkad' is an Assyrian term for Babylonia)
akû(m) weak

alaktu(m) f. way, gait, conduct; *a. parāsu(m)* to block the way
alāku(m) **G** to go (+ vent. to come, see Unit 19.5), to go along (+ acc.) **Gtn** to go repeatedly, back and forth, to and fro **Š** caus.
āle where?
āliku(m) goer
alīlu(m) powerful
allu(m) hoe
alpu(m) ox
ālu(m) town, city
alû(m) (a kind of demon)
amāru(m) (*a/u*) **G** to see, to find, to read, to inspect **N** to be checked, to meet with (*itti*) s/o
amātu(m) see *awātu(m)*
amēlu(m) see *awīlu(m)* and explanation at end of Unit 7.2
amēlūtu(m) see *awīlūtu(m)* and explanation at end of Unit 7.2
ammīni(m) see *ana mīni(m)*
amšāli yesterday
amtu(m) f. female slave, slave girl
ana to(wards), for, against (prep.)
ana libbi into (prep.)
ana mīni(m), ammini(m) why? (lit. for what?, like French *pourquoi*, Italian *perché* and German *warum*)
ana muhhi onto (prep.)
ana qereb into (prep.)
ana ṣēr to (lit. to the back of); *ana ṣēriya* to me (prep.)
anā I (by-form of *anāku*, Unit 37)
anāhu(m) to be tired (*a*) **Št** to weary oneself
anāku I
annû(m), f. *annītu(m)* this
antu(m) f. (name of a goddess)
anu(m) (name of a god)
anumma now
anunnakū (a group of gods)
anzanunzû (pl. only?) (poetic term for the gods of the underworld)
anzû(m) (a mythical bird)
apālu(m) (*a/u*) **G** to answer
apāru(m) **D** to put X (acc.) on head of Y (acc.)
apâtu(m) f. pl. only: numerous
apiltu(m) f. payment
apkallu(m) sage
aplu(m) heir
appu(m) nose
apsû(m) subterranean cosmic waters (see Unit 31.2, Tip box)
aptu(m) f. window
apu(m) reed-bed
aqqullu(m) pl. *-ātu(m)* axe
arahsamna(m) (the eighth Babylonian month); see Reading C, Tip
arāhu(m) **D** to hasten
arallu netherworld
arāmu(m) (*i*) **G** to cover
arāru(m) (*a/u*) **G** to curse
ardatu(m) f. young woman
arhiš quickly
arka, arki see *(w)arki*
armu(m) mountain goat
arnu(m) crime, punishment, fault
arūtu(m) f.? (clay) tube, pipe
asakku(m) (a type of demon)
aslu(m) (a type of sheep)
asû(m) physician
ašar where(ever) (subordinator) (see Unit 36.5)
ašarēdu(m) foremost, pre-eminent (see Unit 6.16)
ašarēdūtu(m) f. pre-eminence
ašāšu(m) **G** to be troubled **D** stat.: to be menacing
āšibu(m) someone who dwells; *āšib X* dweller of X, i.e. who dwells in X
ašlu(m) f. measuring line
ašru(m) place
aššatu(m) f. wife
aššu(m) because of, about (a topic), for the sake of (prep.); because (subordinator); *aššu(m) kīam* this/that is why
aššur Assur (the chief god of Assyria; also the traditional capital of Assyria)
atānu(m) f. female donkey, jenny
athûtu(m) f. (business) partnership
atmû(m) speech
atû(m) doorman
awātu(m), amātu(m) f. word, matter
awīltu(m) f. lady
awīlu(m), amīlu(m) (OB pl. *awīlû*, from stem *awīlā-*) man
awilūtu(m), amīlūtu(m) f. mankind
awû(m) **G** to speak **Gt** to speak to each other
ayyābu(m) enemy
ayyaru(m) (the second Babylonian month); see Reading C, Tip
ayyû (m), f. *ayyītu(m)* which (one)?
azugallatu(m) f. great female physician (epithet of Gula, goddess of healing)

babālu(m) see *(w)abālu(m)*
bābili(m) Babylon (understood in antiquity as *bāb ili(m)* gate of the god)
bābu(m) gate; lid (of box); *bāba(m) (w)aṣû(m)* to leave, to go out, by a gate
bakû(m) (*i*) **G** to weep **Gtn** iter.

balālu(m) **D** to cover, to smear *ina* with, to mix **Dt** pass.
balāṭu(m) (*u*) **G** to be alive, to be healthy **D** to keep (s/o) alive, to provide for (s/o), to revive (s/o)
baltu(m) 1 (a kind of thorny bush)
baltu(m) 2 pride
balṭu(m) alive, living
balṭūtu(m) f. the condition/state of being well
balu(m) without (prep.)
bâlu(m) (*ā*) **G** to supplicate
bamātu(m) f., pl. only open country; *b. šadî* open country of the mountain, i.e. mountain country, mountain slopes
bāmtu(m) f. half
banû(m) 1 (*i*) **G** to build, to beget
banû(m) 2 friendly (face)
baqāmu(m) (*a/u*) **G** to pluck **D** = G **N** to be plucked
barāqu(m) (*i*) **G** to flash, to shine **Ntn** repeatedly to flare up **Š** to cause to shine
barārī (adv.) at dusk
barû(m) (*i*) **G** to see, to look at **Gt** to look carefully at, to inspect **Š** to cause (s/o) to see, to experience (s/th)
bārû(m) diviner (super-lit. seer)
bâru(m) 1 (*ā*) **G** to hunt, to catch
bâru(m) 2 (*ū*) **D** to confirm, to convict **Dt** be established precisely
bâru(m) 3 (*ā*) **G** to rebel against, to stir up
bašālu(m) (*a*, also *i*) **G** to become ripe, cooked **Š** to cook (s/th), to glaze (bricks)
bâšu(m) (*ā*) **G** to be(come) ashamed **D** to dishonour
bašû(m) (*i*) **G** to exist, to be (see Unit 29.1) **N** to come into being **Š** to bring into being
batāqu(m) (*a/u*) **G** to cut off
bâtu(m) (*i*) **G** to spend the night **Gtn** iter.
baṭālu(m) (*i*) **G** to cease
ba'ūlātu(m) f. pl. only: people
bēltu(m) f. lady
belû(m) (*i*) **G** to come to an end **D** to extinguish
bêlu(m) (*ē*) Ass. also *pêlu(m)* **G** to rule
bēlu(m) lord, master, owner
bēlūtu(m) f. lordship
berîš hungrily
berû(m) (*e*) **G** to starve
bēru(m) distant
biblu(m) pl. *-ātu(m)*; thing(s) brought; *b. libbi(m)* heart's desire (lit. brought thing of the heart)
biltu(m), f. tribute, rent yield – related to *(w)abālu(m)*
biri- between (prep.); *birini* between us, *ina birišunu* in their midst
birīt (prep.) between
birītu(m) in-between place; *ina b.* meanwhile
birku(m) knee; dual also: loins
birqu(m) lightning
bīru(m) 1 extispicy
bīru(m) 2 double hour; also a measure of distance (over 10 km), sometimes translated 'league'
biṣṣūru(m) vulva
bītu(m) m., f. pl. *bītātu(m)* house(hold), temple
bubutu(m), *bubūtu(m)* f. hunger
bulṭu(m) life, (medical) remedy
būlu(m) cattle
būnu(m) appearance; pl. face – related to *banû(m)*
būru(m) hunger – related to *berû(m)*
bussuru(m) **D** to deliver good news to
būšu(m), *bušû(m)* goods, property – related to *bašû(m)*
bu''û(m) **D** to look for, to chase

da'(a)tu(m) f. information; *da'at* (can be written *dahat*) *X šâlu(m)* to ask after X
dababu(m) (*u*) **G** to talk, to speak **Gtn** iter. **D** to harass, to pester **Dt** pass.
dābibu(m) speaker
dadmū pl. only: villages, the inhabited world
dādu(m) allure, sex appeal
dagan (name of a god; indeclinable)
dah(a)tu(m) see *da'(a)tu(m)*
dā'išu(m) thresher
dâku(m) (*ū*) **G** to kill **N** to be put to death **Š** to cause s/o to kill
dalāhu(m) (*a/u*) **G** to stir up, to disturb **N** to be disturbed
dalālu(m) (*a/u*) **G** to praise
dalhu(m) muddied
dalpu(m) weary
daltu(m) f. door
damāqu(m) (*i*) **G** to be(come) good **D** to make good, to do good (to s/o, dative)
damqu(m), f. *damiqtu(m)*, *damqatu(m)* good, good-quality, excellent, beautiful, gracious; f. as noun: goodness; f. pl. also: good deeds
dāmu(m) blood
danānu(m) (*i*) **G** to be(come) strong, stat. (OB *dān*) also: to be difficult
dannu(m), f. *dannatu(m)* strong, mighty; f. as noun: i) hardship, harshness, harsh instructions ii) fortress
dânu(m) (*ī*) *dīna d.* to give a verdict
dapnu(m) aggressive
dāriš eternally; *dāriš ūmi* forever (see Unit 36.3)
darû(m), f. *darītu(m)* everlasting
dāṣtu(m) f. disrespect
dâṣu(m) (*ā*) **G** to disrespect
dâšu(m) (*ī*) **G** to thresh
dawdû(m) defeat *d. dâku(m)* bring about a defeat

dayyānu(m) judge; *dayyān dīnāti(m)* decider of verdicts
dekû(m) (*e*, also *i*) **G** to rouse **Š** to incite (heart to do something)
dibbatu(m) f. chatter
dimmatu(m) f. lamentation
dimtu(m) 1 f. (siege) tower
dimtu(m) 2 f. tear
dīnu(m) pl. *-ātu(m)* judgment, verdict, trial
dipāru(m) pl. *-ātu(m)* torch
dirratu(m) f. lash
dullu(m) work, task
dummuqu(m) 1 great goodness
dummuqu(m) 2 very nice
dumqu(m) goodness, good deeds
dunnu(m) strength, hardness
duranki (a Sumerian name of Nippur, literally 'bond of heaven and earth'; indeclinable)
dūru(m) 1 (city) wall
dūru(m) 2 eternity – related to *darû(m)*
du'ūzu(m) (the fourth Babylonian month); see Reading C, Tip

ea (name of the god of wisdom)
ebbu(m) pure, clean; as noun: emissary
ebēbu(m) (*i*) **D** to cleanse
ebēhu(m) (*i*) **G** to gird
ebēru(m) (*i*) **G** to cross **Gtn** iter. **Š** to cause/allow to cross
ebēṭu(m) (*i*) **G** to swell up
ebūru(m) harvest (time)
edēdu(m) (*u*) **G** to be(come) sharp
edēlu(m) **D** to shut
edû(m) 1 **G** to know (irregular; see Unit 27)
edû(m) 2 wave
ēduššu see *(w)ēdu(m)*
e'ēlu(m) (*i*) **G** to bind
egû(m) (*i*, also *u*) **G** to be negligent *ana* about
ēkallu(m) f. palace
ekēku(m) (*i*) **G** to scratch **Dt** to scratch o/s
ekēlu(m) (*i*) **G** to be(come) dark
ekēmu(m) (*i*) **G** to steal (s/th, acc. from s/o, acc.) **N** to be stolen
ekletu(m) f. darkness
ekur (the main temple of Enlil in Nippur; indeclinable)
elamtu(m) f. Elam (part of ancient Iran)
elēlu(m) cheerful song
elēnû(m), f. *elēnītu(m)* upper
eleppu(m) f. ship
elēṣu(m) (*i*) **G** to swell (of heart) **D** = G
eli, *elu* upon, over, above, against, -er … than (prep.)
eliš (or *elîš* or *ēliš*) above (adv.)
ellu(m), f. *elletu(m)* pure
elu see *eli*
elû(m), f. *elītu(m)* upper (sea)
elû(m) (*i*) **G** to go up, to mount **D** to raise
elūlu(m) (the sixth Babylonian month); see Reading C, Tip
ēma (subordinator) wherever
emēdu(m) (*i*) **G** to come into contact with, to lean on, to impose (X, acc., on Y, acc.) **N** to meet (in battle), to seek refuge *ina* in, to jump *eli* onto **Št** to put together
emēmu(m) (*i*) **G** to be(come) hot
enēqu(m) (*i*) **G** to suck
enēšu(m) (*i*) **G** to be(come) weak; for use in verbal couple see Unit 32.4
enšu(m) weak
enû(m) **G** to change (s/th)
enūma see *inūma*
enzu(m) f. nanny goat
eperu(m) see *epru(m)*
epēru(m) **Št** to hurry about
epēšu(m) (*u*) **G** to do, to make, to treat, to take (omens) (stat. *epuš*) **Gtn** iter. **N** to be done, to be made (See Unit 24.1, Tip.)
epištu(m), *epuštu(m)* f. deed
ēpišu(m) f. *ēpištu(m)* doer; f. also means: bewitcher
epru(m), *eperu(m)* earth, earthworks
eqlu(m), f. pl. *eqlētu(m)* field
erbe f. *erbetta* four
erēbu(m) (*u*) **G** to enter (with *ana*) **Š** to cause/allow to enter
erēšu(m) 1 (*i*) **G** to sow
erēšu(m) 2 (*i*) **G** to want, to request (s/th, acc. from s/o, acc.)
eribû(m) locust
erretu(m) f. curse
erṣetu(m) f. the Earth, the netherworld, earth
eršu(m) 1 bed
eršu(m) 2, f. *erištu(m)* wise
erû(m) 1 copper
erû(m) 2 eagle
esagil (the main temple of Marduk, in Babylon; indeclinable)
esēhu(m) (*i*) **G** to gird
esēqu(m) (*i*) **G** to carve
eṣemṣēru(m) backbone (see Unit 6.16)
eṣemtu(m) f. bone
eṣēnu(m) (*i*) **G** to smell (s/th)
ešēru(m) **Št** to lead aright
eširtu(m) f. (pl. *ešrētu(m)*) shrine
eššu(m), f. *eduštu(m)* new
etelliš like a lord
etellu(m) nobleman
etēqu(m) (*i*) **G** to pass (across) **Gtn** iter. **Š** to cause (s/o) to pass (across)

eṭemmu(m) ghost, spirit
eṭēru(m) (*i*) **G** to save
eṭlu(m) pl. *-ūtu(m)* (young) man
eṭû(m) (*i*) **G** to be(come) dark **D** to make dark
ezēbu(m) (*i*) **G** to leave **Š** to save (lit. to help to leave)
ezziš angrily
ezzu(m), f. *ezzetu(m)* angry

gagû(m) convent
galādu(m), galātu(m) (*u*) **G** to tremble, to be(come) afraid
gallābu(m) barber
gallu(m), f. *gallatu(m)* rolling
gallû(m) (a type of demon)
gamālu(m) (*i*) **G** to spare (s/o, acc.), to be kind to **Gtn** iter.
gamāru(m) (*a/u*) **G** to complete, to finish, to use up **Š** stat. to be in complete control of
gāmilu(m) helper
gamru(m) complete
gana come (on)!
gapāšu(m) (*u*) **G** to swell up, to become proud
gapšu, f. *gapuštu(m)* swollen, vast
gašru(m) powerful
gerru(m), girru(m), kerru(m) m. and f. campaign, caravan, journey
gērû(m) enemy
gīdu(m) gristle
gillatu(m) sin
gimillu(m) requital, favour; *g. šakānu(m)* to do a favour *eli* for, to
gimiltu(m) f. favour
gimru(m) all, entirety; *gimir X* all of X, all X, the whole of X
ginâ regularly
gipāru(m) yard, shed
girra (name of the fire god; indeclinable)
girru(m) see *gerru(m)*
gisallû(m) pl. *-ātu(m)* ledge
gišparru(m) snare
gugallu(m) canal controller
gula (name of the goddess of healing)
gulgullu(m) skull
gullubu(m) **D** to shave
gullultu(m) f. sin, misdeed
gullulu(m) **D** to sin *ana* against
gurunnu(m) f. pl. *-ātu(m)* heap

habābu(m) (*u*) **G** to croon *eli* over s/o
habālu(m) (*i/ī*) **G** to do wrong, violence to **N** to be badly treated
habāšu(m) (*u*) **G** to be(come) swollen
habātu(m) (*a/u*) **G** to carry off by force
habbātu(m) robber
hābilu(m) trapper
habru(m) noisy
hadû(m) (*u*) **G** to be(come) glad
hakāmu(m) (*i*) **G** to understand
halālu(m) 1 (*a/u*) **G** to lock (s/o) up
halālu(m) 2 (*a/u*) **G** to creep
halāpu(m) (*u*) **G** to slip into **D** to clothe (s/o, acc.) with (s/th, acc.) **N** to clothe oneself with
halāqu(m) (*i*) **G** to vanish, to be destroyed, to escape **D** to destroy
halṣu(m) district
hamāmu(m) (*a/u*) **G** to collect (in oneself)
hamāṭu(m) (u) **Š** to cause to hasten
hamiš, f. *hamšat* five
hanigalbat (a place name, indeclinable; perhaps originally *hanirabbat*)
hanû(m) Hanean (refers to an Amorite tribe)
harābu(m) (u) **Š** to lay waste
harbu(m) plough
harharu(m) villain
harimtu(m) f. harlot
harrānu(m) f. journey
harru(m) (water) channel
hâru(m) sacrificial donkey
hasāsu(m) (*a/u*) **G** to mention, to think (of) **Gtn** iter. **Gt** to ponder (s/th)
hašāhu(m) (*i*) **G** to need, to want **N** to be necessary
haštu(m) f. hole, pit
hattû(m) Hittite
hâṭu(m) (*ī*) **G** to observe
hāyiṭu(m) espier, watcher
hazannu(m) mayor, city headman
hegallu(m) abundance
hepû(m) (*i*) **D** to smash
herīnu(m) grass seeds
herû(m) (*i*) **G** to dig **D** = G
hibiltu(m) f. pl. *-ētu(m)* crime
himētu(m) ghee, butter
himiltu(m) f. plan
hissatu(m) f. the action of mentioning, the action of remembering
hiṣpatu(m) f. insolence
hiṭītu(m) f. fault, crime, outstanding payment
hubtu(m) m. robbed goods, plundered good(s)
hubullu(m) debt
hubūru(m) noise, din
hūdu(m) joy – related to *hadû(m)*
huhāru(m) bird-snare
hulqu(m) lost property, stolen goods
huppudu(m) **D** to blind
hurāṣu(m) gold
huršānu(m) mountain

ibbaru(m) see *imbaru(m)*
ibru(m) friend
ibrūtu(m) f. friendship
idu(m) f. arm, side, wages
idû(m) see *edû(m)*
igigallu(m) wise one, wisdom
igigū (a group of gods)
ikkibu(m) abomination
ilittu(m) f. offspring – related to *walādu(m)*
ilu(m) god
iltu(m) f. goddess
ilūtu(m) f. divinity
imbaru(m), ibbaru(m) fog
imēru(m) donkey
imittu(m) f. right (hand)
immeru(m) sheep
imtu(m) f. poison
in see *ina*
ina (archaic also *in*) in, at, with (i.e. by means of), from, among
ina libbi(m) as prep.: in, within, into; as adverb: inside, within, there (mimation can only appear if used as adverb, i.e. no genitive or suffix follows)
ina mahar (prep.) in(to) the presence of
ina muhhi(m) as prep.: on, onto, on top of; as adverb: thereupon (mimation can only appear if used as adverb, i.e. no genitive or suffix follows)
ina pan, ina panī before, in front of (prep.)
ina ṣēr on, around; *ina ṣērišu* around him (prep.)
inanna, eninna now
īnu(m) f. eye
inūma when, while
ipru(m) food allowance
iršu(m) desire, want
iṣṣūru(m) pl. *-ātu(m)* bird
iṣu(m) pl. *iṣṣū* or *iṣṣû* tree
išariš straight (adv.)
išaru(m) penis
išātu(m) f. fire
išdu(m) root
išpikku(m) grain bin
išru(m) village
iššiakku(m) (a type of ruler)
ištar (name of the goddess of sex and war); cf. *ištaru*
ištarītu(m) f. hierodule
ištaru(m) pl. *-ū* or *-ātu(m)* goddess (see Unit 19.4, Tip)
ištēn, f. *ištēt* one
ištu, uštu, ultu(m) since, for the past…
ištuhhu(m) (riding) crop
išû(m) **G** to have (irregular; see Unit 27)
itbāru(m) friend, (business) partner
itti together with (prep.)
ittu(m) f., pl. *idātu(m)* ominous sign
itû(m) boundary; f. pl. *itâtu(m)* environs; *itât nawêm* pasturelands
itūlu(m) **Gt** to lie (down)
izuzzu(m) **G** to stand; *ana X i.* to assist in X **Gtn** iter. **Š** to set up (irregular; see Unit 28)
izzimtu(m) f. desire; *izzimta(m) kašādu* to achieve a desire

kabāru(m) (*i*) **D** stat. to be very thick
kabāsu(m) **G** to tread **D** = G
kabattu(m), kabtatu(m) f. liver
kabātu(m) (*i*) **G** to be(come) heavy, difficult **D** to make heavy, to aggravate, to treat as important; *rēš/qaqqad X k.* to honour X
kabtatu(m) see *kabattu(m)*
kabtu(m), f. *kabittu(m)* heavy, important, grave
kadāru(m) (*i*) **G** to rear up
kadru(m), f. *kadirtu(m)* rampaging
kadrû(m) present, gift
kakkabu(m) star
kakku(m) weapon
kalbu(m) dog
kallātu(m) f. daughter-in-law
kalû(m) 1 (*a*) **G** to detain, to restrain **Š** to have (s/o) detained, restrained
kalû(m) 2 all; *mātu(m) kalûša* the entire land
kalūmtu(m) f. lamb
kamāru(m) (*a/u*) **G** to heap up
kamāsu(m) 1 (*i*) **G** to pack, to gather, to finish up
kamāsu(m) 2 (*i*) **G** to kneel down
kamītu(m) f. area outside; *kamêtuš* (to the) outside
kamû(m) (*i*) **G** to bind, to capture
kanāku(m) **G** to seal **D** = G
kanāšu(m) (*u*) **G** to bow (down)
kanīku(m) sealed document
kanšu(m) bowed down, submissive
kânu(m) (*ū*) **G** to be(come) firm **D** to make firm, to prove (guilty), to verify
kanû(m), f. *kanūtu(m)* cherished
kapādu(m) (*u*) **G** to plot **Gt** to devote oneself to something assiduously
kapāru(m) (*a/u*) **G** to peel, to strip
kappu(m) (part or type of) wing
kapru(m) village, settlement
kaqqadu(m) see *qaqqadu(m)*
kaqqaru(m) see *qaqqaru(m)*
karābu(m) (*a/u*) **G** to pray, to bless **Gtn** iter. **Gt** uncl.
karānu(m) wine
karmu(m) hillock, mound, tell
karpatu(m) f. pot
karru(m) mourning garment
karṣu(m) slander; *karṣī X akālu(m)* to slander X
karšu(m) belly
kasāpu(m) (*a/u*) **G** to break into pieces

kaspu(m) silver
kaṣāru(m) (*a/u*) **G** to bind, to knot, to gather **N** to be gathered, to be knotted **D** to fortify **Š** stat. to be tightly bound
kaṣâ(t)ta(m) in the early morning
kaṣû(m) f. *kaṣītu(m)* cold (adj.)
kâṣu(m) (*ū*) **G** to flay
kašādu(m) (*a/u*) **G** to reach, to arrive (at), to go up to (s/o), to conquer **Gtn** iter. **N** to be pursued **Š** to cause s/o to reach, to arrive (at)
kašāru(m) (*a/u*) **G** to repair
kaššāptu(m) f. witch
kašūšu(m) (a type of weapon)
katāmu(m) (*a/u*) **G** to cover **D** to cover, to conceal **Dtn** iter.
katimtu(m) f. something hidden
katû(m) poor
kerru(m) see *gerru(m)*
kezertu(m) f. (a type of cultic prostitute)
kī how?, how come?; prep.: like; subordinator: that (as in: I know that …)
kī'am thus
kibru(m) edge; pl. *-ātu(m)* also the whole world
kibsu(m) footprint, track, sole (of foot)
kidinnu(m) (a person protected by a deity)
kīdu(m) countryside
kikiṭṭû(m) ritual
kilallān both, the two (dual, see Unit 12.1)
kīlu(m), killu(m) confinement, *bīt k.* house (i.e. place) of confinement
kīma prep. like, as, in accordance with, instead of; subordinator: that (as in: I know that …), when
kimiltu(m) f. anger
kimtu(m) f. family
kinātūtu(m) f. the fact of being colleagues
kīniš solemnly
kīnu(m), f. *kīttu(m)* firm, reliable; f. as noun also: truth; *ina kinātim* truly
kinūnu(m) (the tenth Babylonian month, also called *ṭebētu(m)*); see Reading C, Tip
kippatu(m) f. circumference, circle
kirbānu(m) lump
kirhu(m) enclosure wall
kirû(m) garden, orchard
kislīmu(m) (the ninth Babylonian month); see Reading C, Tip
kispu(m) funerary rite
kīsu(m) f. money bag, purse
kiṣru(m) knot; band of men
kišādu(m) neck, bank of river
kišippiš (adv.) with a seal
kišpū pl. only: sorcery, black magic
kiššatu(m) f. entirety, Universe; *kiššat X* all of X, the entirety of X
kišukku(m) captivity
kīttu(m) see *kīnu(m)*
kizû(m) groom
kudurru(m) 1 hod (for bricks)
kudurru(m) 2 boundary, boundary stone
kukkubu(m) (a type of drinking vessel)
kullatu(m) f. all, entirety; the whole world
kullu(m) **D** to hold, to have
kullumu(m) **D** to show s/o (acc.) s/th (acc.), to make s/o experience s/th
kulmašītu(m) f. (a type of temple prostitute)
kūm instead of (prep.)
kunīnu(m) (a type of bowl)
kunukku(m) pl. *-ātu(m)* seal, sealing, sealed document
kuppu(m) (water) spring
kurummatu(m) f. food ration
kusāpu(m) bread; *k. kasāpu(m)* to break bread
kussû(m) throne, sedan chair (stem *kussi-*)
kuṣṣu(m) winter – related to *kaṣû(m)*
kuzbu(m) sex appeal

lā not, non- (see Unit 14.18)
labābu(m) (*a/u*) **G** to be(come) furious
labānu(m) (*i*) **G** to stroke; *appa(m) l.* to stroke the nose, as gesture of submission
labāšu(m) (*a*) **G** to put on (a garment) **Gt** to clothe oneself **D** to clothe (s/o, acc., with s/th, acc.)
labbu(m) lion
labīru(m) old
lahāšu(m) **D** to whisper
lalû(m) desire
lāma before (prep. and subordinator)
lamādu(m) (*a*) **G** to learn, to be informed (of) **D** to inform **Š** to cause (s/o) to learn (s/th), to teach (s/o s/th)
lamassu(m) winged bull
lamû(m) (*i*) **G** to surround
lānu(m) form, body
lapātu(m) (*a/u*) **G** to touch, to stroke, to irrigate (a field, acc.) with (water, acc.), stat. of omens: to be unfavourable **Gt** to smear oneself **D** to touch; to be delayed **Š** to ruin
lapnu(m) poor
larsa(m) (name of a city)
lasāmu(m) (*u*) **G** to run
lāsimu(m) runner
lazzu(m) persistent (of a wound)
lētu(m) f. cheek
lemēnu(m) (*i*) **G** to be(come) evil, to be(come) angry (at s/o, dative) (stat. *lemun*) **D** to trouble stat.: to be very wretched
lemniš badly, cruelly, malevolently
lemnu(m), f. *lemuttu(m)* evil; f. as noun evil(ness); *bēl lemutti(m)* evildoer

leqû(m) (*e*) **G** to take **Š** to cause (s/o) to take (s/th)
lē'û(m) powerful
le'û(m) (*i*) **G** to be able
lē'ûtu(m) f. power
libbātu(m) f. pl. only anger
libbu(m) middle, heart, mind, self
libšu(m) garment, clothing
limītu(m), *limētu(m)* f. vicinity
lipû(m) fat (noun)
lišānu(m) f. tongue
littu(m) f. progeny
lītu(m) 1 f. victory; *līt* X both 'victory over X' (i.e. defeat of X) and 'victory by X' – related to *le'û(m)*
lītu(m) 2 f. cow
līṭu(m) hostage
lū 1 truly 2 see Unit 21 (especially 21.2 and 21.5) for precative function
lû(m) bull
lubāru(m) piece of cloth, rag, garment
lubūšu(m), garment, wool ration
lutu(m) f.? debility

-*ma* connective particle (linking clauses: and, but); for other functions see Units 6.15, 29.3, and 32
ma'ādu(m) see *mâdu(m)*
madādu(m) (*a/u*) **G** to measure out **Gt** pl. stat.: to be commensurate with each other
maddattu(m) f. tribute – related to *nadānu(m)*
mādiš, *madiš* greatly
mâdu(m) (*i*) **G** to be(come) much, numerous **Š** to increase
mādu(m), *madu(m)* f. *māttu(m)*, *ma'attu(m)* sg. much, pl. many
magarru(m) wagon
magāru(m) (*u*) **G** to agree with, stat. to be agreeable **N** to be agreed with **Š** to cause s/o (acc.) to agree
māgiru(m) submissive
magrītu(m) f. slander, malice; pl. words of malice – related to *gerû*
magšaru(m) axe
mahar before (prep.); see also *ina mahar*
mahāru(m) (*a/u*) **G** to receive, to appeal to (s/o, acc.), to meet; *īn X m.* to meet the eye of X = to please X **Gtn** iter. **D** to steer (a boat) upstream **Š** to cause (s/o, acc.) to receive (s/th, acc.)
mahāṣu(m) (*a*) **G** to hit, to smite
mahhûtiš in *m. alāku(m)* to go berserk – related to *mahû(m)*
māhiru(m) recipient, opponent
māhiṣu(m) beater
mahru(m) front
mahrû, f. *mahrītu(m)* previous – see Unit 19.8, Tip
mahû(m) (*i*) **G** to become frenzied
mākālû(m) food
makāru(m) **G** to drench **D** to drench
makkūru(m) property
māku(m) lack; *ina māk* through lack of
mala, *mali* prep.: as much as, as many as; subordinator: everything that
mālaku(m) course, route – related to *alāku(m)*
malāku(m) (*i*) **G** to advise **Gt** to take counsel *itti* with
māliku(m) counsellor
malku(m) ruler, king
mallû(m) (a type of ship)
malû(m) 1 (*a*) **G** to be(come) full (of), **D** to fill
malû(m) 2 matted hair
mamma, *mamman* anyone (this word does not have case endings)
mānahtu(m) tiredness, work, earnings; *mānahāt X leqû* to undertake to reward X – related to *anāhu(m)*
mannu(m) who?
manû(m) 1 (*u*) **G** to count **N** to be delivered (into s/o's hand)
manû(m) 2 (stem: *mana-*) mina (measure of weight)
maqātu(m) (*u*) **G** to fall, to jump down **Š** to fell, to cause the downfall of
maqtu(m), f. *maqittu(m)* fallen
marāṣu(m) (*a*) **G** to be(come) ill, to be(come) sore (stat. Bab. *maruṣ*, Ass. *mariṣ*) **Gtn** iter. **Š** to make sore; stat.: to be very painful, to be very difficult
marhītu(m) f. female consort – related to *rehû(m)*
markasu(m) bond, rope
marru(m) spade
maršu(m) dirty
marṣu(m), f. *maruštu(m)* ill, difficult (terrain); f. as noun: distress
marṣūtu(m) f. the condition/state of being ill
martu(m) f. gall bladder
mārtu(m) f. daughter
māru(m) son; *mār šipri(m)* messenger (for Ass. see Unit 41.1)
maruštu(m) see *marṣu(m)*
marūtuk Marduk (name of chief god of Babylon)
masāku(m) **Š** to consider as bad
maṣṣartu(m) f. guard, watch; *maṣṣarta(m) naṣāru(m)* to keep watch
maṣṣaru(m) guard
maṣṣarūtu(m) f. safekeeping
mašālu(m) (*a*) **G** to be identical *ana* to **D** to make equal
mašā'u(m) (*a/u*) **G** to rob, to ransack
mašku(m) skin, leather, hide
mašmaššu(m) incantation priest
maššakku(m) incense (pl. same meaning)

mašû(m) (*i*) **G** to forget
matāqu(m) (*i*) **G** to be(come) sweet
mati, immati when?, ever
matīma ever, always
mâtu(m) (*ū*) **G** to die **Š** to kill
mātu(m) f. land, country
maṭû(m) (*i*) **G** to become less, to waste away **Št**$_1$ to diminish
mayyālu(m) bed
meat (pronounce *me-at*, not like English 'meat'!) a hundred
mehretu(m) f. front
mehru(m) counterpart, match (i.e. equal person)
mehû(m) storm wind
mekû(m) (*i*) **G** to neglect
melemmu(m), melammu(m) aura, radiance
mēlû(m) high place, height
mēseru(m) imprisonment
mesû(m) **G** to wash (s/th)
mešrêtu(m) f. pl. only limbs
mešrû(m) wealth
mêšu(m) (*i*) **G** to despise
mētequ(m) passage (i.e. the fact of passing), route – related to *etēqu(m)*
-mi (particle) in literature, it marks direct speech; elsewhere, it can imply that the speaker has doubts about what he or she is reporting
mihištu(m) f. bruise – related to *mahāṣu(m)*
mihṣu(m) strike, blow
milku(m) counsel, plan
mīlu(m) flood – related to *malû(m)* 1
mimma at all, anything (indeclinable); *mimma mānahātišu* anthing of his compensations, i.e. his compensation in full
mimmû whatever (subordinator)
minītu(m) f. measure; pl.: limbs, measurements, dimensions – related to *manû(m)*
mīnu(m) what?
miqittu(m) f. fall, death (of cattle)
miqtu(m) m. (a disease)
mīru(m) bull
mīsu(m) (the act of) washing – related to *mesû*
mīšaru(m) justice, law code
miširtu(m) f. produce
mišittu(m) f. paralysis
mithuṣu(m) combat, strife
mītu(m) m. dead
mītūtu(m) f. (the condition of) death
miṭratu(m) f. canal
miṭṭu(m) (a kind of weapon)
mû pl. only: water (stem *mā-*)
mubbiru(m) accuser – related to *abāru(m)*
mūdû(m) knowing – related to *edû* 1
muhhu(m) top (of the head)
mukabbisu(m) treader
mukaššidu(m) pursuer
mukillu holder; construct state *mukīl; mukīl bābi* holder of the gate, i.e. gatekeeper – related to *kullu(m)*
mulmullu(m) arrow
multarhu(m) (from earlier *muštarhu(m)*) arrogant
mūlû(m) ascent – related to *elû(m)*
muparriru(m) scatterer
murṣu(m) disease, soreness; *muruṣ libbi(m)* sorrow
mūru(m) foal
muṣlālu(m) siesta time
mūšabu(m) dwelling – related to *wašābu(m)*
mušaknišu(m) one who causes (s/o) to bow down
mušallimu(m) protector – related to *šalāmu(m)*
mušēbiru(m) someone who enables (s/o else) to cross (a river)
mušēpišūtu(m) f. the duty of overseer; *m. epēšu(m)* to act as overseer
mušītiš at night
mušītu(m) f. night
muškēnu(m) wretch
muštēpištu(m) f. (denotes a type of bewitcher)
muštēširu(m) just
mūšu(m) night; *mūša(m)* at night
muttalliku(m) roaming, restless
mutu(m) m. man, husband
mūtu(m) m. death
mu''uru(m) see *(w)u''uru(m)*

nabalkutu(m) to overturn, to rebel (see Unit 38)
nabāṭu(m) (*u*) **G** to shine **Š** caus.
nablu(m) flame
nabnītu(m) f. form – related to *banû(m)*
nabû(m) (*i*) **G** to name
nadānu(m) (*i*) **G** to give, to grant, to sell
nadû(m) (*i*) **G** to throw, to cast (a spell), *X eli Y n.* to accuse Y of X, stat.: to lie (on bed) **N** pass. to be abandoned (of settlement)
nagāru(m) carpenter
nagāšu(m) **Gtn** (*i*) to wander about
nagbu(m) entirety, depths
nahallu(m) f. wadi
nahāsu(m) (*i*) **G** to collapse, to subside
nahlaptu(m) f. garment – related to *halāpu(m)*
nahšu(m) (meaning unclear)
nâhu(m) (*ū*) **G** to become restful
nā'iru(m), nā'eru(m) roaring
nakādu(m) (*u*) **G** to throb, to be(come) worried **N** to become anxious
nakāmu(m) (*a/u*) **G** to heap up
nakāpu(m) (*i*) **D** to butt, to gore (like a bull)

nakāru(m) (*i*) **G** to be(come) enmitous *itti* towards
nakāsu(m) (*i*) **G** to cut, to slit (throat) **Gtn** iter. **D** to cut
nakmû(m) roasting pot
nakru(m), f. *nakirtu(m)* foreign, hostile; as noun: enemy; construct state: *nakur*
nâku(m) (*i*) **G** to have sex with
namāru(m) (*i*) **G** to be(come) bright, to be(come) healthy, well developed **D** to brighten
namdattu(m) f. amount paid – related to *madādu(m)*
nammaštû(m) wild beasts
namrāṣu(m) difficult territory – related to *marāṣu(m)*
namrīru(m) radiance, radiant auras (pl. with same meaning as sg.)
namru(m), f. *namirtu(m)* bright, friendly (face)
namṣaru(m) sword
namû(m) see *nawû(m)*
namû(m) (from earlier *nawû(m)*) **D** to turn into desert, to devastate
namungatu(m) f. paralysis
nannāru(m) light (of the sky) (epithet of moon god)
napāhu(m) (*a/u*) **G** to kindle (fire) **N** to break out (fire) **D** stat. to be swollen, inflamed
napālu(m) (*a/u*) **D** to gouge out (eyes)
napāšu(m) **D** to ease
napharu(m) totality
naphu(m), f. *napihtu(m)* blazing (fire); f. as noun blazing fire
napištu(m) f. life, throat
napīšu(m) breath
naprušu(m) **N** to fly
napšaštu(m), *napšaltu(m)* f. salve, ointment
napšu(m) abundant
naqāru(m) (*a/u*) **G** to destroy
naqbu(m) cosmic underground waters (synonym for *apsû(m)*), the deep
naqû(m) (*i*) **G** to libate
naquttu(m) f. critical condition
narāmu(m) loved one
nāriṭu(m) swamp (also metaphorically)
narkabtu(m) f. chariot – related to *rakābu(m)*
narû(m) stele
nāru(m) 1 singer
nāru(m) 2 f., pl. *-ātu(m)* river, canal
nâru(m) (*ā*) **G** to kill
naruqqu(m) f. leather bag
nasāhu(m) (*a/u*) **G** to pull out, to wipe out, to transfer
nasāku(m) **Š** to allow to be repealed
nasāqu(m) **Št** to put in order
naṣāru(m) (*a/u*) **G** to guard, to protect
nāṣiru(m) guard, protector
naṣru(m) guarded, protected
našāku(m) (*a/u*) **G** to bite
našāqu(m) (*i*) **G** to kiss
našû(m) (*i*) **G** to lift, to carry, to bear
nāšû(m) bearer
natbāku(m) waterway – related to *tabāku(m)*
naṭālu(m) (*a/u*) **G** to look (at), to observe, to see, to experience **Gtn** iter.
naṭû(m) (*u*) **G** (stative only) to be suitable *ana* to/for
nawû(m), *namû(m)* (stem *nawa-*, *nama-*) desert
nazāqu(m) (*i*) **G** to be(come) annoyed, to squeak **Š** to annoy
nēbaha(m) sash
nēbertu(m) f. crossing, ford – related to *ebēru(m)*
nēmelu(m) earnings
nēmequ(m) wisdom
nēmettu(m) f. cause for complaint – related to *emēdu(m)*
nērāru(m) help, assistance
nêru(m) (*ē*) **G** to kill, to smite
nesû(m) distant
nesû(m) (*i*) **G** to be(come) distant **Š** to keep (s/th, s/o) away
nēšu(m) lion
nikkassu(m) arithmetic, pl.: accounts
niksu(m) (the act of) cutting
nīnu we
nippur (name of a city in Northern Babylonia; often indeclinable)
nipšu(m) scent
nipūtu(m) f. debt slave
niqû(m), *nīqu(m)* libation, sacrifice
nīru(m) yoke
nisaba (name of the grain goddess; indeclinable)
nisannu(m) (the first Babylonian month); see Reading C, Tip
nissatu(m) f. lamentation, wail
niṣirtu(m) f. secret, treasure (house)
niṣru(m) protection
nišītu(m) f. choice; *nišīt* X person/thing chosen by X
nišū pl. only, f. people
nīšu(m) 1 life; *nīš X* oath sworn on the life of X
nīšu(m) 2 (the action of) lifting
niṭlu(m) gaze; *kima n. X* according to X's judgment
niṭûtu(m) f. (a) beating
niziqtu(m) f. worry
nuballu(m) (part or type of) wing
nubālu(m) chariot
nubattu(m) f. resting place; *n. šakānu(m)* to halt for the night – related to *bītu(m)*

nudunnû(m) dowry – related to *nadānu(m)*
nuhatimmu(m) cook
nuhatimmūtu(m) f. duty as cook
nukurtu(m) f. hostility
nullâtu(m) f. almost only pl.: calumny
nūnu(m) fish
nupāru(m), nurpāru(m) prison
nūru(m) light

padānu(m) f. path
pâdu(m) *(ā)* **G** to lock (s/o) up
pādû(m) merciful
pagru(m) body, corpse
pahāru(m) **G** to come together **Gtn** to come together a few at a time, bit by bit **D** to bring together
pāhutu(m) governor (has Assyrian vowel assimilation, see 41.1 number 5; stem *pāhat-*)
palāhu(m) *(a)* **G** to be(come) afraid *ana* of/for; stat.: to be frightening **Gt** to revere **D** to make afraid, to terrify, to intimidate
pālihu(m) fearer
palālu(m) **G** to guard **D** stat. (uncl., perhaps: to see to (s/o))
palāsu(m) *(a/u)* **N** to see, to look at **Ntn** iter. **D** to see to, stat.: to be concerned **Š** to cause (s/o) to see (s/th), to show
palāšu(m) *(a/u)* **G** to pierce **Š** caus.
panānu(m) previously
paniš at the front
panu(m) front, surface; pl. face; *panī X babālu(m)/(w)abālu(m)* to forgive X
panû(m), f. *panītu(m)* past, previous
paphû(m) Paphaean (gentilic adjective; do not pronounce *ph* as in Philip!)
paqādu(m) *(i)* **G** to entrust, to care for
parakku(m) dais
parāku(m) *(i)* **G** to obstruct (s/th), to lie in the way *ana* of
parāsu(m) *(a/u)* **G** to separate, to cut off, to wean, to render a verdict (in a lawsuit) (see Unit 15.5 Tip)
parā'u(m) *(a/u)* **G** to cut off, to slice through
parrisānū pl. only boatmen
parsu(m), f. *paristu(m)* cut off
parṣu(m) rite, (cultic) office
parû(m) mule
parzillu(m) iron
paspasu(m) duck
pašāhu(m) *(a)* **G** to rest **Št$_1$** to be alleviated
pašālatti (adv.) by crawling
pašālu(m) *(i)* **G** to crawl
pašāqu(m) *(u)* **G** to be narrow, difficult **Š** to be in difficulties **Štn** iter.
pašāru(m) *(a/u)* **G** to undo, to interpret (a dream), to ease (anger)
pašāšu(m) *(a)* **G** to anoint **Gt** to anoint oneself **N** to be anointed
pašqu(m), f. *pašuqtu(m)* narrow, difficult
paššūru(m) table; *p. rakāsu(m)* to lay the table
pāšu(m) axe
patāhu(m) **D** to stab **Dt** pl.: to stab each other
patālu(m) *(i)* **G** to twist
patru(m), sword, dagger
paṭāru(m) *(a/u)* **G** to loosen, to undo, to release, to ransom, to go away **N** to be loosened, to be dispelled
pehû(m), f. *pehītu(m)* open (route)
pêlu(m) see *bêlu(m)*
pēmtu(m), pēntu(m) f. embers
pēmu(m) thigh
pērtu(m) f. hair
per'u(m) see *pir'u(m)*
peṣû(m), f. *peṣītu(m)* white
petû(m) *(e)* **G** to open (s/th)
pilludû(m) rite (usually used in plural)
piltu(m) see *pištu(m)*
pirittu(m) f. terror – related to *parādu(m)*
pirṣu(m) breach
pir'u(m) offspring
pīru(m) elephant
pišannu(m) box, chest
pištu(m), piltu(m) f. insult
pitiltu(m) f. string, cord
pizallūru(m) f. gecko
pû(m) mouth, speech (see Unit 11.6, TIP)
puhālu(m) male animal
puhru(m) assembly
pūhu(m) substitute
puhur together
pukkuru(m) **D** to tie up
puluhtu(m) f. fear, reverence, fearsomeness (pl. same meaning)
purussû(m) legal decision
pušqu(m) strait
puzru(m) secrecy

qabaltu(m), qablatu(m) f. middle
qablu(m) battle, onslaught
qabû(m) *(i)* **G** to speak, to say, to declare, to state
qadādu(m) *(u)* **G** to plunge down (of water courses)
qalālu(m) *(i)* **G** to be(come) light **D** to make light, to spoil, to make shabby (clothes); *rēš/qaqqad X q.* to humiliate X

qalliš lightly
qamû(m) (*u*) **G** to burn
qanû(m) (a single) reed
qâpu(m) 1 (*ū*) **G** to collapse
qâpu(m) 2 (*ī*) **G** to believe
qaqqadu(m), kaqqadu(m) head
qaqqaru(m), kaqqaru(m) ground
qardu(m) valiant; as noun: valiant one, warrior
qardūtu(m) f. valour
qarrādūtu(m) f. valour
qaštu(m) f. bow
qâšu(m) (*i*) **G** to give as a gift
qaṭālu(m) **N** to be killed
qatû(m) (*i*) **G** to come to an end
qātu(m) f. hand; transf. also: doings
qebēru(m) (*i*) **G** to bury
qēbiru(m) burier
qerbetu(m) f. meadowland
qerbu(m) middle, inside, interior; pl.: insides (of body); see also *qereb*, *ana qereb*
qereb in, inside (prep.) (see Unit 36.5)
qerēbu(m) (*i*) **G** to approach (*ana* to); stat. (*qerub*) to be near **D** stat. to be very near **Š** to present (a prayer, a plea) to s/o **Štn** iter.
qibītu(m) f. utterance, command – related to *qabû(m)*
qinnatu(m) f. rump, posterior
qinnāzu(m) f. team of workmen, whip
qīptu(m) f. office, appointment
qirtu(m) f. bitumen
qištu(m) f. forest
qīštu(m) f. gift, honorarium, compensation, reward
qīšu(m) forest
qubbû(m) lamentation
quppu(m) basket; box
qurādu(m) warrior
qurunnu(m) f., pl. *-ātu(m)* pile
qu''û(m) **D** to wait

rabāṣu(m) (i) **G** to sit, to lie, to lurk, to lie in wait
rabû(m) 1 (*i*) **G** to be(come) big, great **D** to bring up (a child) **Š** to make big, great
rabû(m) 2, f. *rabītu(m)* big, great
rabû(m) 3 **G** to set (of heavenly bodies)
râbu(m) (*i*) **G** to pay back, to requite (s/th, *ana*, with s/th, acc.)
raggu(m) wicked; as noun: villain
rahāṣu(m) (*i/i*) **G** to flood, to overwhelm like a flood; with storm god as subject: to be in full flood
rāhiṣu(m) flooder (epithet of the storm god); *kīma rāhiṣi(m)* like the storm god in full flood
rāhû(m) see *rehû(m)*
rakābu(m) (*a*) **G** to ride (also sexually) **Gt** pl. to ride each other, to copulate
rakāsu(m) (*a/u*) **G** to bind
rakbû(m) messenger on horseback
raksu(m), f. *rakistu(m)* bound
ramāku(m) (*u*) **G** to bathe (in)
ramāmu(m) (*u*) **G** to roar, to rumble
ramanu(m) self; X *ramanišu* his own X
ramû(m) 1 (*u*) **G** to become slack
ramû(m) 2 (*i*) **G** to sit on
râmu(m) (*ā*) **G** to love
rapāšu(m) (*i*) **G** to be(come) broad **D** to broaden
rapšu(m), f. *rapaštu(m)* broad, vast; of people: numerous
raqādu(m) (*u*) **Gtn** to prance about
râqu(m) (*i*) **G** to be(come) unoccupied
rasābu(m) (*i*) **D** to smite
rašû(m) (*i*) **G** to acquire
rebītu(m) f. (town) square – related to the number four
redû(m) (*i*) **G** to pursue (s/o, acc.), to march, to ride **Š** to cause (liquid) to flow
rēdû(m) soldier (super-lit.: marcher)
rehû(m) (*i*) **G** to seep over (of sleep), to couple with
rēhû(m), rāhû(m), f. *rāhītu(m)* the one who seeps over (s/o, s/th, gen.)
rêmu(m) (*ē*) **G** to have mercy (on s/o, acc.)
rēmu(m) mercy
rêqu(m) (*ū*) **G** to be(come) distant
rēṣu(m) help(er); *rēṣūšu* and *ālik rēṣišu* his helper
rēṣūtu(m) f. help, aid
rēšu(m) head, top, peak, beginning, slave; *r. eqli(m)* destination; dual can be used with same meaning as sg.
reṭû(m) (i) **G** to drive in
rību(m), f. pl. *rībētu(m)* repayment
ridûtu(m) f. succession; *mār r.* crown prince
rigmu(m) shout, cry, noise; *rigma(m) eli X šakānu(m)* to raise a complaint against X
rihiṣtu(m), rihiltu(m) f. devastating inundation
rīhu(m) left over
riksu(m) knot, contract; pl. *-ātu(m)*
rīmtu(m) f. wild cow
rīmu(m) wild bull
rimûtu(m) f. paralysis
rīqu(m) empty
rīqūtu(m) f. emptiness
rubātu(m) f. noblewoman, lady, princess – related to *rabû(m)*
rubṣu(m) bed place, dung
rubû(m) nobleman, lord, prince (stem: *ā*)– related to *rabû(m)*
rubûtu(m) f. lordliness, nobility
ruhû(m) (a type of black magic)
rupšu(m) breadth

rūqu(m) distant; as noun: distance; *ina rūqi(m)* in the distance, in a faraway place; *ana rūqēte* (f. pl. used as noun) from afar
rusû(m) (a type of black magic)
ruššû(m) red
ruteššû(m) **Dtn** to be constantly inconsiderate
ru'tu(m) f. spittle

sābītu(m) f. female tavern keeper, ale wife
sābû(m), sābiu(m) brewer
sadāru(m) (*i*) **G** stat. to be regular
sahālu(m) (*a/u*) **G** to pierce
sahāpu(m) (*a/u*) **G** stat. to be spread over, to cover **D** to overwhelm
saharšubbû(m) (a skin disease, perhaps: leprosy)
sahāru(m) (*u*) **G** to go around, to turn (about), to search for, to threaten **N** to turn towards, to favour **Š** caus.
salāmu(m) **D** to appease
salīmu(m) peace
sallātu(m) family
samānû(m) f. *samānītu(m)* eighth
sâmu(m) (*i*) **G** to be red
sanāqu(m) (*i*) **G** **1** to test, to keep under control **2** to approach (*ana* to)
sapāhu(m) **N** to be dispersed **D** stat.: to be splayed (limbs)
sapānu(m) (*a/u*) **G** to flatten
sartu(m) f. (pl. *sarrātu(m)*) crime, lie, lies
sehû(m) (*i*) **G** to revolt **D** to ruin
sekēru(m) (*i*) **G** to block up
serdû(m) carrying pole (for sedan chair)
sêru(m) (*ē*) **G** to plaster
sihirtu(m) f. entirety, circumference – related to *sahāru(m)*
sihlu(m) thorn
sīhu(m) rebellion – related to *sehû(m)*
sikkatu(m), f. (foundation) peg, pinnacle (of mountain)
sikkūru(m) bolt
silītu(m), f. illness
simanu(m) (the third Babylonian month); see Reading C, Tip
simmu(m) wound
simtu(m), f. fitting thing; *simat X* (that) which befits X, as befits *X*
sîn (name of the moon god)
sinništu(m), f. woman
sippir Sippar (name of city)
sissiktu(m), f. alliance
sisû(m) horse
subartu(m) (a Babylonian word for:) Assyria
sullû(m) 1 **D** to pray
sullû(m) 2 prayer
suluppu(m) date (fruit)
sunqu(m) famine
sūnu(m) lap
suppû(m) prayer
ṣabātu(m) (*a*) **G** to seize, to catch **Gt** to seize each other, to engage in litigation **N** to be caught, to be seized **D** = G **Štn** to constantly cause (s/o, acc.) to seize (s/th, acc.)
ṣābitu(m) m. seizer, catcher
ṣābu(m) troop(s) (of workers, soldiers), work-party
ṣâhu(m) (*ī*) **G** to laugh
ṣalālu(m) (a) to lie (down)
ṣalāmu(m) (*i*) **G** to be(come) black, dark
ṣallu(m) sleeping
ṣalmāt qaqqadi the 'black ones of the head', i.e. black-headed ones (a poetic phrase for 'humanity', based on the idea of people as sheep)
ṣalmu(m) statue
ṣalpu(m) crooked
ṣāltu(m) f. quarrel
ṣalû(m) (*i*) **G** to throw (off)
ṣamādu(m) (*i*) **G** to harness
ṣamāru(m) **D** to strive (for)
ṣarāmu(m) **D** to strive
ṣarāpu(m) 1 (*a/u*) **G** to desire, to burn
ṣarāpu(m) 2 (*u*?) **G** to be loud **Š** to make resound
ṣarpu(m) refined
ṣehēru(m) (*i*) **G** to be(come) little, young
ṣehru(m), f. *ṣehretu(m)*, *ṣehertu(m)* little, small
ṣēnu(m) 1 evil
ṣēnū 2 pl. only, f. sheep and goats
ṣerretu(m) f. nose-rope
ṣerru(m) snake
ṣēru(m) **1** back **2** steppe, open country, the wild; see also *ina ṣēr*, *ana ṣēr*
ṣibûtu(m) f. wish
ṣillu(m) shadow, protection
ṣīru(m) f. *ṣīrtu(m)* exalted
ṣīrūtu(m) f. exaltedness
ṣītu(m) f. exit; *ṣīt X* thing that comes/goes out of X; *ṣīt libbi(m)* offspring
ṣubātu(m) m. garment
ṣuhārtu(m) f. girl
ṣuhāru(m) (OB pl. *ṣuhārû*, stem *ṣuhārā-*) boy
ṣuhru(m) (time of) youth
ṣullulu(m) **D** to cover (a building) with a roof
ṣulūlu(m) shade, protection
ṣumāmu(m) thirst
ṣūmu(m) thirst
ṣurru(m) mind
ša prep.: of; subordinator: which, who, because, although

šabāsu(m) 1 (*u*) **G** to be(come) angry
šabāsu(m) 2 (*a/u*) **G** to gather
šabāṭu(m) (the eleventh Babylonian month); see Reading C, Tip
šadādu(m) (*a/u*) **G** to drag
šadāhu(m) (*i*) **G** to move along, to proceed
šadlu(m), f. *šadiltu(m)* wide
šadû(m) mountain (range)
šagaštu(m), šagaltu(m) f. massacre
šagāšu(m) (*i*) **G** to slaughter
šahāhu(m) (*u*) **G** to be(come) loose (of hair)
šahātu(m) 1 m.? corner, side
šahātu(m) 2 (*u*) **G** to fear
šahāṭu(m) 1 (*a/u*) **G** to tear off
šahāṭu(m) 2 (*i*) **G** to jump; in verbal couple: hurriedly
šā'iltu(m) f. female dream interpreter (super-lit. female questioner)
šakānu(m) (*a/u*) **G** to put, to impose, to set in place, to establish, to appoint, to equip (s/o, acc. with s/th, acc.) to bring about **Gt** = G **N** to be placed, to be appointed, to be equipped with (acc.), to occur **Š** to cause to reside (in heart)
šākinu(m) placer, causer, achiever
šakkanakku(m) governor
šakurru(m) lance, spear
šalālu(m) (*a/u*) **G** to plunder
šalamtu(m) f. corpse
šalāmu(m) (*i*) **G** to be(come) well **D** to make (s/th, acc.) good to s/o (acc.), to lead (s/o) in safety, to keep safe, to repay
šalhû(m) outer wall
šalimtu(m) f. good fortune
šallatu(m) f. plunder; *š. šalālu(m)* to carry off plunder
šalmatu(m) see *šalimtu(m)*
šalmūtu(m) f. the condition/state of being healthy
šalputtu(m) f. ruination
šalšu(m) f. *šaluštu(m)* third; X *šalušti(m)* third-quality X
šâlu(m) (*ā*) **G** to ask, to question
šalultu(m) see *šaluštu(m)*, under *šalšu(m)* (change of *št* to *lt*, as per Unit 47.9)
šalummatu(m) f. radiance
šamāhu(m) **G** to flourish **D** to make flourish
šamāmiš (adv.) heavenwards
šamāmū see *šamû*
šamāru(m) (*u*) **G** to rage
šamaš (name of the sun god)
šamā'ū see *šamû*
šamhu(m), f. *šamuhtu(m)* lush, voluptuous
šammu(m) plant, grass
šamnu(m) oil
šâmu(m) 1 (*ā*) **G** to buy
šâmu(m) 2 (*ī*) **G** to decree (as) a destiny
šamû, šamāū, šamāmū pl. only sky, heaven, the heavens
šanānu(m) (*a/u*) **G** to match, to rival
šanāṣu(m) (*i*) **G** to sneer
šāninu(m) rival
šanû(m) 1 (*i*) **G** to be(come) different; with *ṭēmu(m)* mind: alteration of the mind = madness **D** to repeat
šanû(m) 2 second, other
šapāku(m) (*a/u*) **G** to pour, to heap up, to cast (metal objects) **D** to pour
šapal see *šaplu(m)*
šapālu(m) (*i*) **G** to be(come) low **N** to be cast down **D** to lower
šapāru(m) (*a/u*) **G** to send, to send a letter, to write; stat.: to be in charge of **Gt** (see *šitpuru(m)*) **Gtn** iter. **N** to be sent
šaplānu(m) below
šaplu(m) underside; *šapalšu* under him
šaplû(m), f. *šaplītu(m)* lower (sea)
šāpiru(m) boss
šaptu(m) f. lip, rim (of vessel)
šāptu(m) f. wool (Old Assyrian equivalent of *šīpātu(m)*)
šaqālu(m) (*a/u*) **G** to weigh out, to suspend (i.e. hang)
šaqû(m) 1, f. *šaqūtu(m)* high
šaqû(m) 2 (*u* and *i*) **G** to be(come) high
šaqû(m) 3 (*i*) **G** to give (s/th, acc. to s/o, acc.) to drink
šaqummu(m) utterly silent
šār 3600 (used as a large round number)
šarāhu(m) **G** to be(come) magnificent **D** to glorify
šarāku(m) (*a/u*) **G** to give (as a present), to grant **N** to be given (as a present)
šarku(m) pus
šarāqu(m) (*i*) **G** to steal **Gtn** iter.
šarāṭu(m) (*a/u*) **G** to tear **D** = G
šarqiš (adv.) furtively
šarrābu(m) (a demon)
šarrāqu(m) thief
šarratu(m) f. queen
šarru(m) king
šarrūtu(m) f. kingship
šārtu(m) f. hair (collective)
šāru(m) wind
šasû(m) (*i*) **G** to shout out, to state a (legal) claim *ana* against
šatāhu(m) (*a/u*) **D** to elongate
šatta(m) this year (adverbial accusative of *šattu(m)* year)

šattišam (adv.) year after year (see Unit 36.4)
šattu(m) f. year
šatû(m) (*i*) **G** to drink (**Š** – *šaqû(m)* is usually used instead)
šaṭāru(m) (*a/u*) **G** to incise, to inscribe, to write
šâṭu(m) (*ū*) **G** to despise
šebēru(m) (*i*) **G** to break **D** to smash
šēlūtu(m) f. blade
šemû(m) (*e*) **G** to hear
šēmû(m) hearer
šepṣu(m) obdurate
šēpu(m) f. foot
šeriktu(m) see *širiktu(m)*
šerru(m) child
šērtu(m) 1 f. morning, pl.: the morning hours
šērtu(m) 2 f. bar (as part of lock)
šērtu(m) 3 f. punishment
šēru(m) morning; *tīb š.* dawn
še'u(m) see *û(m)*
še'û(m) (*e*) **G** to seek
šē'û(m) seeker; *šē'i bābi* seeker of the gate, i.e. visitor
šī she, this (f.), that (f.)
šibbu(m) belt
šību(m) old; as noun: old man, witness
šībūtu(m) f. witness-hood, the fact of being a witness, testimony
šigaru(m) bolt
šikaru(m) beer
šikittu(m) f. shape
šiknu(m) form, placement; *nakmû šikin išāti(m)* perhaps: a roasting pot that belongs in the fire
šikru(m) see *šikaru*
šillatu(m) f. shamelessness, sacrilege; pl.: shameless words, sacrilegious words
šīmtu(m), šīmatu(m) f. fate
šīmu(m) price
šina, f. *šitta* two
šinnu(m) f. tooth, tusk
šīpātu(m) f. pl. only: wool
šipru(m) work
šiptu(m) f. spell; *šipat balāṭi(m)* spell of life, i.e. life-giving spell
šir'ānu(m) sinew
širāš beer (the word has no case vowel!)
širiktu(m), šeriktu(m) f. gift, dowry
šīru(m) flesh
šisītu(m) f. shout; *šisīta(m) šakānu(m)* to raise a cry, i.e. to make a scene
šitnunu(m) strife
šitpuru(m) **Gt** stat.: to be clad in
šitta see *šina*
šittu(m) f. sleep
šiṭūtu(m) (or *šiṭûtu(m)*?) f. scorn; *šiṭūt* X *leqû*(m) to scorn X
šizbu(m) milk
šū he, this (m.), that (m.)
šuanna (a poetic name for Babylon); the word has no case vowel, i.e. it is the same in nom., acc. and gen.
šuātu (acc./gen. form of *šū*)
šubtu(m) f. dwelling – related to *wašābu(m)*
šūbu(m) rush (plant)
šubû(m) battering ram
šukênu(m) **Š** to prostrate oneself (pret. *uškīn*)
šuklulu(m) f. *šuklultu(m)* perfect
šukurru(m) spear
šulmannu(m) greeting-gift, bribe
šulmu(m) peace, wellbeing
šulušû(m) f. *šulušītu(m)* three-year-old
šumēlu(m) left (hand)
šumma if; *š. … š.* either … or
šummu **D** to ponder
šumu(m) name
šunatu(m) see *šuttu(m)*
šūnuhiš with great difficulty
šūnuhu(m) exhausted – related to *anāhu(m)*
šupšikku(m) see *tupšikku(m)*
šupšuqu(m) 1 **Š** to be in difficulties, stat.: to be very difficult **Štn** iter.
šupšuqu(m) 2 very difficult
šūquru(m) precious
šurqu(m) stolen goods
šurrû(m) **D** to start (s/th)
šuršu(m) root
šūru(m) reed bundle
šuškallu(m) net
šūt (archaic m. pl. of *ša*) *šūt X* those of X; *šūt rēši* those at (lit. of) the head, i.e. courtiers
šuttatu(m) f. pit
šuttu(m), šunatu(m) f. dream; *š. amāru(m)* to have a dream
šūtu(m) f. the south wind
šūturu(m) very great – related to *(w)atāru(m)*

tabāku(m) (*a/u*) **G** to pour **Š** to cause (s/o) to shed (s/th)
tabālu(m) (*a*) **G** to take (away)
tabāštānu(m) f. excrement
tabrītu(m) f. sighting; pl. *tabrâtu(m)* astonishment – related to *barû(m)*
tabsūtu(m) f. midwife
tāhāzu(m) battle, combat – related to *ahāzu(m)* Gt
tahdītu(m) (the act of) gladdening
tahlīpu(m) armour – related to *halāpu(m)*
takālu(m) (*a*) **G** to trust **N** to trust *ana/eli* in, to
tākulû(m) pain
tamāhu(m) (*a/u*) **G** to seize, to grasp

tāmartu(m) f. audience gift
tamāru(m) **D** stat.: to be covered, referring to words: to be disingenuous
tâmatu(m) see *tâmtu(m)*
tamkāru(m) merchant
tamlû(m) terrace – related to *malû(m)*
tâmtu(m), tâmatu(m) f. sea
tamû(m) **G** to swear (an oath) **D** to make s/o swear (an oath)
tanattu(m) f. praise – related to *nâdu(m)*
taphūru(m) assembly – related to *pahāru(m)*
tappû(m) friend, (business) partner
taqānu(m) (*u*) **G** to be in order, to subside (noise)
tarāku(m) **G** to thump **D** = G
tarāru(m) (*u*) **G** to tremble
tarāṣu(m) 1 (*a/u*) **G** to stretch out
tarāṣu(m) 2 (*u*) **G** to be in good order **D** to put in order
tarbītu(m) f. upbringing
targīgu(m) evil-doer – related to *raggu(m)*
târu(m) (*ū*) **G** to (re)turn, to turn *ana* into; in verbal couple: to do again **D** to turn s/th *ana* into, to return s/th *ana* to s/o
tarû(m) (*u*) **G** to lead (away)
tašīmtu(m) f. reckoning
tašrītu(m) beginning; also the seventh Babylonian month, see Reading C, Tip
tebû(m) 1 erect
tebû(m) 2 (*i*) **G** to rise; to be erect (sexually) **Š** to remove
tēbû(m) rutting; *lā tēbû(m)* incurable
tēnû(m) replacement
terdinnu(m) second son
têrtu(m) f. instruction, omen – related to *wu''uru(m)*
teṣû(m) (*i*) to excrete
tēšû(m) chaos, mêlée
tiāmtu(m) see *tâmtu(m)*
tību(m) rise, attack; *t. tāhāzi(m)* onslaught – related to *tebû(m)*
tibûtu(m) f. swarm (of locusts) – related to *tebû(m)*
tiklu(m) trust
tillû(m) equipment, pl.: tools
tīlu(m) tell, ruin, mound
tinūru(m) oven
titurru(m) bridge, causeway
tiûtu(m) f. food
tukultu(m) f. encouragement, trust
tūltu(m) f. worm
tuppu(m) pl. *-ātu(m)* cuneiform tablet
tupšikku(m), šupšikku(m) earth basket, toil, corvée work
tuquntu(m) f. battle
turbu'tu(m) f. (dust) storm
tūša(m) for sure, suppose
tūšaru(m) plane; *mithuṣ t.* pitched battle
ṭabāhu(m) (*a/u*) **G** to butcher **D** = G
ṭābihu(m) butcher
ṭābtu(m) f. salt
ṭâbu(m) (*i*) **G** to be(come) good, sweet, *eli X ṭ.* to be pleasing to X **D** *šīr X ṭ.* to give bodily well-being to X **Š** to make pleasant
ṭābu(m), f. *ṭābtu(m)* good, kindly; f. as noun: goodness
ṭapultu(m) f. slander
ṭa'tu(m) f. bribe(ry)
ṭarādu(m) (*a/u*) **G** to dispatch **D** to throw (s/o) out
ṭebētu(m) (the tenth Babylonian month, also called *kinūnu(m)*); see Reading C, Tip
ṭehû(m) (*i*) **G** to draw near *ana* to
ṭēmu(m) message, plan, report, matter, mind, news; *ṭ. ṣabātu(m)* to make up one's mind; see also *šanû(m)* 1
ṭênu(m) **G** to grind
ṭiṭṭu(m) m.? clay
ṭūbtu(m) f. peace – related to *ṭâbu(m)*
ṭuppu(m) pl. *-ātu(m)* see *tuppu(m)*

u and, or
ubānu(m) f. finger, pinnacle (of mountain)
ugāru(m) meadow
uggatu(m) f. anger
uklu(m) darkness – related to *ekēlu(m)*
ukullû(m) food, fodder – related to *akālu(m)*
ukultu(m) f. food – related to *akālu(m)*
ul not (see Unit 14.18) *ul ... ul* neither ... nor
uliltu(m) f.? dried fig
ullikīa(m) there
ulṣu(m) delight
ultu see *ištu*
û(m) barley (often preceded by the sumerogram or determinative *še*; this has sometimes been understood as part of the syllabic spelling, but in view of spellings without *še* this seems unlikely)
ūma(m) today (adverbial accusative of *ūmu(m)* day)
ūmakkal(m) a single day
ūmišam(ma) day by day, day after day
umma (introduces direct speech) *umma šū-ma* thus he (spoke/wrote)
ummānu(m) f. army, populace; pl. *-ātu(m)* troops
ummu(m) 1 fever
ummu(m) 2 f. mother
ūmu(m) day
unnīnu(m), unninnu(m) prayer
unūtu(m) f. equipment
upšāšû(m) (a type of black magic, sometimes translated as:) machinations
uqnû(m) lapis lazuli

urhu(m) m. and f. path
urinnu(m) standard
urīṣu(m) male goat
urpatu(m) f. cloud
urrakūtu(m) f. *šipir u.* sculptors' craft
urru(m) day; *urra(m)* by day, tomorrow
urruhiš very quickly
uršānu(m), uršannu(m) warrior
uršu(m) bed
ûrtu(m) see *(w)u"urtu(m)*
ūru(m) 1 roof
ūru(m) 2 vulva
uruk (name of a city)
usātu(m) pl.: help; *bēl u.* doer (lit. owner) of good
uṣultu(m) f. knife
uṣurtu(m) f. ordinance
ušallu(m) f. meadows along river
uššušu(m) **D** to renew
uštu see *ištu*
utlu(m) lap (poetic also of heaven)
utnēnu(m) prayer
utû(m) doorman, gatekeeper
utūnu(m) f. kiln
u"urtu(m) see *(w)u"urtu(m)*
uznu(m) f. ear, attention, wisdom; *uzun X petû(m)* to open the ear of X, i.e. to enlighten X
uzzu(m) anger – related to *ezzu(m)*

(w)abālu(m) **G** to bring, to spend (time), with *libbu(m)* as subject to induce (s/o, acc., to do s/th) **Gtn** iter. **Š** to get (s/o) to bring (s/th), i.e. to have s/th brought, to send
(w)alādu(m) **G** to give birth to
(w)aqāru(m) (*i*) **G** to be(come) precious
(w)arādu(m) **G** to go down
(w)ardu(m) male slave
(w)arhu(m) month
(w)arkatu(m) f. rear; *w. parāsu(m)* to establish the relevant facts
(w)arki, (w)arka after, behind (prep.); afterwards (adv.)
(w)arkû(m) later (adj.)
(w)aršu(m), maršu(m), f. *(w)aruštu(m)* dirty
(w)arû(m) (*u*) **G** to lead **Š** to direct
(w)âru(m) **G** to go (up to); *ašar lā âri* place of non-going up, i.e. inaccessible place
(w)aṣābu(m) **G** to add on, to increase
(w)aṣû(m) **G** to go out, to go away; with ventive: to come forth; *bāba(m) (w)aṣû(m)* to go out through the gate **Š** caus.
(w)ašābu(m) **G** to sit, to dwell, to remain, to be present **Gtn** iter. **Š** to settle (s/o)
(w)ašāru(m) **G** to lower **D** to release
(w)ašāṭu(m) **G** to be(come) difficult (stat. *(w)ašaṭ*)
(w)āšibu(m) dweller; *(w)āšib* X dweller of X, i.e. who dwells X
(w)aštu(m) difficult
(w)atāru(m) **G** to increase (i.e. to become more) **D** to increase (i.e. to make more)
(w)atru(m) surplus (adj.)
(w)ēdu(m) sole, alone; *ēduššu* by himself
(w)uššuru(m) **D** to let go, to release
(w)u"urtu(m) f. command, mission
(w)u"uru(m) **D** to give a task to, to instruct s/o to do something, to dispatch (messenger)

zabālu(m) (*i*) **G** to bear, to bring **Š** to cause to bear
zābilu(m) carrier
zā'erūtu(m) hostile acts (Bab. is singular!)
zakāru(m) (*a/u*) **G** to utter, to swear (an oath) **Gt** = G **Š** to cause (s/o) to swear (an oath)
zakû(m) 1, f. *zakūtu(m)* clean, pure
zakû(m) 2 (*u*) **G** to be(come) clean, pure
zamāru(m) 1 **D** to sing about
zamāru(m) 2 song
zanānu(m) **Š** to cause (s/th) to rain down
zaqāpu(m) (*a/u*) **G** to be(come) pointed, to stick up (mountain peak)
zaqīqu(m) (a dream spirit)
zaqru(m) high
zâqu(m) (*i*) **G** to blow (of wind)
zārû(m) father
zayyāru(m) foe
zâzu(m) (*ū*) **G** to divide
zenû(m) (*i*) **G** to be(come) angry (*itti* with)
zērātu(m) f. pl.: only hostilities; *z. apālu(m)* to reply in a hostile way
zēru(m) seed, progeny
zêru(m) (*ē*) **G** to hate
zikaru(m) man (see Unit 47.4)
zikru(m) utterance, command
zīmu(m) face; pl.: features
ziqtu(m) m. sharp point
zittu(m) f. division
zummû(m) **D** to be deprived of (acc.)
zumru(m) body
zunnu(m) rain – related to *zanānu(m)*
zuqāqīpu(m) scorpion
zuqtu(m) m. peak, spur

Notes to the Poor Man of Nippur

The name Gimil-Ninurta means 'Requital of Ninurta'. The word for 'requital' (*gimillu(m)*) can be either good or bad: it can indicate returning a favour, or taking revenge. Ninurta is a god of Nippur, in which the story is set. The character's name thus speaks volumes about the plot of the story. (Interestingly, Ninurta is not otherwise mentioned, though he may be lost in a break.)

2 *zikrašu* is poetic for *zikiršu* **16** *imtallik* is Gt pret. **17** *a-aṭ-ab-ba-ah*: *aṭ* is probably an error for *ṭa*. **20** *kim-tum* can equally be read *kim-tu*$_4$ **22** reading *dam* as *dama* (see 44.13), the first two words may be infinitives: *ṭâba u damāqa luṣammera ana karšišu,* lit. 'I shall strive becoming good and becoming sweet for his stomach/mood' **28** *bābka* is an adverbial accusative (see 36.5)

36 *ulli* is D pret. of *elû(m)* **41** *ušanna* is D pres. of *šanû* (verbs that introduce speech in Babylonian narrative are usually in the present) **44** *áš-šá-am*: ignore the double *š* **58** *idin* is imp. of *nadānu* **64** *ina aṣêšu* uses the G inf. of *(w)aṣû* (for *ê* see 23.3, Tip) **68** *-tú* see 43.9 **70** (and 72): genitive *malku* (for expected *malki*) is probably a 'honorific nominative' **70** *iltakan* is from *šakānu(m)* (see 47.9) **73** *uškīn* is pret. of *šukênu(m)* **74** *ullâm-ma* is from *elû* **77** *ēma* **wherever**, i.e **whatever**

92 *šum'ud* is Š inf. of *mâdu* (construct state) **93** ki.min **ditto** stands for nu.bàn.da = *hazannu* **94** the import of *ina rēš* is not clear **97** *ittaprašā* is N perf. of *naprušu* **98** *tīb šēri* is an adverbial accusative (see 36.5) **100** *ina nissat libbišu* lit. 'with a wail of his heart' **101** *innemid* is N pret. of *emēdu(m)* **104** the import of *adi* is not clear here, but context suggests *adi puluhtim-ma* means 'in fear' **108** *id-din-šú* apparently represents pl. *iddinūšu* **112** *-tú* see 43.9 **116** *melammē iškunšu* super-literally 'put in place awe-inspiring radiance for him'

117 this line is difficult: the restoration and overall interpretation are tentative **128** ditto on difficulty and tentativeness **132** *hamiš* (m.) *sikkāti* (f.): an example of gender polarity (see Unit 39) **134** note how elsewhere the same phrase is written over two lines (102-103 and 155-156) **142** could also be *bâru(m)* **to catch** **144** *alik* is G imp. of *alāku*; note how there is no phrase or particle introducing the direct speech **145** the chevrons around the *u* at the end of the line indicate that it is thought to be extraneous

147 *irtibiṣ* is for expected *irtabiṣ*, reflecting either Assyrian vowel assimilation (see 41.1 number 5) or (if normalised *irtebiṣ*) *e*-colouring, which in Neo-Babylonian spreads across the language **148** *kamêtuš*: forms like these mix adverbial *-iš* and locative *-um* **149** *sin-ni-šú u zik-ri* probably represents *sinniš u zikar* (see Unit 40); the two words normally go the other way round – the swap may be for comic effect **150** and **151** *ina gi-mir-šú-nu* represents *ina gimrišunu*, with *gi-mir* being a fossilized spelling (see 44.11) **159** *ṣēra* is an adverbial accusative (see 36.5)

Abbreviations

Table 52 lists the abbreviations of English words used throughout the text, and Table 53 gives the abbreviations used to indicate where a Babylonian sentence was taken from.

Table 52

acc.	accusative	N	N system
adj.	adjective	nom.	nominative
adv.	adverb	o/s	oneself
Ass.	Assyrian	OB	Old Babylonian
Bab.	Babylonian	orig.	original(ly)
caus.	causative	pass.	passive
cf.	compare (with)	pers.	person
D	D system	pl.	plural
e.g.	for example	prec.	precative
esp.	especially	prep.	preposition
f.	feminine	pres.	present
G	G system	pret.	preterite
gen.	genitive	Š	Š system
hend.	hendiadys	SB	Standard Babylonian
i.e.	that is	s/o	someone
imp.	imperative	s/th	something
inf.	infinitive	sg.	singular
iter.	iterative (see Unit 33.1)	sp.	spells, spelling
lit.	literally	stat.	stative
m.	masculine	transf.	transferred (meaning)
MB	Middle Babylonian	uncl.	unclear
mill.	millennium	vent.	ventive (see Unit 19.5)

Table 53

AbB	Various authors, *Altbabylonische Briefe in Umschrift und Übersetzung* (Leiden, 1964–; 14 vols.)
Adapa	S. Izre'el, *Adapa and the South Wind* (Winona Lake, 2001)
AfO 17	E. Weidner, 'Hochverrat gegen Nebukadnezar II. Ein Grosswürdenträger vor dem Königsgericht', *Archiv für Orientforschung* (1954–1956), 1–9
AfO 19	W. G. Lambert, 'Three Literary Prayers of the Babylonians', *Archiv für Orientforschung* 19 (1959–1960), 47–66
AH	W. G. Lambert and A. R. Millard, *Atra-Hasis: The Babylonian Story of the Flood* (Oxford, 1969)
Akkade	J. Goodnick Westenholz, *Legends of the Kings of Akkade* (Winona Lake, 1997)
ARM	Various authors, *Archives Royales de Mari* (Paris, 1950; 27 vols.)
Asar.	R. Borger, *Die Inschriften Asarhaddons* (Graz, 1956)
BBSt.	L. W. King, *Babylonian Boundary Stones* (London, 1912) (now rather outdated)
BIWA	R. Borger, *Beiträge zum Inschriftenwerk Assurbanipals* (Wiesbaden, 1996)
BWL	W. G. Lambert, *Babylonian Wisdom Literature* (Oxford, 1960)

BTT	A. George, *Babylonian Topographical Texts* (Leuven, 1992). Freely available online at http://eprints.soas.ac.uk/19287/1/GeorgeOLA40.pdf
CH	The Law Code of Hammurapi, edited in Les.; see also https://www.uni-marburg.de/cnms/forschung/dnms/apps/ast/ob/kh_transliteration.pdf
Chic.	'Chicago Prism' of Sennacherib, edited in Les.
CT 39	C. J. Gadd, *Cuneiform Texts from Babylonian Tablets, & C.*, in the British Museum. Part XXXIX (London, 1926)
En.El.	Ph. Talon, *Enuma Eliš* (Helsinki, 2005)
Erra	L. Cagni, *L'Epopea di Erra* (Rome, 1969)
Etana-Epos	M. Haul, *Das Etana-Epos* (Göttingen, 2000)
GBAO 2	W. Schramm, *Ein Compendium sumerisch-akkadischer Beschwörungen* (Göttingen, 2008)
Gilg.	A. R. George, *The Babylonian Gilgamesh Epic* (Oxford, 2003)
Gula Hymn	W. G. Lambert, 'The Gula Hymn of Bulluṭsa-rabi', *Orientalia* 36 (1967), 105–132
ID	*Ištar's Descent*, edited in Les.
JMC	*Le Journal des Médecines Cunéiformes* (Paris). Volume 5 is freely available online: http://medecinescuneiformes.fr/?page_id=15.
Khorsabad	A. Fuchs, *Die Inschriften Sargons aus Khorsabad* (Göttingen, 1994)
Les.	R. Borger, *Babylonisch-assyrische Lesestücke*, Heft I (3rd ed. Rome, 2006)
Maqlû	T. Abusch, *The Magical Ceremony* Maqlû: *A Critical Edition* (Leiden, 2016)
MARI 5	M.A.R.I.: *Mari, Annales de Recherches Interdisciplinaires,* vol. 5 (Paris, 1987)
OBE	U. Jeyes, *Old Babylonian Extispicy* (Istanbul, 1989)
Poor Man of Nippur	The text offered in Reading H relies on various sources. The most recent edition of the story is B. Ottervanger, *The Tale of the Poor Man of Nippur* (Eisenbrauns, 2016).
RIMA 2	A. K. Grayson, *Assyrian Rulers of the Early First Millennium* BC *I* (Toronto, 1991)
RIMA 3	A. K. Grayson, *Assyrian Rulers of the Early First Millennium* BC *II* (Toronto, 1996)
SAA	State Archives of Assyria (Helsinki, 1987-); vol. 13 is by S. W. Cole and P. Machinist, 16 by M. Luukko and G. Van Buylaere, 17 by M. Dietrich; the complete series has been digitised: http://oracc.museum.upenn.edu/saao/corpus
Schlaf	W. Farber, *Schlaf, Kindchen, Schlaf!* (Winona Lake, 1989)
SEAL	http://www.seal.uni-leipzig.de/
TCL 3	F. Thureau-Dangin, *Une relation de la huitième campagne de Sargon* (Paris, 1912)
TN	P. Machinist, *The Epic of Tukulti-Ninurta I* (unpublished PhD dissertation, Yale, 1983)
VAB 4	S. Langdon (translated by R. Zehnpfund), *Die neubabylonischen Königsinschriften* (Leipzig, 1912) (now rather outdated)
YOS	Several Authors, *Yale Oriental Series* (New Haven)

When reference is made to these works, capital Roman numerals (I, II, III, IV, etc.) refer to Tablets (i.e. 'chapters') of ancient compositions. Lower-case Roman numerals (i, ii, iii, iv, etc.) refer to columns of text on an individual object (e.g. a tablet, a prism, a stele). When an apostrophe appears after the line number, it means that the top part of the object is broken, and some lines are lost. Thus in a reference such as Gilg. VA+BM i.11', what is line 11 currently (i.e. on the broken tablet) was not line 11 originally (i.e. on the pristine tablet).

Assyriologists are very fond of bibliographical abbreviations. Accordingly, while reading their writings you may find it helpful to refer to the following website, where more Assyriological abbreviations are explained:

http://cdli.ucla.edu/wiki/doku.php/abbreviations_for_assyriology.

Index

Numbers refer to units and sections within them. 'TIP' represents a 'Tip' box; 'ex.' represents an exercise; 'pass.' represents a passage.

The contents of Unit 41 ('The main features of Assyrian') have not been indexed individually.

consonants, double: *3.1, 44.7*
construct state: *10*
contagion, awareness of: *ex. 11.2 TIP*
contracted vowels spelled plene: *44.2*
contraction of vowels: *47.1*
'core' of verbal form: *14.2*
couples, verbal: *32.4*
crasis: *47.3*
Cuneiform Digital Library Initiative: *42.3*
cuneiform script, learning: *2.8*
cuneiform script, spelling conventions of: *44*
cuneiform tablets, how to turn: *22.3 TIP*
cuneifyplus: *2.8*
curses: *21*

'dangling' words: *11.12*
dative suffixes: *19*
decipherment: *see What is Babylonian?*
demons: *ex. 17.3 TIP, ex. 30.7*
dentals: *11.7*
determinatives: *see list of sumerograms*
dictionaries: *42.1*
doubling of consonants, purely graphic: *44.7*
Dt system: *34*
Dtn system: *33*
duals: *12*
durative: *(this is what some books call the tense which this book calls 'present')*
durative verbs: *15.1*

e-colouring: *14.13*
e-verbs: *14.13*
edû **to know**: *27.2*
Elamite king: *22.2 TIP, ex. 34.3*
elative: *(this is how some books call the intensifying use of the Š system, see Unit 18.11)*
elephants: *40 pass. 3*
elision of vowels: *47.3–4*
emphatic consonants: *3.1, 47.13*
endingless state: *40*
epēšu, meanings of: *24.1 TIP*
equids, love life of: *ex. 30.7*
Erra, Epic of: *ex. 16.5 TIP, ex. 18.6, ex. 25.6*
errors, ancient: *43.8*
Esarhaddon: *40 pass. 4*
eṣemṣēru **backbone**: *6.17*
eṭlu **young man**: *8.1, 9.6*
eunuchs: *30.3*
exclamation mark: *ex. 15.1*
extispicy: *40 pass. 4*

feminine: *see gender*
feminine *t*: *6.5*
fingerprints rare on tablets: *11.4 TIP*
fossilized spellings: *44.11*
future, conceptualization of: *19.8 TIP*
future, referring to: *15.1, 17.1, 18.3*

Geers' Law: *47.13*
gender: *6.5*
gender, change of from singular to plural: *8.7*
Genesis: *18.5 TIP*
gender polarity (with cardinal numbers larger than 2): *39*
genitive case, function of: *6.3*
genitive constructions: *10.4*
gentilic adjectives: *46.3*
Gilgameš, Epic of: *1.2 TIP, 14.3 TIP, 18.5 TIP, ex. 22.2, ex. 25.6, 42*
Gilgameš, the name: *29.4 TIP*
glottal stop: *3.1, 24.8, 27, 41.3, 47.1*
glottal stop, spellings of: *44.4*
grammatical terminology: *2.5*
grave accents: *4.3*
Gt system: *34*
Gtn system: *33*
guttural consonants: *25, 47.7*
guttural consonants, loss of: *14.13, 47.2, 47.7*

Hammurabi: *see Hammurapi (cf. 40, pass. 1)*
Hammurapi: *24.4*
Hammurapi, Laws of: *22.2 TIP, 40 pass. 1 and 2*
Hanging Gardens: *43 TIP*
helping verbs: *14.19, 21*
hendiadys: *see verbal couples*
hiatus in spelling: *44.4, 44.6*
hollow verbs: *see verbs, II-weak*
honorific nominative: *6.12*
hunting: *40 pass. 3*

II-guttural verbs: *25*
II-vowel verbs: *25*
Iliad: *14.3 TIP*
imperative: *14.19, 20*
impersonal constructions: *14.16*
indeclinable nouns: *6.2*
independent pronouns: *37*
infinitives: *6.10, 22*
infixes: *14.11 TIP*
intonation: *3.1*
Isaiah: *ex. 31.2 TIP*
-iš (adverbial ending): *36.2*
-išam (adverbial ending): *36.4*
Ištar: *6.14 TIP, 19.4 TIP, ex. 25.6*
išû **to have**: *27.2*
iterative meaning: *33.1*

itūlu: *28.3*
izuzzu: *28.2*

Job, Book of: *18.11*

lā: *14.18*
length, metathesis of: *47.8*
libraries at Nineveh: *7.2 TIP*
lipography: *43.8*
locative: *36.9*
logograms: *(this is used by some books to denote certain types of sumerograms)*
longest Babylonian word: *33 TIP*
Louvre Museum: *22.2 TIP*
lt from original *št* *47.9*
lū: *18.9, 21, 27.2, 29.7*

-ma **if**: *32.3*
-ma, connecting clauses: *30.1*
-ma, dash before: *4.4*
-ma, emphatic: *6.15*
-ma, non-connective: *29.3, 30.7*
macron: *3.2*
manû, meanings of: *23.1 TIP*
manuscripts: *1.2, 7.2*
Mari: *ex. 11.2 TIP, 21.4, 47.1*
masculine: *see gender*
measurement, units of: *40*
mediae alef: *see verbs, II-weak*
mediae vocalis: *see verbs, II-weak*
medical prescriptions: *11.12 TIP*
metathesis of length: *47.8*
Middle Babylonian: *1.1*
mimation: *6.11, 36.1 TIP*
month names: *Reading C TIP*
mood: *21 TIP*
moon god: *ex. 25.4 TIP*
morphemes: *15.3 TIP*
morpho-graphemic spellings: *44.5*
morpho-phonological spellings: *44.6*
myths: *1.3*

n-dash: *6.12 TIP*
names: *6.5 TIP, 6.12 TIP*
nasalization: *47.11*
Nebuchadnezzar I: *ex. 24.5*
Nebuchadnezzar II: *40 pass. 5*
negation: *14.18, 29.6, 22*
Neo-Babylonian: *1.1*
-ni (Assyrian verbal suffix in most subordinate clauses): *41.3*
Nineveh: *7.2 TIP, 40 pass. 4*
nisbe adjectives: *46.2*
noise: *ex. 23.2 TIP*
nominative, function of: *6.3*
normalization: *4.4*
nouns, abstract: *46.1*
nouns, formation of: *46*
nouns, indeclinable: *6.2*
nouns occurring in plural only: *8.6*
nouns with stative suffixes: *18.8*
Ntn system: *33*
number differences between Babylonian and English: *6.13*
number in nouns and adjectives: *6.6, 6.13*
number in verbs: *14.3*
numbers: *39*

oblique case: *(some books use this as an umbrella term for accusative pl. and genitive pl.)*
Old Babylonian: *1.1*
or: *6.16*

parāsu, meanings of: *15.5 TIP*
parent verbs: *46 TIP, 46.4*
paronomastic infinitive: *22.6*
participles: *35*
passive: *14.8, 14.16, 18.2, 18.4, 34.6, 34.7*
past, conceptualization of: *19.8 TIP*
patterns: *5*
perfect: *17*
performative utterances: *16.1*
periods of Babylonian: *1.1*
permansive: *(this is what some books call the tense which this book calls 'stative')*
phonetic complements: *4.1*
plague: *ex. 16.5 TIP*
plant of life: *18.5 TIP*
plene spellings: *4.2, 30.9, 44.2, 47.1*
plene spellings marking questions: *44.9*
plural: *see number*
plurale tantum (pl. tant.): *(this is how some books term nouns which occur only in the plural)*
poetry: *6.7, 10.7, 11.1, 14.1, 30.1, 43.7*
Poor Man of Nippur, The: *13.6 TIP, Reading H*
possessive state: *10.4, 11*
possessive suffixes: *6.4, 10.4, 11, 18.8, 22, 29.2, 36.3, 36.7, 36.10*
prayer to gods of the night: *ex. 18.4, ex. 24.4*
precatives: *14.19, 21*
precatives expressing purpose or result: *32.1*
predicative complements: *30.4*
prepositional phrases: *13*
prepositions: *6.3, 11.14, 13, 30.3, 30.5, 31.3, 36.10*
present: *15*
preterite: *16*